Nova Scotia

the Bradt Travel Guide

David Orkin

edition
3

www.bradtguides.com

Bradt Travel Guides Ltd, UK
The Globe Pequot Press Inc, USA

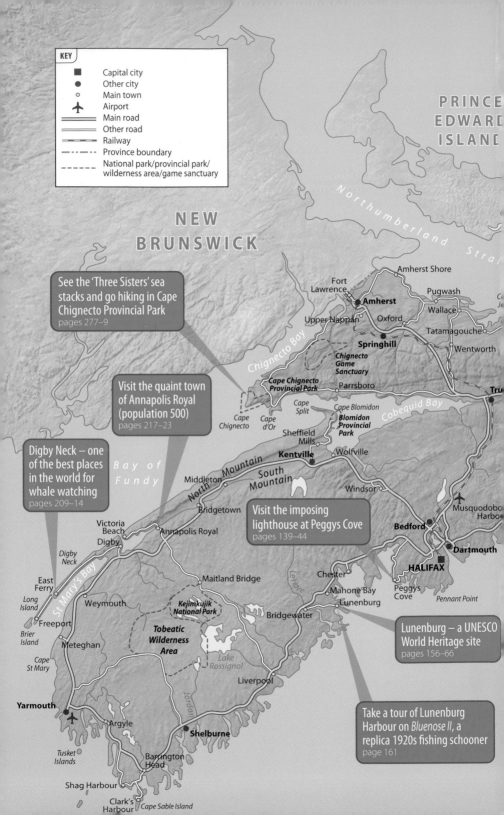

See the 'Three Sisters' sea stacks and go hiking in Cape Chignecto Provincial Park pages 277–9

Visit the quaint town of Annapolis Royal (population 500) pages 217–23

Digby Neck – one of the best places in the world for whale watching pages 209–14

Visit the imposing lighthouse at Peggys Cove pages 139–44

Lunenburg – a UNESCO World Heritage site pages 156–66

Take a tour of Lunenburg Harbour on Bluenose II, a replica 1920s fishing schooner page 161

KEY

- ■ Capital city
- ● Other city
- ○ Main town
- ✈ Airport
- ══ Main road
- ── Other road
- ┼┼ Railway
- ·─··─ Province boundary
- ─ ─ ─ National park/provincial park/ wilderness area/game sanctuary

PRINCE EDWARD ISLAND

NEW BRUNSWICK

Northumberland Strait

Amherst Shore
Fort Lawrence
Pugwash
Amherst
Upper Nappan
Oxford
Wallace
Tatamagouche
Springhill
Wentworth
Chignecto Game Sanctuary
Chignecto Bay
Cape Chignecto Provincial Park
Parrsboro
Cape Split
Cape Blomidon
Cobequid Bay
Tru
Cape Chignecto
Cape d'Or
Blomidon Provincial Park
Sheffield Mills
Kentville
Wolfville
Bay of Fundy
North Mountain
South Mountain
Windsor
Musquodobo Harbo
Middleton
Bridgetown
Bedford
Dartmouth
Victoria Beach
Digby
Annapolis Royal
HALIFAX
Digby Neck
Maitland Bridge
Chester
Peggys Cove
East Ferry
Long Island
Weymouth
Kejimkujik National Park
Mahone Bay
Lunenburg
Pennant Point
St Mary's Bay
Freeport
Brier Island
Meteghan
Tobeatic Wilderness Area
Bridgewater
LaHave
Cape St Mary
Lake Rossignol
Liverpool
Jordan
Yarmouth
Argyle
Shelburne
Tusket Islands
Barrington Head
Shag Harbour
Clark's Harbour
Cape Sable Island

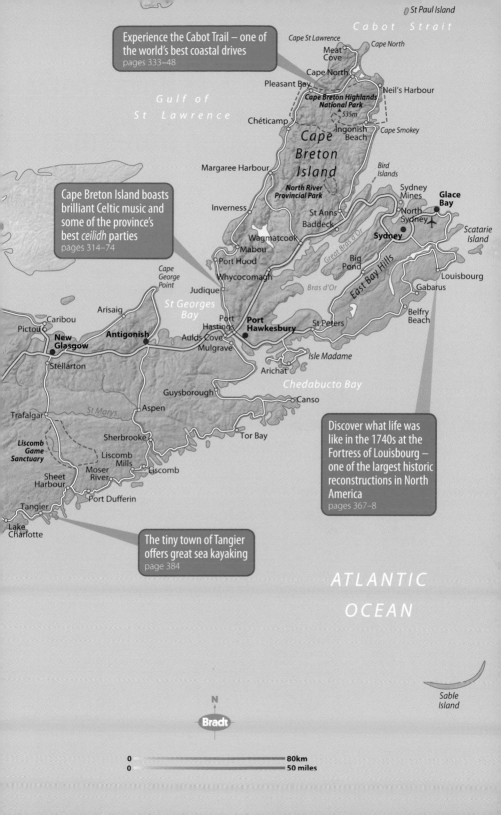

St Paul Island

Cabot Strait

Experience the Cabot Trail – one of the world's best coastal drives pages 333–48

Gulf of St Lawrence

Cape St Lawrence
Cape North
Meat Cove
Cape North
Pleasant Bay
Neil's Harbour
Cape Breton Highlands National Park
535m
Chéticamp
Ingonish Beach
Cape Smokey

Cape Breton Island

Margaree Harbour
Bird Islands
North River Provincial Park
Sydney Mines
Glace Bay
Inverness
St Anns
North Sydney
Scatarie Island
Baddeck
Sydney

Cape Breton Island boasts brilliant Celtic music and some of the province's best *ceilidh* parties pages 314–74

Wagmatcook
Mabou
Port Hood
Whycocomagh
Bras d'Or
East Bay Hills
Cape George Point
Judique
St Georges Bay
Port Hastings
Port Hawkesbury
St Peters
Louisbourg
Arisaig
Caribou
Aulds Cove
St Peters
Gabarus
Pictou
New Glasgow
Antigonish
Mulgrave
Belfry Beach
Stellarton
Isle Madame
Arichat

Chedabucto Bay

St Marys
Aspen
Guysborough
Canso

Trafalgar
Sherbrooke
Tor Bay

Discover what life was like in the 1740s at the Fortress of Louisbourg – one of the largest historic reconstructions in North America pages 367–8

Liscomb Game Sanctuary
Liscomb Mills
Moser River
Liscomb
Sheet Harbour
Tangier
Port Dufferin
Lake Charlotte

The tiny town of Tangier offers great sea kayaking page 384

ATLANTIC OCEAN

N

Bradt

Sable Island

0 ——————— 80km
0 ——————— 50 miles

Nova Scotia
Don't miss...

Halifax's maritime history
The province's most important
metropolis is a testament to its
strong links to the sea: the bustling
waterfront is home to a range of
museums and festivals, such as the
Tall Ships festival held every four
years in July

(AM/A) page 88

Historic colonial
architecture
The Fortress of Louisbourg, the
largest reconstructed 18th-century
French fortified town in North
America, is just one example of
Nova Scotia's colonial past

(TNS) pages 367–8

Stunning geological sites

Locations such as the UNESCO-designated Joggins Fossil Cliffs — a palaeontological site with extensive deposits of 300-million-year-old fossils are a geologist's and fossil hunter's dream
(TNS) pages 279–80

Spectacular whale watching

Digby Neck is one of the best places in the world for sightings — spot smaller finback and minke whales early in the season and enormous humpbacks in the summer
(TNS) pages 9 & 209–14

Drives along the coast

One of the finest coastal drives in the world, the Cabot Trail weaves through miles of untouched wilderness, perfect for spotting moose, bald eagle and whale
(J16/S) pages 325–48

Nova Scotia in colour

above left Fort Anne National Historic Site in Annapolis Royal has a magnificent waterside setting (TNS) pages 222–3

above right Western Light lighthouse on Brier Island is the western-most point in Nova Scotia (WPP/S) pages 212–13

right Visit a replica of the *Hector*, which brought more than 150 Highlanders to Nova Scotia in 1773 (MM/TNS) pages 298–300 & 302

below The colourful town of Lunenburg — the Old Town is one of the province's three UNESCO World Heritage sites (GY/S) pages 156–66

above   Autumn/fall is a great time to explore the Nova Scotian wilderness (DF) page 5

below left   Mayflowers (or trailing arbutus) are the provincial flower of Nova Scotia, and these fragrant blooms appear in forest glades during early spring (JR) pages 4–5

below right   Beautiful forest walks are a highlight of Kejimkujik National Park (SS) pages 223–7

AUTHOR

David Orkin is a freelance travel writer whose work has appeared in leading UK publications such as *The Independent*, *Wanderlust* and *Condé Nast Traveller*. He began writing about travel in 2000 after working in the travel industry for more than 15 years, including eight years co-running his own successful company. He has travelled extensively since the mid 1970s and first visited Nova Scotia in 2004. He returned several times, exploring every corner of the province. He is now a Canadian citizen and has made his home in Nova Scotia.

AUTHOR'S STORY

When I visited Nova Scotia for the first time I looked for a guidebook to help enhance my experience there, but found that most of them lumped the province with its neighbours, Prince Edward Island and New Brunswick, some also including Newfoundland and Labrador. Fine for an overview of the entire region, but of limited use to anyone wanting to focus solely on Nova Scotia. I turned to Nova Scotia's tourism authorities who produced (and still do) *Doers & Dreamers*, a thorough listing of all the province's museums and attractions and virtually all accommodation choices from campgrounds to deluxe resorts, but these are unedited lists.

Each time that I went back to Nova Scotia and explored places – some wonderful, others missable – it became increasingly obvious that there was a need for a more comprehensive, subjective guide. Something to cater to those who wanted to do, those who wanted to dream, and those who wanted to discover the province's highlights, as well as its virtually unknown nooks and crannies. I put a proposal to write a book to the publisher that I thought would be most appropriate for such a guide. Bradt agreed.

Research took place on foot, in canoe and kayak, by ferry, by bike, by coach, and tens of thousands of kilometres by car – and I tried to return everywhere at a different time of year to see if my impressions changed. Now, my Canadian citizenship allows me to spend even more time exploring the province and enjoying long conversations with waiters, fishermen, B&B owners, shopkeepers, park rangers, artists, tourists, birders, musicians and many more – in Nova Scotia it is hard to find someone who doesn't like talking about their fascinating homeland. This guidebook is the collective result of those discussions and my ongoing explorations.

PUBLISHER'S FOREWORD — *Adrian Phillips, Managing Director*

Bradt has built a reputation around publishing guides to destinations off the tourist trail. That can mean places like Rwanda and Ethiopia, of course, but we mustn't forget that there are still areas of mystery and romance in the developed world. As author David Orkin says, despite many visits to Canada over the years, he knew very little about Nova Scotia before going there for the first time – just that it was probably 'cold, wet and windy'. Well, what a land of colour awaited. Who could fail to be enchanted by rugged cliffs, mist-veiled lighthouses and legends of pirates' derring-do? And who could fail to relax in a province where time marches to a slower beat? Nova Scotia – and this third edition of David's excellent book – is very much in the Bradt mould.

Third edition published March 2017   First published 2009

Bradt Travel Guides Ltd
IDC House, The Vale, Chalfont St Peter, Bucks SL9 9RZ, England
www.bradtguides.com
Print edition published in the USA by The Globe Pequot Press Inc,
PO Box 480, Guilford, Connecticut 06437-0480

Text copyright © 2017 David Orkin
Maps copyright © 2017 Bradt Travel Guides Ltd; includes map data © OpenStreetMap contributors
Photographs copyright © 2017 Individual photographers (see below)
Project Manager: Susannah Lord
Cover research: Pepi Bluck

ISBN: 978 1 78477 040 2 (print)
e-ISBN: 978 1 78477 191 1 (e-pub)
e-ISBN: 978 1 78477 292 5 (mobi)

British Library Cataloguing in Publication Data
A catalogue record for this book is available from the British Library

Photographs Aconcagua (A); Alamy: Rolf Hicker Photography (RHP/A), Alexander McClearn (AM/A), Mike Baird (MB); Dreamstime.com: Charles Knox Photo Inc (CKPI/D); www.flpa.co.uk: Tony Hamblin (TH/FLPA); Dan Froese Photography (DF); Sherman Hines (SH); Lost Shores Gallery: Rob Carter (RC/LSG); David Orkin (DO); Qias (Q); Justin Russell (JR); Evan Schiller (ES); Shutterstock.com: Justek16 (J16/S), Vlad G (VG/S), Vadim.Petrov (VP/S), Warren Price Photography (WPP/S), Gary Yim (GY/S); SuperStock (SS); Tourism Nova Scotia (TNS): Izzy Dempsey (ID/TNS), Perry Dyke (PD/TNS), Megan Moss (MM/TNS)
Front cover Peggys Cove Lighthouse (RHP/A)
Back cover Lunenburg's hillside Old Town (GY/S), The Cabot Trail – one of the world's great scenic drives (J16/S)
Title page Drummers at the Fortress of Louisbourg (TNS), Lunenburg's church (VG/S), The delightful Halifax Public Gardens (TNS)

Maps David McCutcheon FBCart.S; colour map base by Nick Rowland FRGS; the Nova Scotia map published by ITMB Publishing (*www.itmb.ca*) was used to produce many of the maps in this book. A map published by All 4 One Graphics was used to produce the maps of Shelburne.

Typeset by Dataworks, and Ian Spick, Bradt Travel Guides
Production managed by Jellyfish Print Solutions; printed in India
Digital conversion by www.dataworks.co.in

Acknowledgements

The list could fill a chapter, so I'll try to concentrate on those who have gone way beyond the call of duty. My thanks go to (those I've omitted accidentally and) Alain Belliveau, Sara Bonnyman, Michele Bourgeois, Silver Donald Cameron, Rob Carter, Bruce & Lisa Chiasson, Julie Cossette, Naomi Cripps, Scott Cunningham, Doug Crowell, Joan Czapalay, Naomi Davidson, Bill Drane, Hilary Drummond, Ashlee Feener, Ray Fraser, Bev Gabriel, Saskia Geerts, Charlotte Hindle, Shalan Joudry, Anne Marie LeBlanc, Krista Lingley, Lori Lynch & David Beattie, Anna Moore, Noella Murphy, June Noble, Carol Nauss, Dorothy Outhouse, Elder Danny Paul, Larry Peach, Doug Reach, Allan Reid, Ashton Rodenhiser, Audrey Sandford, Roger Savage, Maarten & Nelly Schuurmans, Elaine Shanks, Angelo Spinazzola, Lilian Stewart and Thomas Storring.

Thanks to everyone at Bradt, particularly Susannah Lord and Rachel Fielding, and to David McCutcheon for his sterling work in converting my barely legible scribbles into such good maps. Last, but by no means least, special thanks to Vanessa, Oliver and Eleanor for their patience and support.

Contents

LIST OF MAPS

HOW TO USE THIS GUIDE

2017 ADMISSION PRICES As part of the federal 2016 budget, to celebrate Canada's 150th birthday, the Canadian government has announced free admission to all of the country's national parks and national historic sites for 2017. Admission will be charged again from 2018, but rates have not yet been set so the 2016 charge has been shown in the details of the relevant sites for information purposes.

A NOTE ON MAPS
Keys and symbols Maps include alphabetical keys covering the locations of those places to stay, eat and drink that are featured in the book. Note that regional maps may not show all hotels and restaurants in the area: other establishments may be located in towns on the map.

Grids and grid references Several maps use gridlines to allow easy location of sites. Map grid references are listed in square brackets after the name of the place and sight of interest in the text, with page number followed by grid number, eg: [103 C3].

Introduction

By the time I first visited Nova Scotia I had worked in the travel industry for close to 20 years and considered myself well travelled. I had made numerous long trips to Canada, but other than the fact that its airport (and presumably biggest city) was Halifax, I knew very little about Nova Scotia. If pressed, I would have said that I imagined it was cold, wet and windy.

Since then, I've learnt much about the province. Although it always seemed to be lumped in with its maritime neighbours (New Brunswick, Prince Edward Island and Newfoundland and Labrador), it is large enough (55,300km^2) and varied enough (dense forest, countless remote lakes and waterways, a vibrant capital, fabulous music, photogenic fishing villages, towering cliffs and beautiful sandy beaches) to be a popular destination in its own right. Wrapped in 7,400km of coastline and virtually an island, Nova Scotia's culture and heartbeat has always been shaped by the sea. Stories of pirates, buried treasure and ghost-ships abound, and there are stunningly located lighthouses to photograph.

Compared with the UK, it may have relatively cold winters with a fair amount of snow, but Nova Scotia is hardly 'the Frozen North' – the provincial capital, Halifax, is on the same latitude as Bordeaux, France.

When in Nova Scotia, my partner and I liked the contrast of the simple, slow rural lifestyle versus the buzz of Halifax; we were enchanted by the character, comfort (and breakfasts) at the B&Bs; we delighted in the heritage architecture, the music, the seafood, the orchards and the wild flowers; and chatting to the locals – humorous, welcoming and proud of their province – was always entertaining.

We wondered how the kids would enjoy it. Nova Scotia's theme parks are few and far between, and the province's biggest, Upper Clements Amusement Park (page 216), isn't exactly Disneyland. There are only a few cinemas and, with a couple of exceptions, the museums aren't exactly hi-tech. Apart from the Northumberland Strait (and a few other hotspots) the sea isn't warm enough for swimming.

But they loved watching a blacksmith at work and wool being spun at the living museums, taking a boat trip in search of whales, paddling a canoe, and gorging themselves on berries at a U-pick (pick-your-own) farm. On Cape Breton Island we had moose-spotting competitions, sailed on the Bras d'Or Lake, explored the fortress at Louisbourg and swapped four wheels for two on Isle Madame.

The kids played soldiers at the Halifax Citadel, and rolled down the grassy ramparts at Annapolis Royal's Fort Anne. Ice creams made up for the disappointment of failing to find any fossils or gemstones on the beach at Scots Bay.

After several visits we decided to save the time and expense of crossing and re-crossing the Atlantic. We bought a big souvenir – a house overlooking the sea – and have now called Nova Scotia home for more than seven years.

Part One

GENERAL INFORMATION

Name of province Nova Scotia
Country name Canada
Languages English, French
Population 943,000 (Statistics Canada, 2016)
People Scottish 29%, English 27%, Irish 19%, French/Acadian 12%, German 8%, Mi'kmaq 2%, others 3%
Religion Roman Catholic 33%, United Church 16%, Anglican 13%, Baptist 11%, Presbyterian 3%, Lutheran 1%, Pentecostal 1%, other or no religious affiliation 22%
Canadian Prime Minister Justin Trudeau
Nova Scotia Premier Stephen McNeil
Nova Scotia ruling political party Liberal Party
Neighbouring provinces and states Land border with New Brunswick, Canada; nearby Canadian provinces Prince Edward Island and Newfoundland and Labrador. Nearest US state: Maine.
Area 55,300km²
Time Atlantic Standard Time Zone (AST). Winter GMT −4; summer GMT −3 (clocks adjusted second Sunday in March and first Sunday in November).
Currency Canadian dollar (CAN$ or CAD)
Exchange rate £1=CAN$1.66, US$1=CAN$1.33, €1=CAN$1.38 (December 2016)
Flag An extended blue cross on a white background superimposed with a shield bearing the Royal Arms of Scotland
Telephone codes Canada +1 (international code); Nova Scotia 902 (also 782; see box, page 75)
Electricity supply 110v 60Hz
Public holidays 1 January (New Year's Day), February (Nova Scotia Heritage Day; third Monday in February), March/April (Good Friday), March/April (Easter Monday), May (Victoria Day; first Monday after 25 May), 1 July (Canada Day), August (Natal Day; first Monday in August), September (Labour Day; first Monday in September), October (Thanksgiving Day; second Monday in October), 11 November (Remembrance Day), 25 December (Christmas Day), 26 December (Boxing Day)

1

Background Information

GEOGRAPHY

With an area of 55,300km², Nova Scotia is the second smallest of Canada's 13 provinces and territories – only nearby Prince Edward Island (at 5,660km²) is smaller. For a European comparison, Nova Scotia is larger than Denmark (approx 43,000km²) but much smaller than Scotland (approx 79,000km²).

Connected to mainland Canada only by a narrow isthmus, it is almost surrounded by the sea. To the south and east is the Atlantic Ocean; to the northeast is the Cabot Strait; to the north the Northumberland Strait; and to the northwest the Bay of Fundy. Although it measures over 550km in length, with an average width of 130km, Nova Scotia has 7,400km of coastline. No point of land is more than 60km from the sea. The shape of the province has been likened to that of a lobster, with Cape Breton Island to the northeast forming the claws.

Halifax is Nova Scotia's capital and is situated at the head of a huge natural harbour on the southeastern coast of the province. In terms of latitude, Halifax is further south than both Paris and Vienna. In fact, the province lies halfway between the North Pole and the Equator, straddling the 45th parallel.

Thick forests – with pine, spruce, fir, hemlock, birch and maple dominating – dotted with lakes cover 80% of the land, but there are also blossom-covered orchards, blueberry fields, and rolling farmland. Much of the best farmland is found in the Annapolis Valley, sheltered by hills to both the north and south.

In general, elevations do not exceed 200m. The main exception is on Cape Breton Island, where 535m-high White Hill forms the province's highest point.

CLIMATE

Nova Scotia lies within the Northern Temperate Zone. The climate is more typically continental than maritime, although the sea has an attenuating effect on the temperature highs and lows. Cape Breton Island experiences much more extreme weather patterns than mainland Nova Scotia. In general, sea temperatures are too low for enjoyable swimming: the main exceptions to this are the coastal waters of the Northumberland Strait and northwest Cape Breton Island, particularly in August.

Annual precipitation averages 1,200mm, falling mainly as rain during autumn and as snow in winter. Boosting the average are the highlands of Cape Breton Island (an average of over1,600mm of precipitation per year) and the southwest (1,500mm): in comparison, the Northumberland Strait receives less than 1,000mm a year.

The summer of 2016 was particularly dry, with the southwest of the province experiencing its lowest rainfall levels for more than 70 years.

The merging of warm, moisture-laden air above the Gulf Stream with the far cooler air above the Labrador Current results in a lot of fog: this can often blanket coastal regions, particularly in the morning between mid spring and early summer. The good news is that the fog is often localised, and more often than not dissipates by late morning. Some of the foggiest parts of the province are Halifax, Yarmouth, Canso, Sydney and Sable Island.

Although most fizzle out before they reach Nova Scotia, some hurricanes and tropical storms do stay the distance and sweep across the province, uprooting trees, knocking down power lines and washing away bridges. The worst in recent years was Hurricane Juan (September 2003) which caused vast amounts of damage.

Environment Canada's website (*weather.gc.ca/canada_e.html*) offers weather forecasts for more than 40 towns across the province. Current weather forecasts can also be obtained by phone (✆ *902 426 9090*).

WINTER (*early November–mid April*) Winter is moderately cold with high temperatures ranging from an average of −4°C to 5°C. At this time of year, freezing rain is a Nova Scotia speciality. There are a fair number of bright, sunny (albeit cold) days. The Northumberland Strait and Gulf of St Lawrence are ice-covered during much of the winter, cooling down nearby coastal areas.

SPRING (*mid April–mid June*) During spring, average high temperatures range from 4°C to 14°C inland, and a couple of degrees cooler in coastal areas.

SUMMER (*mid June–mid September*) Summer temperatures range from daytime highs of 18°C to 25°C (occasionally reaching 30°C) to evening lows of 9°C to 14°C. Further inland, the air is typically about 5°C warmer.

AUTUMN (*mid September–early November*) Early autumn is often mild, and the warm Gulf Stream extends the season, but days become cooler as winter approaches.

NATURAL HISTORY

FLORA The province offers a range of habitats from the Atlantic Coastal Plain to the high plateaux of Cape Breton's northern highlands, and these support a wide variety of flora – including more than 1,650 vascular plants. Trees cover close to 80% of Nova Scotia, but aren't just evergreen conifers, something that becomes even more apparent if you visit in the autumn. At this time, hardwoods such as maple, birch, oak, aspen and mountain ash burst into an explosion of brilliant colour. It is a conifer, however, the red spruce (*Picea rubens*), which has been designated Nova Scotia's provincial tree.

In exposed coastal areas, stunted trees such as black spruce, often bent by the wind, are common as are shrubs like creeping juniper, common juniper and black crowberry. Sand dunes are usually covered with marram grass (also known as American beach grass). You're also likely to see seaside plantain, beach pea, sea rocket and seaside goldenrod: look out too for the aromatic northern bayberry and beautiful wild roses.

Nova Scotia's provincial flower is the mayflower, or trailing arbutus, which blooms (with delicately scented pink flowers) in the forest glades in early spring, often amid the last remaining snows of winter. From then until early autumn a range of species will be in bloom – the visitor will often see carpets of colour by the roadside. Stands of lupins, for example, are stunning in June. Some of the more common summer-flowering species include Queen Anne's lace, ox-eye daisy, pearly everlasting and yarrow. Purple loosestrife may be an aggressive weed, but still contributes to the floral colour show.

As summer begins to give way to autumn, days become shorter and nights become cooler. The colour of the leaves of deciduous trees and shrubs, dark green with chlorophyll in summer, also begins to change. Chlorophyll production declines, and the green colour fades. Whilst the leaves of many species turn yellow, the colour pigmentation of red oak, mountain ash, blueberry and huckleberry leaves, for example, turn red, whilst the colour of sugar and red maple leaves runs the range from yellow to purple.

When contrasted with the dark green of the evergreens and the blue (hopefully) of the sky, the result is one of nature's most stunning displays.

In a typical year, the 'leaf-peeping' season runs from the end of September until late October, and is at its height in the second week of October. Nature being nature, not all years are typical: summer 2016, for example, was sunnier and far drier than the norm, confusing the leaves into turning weeks earlier.

Where are the best viewing areas? Personal favourites (if you time it right) are Milton (page 177), Kejimkujik National Park (if it is open; see pages 223–7), Bear River (pages 214–15), Wentworth (pages 293–4) and Cape George (page 311). There are many wonderful areas on Cape Breton Island, too – try to time your visit to coincide with the wonderful Celtic Colours Festival (box, page 318).

Bog plants typically include various mosses, cranberries and liverwort. Many types of orchid can also be seen. Some bogs are also home to insectivorous plants such as sundew, butterwort, pitcher plant and bladderwort.

Seaweeds Many of the algae found on the beaches and shores are put to good use. Rockweed is the dominant brown seaweed found intertidally along the province's coast. Hand-harvested, its main use is as a fertiliser. Irish moss has long been harvested for use as a food source: it contains high amounts of carrageenan, used in the manufacture of dairy products, cosmetics and more.

Dulse has reddish-purple, somewhat leathery fronds. Rich in minerals and vitamins and with a high protein content, it is often dried and sold as a snack food (something of an acquired taste which I am yet to acquire!).

SLIMY SUCCESS STORY

Dartmouth-based Acadian Seaplants (☎ 902 468 2840; www.acadianseaplants. com) has come a long way in a couple of decades. Based near Lower East Pubnico (page 189), it now has five seaweed-processing plants including three in Nova Scotia (and one in Ireland). Today, it's a multi-national, biotechnology exporter that also operates the largest land-based commercial seaweed cultivation facility in the world. It sustainably harvests *Ascophyllum nodosum* employing world-leading resource management practices and resource scientists. Irish moss, rockweed and other algae are used to produce a range of agricultural, health and beauty and brewing products, including an 'instant sea-vegetable bouquet salad' called Hana Tsunomata™, which is very popular in Japan.

FAUNA

Mammals You're too late for the woodland caribou (hunted to extinction here by the 1920s), but Nova Scotia is home to almost 70 different land mammals. The most common large mammal is the white-tailed deer, which, when disturbed, will 'flash' the white underside of its distinctive tail. The deer are often seen prancing across the road in wooded rural areas, particularly early or late in the day. Other species include mink, river otter, red fox, coyote (similar to a large, grey-brown fox), red squirrel, seven types of bat, eastern chipmunk (reddish-brown in colour with five distinct black stripes down its back and a member of the squirrel family), and various members of the weasel family including the American marten.

Mammals with which visitors from the UK may be less familiar include the porcupine, common on the mainland. The porcupine – the province's second-largest rodent after the beaver – is an excellent climber. It has strong, short legs with powerful claws and is covered with thousands of sharp quills. Porcupines feed on twigs, leaves, buds and the inner bark of trees and are nocturnal (so I was surprised to find two up one of my apple trees recently). If you travel off the major highways, you're likely to see porcupines, but sadly they will almost always be roadkill (killed by traffic). Kejimkujik National Park is a good place to try and spot a live one.

Another common species is the eastern striped skunk, easily recognised by its long, black fur, long, bushy tail, and two white stripes that run along its back. It can grow up to 1m in length. If a skunk turns its back on you and raises its tail, run – or at least cover your eyes: it is about to squirt from its anal glands a particularly malodorous and long-lasting spray. Racoons are found throughout the province: excellent climbers and generally nocturnal, they have small pointed ears, greyish fur, a black mask around the eyes and black rings around a long, bushy tail.

Also known as a groundhog, the woodchuck is the largest member of the squirrel family and grows up to 40–50cm in length. It has a stocky build with a flattened head and short tail. The muskrat is a large (40–50cm) rodent with brown to black fur, webbed feet and a long, scaly tail flattened on both sides. It is an excellent swimmer. The northern flying squirrel is common throughout the forests of Nova Scotia; the smaller and much rarer southern flying squirrel is thought to be limited to parts of the Gaspereau Valley and Kejimkujik National Park. The squirrels have a pair of skin membranes which enable them to glide (rather than fly) up to 35m.

Approximately 100–500 lynx live on Cape Breton Island, the majority in remote areas of the island's northern highlands. Sometimes mistaken for a bobcat, the lynx has larger paws, longer ear tufts and a totally black-tipped tail. Bobcats have stumpy tails, with a dark tip on top. Their hind legs are noticeably longer than the forelegs, and their coats tend to be more patterned than the lynx.

MYSTERY CAT

Although (supposedly) hunted to extinction in the province over a century ago, no-one is too sure whether cougars (known elsewhere in North America as mountain lions) exist in Nova Scotia. There are about 100 reported sightings a year (one man alone has claimed five separate sightings between 1991 and 2009), but as yet no physical proof. In 2016, the Resource Conservation Manager at Kejimkujik National Park decided to use his resources for other things after a fruitless ten-year search for hard evidence of cougar presence in the park. The Department of Natural Resources sits on the fence: apparently the animal has been included on the Department's 'protected' list 'just in case'.

Having survived the days when their pelts were the mainstay of Nova Scotia's economy, the beaver is common throughout the province, and is Nova Scotia's largest rodent. It is known for its habit of building dams (and dome-shaped lodges) on streams to form ponds.

There are not thought to be any wolves in Nova Scotia, and the first reports of coyotes in the province date from the late 1970s. Now they are a common feature of the environment. In recent years, there have been a handful of high-profile interactions between coyotes and humans, culminating in a tragedy on Cape Breton Island in October 2009 when two coyotes attacked and killed a 19-year-old lone female hiker. That was only North America's second reported fatal coyote attack on a human (the other victim was a three-year-old in California in 1981).

The type of coyote (*Canis latrans var.*) found in the region is said to be more of a coyote/wolf hybrid, and is approximately 20% larger and heavier than its counterpart in western Canada. Male coyotes in Nova Scotia average 15kg but can weigh over 20kg. They generally eat deer, squirrels, rabbits, hares and fruit, and are excellent scavengers. The coyote population in Nova Scotia is estimated to be around 8,000. In 2010, the provincial government introduced a five-year CAN$20 per pelt bounty to encourage hunters to 'harvest' coyotes during the hunting season.

In the unlikely event that you encounter a coyote at close range, official advice includes 'don't try to feed or photograph the coyote(s)' and 'remain calm and remove yourself from the area by backing away slowly – do not turn and run'.

With the possible exception of the black bear, the land mammal that most visitors want to see is the largest member of the deer family, the moose. Dark brown and awkward-looking, moose have humped shoulders, spindly legs, a drooping muzzle, and a bell – a flap of skin hanging from the throat. An adult male (bull) moose stands approximately 2m tall at the shoulder and weighs around 500kg. In spring, bulls grow (often huge) antlers that are shed late in winter. Moose can be dangerous if approached too closely, especially during mating season (September–October) or calving season (late May–early June). There are two moose sub-species in the province: the mainland moose and the Cape Breton moose. Approximately 5,000 moose live on Cape Breton Island, which offers the highest chance of a sighting, whereas fewer than 1,000 individuals are thought to survive in isolated areas of the mainland.

The black bear is usually (but not necessarily) black, and is the only type of bear found in Nova Scotia. Though widespread, it is not often seen by visitors. Although not true hibernators, bears tend to stay in their dens from mid November to early spring. During this period, their metabolism slows and they are unconscious but will wake and respond to danger. Adult males stand at about 1m high at the shoulder and can weigh 200kg. They are said to be nocturnal, but I have seen black bears crossing backroads and walking along the edge of woodland in the middle of the day. Whilst undoubtedly dangerous, there have been no records of anyone even being scratched by a bear in Nova Scotia. Don't be the first, though – be aware.

Finally, the only wild horses to be found in Nova Scotia are Sable Island horses (see box, page 399, for further information).

Reptiles and amphibians
Nova Scotia has no poisonous snakes: the largest (rarely over 1m in length) and most widespread is the maritime garter snake.

Seven species of turtle can be found off Nova Scotia's shores at different periods of the year. During summer, there are sightings of the Atlantic leatherback, Ridley and loggerhead turtles.

Four species of (harmless) salamander live in the province, the rarest of which is the four-toed salamander, which is orange to reddish brown with black spots and is the only white-bellied salamander. In addition, there's just one type of toad (the eastern American) and seven frog species – the largest of which is the bullfrog.

Birds *with Joan Czapalay and the late Blake Maybank (author of* Birding Sites of Nova Scotia)

Nova Scotia is a superb birdwatching (we call it '*birding*') destination. Despite being the second-smallest province in Canada, it boasts the country's third-highest bird species' total; only British Columbia and Ontario, Canada's largest provinces, have more.

While there are no species endemic to Nova Scotia, the province is a reliable and logistically friendly base to seek out certain sought-after birds, including boreal forest specialities (spruce grouse, boreal chickadee, black-backed woodpecker and white-winged crossbill), winter birds from the high arctic (dovekie and black-headed gull), seabirds (Manx shearwater and great skua), and regional specialities (Bicknell's thrush, which breeds in the Cape Breton Highlands, and the Ipswich race of savannah sparrow, which breeds only on Sable Island).

The province is well situated in all seasons. The surrounding ocean moderates the climate, and the cooler summers mean that northern species can breed – among the 150-plus breeding species are 22 warblers, nine flycatchers and 20 sparrows and finches. The ocean also moderates the winter, with nearly 200 species sighted each year between December and February (see *tinyurl.com/nswinter*). And because Nova Scotia lies at the eastern end of the continent, halfway between the Pole and the Equator, many waifs and rarities have visited, comprising more than 35% of the province's impressive total of 486 species plus several subspecies (as stated in McLaren, I *All the Birds of Nova Scotia* Gaspereau Press, 2012). A notable subspecies, the Ipswich sparrow breeds only on Sable Island, but is frequently found during migration on coastal beaches.

Visitors are also drawn to the province's birding spectacles. From June to October the Bay of Fundy offers superb whale watching, and the abundant food that attracts the whales also lures large numbers of seabirds, making Nova Scotia the most affordable and reliable spot in eastern North America to see thousands of shearwaters (great, sooty and Manx), storm petrels (both Wilson's and Leach's) and phalaropes (red and red-necked), as well as numerous puffins, razorbills, fulmar, jaegers and, occasionally, south polar skuas.

Nova Scotia has its own seabird colonies. Atlantic puffins, razorbills and black-legged kittiwakes reign over the Bird Islands in Cape Breton, accessible by daily guided boat tour, and Canada's largest roseate tern colony lies on The Brothers Islands, off the village of Lower West Pubnico in Yarmouth County. Another great avian display is the southward migration of arctic-nesting shorebirds. Millions of sandpipers refuel in the rich Bay of Fundy mudflats exposed by the world's highest tides. The largest flocks, primarily semipalmated sandpipers and sometimes in excess of half a million birds, typically occur in the second and third weeks of August. Along the Atlantic coast shorebird flocks are smaller, but contain more species.

Winter offers its own spectacle, when nearly 1,000 bald eagles descend on the Annapolis Valley (page 38).

The search for bird species and spectacles occurs against a backdrop of uncommon beauty – visiting birdwatchers, especially those from Europe or the urban United States, enjoy the absence of crowds, and the freedom to wander almost anywhere the urge takes them. The joy of watching shorebirds on a nearly deserted pristine beach, or listening to warblers sing along well-maintained and secure trails, is an experience rare or absent in much of the world.

During the breeding season the best sites are in the interior, where the diversity of breeding birds is the greatest. The two national parks, Kejimkujik (pages 223–7) in the south and Cape Breton Highlands (pages 331–3) in the north, and Cape Chignecto Provincial Park (the largest of the provincial parks; see pages 277–9) are all rewarding, with extensive trail systems, visitor facilities, and informed staff. Elsewhere there are dozens of smaller provincial and regional parks, trails, and freshwater marshes. Try, for example, the Uniacke Estate (page 125), Annapolis Royal's French Basin Trail (page 222), Amherst Point (pages 288–9), the Fairmont Ridge Trail (page 311) and the Musquodoboit Trailway (page 380). For spring and autumn land bird migration the best sites are the Canso Peninsula (pages 391–4), Hartlen Point (page 132), Cape Sable Island (pages 188–9) and Long and Brier islands (pages 211–14).

Autumn shorebirds are best viewed at Cherry Hill Beach (page 173), Cape Sable Island (pages 188–9) and inner Cole Harbour (page 377). The finest autumn hawk-watching site is on Brier Island (pages 212–14).

Winter birding (see *tinyurl.com/nswinter*) is primarily a coastal experience, with popular areas including Halifax Harbour (pages 83–4) and the Eastern Shore, Pictou Harbour (page 298), Cape Sable Island, Canso Harbour (pages 391–2), Brier Island, and Sydney Harbour (page 355).

If you want to go birding with a guide, consider going out with a local birdwatcher: several are usually listed on birdingpal.org, or contact the Nova Scotia Bird Society (*www.nsbirdsociety.ca*).

MARINE WILDLIFE

Whales Whilst man has been instrumental in wiping out over 90% of the world's whale population in the last couple of centuries, the good news is that Nova Scotia is one of the best places in the world to go whale watching, both in terms of quantity, and variety – 21 whale species cruise the province's coastal waters. Baleen whales (such as minke, humpback, fin and the critically endangered north Atlantic right whales) are drawn by huge amounts of plankton, krill and schools of small fish, particularly where the cold outflow of the Bay of Fundy meets the warm Gulf Stream waters. Toothed whales (such as pilot, killer (orca) and sperm whales) tend to eat fish and squid and are common in the Gulf of St Lawrence and Cabot Strait. Although it varies from species to species, whale numbers tend to be highest from late July to mid September.

For many visitors, a tour on a whale-watching boat is a must-do (and highlight) of a summer or early autumn visit to Nova Scotia. Seeing a huge humpback whale breaching at close quarters or watching a huge fluked tail disappear into the sea are memories that will last a lifetime. On many tours, porpoises, dolphins, seals and pelagic seabirds join in the action and are added bonuses.

Although trips are offered from various places in the province, two areas stand out. One is northern Cape Breton Island, but, for me, the best whale-watching trips depart from Westport (page 212) on Brier Island, and Freeport and Tiverton (pages 211–12) on adjacent Long Island. Boat trips apart, it is not unusual to spot whales from the land, especially in the areas just mentioned.

Seals Two seal species are commonly found in the coastal waters of Nova Scotia: harbour, and grey seals. Harp and hooded seals are far rarer here. Don't be surprised to see a harbour seal pop its head out of the water in Halifax Harbour; otherwise good places to see seals include Kejimkujik Seaside (page 178), Brier Island (pages 212–14), northeast Cape Breton Island (page 333), and Sable Island (page 399) – home to the world's largest breeding colony of grey seals. Most maritime fishermen blame seals for decimating fish stocks in the region.

Fish, shellfish and molluscs For centuries, incredible quantities of fish – particularly cod – drew fishermen from near and far to the region's waters. As recently as the last few decades, cod numbers have dropped alarmingly, largely because of overfishing. Dozens of other species live in the province's coastal waters, streams, rivers and lakes: these include Atlantic salmon, mackerel, pollock, haddock, flounder, hake, herring, monkfish, perch, pickerel, trout and eel. Bluefin tuna, porbeagle and blue shark are popular targets for deep-sea sport-fishing.

Despite the (near) death of groundfishing, shellfish and molluscs – particularly lobster, scallop, shrimp, clam and crab – are now the focus of the fishermen's attention, and grace many a table in the province's eateries.

NATIONAL PARKS Nova Scotia boasts three of Canada's 47 national parks and national park reserves: Kejimkujik National Park & National Historic Site, Cape Breton Highlands National Park, and Sable Island National Park Reserve. As part of the federal 2016 budget, to celebrate Canada's 150th birthday, the Canadian government announced free admission to all of the country's national parks and national historic sites for 2017. Admission will be charged again from 2018, but rates have not yet been set so the 2016 charge has been shown for information purposes.

Kejimkujik National Park & National Historic Site (pages 223–7) 'Keji' – as it is more commonly known – is accessed by Highway 8, which connects Liverpool and Annapolis Royal. The largest inland national park in Atlantic Canada draws lovers of the outdoors for hiking, lake swimming, mountain biking, canoeing and kayaking. The park has another section (Kejimkujik Seaside; page 178), approximately 100km away on the coast.

Cape Breton Highlands National Park (pages 331–8) Completely different in character from Keji, this national park is situated in northern Cape Breton Island. Boasting magnificent coastal and mountain scenery and superb hiking, it is accessed by a dramatic scenic drive, the Cabot Trail.

Sable Island National Park Reserve (pages 398–401) Those lucky enough to get to one of Canada's newest national parks, a narrow, windswept crescent and one of Canada's furthest offshore islands, will be rewarded with shifting sand dunes, seals and wild horses.

UNESCO SITES AND RESERVES Three of Canada's 18 UNESCO World Heritage sites are found in the province: Old Town Lunenburg (pages 156–66), Grand Pré (pages 244–6), and the Joggins Fossil Cliffs (pages 279–80). Nova Scotia is also home to two **UNESCO Biosphere Reserves**: such reserves are described as 'sites established … to promote sustainable development based on local community efforts and sound science'. One – the **Southwest Nova Biosphere Reserve** (*swnovabiosphere.ca*) – encompasses (as you might have guessed) most of the province's southwest, and occupies over 1.5 million hectares. The other is Cape Breton Island's **Bras d'Or Lake**

Biosphere Reserve (*blbra.ca*), which includes the Bras d'Or Lake and its watershed, encompassing approximately 360,000ha.

A vast area in the southwest of the province has been labelled 'Acadian Skies & Mi'kmaq Lands' (*www.acadianskies.com*) and as 'a site where a commitment to defend the night sky quality and the access to starlight has been established' was designated North America's first '**Starlight Reserve & Destination**' in 2014. Though sometimes marketed as a 'UNESCO Starlight Reserve', UNESCO doesn't actually dish out labels for the sky.

PROVINCIAL PARKS Nova Scotia also has almost 130 provincial parks (*parks. novascotia.ca*) administered by the Parks and Recreation section of the Department of Natural Resources. These vary from parks with a few picnic tables and interpretive panels, to magnificent stretches of coastal scenery peppered with hiking trails.

The majority of provincial parks are day-use only and are open between mid May and mid October: about 20 others have campgrounds – reservations can be made online or by phone (**tf** *1 888 544 3434*) – and generally shorter seasons. Sadly, some are only open between late June and the beginning of September. When parks are closed for the season, barriers prevent vehicular entry: grounds, trails and roads are not maintained and no services are provided (water is turned off and toilets locked). However, it is almost always possible to park outside and enter the parks on foot – but be aware that you do so at your own risk.

Admission is charged at just one of the parks: Shubenacadie Wildlife Park (page 260). For wonderful coastal hiking, try for example Cape Chignecto (pages 277–9), Blomidon (pages 237–9) or Taylor Head (page 385): beach fans will enjoy Rissers Beach (page 173), Summerville (pages 177–8), Thomas Raddall (page 179), Mavillette Beach (page 200), the beach parks of the Northumberland Shore (pages 282–313), and Martinique Beach (page 381). Look for moose in the park at Cape Smokey (page 338).

CONSERVATION AND ENVIRONMENTAL ISSUES

Nova Scotia has a strong and enduring tradition of environmental activism. With its forests, lakes, and compelling intricate coastline of peninsulas, coves and harbours comes a history of human habitation that goes back more than 10,000 years. The various settler groups (from the Mi'kmaq, through the 17th- and 18th-century French and English colonisers, to 'recent' immigrants from around the world) have found their livelihood in the natural abundance of the region. Forestry, hunting, fishing and trapping have provided shelter and food and a basis for trade and commerce that endure, to varying degrees, to this day.

The population grew and technological advances provided the means of sourcing, harvesting and exploiting the natural resources, but awareness of the systematic degradation of the environment and its natural species didn't really start surfacing until the 1970s. City sewage was being pumped into the harbours of Halifax and Sydney. The aggressive harvesting and destruction of the once vast cod fish populations; the clear-cutting of forests to produce pulp and paper; the accumulation of noxious by-products of steel manufacturing residue in Sydney's tar ponds (page 354) are all examples of short term economic gains at the expense of the environment and future generations.

In recent decades, Nova Scotians have increasingly come together in alliances and coalitions to fight for the protection of their environment and the reversal of environmentally damaging practices. The province has a waste diversion rate higher than any industrialised nation and has many other emerging success stories.

After a CAN$400 million clean-up, which has taken years of fighting and false starts to get off the ground – and around six years to execute – the tar ponds of Sydney (page 354) are now covered by a 32ha green belt. Three fully operational water treatment plants have improved the water quality in the once polluted Halifax Harbour, to the extent that some city beaches have reopened for swimming. Provincial law now requires that 40% of electricity sold by the monopoly provider, Nova Scotia Power, be generated from renewable resources by 2020. This is one of the most ambitious targets in North America and, with its abundant wind, tidal, biomass (and even solar resources), the target is achievable. However, some environmental advocates are concerned that to meet this target the government will include large-scale forest biomass. After years of overcutting to feed the (now failed) paper pulp mills, the controversy regarding clear-cutting, how it is defined, and how forest harvesting will be managed and monitored, will continue to cause tension between politicians and environmentalists. Finally in 2016, the contentious 'must-run' designation of the Nova Scotia Power Biomass plant was changed to a run on an 'as-needed' basis.

There are now six wind farms operating in evidence across the province. An additional potential source of renewable energy is the power generated by the Bay of Fundy tides (pages 259 and 260), and June 2016 saw the long-anticipated installation of the first of the immense turbines (box, page 24). Environmentalists in Nova Scotia are constantly monitoring the impacts of tidal energy on the marine ecosystems and livelihoods that rely on these systems. The switch to renewables, energy-efficiency programs and the closure of at least one pulp mill has reduced demand for electricity, and Nova Scotia has reduced its reliance on coal by 20%. However, the Donkin Coal Mine (near Glace Bay; pages 361–2) in Cape Breton Island is slated to reopen as a viable source of coal for the province.

Nova Scotia is now in third place in Canada for the total percentage of land protected (12.26%). A deep decline in the global pulp and paper market has led to the closure of some of the largest paper mills in the province. In the case of one of the mills, this will trigger the sale of vast tracts of forest – known as the Bowater-Mersey lands – throughout Nova Scotia. The sale of the Bowater-Mersey to the province in 2015 added 555,000 acres of Crown Land to Nova Scotia.

Active campaigns are running in a co-ordinated effort by a coalition of citizens' groups, residents' associations, environmentalists and historians to reclaim still more of these lands from private ownership, to be 'returned to the people of Nova Scotia' for sustainable commercial and recreational use and for the preservation of historical sites, with hopes that some of the land will be added to the other protected areas (see page 13). If this campaign succeeds, Nova Scotia will become an even more highly accessible wilderness tourism destination, with a range of back-country experiences awaiting the fishing, canoeing, hiking and camping tourists of tomorrow.

Over the past several decades, the province has seen an increase in reliance on imported foods and consequently its food transport carbon footprint. To try to counter this, the environmental movement is actively engaged in protecting farmlands from development (300ha have been protected through working land conservation easements) and there are campaigns supporting organic farming and sustainable fishing practices, and experimentation with urban agriculture projects. There is growing public interest in home-grown foods, composting and community gardening, with environmentalists engaging schools and communities to build awareness and competence. The province now has more than 40 farmers' markets.

When travelling along the coastline, you may see open net-fish-farming pens. Fish farms grow and produce Atlantic salmon by the hundreds of thousands. Once cod and haddock were the staple fish on offer in Nova Scotia's supermarkets, with salmon a premium-priced rarity, but nowadays the salmon price has shot down (it is still relatively high when compared to, say, the UK) and is far from rare.

However, the expansion of open-pen finfish aquaculture has generated a great deal of environmental and political heat. Opponents of these fish farms say that they cause destruction of the ocean habitat underneath pens. The use of antibiotics and pesticides is known to cause the proliferation of viruses and parasites. Health Canada and the Canadian Food Inspection Agency announced in 2016 the approval for sale of genetically modified salmon (without appropriate GM labelling) in Canada. Two court challenges against the fish have been launched in Nova Scotia against this commercial production.

There is now one land closed-containment fish farm in the province that now is bringing organic salmon to market.

Environmental groups have advocated for a moratorium on the expansion of what they call 'feed-lots' until comprehensive environmental impact studies can be conducted and concluded. There is evidence of a profoundly negative impact on wild Atlantic salmon stock through sea lice contamination and cross-breeding with the thousands of regular escapees from the open net pens, as well as what appears to be a negative impact on lobsters. Yet, in the short term, the establishment of fish farms, packing plants and transportation of processed salmon provides jobs in communities where unemployment is rife (and from which young people are moving away in a search for work). So the battle will continue between government, private investors and community groups for some time to come.

In 2014, Bill 6 placed a moratorium on high-volume hydraulic fracking in Nova Scotia until the government could develop regulations and an onshore atlas of available natural gas resources. No regulations have yet been forthcoming, nor has an atlas has been created.

Other ongoing environmental campaigns include the removal of lawn pesticides from the shelves of local stores. Green construction and renovation methods are on the increase. And though this is no Holland, there has been an increase in the number of cycle lanes; in 2010 the province introduced a 'one-metre rule' compelling drivers to give cyclists they were passing a wider berth.

The province's major environmental group is the **Ecology Action Centre** (*2705 Fern Lane, Halifax;* ☏ *902 429 2202; www.ecologyaction.ca*), established in 1971 and now with more than 4,000 members, 1,500 volunteers and staff, and seven active teams and committees.

PROTECTED LAND
Approximately 30% of land in Nova Scotia is Crown (or public) land. The province has close to 40 'Protected Areas' (the largest of which being the Tobeatic Wilderness Area, known as the 'Toby'; box, pages 186–7), more than 20 nature reserves and two heritage rivers (the Margaree and the Shelburne).

Mining, forestry and the like are prohibited in Protected Areas (except where pre-existing commitments were made), which is all well and good. There are, however, many other areas of public land which concerned citizens believe should be protected from such things as industrial forestry and exploitative mining. In Nova Scotia, game sanctuaries don't protect habitat; they only curtail certain types of hunting activities. By contrast, protected wilderness areas protect habitat and prevent forest harvesting, mining, road building, and other types of development.

HISTORY

Note: Nova Scotia was not thus named until 1621, and was not declared a province until 1867. Nevertheless, I have used this designation for history before those dates to save repetition of the phrase 'what is now called'. Similarly, current place names have been used to describe events in areas that were at the time unnamed or known by a different name.

THE FIRST INHABITANTS The earliest evidence of human habitation found in Nova Scotia was discovered in 1948 at Debert, near Truro. Thousands of Paleo-Indian artefacts were later unearthed, and some were radiocarbon-dated to 8,600BC. Paleo-Indians are believed to have crossed to the North American continent from Siberia. Over the years, as temperatures in the region waxed and waned, the inhabitants of the area are likely to have retreated south, returning perhaps a few centuries later: this cycle was probably repeated a few times. The native people living in Nova Scotia were the Mi'kmaq, members of the Algonquian-speaking Abenaki Confederacy.

EARLY VISITORS? There is much speculation – and the occasional shred of evidence – to suggest that various outsiders visited Nova Scotia well before French settlement.

Irish-born St Brendan the Navigator may have stopped by early in the 6th century. Vikings almost certainly visited nearby Newfoundland very early in the 11th century, and there have been several claims that Iceland-born Leif Ericsson stopped at several places on Nova Scotia's southwest coast in 1007.

Some say Prince Henry Sinclair from Scotland landed in 1398, and the Venetian Zeno brothers may have visited soon after. One man claimed to have found ruins of a 15th-century Chinese settlement on Cape Breton Island.

Basque fishermen are certain to have made landfall in Nova Scotia during whaling and cod-fishing trips in the province's waters, possibly as early as the 15th century.

NEW SCOTLAND

Sir William Alexander, a member of the court of King James I, proposed establishing a New Scotland in North America and put his idea to HRH in 1621. In a generous mood, the king granted Sir William most of the northeast American continent. The land was to be named 'Nova Scotia' and in return, Sir William had to pay 'one penny of Scottish money'.

After failed attempts to get shiploads of immigrants to his land in both 1622 and 1623, he came up with another scheme. In 1624, Sir William persuaded the king to create 150 Baronets of the Kingdom of New Scotland: in return for a substantial amount of money, those so honoured would receive a land grant in the new kingdom, a knighthood, and several other privileges. Barons did not even have to cross the Atlantic to receive their titles – a small patch of Edinburgh Castle's parade ground was declared to be part of Nova Scotia and set aside for the purpose (to this day a little bit of Nova Scotia lies under Edinburgh Castle's Esplanade). Finally, in 1628, he sent his (Baronet) son in command of four vessels to Port-Royal, but soon after, King Charles, who had succeeded James, instructed Sir William to demolish all New Scotland's buildings and remove all his people from it. Sir William complied, but never received the £10,000 compensation promised. He died bankrupt in 1640.

THE MI'KMAQ

Pre-colonisation, Mi'kmaq territory included all of Nova Scotia and Prince Edward Island, and parts of Quebec, New Brunswick and Maine. The Mi'kmaq practised a religion based on Mother Nature, deeply tied to the land. Mythology also played an important part in spiritual life. They lived in conical birch-bark wigwams; birch bark was also used to make canoes in which to travel the waterways. The Mi'kmaq were also at home on the sea, travelling in ocean-going versions of their light canoes.

For centuries, they lived along the shoreline in summer, fishing, gathering shellfish, and hunting seals and whales. In the winter, most moved inland, setting up settlements in sheltered forested areas. Moose, bear, caribou, and smaller game provided food and clothing, supplemented by wild berries: plants and herbs were used for teas and medicinal purposes.

They respected their environment and only killed, took or used what they needed. When Europeans first settled Nova Scotia, the natural resources were virtually untouched. They befriended the first French settlers, acting as guides, teaching them to live off the land and showing them how to make fish-weirs and eel-traps, how to ice-fish, which wild berries were safe to eat and how to prepare them, how to cure and prevent scurvy, and more.

The Mi'kmaq began to convert to Christianity in 1610, and their way of life underwent other major changes as they abandoned many traditional customs and focused on gathering furs and hides for trade purposes. The French gave them weapons, and both French and English passed on diseases such as smallpox which killed hundreds – if not thousands. Distrustful and fearful, the English and New Englanders saw the Mi'kmaq not as allies but hostile savages, and decided that forceful subjugation and assimilation would be the best course of action. In 1744, British Governor William Shirley of the Massachusetts Bay colony, responding to a request from Nova Scotia's Governor, Jean Paul Mascarene, declared war upon the Mi'kmaq and Maliseet Nations, in which he offered a bounty for the scalps of Mi'kmaq and Maliseet men, women and children, and, in 1749, Governor Cornwallis put a bounty on the head (or scalp) of every Mi'kmaq, man, woman or child. The amount of the bounty was increased the following year.

Although a proclamation by King George III in 1763 promised protection for the Mi'kmaq and their hunting grounds, they suffered a similar fate to that of First Nations people and Native Americans across the continent. Often caught between the French and the English/British power struggle for North America, they were robbed of their land, persecuted, forced to live with virtually no rights, and herded onto reserves. For decades, the federal government actively suppressed Mi'kmaq traditions. For example, in 1885, religious ceremonies were prohibited. In 1927, Canadian government legislation forbade aboriginals in Canada from forming political organisations, as well as practising their traditional culture and language.

In the 19th century, the Mi'kmaq were confined to about 60 locations, both on and off reserves, dotted about the province. In the 1940s, the Canadians implemented a Centralisation Policy, which mandated that they be moved against their will to just two reserves. Young Mi'kmaq children were taken away from their families and taught the 'white-man's ways', to integrate them into mainstream society – and rapidly lose the culture and heritage of their ancient way of life.

See also box, page 26.

In 1497, John Cabot crossed the Atlantic from England. None of Cabot's own records has survived, but a map drawn 45 years later by his son suggests that Cabot landed at northern Cape Breton Island.

In the early 1520s, the Portuguese probably had a seasonal fishing colony at the site of present-day Ingonish.

THE FRENCH AND ENGLISH In 1603, the French were looking to plant Gallic seeds in the New World. French nobleman Pierre du Gua, Sieur de Mons (sometimes written as 'de Monts'), was awarded a monopoly to trade fur across a vast swathe of North America on the condition that he would establish a colony there. In 1604, he and Samuel de Champlain established the first permanent European settlement north of St Augustine, Florida, at Port-Royal (page 217). They were befriended by Mi'kmaq in the area. The French named the entire region 'Acadie', anglicised as Acadia.

At roughly the same time, England began to colonise some of the eastern parts of the United States of America. For more than 150 years the English and these settlers were allies: English ships under Samuel Argall from Virginia destroyed the Port-Royal settlement in 1614. A 1632 treaty returned Acadia to the French who made another attempt to colonise, establishing a settlement on the LaHave River (page 167), and re-establishing Port-Royal close to its original site. As French presence in – and colonisation of – Acadia grew slowly, one man in particular, **Nicolas Denys** (box, page 349) was instrumental in establishing settlements both on mainland Nova Scotia and on Cape Breton Island.

Treaties between the English and French continued to pass Nova Scotia back and forth, and in the late 1680s, the French in Quebec attacked New England. This prompted the New Englanders to attack the Acadians, who were far more interested in farming than fighting. Each time the French attacked New England from Quebec or New Brunswick, the New Englanders ransacked a few more Acadian villages in misguided revenge. The Treaty of Utrecht in 1713 gave most of Acadia to the British, but left Cape Breton Island in French hands. Nova Scotia became an official colony, and Annapolis Royal its capital.

LOUISBOURG AND HALIFAX The French decided that they had to build a mighty fort on Cape Breton Island, to protect their fishing interests and help guard Quebec from prospective attacks by the British navy. The chosen site was Louisbourg, named for Louis XV.

War broke out again in 1744, and the French attacked Canso. Effectively, they now controlled the region's highly lucrative fishing industry. This was not good for the New Englanders who attacked and took the fortress of Louisbourg in 1745: in 1748, a treaty returned it and Cape Breton Island to the French.

Halifax was founded by **General Edward Cornwallis** in 1749, partly as a secure base from which the British could attack the French. It was declared Nova Scotia's capital. Attempts to increase the population went into overdrive: land, rations, equipment, support and military protection were all promised to those prepared to start a new life in Nova Scotia.

Beyond Halifax Shiploads of new immigrants began to arrive in Halifax, the vast majority foreign Protestants predominantly from German-speaking parts of modern-day France, Switzerland and Germany.

When they reached Halifax, they found that land grants were far smaller than had been advertised, rations and supplies were meagre, and wages were set so low that paying off passages would take a lifetime. The British kept them quiet and created another base by shipping many of the German-speakers to Lunenburg.

Oaths of allegiance In general, the Acadians had tried to get on with their lives (whether the land was called Acadia or Nova Scotia), building dykes in order to reclaim the marshlands and wetlands around tidal river estuaries, and farming the fertile results. They planted orchards and the odd vineyard. However, they spoke French, were friendly with the Mi'kmaq – with whom the French were still closely allied – and were not trusted by the British.

Governor Cornwallis had demanded an oath of allegiance from them, but terms were not agreed. When Charles Lawrence became lieutenant-governor in 1753, approximately 10,000 Acadians lived in Nova Scotia. In 1755, they were asked to sign another oath of allegiance to the British, this one even stronger, stating that in the case of war, the Acadians could be told to fight with the British against the French. Again, they refused to sign.

LE GRAND DERANGEMENT – THE GREAT UPHEAVAL On 28 July 1755, Lawrence and the rest of the governing council in Halifax called for the deportation of 'French inhabitants'. Orders were sent to the major British forts, and the operation began in mid August. The Acadians were to be sent off on ships and could take with them only what they could carry: land and livestock would become the property of the Crown.

Almost 3,000 Acadians were deported from one area alone – Grand Pré – and in all around 10,000 were herded onto ships and banished to colonies along the eastern American seaboard, to French colonies in the Caribbean, some even to Europe. In many cases, families became separated in the huge operation. Troops burned all the Acadians' buildings so that they would have nothing to return to.

Some Acadians adapted to their new lives. Some drifted south and reached Louisiana, then under French control. Many others never lost their attachment to their former homeland, and survived from day to day, hoping for an opportunity to return from Expulsion. Another British–French war started in 1756, and the supposedly invincible French fortress at Louisbourg fell again in 1758.

FILLING THE VACUUM The flow of immigrants increased significantly with the signing of the Treaty of Paris in 1763, after which the French were no longer seen as a threat in Nova Scotia.

The Planters In its efforts to re-populate Nova Scotia – and increase and improve the food supply – the government attempted to attract New Englanders with free grants of rich farmland (stolen from the Acadians) and other benefits. The first such land grants were in two dykeland areas near modern-day Wolfville and the first Planters – as these immigrants were called – arrived from Connecticut, Rhode Island and Massachusetts in 1760.

Returning Acadians From 1763, the British allowed exiled Acadians to return to Nova Scotia. Unable to pay for passage by sea, hundreds returned on foot to find that their old lands had been given away to other immigrants. They walked on and settled eventually in less desirable areas with poor-quality soil, such as the Bay of Fundy coast between Yarmouth and Digby, part of which is still known as the French Shore. Many former farmers turned to fishing.

The Scots After the Battle of Culloden in 1746, the British authorities began to stamp out all aspects of Scottish Highland culture. Those that could afford to do so moved away, and many headed for the New World. The major influx to Nova Scotia began in 1763 when the *Hector* sailed into Pictou.

Back home, the Highland Clearances forced tens of thousands off the land they had long called home: many followed in the wake of the *Hector* and headed for Pictou. On arrival, they dispersed along the Northumberland Strait shore (by 1830 there were around 50,000 Scots in Pictou and Antigonish counties) and on to Cape Breton Island, which became part of Nova Scotia in 1820.

The Irish By 1760, the Irish (mostly Catholics) made up about 20–25% of the population of Halifax. This was thanks in large part to Alexander McNutt – born in Londonderry, Northern Ireland – who emigrated to America in the early 1750s, and was stationed in Nova Scotia whilst in the army. Simply by applying to the governor, he received generous (free) land grants on both sides of the Minas Basin, and on the South Shore. He dreamt of turning Nova Scotia into 'New Ireland' and invited primarily Presbyterians from the country of his birth to come over and buy their own plot of land from him. Almost 300 arrived in Halifax from Londonderry in 1761, and another 150 or so followed. The Irish Privy Council didn't want a mass exodus of its citizens and stopped McNutt from emptying (old) Ireland. (Incidentally, McNutt then turned his attention to building a New Jerusalem on the South Shore – but that's another story.)

Economic conditions were not good in Ireland even before the devastation resulting from failed potato crops in the 1840s. North America offered hope, possibilities, dreams, and (sometimes) work. A fair share of the hundreds of thousands of Irish who emigrated across the Atlantic in the 19th century made Nova Scotia their new home.

Loyalists When the American Revolution started in 1775, a good chunk of the population of the colonies preferred to remain loyal to the British Crown, but understandably were far from popular in the United States. From 1783, tens of thousands of 'Loyalists' emigrated, with around 20,000 going to Nova Scotia. Some 10,000 went to Shelburne, instantly creating (what was then) North America's fourth-largest city.

Comparatively wealthy – even aristocratic – and well educated, many Loyalists were not best suited to pioneer life and moved on to pastures new. The remainder persevered and, in general, adapted well to Nova Scotia.

SHIPBUILDING – THEN

With Halifax beginning to grow, Governor Cornwallis (see page 15) introduced a bounty for every new vessel built. Vessels were needed for trade, transport, and – in times of war – as privateers (box, page 19).

Between 1800 and 1875, thousands of vessels were built in hundreds of shipyards all around the province. Nova Scotia had safe harbours and river mouths, plentiful timber and sawmills, and some of the world's best ship designers, craftsmen and shipwrights. However, from the late 1870s onward the demand for wooden ships began to slow down, not helped by the use of the new railways and the increasing use of steel in shipbuilding. The Golden Age of Sail was over.

Over the years, nature, time and recycling of building materials have removed most traces of those shipyards.

PRIVATEERS – OR PIRATES?

War, particularly sea battles, dominated much of Nova Scotia's early history, with almost constant conflict between the colony's 'Anglo' settlers and either (sometimes both) the French and the Americans.

Privateers – privately owned vessels which would attack the enemy's merchant ships, allowing the navies to concentrate on fighting each other – took to the seas. This form of 'legalised piracy', which reached a peak between 1760 and 1815, had strict rules: captains (usually backed by private investors) had to register full details of their vessel and its owners, and a bond was payable. The captain would then receive a *letter of marque*, an official licence to set out to harass the enemy, and capture every enemy vessel ('prize') he could. Privateers often strayed far from Nova Scotia's coastal waters, hunting American ships along the eastern seaboard and seeking out French vessels trading in the Caribbean.

When a prize was captured, it and at least one member of its crew would be taken to naval officials. Nova Scotia's privateers were required to take prizes to Halifax's Privateers Wharf where they would be inspected. Legally captured prizes – no enemy men were to be killed in cold blood or inhumanely treated, and the prize had to be an enemy, rather than a neutral, ship – were sold at auction and the money was split between (in descending order) the authorities, the privateer's owners, the captain and his officers, and perhaps a few coins for the rest of the crew. The highest bidders were privateer investors who bought the captured ships to put back to use in their own privateer fleets. Consequently, some vessels changed sides frequently.

Privateers didn't restrict themselves to the sea when seeking bounty, often putting in to feebly defended ports and harbours where armed raiders would rush ashore and strip the settlement of anything of value. Louisbourg was a haven for French privateers, but the Nova Scotia port most associated with privateers was Liverpool.

At an auction in 1811, Liverpool-born Enos Collins purchased a captured slave-smuggling schooner, to convert and use as a privateer vessel: he named her the *Liverpool Packet*, and put her under the command of Joseph Barss. The *Liverpool Packet* wreaked havoc on American shipping between 1812 and 1814 and by the end of the conflict had taken over 50 prizes. When he died in 1871, Collins, who had been a shrewd banker, merchant and investor, was said to be the richest man in Canada. Most of those who invested in privateers, however, made little or no money at all.

Privateering was abolished in 1856 by the Declaration of Paris, but its memory lives on – each July Liverpool celebrates 'Privateer Days'.

Nova Scotia is incredibly rich in pirate folklore and it seems that there is a tale of buried treasure for almost every one of the province's multitude of beaches, coves and islands. Most pirate activity took place between the late 17th and mid 18th centuries, but the vast majority of pirate tales told these days are probably better filed under 'fiction' than 'fact'.

Germans   The first wave of German immigrants arrived in the early 1750s: after the American Revolution, there was a second wave when soldiers in German regiments hired to fight by the British Crown were offered land and provisions to start a new life in Nova Scotia. These men were mostly from Hesse, Brunswick, Anspach-Bayreuth and Waldeck; many settled between Digby and Annapolis Royal.

Black immigration There were three significant tranches of black immigration to Nova Scotia.

When the Loyalists left the United States in the aftermath of the American Revolution, they were joined by their slaves and former slaves who had fought on the Loyalist side in return for their freedom. About 3,000 blacks came to Nova Scotia, many settling at Burchtown (later Birchtown; box, page 184). Some went to Halifax, settling near Dartmouth in Preston – which to this day has a sizeable black population.

In 1796, more than 500 Trelawny Maroons (maroons were runaway slaves and/ or their descendants) were sent to Halifax from Jamaica.

Another wave of black immigration came during the 1812–15 Anglo-American War: American slaves who deserted to the British side were offered the opportunity to serve with the British military service or go as free settlers to a British colony. In this time, approximately 1,500 former slaves settled in Nova Scotia.

It is recorded that in the 1820s, Halifax had at least one black policeman, a Constable Septemus Hawkins.

PEACE AND CONFEDERATION After so much conflict, from 1815 Nova Scotia enjoyed a rare long period of peace. In the 1820s, a British company, the **General Mining Association (GMA)**, won control of mining leases in the colonies – and a monopoly over coal mining in Nova Scotia. It invested large sums of money into the mines and the mining infrastructure.

Having been stung by its American colonies, the British government was reluctant to let colonies have too much power, and did its best to ensure that major decisions were always along the lines of what London (rather than the colonists) might want.

However, during the 1830s and 1840s, **Joseph Howe**, a newspaper owner and politician, led a group of political reformers. Through his efforts, Nova Scotia became the first colony in the British Empire to become self-governing and to achieve responsible government based on parliamentary accountability. Howe later became premier of Nova Scotia from 1860 to 1862.

Nova Scotia had long been only too happy to stand alone politically, but the idea of joining together with neighbouring New Brunswick and Prince Edward Island had begun to sound a lot more attractive. As it turned out, within a few years the Dominion of Canada was created (box, below).

Many people in Nova Scotia were anti-Confederation, but it did bring the province benefits – including a railway connection with the rest of Canada. Steel was first produced commercially in 1883, and many more coal mines were opening, particularly in Pictou and Cumberland counties, and on Cape Breton Island.

THE 20TH CENTURY AND BEYOND The new century brought two tragic events which put Halifax in the news: the aftermath of the sinking of the *Titanic* in 1912 (box, page 92), and 1917's Halifax Explosion (box, page 93). The latter (in particular) left a big grey cloud over the province, and for many years the people's mood remained sombre. Times continued to be hard, and worsened as Nova Scotia suffered its own elongated Great Depression.

One of the few bright lights shining through those gloomy times came in the unlikely form of a fishing vessel, the *Bluenose* (box, page 161). Through a long and difficult period, this racing champion's successes gave the people a reason to be proud, and lifted the spirits of many.

Halifax was a very important port during World War I. In World War II, it was again a crucial part of the Allied war effort as a gathering point for convoys heading across the Atlantic, a 'holding area' for neutral ships, and the departure point for Canadian forces heading out by sea.

The post-war years brought the opening of the **Canso Causeway** (box, page 315) providing a land link between mainland Nova Scotia and Cape Breton Island. In general, though, the economy was in poor shape, and thousands left the province to seek greener grass elsewhere.

In the late 1950s and 1960s, workers left farming and fishing for new jobs in manufacturing and there was a big population shift from rural to urban areas. Coal mining – long a mainstay of the economy – began to die as the cost of obtaining the coal made it uncompetitive compared with oil and gas. Just a few small mines hung on, but most were closed.

Then the fishing industry – a major contributor to Nova Scotia's economy for centuries – hit serious problems. Overfishing had resulted in massive drops in catch sizes, and by the early 1990s, tens of thousands of jobs were lost – not just by those

FATHERS OF CONFEDERATION

In the mid 1860s, conferences were held in Charlottetown (Prince Edward Island), Quebec City and London, England. These gave birth to the British North America Act to which Queen Victoria gave royal assent. The act, which united the Province of Canada with New Brunswick and Nova Scotia to form the Dominion of Canada, came into effect on 1 July 1867: 1 July is still celebrated as Canada Day. The 36 attendees at the historic conferences, six of whom were from Nova Scotia, are known as the Fathers of Confederation.

In 1982, the British Parliament passed the Canada Act which left Canada as part of the Commonwealth, but finally severed all Canada's remaining legislative dependence on the United Kingdom.

As the 19th century progressed, the temperance movement had been gaining strength across North America. Prohibition laws were introduced in Canada in 1878, but individual areas could choose to opt out of the legislation.

When the US government introduced (stricter) Prohibition in 1920, Canadian distillers were permitted to export to non-Prohibition nations, the nearest being the French-owned islands of St Pierre and Miquelon (off the southeast coast of Newfoundland), and vast quantities of alcohol were sent there.

Nova Scotia's coastal waters were the perfect secret sea route between the islands and the east coast of the USA, and many fishing-boat owners adapted their vessels to carry liquid contraband. When the US authorities began to use faster craft, the province's boatbuilders designed more efficient purpose-built vessels in which to evade their pursuers.

Ports such as Mahone Bay, Lunenburg, Liverpool, Yarmouth and Meteghan were home to dozens of 'rum-running' vessels. Rum, in fact, was very rarely part of the cargo but was used as a generic term for the alcoholic drinks that were carried.

Sometimes vessels failed to evade the American or Canadian authorities and the boat's captain would normally be jailed, but – until 1933 when prohibition was repealed in the USA – Nova Scotia's skilled seafarers enjoyed a very profitable, albeit illegal, period.

who fished for cod and flat-fish, but in the processing plants, boatbuilders, and those who serviced them.

Natural gas was discovered off Sable Island in 1968, but at that time, developing costs were prohibitive. However, oil was discovered in the same region and was drilled from 1992 to 1999 – Canada's first offshore oil project. The first gas was finally shipped to market in December 1999 via the Sable Offshore Energy Project, and production is still going.

The consequences of Nova Scotia's economic woes through much of the 20th century haven't all been bad. Outside a few urban areas, there has been precious little development. Forests still cover the majority of the land, and – in the main – the coastline is generally unspoilt. Another positive trend is just beginning as former fishermen are beginning to look at tourism as a way to make use of their boats.

The economy was given (what should turn out to be) a huge economic boost when a Halifax shipyard won a huge naval contract late in 2011 (box, page 25); the mood stayed positive even with the closure of some of the province's largest paper mills a few weeks later.

Much of Canada celebrated the election of Justin Trudeau's Liberals in the 2015 federal elections, but those living in these parts often say that other Canadian provinces (eg: Ontario, British Columbia and Alberta) see benefits long before any filter through to the eastern side of the country.

GOVERNMENT AND POLITICS

A member of the Commonwealth, Canada is a constitutional monarchy, with Queen Elizabeth II the sovereign and head of state. The queen appoints a governor-general to represent her for a five-year term. Canada's federation of ten provinces and three territories operates under a parliamentary democracy in which power is shared between the federal government, based in Ottawa, and the provincial governments.

THE FEDERAL GOVERNMENT The head of government is the prime minister, who is the leader of the majority party or party coalition in the House of Commons.

The Canadian Parliament comprises two houses: the House of Commons, with 338 members (11 from Nova Scotia), is apportioned by provincial population and elected by plurality from the country's districts; the Senate comprises 105 members (eight from Nova Scotia) appointed by the governor-general on the advice of the prime minister. Legislation must be passed by both houses and signed by the governor-general to become law.

The federal government has authority over defence, criminal law, trade, banking, and other affairs of national interest.

PROVINCIAL GOVERNMENT Responsible for civil services, health, education, natural resources and local government, Nova Scotia's Legislative Assembly consists of a one-house legislative body with members elected every four years. Although there is a nominal head of government (the lieutenant-governor, appointed by the Governor-General of Canada), executive power rests with the 52-member Halifax-based Nova Scotia House of Assembly, headed by a premier, the leader of the majority party. At the time of writing, the lieutenant-governor is Brigadier-General The Honourable J J Grant, CMM, ONS, CD (Ret'd).

For many years, the people of Nova Scotia have been ruled by a minority government. In 2009, the Nova Scotia Progressive Conservative Party ('Tories') lost a vote of confidence over financial policy. Elections the following month saw a huge swing to the left, with the New Democratic Party (NDP) sweeping to power. The Tories were reduced to just ten seats. The NDP win ended ten years of Tory rule.

But in the 2013 election, Stephen McNeil and his Liberal Party trounced both the NDP and the Tories. The next elections are scheduled for 2017.

In an effort to reduce bureaucracy, the government did away with incorporated cities in the 1990s forming the Halifax Regional Municipality (HRM) through the amalgamation of the former cities of Halifax and Dartmouth and the town of Bedford and the municipality of Halifax County, and the Cape Breton Regional Municipality (CBRM) by amalgamating the former city of Sydney, six towns and the municipality of the county of Cape Breton. In 2016, there was a 'no' vote by residents when offered the chance to amalgamate the towns of Pictou, Stellarton, New Glasgow and the County of Pictou. But towns seeking dissolution also seems the 'in thing': in recent times, Bridgetown (pages 230–1), Springhill (pages 280–1) and Mulgrave (page 398) have also been among those applying to dissolve.

ECONOMY

Traditionally, Nova Scotia's economy has been based on natural resources. Fishing has been important since the days of pre-European settlement, and the profusion of forest was the basis for a strong lumber industry and shipbuilding. Coal mining took off in the mid 19th century, and flourished for a century – it is said that the province contains more coal fields for its area than any other part of the world. Iron mines were in operation between 1825 and 1920, and the province had a gold rush in the 1860s, though gold mining's best years proved to be from 1885 to 1903.

HIGH TIDES, GREEN ENERGY

The Bay of Fundy tides are the highest in the world, with more than four times the combined flow of all the world's freshwater rivers during the same 6-hour interval. The power of these tides is so great that scientific experts and engineers continue to work on turbine designs to successfully harness it and produce clean energy.

The Annapolis Tidal Power Plant was built in the 1980s using a barrage design that blocks the flow of water with a dam. This design has mixed results, and while it generates electricity, it also incurs soil erosion and high fish mortality. Currently the only such plant in the western hemisphere, it has a capacity of 20 megawatts and a daily output of roughly 80–100 megawatt hours, depending on the tides.

In 2009, North America's first and only commercial-scale in-stream tidal turbine was deployed in Minas Passage. Within three weeks, the power of the Bay of Fundy tides tore the blades from the turbine. Since then, in-stream turbine energy extraction has been under intensive study involving the Nova Scotia Department of Energy, the Fundy Ocean Research Centre for Energy (FORCE), the Offshore Energy Research Association, major universities in the province, and various commercial companies. Not only is the possibility of 200 megawatts of energy extraction being studied, but just as important, is the research to determine what environmental impacts the turbines may have on the Bay of Fundy, home to many fish species, lobster, porpoises and more.

2016 is slated for the deployment at the FORCE test site of two large in-stream turbines built in Pictou. The life of the turbines depends on a successful environmental monitoring program, extraction of clean energy and its economic benefits to Nova Scotians, and, of course, the incredible power of the Bay of Fundy tides.

Gypsum has been mined since the 1770s (the province is the leading Canadian producer), salt since 1918, first at Malagash (page 293), then at Pugwash (see pages 289–90), and barytes, primarily around the Minas Basin, since the 1860s.

In the main, the economy continues to transition from industrial to more service-oriented. Private services now account for more than half of Nova Scotia's output, while health, education and public administration account for another third.

Overfishing and poor resource management from the 1970s to the early 1990s had devastating effects on the region's cod-fishing industry. Fishing bans, quotas and other attempts to turn things around seem to be having little effect. More important to the sector today are shellfish: shrimps, crabs and scallops – oh, and lobster: Nova Scotia is the world's largest exporter of the crustacean.

The waters off Sable Island (pages 398–401) are the site of offshore **natural gas-drilling platforms**. The Sable Offshore Energy Project (SOEP) started production in 1999, and at its height was pumping around 500 million cubic feet of gas per day. In 2016, production dropped to under 4.25 million m³ of gas per day and there is speculation that the site could be closed as early as 2018. ExxonMobil Canada is the majority shareholder. Encana's gas production at Deep Panuke, a little bit further to the southwest, began in 2013 and the site is estimated to be productive until around 2026, with peak production of 8.5 million m³ of gas a day.

Although less than 10% of Nova Scotia's land is arable, **agriculture** contributes heavily to the economy. Significant crops include apples, cranberries and wild

In 2011, the federal government decided that new vessels would be required for the Canadian navy for the coming decades. Once the programme had been announced, bids (for a contract said to be worth CAN$25 billion) were invited from interested parties. In the end, there was a three-horse race between a shipyard in British Columbia, one in Quebec, and Nova Scotia's Halifax Shipyard. In addition to the contract itself, spin-offs were estimated to include close to 12,000 new jobs.

Committees examined every aspect of each bid with fine-toothed combs and deliberated for ages. After a three-horse race, Irving Shipbuilding was selected by the Canadian government, and you can barely imagine the wave of euphoria that swept through Halifax and beyond on that October day.

Since then a lot has happened at the company's Halifax Shipyard. More than CAN$350 million have been invested to build North America's most modern shipyard, and in September 2015 construction started on the first Arctic Offshore Patrol Ship (AOPS). With a streamlined procurement approach, construction of a Canadian Surface Combatant (CSC) vessel could start at Halifax Shipyard in 2020.

As a result of the National Shipbuilding Strategy (as of June 2016), Irving Shipbuilding has awarded in excess of CAN$1 billion in contracts to more than 200 companies across Canada.

Will 19 October 2011 turn out to be one of the most important days in the province's history? 'Fair winds and following seas', as they say.

blueberries; and poultry and dairy products figure strongly. More than two-thirds of the province is covered by productive forest, some of which is harvested for lumber and pulp. Nova Scotia is the world's largest exporter of wild blueberries and Christmas trees. Acadian Seaplants, based in the province (box, page 5), is the world's largest manufacturer of seaweed-based speciality products.

There are both hydro-electric and – harnessing the power of the sea – tidal-power generating plants (pages 222 and 271). Manufacturing is also a major contributor, but it is small businesses that make up over 90% of the province's economy. Tourism continues to be a growing contributor, but the world economic situation and the strength of the Canadian dollar against the US dollar, sterling and the euro have meant reduced visitor numbers in the last few years.

In 2014, Nova Scotia's per-capita GDP was $37,944 (the average across Canada was $47,171). The province's economic output has been lower than the national average for most years of the past decade. Nova Scotia did improve on the national average during the 2008–09 financial crisis and recession, but prior to that, it was only during the construction and initial (peak) production of the Sable Offshore Energy Project that the province's real GDP growth exceeded the national average.

Companies, including Shell Canada, continue to spend hundreds of millions of CAN$ in the search for offshore oil.

At the time of writing, the latest private sector consensus for Nova Scotia's growth for 2015 is +1.2%, though the private sector is more optimistic about the outlook for 2016, with the expectation of +1.6% for that year.

In 2014, Nova Scotia's (nominal) gross domestic product (GDP) was CAN$39.007 billion (real GDP CAN$29.951 billion). The first effects from the construction activity related to the shipbuilding project (box, above) should continue to boost

1

growth for several years, as well a number of other large construction projects, including a new convention centre in Halifax, and the possibility of a 'super' container terminal on the Strait of Canso (page 397).

PEOPLE

Nova Scotia is home to approximately 943,000 people: the majority live in urban centres, with approximately 40% living in the Halifax Regional Municipality. This means the province's population density is 17.4 people/km² (England's is approx 413 people/km²). Official figures released early in 2016 showed deaths outnumbering births.

Almost 80% of the population can trace their ancestry to Scotland, England or Ireland; France and Germany are next on the list. Although the highest number of immigrants continue to arrive from the UK and Ireland, arrival numbers from eastern Europe, the Middle East, and southeast Asia and the Far East are not insignificant. By March 2016, the province had taken in more than 1,000 refugees from Syria. Having said that, Nova Scotia still has one of the smallest percentages of 'visible minorities' of any Canadian province/territory. Recent years have also seen many Canadians move here from the provinces of Ontario, Alberta and British Columbia: many sold their homes and realised that – in terms of buying property – their dollars will go much further in Nova Scotia.

As is generally the case, life in the big urban centres is lived at a much faster pace than in small towns and rural areas: if you've been exploring the province for a few days, coming back to Halifax can seem like jumping forward a few decades.

The population has a median age of 43.7 years, but the number of younger people in the big urban centres means that in less built-up areas, there is a far higher proportion of senior citizens. Visitors will find most locals approachable, friendly and helpful – 'old timers' in particular love to talk, so if you ask one for directions you may also get their (usually fascinating) life histories.

THE MI'KMAQ IN THE 21ST CENTURY

Today, approximately 16,000 Mi'kmaq (box, page 15) live in the province. They are divided into 13 Mi'kmaq First Nation Bands, whose members have usufructuary rights (rights to enjoy and benefit from property that belongs to someone else) to approximately 11,200ha of mostly unproductive land (the title of Reserve Land is held by the Canadian Crown). About 60% live on 32 widely scattered Indian reserves. In recent years, in a few cases the Mi'kmaq have used their Aboriginal Rights, supported by the Royal Proclamation of 1763, to try to reclaim their hunting and fishing rights – albeit to the annoyance of some in the province's heavily regulated mainstream fishing industry.

After centuries of suffering suppression, persecution and attempted genocide, there are attempts to put the historical record straight. Daniel N Paul's *We Were Not the Savages* (*www.danielnpaul.com*) is a must-read for anyone interested in the history of the province from a Mi'kmaq perspective. The author was also behind a petition to rename all of the province's public entities that had been named in honour of Governor Edward Cornwallis who founded Halifax in 1749 and who offered bounties for the scalps of Mi'kmaq men, women and children. A hopeful sign for the future is that many younger Mi'kmaq are rediscovering their language, culture and heritage.

Just occasionally, the visitor may be thrown by an unusual word or expression. A resident of Nova Scotia is a Bluenose (or Bluenoser). There are different versions of the origin: these include the coloured marks left on their noses by fishermen wearing (poorly dyed) blue mittens, and a variety of knobbly potato, blueish in colour, grown in (and exported from) the province early in the 19th century. Nova Scotia's most famous sailing vessel (box, page 161) was named the *Bluenose*.

Someone from elsewhere who now lives in the province is a Come-From-Away (CFA). All over Canada a 'looney' (or 'loonie') is a Canadian one-dollar coin (a bird, the loon, has for many years appeared on the tails side of the coin) and a 'twoonie' (or 'tooney' or 'toonie') is a two-dollar coin. Furthermore, a take-away is referred to as a 'take-out'; and a look-out is called a 'look-off'. Finally, dates are written numerically (MM/DD/YY), so 18 March 2017 would be written 03/18/17. 'Quite nice', when used by your average British person, equates to a Nova Scotian saying something is 'awesome'.

GENEALOGY There is far more interest in genealogy in Nova Scotia (and North America in general) than in Europe. The Mi'kmaq apart, everyone is – or descends from – an immigrant, and perhaps because people's ancestors only started arriving here in the last four centuries, tracing roots is more manageable. You'll find genealogical research facilities and archives all over the province.

LANGUAGE

Canada is bilingual (English and French) by constitution, but less than 11% of Nova Scotia's residents are bilingual. English is the language of choice for almost 90% of the population, while just under 0.1% call French their mother tongue. In some places (Pugwash and Antigonish, for example; see pages 289–91 and 306–12, respectively) street signs are in Scottish Gaelic (Gáidhlig), the language brought over by the Scottish Highlanders: in recent years many community name signs on Cape Breton Island have been replaced with signs showing both the English and Scottish Gaelic names.

RELIGION

Church affiliation in Nova Scotia is higher than elsewhere in Canada. Roman Catholics are the largest group, making up almost 33% of the population. Next (in descending order) are the United Church of Canada, Anglicans and Baptists. There are smaller percentages of Lutheran, Presbyterian, Greek Orthodox and other Christian denominations. The province has a fast-growing Muslim population, and small populations of Hindus, Buddhists and Jews. Pockets of (Protestant) Mennonites are dotted about rural areas.

At Port-Royal in 1607, Frenchman Marc Lescarbot taught the Mi'kmaq about Christianity and is credited with establishing Canada's first Sunday School.

It is told that a few decades back, the Pentecostal pastor at the Bethel Mission near Mahone Bay (on the province's South Shore) decided to hold a Divine Healing service. Preacher Burton Shupe led the prayers, and called for those in need of more curative medical treatment than the health services had managed to provide to come forward. One Letitia Sawler, mother of 14 and dependent on crutches, was helped onto the dais by some of the faithful. Preacher Shupe spoke in tongues, and then ordered Lettie to throw away her crutches. There was an audible gasp as two walking aids were cast away. Lettie teetered for a moment, then lost her balance and fell to the ground, prompting another gasp. Some members of the congregation rushed to try and help her, but Preacher Shupe – who had had a moment to gather his thoughts – commanded 'Leaver 'er layin' where Jesus flang 'er'.

EDUCATION

Nova Scotia has more than 440 public (state) schools. These are under the auspices of seven regional school boards, and one school board which is responsible for the province's 20 French-language schools. Private schools include Halifax Grammar and Windsor's Kings Edgehill, and there are Montessori schools (where tuition is based on the child-development theories of Maria Montessori, who advocated that the teacher's role is to introduce children to materials and then remain a silent presence in the classroom, whilst the children direct their own learning) in Halifax, Windsor, Wolfville and Sydney.

Children normally begin school in September if their fifth birthday is before 31 December. Parents are allowed to home school if they wish. The first year is called Primary and the next year is Grade 1 and so on to Grade 12, the final year of high school. There are no equivalents to the UK's Ofsted reports or school 'league tables'. In addition to ten universities, the Nova Scotia Community College (NSCC) has 13 campuses around the province.

CULTURE

LITERATURE with Hilary Drummond

As one of the oldest Canadian provinces, Nova Scotia enjoys a rich and varied literary heritage beginning with the ancient **oral storytelling** traditions of its First Nations peoples. The first written accounts of Mi'kmaq literature in Nova Scotia are credited to French missionary Pierre Maillard (1710–62), and Mi'kmaq Glooscap legends were retold by acclaimed Nova Scotian author Alden Nowlan (1933–83). Cape Breton poet Rita Joe (1932–2007) is known as the Poet Laureate of the Mi'kmaq and was awarded the Order of Canada in 1989. If you're interested in reading more about the Mi'kmaq, anthropologist Ruth Holmes Whitehead researched and compiled Mi'kmaq mythology in *Six Mi'kmaq Stories* and *The Old Man Told Us*; and journalist and activist Daniel Paul offers a Mi'kmaq perspective on Nova Scotian history in his book *We Were Not the Savages*. *Bear River* author Shalan Joudry's *Generations Re-merging* is a collection of poems exploring cultural issues encountered by Mi'kmaq women in a modern context.

European colonisation brought a wealth of literary talent to the province, beginning in 1609 with Marc Lescarbot, who wrote *Histoire de la Nouvelle-*

France, an account of a French, late 16th-century exploratory voyage. Although Henry Wadsworth Longfellow (1807–82) never visited Nova Scotia, his epic poem *Evangeline* brought international attention to the 1755 Expulsion of the Acadians by the British (page 17). One of the first notable authors writing in English was Windsor native Thomas Chandler Haliburton (1796–1865), a political satirist and the creator of Sam Slick, the wisecracking protagonist of his *Clockmaker* books (box, page 252). Thomas H Raddall (1903–94) was the author of more than 30 works of fiction and non-fiction including *Halifax, Warden of the North*, an excellent history of the province's capital. Pulitzer Prize-winner Elizabeth Bishop spent some of her childhood in Great Village (pages 267–8), and much of her work was inspired by her time in Nova Scotia.

More recently, Lawrence Hill's *The Book of Negroes* attracted international attention on a period of Nova Scotian history. And George Elliott Clarke (*Execution Poems; The Motorcyclist*) was appointed Poet Laureate of Canada in 2016.

A list of recommended Nova Scotia-related literature can be found in the Appendix (pages 402–4).

ART Nova Scotia has a vibrant artistic community with artists and creators of fine art, folk art, and crafts to be found in countless nooks and crannies.

The province has been home to some impressive fine artists such as Helsinki-born William deGarthe (1907–83) who lived in Peggys Cove for almost 30 years: much of his work had a marine theme. His home is now a gallery. Willard M

MAUD LEWIS

Born in rural Yarmouth County in 1903, Maud Dowley suffered birth defects that gave her hunched shoulders and pressed her chin into her chest. She was very small and developed rheumatoid arthritis in childhood. Maud had no formal art training and dropped out of school (where she had been teased incessantly) at 14. When her parents died in the late 1930s, their 'estate' was left to their son, and he made no provision for his sister. She answered an advert for a housekeeper and moved to the home of Everett Lewis, a door-to-door fish seller. The two lived in his simple one-room home in Marshalltown (near Digby), and were married soon afterwards. Here, despite worsening arthritis, Maud painted and painted. Every surface in the house became her canvas, as did any scraps of cardboard or wallpaper. Everett sold Maud's paintings of colourful scenes of rural Nova Scotia whilst on his fish rounds, and later to tourists in the area. Most sold for a dollar or two.

In 1965, still living in the tiny hut – Everett didn't want to waste money on running water or electricity – Maud was featured on a television documentary, and soon after, in a Toronto paper. Her fame began to spread rapidly: in 1969, a White House aide commissioned two of her paintings for Richard Nixon (Maud asked for payment in advance). Sadly, her arthritis prevented her from being able to fulfil most of the orders that fame had finally brought.

She died of pneumonia in 1970 and was buried in a pauper's grave. Everett tried forging a few paintings and died in 1979: the Lewis shack was acquired by the Art Gallery of Nova Scotia (page 117) where it is now on display.

Shot in Newfoundland and set in Nova Scotia, a new film (starring Ethan Hawke and Sally Hawkins) depicting the life of Maud Lewis premiered at the Toronto International Film Festival in September 2016.

Mitchell (1881–1955) lived in Amherst for about 20 years and is best known for his miniature landscape watercolours. Much of the work by Robert Pope (1956–92) who died aged just 35 was inspired by his experience of healthcare and life as a cancer patient. One of Canada's greatest contemporary artists, Alex Colville (b1920) has spent most of his life in Nova Scotia and has lived in Wolfville for the last three decades.

The province has produced some renowned folk artists including Maud Lewis (box, page 29) and Joe Norris (1924–96), both of whose work can be seen at the Art Gallery of Nova Scotia (page 117). In the 21st century, the tradition continues. Dotted around the province, you'll find some excellent folk art galleries, and the genre is celebrated with an annual festival in Lunenburg (page 162).

Aboriginal art is also well worth seeking out: Alan Syliboy is the best-known contemporary Mi'kmaq artist. Up-and-coming, edgier Mi'kmaq artists include Charles Doucette of Potlotek (page 351). Liverpool now has a Mi'kmaq art gallery (page 175).

MUSIC Music has always been an important part of life in Nova Scotia, particularly since the Scots began to pour into Pictou in the 1770s (page 298). Whilst a wide variety of musical genres has begun to take off, this has not been at the expense of the popularity of Celtic music: whether traditional or fused with other styles, Celtic music is very much alive, well, and thriving in 21st-century Nova Scotia. Some visitors come primarily for the music; others look back on their time in Nova Scotia and realise what a highlight the music was.

Celtic music The Scottish Highlanders who arrived in the late 18th and early 19th centuries brought their music with them, and all these years later the highest concentration of Celtic music and dancing is to be found in the region where so many of those immigrants settled: Cape Breton Island.

The term 'Celtic music' covers a broad spectrum. Pure traditional tunes are still played, virtually unchanged from when they were learnt in Scotland, but the music has evolved its own identity too, in forms such as Cape Breton fiddle music. Some musicians add a dollop of other musical influences into the Celtic mix.

You can hear wonderful Celtic music throughout the year on Cape Breton Island, but opportunities increase dramatically in the summer, when there's a kitchen party or *ceilidh* (pronounced 'kay-lee' – a Gaelic word which refers to a traditional dance or music gathering) almost every evening somewhere in easy reach. That is definitely the case during October's joyous Celtic Colours International Festival (box, page 318), timed to coincide with nature's brilliant autumn leaf display. Celtic music aficionados should not miss this festival. Look out for ceilidhs all over the province – they aren't exclusive to Cape Breton Island.

So who are the people to watch out for? Top names include former members of the Rankin Family, particularly Jimmy Rankin: in October 2012, cancer accounted for his sister (and fellow group founder) Raylene. Gordie Sampson is a multi-award-winning singer-songwriter. Natalie MacMaster is Cape Breton Island's best-known fiddler – one of her cousins is Ashley MacIsaac, also a master of the instrument. Other big names include The Cottars and The Barra MacNeils. McGinty have been playing Celtic-influenced ballads, traditional, folk and bar tunes for almost four decades. John Allan Cameron (1938–2006) released ten albums between 1968 and 1996 and was known as 'The Godfather of Celtic Music'.

Those well established, but less well known on the international circuit include guitarist Brian Doyle, Mary Jane Lamond who fuses Gaelic music and contemporary pop, fiddler Andrea Beaton, Troy MacGillivray, stringed-instrument maestro Dave MacIsaac, Celtic harpist Alys Howe, and a band, Celtic Rant. But don't just look for those who have made it – in general, the standard of playing is so high that you're unlikely to be disappointed whoever you see. And where there's music, feet start tapping: step dancing, square dancing, highland dancing – and 'enthusiastic-but-unco-ordinated-tourists-forgetting-inhibitions dancing'. Those interested in Celtic music should ensure that they visit the Celtic Music Interpretive Centre in Judique (page 315).

Classical and choral Nova Scotia has produced one of the greatest contraltos in Canadian music history. Portia White (1911–68) was born in Truro and received international acclaim in the 1950s and 1960s. She was also an inspiration for the province's black community.

Established more than a quarter of a century ago, Halifax-based Symphony Nova Scotia (*www.symphonynovascotia.ca*) is the province's top chamber orchestra. Peter Allen is the province's leading classical pianist. Comprising coal miners from Cape Breton Island, male choral ensemble The Men of the Deeps has been entertaining audiences for more than four decades (page 362).

Country, folk, pop and rock The province has produced some country megastars including Hank Snow (page 176), Wilf Carter and more recently Anne Murray (page 280). Folk singer Rita MacNeil had been wowing audiences since the 1970s, but passed away in 2013. Folk legend Stan Rogers (who died in a plane crash in 1983, aged just 33) spent many summers in Nova Scotian and is commemorated in an annual festival (page 392). Sarah McLachlan was born in Halifax in 1968 and spent almost 20 years in the province before moving to Vancouver.

Country music is alive today with the flag flown by artists and bands such as George Canyon, Joyce Seamone, RyLee Madison and Jesse Beck, but is often blended with roots, folk and rock by bands such as the Moonshine Ramblers. Yarmouth's Ryan Cook is more country than folk. Up-and-coming Nova Scotian country 'stars' include Jason Price, J D Clarke, Chad Brownlee, and Makayla Lynn, and 2016 saw the province's inaugural Canaan Country Music Fest (page 237).

Old Man Luedecke sings fun songs, serious songs, and plays the banjo, and Truro's James Hill is a ukulele maestro.

Toronto-based pop-rockers Sloan started out in Nova Scotia, as did April Wine (big in the late 1970s and early 80s): these days, the closest thing that Nova Scotia has to an international rock star is Joel Plaskett (either solo or with band). One of his protegées is singer-songwriter Mo Kenney.

In no particular order, and often crossing genres, here are some names to look out for: Wintersleep, roots singer-songwriters Dave Gunning, Jenn Grant and Christina Martin, J P Cormier (who plays guitar and dobro mixing genres including Celtic, folk and bluegrass), and Lennie Gallant. The Stanfields blend heavy rock, bluegrass and Celtic music. Quiet Parade cover the range from gentle acoustic pop to more anthemic rock. Crowdis Bridge are very easy on the ear, Breagh MacKinnon plays folk-pop, and Rich Aucoin is definitely worth seeing (you'll love him or hate him). Ben Caplan offers a fab cocktail of blues, klezmer, rock and more, and Keith Mullins describes his own music as 'Folk Soul', there's the Django Rheinhardt-style gypsy swing Swingology, Matt Minglewood also crosses several genres, and The Town Heroes are a drum and guitar duo. Dog Day is an indie-rock duo, Gloryhound an old-fashioned rock band, Tuns is a rock/pop 'supergroup' trio, The Trews play hard rock, and Last Call Chernobyl's music tends to be metal (often with a lighter touch).

Born in 1810, Silas Tertius Rand became a Baptist missionary largely by self-education. Rather than go overseas, he lived with the local Mi'kmaq for more than 40 years, attempting to show them the way to heaven. He had to master their language and in thus doing, compiled a dictionary and wrote a grammar, and recorded a collection of 80 Mi'kmaq stories and legends. These actions are said to have saved the Mi'kmaq language (and some more of their tales) from oblivion. Much of what we know today about Mi'kmaq traditions is a direct result of his work.

Oh, and I nearly forgot to mention Charlie A'Court, Dali Van Gogh, Dylan Guthro, Steven Gates, Hillsburn and Tim Crabtree's Paper Beat Scissors. Making a name for herself too is Halifax's Ria Mae, who blends pop, folk and alternative.

On the **jazz and blues** front, a sad loss was the passing in 2012 (at age 75) of Halifax saxophonist Bucky Adams. Other heroes from the past include 'The Prime Minister of the Blues', Dutch Mason (1938–2006) – his son, Garrett Mason, looked set to follow in his father's footsteps but has been out of the limelight for a while. Joe Murphy has been entertaining blues lovers since the 1970s, and switches between harmonica, guitar and accordion. Keith Hallett has established himself as a powerful blues guitar man and Scott Macmillan's composing and guitar playing cross all the main genres, and the same could be said for finger-style guitarist Don Ross. John Campbell sings and plays slide guitar, and Detroit-born blues guitarist Morgan Davis has played with all the greats and has been living in Nova Scotia for over a decade. Another guitarist, Roger Howse's music straddles the blues, roots and Americana genres, and Dan Doiron has many fans. Drumlin (page 34) play

THE BEGINNING AND THE END

According to Mi'kmaq tradition, there were seven stages in the creation of the world (seven is an important recurring number in Mi'kmaq mythology). First there was Kisu'lkw, the Giver of Life, followed by Na'ku'set, the Sun (also called Grandfather). Created by bolts of lightning were both Sitgamu'k, Mother Earth, and the fourth stage of creation, Glooscap, who was later charged with passing on his knowledge to the Mi'kmaq people. He was followed by his Grandmother, Nokami (or Nugumi), with Glooscap's nephew, Netaoansum, and mother, Ni'kanaptekewi'sqw, completing the set.

When it was time for Glooscap to leave his people, he chanted and called for a whale to carry him to a land far to the west. The first whale to respond was rejected as being too small, but one of the desired proportions was the next to appear. Glooscap climbed onto its huge back, and the pair headed off through the sea.

When they reached their destination, Glooscap bade farewell to the whale, and offered the creature a pipe to smoke. The whale put the pipe in its huge mouth and swam off back towards its distant home: Glooscap climbed a hill and watched its progress, smiling as he saw the whale puffing out plumes of smoke at intervals.

Glooscap still lives away to the west: it is hoped that he will return to ease his people's troubles when the time is right.

folk-rock infused with 'Nova Scotia heritage music'. The Hupman Brothers play folky blues, and saxophonist and singer Shirley Jackson is worth seeing with or without 'Her Good Rockin' Daddys'. Steve Dooks plays smooth and easy piano, Thom Swift rootsy blues, and Shan Arsenault is an excellent jazz improv guitarist.

Halifax, in particular, has a powerful **hip-hop** scene. Important artists include Three Sheet, Something Good, Anonamyss, and Buck 65: on the rise are Quake Matthews, Thrillah, Shevy Price and more. Happy listening!

FOLKLORE Long before the Europeans arrived, the Mi'kmaq had their customs, tales – most of which involved Glooscap (sometimes written as 'Kluscap'), a mythical demi-god who slept using Nova Scotia as a bed and Prince Edward Island as a pillow – beliefs and sayings. As a consequence of the trials and tribulations of having to share their land for more than four centuries, some of their folklore was lost forever. The work of people such as **Silas Tertius Rand** (box, page 32) has helped to stop even more being forgotten.

The Europeans – particularly those of Celtic origin – brought their own folklore with them, and over time this has been shaped by their lives and surroundings in Nova Scotia, with the sea perhaps the biggest influence. Most early immigrants from Scotland and Ireland in particular arrived with a belief in God and the supernatural: they were no strangers to stories of mysterious unworldly creatures inhabiting hills, valleys and dark forests (of which Nova Scotia has many). Sprinkle into the mix the (supposedly hostile) local people who lived in tepees, spoke a strange language and had strange customs. Then add the sea: fog and sea mists, huge tides, howling wind, pirates. The result is an incredibly rich folklore of sea shanties, songs and ballads, proverbs, tales of buried treasure, witches, all manner of superstitions – and so much more.

Much of this has been lost, but Nova Scotia has benefited from the work of some forward-thinking folklorists who realised that records had to be made before it was too late. The province's best-known folklorist was Dartmouth-native

1

FORERUNNERS

In Nova Scotia, supernatural warnings of approaching (generally bad) events are most commonly known as 'forerunners'. There are several types, including unexplained knocks-on-doors or walls (typically of bedrooms), or pictures or mirrors suddenly falling down and smashing. There was, for example, a man who lived alone in a fishing shack and regularly complained of hearing screams and moans. Eventually these bothered the man so much that he moved away. Shortly afterwards, a ship was blown onto the rocks near the shack, and despite attempts to rescue those on board, they were thrown from the vessel and dashed against the rocks, their screams of pain and terror being carried on the howling wind to the onlookers. Whilst graves were dug the victims' bodies were placed in a temporary morgue – the very hut where the screams had previously been heard.

Forerunners mostly deal with sound, but visual signs are labelled foresight too. In a typical example, someone would have a vision of a funeral for a particular person before the 'deceased-to-be' had even fallen sick.

Even those who proclaim themselves non-believers in ghosts having no time for that 'stuff-and-nonsense' seem to find it acceptable to believe in forerunners and foresight.

Those born (or who lived) in Nova Scotia include: shipping magnate Sir Samuel Cunard, Alexander Graham Bell, actor Donald Sutherland, Pulitzer Prize-winning poet Elizabeth Bishop, singers Anne Murray, Hank Snow, Denny Doherty (of the Mamas & the Papas), Sarah McLachlan, Sara Vaughan, Rita MacNeil, (Leslie) Feist, the Rankin Family, fiddler Natalie MacMaster and ice hockey star Sidney Crosby.

Helen Creighton (1899–1989) who collected folk songs and tales across the province and further afield for more than 50 years. She wrote 13 books on the subject and recorded more than 15,000 songs and ballads. In 2008, Bridgewater-based family band Drumlin (*drumlin.ca*) released *Mackerel Skies*, an excellent CD of 12 of the heritage songs collected by Helen Creighton.

Many of her books are collections of tales of ghostly (or at least unexplained) happenings. These tell of 'forerunners' (box, page 33), phantom ships, ghosts guarding buried treasure, and non-threatening spectres who just pass by. And her material didn't just come from the Scots and Irish: she collected many stories from those of German, Acadian (in the 1830s, a French missionary recorded that some of the Acadians in Yarmouth County used books of spells regularly), Mi'kmaq and English origin.

ARCHITECTURE The history of Nova Scotia's early architecture and town planning is more varied (and complex) than you find in any other Canadian province, with strong French, British, German/European, pre- and post-revolution American, and Scottish influences. Through time – and British thoroughness in razing everything Acadian to the ground in the 1750s – no Acadian buildings remain from pre-Expulsion, although the Habitation (page 228) is a pretty accurate reconstruction of the original (1605) French fur-trading post.

Most of the earliest-surviving edifices were built by Loyalists (page 18) from New England. In some cases, timber frames for the houses were cut in Boston, Massachusetts, and shipped to Nova Scotia where local materials were used to complete the structure: such was the case with St Paul's Church in Halifax (page 120). The Loyalists also introduced the popular Cape Cod design, a simple wood-frame house with a gabled roof and shingle siding.

Fine mansions were later built from the profits of shipbuilding and shipping. Be sure to visit Lunenburg, the best-surviving example of a planned British colonial settlement in North America – though the buildings themselves show a strong European influence. A particular feature to look out for is the Lunenburg 'bump' (page 158). Liverpool, Shelburne, Yarmouth and Annapolis Royal should all be included in your itinerary.

Prescott House (page 244), Province House in Halifax (page 119) and Uniacke House (page 125) are all excellent examples of Georgian architecture. Other styles frequently occurring include Queen Anne Revival, Second Empire, Gothic Revival and Victorian Italianate. Amherst has numerous impressive 19th- and early 20th-century public buildings constructed from local sandstone in a variety of styles. You often hear the term 'century house' in Nova Scotia – this tends to be used when describing houses constructed in the late 1800s (presumably because they are more than 100 years old).

Although there have been many cases of ships 'disappearing', they are almost always found in pieces, run aground, damaged but still afloat – or, like the *Mary Celeste* (box, page 276) empty and off-course – at a later date. The largest vessel to disappear without trace in Nova Scotia's waters – I suppose the MH370 of its time – was the SS *City of Boston* which left Halifax for Liverpool, England, late in January 1870 but wasn't seen again. No trace of the Inman Line's ship – or the 207 people on board – has yet been found.

SHIPWRECKS For centuries, attempting to navigate round the coastal waters, rocky shores and islands of Nova Scotia – especially in darkness, fog, blinding blizzards and/or raging seas – proved too much for countless vessels. Almost 5,000 wrecks have been recorded (you wonder how many more haven't made it onto the lists).

Some areas in particular have seen alarming numbers of wrecks. Sable Island (pages 398–401) has long been known as the 'Graveyard of the Atlantic'. St Paul Island (pages 335–6) the 'Graveyard of the Gulf'. Dozens of vessels have gone down in the Cape Sable Island (pages 188–9) area, and, in truth, there are few parts of the province's coastline that haven't seen a shipwreck. Lighthouses, their foghorns and technological improvements were great navigational steps forward, but the boom in the quantity of shipping, particularly in the second half of the 19th century, kept wreck numbers high. The good news was that on many occasions, a higher proportion of those on board survived.

The RMS *Titanic* (box, page 92) is closely associated with Nova Scotia, but actually went down over 900km east–southeast of the province. Almost 40 years earlier, however, another White Star Line ship, the SS *Atlantic* (box, page 138) met her end near Lower Prospect, with more than 560 lives lost: it was at the time the world's worst merchant shipwreck.

In many cases, a ship's unfortunate end brought some good to local residents: valuable cargo was often washed ashore, and salvaging wreckage provided a living in some areas. So much so that there were several cases where ships were lured deliberately onto rocks by those hoping to reap reward from the resulting wrecks. Many of the wrecks now attract recreational divers (page 70), and there are still those who seek treasure – though legislation was introduced in the 1960s to prohibit salvage work on old shipwrecks without a permit. Late in 2011, the 225m-long MV *Miner* – under tow, and Turkey-bound – was shipwrecked off the southeast coast of Cape Breton Island, and in July 2015, a huge wreck was discovered on the bottom of Pictou Harbour. It turned out to be the *Dieuze*, which sank on 25 September 1925 after a fire broke out near the galley.

Background Information   CULTURE

1

Practical Information

WHEN TO VISIT

Whilst there are reasons to visit Nova Scotia in the winter – a few festivals, some wildlife-spotting opportunities, and some minor ski resorts – there can be a lot of snow and it can get very cold. Most attractions, many eateries and places to stay outside the biggest urban centres are closed. More doors begin to open after Canadian Mother's Day (the second Sunday in May).

Realistically, those considering a visit to the province should concentrate on the period between May and late October. May is quiet, though the days are long and the weather is warming up. Later in the month, apple blossom covers much of the Annapolis Valley, and flowers begin to bloom. By the beginning of June the weather is generally good for outdoor activities such as hiking, cycling, swimming, kayaking, etc, though late spring and early summer can be foggy. The golf courses and most provincial parks are open, more attractions are opening by the day, the festival season is well underway, and by the middle of June whale-watching trips have begun.

July, August and early September are relatively busy; everything is open, though high-season pricing is in effect. Those who enjoy swimming in the sea will find that August and early September offer the warmest air and water temperatures. If you will be visiting at these times, book your accommodation well in advance, and bear in mind that things will be busier. You can still find uncrowded beaches – though you'll have to walk away from the parking areas – but bear in mind that a crowded beach by Nova Scotia standards would seem relatively quiet in many other places.

WHY THE 'CLOSED' SIGN?

If you are visiting outside July, August or early September, a consequence of the worldwide economic downturn seems to be some B&Bs, restaurants, parks and attractions opening later in the (day or) year, and closing earlier. This can also be true of tourist information offices – lack of volunteers (or funds for staff and premises) can mean that communities forsake these centres for the season. Decisions can also be weather-dependent: a good spring (for example) can mean things opening earlier in the year but a quiet, wet summer may mean people shut up shop earlier in the year than usual. Similarly, the staff at a café or restaurant due to be open until (say) 20.00 may make an ad hoc decision to close an hour or two early if traffic has been slow. If you are making a special journey – or, for example, depending on a restaurant to be open for supper – it is prudent to call ahead to be sure.

Listings in this guide are open year-round, unless otherwise stated.

By the second week of September things quiet down: many attractions have already started to close (their first trigger is Labour Day, the first Monday in September), and kids are back at school. Having said that, if your travel is not restricted to school holidays, it is a good time to visit. The daytime weather generally remains good, though night-time temperatures begin to drop. Another wave of visitors then arrives to enjoy the magnificent autumn colours – and to attend the Celtic Colours International Festival (box, page 318) on Cape Breton Island.

HIGHLIGHTS

'Something for everyone' is a much-used phrase in guidebooks and destination-based travel articles. Does it apply to Nova Scotia? Almost. But don't come for nightlife (limited) or hi-tech theme parks (the one major theme park doesn't have state-of-the-art rides), and don't come for bustling resorts with beach bars and lines of sunlounger chairs and parasols on the sand.

CULTURE Nova Scotia is proud of its cultural heritage. Numerous centres and festivals have been established to educate and celebrate Celtic, Gaelic, Acadian and Mi'kmaq (aboriginal) cultures. In all, there are more than 550 festivals, most of which are held during the summer, celebrating everything from garlic to all things Gaelic, black flies to blueberries. Celtic music fans should make a beeline for Cape Breton Island Celtic Colours International Festival (box, page 318), but a wide variety of musical genres can be heard at music festivals held all over the province (see individual chapters). Halifax has a particularly strong live music scene, which spans the range from rap to classical.

FOLKLORE Dozens of locations, including a university, schools, inns, B&Bs and restaurants, are said to be haunted, and several towns host ghost walk tours – even candlelit graveyard tours – in case you fancy rubbing shoulders with ghouls. Shag Harbour (box, page 188) was the site of an as yet unexplained UFO crash in 1967. Several places are associated with tales of buried treasure too – none more so than Oak Island.

FOOD AND DRINK Long known for sublime seafood – particularly scallops, clams and lobster – the province has developed a good little wine industry. Tour its wineries and sample their produce. Wolfville and the Gaspereau Valley have a particularly high concentration of wineries.

ACCOMMODATION WITH CHARACTER There are a few high-rise hotels in the biggest urban centres, but far better are the delightful B&Bs and inns, many of which occupy beautifully restored century-old houses and mansions.

HISTORICAL SITES Nova Scotia is very rich in historical sites compared with much of North America. The most important sites include: Halifax Citadel, one of the largest British fortresses on the North American continent (pages 114–15); Port-Royal, the earliest European settlement in North America north of Florida (pages 228–9); Fort Anne, which contains the oldest building in any Canadian National Historic Site (pages 222–3); the Alexander Graham Bell National Historic Site (pages 346–7); and the Fortress of Louisbourg, one of the largest historic reconstructions in North America (pages 367–8). There are numerous lighthouses (including Canada's first), and countless examples of well-preserved Victorian and

Georgian architecture. Old Town Lunenburg is a UNESCO World Heritage site, as is the Grand Pré region (pages 156–7 and 244–7).

NATURAL HISTORY Geologists and fossil fans will want to visit the Joggins Fossil Cliffs – designated a UNESCO World Natural Heritage site in 2008 – a world-renowned palaeontological site with extensive deposits of 300-million-year-old fossils (pages 279–80). There are a number of other major fossil sites in Nova Scotia (note: unless you have a Heritage Research Permit – for details search for 'fossils' at cch.novascotia.ca – you're not allowed to take the fossils away with you). In addition, Parrsboro is home to the Fundy Geological Museum, and some beaches on the Bay of Fundy's shores can be good hunting grounds for those in search of semi-precious stones.

OUTDOOR ACTIVITIES For outdoor types, there is superb hiking, particularly on Cape Breton Island. Waterways in remote parts of the province such as the Tobeatic Wilderness Area and Kejimkujik National Park attract adventurous get-away-from-it-all canoeists.

There are numerous golf courses; two on Cape Breton Island are rated amongst Canada's best.

Choose from more than 100 beaches, many beautiful, most almost deserted and with virtually no development, or cool off in one of the multitude of lakes. Water-based activities include world-class sea kayaking, sailing and tidal-bore rafting. Surfing and scuba diving (primarily wreck diving) are also popular. Fish numbers have dropped, but both deep-sea sport-fishing and freshwater angling continue to be popular, as does (rightly or wrongly) hunting.

The terrain in many parts of Nova Scotia, including the Yarmouth area and Cape Breton Island's Isle Madame, lends itself to cycling holidays. If you prefer four wheels, the province offers several lovely drives, the majority overlooking the sea. One – the Cabot Trail – ranks amongst the world's best coastal drives.

WILDLIFE AND NATURE For wildlife enthusiasts, the Digby Neck in particular offers some of the world's best whale-watching opportunities. In addition, there are several seal colonies just off Brier Island (pages 212–14). From the few roads which pass through the province's densely forested interior you may be lucky to spot black bear. If you want to see moose, head for the Cape Breton Highlands National Park (pages 331–3).

Birdwatchers are spoilt for choice: bald eagles can be seen around the Bras d'Or Lake in summer and autumn, and in huge numbers near Sheffield Mills in the winter. August is the best time to see the southward migration of arctic-nesting shorebirds.

New England might be better known for its autumn colours, but they can be pretty impressive here, too. Combine leaf-peeping with some of the world's best Celtic music at Cape Breton Island's annual Celtic Colours International Festival in October.

SUGGESTED ITINERARIES

As everyone has their likes and dislikes and their own preferred way of travel, use these basic itineraries as starting points and tailor them to your own preferences. Personally, I prefer to spend more time in fewer places, but I appreciate that others may wish to pack as much of the province as possible into their trip. Keep your fingers crossed for good weather: like many other places, too many grey, wet days can easily take the gloss off a holiday.

A WEEKEND   Stay in Halifax and take a day trip out to Mahone Bay and Lunenburg.

A WEEK   Stay a couple of nights in Halifax, a couple of nights in Lunenburg (visiting Chester and Mahone Bay *en route*), relax on one of the beaches near Liverpool or explore Kejimkujik National Park *en route* to Annapolis Royal: spend two nights there, taking a whale-watching tour from Brier Island, then a night in Wolfville (visiting Grand Pré). Or, stay a couple of nights in Halifax, a night in Antigonish, head to Cape Breton Island and start driving the Cabot Trail clockwise, stay a couple of nights in the Ingonishes, a night in Sydney or Louisbourg and a night on Isle Madame.

TWO WEEKS   Combine the two one-week suggestions, replacing two of the Halifax nights with a night in Parrsboro (between Wolfville and Antigonish) and a night in Guysborough (after Isle Madame).

Any extra days will allow you to include Shelburne, Yarmouth, Cape Chignecto, and more of the Eastern Shore. Ideally, take longer and cover less distance. Don't rush Nova Scotia!

TOUR OPERATORS

Any decent travel agent in the UK should be able to book you a flight to Nova Scotia, book rooms at the big hotels and arrange car (or motorhome) hire. There isn't a company that focuses solely on the province, but some know it better than others.

Some of the **UK operators** mentioned below offer suggested self-drive itineraries around the province, and should also be able to organise a tailor-made itinerary to suit your needs. Note that UK operators don't offer multi-day escorted trips just around Nova Scotia – most combine a few days exploring the province with time also in New Brunswick and Prince Edward Island. The operators starred below (*) – all of whom will tailor-make itineraries for you – are those with good Nova Scotia content in their programmes. The rest are strong on Canada, but have more limited Nova Scotia product.

The companies listed under **Europe** specialise in holidays in North America and can advise on and arrange Nova Scotia itineraries. Few **Australian** tour operators know Nova Scotia well, or even include much about the province in their brochures, but your best bet is listed below.

You're unlikely to save much money, but you can of course **tailor-make your own trip** by booking flights through an operator or direct with the airline and hiring a vehicle through an operator, car-hire broker or direct with the car-hire (or motorhome) company. Larger hotels can be booked through a travel company or direct with the hotel, an increasing number are available through Airbnb (*www. airbnb.ca*), but for many inns and B&Bs you'll need to contact the property directly.

UK

1st Class Holidays   +44 (0)161 888 5606; www.1stclassholidays.com
*Audley Travel   New Mill, New Mill Lane, Witney, Oxfordshire OX29 9SX or Monsoon Building,

1 Nicholas Rd, London W11 4AN; +44 (0)1993 838 700; www.audleytravel.com
*Bridge & Wickers/The Ultimate Travel Company   25–27 Vanston Pl, London SW6 1AZ; +44 (0)20 3131 5588;

www.theultimatetravelcompany.co.uk. 6- &
7-night self-drive Nova Scotia itineraries, plus
longer trips combining the Maritime provinces.
Canada Travel Specialists 📞0800 033 4782;
www.canadatravelspecialists.com
Flight Centre 📞0808 260 9979; www.
flightcentre.co.uk
Frontier Canada 61A High Street, Orpington,
Kent BR6 0JF; 📞+44 (0)20 8776 8709; www.
frontier-canada.co.uk. Tailor-made holidays to
Canada: 6-night walking holidays in Nova Scotia,
8- & 14-night self-drive holidays in the province.
*Independent Traveller Devonshire Hse,
Devonshire Lane, Loughborough, Leicestershire
LE11 3DF; 📞+44 (0)1509 618800; www.
itiscanada.co.uk
Kuoni 📞0800 140 4777; www.kuoni.co.uk.
13-night Nova Scotia self-drive tours.
North America Travel Service 📞0333 323
9099; www.northamericatravelservice.co.uk
Titan 📞0808 163 6217; www.titantravel.co.uk.
Focuses on escorted coach tours.
Trailfinders 📞+44 (0)20 7368 1200; www.
trailfinders.com. 13-night Nova Scotia self-drive
tours.
Travel 2 Bookable only through travel agents.
Travelbag 📞0871 402 1634; www.travelbag.
co.uk

USA *Some tours are Nova Scotia-only, many have
strong Nova Scotia content.*
Backroads tf 1 800 462 2848; www.backroads.
com. Offers hiking & biking tours.
Caravan tf 1 800 227 2826; www.caravan.com
Collette Tours tf 1 844 269 4583; www.
gocollette.com
Field Guides tf 1 800 728 4953; fieldguides.
com. Offers tours for birdwatchers, combining Nova
Scotia & Newfoundland.
Globus 📞1 800 268 3636; www.globusjourneys.ca
Grand Circle Travel tf 1 800 221 2610; www.
gct.com. Offers escorted tours with good Nova
Scotia content.
Road Scholar tf 1 800 454 5768; www.
roadscholar.org. A Boston-based non-profit
organisation offering 'learning adventures' &
educational tour programmes for those aged 55 or
over. Formerly branded as 'Elderhostel'.
Tauck tf 1 800 788 7885; www.tauck.com. Offers
escorted tours with good Nova Scotia content.

EUROPE
Austria
canadareisen.at 📞+43 (0)2243 25994;
canadareisen.at
CanAmDreams 📞+43 (0)1 907 66 21; www.
canamdreams.at

SPECIALIST TOUR OPERATORS

CYCLING AND SEA KAYAKING TOURS Excellent cycle-tour companies offer both
guided small group trips and self-guided tours through some of Nova Scotia's
prettiest countryside. And you won't be roughing it at night – the companies
tend to use some of the province's wonderful B&Bs and inns for overnight
accommodation. Some tours are accompanied by a support vehicle to carry
luggage (and saddle-weary tour participants). Bike hire is included, or you can
use your own. With the exception of Eastwind, all the following companies
also offer sea kayaking holidays.

Coastal Adventures 📞902 772 2774; tf 1 877 404 2774; www.coastaladventures.com
Eastwind Cycle 📞902 471 4424; tf 1 866 447 7468; www.eastwindcycle.com
Freewheeling Adventures 📞902 857 3600; tf 1 800 672 0775; www.freewheeling.ca
Pedal & Sea Adventures tf 1 877 777 5699; www.pedalandseaadventures.com

WINE TOURS A variety of vineyard and winery tours are offered by:

Uncorked Wine Tours 📞902 352 2552; tf 1 877 365 2552; wp.winetoursns.com
Grape Escapes 📞902 446 9463; tf 1 855 850 9463; www.novascotiawinetours.com

Germany

America Unlimited Hanover; ☎+49 (0)511 3744 4750; www.america-unlimited.de
Canusa Touristik Hamburg; ☎+49 (0)40 22 72 530; www.canusa.de
Dertour Frankfurt ☎+49 (0)69 153 22 55 33; www.dertour.de

Netherlands

Jan Doets America Tours Heerhugowaard; ☎+31 (0)7257 53333; www.jandoets.nl

Switzerland

Kuoni Reisen ☎+41 (0)1 277 4444; www.kuoni.ch
Schär-Reisen ☎+41 (0)1 318 5757; www.schaerreisen.ch

Australia

Fresh Tracks Canada ☎+61 (0)808 149 2580; www.freshtrackscanada.com

NOVA SCOTIA AND CANADA *See also Backroads, listed under USA.*

Atlantic Tours ☎902 423 7172; tf 1 800 565 7173; www.atlantictours.com. One of the province's biggest tour operators: wide range of day, escorted & customised tours.
Bootprints Hiking Tours ☎902 478 6145; bootprintshikingtours.ca. Multi-day guided & self-guided hiking tours with some budget-friendly options.
Great E.A.R.T.H Expeditions ☎902 223 2409; greatearthexpeditions.com. Offers eco-adventures, hiking, camping, kayaking & more to out-of-the-way areas.
Maxxim Vacations tf 1 800 567 6666; www.maxximvacations.com. Offers guided & independent packages.
Nova Scotia Travel novascotiatravel.ca. Offers packaged & custom tours.
TayMac Tours ☎902 422 4861; tf 1 800 565 8296; taymactours.com. Offers guided & independent packages.
Ukaliq ☎902 789 7471; www.ukaliq.com. Customised guided wilderness tours.

TOURIST INFORMATION

You can contact Nova Scotia's tourist information department (Tourism Nova Scotia) by phone (☎ *902 425 5781;* tf *1 800 565 0000*) or email (e *explore@novascotia. ca*). Nova Scotia's official tourism website (*www.novascotia.com*) is a good source of information and (during some of the working day) offers a free 'live chat' option, via which an operator helps direct you to the information you're after (if it is on the website). The organisation publishes the (free) annual *Doers & Dreamers* services guide in the early spring packed with listings, articles and advertisements. Canada has tourist offices in about a dozen of the world's major cities, but in my experience these offices provide pretty limited information on Nova Scotia.

In Nova Scotia, just three provincial visitor information centres are open year-round: one at Halifax Airport (page 45), one on Halifax's waterfront (page 92), and the other at Amherst (page 287), near the Nova Scotia–New Brunswick border. Between mid May and mid October (hitting a peak in July and August), many more locally operated tourist information offices open, and these are listed under the relevant towns later on in the book. Within North America (and, of course, Nova Scotia) you can obtain tourist information and assistance, make reservations and more by phoning tf 1 800 565 0000.

RED TAPE

NOTE This information is correct at the time of writing, but rules and practices change, so do check the current situation (www.cic.gc.ca/english/visit/tourist.asp) before buying your ticket.

As of 29 September 2016, most international visitors intending to fly to (or transit) Canada need an Electronic Travel Authorisation (eTA). Exceptions include

US citizens, and travellers with a valid Canadian visa. At the time of writing, if you are entering Canada by land or sea, an eTA is not required.

eTAs will allow the Canadian authorities to screen travellers before they arrive. The eTA is electronically linked to your passport and is valid for five years or until your passport expires, whichever comes first. As it is passport-linked, you must travel using the passport with which you applied for your eTA.

Applying for the eTA is a simple online process and should only take minutes. The charge for the eTA is CAN$7. Although it may change, at the time of writing the correct website to apply for an eTA is: www.cic.gc.ca/english/visit/eta-start.asp. Be aware that some fake 'eTA' websites have been set up.

The eTA doesn't guarantee you entry to Canada – you'll still need to meet certain criteria (eg: good health, enough money for your stay, ability to satisfy the immigration officer that you'll leave Canada at the end of your visit). Most visitors are permitted to stay in Canada for up to six months. If you wish to extend your stay once in Canada, you must apply at least 30 days before the stamp in your passport expires. There is a form to complete (this can be done online), and a fee (*currently CAN$100*) to pay.

Unless you are a citizen of the USA, you will need a valid passport to enter Canada and it should be valid for at least as long as your intended period of stay. If you are a US citizen, you do not need a passport to enter Canada (unless arriving in Canada from a third country), but you now need a passport to re-enter the USA, and those travelling by land or sea need a passport, or other appropriate secure document like a NEXUS card. If you are a permanent resident of the USA, you must bring your permanent resident card (ie: Green Card) with you. The US Department of State website (*www.travel.state.gov/travel*) will have the latest information.

Most visitors to Canada are not allowed to work or study in Canada without permission. You must apply for a work or study permit before coming to Canada. If you are visiting Canada and you want to apply to work or study, you must leave Canada and apply from your home country. The Canadian government's Citizenship and Immigration website (*www.cic.gc.ca*) should answer most questions.

Note: This information is correct at the time of writing, but rules and practices change so do check the current situation before buying your ticket.

CUSTOMS REGULATIONS Visitors to Nova Scotia (and Canada in general) are permitted to bring in personal items such as clothing, camping and sports equipment, cameras and personal computers that will be used during a visit. Gifts (each valued at CAN$60 or less) for friends or family can be brought in duty- and tax-free, but alcohol and tobacco products are not classed as gifts.

Those aged over 18 (19 for alcohol) can bring in the following duty-free: either 1.5 litres of wine or 1.14 litres of liquor (maximum 1.14 litres if you're bringing wine and liquor) or 24 (355ml) cans (maximum 8.5 litres) of beer or ale. Despite the ban on smoking in public places, you can bring in 200 cigarettes, 50 cigars/cigarillos, and 200g of manufactured tobacco duty-free. If you wish to avoid paying duty, the cigarette/tobacco packaging must be stamped 'duty paid Canada *droit acquitté*'.

Born near Halifax in 1971, Jeffrey Delisle joined the Canadian forces reserves in 1996, and became a regular member of the Canadian army in 2001, working in intelligence. In 2007, dressed not in a tuxedo and bow tie but a red baseball cap and anorak, and rather than parachuting onto the roof, Delisle walked into the Russian Embassy in Ottawa and offered to sell secrets to that country's military intelligence agency.

Delisle worked at a secret super-high-security location in Halifax on an assignment called the *Stone Ghost*: the ultra-sensitive project involved the intelligence services of the 'Five Eyes' – Canada, the USA, the UK, Australia and New Zealand. Although the computer he worked on had highly elaborate security, apparently there was another computer alongside it that was totally un-monitored. It is said that Delisle simply copied reams of classified, top-secret information onto a disk, transferred it to the second computer, copied the data onto a memory stick and carried that out of the building to collate at home. Once a month – in return for a payment of CAN$3,000 per batch – he would send a package of *Stone Ghost* intelligence information to the Russians.

In 2009, Delisle contacted the Russians and told them that he wanted to stop the arrangement: shortly afterwards, he received an envelope in the mail containing a photo of his daughter walking to school in Halifax. Delisle was instructed to fly to Brazil to meet his Russian 'handler': alarm bells finally rang when he was stopped on his return by Canadian customs officials who were suspicious because he had been away only a few days and was carrying almost CAN$50,000. However, Delisle continued to pass secret data onto the Russians until his arrest in January 2012. Rather than being suspended over a shark pool and left to die (or escape and just manage to stop a timing device before it blew up the Western world), he was imprisoned. At his Halifax court appearance in October 2012, he pleaded guilty to breach of trust, and two counts of passing information to a foreign entity. The first Canadian to be convicted of spying in decades is serving a 20-year sentence in a federal prison for betraying his country.

There are strict rules concerning the import of numerous things from food products to firearms, plants to prescription drugs. For full information, see the guide for 'Visitors to Canada' at www.cbsa-asfc.gc.ca.

EMBASSIES Although the Canadian Government has more than 260 offices in about 150 countries around the world (including embassies, consulates, high commissions and trade offices), for most people the visa-issuing centres are the most relevant. The contact details for each office is listed at www.cic.gc.ca/english/information/offices/vac.asp.

Consulates in Nova Scotia

E Austria 1096 Marginal Rd, Halifax B3H 4N4; ☎902 431 3102

E Germany Suite 1100, Purdy's Wharf Tower 1, 1959 Upper Water St, Halifax B3J 3N7; ☎902 491 4106

E The Netherlands 2000 Barrington St, Halifax, B3J 3K1; ☎902 422 1485

E UK British Honorary Consul: 1 Canal St, Dartmouth B2Y 2W1; www.gov.uk/government/world/canada

E USA Suite 904, Purdy's Wharf Tower 2, 1969 Upper Water St, Halifax B3J 3E5; ☎902 429 2480; https://ca.usembassy.gov/embassy-consulates/halifax/

Practical Information RED TAPE

2

Most European visitors arrive into Nova Scotia by air, flying into Halifax Robert L Stanfield International Airport. For those coming from (or going to) other parts of Canada, there are a few other options: one rail connection, and two road crossings from the neighbouring province of New Brunswick (itself connected by road to the Canadian province of Quebec, and to Maine in the United States). There is a ferry connection with Maine, USA, as well as ones with New Brunswick, Prince Edward Island and Newfoundland.

Travellers from the USA have the choice of flying, taking the ferry from Portland, Maine, driving to Saint John, New Brunswick, and taking the ferry from there, driving through New Brunswick to take the land route in to Nova Scotia, or some combination of the above (eg: ferry one way, drive the other). By road, Portland to Saint John is just over 480km by road: Portland to the New Brunswick–Nova Scotia border, near Amherst, is 750km.

BY AIR Air Canada is the only airline to offer non-stop year-round flights between the **UK** and Nova Scotia (London Heathrow to Halifax). Between spring and early autumn, Canadian airline Westjet offers direct flights between both Glasgow and Dublin and Halifax. Flying time from London to Halifax is around 6½ hours (the Gulf Stream winds mean that the return journey is usually about 45 minutes quicker). If you are having problems finding seats at a competitive fare, try looking beyond direct flights – more options exist if you are prepared to change planes. Westjet, for example, often offers good deals from London Gatwick to Halifax changing planes in St John's (Newfoundland) or Toronto. However, it's

worth comparing any savings in cost against the extra time and inconvenience the stopovers will incur. The most expensive time to fly is in July and August.

If you're coming from elsewhere in Canada, options also exist in the summer to fly direct to Sydney (on Cape Breton Island) from Toronto.

In addition to the daily (except where specified) direct flights between **US** airports and Halifax, if you are prepared to change planes, there are more possibilities. Incidentally, if you are flying directly to the USA, Halifax Airport has a US Customs pre-clearance facility allowing you to go through US Customs and Border Protection before your flight – saving quite a bit of time at the other end (note though that this is not offered 24/7).

There are no direct flights between **Australia** and Nova Scotia – you will have to change planes at least twice. A couple of airlines offer through fares, for example **Air Canada** (↘ *1300 655 767; www.aircanada.com/au/en/home.html*) and **United** (↘ *131 777; www.unitedairlines.com.au*). It is often cheaper to buy a ticket to (say) New York, and a separate ticket New York–Halifax.

From the UK & Ireland
✈ **Air Canada** ↘0871 220 1111; www. aircanada.co.uk. Daily flights between London

Heathrow & Halifax (*Apr–Oct; 3–4 times weekly Nov–Mar*). In general, if direct flights are full or don't operate on a particular day, it is possible to change planes in Toronto or Montreal for the same fare.

✈ **Condor** www.condor.com. Between late spring & autumn, this German airline (part of the Thomas Cook group) flies to Halifax from Frankfurt or Munich. Through fares from Heathrow, Birmingham & Manchester are usually offered.

✈ **Icelandair** ✆0844 811 1190; www.icelandair. co.uk. Offer flights 2–3 times weekly (*early Jun– early Oct*) from Heathrow, Manchester & Glasgow with a plane change in Reykjavik.

✈ **Westjet** tf 1 888 937 8538; www.westjet. com. Direct flights to Halifax from Glasgow & Dublin (plus flights from Gatwick changing planes in St John's (Newfoundland) or Toronto).

From elsewhere in Europe
✈ **Air Canada** www.aircanada.com. Daily flights from Paris, Frankfurt, Munich, Rome & Zurich with a change in Toronto or Montreal.

✈ **Condor** ✆+49 (0) 6171 698 8920 (in Germany); www.condor.com. Thrice-weekly direct flights between Frankfurt & Halifax,weekly between Munich & Halifax (*mid May–late Oct*).

✈ **Icelandair** www.icelandair.com. Flights via Reykjavik (*early Jun–early Oct*), with a plane change, from various European cities including Madrid, Paris, Amsterdam, Milan, Munich, Frankfurt & Berlin.

From elsewhere in Canada
✈ **Air Canada & Air Canada Jazz** tf 1 888 247 2262; www.aircanada.com. Direct flights to Halifax

from Calgary (summer only), Charlottetown, Deer Lake, Fredericton, Gander, Goose Bay, Montreal, Moncton, Ottawa, Saint John, St John's, Toronto & Vancouver. Also a Toronto–Sydney service (*May–Oct*).

✈ **Air St Pierre** tf 1 877 277 7765; www. airsaintpierre.com. Flights between Saint Pierre (St Pierre & Miquelon islands, just south of Newfoundland) & Halifax year-round, & Sydney (*early Jul–early Sep*).

✈ **Porter Airlines** tf 1 888 619 8622; www. flyporter.com. Flights between Halifax & Montreal, St John's, Ottawa & Stephenville (summer only).

✈ **Westjet** tf 1 888 937 8538; www.westjet. com. Flights to Halifax daily year-round from Calgary, Deer Lake, Edmonton, Ottawa, St John's & Toronto, & in the summer to Halifax from Hamilton, Vancouver & Winnipeg, & to Sydney from Toronto.

From the USA
✈ **Air Canada** tf 1 888 247 2262; www. aircanada.com. Direct flights to Halifax from Boston.

✈ **Delta** tf 1 800 221 1212; www.delta.com. Direct summer flights between New York (JFK) & Halifax.

✈ **United** tf 1 800 538 2929; www.united.com. Direct flights between Newark & Halifax.

✈ **Westjet** tf 1 888 937 8538; www.westjet. com. Weekly flight between Orlando & Halifax.

✈ **Westjet Encore** tf 1 888 937 8538; www. westjet.com. Direct flights to Halifax from Boston.

Airports
Halifax Robert L Stanfield International Airport (✆ 902 873 4422; hiaa.ca)
Not surprisingly, this tends to be referred to as Halifax Airport or 'the airport': its IATA code is YHZ. Modern and efficient, it processes some 3.7 million passengers annually. There's a well-stocked tourist information office just outside the arrivals hall (⌚ 09.00–21.00 daily), as well as ATMs, bureaux de change, car-hire and ground-transportation desks, and shops and cafés. There's a 2,300-space multi-storey car park (take care to choose either hourly or daily parking) and one on-airport hotel (page 99) which is actually connected to the terminal by covered walkway. The airport is situated just off Exit 6 of Highway 102, approximately 35km from downtown Halifax. In general, the journey to or from the city should take 30–45 minutes, but traffic can be bad going into Halifax between 08.00 and 09.30, and leaving the city between 16.30 and 18.00, so allow perhaps 80 minutes at these times. Incidentally, between Exit 6 and the airport you'll pass a Tim Horton's (it's on your right if coming from the highway). Inside are (coffee, doughnuts and) flight departures and arrivals boards. Savvy drivers who don't want to overspend on airport parking often hang out here, for example when

2

waiting to meet someone off an incoming flight. For details of transport to and from the airport, see below.

Sydney Airport (✆ *902 564 7720; sydneyairport.ca*) Sydney Airport is 9km from Sydney, Cape Breton Island. The airport's IATA code is YQY. Few flights come and go, but there's a restaurant, ATM and car-hire desks.

BY CAR Whether driving from the USA or Canada (unless you take a ferry; see opposite), you'll pass through New Brunswick and cross in to Nova Scotia near Amherst (pages 283–8). From there it is 215km/134 miles – about a 2½–3-hour drive – to Halifax. Montreal is about 1,250km/777 miles from Halifax by road, and (again if you don't take a ferry) Boston is 1,120km/700 miles. For more on driving in Nova Scotia, see pages 54–7.

BY COACH **Maritime Bus** (tf *1 800 575 1807; maritimebus.com*) took over long-distance coach services in December 2012. They usually operate three services daily in each direction between Halifax (calling at various places in Nova Scotia including Dartmouth, Halifax Airport, Truro and Amherst) and Sackville and Moncton (both in New Brunswick): Halifax to Moncton usually takes just over 4 hours. From Moncton there are connecting services through New Brunswick to Quebec. Those wishing to connect to/from Prince Edward Island should change buses in Amherst.

Advance Shuttle (✆ *902 888 3353*; tf *1 877 886 3322; www.advanceshuttle. ca*) operates 11-passenger air-conditioned vans once daily in each direction between Nova Scotia and Prince Edward Island (*4–5hrs; CAN$69 one-way*) via the Confederation Bridge (which connects New Brunswick and Prince Edward Island). The route is Charlottetown–Summerside–Borden (all in Prince Edward Island), then Amherst–Oxford–Truro–Elmsdale–Enfield–Halifax Airport–Halifax City–Dartmouth.

BY TRAIN **VIA Rail** (tf *1 888 842 7245; www.viarail.ca*) operates an overnight train, *The Ocean*, three times a week between Montreal and Halifax. The train leaves Montreal in the evening, travels via Moncton and New Brunswick, arriving in Halifax mid afternoon. In the other direction, afternoon departures from Halifax reach Montreal the next morning.

Year-round, the train offers standard economy class and sleeper class; the latter affords you a bed in private accommodation. Between mid June and mid October, you can also travel in sleeper touring class. Extra benefits, instead of standard sleeper class, include on-train presentations with cultural and historical insights to the Maritimes, exclusive access to the train's lounges and panoramic section of the luxurious Park Car, breakfast, lunch and a three-course dinner. Regular fares are CAN$218 each way in economy class, but a limited number of no change, no refund 'Economy Saver' tickets are sold for each journey at just CAN$135. Look out, too, for special sales.

BY SEA Bay Ferries (tf *1 877 762 7245; www.ferries.ca*) operates *The CAT*, a high-speed catamaran ferry, daily (each way) between Portland, Maine, and Yarmouth. The 2016 season ran from 15 June to 1 October with a morning departure from Yarmouth and an afternoon departure from Portland (*5½hrs; US$107 one-way per passenger, from US$199 one-way per vehicle excluding driver*).

The company also operates Digby–Saint John (New Brunswick) on the *Fundy Rose* year-round (*1–2 times daily; 3hrs; passenger fares from CAN$46 one-way, vehicle cost from CAN$112*); and Caribou (near Pictou)–Wood Island (Prince Edward Island) on NFL Ferries MV *Confederation* and MV *Holiday Island* from May to mid December (*3–8 times daily; 75mins; fares from CAN$19 round-trip for passengers, from CAN$81 round-trip – including passengers – for a vehicle*).

Marine Atlantic (tf *1 800 341 7981; www.marineatlantic.ca*) offers two connections between Nova Scotia's Cape Breton Island and the Canadian province of Newfoundland: North Sydney–Port aux Basques (Newfoundland) year-round (*6–8hrs; passenger fares from CAN$43, vehicle from CAN$113*); and North Sydney–Argentia (Newfoundland) three sailings a week from late June to late September (*16hrs; passenger fares from CAN$115, vehicle from CAN$232*). Fares shown are one-way. Note that the vehicle rate does not include driver or passengers.

HEALTH   *with Dr Felicity Nicholson*

The standard of public health in Canada is excellent, but very expensive for non-residents. If you become ill in Nova Scotia, for minor ailments, seek out a pharmacy. If it is something more serious, your next step is to go to one of the few walk-in clinics or to the emergency department of a hospital. You will have to pay at both to use the facilities and to see a doctor, and for any treatment and/or medicines that may be required. It is a similar story for emergency dental work. Consequently, it would be foolhardy to visit Nova Scotia (and anywhere in North America) without comprehensive medical insurance (check that your travel insurance policy includes adequate cover).

If you take prescription medicines to Nova Scotia, make sure that they are in their original packaging (with a label that specifies what they are and that they are being used under prescription). If that is not possible, carry a copy of the prescription or a letter from your doctor. Otherwise, they may be confiscated by customs officials. No vaccinations are legally required, but it is always wise to be up to date with routine vaccinations such as diphtheria, tetanus and polio. Tap water is safe to drink.

BLACK FLIES AND MOSQUITOES Tiny, biting black flies appear in the spring and (though everyone says that they go by early to mid June) may hang around into July. They cannot bite through clothing, but sometimes bite above the hairline, or below the collar line. They don't bite after dark. In rural areas in May and early June, it is not uncommon to see locals who are working outside wearing head nets.

Just before the black flies start to die down for the year, mosquitoes make their appearance, and buzz around until late summer – even longer in swampy areas. Whereas in many places mosquitoes are creatures of the night, in Nova Scotia they are just as evident in the daytime. In theory, coastal areas are less badly affected, but I've seen plenty of evidence to the contrary. Mosquitoes here do not carry malaria, but there is said to be a tiny risk of West Nile virus. However, as of June 2016, no humans have ever been recorded as having acquired West Nile virus in the province.

Help protect against black flies and mosquitoes by covering up: wear light-coloured long-sleeved shirts and trousers and cover exposed skin with a DEET-based insect repellent.

TICKS Forests and areas with long grass can be home to ticks, particularly in spring and early summer. Some black-legged ticks carry the bacteria which could cause **Lyme disease**. Both black-legged and dog (or wood) ticks are found in many parts of Nova Scotia. In 2015, there were 245 reported cases of Lyme disease, more than double the 2014 figure. If you go walking in tick country, try to avoid tall grasses and shrubby areas. Wear long trousers tucked into socks, a long-sleeved shirt and a hat, and spray a DEET-based insect repellent on outer clothing. After leaving the area, carefully examine yourself all over as soon as it is practical. If you find a tick they should be removed with special tick tweezers that can be bought in good travel shops. Failing that you can use your fingernails: grasp the tick as close to your body as possible and pull steadily and firmly away at right angles to your skin. The tick will then come away complete, as long as you do not jerk or twist. If possible douse the wound with alcohol (any spirit will do) or iodine. Irritants (eg: Olbas oil) or lit cigarettes are to be discouraged since they can cause the ticks to regurgitate and therefore increase the risk of disease. It is best to get a travelling companion to check you for ticks; if you are travelling with small children, remember to check

> **EMERGENCY**
>
> Owing to a shortage of funds, not all hospital departments are open 24/7: in the case of a medical emergency, phone ⟍ 911 – the ambulance crew will know where to take you. It is important that you have adequate travel/medical insurance: unless you're from the province with a valid health card, an ambulance trip to the nearest hospital can cost well over CAN$700.

their heads, and particularly behind the ears. Spreading redness around the bite and/or fever and/or aching joints after a tick bite imply that you have an infection that requires antibiotic treatment, so seek advice.

LEECHES Leeches can occur in still or slow-moving water, such as the shallow edges of lakes. Many locals carry salt shakers with them when going on swimming (or paddling) trips to a lake, and if a leech attaches itself, a sprinkle of salt will usually make the creature dislodge. Leeches do not carry disease but do inject an anti-coagulant agent into the wound, so try to clean the wound, put on a dab of antiseptic cream, and cover with a plaster.

RABIES Rabies is spread through the saliva of an infected animal. It is usually transmitted through a bite or a scratch but can be transmitted by licks over broken skin or saliva getting into the eyes or mouth. The risk in terrestrial animals in Canada is low but not non-existent, so it is always wise to seek medical advice if you have a potential exposure from any warm-blooded mammal, including bats. However, the first thing to do before you seek advice is to thoroughly wash the wound with soap and water for a good ten to 15 minutes.

POISON IVY This toxic plant is found here and there in Nova Scotia (and in most of North America): it produces urushiol, an irritant which causes an allergic reaction to most of those who come in contact with it. The reaction takes the form of itching and inflammation and can be severe. I've only seen poison ivy once in Nova Scotia, and there were several big 'Warning! Poison Ivy' signs all around.

SUN Especially with cooling coastal breezes or thin layers of cloud, it is easy to get sunburned in Nova Scotia. Cover up and use sun cream.

SAFETY

Canada is politically stable and one of the world's safer places, and – Halifax and Dartmouth apart – Nova Scotia's crime rates are about average for the country (they have been on a downward trend for the last few years). Halifax (including Dartmouth) is second to Winnipeg as the Canadian city with the highest murder rate, and violent crime figures in the city are bucking the national trend and are on the increase. Having said that, you would have to be exceedingly unlucky to be in the wrong place at the wrong time.

Crimes tend to be a different story outside the city. Rightly or wrongly, many people in rural areas still don't lock their doors. I don't suggest that you follow their example, however romantic the notion might be.

Violent crimes are infrequent; far more common is petty theft. Some parts of the big urban areas are troubled by youth crime, often drug- or drink-inspired, but probably to a lesser degree than in equivalent cities in Europe or the USA.

Outside the urban centres, things seem so laid-back that it is easy to forget common sense. For instance, if you must leave valuable items in your car unattended, keep them out of sight, preferably locked in the vehicle's boot. And wherever you are in the world, carrying large amounts of cash around isn't a great idea.

THE LAW If you steer clear of drugs, you are unlikely to have unsolicited contact with the police in Nova Scotia. Pedestrians should be aware that, although in the UK, crossing the road safely is considered a personal responsibility, in Canada and the USA jaywalking (crossing a road without regard to traffic regulations) is a crime – albeit one that dozens of people in the province commit regularly, often in view of the police. Once behind a wheel, your chances of attracting the attention of local law enforcers do increase (see pages 55–6).

THE POLICE You won't see red-jacketed, horseriding Mounties in Nova Scotia – here the Royal Canadian Mounted Police (RCMP) dress less garishly and travel in police cars.

Municipal governments around the province are responsible for policing, and can choose if they want policing to be done by the RCMP or their own force. There are municipal forces in the two major urban centres (the central core of the Halifax Regional Municipality and Cape Breton Regional Municipality) and ten other towns, while the RCMP provides policing elsewhere in the province and in rural areas. It also performs the vast majority of highway policing. According to CBC news in July 2016, Halifax is the only major city in Canada to staff a police force that is as racially diverse as its community. Outside the HRM, some communities have their own local numbers on which to contact the police for non-emergencies. These can be found in the phone directory, or online at www.411.ca. The standard number to call for police assistance (and the fire or ambulance service) is ☏911.

TERRORISM No recent terrorism events have occurred in the province (unlike in 1883; box, below). Having said that, in 2015 a trio who (apparently) plotted a Valentine's Day mass shooting at a Halifax mall were deemed not to be terrorists but 'murderous misfits' because the attack they were planning did not appear to have been 'culturally motivated'.

WOMEN TRAVELLERS Women using their common sense are unlikely to have any problems in Nova Scotia, even if travelling alone. There have been claims that immigration officials give solo female travellers more of a grilling than others. Other than that it's just a case of being sensible: don't wander in dodgy areas at night, hitchhike alone, etc.

GAY AND LESBIAN TRAVELLERS Attitudes to gays and lesbians (not forgetting BTQ+) vary across the province. The Halifax Pride Festival (*halifaxpride.com*), for example, is Atlantic Canada's largest Pride celebration. On the other hand, for years Truro's mayor and council refused requests to raise the Gay Pride flag at the town hall and opposed a local Gay Pride parade. It takes time for embedded conservative beliefs to change, but thousands attended when the town finally held its first-ever Pride parade on a sunny July day in 2016. Truro's officials apart, in general there is greater acceptance in the big urban centres and more tourist-orientated and/or arts-focused communities.

POWER BEATS TERRORISTS

In 1883, Chief Constable Nicholas Power arrested two men in possession of explosives suspected of planning to blow up the HMS *Canada* in Halifax Harbour. At the time, Prince George, who would later become King George V, was serving on that very ship. Power was awarded the King's Police Medal (the police equivalent of the Armed Forces' Victoria Cross) in 1915.

Look out for *Wayves* magazine (*www.wayves.ca*), published 11 times yearly in Halifax for gays across the Atlantic Canada region. NSRAP, the Nova Scotia Rainbow Action Project (*nsrap.ca*), and the Nova Scotia section of gay-travel resource Purple Roofs (*www.purpleroofs.com*) may also be of interest.

TRAVELLERS WITH A DISABILITY Canada, including Nova Scotia, has relatively high accessibility standards. There has been an increasing awareness that many people need special services, from various diet requirements to accessibility arrangements and protection from animal allergies. As such, its beach resorts as well as its wilderness are becoming a joy for everyone. The most comprehensive accessibility information website is offered by **Access Guide Canada** (*www.abilities.ca*), a voluntary programme compiling information on a wide variety of services, from transportation to lodgings and entertainment venues. Contact the **Nova Scotia League for Equal Opportunities** (*5251 Duke St, Suite 1211, Halifax B3K 4E1;* \ *902 455 6942;* e *nsleo@eastlink.ca; www.novascotialeo.org*) with enquiries regarding transportation services, access to recreational facilities, or other services and referrals. Information may also be obtained via www.gov.uk/guidance/foreign-travel-for-disabled-people.

WHAT TO TAKE

Choose your clothes on the basis that temperatures and weather conditions can change quickly and dramatically even in summer. A sudden sea mist can block out the sun and cause the temperature to drop a number of degrees – dress in layers.

Rain- and wind-proof gear is useful at any time of year, and a sturdy, fold-up umbrella (which doesn't blow inside-out at the first hint of a breeze) can be useful for summer showers, or if the sun gets too strong. In addition to comfortable walking shoes, hiking boots or shoes (with a good grip) will enable you to better enjoy the many beautiful trails.

Long-sleeved shirts and blouses can help protect against mosquitoes and tiny black flies: insect repellent can be a necessity in some areas at some times of the year, though it can be purchased locally. Binoculars can be useful for wildlife spotting, and if you're taking electrical goods, or those that operate on rechargeable batteries.

Take out comprehensive travel insurance when you book your travel arrangements – this should cover cancellation, lost or stolen baggage, and – most importantly – medical emergencies.

ELECTRICITY Canada's electrical sockets are the same as those found in the USA, ie: two flat-pin plugs. Occasionally, some have a third round earth pin. The electrical supply is 110 volts and 60 hertz (cycles per second).

Many, but not all, electrical appliances sold in the UK have dual voltage power supplies and will work happily in Canada once you attach a UK–US/Canada adaptor. If the appliance rating plate on your device does not say something like 'input 100–240V', you may need a transformer or converter and an adaptor: check with an electrical shop to be sure.

UK–US/Canada adaptors are surprisingly difficult to find in Nova Scotia, so take what you'll need with you.

MONEY

CASH The Canadian dollar (CAN$) is Canada's official unit of currency. One dollar equals 100 cents. Dollars are issued in banknote denominations of 5, 10, 20,

50 and 100 and coins of 1 (often called a 'looney'; box, page 27) and 2 dollars (a 'toonie'). Cent coin denominations are 5 (nickel), 10 (dime), 25 (quarter) and 50.

US dollars are widely accepted, but change (if any) will be given in Canadian dollars, and the exchange rate will almost always be worse than that offered by banks. In recent years, the Canadian dollar exchange rate has rollercoasted against the US dollar, and I'm not even going to try to guess what Brexit will do to the pound. The current exchange rates are £1=CAN$1.66, US$1=CAN$1.33 and €1=CAN$1.38 (December 2016).

CREDIT AND DEBIT CARDS Virtually all major credit and debit cards are quite widely accepted in Nova Scotia, but some businesses are still cash only. As is the case in the UK, at some ATMs (for example, those in petrol stations or general stores) there may be a charge for using the machine, in addition to the fee charged by most UK banks each time that a debit card is used abroad. Check with your bank as other fees (for example, exchange-rate loading) may also apply. Using a credit card for purchases and a debit card for getting cash is now the most popular combination for those visiting the province. An ever-increasing number of businesses now use tap credit/debit card machines. More than once I've had a UK card that just wouldn't work in any of these machines, but was fortunate that another of my cards (attached to another account) did work.

I find the 'Cheap Travel Money' section at www.moneysavingexpert.com to be a very useful resource for the latest and best ways of getting the best rates whilst incurring the least charges.

It is worth notifying your bank where you will be going and for how long at least a week or so before you leave home: at the same time, make a note of the phone numbers to use if your card(s) are lost or stolen whilst in Nova Scotia.

EXCHANGING CURRENCY Currency can be exchanged in banks, credit unions, trust companies, larger hotels and at currency-exchange bureaux. Check not only the exchange rate, but also any commission charges. Most travellers to Nova Scotia now rely on credit cards, and ATMs (often referred to as ABMs in Nova Scotia) for cash withdrawals with debit cards.

PRE-PAID TRAVEL MONEY CARDS These are a relatively recent phenomenon and are designed to give the security of travellers' cheques with the convenience of a plastic debit card. You apply for a card, load it up with funds before you go, and use your card to withdraw cash at the province's ATMs, or to pay at most businesses that accept credit cards. You can even top the card up whilst you are away.

HARMONISED SALES TAX (HST)

Nova Scotia leads Canada by having the highest sales tax. Harmonised Sales Tax (HST) of 15% is added to the price of most goods and services in Nova Scotia. Exceptions include basic groceries (milk, bread, vegetables) and items bought at farmers' markets and yard sales. But in most cases whenever you see a price in Nova Scotia – on a menu, in a shop, for a hotel room, etc – expect an extra 15% to be added. Occasionally, something is listed as 'taxes in', which means the tax has already been added. There used to be a program where visitors could claim back some (or all) of the HST they had paid when in Nova Scotia, but no longer. Unless stated otherwise, prices shown in this book include HST.

DISCOUNT CARDS

If you have an International Student Card (ISIC), or International Youth Travel Card (IYTC), or are a 'senior', it is always worth asking for a discount at attractions, for tours, even for accommodation. Students, youths and seniors (60+) are entitled to reduced rates on VIA Rail.

The downside is that again there are fees to watch out for. Some providers charge for card applications, ATM withdrawals and top-ups. However, as more players come into the market, it is likely that these cards will become more competitive and user-friendly. Once again, check the 'Cheap Travel Money' section at www.moneysavingexpert.com for current best buys (and their pros and cons).

BANKS Banking hours vary, but in general are 10.00–16.00 Monday–Friday. Some banks stay open later on Fridays, and a few may open on Saturday mornings. In terms of their networks, the province's main banks are **Scotiabank** (*www.scotiabank.com*) and **Royal Bank** (*www.rbcroyalbank.com*). Twenty-four-hour ATMs (often called ABMs) are commonplace. Larger supermarkets almost always have ATMs, and many offer some banking services. Many bigger stores offer cashback.

BUDGETING

So how expensive is a holiday in Nova Scotia going to be? Some things are easy to work out – air fares (including all the taxes), car hire (if you pre-pay) – whilst others are of course more variable. A lot, too, depends on the vagaries of fluctuating exchange rates.

In general, you'll find grocery prices higher than in both the UK and the USA. Grocery bills can be reduced by taking advantage of the range of goods on special offer each week – these are listed in newspaper-like flyers which come out every Thursday. Eating out in most cafés and restaurants tends to be on par with the UK, cheaper for shellfish (eg: lobster, mussels, clams, etc).

Petrol (gas) prices have fluctuated a lot of late, but are usually significantly cheaper than the UK (see *www.novascotiagasprices.com*). Compared with provinces (and American states) on the west of the continent, Nova Scotia is quite compact, so driving distances tend to be shorter too.

Although there aren't many youth (or backpacker) hostels, there are plenty of cheap motels, and most B&Bs are very well priced (especially when you take

SAMPLE PRICES (JULY 2016) INCLUDING TAX WHERE RELEVANT	
A litre of (regular) petrol	CAN$1
A litre of milk	CAN$2.30
A (473ml) can of beer (Keith's IPA)	CAN$3.49
A dinner main course (including vegetables) at a reasonable restaurant	CAN$18–28
A bus (or ferry) ticket in Halifax	CAN$2.50
A three- to five-hour whale-watching trip from Brier Island (box, page 211)	CAN$49–65
A dormitory bed in a backpackers' hostel	CAN$30
A daily newspaper (the *Chronicle Herald*)	CAN$2

Practical Information BUDGETING

2

the quality breakfasts into account), and tend to be cheaper than in many other Canadian provinces. A range of accommodation is available for those who are happy to spend more for more space, better facilities, etc.

GETTING AROUND

It is easy to travel around Nova Scotia – if you have a vehicle. Sadly, public transport is quite limited, and virtually non-existent in many areas.

BY AIR Air Canada (tf *1 888 247 2262; www.aircanada.com*) offers a few flights a day between Halifax and Sydney, Cape Breton Island, as does Westjet (tf *1 888 937 8538; www.westjet.com*).

BY CAR For the freedom it gives you, the (generally) good roads, and – compared with much of Europe and urban North America – the (generally) very light traffic, driving is by far the best way to get around the province. British motorists, used to driving on the left, will quickly adapt to driving on the right. Most drivers in Nova Scotia are courteous, patient and observant of speed limits. Outside downtown Halifax, parking is rarely a problem.

Traffic jams are not unheard of, particularly during rush hour on the approaches to and from Halifax and Dartmouth, and the motorway (Hwy 102) which links them with the airport.

Everywhere is well within a day's drive of Halifax. You could easily reach Yarmouth in three–four hours, and Sydney (on the east coast of Cape Breton Island) in four–five hours. But Nova Scotia is not about rushing from A to B: in fact, quite the opposite. Where possible, try to avoid the motorways and aim instead for the smaller, often much more scenic – albeit slower – alternatives. Try to allow far more time than distances on the map might suggest. One of the joys of touring the province is discovering what lies beyond the main roads: making side trips down virtually uninhabited peninsulas, trying to spot whales from a headland, stopping to pick your own strawberries, to wander deserted beaches, take in the view from a look-out, or to watch boats bobbing in the harbour at tiny fishing villages.

If you're a member of an automobile association such as the AAA, AA or RAC, you should be able to take advantage of the services of the **Canadian Automobile Association (Atlantic)** (*www.atlantic.caa.ca*) which has offices in Halifax (✆ *902 443 5530*) and Dartmouth (✆ *902 468 6306*). Members of related overseas associations can enjoy many benefits including free maps and guides, travel agency services, and emergency road services.

DRIVING THROUGH HISTORY

In September 1899, The *Halifax Echo* reported the arrival (from Liverpool, England) of a ship carrying the first car ever seen in Nova Scotia.

Until 14 April 1923, driving was on the left-hand side of the road. At that time, teams of oxen (pulling wagons) were common on the province's roads, but it proved almost impossible to retrain them to walk on the other side of the road. So many redundant oxen were sent to the slaughterhouse as a result, that there was a dramatic reduction in the price of beef. Horses proved a bit more adaptable: almost nine decades later, it is only the occasional absent-minded driver visiting from the UK who gets it wrong.

Roads Nova Scotia has some 23,000km of roads, and 4,100 road bridges. Officially, all named roads in Nova Scotia are 'highways' whether they are (what we would call) motorways or narrow country roads. Limited-access motorways (usually blue or green on road maps, and numbered 100–199) are usually two lanes in each direction, sometimes dual carriageways, but sometimes just a single lane in each direction.

The vast majority of those entering the province by road will do so near Amherst on the Trans Canada Highway (TCH), Highway 104. Between exits 8 and 10, a toll (*from CAN$4*) is levied. The TCH heads east to Cape Breton Island (*en route* a short spur, Highway 106, leads to the Caribou ferry terminal) where it connects with Highway 105. Highway 104 continues to St Peter's, whereas Highway 105 leads to North Sydney.

For those renting a car at Halifax Airport, the airport is off Highway 102, which connects Halifax with the TCH, meeting it near Truro.

Highway 101 runs between Halifax and Yarmouth via the Annapolis Valley, and Highway 103 connects the same end points via the South Shore.

The old (pre-motorway) single-digit main roads tend to run almost parallel with their motorway counterparts (eg: highways 1 and 101, 2 and 102, etc).

Most other roads are one lane in each direction, with soft (gravel) shoulders. Be prepared for some rough surfaces and potholes – a combination of winter weather and the cost of maintaining thousands of kilometres of backroads. In rural areas (much of the province!) watch out for wildlife (eg: deer, racoons, porcupine) particularly if driving at dusk or after dark.

Petrol (gas) is sold by the litre. At some garages (gas stations) small discounts are sometimes offered to those paying in cash or by debit card; at some others, companies may offer a couple of cents per litre off to customers who have (or apply for) a (free) loyalty card. Where offered, 'full-serve' (someone pumping for you) is usually a couple of cents per litre more than 'self-serve'. Prices at the pumps change at midnight on Thursday. You should bear in mind that few rural petrol stations are open 24/7. Similarly, not all rural petrol stations open on Sundays or holidays. The (self-explanatory) website www.novascotiagasprices.com may also be of interest.

Licences Full national driving licences from most major countries of the world, including the UK, Australia and the USA, are valid in Nova Scotia. If your licence is not in English or French, I'd recommend obtaining an International Driving Permit. UK drivers with two-part (photocard and paper) licences should take both parts with them, though the paper part is rarely asked for. Those who are staying long-term and working in Nova Scotia, or whose children will be attending school in the province, should check at what stage they need to exchange their 'foreign' licence for a Nova Scotia licence (Nova Scotia has a licence reciprocity agreement with the UK).

Driving laws Wearing of safety belts is compulsory for all passengers, and motorcyclists and any pillion passengers must wear helmets. Infants weighing under 10kg must be strapped into a rear-facing secured approved seat: toddlers weighing 10–18kg must be strapped into an appropriate forward-facing child's seat. Children weighing over 18kg, but less than 145cm tall, must use a booster seat. Those hiring cars can request these seats to be included at extra cost: I've found it easier to take them with me from the UK.

Speed limits are generally 100km/h on the Trans Canada Highway and 100-series roads, 80km/h on other highways, 50km/h in cities and towns, and 30km/h when children are present.

The province's highways are patrolled by the Royal Canadian Mounted Police (RCMP) and by air patrol: substantial fines are imposed for violating speed limits.

Be very careful around yellow, old-fashioned school buses: you must stop at least 20m from a school bus, on either side of the road, which is loading or unloading passengers (this will be indicated by flashing red lights, or 'stop flags' on the side of the bus). Do not proceed until the lights are switched off, or flags lifted.

When driving in towns and cities, take great care when you see pedestrians anywhere near the kerb: it is compulsory to stop for pedestrians at a crosswalk (like a zebra crossing but without the Belisha beacons), and some pedestrians have become so used to courteous local drivers stopping and waving them across the road that they may step out into the road without looking.

You must stop completely at a stop sign (traffic police aren't impressed by 'rolling stops'), but – unless signs say otherwise – you are permitted to turn right at a red traffic light, having first stopped and checked that it is safe to do so. When turning left at a junction, turn in front of a car coming from the opposite direction which is also turning left.

When overtaking (passing), you are supposed to sound your horn (though almost nobody does).

In an emergency, pull as far away from the driving lanes as possible, and switch on your hazard lights. If you are involved in a collision, within 24 hours you must notify the RCMP, local police, or the Registry of Motor Vehicles if the accident involves injury, death or damage of more than CAN$1,000.

Authorities in Nova Scotia regard drinking and driving (with a blood-alcohol level of 0.08% or higher), or driving whilst under the influence of drugs, as very serious offences. You could be imprisoned for up to five years even on a first offence.

For further information, see the provincial government-produced *Nova Scotia Driver's Handbook*, at novascotia.ca/sns/rmv/licence/handbook.asp.

Insurance for US drivers If you are driving your vehicle in Nova Scotia, proof of auto insurance is required. US auto insurance is accepted as long as you are visiting as a tourist. US insurance firms will issue a Canadian insurance card, which should be obtained prior to departure from the USA and carried with you when driving in Nova Scotia. You may also be asked to prove vehicle ownership, so it is wise to carry your vehicle registration form.

Car hire Most visitors driving in Nova Scotia will need to hire (or rent) a vehicle. You will need to be 21 or over: most rental companies apply a Young Driver Surcharge for under 25s, present a passport, full driving licence, and – even if you have pre-paid for your vehicle hire – will be asked for a credit card to cover any incidental charges.

All major car-hire companies have outlets at Halifax International Airport and in (or close to) downtown Halifax. For other locations, see opposite. Most companies will allow you to pick-up in downtown Halifax and drop-off at Halifax International Airport at no extra cost. If, however, you want to pick-up in Halifax and drop-off in, say, Sydney, check for one-way rental surcharges.

When comparing prices, there are numerous factors to take into consideration: check inclusions and exclusions, extra driver charges if more than one of you will take the wheel, taxes and more. All-inclusive pre-paid rates, especially when booked via the internet, are often the best value. Using an internet car broker (eg: www.carrentals.co.uk or www.rentalcars.com) can save a lot of searching time. Tour operators are also worth checking: I've found ebookers.com to be competitive.

Major rental companies (and locations of their depots) include:

🚗 **Avis** 📞0808 284 0014; www.avis.co.uk. Halifax & airport, Dartmouth, Westville &, Sydney, North Sydney.

🚗 **Budget** 📞0844 544 3439; www.budget. co.uk. Halifax & airport & Sydney.

🚗 **Enterprise** www.enterprise.co.uk. Halifax & airport, Dartmouth, Falmouth, New Glasgow, Sydney, Bridgewater, Yarmouth, Amherst, Antigonish, Digby, Lower Sackville, Middleton & New Minas.

🚗 **Hertz** www.hertz.co.uk. Halifax & airport.

Motorhome rental Another option is to hire a motorhome (campervan) or RV (recreational vehicle) as they're often known in North America. You can then reduce costs by sleeping (comfortably) and even cooking in your vehicle. Prices aren't particularly cheap, and there are extras to add. Personally, I think western Canada is better suited to motorhome holidays, but it is something to consider.

Canadream 📞902 435 3276; **tf** 1 8888 480 97268; www.canadream.com. Bookable in the UK (📞0808 168 0045) & based in Dartmouth, NS.

Cruise Canada 📞902 865 0639; **tf** 1 800 671 8042; www.cruisecanada.com. Bookable in the UK through North America Travel Service or Trailfinders (page 40) & based in Upper Sackville.

BY COACH With the exceptions of one section of railway line (serving just four stations thrice-weekly), a few local public bus services and private shuttle companies, Nova Scotia's primary public transport network consists of coach services offered by **Maritime Bus** (**tf** *1 800 575 1807; maritimebus.com*). The network includes a daily (or more frequent) service in each direction between Halifax and Kentville stopping at Dartmouth, Lower Sackville, Falmouth (for Windsor), Wolfville and New Minas. Halifax is also connected a few times daily with Dartmouth, Halifax Airport, Truro, Amherst and Moncton, New Brunswick.

Maritime Bus stops on once- or twice-daily services between Halifax and Sydney (Cape Breton Island) include Dartmouth, Halifax Airport, Elmsdale, Stewiacke, Truro, New Glasgow, Antigonish, Port Hawkesbury, Whycocomagh, Baddeck and North Sydney. To stop at certain places (eg: Falmouth and Baddeck) your ticket must be purchased at least 24 hours before the journey. Sample one-way are: Halifax–Wolfville CAN$27, Halifax–Sydney CAN$86.

BY SHUTTLE Shuttle services, usually in comfortable minivans, are another option. Most shuttle operators will also do pick-ups/drop-offs at Halifax International Airport. For services between Halifax International Airport and downtown Halifax/Dartmouth, see pages 84–5. Most services between Halifax and Cape Breton Island will allow pick-ups and drop-offs at Dartmouth, Halifax Airport, Truro, New Glasgow, Antigonish, Port Hastings, Whycocomagh and Baddeck.

KEEPING UP APPEARANCES

By the 1840s there was a regular stagecoach service between Halifax and Truro. On leaving Halifax, the coach was pulled by six grey horses. However, this was mainly for show: just a few miles after leaving Halifax, the handsome horses were changed and replaced with (less eye-catching) heavier and more powerful beasts. Strength was needed – the road was often axle-deep in mud.

Various shuttle operators/guides will customise tours for you: try for example Digby-based **Kathleen's Shuttle and Tours**.

Shuttle services & operators

Between Halifax & Yarmouth
Daily service; approx CAN$75–85 one-way
Cloud Nine Shuttle ☎ 902 742 3992; www.thecloudnineshuttle.com. Via the South Shore or Annapolis Valley.
Mariner Shuttle tf 1 855 586 6140; www.marinershuttle.co. Via the French Shore, Digby & the Annapolis Valley.

Between Halifax & Mahone Bay, Lunenburg & Bridgewater
Daily service by advance reservation
Try Town Transit ☎ 902 521 0855

Between Digby, Yarmouth & Halifax *Daily service by advance reservation*

Kathleen's Shuttle and Tours ☎ 902 834 2024; tf 1 877 720 8747; kathleensshuttleandtours.webs.com

Between Halifax and Cape Breton Island *Daily service; approx CAN$60–80 one-way*
Bay Luxury Shuttle ☎ 902 849 8083; tf 1 855 673 8083; www.capebretonshuttle.ca
Cape Shuttle Service ☎ 902 539 8585; tf 1 800 349 1698; www.capeshuttleservice.com
East Coast Shuttle ☎ 902 794 1512; tf 1 800 873 5551; www.eastcoastshuttle.com
MacLeod's Shuttle ☎ 902 539 2700; www.macleodsshuttle.ca
Nova Shuttle/Scotia Shuttle ☎ 902 539 8585; tf 1 800 349 1698; www.scotiashuttle.ca

BY BUS Local public bus services cover the most populated parts of the Halifax Regional Municipality (page 86), the Cape Breton Regional Municipality (page 355), and the stretch of the Annapolis Valley and environs between Weymouth and Brooklyn (page 204).

BY TRAIN Passenger rail travel is very limited, but possible: three days a week, **VIA Rail** (tf *1 888 842 7245; www.viarail.ca*) runs a service between Montreal, Quebec and Halifax, and this stops at Amherst, Springhill Junction and Truro. See pages 46–7 for more information.

BY BIKE Cyclists are permitted on all Nova Scotia's roads, including motorways. Helmets must be worn. When riding at night you must use a white front light and a red rear reflector (a rear-facing, flashing red light is acceptable). Reflectors and reflective clothing are also advisable. Most airlines allow bikes as checked baggage, but will have rules as to how the bike should be packed: a handling fee may apply. Check and re-check before booking your ticket. For more on cycling, see pages 69–70.

HITCHHIKING Hitchhiking is not allowed on 100-series major (controlled-access) motorways. Whilst chances are that all will go well and that you'll meet some interesting people, climbing into a stranger's vehicle always carries some degree of risk. Police may also pull over and chat to hitchers to check that they are not missing persons or runaways. As in much of the world, hitching isn't as easy (or as safe) as it used to be – and the release in 2007 of a remake of a 1986 film, *The Hitcher*, hasn't helped. Storylines of psychopathic, murderous hitchhikers don't exactly encourage drivers to pick up strangers.

ACCOMMODATION

The province offers a range of places to stay, from wilderness campsites through to deluxe hotels and resorts. Virtually all of these are listed on Nova Scotia's official

Some love it, some don't trust it: most of the bookings I've made with Airbnb (*www.airbnb.ca*) have turned out well, but I've heard from others who weren't so lucky. In case you don't know, Airbnb is an online community marketplace that tries to connect owners looking to rent out one or more rooms – or whole buildings – with people who are looking for accommodation. Some prestigious establishments have signed up to the service, and are often listed alongside a property where someone has an extra bedroom that they think they can get an income from. The internet is full of pages of pro/anti comments and tips on how best to use the service. Several of the B&Bs, motels, hotels, etc, recommended in this book market themselves through Airbnb (and other channels); conversely, just because somewhere on Airbnb isn't recommended in this guide doesn't mean that there is something wrong with it.

tourism website (*www.novascotia.com*), and also appear in the official annual *Doers & Dreamers* guide (page 41). Outside the biggest urban centres, relatively few properties are open year-round: for most, the season runs mid May to early October. In listings, we have noted those places only open in season; otherwise, assume they are open year-round.

High season (with the highest prices) is July and early to mid September, but advance reservations are recommended for stays between late June and the end of September, and during the Celtic Colours Festival in Cape Breton in October. Outside these dates, festivals apart, you should be able to find something in the area. You won't find all the motels, B&Bs, guesthouses, etc, in this book listed on such websites as www.booking.com, www.expedia.ca or www.airbnb.ca but all three – plus www.bbcanada.com/nova_scotia, for B&Bs – are worth trying anyway. Unless stated otherwise, the prices quoted in this book are high-season rates for a single night's stay in a room for two people. Many properties offer significantly cheaper rates out of season: others may give discounts for stays of more than a couple of nights. In my opinion, it is always worth asking about discounts – they are sometimes given to students, seniors, Automobile Association members, those wanting more than one room, etc – but don't expect reductions in high season.

HOTELS Halifax and Sydney are home to the big-name (relatively) high-rise hotels. Dotted about the province's shoreline are resorts offering everything from standard rooms to three- or four-bedroom private chalets, and numerous activities, which often include a golf course.

MOTELS Motels range from traditional family-owned single-storey buildings (some have seen better days) where you can park right outside the door of your room, to brand-new international chains, often with heated indoor swimming pools.

B&BS For me, one of the joys of travelling around Nova Scotia is its B&Bs and small inns. Several are housed in beautifully renovated historic buildings, many of which are heritage properties, and are tastefully decorated with period(ish) antiques. Despite the historical surroundings, amenities are modern and the plumbing works well. Each property is unique and full of character, and good hosts can quickly recognise whether you want your own space, or whether you'd like to sit, chat and perhaps benefit from their local knowledge. Breakfasts are generally superb. A good place to start looking is the website www.bbcanada.com/nova_scotia.

Bathrooms can be shared, private or en suite. Occasionally, the terminology can cause confusion: where a property has a shared bathroom, that bathroom is for the use of the occupants of more than one guestroom; a private bathroom is solely for the use of guests in a particular room, but guests will have to go out of their room and across the corridor or down the hall to the bathroom; if a bathroom is en suite, you will be able to access your own bathroom by opening a door in your guestroom. All (non-camping) accommodation listed in this book offers en-suite or private bathrooms unless otherwise noted.

Also be aware that some inns and B&B owners have pets and there may be dogs or cats on the premises: check before booking if that might bother you.

HOSTELS AND BACKPACKERS These are somewhat limited. There are Hostelling International (HI) hostels in Halifax, at South Milford near Kejimkujik National Park, at Wentworth, on Cape Breton Island at Pleasant Bay and Aberdeen. There are also private hostels in Halifax, near Lunenburg/Mahone Bay, at Port Mouton, just outside Kejimkujik National Park in Caledonia, in Digby, and in Parrsboro. If there are two (or more) of you, a cheap room in a motel or simple B&B often won't cost much more than a couple of dormitory beds would.

CAMPING If you're looking to spend your nights under canvas – well, nylon – Nova Scotia has both province-run and privately owned campgrounds. The former are in the two mainland national parks and over 20 provincial parks (see *parks.novascotia. ca*) – but note that many provincial parks close in early September. There are

---

RATING THE RATINGS

In the absence of a standard international rating system for hotels, inns, B&Bs and other accommodation, Canada uses a star system under the auspices of **Canada Select** (*www.canadaselect.com*), administered in Nova Scotia by **Quality Visitor Services** (↳ 902 406 4747; *www.qvs.ca*). The programme is voluntary in Nova Scotia. Accommodations are divided into various categories (eg: Hotel/Motel, Inn, Resort, B&B/Tourist Home, Cottage/Vacation Home) – plus camping. Several of these categories have further subdivisions. Properties are evaluated by an inspector who takes several factors (including facilities, services and amenities provided) into account, and a star rating from 1 to 5, in ½-star increments is awarded.

This works fine for many types of accommodation, but doesn't work very well for B&Bs and inns. Under the rating system for B&Bs, an establishment that chooses to have a television in a lounge (rather than in each guestroom) drops one star. If it decides not to have a phone in every guestroom, another star disappears. Many people spend a couple of nights at a five-star-rated B&B or inn, then transfer to a three-star and are surprised to find it a lot better. For me, the system focuses too heavily on facilities/amenities offered, too lightly on individuality, ambience, charm, service and quality, and not at all on comfort or the hospitality offered. A number of inn and B&B owners agree, and – rather than receive a lower star rating based on a checklist of amenities – have withdrawn from the Canada Select programme. Don't rush to select or omit a property based just on its star rating (or lack thereof).

about 120 privately owned campgrounds, more than 70 of which are listed on the **Campground Owners Association of Nova Scotia** website (*www.campingnovascotia. com*). In addition to standard sites, many campgrounds have serviced sites where those with motorhomes can hook up to water, electricity and a sewer. Many private sites have sliding costs depending on site location – in other words, seafront sites, for example, may cost a lot more than those a few rows back. At both of the national parks, Parks Canada offers you the chance to stay in an **oTENTik**, a spacious blend of tent and rustic cabin equipped with beds and furniture on a raised floor. At the other end of the scale, there are also opportunities for wilderness or back-country camping.

RENTALS Those looking for more space will find a variety of places to rent, from studio apartments to large multi-bedroom houses. Confusingly, these are often referred to as housekeeping units, vacation homes or cottages. They will have equipped kitchens or kitchenettes, and towels and bedding will be provided. How well equipped they are varies from place to place. Often a minimum rental of three or more nights applies, and in summer a minimum of a week is the norm, usually starting on a Saturday.

Many are marketed by **Cottage Connection** (**tf** *1 800 780 3682; www.stayinnovascotia. com*), but also try **Sandy Lane Vacations** (\ *902 875 2729;* **tf** *1 800 646 1577; www. sandylanevacations.com*), who focus on the South Shore west of Bridgewater. Rentals of all shapes and sizes are also offered through the 'real estate: rental' section of www. kijiji.ca, and don't forget the ever-growing Airbnb (box, page 59).

HOMESTAYS WITH THE MI'KMAQ As yet, there are no organised programmes for those who wish to stay overnight (or longer) with a Mi'kmaq family. However, it may be possible to arrange homestays on an ad hoc basis by contacting either the **Millbrook Cultural and Heritage Centre** (page 267) or **Eskasoni Cultural Journeys** (box, page 353).

Practical Information ACCOMMODATION

2

William Deer, who lives here, keeps the best of wine and beer, brandy, and cider, and other good cheer. Fish, and ducks, and moose and deer, caught or shot in the woods near here, with cutlets, or steaks, as will appear; If you will stop you need not fear But you will be well treated by William Deer, And by Mrs Deer, his dearest, deary dear!

Sign outside an inn in Preston, Nova Scotia, in the 1850s

FOOD Visitors who enjoy **seafood** will be in gastronomic nirvana everywhere in Nova Scotia. The price may have crept up over the years, but fish (usually haddock) and chips is almost always done well, freshly cooked and not too greasy. You'll also see a lot of flounder, halibut and salmon: plank (or planked) salmon – where the fish is slow-cooked on a wood plank (usually cedar) – is a highlight.

Then there's the **shellfish**. Top of the pile is lobster – Nova Scotia is the world's largest exporter of the crustacean, but more than enough remains to grace menus throughout the province. It is usually steamed or boiled in seawater, then served with butter – fancier methods of presentation, such as lobster thermidor or lobster Newburg, are seen less often. The larger supermarkets often have glass lobster tanks – at Sobeys stores (page 67) you can choose a lobster and have it cooked whilst you wait, at no extra cost.

But the province's waters offer other treats, too. Enjoy some of the world's most delicious scallops, plus tasty mussels, oysters, crab and clams. Seafood chowder (a thick, chunky creamy seafood soup) can be a meal in itself.

Those who choose not to eat, or want a change from, seafood need not worry. You will usually find a reasonable selection of chicken, turkey, pork, beef and (to a lesser degree) lamb dishes. Upmarket steak restaurants tend to use beef flown in from Alberta, Canada, or the USA.

ACADIAN CUISINE AND OTHER LOCAL SPECIALITIES

The province's earliest European settlers left a gastronomic legacy that still lives on. Order Solomon Gundy and you'll be presented with pickled herring; fiddleheads are the unfurled fronds of ostrich ferns, delicious steamed and served with a squeeze of lemon juice and a dab of butter. Dulse is dried, purple seaweed, usually nibbled as a snack. Lunenburg pudding is a kind of meat-based pâté. Blueberry grunt is a much-loved summer dessert. Although many dishes focus on seafood, there are several to look out for which are land-based: *chicken fricot* (stew), *tourtiere* (meat pie), *pâte à la rapure* (often called 'rappie pie'), and butterscotch pie. Particularly popular with the junk-food crowd are *donair* (a Nova Scotia version of the doner kebab) and *poutine* – chips (fries) topped with cheese curds and brown gravy. Taste buds tingling yet?

SOLOMON GUNDY
Ingredients
Six salt herring (heads and tails removed, cleaned, skinned and deboned)
Three medium onions, thinly sliced
Two cups vinegar
Two tablespoons pickling spice
Half a cup caster sugar

With a few exceptions (notably Pictou County), sheep are pretty scarce in Nova Scotia. There are a number of reasons for this: for example, much of the land is forested, the difficulty in protecting flocks from coyote predation, and higher returns from using pasture for cattle. It is also said that – unlike coyotes – most Nova Scotians just aren't all that keen on the taste of lamb.

In the summer and autumn, **fruit** is fresh and plentiful, and apples and blueberries in particular make their way onto many menus, and not just in the dessert section. For example, apple sauce is a perfect accompaniment to roast pork, whilst blueberry sauce works well with red meat.

Outside Halifax and Dartmouth, the university towns of Wolfville and Antigonish, and places that attract a high number of visitors, the majority of restaurateurs still seem to care little about their restaurant's aesthetics or their food's cholesterol levels. Less than a decade ago, those who wanted to avoid deep-fried food were looked upon with bewilderment.

The good news is that recent years have seen some changes. Driven by a combination of factors – the theory of healthy eating slowly filtering through to Nova Scotia, the culinary wishes expressed by visitors, and an increase in new restaurateurs from outside the province – many more establishments have learnt to use cooking methods other than the deep-fryer and use fresh, often organic, locally grown produce. Thought is given to the look of the establishment's interior, and food presentation, and the menus themselves are more varied and creative. Many of the old-style eateries have begun to join the revolution and will now grill (or at least) pan-fry fish for you – although this may add a dollar or two to the price. More sophisticated cuisine also tends to mean slightly smaller portions.

Directions Cut the herring into approximately 2cm pieces and soak for 24 hours in cold water. Squeeze the water from the herring. Place in jar with slices of onion, in alternate layers. Heat vinegar, pickling spice and sugar, stirring. Allow to cool, pour into jar. Seal jar and keep in fridge for eight to ten days.

BLUEBERRY GRUNT
Fruit mix ingredients
Four cups blueberries
Two-thirds of a cup caster sugar
Half a cup water
One tablespoon lemon juice

Dumpling ingredients
Two cups plain flour
Four teaspoons baking powder
One tablespoon caster sugar
Half a teaspoon salt
Two tablespoons butter
Milk

Directions Combine fruit mix ingredients and bring to the boil in a large saucepan. Reduce heat and simmer until berries are soft and sauce begins to thicken, about five minutes. Sift flour, baking powder, sugar and salt into a bowl. Cut in butter and stir in just enough milk to make a soft dough. Mix well, then drop spoonfuls of batter onto the simmering berry sauce. Immediately cover saucepan and simmer without removing cover for 15 minutes. Serve warm with whipped cream.

Practical Information EATING AND DRINKING

2

If you prefer fast and/or junk food, you need not worry: McDonald's (where the summer menu usually includes a McLobster roll!), KFC, Subway, Dairy Queen, Taco Bell and many other burger chains (eg: A&W) are well represented, and there are numerous pizza joints and take-aways.

Look, too, beyond traditional restaurants, cafés, dining rooms and bistros: community breakfasts and suppers may not offer *haute cuisine* but are almost always excellent value (breakfasts around CAN$8, dinners around CAN$12), and a great way to meet (and chat to) the locals. Farmers' markets and supermarket deli counters are good places to put a picnic together, and – in season – you can pick your own fresh berries for dessert.

Bear in mind that outside the biggest cities it may be hard to find restaurants open much past 20.00 (or earlier!). Be aware too that away from the capital, some of the province's best eateries are actually inn restaurants.

Vegetarians Whilst vegetarian restaurants are few and far between, vegetarian choices are usually offered, although they may not be more exciting than pasta or pizza. In general, the new-wave, more sophisticated cafés, bistros and restaurants will be more vegetarian-friendly.

BEER AND BEANS BOOM

Recent years have seen such a rapid growth in the numbers of both microbreweries and coffee roasteries that one could almost dedicate an entire Nova Scotia guide just to coffee and beer. Coffee aficionados should look out for names such as Just Us!, Laughing Whale, Sissiboo, T.A.N., North Mountain, Full Steam and Puddle Jump.

Independent beer producers are dotted about the province: in the regional sections I have tried to include breweries that are open for tours/tastings and or brewpubs. Halifax/Dartmouth is home both to the relatively big guys such as **Propeller Brewing Co** (*www.drinkpropeller.ca*) and the young upstarts like the **Good Robot Brewing Company** (*goodrobotbrewing.ca*). Every month, it seems, a new craft brewery opens, and it is the same province-wide. Head to Guysborough for the **Authentic Seacoast Brewing Co** (*www.rarebirdpub. com/brewery*), to **Mahone Bay** for the Saltbox Brewing Company (*www. saltboxbrewingcompany.ca*), to Port Williams (near Wolfville) for **Sea Level Brewing** (*www.sealevelbrewing.com*) and **Wayfarers' Ale** (*wayfarersale.ca*). Tatamagouche has the **Tatamagouche Brewing Co** (*tatabrew.com*), and Cape Breton Island breweries include **Big Spruce Brewing** (*bigspruce.ca*) and **Breton Brewing** (*bretonbrewing.ca*). The list could go on and on. Cheers!

In recent years, Nova Scotian wines have begun to make their mark, both at home and on the international stage. The long-established wineries of Domaine de Grand Pré (page 247) and Jost Vineyards (pages 292–3) continue to deliver quality wines, whilst seemingly more and more other wineries scattered across the province are producing a variety of wines and wine styles. Nova Scotia excels at crisp, refreshing white wines made from L'Acadie Blanc, Seyval Blanc and Muscat grapes, all terrific with the local fresh seafood.

The province's wine industry was thrilled to introduce a new appellation wine called Tidal Bay. Stylistically, a wine bearing the 'Tidal Bay' appellation on its label is a fresh, crisp, off-dry, still, white wine that must meet a set of standards (like any established world-class wine-producing region).

Wineries such as L'Acadie Vineyards and Benjamin Bridge are making world-class traditional-method sparkling wines that (some experts say) could be mistaken for French Champagne in a blind tasting.

Though Nova Scotia also makes red wines from (mainly) Marechal Foch, Leon Milot and Baco Noir grapes that range from light, fresh and juicy to full and earthy, the focus is clearly on their fresh whites and traditional method sparkling wines.

Oenophiles may wish to subscribe (free) to Canada's best wine e-newsletter (*www.nataliemaclean.com*). Its author, sommelier and award-winning wine writer Natalie MacLean, is particularly impressed by the province's sparkling wines and crisp whites, but adds that their production may still be too small for widespread national or international distribution.

A good time for wine aficionados to visit the province is mid September to mid October, to tie in with the month-long Nova Scotia Fall Wine Festival.. For more about this – and the latest on what's what on the Nova Scotia wine scene – see the website winesofnovascotia.ca.

For companies offering wine tours in Nova Scotia, see box, page 40.

Gluten-intolerants The types of cafés and restaurants who recognise that not everyone wants to eat meat, plus supermarkets, delis, and some bakeries have become aware of the boom in the number of people looking to avoid gluten. You may not find gluten-free products everywhere, but you shouldn't have to go too far.

DRINK You'll find big-name Canadian and American beers everywhere, but even more popular are Nova Scotia-produced brands. Best known (and much-loved locally) is **Keith's**, and the love affair continues even though the brewery is now owned by Labatt's, a subsidiary of Anheuser-Busch InBev. Beer fans are spoilt for choice with an increasing number of microbreweries and brewpubs dotted around both Halifax and the rest of the province (box, page 64).

Another tipple that you should sample is Nova Scotia's **single malt whisky**, distilled on Cape Breton Island (page 322). Whisky is now also distilled in Guysborough (page 396) and River John (page 298).

Other good distilleries include those in Lunenburg (page 166) and Lequille (near Annapolis Royal; page 222).

With an abundance of delicious apples, you won't be surprised to hear that very good **cider** is produced locally. Visitors from the UK may get a surprise when they taste it though: unless called hard cider, it will be nothing stronger than sweet, refreshing apple juice.

The legal drinking age is 19 years. Accompanied children and those under 19 are allowed in licensed restaurants and pubs up to 21.00. Whilst it is generally not as bad as in the USA (where I – three decades over the minimum drinking age – have often been asked for photo ID to confirm I'm legal to drink), if you are (or look) young, you may be asked to prove your age.

With a few exceptions (eg: vineyard shops), alcohol is only sold at government-licensed liquor stores (page 67).

A recent change in the provincial law means that licensed restaurants are allowed to operate a 'bring your own wine' policy: some have taken up the opportunity, but many of these charge outrageously for corkage – CAN$25 per bottle is not unknown. Licensed restaurants can serve alcoholic drinks from 10.00 to 02.00 daily.

PUBLIC HOLIDAYS AND FESTIVALS

Nova Scotia's calendar has long been packed with all manner of festivals (especially between late spring and autumn) celebrating the province's music, food, arts, heritage, history and more. In fact, Nova Scotia likes the tag 'Canada's Official Festival Province'. In recent years, more festivals have been added, and attempts have been made to hold some of these in traditional off-season periods.

Information on the best regional festivals and events is included under the relevant regional section. The following public holidays are celebrated annually (note that many businesses and shops may close on these days).

1 January	New Year's Day
February	Nova Scotia Heritage Day (third Monday in February)
March/April	Good Friday
March/April	Easter Monday
May	Victoria Day (the Monday preceding 25 May)
1 July	Canada Day
August	Natal Day (first Monday in August)
September	Labour Day (first Monday in September)
October	Thanksgiving Day (second Monday in October)
11 November	Remembrance Day
25 December	Christmas Day
26 December	Boxing Day

SHOPPING

Popular gifts or souvenirs include locally produced wine, especially ice wine (box, page 293), whisky, maple syrup, Nova Scotia tartan, and all manner of arts and crafts. Recent years have seen a boom in the quantity and quality of artists and artisans in the province. So in addition to cuddly moose, whales and red plastic lobsters all mass-produced in factories on the other side of the world, visitors can take home a locally made individually crafted work of art.

For the last few years, Sunday shopping has been legal, though in general it is mainly supermarkets and big mall stores that open on Sundays. Remember that in most cases, 15% tax will be added to prices (box, page 52).

ANTIQUES You'll also see plenty of antique shops – plus those that cross the line that divides antiques from junk. If you are interested in the former, you may find the website www.antiquesnovascotia.com of interest. Yard sales are very popular on weekends between spring and autumn: some are advertised in provincial papers, but in most cases just by hand-written fluorescent signs stuck up around the relevant town or village giving the address and time of the sale. These vary from a family clear-out held in an attempt to earn a few dollars for what they would otherwise throw out, to the disposal of the entire contents of an impressive, well-furnished old house. They can be rich hunting grounds or a waste of time. Get there early for the best stuff.

FOOD SHOPPING For food shopping, self-caterers will probably look to stock up at the huge supermarkets, **Atlantic Superstore** (*www.atlanticsuperstore.ca*) and **Sobeys** (*www.sobeys.com*). In general, these are open 07.30–22.00 Monday–Saturday and 10.00–17.00 Sunday, but check specific store hours for early mornings and late evenings. There are also smaller chains (Independent is a 'daughter' of Atlantic Superstore, Foodland of Sobey's), and a seemingly ever-decreasing number of general stores. **Farmers' markets** – usually held one morning a week – are well worth visiting, not just for fresh local produce and baked goods, but often, too, for arts and crafts. There are more than 40 and some of the best include those at Halifax (page 111), Hubbards (page 145), Wolfville (page 243) and Annapolis Royal (page 221).

The summer offers numerous **U-pick** ('pick-your-own') fruit possibilities. Prices are low and a certain amount of 'eating-as-you-pick' expected and tolerated.

With a few exceptions (eg: vineyard shops), alcohol is sold only at government-licensed liquor, beer and wine stores – and only to persons aged 19 and above. Expect to be asked for photo ID if you're under 40! A list of all Nova Scotia Liquor Commission (NSLC) stores and their opening hours – usually 10.00–21.00 Monday–Saturday, noon–17.00 Sunday – can be seen at the 'store information' section of the website www.mynslc.com.

SHOPPING MALLS Many people head out to the big malls to do their shopping. Apart from plenty of free parking and convenience, these tend to stay open later than downtown shops. Alongside the malls you'll usually find big 'box' stores (such as Canadian Tire and Wal-Mart).

Practical Information SHOPPING

2

SOUVENIR GOODS Studios and galleries are to be found all over the province, but some areas and communities, such as Bear River (pages 214–15) and North River on Cape Breton Island (pages 339–40) are particularly popular. Often you'll be able to watch artisans creating pottery, working glass, carving wood or painting. A piece of whimsical folk art, a stained glass sun-catcher, a handcrafted walking stick, or a hooked rug, all make excellent presents or keepsakes. In tourist offices, look out for the (free) Studio Map: produced annually, it lists art and craft studios and galleries all over the province and can also be viewed at www.studiorally.ca.

ARTS AND ENTERTAINMENT

CINEMA The province has just 14 cinemas, all owned by Cineplex Cinemas (*www. cineplex.com*), many of which are in and around Halifax. In many towns, films are screened from time to time in theatres or community/cultural centres.

Before films can be screened, they have to be made: Halifax – home to the ten-day Atlantic Film Festival (page 89) – is the hub of east-coast Canada's film industry. However, the province's burgeoning film industry has recently been hit hard by 2016 changes to Nova Scotia's film tax credit. Film-making was contributing about CAN$100 million annually to the province's economy and employing close to 2,000 people, but now those figures are likely to drop. **Screen Nova Scotia** (📞 *902 229 3793*, 📘) is the starting point for those wanting to learn more.

Films shot in the province include *The Scarlet Letter* (1995), *Dolores Claiborne* (1995) and parts of *Titanic* (1997).

MUSEUMS Nova Scotia has well over 100 museums, ranging from little one-room schoolhouses to the Nova Scotia Museum of Industry, one of the biggest museums in Atlantic Canada. Many are themed, with subjects covering, for example, fishing, mining, lighthouses, Acadian history, the Age of Sail, or individuals such as country

> ## TITANIC TRIP
>
> Various scenes from the 1997 blockbuster *Titanic* were shot on a Russian ship in Halifax's harbour in the summer of 1996. At the evening meal on the last day of filming, a disgruntled crew member (who is yet to be identified) added a strong dose of a hallucinogenic drug to one of the repast's first courses, lobster chowder. Around 80 crew and cast were affected, and over 50 taken to hospital. One – who had had seconds of the chowder – was still feeling the effects five days later. Apparently the director, James Cameron, was spared somewhat as he vomited before his digestive system absorbed too much of the hallucinogen.

singer Hank Snow. Popular too are the 'living museums', staffed by costumed interpreters who demonstrate the almost-forgotten skills of the blacksmith, the wool carder, the potter, the wooden boatbuilder and the lobster plug carver.

A total of 28 of the province's museums make up the diverse family of the **Nova Scotia Museum** (*museum.novascotia.ca*): admission at each varies from CAN$2 to CAN$11. A pass is available covering admission to all 28 museums for CAN$46.85. At many other of the museums, often community-run and staffed by volunteers, entrance is free, but donations are encouraged. Consequently, if no admission price is shown in this guide, assume that entry is 'by donation'. These museums rely on the generosity of visitors – and volunteers giving up their time – to keep going, so try to chip in at least a couple of dollars a person where possible.

NIGHTLIFE Nightlife is best in Halifax and environs, and to a far lesser degree Sydney and the university towns of Wolfville and Antigonish. Other than that, you're probably looking at pubs and bars, a disco (if you're very lucky), or stargazing.

THEATRE During their time at Port-Royal, one of the French party, lawyer, author and explorer Marc Lescarbot, wrote a play. *Le Théâtre de Neptune* had its world première when performed in the shallows between ships and shore in 1607. This was the first recorded dramatic production in Canada. Lescarbot was something of a poet, and in addition wrote at least once weekly on events at the little French Habitation. On this basis, it is said that Canadian drama, verse and prose were first created at Port-Royal.

Theatre still plays a big part in the province's arts scene: Halifax, Liverpool, Wolfville and Antigonish are some of the places with annual theatre festivals: calendars of events at theatres in many other communities mix performing arts with film screenings.

SPORTS AND ACTIVITIES

CANOEING AND RIVER KAYAKING An abundance of unspoilt (almost untouched) wilderness, lakes, ponds and rivers draw those wishing to explore the inland waters by canoe or kayak. In season, various commercial operators offer hourly rentals: to venture into the back country on a multi-day trip, it is worth consulting a specialist outfit such as **Hinterland Adventures** (✆ *902 837 4092;* ☏ *1 800 378 8177; www. kayakingnovascotia.com*).

CYCLING A good network of largely empty roads and (northern Cape Breton Island apart) low hills means wonderful cycling opportunities. In addition to magnificent and varied coastal scenery, there are fertile valleys and many historic towns to explore.

Practical Information   SPORTS AND ACTIVITIES

2

69

Either build an itinerary around one of the province's scenic trails or base yourself somewhere such as Hubbards, Lunenburg, Yarmouth or Wolfville for a few days, head out on day trips and return each evening to your accommodation.

Hundreds of old logging and mining roads and long-forgotten centuries-old footpaths cover much of rural Nova Scotia and provide excellent possibilities for mountain biking.

A few shops and companies around the province hire out road and mountain bikes for anything from an hour or two, allowing you to potter around the local area. These are listed in the following chapters.

DIVING The waters around Nova Scotia offer some of the very best cold-water wreck-diving places in the world (you'll need either a drysuit, or a warm wetsuit). Most diving is done in the summer months, when the winds are down and the water is at its warmest. A few hardy locals dive year-round.

The Atlantic Ocean and the Gulf of St Lawrence offer particularly good underwater visibility and the waters are home to a great variety of marine life and an incredible collection of shipwrecks.

There are a number of diving shops in Halifax/Dartmouth and elsewhere, of which the best is probably **Torpedo Rays** (*625 Windmill Rd, Dartmouth;* \ *902 481 0444; www.torpedorays.com*).

FISHING Deep-sea fishing tours in search of blue shark, or the increasingly rare bluefin tuna, are easily arranged on licensed charter boats berthed at many of the

---

SEA KAYAKING *with Dr Scott Cunningham*

Sea kayaking has become increasingly popular in recent years and Nova Scotia, with its countless harbours and headlands, inlets and islands, offers a world-class destination. The meandering shoreline is extensive, access is easy and the contrasts are exceptional. There is something for paddlers of every taste and skill level. You will find protected day trips for the beginner as well as challenging multi-day routes, and everything in between. And thousands of kilometres of coastline means that you can explore all this in relative solitude.

My favourite realm, and my home, is along the rugged **Eastern Shore**, where an isolated band of islands stretches from Clam Harbour to Canso. This forgotten wilderness forms a compelling mix of natural and human history. Some of these outposts are just tiny specks, scarcely breathing air at high water, whilst others are huge forest-covered expanses that dominate the horizon, and beckon to the inquisitive traveller. Explore abandoned lighthouses and shipwrecks, uncover those vanishing signs of our own transient history, or camp on a deserted isle where your only companions are the seals and the seabirds, far from the summer bustle. Tangier is an ideal place from which to start. On the other side of Halifax, the **South Shore** offers dozens of places to put in and explore, especially the Kejimkujik Seaside, the LaHave Islands, Blue Rocks, and Prospect. Even Halifax, with its eclectic waterfront and harbour islands, merits a visit by kayak.

Further north, on **Cape Breton Island**, the majestic Highlands rising abruptly from the Gulf of St Lawrence are particularly imposing when viewed from the perspective of a sea kayak. Sea spires, caves and a colourful geology decorate the perimeter, while the Cabot Trail winds out of sight and sound far above. Rich deciduous valleys alternate with barren vertical cliffs, washed by waterfalls and

province's harbours. Try for example **Lunenburg Ocean Adventures** (♦ *902 634 4833; www.lunenburgoceanadventures.com*) in Lunenburg for shark and more. Based near Antigonish, **Zappa Charters** (♦ *902 386 2669;* e *the-tuna-hunter@live.com*) specialise in bluefin tuna.

Freshwater anglers try for brook, rainbow and brown trout, Atlantic whitefish, yellow perch, shad, smallmouth bass and – the once mighty – Atlantic salmon. For much of the past two decades, salmon numbers have been dropping towards critical levels. For more on Atlantic salmon and trout fishing in the province, see the **Nova Scotia Salmon Association's** website (*www.nssalmon.ca*).If you are thinking of fishing whilst in the province, get clued up on the regulations via the **Department of Fisheries and Aquaculture** website (novascotia.ca/fish).

For **fishing guides**, try Hunt's Point-based Vinal Smith (♦ *902 356 2498; www. vinalsmith.com*) on the South Shore or Dave Doggett (♦ *902 299 0191; www. novascotiafishingguide.com*) based near Chester on the South Shore. Local general stores and outfitters are often good sources of advice. A list of fishing guides can be found on the Department of Fisheries and Aquaculture website.

GEOCACHING Geocaching (*geocachingnovascotia.ca*) – a type of treasure hunt game using a Global Positioning System (GPS) device – is quite popular in the province. The idea is to find a treasure or cache placed in a specific location using only GPS co-ordinates. Tales of buried treasure abound in the province, and there have been a handful of finds over the centuries. However, I have decided to leave 'metal detector' off the 'what to take' list.

you will certainly spot bald eagles and seals. If lucky you will also paddle with the whales, as I have done many a time. By midsummer the water can warm up considerably, to 20°C, but this is an open coast and experience is advised.

The **Bay of Fundy** is perhaps the most distinctive region. The highest tides ever recorded on earth wash these shores, sculpting cliffs and inundating massive salt marshes and mud banks with surprising speed. Experience here is essential. Cape Chignecto's long and rich geological history has resulted in a striking melange of colours, textures and forms. The abrupt cliffs, numerous pinnacles and sea caves, combine with tides exceeding 12m to create a spectacular land/seascape.

If you arrive early in the season when the Atlantic coast may be draped in fog (the best times are early July to October), or if the Highlands and the Fundy are too exposed for your taste, you should try the province's **Northumberland Strait** shore where you will be treated to the warmest salt water north of the Carolinas. Fog has been banned, and the miles of sandy shores and salt-marsh estuaries offer protected paddling for the entire family. Kayakers are not the only ones who enjoy soaking up a few summer rays and this shore has become a mecca for the vacation crowd. However, secluded corners can still be found.

There are many other exciting areas of our coastline to entice you and your sea kayak. A comprehensive guide, *Sea Kayaking in Nova Scotia*, available at most bookshops, will help with detailed descriptions of more than 40 routes. Bring your own boat and paddle on your own, or accompany a local outfit who can introduce you to the biology, geology and human history of this fascinating environment where the land meets the sea. Happy paddling!

For more information visit www.coastaladventures.com.

GOLF Nova Scotia now has more than 60 golf courses including world-renowned Highland Links (page 338) and Bell Bay (page 347), both on Cape Breton Island. There are also fabulous new links courses at Inverness, Cabot Links and Cabot Cliffs. Depending on their location, and the weather, the season can start as early as April and run to the end of October. Standard high-season green fees (including tax) for 2016 are shown in this guide, although almost all courses offer discounts – often substantial – for early or late season, later tee offs, etc. Quite often courses work together with certain local accommodation to offer stay-and-play packages.

Golf Nova Scotia (*www.golfnovascotia.com*) markets over 20 of the province's well-regarded courses, publishes a guide to golf in Nova Scotia, and offers stay-and-play packages.

HIKING AND WALKING With fabulous varied coastal and mountain scenery, inland valleys, pristine rivers, dozens of lakes and waterfalls, wild flowers and abundant wildlife, Nova Scotia is a delight for the hiker.

The trails of the Cape Breton Highlands National Park are justifiably popular, but so many more areas are wonderful to explore on foot. Also on Cape Breton Island, there are a number of superb hikes in the Mabou area, whilst on the 'mainland', Cape Chignecto Provincial Park and the Cape Split Trail are hiking highlights. Several sections of the province's old disused railway lines have been converted to multi-use trails.

RAFTING Whilst you won't find organised white-water rafting here, Nova Scotia offers a unique alternative. Several commercial operators take raftloads of (soft) adventure-seekers onto the Shubenacadie River to ride the tidal bore (box, page 261).

ROCKHOUNDING The richest areas for rockhounding (looking for rocks, semi-precious stones and minerals in their natural environment) are the beaches of the Minas Basin and the Bay of Fundy. In fact, the annual Gem and Mineral Show, held in August in Parrsboro (page 271) used to be called the Rockhound Roundup. The region's extreme tides erode cliff faces that may contain jasper, amethyst, agates, zeolites and more, sometimes depositing the semi-precious stones in amongst other pebbles.

SAILING The waters of Nova Scotia are actively used by a 40,000-vessel fishery and a range of commercial and military vessels. However, the density of boats is low and few spots are busy or crowded. Even in relatively busy harbours and bays, sailors can quickly get away to pristine waters, uninhabited islands and secluded anchorages.

The vast Bras d'Or Lake of Cape Breton Island is a renowned cruising destination for larger sailboats and mega-yachts because of its beauty and its accessibility (north and south) from the ocean. Other noted cruising destinations include Mahone Bay, St Margarets Bay and Halifax Harbour.

Nova Scotia is still one of the best-kept secrets for sailors, whether out for a day or a cruising adventure. Whilst there are very few, if any, Nova Scotia businesses that offer bareboat (where you skipper and crew the yacht) charters, sailing and cruising training is readily available. A full range of courses with certified instructors is offered by Sail Nova Scotia (*www.sailnovascotia.ca*) lasting from a few hours to a week. Try, for example, **Sou'Wester Adventures** (902 627 4004; tf 1 877 665 4004; *souwesteradventures.com/*).

SKATING There are ice rinks all over the province, but the majority are only open between late autumn and early spring. Unfortunately, very few offer ice-skate hire. Many locals prefer outdoor skating (on frozen ponds and lakes) to arena rinks.

Be aware that (like it or not) hunting is legal in Nova Scotia, and enjoyed by many. To avoid being mistaken for a black bear, moose or white-tailed deer, wear something brightly coloured if you go walking in the woods between September and mid December.

Hunting is regulated by the provincial government's Department of Natural Resources (*novascotia.ca/natr/hunt*). The following operators organise hunting trips:

Farmland Outfitters 902 899 3144; farmlandoutfitters.com. Based in Millbrook, near Truro.
Purcell's Hunting Excursions 902 483 1594; www.purcellshunting.com. Based near Halifax.

SKIING AND SNOWBOARDING Winter visitors do have some opportunities to strap on the skis (or a snowboard) and take to the slopes. Whilst vertical rises don't break any records, rentals and lift passes are cheap, and the resort staff – and other skiers – friendly.

The main downhill resorts are Ski Martock (pages 252–3) near Windsor, Ski Wentworth (page 293) between Truro and Amherst, and Cape Smokey (page 338) and Ski Ben Eoin (page 352), both on Cape Breton Island. Cross-country skiing is widespread, and snowmobiles are popular for whizzing across the white stuff.

STARGAZING Kejimkujik National Park (pages 223–7) is an official 'Dark Sky Preserve', but countless parts of the province have minimal light pollution. Incidentally, you may remember that the protagonist in Carly Simon's 1972 hit *You're So Vain* flew to Nova Scotia to see the total eclipse of the sun (there were such eclipses in 1970 and 1972, and the next one is due in August 2017). Get an astronomy book or just look up and enjoy.

SURFING, STAND-UP PADDLEBOARDING (SUP) AND WINDSURFING Nova Scotia ain't Hawaii (at least in terms of weather), but adventure-loving locals – and a few visitors – love to slip into a wetsuit and climb onto a board year-round. The most popular base for surfers and SUPers is Lawrencetown (pages 376–7) on the Eastern Shore, though you can find a couple of surf shops on the South Shore (pages 137–78). In general, the waves are best between September and May. Isle Madame (pages 369–73) has also started attracting SUPers.

SWIMMING With over 7,000km of coastline, the province has a number of magnificent beaches. However, with a few exceptions (noted in the text) not all are ideal for swimming. Even when the air temperature rises, sea swimming can often be too nippy. Luckily, those wishing to cool off without freezing have numerous opportunities for freshwater dipping. Good lakes for a swim are dotted about the province and include Chocolate Lake (page 113), Dollar Lake (page 382), Sandy Bottom Lake (page 224), Lake Midway (page 210), Bras d'Or Lake (page 342), and Porter's Lake Provincial Park (page 377).

Some hotels, and most resorts, have heated outdoor pools, and many towns have outdoor pools that may or may not be heated. Indoor pools are relatively rare.

ZIPLINING A relatively recent addition to the province's outdoor adventure possibilities involves whizzing along whilst attached to an inclined cable high above the ground. You can zipline at OnTree Park (page 253), Anchors Above (page 306), and – as part of a longer course – at Upper Clements Tree Topper Adventure Park (pages 216–17).

TIME, MEDIA AND COMMUNICATIONS

TIME Nova Scotia is in the Atlantic Time Zone. This is four hours behind Greenwich Mean Time (GMT) but Daylight Saving Time is observed between the second Sunday in March and the first Sunday in November. During this period, the province is three hours behind GMT. The Atlantic Time Zone is one hour ahead of Eastern Standard Time and four hours ahead of Pacific Time.

PRINT The province's leading newspaper is the independently owned *Chronicle Herald*, which first appeared in 1875. Daily print copy circulation is now close to 70,000, and the Sunday version, the *Sunday Herald*, sells about 72,000 copies. In general, editorial policy tends to be moderate conservative.

The TC Transcontinental media group publishes a number of regional weekly titles and four regional dailies: the *Amherst Daily News*, *Cape Breton Post*, *The News* (New Glasgow) and the *Truro Daily News*.

The free *Metro* is published on weekdays and distributed through much of the Halifax Regional Municipality (HRM).

The Coast (also free and available online; *www.thecoast.ca*) is published on Thursday and distributed in Halifax, Dartmouth, and some nearby communities: it focuses primarily on Halifax. There are excellent listings pages, and reviews, including restaurants, music, performing arts and more. Editorial policy tends to be slightly left-wing.

Almost 30 other local newspapers are published including one in French, *Le Courrier* (published monthly). Inspired by the UK's *Private Eye*, the fortnightly *Frank* magazine mixes humour, news and satire.

TELEVISION In addition to the Canadian Broadcasting Corporation's (CBC's) English- and French-language channels, other terrestrial television stations include CTV, Global, City and TVA. Catch up with the news on CBC at 06.00, noon or at 18.00. Most tourist accommodations offer cable/satellite television.

RADIO The Canadian Broadcasting Corporation offers five terrestrial networks: CBC Radio One, CBC Radio 2, CBC Radio 3, and two French-language networks, Ici Radio and Ici Musique. You can tune in to a range of English and French radio stations in the province, though reception can be poor in some areas.

Some hire cars are equipped with satellite radio, opening up a host of other stations.

USEFUL TELEPHONE NUMBERS

Fire, police, medical ╲911
Operator ╲0
Local directory assistance ╲411
Assistance with navigating the network of community and social services provided by government and the not-for-profit sector ╲211
Long-distance directory assistance ╲1 + the area code, if you know it, + 555 1212
(directory assistance is free from a payphone)

TELEPHONE There are still some public telephones (pay phones) in Nova Scotia: these can be operated by phonecard. Some accept credit cards, and a decreasing number take coins. Sold at newsagents, general stores, petrol stations, post offices and many other places, phonecards come in various denominations (eg: CAN$5, CAN$10 or CAN$20). Some may be better than others depending on your requirements (for example, if you're likely to make a high proportion of calls to numbers outside the province). I've found the President's Choice cards sold at Atlantic Superstores to be a good all-rounder.

The area code for the whole of Nova Scotia is ✎902 (but see box, below) and the international access code for Canada, like the USA, is ✎+1. If you're calling overseas from the province other than within Canada, to the USA or Caribbean, the outgoing code is ✎011 followed by the relevant country code. Common country codes are: Australia +61, France +33, Germany +49, Ireland +353, UK +44. If you are calling the UK from Nova Scotia, prefix the number you are calling – less its initial zero – with 011 44.

Mobile phones Not all mobile (they are called 'cell' in Nova Scotia) phones are enabled for international roaming, and (more importantly), not all handsets work in Canada. If your phone is enabled and compatible with the Canadian mobile-phone providers, check with your provider for the charges for making and receiving calls and texts. Alternatively, you can buy a pay-as-you-go SIM card either in the UK before you go or once in Nova Scotia from **Rogers** (see the 'store locator' section of www.rogers.com for branches and phone numbers in the province). Do read the 'Mobile Roaming' page in the 'Travel and Motoring' section of www. moneysavingexpert.com. When I think how far we should've come since the days of Alexander Graham Bell, inventor of the telephone, who lived near Baddeck on Cape Breton Island, I must admit to getting frustrated when I lose mobile-phone contact when in some of the province's not all that far-flung areas.

POST OFFICES City and town post offices (tf *1 866 607 6301*) are usually open 08.00–17.00 Monday–Friday, whilst rural outlets have varying hours (they may well close for lunch) and some may open on Saturday mornings. To confuse matters, in the biggest urban areas some larger shops have post office counters which operate

NOVA SCOTIA PHONE NUMBERS

The vast majority of Nova Scotia phone numbers listed in this guide are standard ten-digit numbers. If calling these numbers from anywhere in the province outside the immediate area, Canada or the USA, you may hear a message telling you to redial, prefixing the 902 with a 1. If dialling from outside these areas, you'll need to add the international code for North America (00). Numbers listed as tf (which begin 1 8XX) are (in theory) toll-free. Some are toll-free from outside North America, but if you try to call others from abroad, you will be intercepted by a message telling you your call is not toll-free: you can proceed with the call and should be charged the normal tariff. To call these 1 8XX numbers from outside North America, dial 00 first (eg: 00 1 8XX etc).

Nova Scotia shares the 902 code with the neighbouring province of Prince Edward Island, and in mid 2012 it was reported that there would not be enough seven digit phone numbers left to handle new business by perhaps 2015.

Although new numbers allocated from 2014 were supposed to be prefixed by 782 rather than 902, I am yet to come across a '782' number.

different hours. Canada Post's website (*www.canadapost.ca*) has a 'find a post office' section which gives each office's location and opening hours.

Postage prices are determined by weight and size of the item, and destination: standard-size letters within Canada cost CAN$1.15, to send to the USA it is CAN$1.38, and internationally CAN$2.88.

INTERNET A decreasing number of internet cafés are still to be found in some of the biggest urban centres, and the network of Wi-Fi hotspots is ever-growing. Many accommodations offer Wi-Fi for those travelling with a laptop, or have a computer terminal for guests' use.

Many public buildings, especially libraries and tourist offices, offer free public internet access: look for a sign saying C@P site or check www.nscap.ca. Unfortunately, the federal government cut funding for C@P (Community Access Program) sites, so the list might not be up to date.

MAPS The provincial and regional tourist offices offer a range of free maps that might well be all you need on a holiday in the province.

The provincial government's **GeoNOVA** department (*160 Willow St;* ☏ *902 667 7231;* **tf** *1 800 798 0706; geonova.novascotia.ca/maps*) produces and sells a range of regional atlases, maps and guidebooks. These are available online, by phone, or in person.

More detailed road atlases, often including New Brunswick and Prince Edward Island, can be purchased at bookshops and petrol stations for about CAN$20.

International Travel Maps (☏ *1 604 273 1400; www.itmb.ca*) publishes a good 1:400,000-scale map of Nova Scotia which has been used to produce several of the maps in this guide.

For shops selling specialised maps in Halifax, see page 110.

BUSINESS

Business etiquette is similar to that in western Europe and the USA. Suits are common for men, but staff at many companies dress more casually. Business hours tend to be 08.00–09.00 to 16.00–17.00, with a break of 30–60 minutes at lunch. Many companies offer flexible working hours, and an increasing number of staff work from home. Halifax is a popular place for international business conferences and conventions, and several hotels and resorts around the province endeavour to attract the convention market.

Many global companies are represented in Nova Scotia including Stelia Aerospace and Michelin. It is home to world-renowned research facilities such as the National Research Council's Institute for Marine Biosciences and the Bedford Institute of Oceanography. Defence, security and aerospace companies include Lockheed Martin, General Dynamics, IMP Group and Pratt and Whitney. The province is one of North America's leading emerging IT and business process outsourcing (BPO) destinations: CGI, Convergys, IBM, Unisys and Xerox all have bases here.

A list of all the province's main Chambers of Commerce and Boards of Trade can be found at the Atlantic Chamber of Commerce website (*www.apcc.ca*). The UK-based Canada–United Kingdom Chamber of Commerce (*Canada Hse, Trafalgar Square, London SW1Y 5BJ;* ☏ *020 7930 4553; www.canada-uk.org*) might also be of use.

BUYING PROPERTY

Many visitors come to Nova Scotia, happen to glance in an estate agent's (real estate brokerage's) window, and wonder if they are seeing things. Magnificent houses on large acreages can still be found for the sort of price you might expect for a run-down house in rural eastern Europe. People say that Nova Scotia is a Canadian version of New England, but even with the recent house-price crash in the USA, prices here are still a fraction of those in Maine, New Hampshire or Connecticut. You can start house hunting long before you leave home: just go to www.realtor.ca.

If you see something you like, or – when in the province – are tempted by a 'For Sale' sign as you drive by a beautiful house on a bluff overlooking the ocean, you can contact the real estate brokerage directly (the phone number will be on the website or sign). However, I would suggest approaching another realtor (real estate broker) at a different company in the same area (for an explanation, see later in this section). You can always try more than one company until you find someone with whom you feel you have a rapport. They will work on your behalf as a purchasing agent, at no cost to you, as all the brokerage companies have access to competitors' listed properties. Give your chosen realtor a list of the properties in which you are interested and they will arrange viewing appointments. They may also suggest other properties which they feel may interest you. In general, the owners are usually out when you view a house, and your realtor is your guide through as many homes as you wish to view.

They will advise you on some of their pros and cons, and – if something interests you – will negotiate with the seller's realtor on your behalf. They act as the conduit between the buyer and the home owner. That is why I suggest avoiding the situation where your realtor is the listing realtor for the property in which you are interested: rightly or wrongly it is the perception that realtors will work harder for the seller than the buyer in such circumstances (though realtors work under a strict code of ethics, imposed by the Canadian Real Estate Association (CREA), requiring them to follow a set of guidelines when representing both buyer and seller in the same transaction). Remember that even if the realtor is working for you, they are in business to make a sale, not to be your friend. Rely solely on realtors' advice or opinions at your peril.

If you are considering making an offer well below the asking price, different realtors work in different ways. Some will have an informal chat with the seller's listing realtor or if it is their own listing, directly with the homeowner; whilst others will insist that you make a formal offer in writing. Either way is appropriate.

All Nova Scotia Purchase and Sale agreements now have a pre-written clause making it advisable to contact an experienced property (real estate) lawyer after signing your Agreement of Purchase and Sale and allowing them time to review the fine print and comment or recommend changes to the transaction. Any realtor should be able to point you in the direction of a good lawyer.

Your offer should include certain conditions: these will vary from purchase to purchase. They might relate to timing – don't be rushed as you are likely to need time to arrange financing (and, probably transfer of funds from the UK to Nova Scotia) before you are bound to the contract. It should be made clear that your offer is subject to a satisfactory home inspection (what is called a survey in the UK) and, perhaps a land survey, which confirms that the home is located on the land described in the deed. If the property relies on a well for its water supply and/or a septic tank for sewage disposal – as many do outside cities and towns – I suggest that you include having those checked as a condition to be included in the agreement.

Another condition might be that the sale is dependent on your being able to obtain insurance for the property: some insurance companies will refuse to insure certain properties, or (more likely) may insist that certain changes are made before the cover that they offer will take effect.

In the vast majority of cases, either prior to making an offer to purchase or upon making the offer to purchase, you will be given a Property Disclosure Statement

A NEW LIFE IN NOVA SCOTIA

Thinking of emigrating to Nova Scotia? Before you can become a Canadian citizen, you have to apply for Permanent Residence. To do this, you can be sponsored by a family member who is a Canadian citizen (or Permanent Resident) or apply under one of the following categories:

- Skilled workers and professionals (this category has an Express Entry Scheme)
- Investors, entrepreneurs, caregivers and self-employed people

The **Citizenship and Immigration Canada** website (*www.cic.gc.ca*) has a useful 'check your eligibility' section. Successful candidates should expect to have to wait two years or more from when they submit their initial application until they receive their Permanent Residence.

A quicker method - especially if you are eligible for Express Entry via the Nova Scotia Demand or Nova Scotia Experience categories – is likely to be via the **Nova Scotia Nominee Program** (*novascotiaimmigration.com*). Here you apply to the Nova Scotia Office of Immigration: if you are considered worthy, you will receive a Letter of Nomination. You then apply via the Federal scheme as above, but will hopefully have been 'fast-tracked'.

Either way, there will be fees to pay: from CAN$475 for Right of Permanent Residence (PR), then CAN$550–1,050 depending on the category. You'll also have to fork out for a private medical.

Do the paperwork yourself, or engage the services of an immigration lawyer: try, for example, Cox & Palmer (✆ *902 421 6262; www.coxandpalmerlaw. com*) or Nova Scotia Immigration Lawyers (✆ *902 446 4747; nsimmigration.ca*).

Moving to a foreign (albeit English-speaking) country is something of a minefield, and you may wish to seek help from a couple of commercial organisations who specialise in the field. Try **UK2NovaScotia** (e *info@ uk2novascotia.com; www.uk2novascotia.com*). Most counties in the province have offices whose brief it is to help new arrivals settle.

If you are successful, you have to 'land' in Nova Scotia within a certain amount of time (usually within a year of the date of your medical). You can then apply for a Social Insurance Number (SIN), and a Nova Scotia Health Card (benefits under the health card do not apply for six months). To maintain your PR status, you must spend at least 730 days out of five years in Canada. You can apply for Canadian citizenship if you have PR status and have spent at least three out of four years in Canada.

(PDS) which the seller has completed. In this, the seller must disclose (to the best of his or her knowledge) information about the property, even if these may be damaging to the sale. Topics covered include recent repairs, water supply, electrical services, plumbing, water leakage issues, rights of way and building restrictions. You will be allowed a certain amount of time to check this through.

It is very important that you go through the PDS carefully, clarifying anything that is unclear, ambiguous or has been left blank. In my opinion, I think that it is worth ensuring that your home inspector has a copy of the PDS so that they can also comment on any specific problems that have been noted thereon. Ensure also that your lawyer sees the PDS, if available, before you go ahead with the purchase.

Once all has been settled, you pay the agreed down payment (a negotiated amount, which may be as much as 10% of the sale price) on a pre-arranged date if all the conditions have been met. Note that if you then get cold feet, you will not only lose your deposit but could be sued for damages.

Don't get carried away, and do think things through. How much will the house and grounds cost to maintain? What will happen to the property when you're not using it? Are you thinking of buying to let? Outside Halifax and Wolfville (university towns), the rental season doesn't stretch much beyond July and August. You are likely to need a property manager, or property maintenance company. Bear extra costs – such as legal fees, deed transfer tax, home inspection, adjustments (including your share of property taxes and fuel pre-paid by the seller), all plus 15% Harmonised Sales Tax (HST) – in mind. HST only applies to the purchase price of the property if you are buying a new home from a developer – but not if you are buying a home that has been owned/inhabited previously.

If you are buying a home that needs work, remember the message from all of those property programmes – repairs and renovations almost always cost far more than the amount for which one budgets.

Recommended realtors include **Tradewinds Realty Inc** (*www.tradewindsrealty. com*) and **RE/MAX** (*www.remax.ca*). For home inspectors, choose a member of the **Canadian Association of Home and Property Inspectors** (*www.cahpi-atl.com*).

CULTURAL ETIQUETTE

TIPPING As in the USA, tipping is a common practice in Canada. Taxi drivers are normally tipped 15% of the fare, hairdressers and barbers also 15%, airport/hotel porters CAN$2–3 per bag, and valet parkers CAN$3–5. Tour guides and bus drivers normally receive CAN$5 per day. Tipping your server, a couple of dollars per round, whether at the bar or at your table, is common in bars.

In cafés and restaurants, you don't need to tip if eating at the counter (but of course you can do if the service is particularly good), but you are expected to tip 15–20% for meals.

SMOKING Smoking is not permitted in indoor public areas, bars and restaurants, or on restaurant and bar patios. It is illegal to smoke in a vehicle with passengers under the age of 19.

VISITING SOMEONE'S HOME Many people in Nova Scotia take their shoes off when they enter their homes: be aware of this, and perhaps ask your host if you should de-shoe.

TRAVELLING POSITIVELY

Whilst Canada has many worthy countrywide charities, specific to the province is **Feed Nova Scotia** (*213 Bedford Hwy, Halifax B3M 2J9;* \ *902 457 1900; www. feednovascotia.ca*), which aims to feed hungry people by providing year-round food deliveries to a network of 150 food banks across the province. The organisation's ultimate aim is to eliminate chronic hunger and alleviate poverty.

Shelter Nova Scotia (\ *902 406 3631; www.shelternovascotia.com*) works to end homelessness in the province, and provides assistance for men and women attempting to make the change from prison living to community living.

Angeline Publicover was due to be married. Early in December 1868 she boarded a schooner, the *Industry*, in LaHave (box, page 172), bound for Halifax, where she wanted to buy her wedding dress. What should have been a simple day's sail for the seven people on board didn't turn out that way as unexpected winds came up when the ship neared Sambro. The captain tried to return to port, but the vessel was blown out to the open sea, where more gales, storms and winds blew the helpless *Industry* further and further out. Days passed with little let-up in the conditions: the crew and passengers subsisted on (rationed) water, melted hailstones and a handful of biscuits. Their Christmas Day dinner was one rotten potato divided into seven. On 29 December, a barque named *Providence* sighted the crippled schooner in the mid Atlantic: the survivors managed to transfer boats in rough seas, and just in time – the battered *Industry* sank less than an hour later. Angeline and her fellow survivors were taken on the *Providence* to London, England and then returned to Halifax on a steamer, finally arriving in Nova Scotia on 12 February 1869.

For those who prefer happy endings, Angeline's fiancé was waiting by the dockside, and the happy couple were married a few days later. But the truth is that by the time she returned to Nova Scotia, he had changed his mind, and the wedding was not just delayed but called off.

Despite many hours of research, I could not find out if Angeline bought a wedding dress during her time in London or Halifax, or where she obtained the dress that she wore for her marriage (to a less fickle man) four years later. Plenty of other fish in the sea, as they say.

An increasing number of musicians and creative artists from the province work with the **ArtsCan Circle** (*www.artscancircle.ca*), travelling to remote northern Canadian First Nations communities to encourage self-esteem amongst indigenous youth through music and art workshops.

For over 250 years, lighthouses helped reduce the high number of wrecked ships in the province's coastal waters. Unfortunately, the majority of the 350-plus lighthouses are now gone or in ruinous states. The **Nova Scotia Lighthouse Preservation Society** (*www.nslps.com*) does valiant work ploughing time, effort and money into preserving the province's lighthouse heritage.

The **Nova Scotia Nature Trust** (☏ *902 425 5263; www.nsnt.ca*) works to conserve the province's increasingly threatened ecologically significant lands.

There are Nova Scotia chapters of **both** the **Canadian Parks and Wilderness Society** (*5435 Portland Pl, Suite 101, Halifax B3K 6R7;* ☏ *902 446 4155; www.cpawsns. org*), Canada's leading grass-roots non-government organisation for wilderness conservation, and Canada's **Society for the Prevention of Cruelty to Animals** (*SPCA;* ☏ *902 835 4798; spcans.ca*).

Please remember that the majority of the province's museums are staffed by volunteers and offer free admission: they rely (in varying degrees) on donations from visitors.

Part Two

THE GUIDE

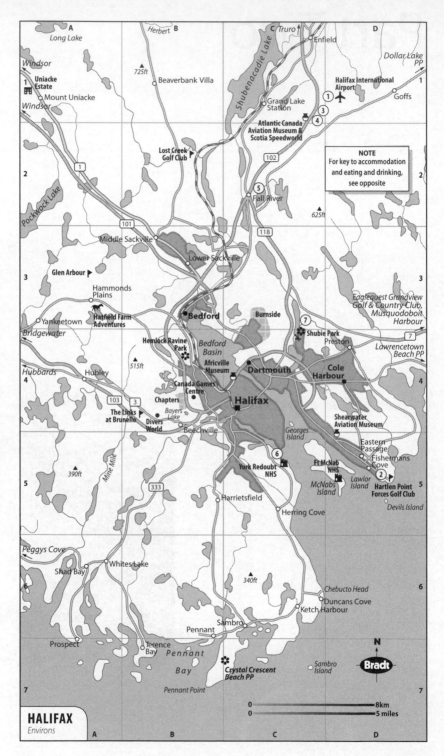

NOTE
For key to accommodation
and eating and drinking,
see opposite

HALIFAX
Environs

0 ——————————— 8km
0 ——————————— 5 miles

3

Halifax, Dartmouth and Around

Nova Scotia's capital is not a city as such, but a municipality. The cities of Halifax and Dartmouth, the town of Bedford and the municipality of the county of Halifax were dissolved and amalgamated into the Halifax Regional Municipality (HRM) in 1996. The HRM has a population of close to 390,000 (of whom approx 298,000 live in urban areas) and is home to over 40% of Nova Scotia's population. Despite the urban consolidation, virtually everyone still talks about the different entities as though nothing has changed.

Halifax (pages 89–125) – which has the largest component population (approx 125,000) and is home to the majority of the government buildings and offices – sits at the heart of the HRM. It is here that you find the majority of the HRM's hotels, restaurants and best museums and attractions. Dartmouth (with a population of approx 72,000; pages 125–33) is across the harbour from Halifax – a short ride by regular ferry.

At the head of the harbour is Bedford (population: approaching 30,000). Compared with much of the rest of the province, the area to the north, northeast and northwest of Bedford is also quite densely populated, the major communities being the Sackvilles, Fall River and Waverley.

Visitors should try and head beyond the urban centres to explore areas such as the Northwest Arm (pages 123–4), the Eastern Passage (pages 131–3) and the Uniacke Estate (page 125).

Although its official boundaries stretch as far to the southwest as Hubbards (pages 144–6) and to the east as Ecum Secum (page 388), this chapter focuses on the heart of the HRM.

ORIENTATION

Halifax's *raison d'être* was its harbour, which is still a major part of life for Halifax, Dartmouth and Bedford. At the mouth of the harbour are Chebucto Head on the Halifax side and Hartlen Point on the Dartmouth side. Herring Cove Road and Purcells Cove Road lead towards the downtown area from Chebucto Head, passing fjord-like Northwest Arm, and on the Dartmouth side, Shore Road and Eastern Passage Road run close to the waterfront, with McNabs and Lawlor islands just offshore.

Connected by passenger ferry, downtown Halifax and downtown Dartmouth face each other across the harbour, which then narrows through

HALIFAX Environs
For listings, see page 99,
unless otherwise stated

🛏 **Where to stay and eat**
1 ALT Hotel Halifax Airport.....................D1
2 Eastern Passage B&B *p132*.................D5
3 Hilton Garden Inn Halifax Airport......C1
4 Holiday Inn Express Halifax
    Hotel & Suites.....................................C1
5 Inn on the Lake....................................C2
6 SeaWatch B&B......................................C5
7 Shubie Park Campground *p127*.........C3

a stretch aptly called The Narrows, before opening up into the expanse of the 40km² Bedford Basin. Two toll bridges – the MacDonald to the south and MacKay slightly further north – cross The Narrows, providing road links between the two communities. The MacDonald has cycle lanes, a pedestrian walkway, and great views.

Near Bedford, which is at the head of the Bedford Basin, two of the province's major motorways meet. Highway 102 leads southwest to Halifax and northeast to Halifax International Airport, approximately 38km from downtown, and Truro. Highway 101 leads southwest to Dartmouth, and northeast to Windsor, Wolfville and Yarmouth, via the Annapolis Valley.

The region's other major motorway, Highway 103, leads west from Halifax towards Liverpool, Bridgewater and Yarmouth, via the South Shore.

The layout of downtown Halifax is relatively simple, with a series of short streets rising up from the western side of Halifax Harbour towards Citadel Hill. On the waterfront itself, most of the tourist sites are between Casino Nova Scotia to the north, and the cruise ship dock to the south. Lower and Upper Water streets connect and run parallel to the water, with Barrington Street two to three blocks inland.

En route up to Citadel Hill, grassy Grand Parade is bordered by Barrington, Argyle, Duke and Prince streets. Around Citadel Hill are large green areas with individual names, but collectively referred to as The Commons, and bordered by Robie Street. Cogswell Street runs from Barrington Street to Robie Street, continuing on as Quinpool Road before reaching the Armdale Rotary.

Locals tend to refer to everything south of The Commons as the South End, and everything to the north as the North End. The North End – much of which was flattened by the Halifax Explosion in 1917 (box, page 93) – includes the Hydrostone district, bordered by Young, Agricola, Duffus and Gottingen streets. This European-style district was built in the aftermath of the Halifax Explosion using hydrostone, a special kind of masonry. Completed in 1920, the district includes a market with a collection of shops and eateries.

In the South End (the southernmost part of which is occupied by beautiful Point Pleasant Park) is the city's academic area, site of Dalhousie University, University of King's College, St Mary's University and the Nova Scotia College of Art & Design University.

GETTING THERE

For international and inter-provincial services, see pages 44–7.

BY AIR Flights connect Halifax with Sydney (page 54).

Airport transfers
Taxi You can reach the centre of Halifax by taxi or limousine in about 30–35 minutes (*CAN$63*). You'll see 'Ground transportation' booths as you emerge from the arrivals hall.

Bus If you're not in a hurry and don't have much luggage, **MetroX** (page 86) route 320 connects the airport with Dartmouth and Halifax (Albemarle Street, near the Metro Centre) with departures once or twice per hour between approximately 05.45 and midnight. The fare is CAN$3.50 (note: exact change is required), and transfer onto Metro Transit bus/ferry is permitted. Note that this service is aimed at commuters, so luggage space may be limited. **Maritime Bus** (page 57) connects the airport (1–3 times daily) with destinations such as Wolfville (change of coach required), Truro, Amherst, New Glasgow, Antigonish, Baddeck and Sydney.

Shuttle Between May and October, **Airport Express** (**tf** *1 800 350 6945; maritimebus.com/halifax-airport-shuttle; one way CAN$22, return CAN$40*) operates around seven services each way daily between various Halifax (and a couple of Dartmouth) hotels and the airport. Between November and April, **Maritime Bus** coaches (page 46) connect the airport with the Maritime Bus terminal in Halifax (see below). The one-way fare is CAN$19.50. In both cases, tickets must be pre-purchased prior to travel: you can do this online or at the 'Ground transportation' booth at the airport.

BY CAR If you are travelling by car from the north and/or the airport, Highway 102 brings you into downtown Halifax via Bayers Road (avoiding the toll bridges). If you are heading for Windsor or the Annapolis Valley, or the South Shore from the airport, head towards Halifax on Highway 102, then follow signs to highways 101 or 103 respectively.

Coming from Dartmouth and/or the Eastern Shore, it makes most sense to take one of the toll bridges: the A Murray MacKay Bridge and Angus L MacDonald Bridge (the latter has pedestrian and bicycle access). The toll is CAN$1 and some booths are designated for those without exact change.

Car hire Car-hire companies offer rentals at the airport and other locations including downtown Halifax and Dartmouth (see pages 56–7 for further information).

BY BUS Long-distance bus services (page 57) arrive and depart from the VIA Rail Station [101 G4] (*1161 Hollis St*), 1km south of downtown and next to the Westin Nova Scotian hotel. **Maritime Bus** (page 46) offer departures from Halifax to various points throughout the province and beyond.

BY TRAIN Don't be fooled by the size and grandeur of the VIA Rail Station [101 G4] – there's just one departure and arrival three days a week, a service which connects Halifax with Montreal, Quebec. Stops in Nova Scotia are at Truro, Springhill Junction and Amherst. For fares and times contact **VIA Rail** (**tf** *1 888 842 7245; www.viarail.ca*).

GETTING AROUND

BY CAR The downtown core of Halifax is quite compact, and parking can be hard to find. Colour-coded parking meters (*red: max 30mins; grey: max 1hr; green: max 2hrs; yellow: max 3–5hrs*) charge CAN$0.25/10 minutes and are strictly monitored by a very enthusiastic enforcement team. Downtown Dartmouth has only grey and green meters, but there is talk of bringing in full colour-coding here, too. Meters are in effect 08.00–18.00 Monday–Friday, which means you can park free at meters outside these times (unless signs say otherwise). See www.halifax.ca/ParkingEnforcement/Meters.php for more information, anden.parkopedia.ca may also be useful.

Some car parks (Halifax waterfront and other) have 'Pay by Plate' signs at their entrance: this just means that instead of a paper ticket, you enter your licence plate number in the 'pay' machine. Rates are CAN$3/hour.

There are several underground or multi-storey garages (look for the blue 'P' sign) that charge around CAN$3–4/hour, for example at the Scotia Square Mall [94 E3], the Prince George Hotel [94 D4] or 1557 Granville Street [95 E6]. Hotels charge guests around CAN$20/day for parking.

By and large, Haligonians (as residents of Halifax are known) drive slowly and considerately: they will allow traffic to merge and often stop at the first sign of a pedestrian near a kerb (you are obliged to stop for pedestrians at crosswalks). There are several one-way streets to watch out for, and the Armdale Rotary – basically just a simple roundabout – often causes locals vast amounts of confusion.

BY TAXI Taxis are easiest to find outside major hotels, shopping malls and the VIA Rail Station [101 G4]. You may be able to flag down a cruising taxi, but two useful firms are listed below. Fares start at CAN$3.20, with CAN$1.70/km added after that, and each extra passenger is charged CAN$0.70. A ride from the Halifax waterfront to Citadel Hill, for example, will cost about CAN$10. There are no signs that Uber – which operates in some cities as a competitor to traditional taxi services – will start up in Halifax.

Casino Taxi ☏ 902 429 6666   **Yellow Cab** ☏ 902 420 0000

BY BUS Metro Transit (☏ *902 490 4000; www.halifax.ca/metrotransit*) operates public transport in Halifax, Dartmouth and to some other parts of the HRM – see the website for schedules, route maps and more. Almost all tickets (including free transfers) cost: CAN$2.50 for adults, CAN$1.75 for seniors and children (aged five–15), and under fives go free. A book of ten tickets costs CAN$20 (senior and child CAN$14.50). Conductors prefer exact change only. If you are changing buses, or will be travelling by both bus and ferry, ask for a (free) transfer ticket – valid for 90 minutes.

There are also a few **MetroX** express commuter routes (eg: Metro Transit bus route 320 between Halifax city centre and Halifax airport) on which the fare is CAN$3.50, or one transit ticket or transfer plus CAN$1.

If you're at a stop waiting for a bus, dial 480 followed by the four-digit bus stop number (marked in red at every stop) for real-time information on when the next bus will be arriving.

Many bus routes use accessible low-floor buses (ALF), and the ferries are also accessible. There is also an Access-A-Bus service providing door-to-door accessible transportation throughout the city. If you might use the service, contact Metro Transit in advance to register.

Need-A-Lift (☏ *902 222 5438; www.needalift.ca*) offers a wheelchair-accessible bus and taxi service in many HRM areas (prices start at CAN$29).

BY FERRY Metro Transit (above) also runs the Halifax–Dartmouth ferry (the oldest saltwater passenger service in North America) from the foot of George Street [94 G4] to Alderney Drive in Dartmouth [129 B2] (⊕ *06.30–23.30 daily, departures every 15–30mins*). Not that I want to take business away from Halifax's boat tour operators, but for CAN$2.50 each way, the 8–10-minute crossing makes an excellent, cheap harbour ride. There is also a similarly priced ferry service (⊕ *06.30–20.30 weekdays only*) between Halifax and Woodside (on the Dartmouth side).

BY BIKE Over the past few years, the HRM has made efforts to make the city more bike-friendly, and renting a bike (or riding your own) can be a good way to explore the area (with some steep hills to keep you fit). Best bet for rentals is **Idealbikes** [95 E5] (*1678 Barrington St;* ☎ *902 444 7433; www.idealbikes.ca*) or **I Heart Bikes** [101 G3] (*1325 Lower Water St;* ☎ *902 406 7774; www.iheartbikeshfx.com;* ⊕ *seasonally*). **Pedal and Sea Adventures** (tf *1 877 777 5699; www.pedalandseaadventures.com*) and **Freewheeling Adventures** (☎ *902 857 3600;* tf *1 800 672 0775*) are based in Hubbards (page 325) but offer free delivery to the Halifax area.

ON FOOT The downtown area is easily explored on foot, though Citadel Hill [94 B3] and the Public Gardens [95 A6] are a long way uphill from the waterfront. In the downtown area, many hotels and shops are connected by covered pedestrian walkways (pedways).

FESTIVALS AND EVENTS

Halifax, Dartmouth and the surrounding communities have an event-packed calendar. Although (not surprisingly) anything with an outdoor focus is held in the summer months, it seems that there is something going on throughout the year. Tickets for some of the bigger events are available through companies such as **Ticket Atlantic** (☎ *902 451 1221;* tf *1 877 451 1221; www.ticketatlantic.com*) and **Ticketpro** (tf *1 888 311 9090; www.ticketpro.ca*) – phone or see their websites for the nearest outlet.

JANUARY
In the Dead of Winter (*www.inthedeadofwinter.com*) Acoustic music festival held on the last weekend in January. Top singer-songwriter talent.

Savour Food and Wine Festival (☎ *902 429 5343;* tf *1 800 665 3463; www. savourfoodandwine.com*) Running between January and March, this Festival has a growing number of culinary experiences: many of the city's best restaurants offer special fixed-price menus to mark the occasion.

MARCH
Halifax Burger Week (*burgerweek.co/*) Week-long event celebrating ground meat (or vegetarian equivalent) stuffed in a bun. *Ich bin ein Halifaxer!*

APRIL
Halifax Comedy Fest (*halifaxcomedyfest.ca*) A four-day festival of laughs. Prices for shows range from free to CAN$50.

MAY
Scotiabank Bluenose Marathon (*bluenosemarathon.com*) Marathon, half-marathon and 5km and 10km events, plus a popular youth run.

NOVAFest (*nsccnovafest.wordpress.com*) Students of the NSCC Music Arts program are behind this genre-crossing 'new music' festival.

STAGES Theatre Festival (*www.easternfronttheatre.com*). Almost two weeks of new full-length and 10-minute plays at various venues. Tickets CAN$5–$30.

JUNE
Doors Open Halifax (*doorsopenhalifax.com*) The chance to visit around 30 of the city's buildings, many not usually open to the public.

Greek Festival (*www.greekfest.org*) Very popular even with those who don't have Hellenic roots. Held early to mid June.

The Scotia Festival of Music (✆ *902 429 9467;* **tf** *1 800 528 9883; www. scotiafestival.ns.ca*) A celebration of chamber music over two weeks in early June. Concert tickets CAN$30, discounted multi-concert tickets available.

JULY
Halifax Jazz Festival (*www.halifaxjazzfestival.ca*) Held over eight days, this is the largest Canadian music festival east of Montreal, and one of North America's major jazz events. Performances are held in a range of venues – in a variety of music styles. Many of the world's big names come to play, but it is also a reminder of the breadth and depth of local talent. Some free shows. In general tickets are CAN$15 and up: day passes and festival passes available.

Halifax Pride (*halifaxpride.com*) Atlantic Canada's largest Pride celebration is aimed at (in the words of the organisers): 'Lesbian, Gay, Bisexual, Transsexual, Transgender, Intersex, Queer, Questioning, 2 Spirited, Asexual, and Allies'. Accessible to all.

Maritime Fiddle Festival (*maritimefiddlefestival.ca*) Held in Dartmouth, Canada's longest running old-time fiddle festival also includes a step-dance competition and music workshops.

Royal Nova Scotia International Tattoo (✆ *902 420 1114;* **tf** *1 800 563 1114; www.nstattoo.ca; tickets CAN$35–72*) Billing itself 'the world's largest annual indoor show', this is a fantastic eight-day mix of marching bands, gymnastics, pageantry, dance, military competitions, music and more held in early July. And the organisers keep trying to push the barriers further. Performers come from the world over, and previous tattoos have seen 20 Swiss Elvis impersonators performing on parallel bars, and regular favourites include the Gun Run. A great – and very popular – family event. Held at the Scotiabank Centre [94 D4], there is one performance daily (either a matinee at 14.30, or in the evening at 19.30).

Shakespeare by the Sea (✆ *902 422 0295; www.shakespearebythesea.ca; admission by donation – CAN$20 suggested*) Between July and early September a selection of the Bard's (and other) works performed outdoors in an amphitheatre at an old gun battery in Point Pleasant Park [101 H6].

Tall Ships (*my-waterfront.ca*) This event – where beautiful sailing ships from around the world join many of Canada's finest sailing vessels in Halifax Harbour – only takes place every three to five years: it is due to be hosted here in 2017, but may not be back for a few years after that.

AUGUST
International Busker Festival (*www.buskers.ca*) Those to whom a busker is just a one-man band covering a 1960s' Bob Dylan song (badly) will have their eyes opened at this ten-day celebration of 'street theatre'. See jugglers, mime artists and fire-eaters from all over the world – and a whole lot more – at six waterfront properties. Free and great fun.

Natal Day (*www.natalday.org*) The communities of Halifax and Dartmouth come together in early August to celebrate their birthdays with a civic holiday long known as Natal Day. It is held over five days: expect parades, running races, live entertainment, fireworks and more.

SEPTEMBER
Atlantic Film Festival (☎ *902 422 3456*; **tf** *1 877 611 4244*; *www.atlanticfilm. com*) This ten-day mid September celebration of film and video from the Atlantic Provinces, Canada and around the world offers screenings of more than 150 films. These are shown in cinemas in and around town. Tickets cost CAN$12.50 per screening (more on opening nights).

Atlantic Fringe Festival (☎ *902 422 7604*; *www.atlanticfringe.ca*) Held over a period of ten days (or more) in early September, this festival offers a programme of more than 50 performing arts shows at various downtown venues. Ticket prices tend to be CAN$5–12 per show.

Prismatic Arts Festival (*prismaticfestival.com*) Canada's only multi-arts festival, featuring culturally diverse and Aboriginal artists. Held over five days at multiple downtown locations.

Word on the Street (*thewordonthestreet.ca*) Literary festival – listen to readings or pitch to publishers. Admission is usually free to all events.

OCTOBER
Halifax Pop Explosion (☎ *902 482 8176*; *www.halifaxpopexplosion.com*) A five-day festival featuring a range of music from folk-rock to hip-hop, with 150 bands over 18 venues. Music fans won't want to miss the party.

Nocturne: Art at Night (*nocturnehalifax.ca*) Fab three-night event that showcases and celebrates the visual arts scene in Halifax.

NOVEMBER
Hal-Con (**f** *halconscificon*) Join comic-lovers at the largest sci-fi, fantasy and gaming convention in Atlantic Canada.

Christmas at the Forum (*Halifax Forum, 2901 Windsor St*; **tf** *1 866 995 7469*; *www.christmasattheforum.com*) A festival of crafts, antiques, art and food held over three days at the beginning of the month.

HALIFAX

The province's most important metropolis was once the major point of entry to Canada for more than a million immigrants and refugees (page 116), and the port remains a busy centre for shipping today. Much attention focuses on the bustling waterfront, and traffic in the harbour is a mix of ferries, yachts, tugs, container ships, naval vessels and ocean cruisers.

Halifax (and Nova Scotia's) strong links to the sea are recognised at the absorbing Maritime Museum of the Atlantic [95 F5] (page 115), whilst high up the hill is the impressive Halifax Citadel National Historic Site of Canada [94 B3] (pages 114–15).

In an attempt to harass the British and the New Englanders who had taken Louisbourg (pages 363–4), in 1746, Louis XV sent a huge naval expedition to seek revenge. Under the command of the Duc d'Anville (who had little naval experience), a fleet of more than 70 sailing vessels and thousands of men endured an awful ten-week crossing of the Atlantic – including losing ships off Sable Island (pages 398–401) – before reaching what is now Halifax Harbour. The Duc himself died within a week of the arrival and was buried on Georges Island [101 H3] (page 123). Typhoid continued to claim lives, and when the men went ashore to bury their dead, the disease was passed on to the local Mi'kmaq population with devastating results.

The battered French fleet limped out of the harbour with the intention of sailing round and attacking Annapolis Royal (page 217) but turned back and headed for home. Less than a fifth of the original party reached France alive.

A range of museums, galleries and indoor attractions – not to mention shopping, particularly on lively Spring Garden Road [95 D7] – will occupy you if the weather isn't at its best, but when the sun comes out and the mercury rises you'll want to wander the beautiful Halifax Public Gardens [95 A6] (page 115) and hike along the seafront at Point Pleasant Park [101 H6] (page 119), take a boat on the harbour [94 G4], or go for a picnic. Summer is the time for an array of festivals, many of which are free.

Although hills may put some off, the downtown area is easily explored on foot – just as well bearing in mind that parking spots can be hard to find. Try to go beyond the downtown area to sample the shops and eateries of cosmopolitan Quinpool Road [100 C4], or the Hydrostone district [100 B1] (page 109).

Halifax continues to evolve. Built for the 2011 Canada Winter Games, the Emera Oval [100 D3] (page 113) is the largest outdoor, artificially refrigerated ice surface in Atlantic Canada. More major changes are underway: two complete city blocks (bordered by Prince, Argyle, Sackville and Market streets) are being transformed into the futuristic Nova Centre [95 D5] (*www.novacentre.ca*) which is set to house a financial centre, luxury hotel, residences, retail and entertainment amenities and a convention centre, parking, and public space: it might even be completed by the time you read this. A stunning, new CAN$58 million Halifax Central Library [95 C7] opened in late 2014.

Whilst first impressions will suggest that Halifax is friendly, charming and relaxed, dig deeper and you'll also find a well-developed music scene, lively pubs, and restaurants and bars to suit most palates and budgets. The two universities keep the atmosphere youthful – but rarely rowdy.

HISTORY Late in the 1740s, the British were looking for a site for a garrison as a base from which to defeat the French at Louisbourg, now back in French hands. They saw the potential of the area known to the Mi'kmaq as Jipugtug ('the great long harbour'), which was later anglicised as Chebucto. On one side of the wonderful harbour was a drumlin on which a fortress could be built. In 1749, General Edward Cornwallis arrived with about 2,500 settlers on 13 ships, and founded a settlement. The Earl of Halifax, President of the Board of Trade and Plantations, had been instrumental in obtaining British government approval for the projected town, and it was named Halifax in his honour.

HANGING AROUND IN HALIFAX

In days long gone by, criminals were often flogged, then branded on the ball of a thumb. Second offenders often faced the noose. In Halifax, there were central gallows at the foot of George Street [94 G4] (near the modern-day ferry terminal) and military gallows in the middle of the Citadel Hill parade ground [94 B3].

At the mouth of Halifax Harbour, a small, open cove named Black Rock Beach was the site of one of Halifax's earliest public gallows. Years later, these gallows were dismantled, relocated to McNabs Island and reassembled on a beach there. To this day, that stretch of sand is known as Hangmans Beach.

Immediately, the first fortress was built on the hilltop: this later developed into the Citadel [94 B3] (pages 114–15). St Paul's Church [95 E5] (page 120), Canada's first Anglican sanctuary, was constructed in 1750: that year, more settlers arrived and founded Dartmouth across the harbour. By 1752, the two towns were linked by a ferry system, the oldest saltwater ferry system in North America.

Protestants were recruited from mainland Europe in an attempt to counter the French and Catholic presence in Nova Scotia and between 1776 and 1783, population in the settlement was further boosted with the arrival of thousands of Loyalists from America.

Realising Halifax's strategic importance, in the years that followed, fortifications went up along the harbour approaches: these included batteries at McNabs Island, a Martello tower at Point Pleasant [101 H6], and forts at Georges Island [101 H3] and York Redoubt [82 C5].

St Mary's University [101 F5] was established in 1802 and Dalhousie University [100 D5] opened in 1818. Alexander Keith's brewing company [95 F7] (page 118) opened in 1820. In 1834, a cholera epidemic killed over 600 people in Halifax.

Native Haligonian Samuel Cunard was the leading figure in the city's shipping business, and in 1840, the Cunard Steamship Company's *Britannia* became the first vessel to offer a regular passenger service between Liverpool, UK, and Halifax.

Halifax is the only North American city founded by the British government (as opposed to British merchants or individuals), and was incorporated in 1841, and was connected by rail to Windsor (pages 247–53) and Truro (pages 262–7) in 1858.

After Canadian confederation in 1867, the city retained its British military garrison until British troops were replaced by the Canadian army in 1906. The British Royal Navy remained until 1910 when the newly created Royal Canadian Navy took over the Naval Dockyard.

The city leapt into the international spotlight in 1912 when the RMS *Titanic* sank northeast of Nova Scotia (box, page 92). The harbour, ice-free year-round, had long been recognised as one of the best deep-water ports in all of eastern North America. Opening into the expanse of Bedford Basin, this was a sanctuary where literally hundreds of ships could moor in safety.

During both World Wars, Halifax Harbour was of great strategic importance as it sheltered convoys from German U-boat attack before they headed out across the Atlantic and acted as the departure point for Canadian soldiers heading overseas. The devastating Halifax Explosion occurred in December 1917 – 2017 will mark its 100th anniversary (box, page 93).

Sir Winston Churchill visited Halifax twice during World War II. Having been shown the Public Gardens and Citadel Hill, he told the mayor: 'Now, sir, we know your city is something more than a shed on a wharf.'

On 10 April 1912, the White Star Line's RMS *Titanic* – at that time the largest passenger steamship in the world – left Southampton, England, on her maiden voyage to New York, carrying more than 1,300 passengers and 900 crew. Just before midnight on 14 April, she struck an iceberg south of Newfoundland, and sunk in less than 3 hours. Although 706 survivors were rescued, well over 1,500 men, women and children died. Some victims' bodies were recovered and buried at sea: 209 bodies were brought to Halifax. A temporary morgue was established in a curling rink (now an Army Surplus store): 150 victims were buried in three Halifax cemeteries between May and early June (121 in the Fairview Lawn Cemetery, 19 in the Mount Olivet Cemetery, and ten in the Baron de Hirsch Private Cemetery).

The Maritime Museum of the Atlantic (page 115) has a special section devoted to the *Titanic* disaster and its aftermath.

By the 1960s, Halifax was looking more than a little run down. Just in time, there was massive investment from federal, provincial and private sectors: several old buildings were renovated, the waterfront tastefully and imaginatively brought back to life, and many new hotels built. Care was taken to limit the height of high-rise buildings, and to preserve sight-lines.

Recent years saw another disaster, when huge amounts of damage were caused, but (thankfully) only eight people lost their lives. Tens of thousands of trees were knocked down, many in Point Pleasant Park: there was extensive damage to buildings, and many homes had no electricity for a fortnight. All this was a result of Hurricane Juan, which arrived in the early hours of 29 September 2003 and lashed Halifax with sustained wind gusts of over 180km/h. To date, this was the most damaging storm in modern history for the city.

TOURIST INFORMATION AND TOUR OPERATORS The tourist information centre [95 G5] is located at 1655 Lower Water St (✆ *902 424 4248;* ⊕ *Jul–mid Oct 08.30–19.00 daily; mid Oct–Jun 09.00–17.00 daily*). Staff offer a plethora of leaflets and brochures and will endeavour to answer your questions.

Local tour operators There are various good options for those who wish to be driven around the highlights of Halifax (and vicinity), and guides/drivers tend to be knowledgeable and entertaining. They may be geared towards cruise-ship passengers, but will happily take land-based folk; good suggestions are **Halifax Titanic Tours** (✆ *902 292 6780; www.halifaxtitanictours.ca*), **Halifax Taxi Tours** (✆ *902 489 8294; www.halifaxtaxitours.com*) or **Picture Perfect Tours** (✆ *902 292 6688; pictureperfecttours.ca*).

At 20.30 on certain dark evenings (see website for dates) between July and October, a guided 2-hour **Halifax Ghost Walk** (✆ *902 466 1060; www.thehalifaxghostwalk.com; CAN$15*) sets off from the Old Town clock. It's interesting – and fun, with a mix of folklore, historic sites and ghostly tales as you wend your way down to the waterfront.

Other recommended operators are:

Segway Tours ✆ 902 880 6630; www.segwayns.com. Those who prefer to sightsee by less mainstream methods of transport should consider this company, who operate their tours

In winter 1917, Halifax Harbour was alive with activity as heavily armed warships prepared to escort convoys carrying troops, munitions and supplies on the dangerous crossing of the Atlantic, neutral vessels waited at anchor, and the usual shipping traffic buzzed around.

On the morning of 6 December, the French ship *Mont-Blanc* left her anchorage outside the mouth of the harbour to join one of the convoys. She was loaded with hundreds of tons of TNT, picric acid, benzene and other explosives. At the same time, the *Imo*, a Norwegian ship in service of the Belgian Relief, was headed in the opposite direction. To cut a long story (and much speculation) short, the *Imo* struck the *Mont-Blanc* on the bow. Fire immediately broke out on board the *Mont-Blanc* and her terrified captain and crew took to the lifeboats and rowed for their lives to the Dartmouth shore.

The abandoned *Mont-Blanc* drifted toward the Halifax docks. At 09.05, what was at the time the largest manmade explosion in history – unrivalled until the detonation of the first atomic bomb – occurred. About 130ha of the city's North End was flattened, more than 10,000 people were wounded (many blinded by glass from shattered windows), and almost 2,000 were killed. Around 8,000 people's homes were destroyed, and tens of millions of dollars of damage done. The shock wave of the blast was felt over 400km away in Sydney on Cape Breton Island.

Fort Needham Memorial Park on Needham Street is home to a memorial carillon dedicated in 1984 to the memory of those who died in the explosion.

Incidentally, in World War II, three other potentially huge explosions involving vessels carrying munitions were narrowly avoided.

by 2-wheeled self-balancing battery-powered scooter.

I Heart Bikes 902 406 7774; www. iheartbikeshfx.com/tours; May–Oct. Offer good 2hr cycle tours of the city: price includes guide, helmet & bike hire.

Murphy's the Cable Wharf 902 420 1015; www.mtcw.ca; May–late Oct. Offer a wide range of bus/coach sightseeing tours in the city & further afield. Perhaps more interesting – as a harbour tour is something of a must – there are trips to choose from on a variety of vessels including the tugboat *Theodore Too*, the Nova Scotia maritime equivalent of *Thomas the Tank Engine*. One of their offerings – Harbour Hopper Tours – lets you combine land & sea with 55min tours in a brightly coloured amphibious vehicle. Or, go back in time & board the beautiful Tall Ship *Silva* for a 90min trip (using sail power where possible).

Kayak Halifax 902 210 7728; kayakhalifax. com. Action seekers might want to propel themselves across Halifax Harbour, (hopefully) avoiding ferries, amphibious vehicles, cruise ships, tugboats with hats on, & other water traffic. If so, these are the people to contact.

Local travel agents

Flight Centre [94 E3] Halifax Shopping Centre, 7001 Mumford Rd; tf 1 866 581 7769; www. flightcentre.ca

Maritime Travel [100 A4] Halifax Shopping Centre, 7001 Mumford Rd; 902 455 7856; tf 1 888 527 1444; www.maritimetravel.ca

WHERE TO STAY All too often, conventions or major events can fill all hotel beds in and close to downtown. Many of the bigger hotels are geared to business travellers and may offer cheaper rates on Friday and Saturday nights. It is always worth asking for a discount, especially if you're staying out of season or for more than a

Halifax, Dartmouth and Around HALIFAX

3

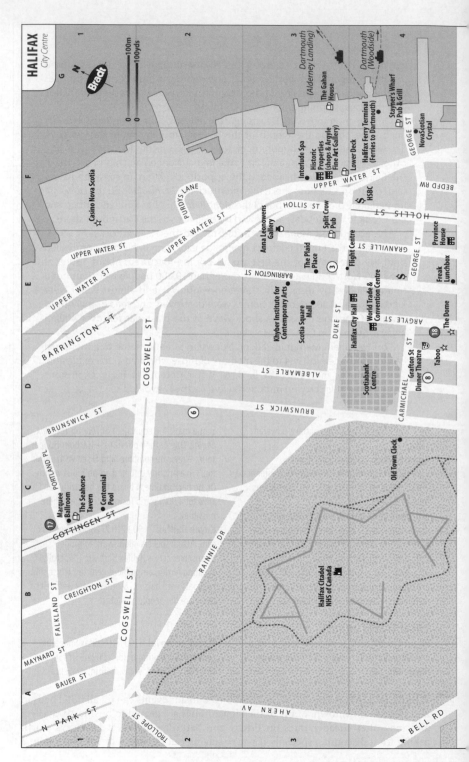

G   1

100m
100yds

N

Bradt

2

Dartmouth
(Alderney Landing)   3

The Gahan
House

Dartmouth
(Woodside)

Stayner's Wharf
Pub & Grill   4

NovaScotian
Crystal

Interlude Spa
Historic
Properties
(shops & Argyle
Fine Art Gallery)

Lower Deck

Halifax Ferry Terminal
(Ferries to Dartmouth)

GEORGE ST

F

UPPER WATER ST

Casino Nova Scotia

HOLLIS ST

HSBC

BEDFD RW

Anna Leonowens
Gallery

Split Crow
Pub

HOLLIS ST

The Plaid
Place

Flight Centre

GRANVILLE ST

GEORGE ST

Province
House

E

UPPER WATER ST

UPPER WATER ST

PURDY'S LANE

BARRINGTON ST

3

World Trade &
Convention Centre

ARGYLE ST

Freak
Lunchbox

UPPER WATER ST

Khyber Institute for
Contemporary Arts

Scotia Square
Mall

DUKE ST

Halifax City Hall

ARGYLE ST

18

The Dome

Taboo

BARRINGTON ST

COGSWELL ST

ALBEMARLE ST

Scotiabank
Centre

CARMICHAEL

Grafton St
Dinner Theatre

8

D

BRUNSWICK ST

6

BRUNSWICK ST

C

Marquee
Ballroom

PORTLAND PL

The Seahorse
Tavern

Centennial
Pool

Old Town Clock

GOTTINGEN ST

17

COGSWELL ST

RAINNIE DR

B

FALKLAND ST

CREIGHTON ST

Halifax Citadel
NHS of Canada

A

MAYNARD ST

BAUER ST

COGSWELL ST

N PARK ST

TROLLOPE ST

AHERN AV

1

2

BELL RD

4

3

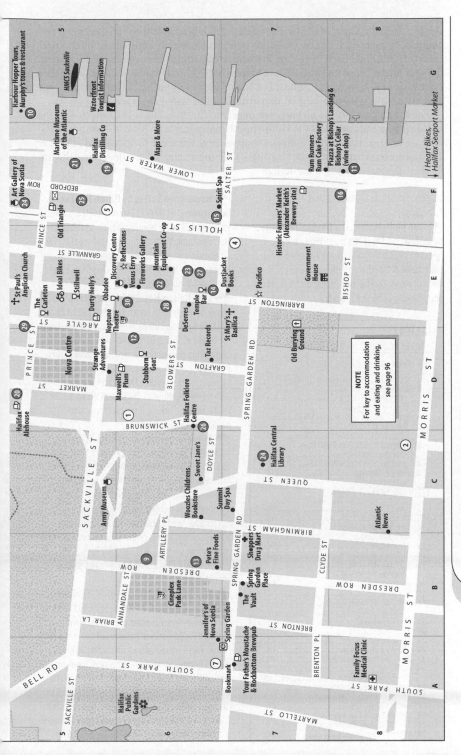

Harbour Hopper Tours,
Murphy's tours & restaurant
HMCS Sackville
10
Wateffront
Tourist Information

Art Gallery of
Nova Scotia
24
BEDFORD ROW
Maritime Museum
of the Atlantic
21
Halifax
Distilling Co
19
Maps & More

Old Triangle
25
5
LOWER WATER ST
HOLLIS ST
SALTER ST

Rum Runners
Rum Cake Factory
Piazza at Bishop's Landing &
Bishop's Cellar
(wine shop)
11

Spirit Spa
15

Historic Farmers' Market
(Alexander Keith's
Brewery site)
16
BISHOP ST

St Paul's
Anglican Church
PRINCE ST
GRANVILLE ST
Ideal Bikes
Stillwell
Durty Nelly's
Obladee
The
Carleton
29
ARGYLE ST

Discovery Centre
☆ Reflections
Venus Envy
Fireworks Gallery
Mountain
Equipment Co-op
22
23 27
Dustjacket
Books
14
Pacifico
Government
House

Neptune
Theatre
30
28
DeSerres
Temple
Bar
Taz Records
St Mary's ✝
Basilica
BARRINGTON ST

Strange
Adventures
12
Stubborn
Goat
Maxwell's
Plum
BLOWERS ST
GRAFTON ST
SPRING GARDEN RD
Old Burying
Ground

Nova Centre
MARKET ST
PRINCE ST

Halifax
Alehouse
20
Halifax Folklore
Centre
26
BRUNSWICK ST
DOYLE ST
Halifax Central
Library
24
2

Army Museum
SACKVILLE ST

NOTE
For key to accommodation
and eating and drinking,
see page 96

MORRIS ST

Woozles Childrens
Bookstore
Sweet Jane's
Summit
Day Spa
QUEEN ST
Atlantic
News
BIRMINGHAM ST
CLYDE ST

ARTILLERY PL
DRESDEN ROW
Pete's
Fine Foods
13
9
Sheppers
Drug Mart
Spring
Garden
Place
The
Spring
Vault
SPRING GARDEN RD
BRENTON ST
DRESDEN ROW

ANNANDALE ST
BRIAR LA
Cineplex
Park Lane
Jennifer's
of Nova Scotia
Spring Garden
7
Your Father's Moustache
& Rockbottom Brewpub
Bookmark
SOUTH PARK ST
BRENTON PL
Family Focus
Medical Clinic
MORRIS ST

BELL RD
SACKVILLE ST
Halifax Public
Gardens
SOUTH PARK ST
MARTELLO ST

I Heart Bikes,
Halifax Seaport Market

95

couple of nights. Many of the larger hotels are also bookable through internet travel companies such as Expedia (*www.expedia.co.uk*), which sometimes offer lower rates than the hotel itself. If you are looking to stay somewhere upmarket for several days (or longer), also consider **Moore Suites** (✆ *902 407 5111; mooresuites.com*): they offer various downtown locations. For the nearest camping to downtown, see page 127. All accommodation is open year-round unless stated otherwise.

For hotels close to the **airport**, see page 99. The ALT Hotel is connected to the terminal by a walkway, and the Hilton and Holiday Inn both have indoor pools and offer 24-hour complimentary airport shuttles. Both are close to Exit 5A of Highway 102 and are less than 4km to the terminals. Offering an airport shuttle service, the Inn on the Lake is also worth considering.

Waterfront & downtown
Luxury

🏠 **The Hollis Halifax – a DoubleTree Suites by Hilton** [95 F5] (120 suites) 1649 Hollis St; ✆902 429 7233; thehollis.ca. Well-located hotel with studio & 1-bedroom suites with city or harbour views. Cocktail bar, fitness centre & indoor pool. Parking CAN$18.95. **$$$$**

🏠 **Homewood Suites by Hilton Halifax-Downtown** [94 D2] (135 suites) 1960 Brunswick St; ✆902 429 6620; homewoodsuites3.hilton.com/en/index.html. Modern, comfortable studio, 1- & 2-bedroom suites with well-equipped kitchens. Fitness centre & indoor pool. Parking CAN$19.95/day. Rate inc hot b/fast. **$$$$**

🏠 **Lord Nelson Hotel & Suites** [95 A6] (262 rooms & suites) 1515 South Park St; ✆902 423 6331; tf 1 800 565 2020; lordnelsonhotel.ca. On the corner of Spring Garden Rd with many rooms overlooking the Public Gardens, the décor in this grandiose c1928 hotel is contemporary in style: bathrooms are spacious. There's a fitness room, & an on-site traditional-English style pub where food is served. Parking is CAN$28/day, valet parking CAN$40. **$$$$**

🏠 **Prince George Hotel** [94 D4] (186 rooms & 15 suites) 1725 Market St; ✆902 425 1986; tf 1 800 565 1567; www.princegeorgehotel.com. Close to the Halifax Citadel (& uphill from the centre of downtown), this was completely renovated in 2015. It is another good choice for those who like big, comfortable hotels. Good concierge service, plus business centre, fitness centre & indoor pool, & 3 fine eateries (Gio, see page 103, LevelBar Patio & Terrace). Underground parking CAN$22/day, valet parking offered. **$$$$**

🏠 **Westin Nova Scotian** [101 G3] (310 units) 1181 Hollis St; ✆902 421 1000 tf 1 877 993 7846; www.thewestinnovascotian.com. Built by the Canadian Pacific National Railway in 1930 as the Nova Scotian (adjacent to Halifax Railway Station), this grand 11-storey hotel has recently undergone major renovations & is looking good outside & 'urban chic' within. It has all the facilities you'd expect from a top city hotel (indoor pool, fitness centre, business centre & more), a stylish bar & more casual, highly regarded restaurant. Parking from CAN$18/day. **$$$$**

THE COMMUNITY THAT DISAPPEARED

Compared with the thousands of Acadians deported from Nova Scotia for refusing to sign an oath of allegiance to the British (page 17), the eviction of 400 townsfolk might not seem a lot. The residents of Africville, a shanty town on the edge of Halifax, weren't turfed out of their homes in the 18th century, however, but in the 1960s.

Africville was founded in the 1840s by people living in very poor black communities seeking a better life. Railway lines were built right through the centre of the town and later a slaughterhouse, fertiliser plant and factories went up immediately adjacent to it.

Although the residents paid taxes, at no stage did the city of Halifax provide basic services such as running water, sewage or paved roads. The community had a school, post office, and its focus, the church. But in the 1950s, the large, open city dump was moved to within a few hundred metres of Africville.

Then in 1962, the city government announced it was expropriating the land on which Africville stood as part of an Urban Renewal programme. In 1964, rubbish trucks arrived to remove the first residents. Most had no way to prove that they owned the run-down houses that they occupied, and were given CAN$50 as a goodwill compensatory gesture. In 1970, the last property was bulldozed.

In February 2010, Halifax's Mayor apologised to the people of Africville for the destruction of their community nearly 40 years before. The apology was supported by the allocation of land and CAN$3 million for the construction of a replica of the church that had stood at the geographic and emotional heart of Africville. The Africville Museum (page 116) opened in 2012.

Upmarket

Cambridge Suites Hotel Halifax [95 D6] (200 suites) 1583 Brunswick St; 902 420 0555; tf 1 800 565 1263; www.cambridgesuiteshalifax.com. In addition to comfortable, well-equipped roomy suites (all rooms have microwave & fridge) this modern, well-located property has a licensed restaurant, rooftop fitness centre & sundeck. A good choice for families. Indoor parking CAN$20/day. Rate inc hot b/fast. **$$$**

Delta Barrington [94 E3] (200 rooms) 1875 Barrington St; 902 429 7410; tf 1 800 268 1133; .www.marriott.com/hotels/travel/yhzdb-delta-barrington. This upscale boutique hotel close to the waterfront has a business centre, indoor pool, fitness centre, & restaurant & bar (Tempo Food & Drink). It might look old from the Granville St side but that's just the result of a painstaking restoration of the building's original façade. Valet parking available at CAN$25/day. **$$$**

Four Points by Sheraton Halifax [95 E7] (159 rooms & 18 suites) 1496 Hollis St; 902 423 4444; tf 1 866 444 9494; www.starwoodhotels.com. This conveniently located, modern (c2002),

7-storey hotel is another good well-equipped choice. There's an indoor pool, fitness room & the Niche Restaurant. Underground parking at CAN$19.95/day. **$$$**

The Halliburton [101 F3] (25 rooms & 4 suites) 5184 Morris St; 902 420 0658; tf 1 888 512 3344; www.thehalliburton.com. Occupying 3 adjoining c1809 properties, the beautifully restored Halliburton successfully blends B&B & boutique hotel. It is elegant & very comfortable, & when the sun comes out the courtyard garden is very pleasant. The on-site restaurant, Stories (page 102), offers dinner Tue–Sat . There is also (limited) free parking. Light buffet b/fast inc. **$$$**

Waverley Inn [101 F3] (34 rooms) 1266 Barrington St; 902 423 9346; tf 1 800 565 9346; waverleyinn.com. This delightful c1866 property has included Oscar Wilde amongst its guests. Expect hardwood floors & antiques. As the cheapest 'Traditional' rooms are on the small side, you may want to consider upgrading. Rooms on 3 floors (no lifts). Free parking is a bonus. Hot b/fast buffet & snacks inc. **$$$**

Budget

🏠 **HI-Halifax: Halifax Heritage House Hostel** [101 F3] (75 beds) 1253 Barrington St; ☎902 422 3863; www.hihostels.ca. Probably the better located of the city's hostels, this is close to the waterfront within walking distance of many attractions & the bus/train station. In addition to dorm beds, there are a couple of private/family rooms with private baths & also shared bathrooms, a kitchen, common room & laundry. Discounts for YHA/HI members. *Dorm CAN$35, private room CAN$72.* **$**

Central Halifax
Mid range

🏠 **Atlantica Hotel Halifax** [100 D3] (230 units) 1980 Robie St; ☎902 423 1161; tf 1 888 810 7288; www.atlanticahotelhalifax.com. Located at Robie St's junction with Quinpool Rd, directly across from the Halifax Commons. Restaurant & lounge, indoor pool, whirlpool, sauna, fitness equipment (seasonal) sundeck & business centre. Free Wi-Fi. On-site parking CAN$20/day. **$$–$$$**

🏠 **Commons Inn** [100 C2] (41 units) 5780 West St; ☎902 484 3466; tf 1 877 797 7999; www.commonsinn.ca. Accommodation at this Edwardian building within a 15-min walk of many downtown attractions includes simple standard rooms, larger deluxe rooms with microwave & fridge, & a suite. There are also 2 rooftop patios. Free parking. Light b/fast inc. **$$**

Budget

🏠 **Marigold B&B** [100 C4] (2 rooms) 6318 Norwood St; ☎902 423 4798; www.marigoldbedandbreakfast.com. If you don't mind sharing a bathroom, this uncluttered c1893 house on a residential street approx 25mins' walk or a short bus ride from downtown – & well placed for shopping/dining on Quinpool Rd – is a good choice. Free off-road parking. Wi-Fi. Full b/fast inc.**$**

North Halifax
Budget

🏠 **Halifax Backpackers Hostel** [100 D2] (30 beds) 2193 Gottingen St; ☎902 431 3170; tf 1 888 431 3170;www.halifaxbackpackers.com. This friendly hostel is not far from things, but neither is it in the most salubrious part of town. Located in an old building with dorms that are a little cramped. Communal kitchen, laundry, lounge & on-site licensed organic fairtrade café. *Dorm CAN$23, private room CAN$55-65.* **$**

South Halifax
Mid range

🏠 **At Robie's End B&B** [101 F6] (2 rooms) 836 Robie St; ☎902 405 2424; www.robiesend.com. Both of the guestrooms at this quiet B&B near St Mary's University & Point Pleasant Park have private entrances & mini fridges. Continental b/fast inc or, for a surcharge, an excellent full b/fast. **$$**

Budget

🏠 **Dalhousie University** ☎902 494 8840; tf 1 888 271 9222; www.dal.ca/dept/summer-accommodations.html; ⊕ early May–late Aug. During the summer break, this university rents out sgl & twin rooms (shared facilities) at 3 locations: Howe Hall [100 D5] (*6230 Coburg Rd*), Gerard Hall [95 C8] (*5303 Morris St*) & Risley Hall [100 D5] (*1233 LeMarchant St*). Or, opt for a 2-, 3- or 4-bedroom suite at LeMarchant Place [100 D5] (*1246 LeMarchant St*). Rates include use of the university recreation facilities. **$**

Near Northwest Arm
Luxury

🏠 **The Pebble B&B** [100 B5] (2 suites) 1839 Armview Terrace; ☎902 423 3669; tf 1 888 303 5056; www.thepebble.ca. On a quiet cul-de-sac with fine views over the lovely Northwest Arm, especially from the terrace. Bright, spacious,

REDS IN THE BED

In 1917, during her husband's time in Amherst (box, page 284), Mrs Trotsky and the boys stayed in Halifax, first at the home of the local man who had been assigned as Trotsky's interpreter when he first came ashore, and later at the Prince George Hotel which was on the corner of Sackville and Hollis streets. That hotel burned down a few months after the Trotskys checked out and is connected in name alone with today's Prince George Hotel on Market Street.

comfortable suites, emphasis on details & comfort. Pet friendly. Rate includes parking, afternoon tea on arrival & full b/fast. **$$$$**

Mid range
🛏 **SeaWatch B&B** [82 C5] (2 suites) 139 Ferguson's Cove Rd; ☎ 902 477 1506; seawatch.ca. Both suites at this modern, nautically themed B&B have private entrances & decks with a panoramic view of Halifax Harbour. Approx 15mins' drive from downtown Halifax, near York Redoubt. Free parking & rate includes light hot b/fast. **$$**

Near the airport
🛏 **ALT Hotel Halifax Airport** [82 D1] 40 Silver Dart Dr; ☎ 902 334 0136; **tf** 1 855 258 5775; www.althotels.com. Modern, European-style hotel a short walk from the terminals. Friendly staff, clean, comfortable. There is a bar & vending area but my only thumbs-down is that to eat more substantially you have to go back to the airport terminal. **$$**

🛏 **Hilton Garden Inn Halifax Airport** [82 C1] (145 rooms) 200 Pratt & Whitney Dr, Enfield; ☎ 902 873 1400; www.halifaxairport.stayhgi.com. Some rates include b/fast. **$$**

🛏 **Holiday Inn Express Halifax Hotel & Suites** [82 C1] (96 rooms & 23 suites) 180 Pratt & Whitney Dr, Enfield; ☎ 902 576 7600; www. hiexpress.com. Hot b/fast buffet inc. **$$**

🛏 **Inn on the Lake** [82 C2] (39 units) 3009 Hwy 2, Fall River; ☎ 902 861 3480; **tf** 1 800 463 6465; www.innonthelake.com. With 20 rooms & 19 executive rooms/suites (with whirlpool baths), this establishment just off Hwy 102 Exit 5 (approx 10mins to airport and 18mins to downtown Halifax) offers more than most airport hotels including an outdoor (seasonal) pool & acres of groomed lakefront parkland. A complimentary airport shuttle is offered 05.00–midnight daily. Olivers gastropub (🕐 14.00–21.00 daily) offers food, as does the rather good licensed Encore Restaurant (🕐 07.00–21.00 daily). **$$**

✖ **WHERE TO EAT AND DRINK** In recent years, the food scene in Halifax has seen great and wondrous changes. A new breed of entrepreneur restaurateurs have already made their mark, transforming what wasn't (with the odd exception) a place with the most exciting dining choices in the world.

Today's Halifax (and environs) paints a different story, and one is almost spoilt for choice. Whether you want to eat in a café, pub, old-style diner or zanily designed trendy upmarket restaurant, in general standards are high and prices reasonable. Hotel restaurants in particular have come forward in leaps and bounds. The area's multi-cultural vibe also means a wide range of ethnic restaurants – always a good thing for the adventurous eater. 'Fill yer boots' (as they say) here, as you won't find much ethnic food outside the HRM. Virtually all of the better restaurants accept reservations – some are so popular that these are a necessity. Note that many restaurants charge significantly less for the same dish at lunch than in the evening.

LocalTastingTours (☎ 902 818 9055; www.localtastingtours.com) offer guided walking tours (including free tastings) of selected highlights of downtown and the waterfront's food shops, breweries and eateries, while **Taste Halifax Food Tours** (☎ 902 446 9463; www.halifaxfoodtours.com) offer similar – but chauffeured – experiences. Both are recommended.

If you find downtown/waterfront prices too high, or fancy a wander past a varied selection of ethnic and/or budget eateries, head along **Quinpool Road**. A few highlights are listed on pages 105–6.

Waterfront & downtown
Luxury
✖ **CUT Steakhouse, Shuck Seafood & Raw Bar** [95 F6] 5120 Salter St; ☎ 902 429 5120; www.cutsteakhouse.ca; 🕐 (Shuck) 11.30–14.30 daily, (Shuck & CUT) 17.30–21.00 or later daily.

There are 2 different dining experiences here: the downstairs bar exhibits a traditional yet modern East Coast vibe & serves up dishes chosen to highlight the quality & freshness of the shellfish/ seafood. Upstairs, the house specialty is the finest USDA Prime Beef, dry-aged on site, paired

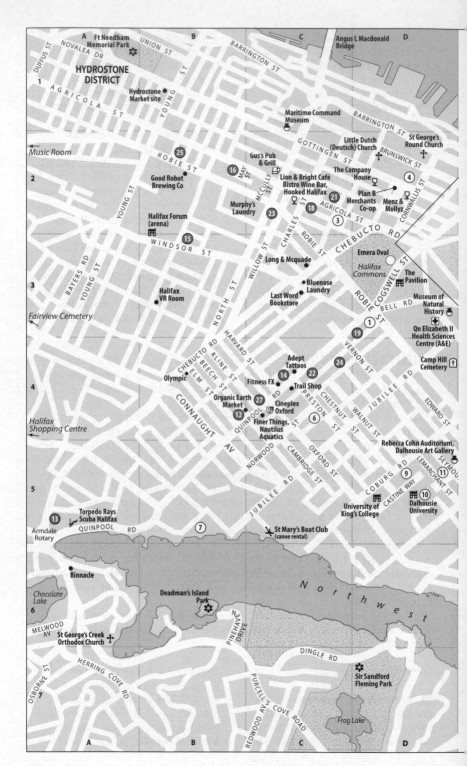

A · Ft Needham Memorial Park
UNION ST
BARRINGTON ST
Angus L Macdonald Bridge
NOVALEA DR
DUFFUS ST
YOUNG ST
HYDROSTONE DISTRICT
1
AGRICOLA ST
Hydrostone Market site
BARRINGTON ST
Maritime Command Museum
Little Dutch (Deutsch) Church
St George's Round Church
Music Room
ROBIE ST
(25)
MAY ST
Gus's Pub & Grill
GOTTINGEN ST
The Company House
BRUNSWICK ST
2
(16)
Good Robot Brewing Co
McCULLY ST
Lion & Bright Café Bistro Wine Bar, Hooked Halifax
(21)
Plan B Merchants Co-op
Menz & Mollyz
CORNWALLIS ST
(4)
YOUNG ST
Murphy's Laundry
(23)
(18)
AGRICOLA ST
(3)
CHARLES ST
CHEBUCTO RD
Halifax Forum (arena)
(15)
WINDSOR ST
WILLOW ST
Long & Mcquade
ROBIE ST
Emera Oval
Halifax Commons
COGSWELL ST
The Pavilion
BAYERS RD
YOUNG ST
3
Fairview Cemetery
NORTH ST
Halifax VR Room
Bluenose Laundry
Last Word Bookstore
ROBIE ST
BELL RD
Museum of Natural History
Qn Elizabeth II Health Sciences Centre (A&E)
HARVARD ST
(1)
(19)
VERNON ST
Camp Hill Cemetery
CHEBUCTO RD
KLINE ST
BEECH ST
Adept Tattoos
(14)
(22)
(24)
CHESTNUT ST
JUBILEE RD
EDWARD ST
4
Olympic
ELM ST
Fitness FX
Trail Shop
PRESTON ST
WALNUT ST
Halifax Shopping Centre
Organic Earth Market
(27)
QUINPOOL RD
(12)
Cineplex Oxford
Finer Things, Nautilus Aquatics
(6)
OXFORD ST
Rebecca Cohn Auditorium, Dalhousie Art Gallery
SEYMOUR
CONNAUGHT AV
NORWOOD ST
CAMBRIDGE ST
COBURG RD
CASTINE WAY
(9)
(11)
LEMARCHANT ST
5
JUBILEE RD
(10)
Torpedo Rays Scuba Halifax
(13)
(7)
University of King's College
Dalhousie University
Armdale Rotary
QUINPOOL RD
St Mary's Boat Club (canoe rental)
Binnacle
N o r t h w e s t
Chocolate Lake
6
Deadman's Island Park
MELWOOD AV
PINEHAVEN DRIVE
St George's Creek Orthodox Church
DINGLE RD
Sir Sandford Fleming Park
OSBORNE ST
7
HERRING COVE RD
PURCELL'S COVE ROAD
REDWOOD AV
Frog Lake

100

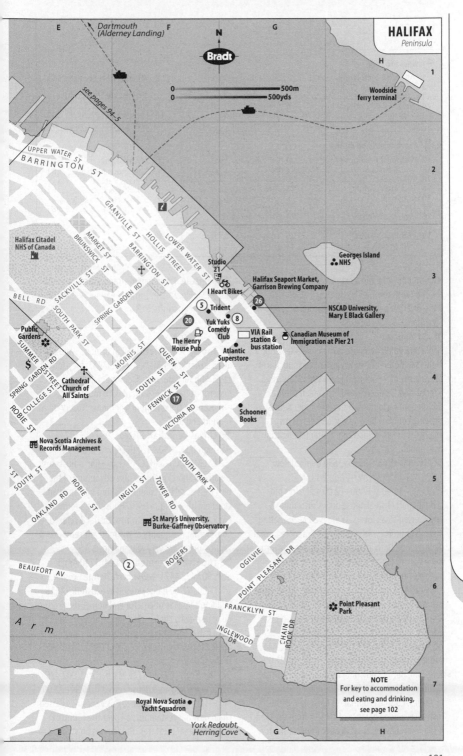

N

Bradt

Dartmouth
(Alderney Landing)

see pages 94–5

0 ————————— 500m
0 ————————— 500yds

Woodside
ferry terminal

UPPER WATER ST
BARRINGTON ST

Halifax Citadel
NHS of Canada

GRANVILLE STREET
HOLLIS STREET
LOWER WATER ST
BRUNSWICK ST
MARKET ST
BARRINGTON ST
SPRING GARDEN RD

BELL RD
SACKVILLE ST

Studio
21

Georges Island
NHS

I Heart Bikes

Halifax Seaport Market,
Garrison Brewing Company

26

5 Trident

8

20

Yuk Yuks
Comedy
Club

NSCAD University,
Mary E Black Gallery

Public
Gardens

SOUTH PARK ST

The Henry
House Pub

VIA Rail
station &
bus station

Atlantic
Superstore

Canadian Museum of
Immigration at Pier 21

SUMMER ST

SPRING GARDEN ST

MORRIS ST

QUEEN ST

ROBIE ST
COLLEGE ST

Cathedral
Church of
All Saints

Nova Scotia Archives &
Records Management

SOUTH ST

FENWICK ST

17

VICTORIA RD

Schooner
Books

OAKLAND RD
ROBIE ST

INGLIS ST

TOWER RD

SOUTH PARK ST

St Mary's University,
Burke-Gaffney Observatory

BEAUFORT AV

2

ROGERS ST

OGILVIE ST

POINT PLEASANT DR

FRANCKLYN ST

INGLEWOOD DR

CHAIN ROCK DR

Point Pleasant
Park

Arm

Royal Nova Scotia
Yacht Squadron

York Redoubt,
Herring Cove

NOTE
For key to accommodation
and eating and drinking,
see page 102

HALIFAX *Peninsula*
For listings, see pages 96–8 & 102–6

Where to stay

1	Atlantica Hotel Halifax.....D3		HI-Halifax: Halifax	8	Westin Nova Scotian.....G3	
2	At Robie's End B&B............F6		Heritage House			
3	Commons Inn.....................C2		Hostel.....................(see 5)		*Dalhousie University:*	
4	Halifax Backpackers	6	Marigold B&B..................C4	9	Howe Hall..........................D5	
	Hostel...............................D2	7	The Pebble B&B..............B5	10	LeMarchant Place..........D5	
5	The Halliburton.................F3		Waverley Inn............(see 5)	11	Risley Hall.........................D5	

Where to eat and drink

12	Ardmore Tea Room..........B4	20	Gingergrass......................F3		*Hydrostone:*	
13	The Armview.....................A5	21	Hali Deli............................C2		Epicurious Morsels.........B1	
14	Athens................................C4	22	Heartwood........................C4		Julien's Patisserie,	
15	Brooklyn Warehouse........B3	23	Java Blend.........................C2		Bakery & Café.................B1	
16	Coastal Café......................B2		Phil's Seafood.........(see 2)		Salvatore's Pizzaiolo	
17	Darrell's.............................F4		Stories......................(see 5)		Trattoria...........................B1	
18	enVie – A Vegan	24	Sweet Hereafter..............C4			
	Kitchen.............................C2	25	Tarek's Café......................B2			
19	Freeman's Little	26	Tomavino's Pizza............G3			
	New York.........................D3	27	Wasabi House...................C4			

with probably the most extensive wine list in the city (with sommeliers on site). Eat alfresco if the weather permits. Shuck Seafood $$; CUT Steakhouse $$$–$$$$

✘ **da Maurizio's** [95 F8] 1496 Lower Water St; ☎ 902 423 0859; damaurizio.ca; ⏰ 17.00–22.00 Mon–Sat. Before the new wave of exciting places to eat arrived in Halifax, there was da Maurizio's. Specialising in superb northern Italian cuisine, this elegant restaurant in the Alexander Keith's Brewery complex has more than held its own against some very good competition. Delightful fine-dining. $$$$

✘ **Ryan Duffy's** [95 F5] 1650 Bedford Row; ☎ 902 421 1116; www.ryanduffys.ca; ⏰ 11.30–14.00 & 17.00–22.00 daily. This old-style upmarket steakhouse draws discerning & well-heeled steak lovers. There is a bar & 2 eating areas, a lounge – with fireplace – & a more formal dining room: both are simple & elegant, the former more casual. Top-notch steak apart, seafood is strongly promoted too, but with slabs of (albeit high-quality) beef being carved table-side (before being wheeled away to be cooked over charcoal) it's probably not the first choice for vegetarians. $$$$

✘ **Stories** [101 F3] 5184 Morris St; ☎ 902 444 4400; www.storiesdining.com; ⏰ 17.30–21.00 Tue–Sun. Better known for its guestrooms, The Halliburton (page 97) has a fine-dining winner in Stories. Cuisine is upmarket Canadian, & the menu has a good balance of choices from the land & sea. Presentation & service are impeccable: try the pan-seared, rice paper-wrapped scallops with ginger vinaigrette. In summer eat on the patio if the weather permits. $$$

Upmarket

✘ **The Bicycle Thief** [95 F8] Bishop's Landing, 1475 Lower Water St; ☎ 902 425 7993; bicyclethief. ca; ⏰ 11.30–late daily. Fashionable, upscale waterfront Italian restaurant with nice views & atmosphere. Good for lunch or dinner: reservations recommended. $$$

✘ **Chives Canadian Bistro** [95 E6] 1537 Barrington St; ☎ 902 420 9626; www.chives.ca; ⏰ 17.00–21.00 daily. Chef Craig Flinn adjusts his (relatively short) menu to take advantage of the best fresh local ingredients, dishing up Canadian cuisine with a unique twist. Housed in a former bank, the atmosphere is warm, casual & relaxed. Considering the quality of the food, presentation & service, prices are very reasonable. $$$

✘ **The Five Fishermen** [94 E4] 1740 Argyle St; ☎ 902 422 4421; www.fivefishermen.com; ⏰ 17.00–22.00 daily. Housed in a historic c1816 building that was once a funeral home. There are good non-fishy choices, but beautifully prepared fresh fish & shellfish – locally grown & caught – are the focus. Try The Five Fish, or lobster-stuffed Digby scallops. $$$

✘ **The Keg** [95 D5] 1712 Market St; ☎ 902 425 8355; www.kegsteakhouse.com; ⏰ 16.30–22.00 Mon–Sat, 16.30–21.30 Sun. This Vancouver-based chain now has restaurants all over the country & in a number of US states. The focus is on steaks &

TIME FOR A CUPPA

Halifax has plenty of choices for those just looking for a coffee or tea (and perhaps something sweet to nibble on or dunk. My favourites include:

DOWNTOWN

💻 **The Old Apothecary** [95 E6] 1549 Barrington St; 📞 902 423 1500; www. theoldapothecary.com. Exquisite baked goods.

💻 **Pavia** 📞 902 497 4008; www.paviagallery.com; Art Gallery of Nova Scotia [94 F5] ⊕ 08.00–17.00 Mon–Fri, until 21.00 Thu (page 117) & Halifax Central Library [95 C7] ⊕ 08.00–21.00 Mon–Thu, 09.00–18.00 Fri–Sun (page 118). All locations (there are 2 at the library: ground floor & top floor) are bright espresso bars with small menus (paninis, baked goods, etc).

💻 **Steve-O-Reno's Cappuccino** [95 D6] 1536 Brunswick St; 📞 902 429 3034; www. steveorenos.com. Good b/fasts & brunches.

💻 **World Tea House** [95 E6] 1592 Argyle St; 📞 902 422 8327; worldteahouse.ca. Relax and sip a 'cuppa' at Halifax's top loose-leaf organic tea retailer.

NORTH END/HYDROSTONE

💻 **Java Blend** [100 C2] 6027 North St; 📞 902 423 6944; **tf** 1 877 596 5282; javablendcoffee.com It can be hard to find a table at this bustling coffee shop & roastery. Good muffins.

💻 **Julien's Patisserie, Bakery & Café** [100 B1] 5517 Young St; 📞 902 455 9717; julienshydrostone.ca. This French-style eatery is a popular Hydrostone coffee/light-lunch spot.

---

prime rib, but there's also chicken, seafood, etc. Try a Keg Caesar cocktail, & – if there's still room – finish off with a wedge of (outrageously yummy) Billy Miner Pie. **$$$**

✖ **McKelvie's** [95 F5] 1680 Lower Water St; 📞 902 421 6161; mckelvies.com; ⊕ 11.00–21.30 Mon–Fri, 16.00–21.30 Sat & Sun. The menu heading is 'delishes fishes dishes' but this isn't some awful themed restaurant where the descriptions are peppered (ha) with bad puns. There are decent alternatives that didn't originate underwater, a family-friendly-but-still-formal-enough-for-business-meetings atmosphere, & a decent wine list. Best of all, the fish & shellfish – cooked in a wide variety of ways – are, indeed, 'delishes'. **$$$**

✖ **Gio** [94 D4] 1725 Market St; 📞 902 425 1987; giohalifax.com; ⊕ 11.00–23.00 Mon–Fri, 17.00–23.00 Sat. Not your typical hotel restaurant, this chic, modern, fine/casual dining experience located within the Prince George (page 96) never seems to disappoint. Ingredients are high quality & fresh, service & presentation delightful. The menu often includes more exotic meat & fish selections. *Lunch* **$$**, *Dinner* **$$$**

✖ **The Middle Spoon** [95 E6] 1559 Barrington St; 📞 902 407 4002; www. themiddlespoon.ca; ⊕ 16.00–23.00 Mon–Thu, 16.00–01.00 Fri & Sat. How can a self-confessed sweet-toother not include a 'desserterie' on their list, where the vast majority of the menu is homemade desserts & innovative cocktails (there's also wine & coffee). Trendy, modern, comfortable, & (the downside) all too easy to walk out tens of dollars lighter & tens of pounds heavier. **$$–$$$**

Mid range

✖ **Baan Thai** [95 B6] 5324 Blowers St; 📞 902 446 4301; baanthai.ca; ⊕ 11.30–22.00 Mon–Fri, 15.00–22.00 Sat & Sun. The exterior isn't all that promising, but the interior is pleasant, & the Thai food authentic & high quality. **$$**

✖ **Bistro Le Coq** [95 D6] 1584 Argyle St; 📞 902 407 4564; bistrocoq.ca; ⊕ noon–22.00 Tue–Fri (til midnight Fri), 11.30–midnight Sat, 11.30–22.00 Sun. Bright, authentic-looking French bistro. It's not just the décor that transports you to la belle Paris – the menu & food both help to enhance the impression. **$$–$$$**

✕ Gingergrass [101 F3] 1284 Barrington St; ☎ 902 425 8555; gingergrass.ca; ⏰ 11.30–14.00 & 16.30–20.00 Mon–Sat. Simple, sensibly priced traditional Vietnamese & Thai cuisine to tempt your taste buds. Friendly & relaxed. $$

✕ Ristorante a Mano [95 F8] Bishop's Landing, 1477 Lower Water St; ☎ 902 423 6266; www. ristoranteamano.ca; ⏰ 11.30–22.00 Mon–Sat. Good Italian restaurant offering well-made pasta, poultry, meat & fish. Nice terrace, friendly service. The antipasto is a good starter. Same ownership as The Bicycle Thief (page 102). $$–$$$

✕ Sushi Shige [95 E6] 1532 Granville St; ☎ 902 422 0740; ⏰ 11.30–14.00 & 17.00–21.30 Mon–Fri, 17.00–21.30 Sat. In the main, good, traditional-style Japanese favourites (eg: sushi, sashimi, yakitori, tempura) are all well executed. Plus something less traditional but very popular – sushi pizza (salmon, tuna or mixed seafood with toppings on a deep-fried rice cake). $$

✕ The Wooden Monkey [95 E5] 1707 Grafton St; ☎ 902 444 3844; www.thewoodenmonkey. ca; ⏰ 11.30–22.00 Sun–Thu, 11.30–23.00 Fri & Sat. Health- & environment-conscious diners will enjoy this eatery where just about everything is organic, macrobiotic, locally grown & very tasty. The sweet apple salad is a winner, & I'm told that Jerry Seinfeld loved the sesame-crusted haddock. Offers vegetarian – plus vegan & gluten-free – & meat options. As they have done since the 1960s, such places attract artists, musicians & other bohemians. And of course, Jerry Seinfeld. $$

Budget

✕ The Battered Fish [95 G5] 1751 Lower Water St; ☎ 902 492 8898; thebatteredfish.ca; ⏰ May–Oct 11.00–dusk daily. Despite the touristy location, this franchise chain eatery isn't a bad option if you stick to fish & chips. $–$$

✕ Chez Cora [95 B6] 1535 Dresden Row; ☎ 902 490 2672; www.chezcora.com; ⏰ 06.00–15.00 Mon–Sat, 07.00–15.00 Sun. What started off in a former snack bar in Montreal has rapidly grown to become a chain of more than 120 eateries countrywide. This one, just off Spring Garden Rd, is one of the most convenient. Expect bright, cheery décor, hearty servings of omelettes, waffles, pancakes & crêpes (balanced by lots of fresh fruit). $

✕ The Great Wall [95 F5] 1649 Bedford Row; ☎ 902 422 6153; www.thegreatwall.ca; ⏰ 11.30–22.00 daily. Everything is made from scratch in this well-established Chinese restaurant. The dim sum session (⏰ *11.30–15.00 Sun*) is justifiably popular. Flavoursome & good value. $

✕ Willy's Fresh Cut Fries & Burgers [95 E6] 5239 Blowers St; ☎ 902 402 3365; www. willysfreshcut.ca; ⏰ noon–04.00 Tue–Sat, 22.00–04.00 Sun & Mon. After years of success catering to nightbirds/the 'after-bar' crowd, this take-out has begun feeding good burgers & its signature dish – poutine (box, page 62) – to those with standard bedtimes. Cheap & cheerful. $–$$

North End & Hydrostone
Upmarket

✕ Brooklyn Warehouse [100 B3] 2795 Windsor St; ☎ 902 446 8181; www.brooklynwarehouse. ca; ⏰ 11.30–15.30 & 16.30–21.00 Mon–Sat (til 22.00 Fri & Sat). A hit since opening in 2007 for its use of fresh, seasonal, local ingredients to create a varied & award-winning menu which blends & twists Canadian classics, hints of the Mediterranean, & Asia. The (short) menu changes daily, & some options sell out. $$$

✕ EDNA [94 C1] 2053 Gottingen St; ☎ 902 431 5683; ednarestaurant.com; ⏰ 17.00–22.00 Tue–Sun (Fri & Sat til 23.00), plus brunch 10.00–14.30 Sat & Sun. Sophisticated, trendy, upmarket bistro where the focus is on preparation & taste rather than big portions. No reservations. $$$

✕ Epicurious Morsels [100 B1] 5529 Young St; ☎ 902 455 0955; epicuriousmorsels.com; ⏰ 11.30–15.00 & 17.00–20.00 Tue–Fri, 10.30–14.30 & 17.00–21.00 Sat, 10.30–14.30 & 17.00–20.00 Sun. Chef Jim Hanusiak has an interesting little place in the Hydrostone, tastefully decorated & comfortable – romantic even. Serves French–Mediterranean-inspired dishes – be sure to try some in-house-smoked Atlantic salmon or *gravad lax* – oh, & leave room for dessert. *Lunch/ brunch* $$; *dinner* $$–$$$

Mid range

✕ Coastal Café [100 B2] 2731 Robie St; ☎ 902 405 4022; www.thecoastal.ca; ⏰ 08.00–14.15 daily (from 10.00 Sun). This North End award winner is getting too popular & can feel overcrowded. Exotic & exciting takes on b/fasts/ diner food. $$

✕ enVie – A Vegan Kitchen [100 C2] 5775 Charles St; ☎ 902 492 4077; enviehalifax.com; ⏰ 11.00–21.00 Tue–Fri, 10.00–22.00 Sat,

10.00–21.00 Sun. Tasty vegan food, & various meat-style dishes (eg: double bacon cheeseburger) using mushrooms, seitan or tempeh. Uses GMO-free ingredients, organic nuts, grains, pulses, etc. Suggested beer or wine pairings. Take-home meals, too. $$

Budget

✖ **Hali Deli** [100 C2] 2389 Agricola St; ✆ 902 406 2500; halideli.com; ⊕ 10.00–15.00 Mon–Wed, 10.00–19.00 Thu & Fri, 09.00–19.00 Sat, 10.00–17.00 Sun. Old Jewish-style deli serving heart breakfasts, overstuffed smoked meat sandwiches, borscht, latkes (potato pancakes) & more. Half a sandwich and a serving of chicken matzah ball soup is a great lunch special. $–$$

✖ **Salvatore's Pizzaiolo Trattoria** [100 B1] 5541 Young St; ✆ 902 455 1133; www.salvatorespizza.ca; ⊕ 11.30–22.00 Mon–Sat, 16.00–22.00 Sun. NY-style 'hero' sandwiches, plus very good pizzas with thin-crust bases & high quality ingredients. Loads of toppings to choose from, but I like to keep it simple & stick to the roasted garlic & sautéed mushrooms. In the Hydrostone. $–$$

🖵 **Tarek's Café** [100 B2] 3045 Robie St; ✆ 902 454 8723; www.tarekscafe.ca; ⊕ 11.30–19.30 Mon–Sat. Come for good, low-budget Lebanese/Greek food (dips, salads, pita sandwiches, etc), with some non-Mediterranean fillings (eg: Philly steak) & dishes (eg: curry ginger chicken). $–$$

Quinpool Rd
Mid range

✖ **The Armview** [100 A5] 7156 Chebucto Rd; ✆ 902 455 4395; www.thearmview.com;

⊕ 11.00–22.00 Mon–Wed, 08.30–22.00 Thu–Sun. The décor is late 1950s, the menu long & varied, the service friendly, & the food – diner meets *haute cuisine* – very good. Near the Armdale Rotary. $$

✖ **Athens** [100 C4] 6273 Quinpool Rd; ✆ 902 422 1595; www.athensrestaurant.com; ⊕ 08.00–21.00 daily, til 22.00 Thu–Sat. The Greek food is usually very good & the portions generous. $$

✖ **Freeman's Little New York** [100 D3] 6092 Quinpool Rd; ✆ 902 429 0241; www.freemanspizza.ca; ⊕ 10.00–05.00 daily. Nightbirds who feel like something to eat in the wee small hours are best off at this Quinpool Rd institution. Pizzas, burgers, pastas, nachos & more. $$

✖ **Heartwood** [100 C4] 6250 Quinpool Rd; ✆ 902 425 2808; www.iloveheartwood.ca; ⊕ 11.00–21.00 daily (til 22.00 Fri & Sat). Organic vegetarian/vegan food, local beers on tap. Pop in for a bite – try the Heartwood Bowl (brown rice or vermicelli noodles, topped with seasonal vegetables, mixed greens & sauce of your choice) – or just to grab a decadent-looking but apparently healthy hazelnut brownie or other treat. Outdoor patio. $$

✖ **Wasabi House** [100 C4] 6403 Quinpool Rd; ✆ 902 429 3300; wasabihouse.ca; ⊕ 11.00–23.00 daily. Good service, fresh sushi, & often a line of locals waiting for a table. $$

Budget

🖵 **Ardmore Tea Room** [100 B4] 6499 Quinpool Rd; ✆ 902 423 7523; ⬛; ⊕ 05.00–20.00

Halifax, Dartmouth and Around HALIFAX

3

BUCK STARS IN COFFEE SHOP – AND OTHER CERVINE CAPERS

On a Monday morning in June 2011, a young deer crashed through the window of the Uncommon Grounds coffee shop on Halifax's South Park Street. The poor creature thrashed around, jumping on tables and knocking over chairs before crashing out through another window pane. A year later, another deer explored the Dalhousie University campus, passed a few shops along Quinpool Road, and then walked up Citadel Hill. And, not to be outdone by its far more common cousins, a moose – very rarely seen in mainland Nova Scotia – was found wandering the streets not far from the Fairview Cemetery. Unfortunately for the glazier, officials reached the animal before it found a coffee shop. In all three cases, Department of Natural Resources staff tranquilised the animals and later released them back into woodland well outside the urban centre.

daily. The Ardmore – going for over half a century – just keeps on dishing out the all-day b/fasts & more. Come for huge, cholesterol-packed portions & low prices – not décor, sophistication or linen tablecloths. Small & ever-popular. $

✗ **Phil's Seafood** [100 C4] 6285 Quinpool Rd; ☎ 902 431 3474; philsseafood.ca; ⏰ 11.30–20.00 Tue–Sat, 11.30–19.30 Sun. A great fish & chip shop especially if you prefer lots of fish to lots of batter. There are scallops, shrimps & more, too – & it doesn't have to be fried. Good value, especially the large fish & chips. $

🖵 **Sweet Hereafter** [100 C4] 6148 Quinpool Rd; ☎ 902 404 8001; www.sweethereafter.ca; ⏰ noon–22.00 Mon–Sat (til 23.00 Thu–Sat). This striking, modern 'cheesecakery' (their description, not mine) offers decent beverages & all sorts of flavours of premium (you guessed it) cheesecake, including dozens of gluten-free &/or vegan options. $

South End
Mid range

✗ **Darrell's** [101 F4] 5576 Fenwick St; ☎ 902 492 2344; www.darrellsrestaurants.com; ⏰ 11.00–22.00 daily. There are salads, very good pita bread wraps, sandwiches & more, but the burgers are hard to resist (except perhaps for the bizarrely popular, multi-award-winning peanut butter-smothered one). Attempt to wash it down with a super-thick milkshake. Close to the universities & with a downstairs area where sport is shown on a large-screen TV, it is understandably popular with students. $$

✗ **Tomavino's Pizza** [101 G3] 1113 Marginal Rd; ☎ 902 425 7111; www.tomavinos.ca; ⏰ 11.00–22.00 Mon–Thu, noon–23.00 Fri & Sat, 16.00–22.00 Sun. Next to the Garrison Brewery near Pier 21. Excellent pizzas: the Ambrosia (mushrooms, fresh spinach & Italian sausage) has countless admirers. $$

ENTERTAINMENT AND NIGHTLIFE

Bars, pubs and clubs It is often said that Halifax has more pubs/bars per capita than anywhere else in Canada. Several of the region's better **pubs** serve good-value, sometimes quite upmarket, pub food, and many of the following could also be listed in the *Where to eat and drink* section. Halifax's most famous **brewery** is Alexander Keith's (page 118): within that complex is the Stag's Head Tavern. You'll visit it if you do the brewery tour, but can also just pop in for (for example) a glass of Keith's celebrated India Pale Ale. The atmosphere is friendly, but rarely raucous.

Currently, the HRM has just one out-and-out **gay bar** (page 107), but there is also the gay-friendly **Reflections Cabaret** (page 108) and **The Company House** (page 107). In addition, **Venus Envy** (page 110) can be a useful source of local gay event info.

Far and away the best source of information for **live music** listings of all genres is the weekly free newspaper, *The Coast* (www.thecoast.ca), also available in an online format. Many of the eateries, pubs and bars mentioned host live music, as does the casino (page 109). The downtown **Scotiabank Centre** [94 D4] (*1800 Argyle St;* ☎ *902 451 1221; www.halifaxmetrocentre.com;* formerly the Halifax Metro Centre) hosts major sporting events and concerts.

Pubs & brewpubs

🍺 **Durty Nelly's** [95 E5] Cnr Argyle & Sackville sts; ☎ 902 406 7640; www.durtynellys.ca; ⏰ 11.30–01.00 (or later) daily. This place prides itself so much on being authentic that it was designed & built in Ireland, shipped to Halifax & put together piece by piece.

🍺 **The Gahan House** [94 F3] 1869 Upper Water St; ☎ 902 444 3060; halifax.gahan.ca; ⏰ daily from 11.00. Brewpub with great waterfront location: the food is usually good. Can be very busy.

🍺 **The Henry House Pub** [101 F4] 1222 Barrington St; ☎ 902 423 5660; www.henryhouse. ca; ⏰ 11.30–midnight Mon–Thu, 11.30–00.45 Fri & Sat, 11.30–23.30 Sun. In a lovely historic 1834 building, this is a must-visit for fans of traditional British pubs. The lower level is more pubby, & the main dining area upstairs turns out well above average old-style dishes, supplemented by Maritime favourites. Among many other tipples, 6 locally brewed (Granite Brewery) British-style ales are offered – sample the Peculiar.

🍺 **Lower Deck** [94 F3] 1869 Upper Water St; 📞902 425 1501; www.lowerdeck.ca; ⏲ in season 11.30–00.30 daily, off-season 17.00–midnight Mon–Wed, 17.00–00.30 Thu, Fri & Sun, 14.00–00.30 Sat. Another well-patronised place with regular generally high-quality live music & entertainment. Good food helps make this one of the waterfront's most popular venues.

🍺 **Maxwell's Plum** [95 D6] 1600 Grafton St; 📞902 423 5090; www.themaxwellsplum.com; ⏲ 11.00–midnight daily (til 02.00 Thu–Sat). One of the largest selections of on-tap beers in the country, plus dozens of bottled varieties. A good place to try the produce of microbreweries, local & otherwise. 4 large-screen TVs, so often lively.

🍺 **Old Triangle Irish Ale House** [95 F5] 5136 Prince St; 📞902 492 4900; www.oldtriangle.com; ⏲ 11.00–midnight Sun–Tue, 11.00–01.00 Wed & Thu, 11.00–02.00 Fri & Sat. Equally good for a bite to eat, a drink, or live music. The sweet potato fries may be less authentic than, say, the steak & kidney pie, but boy are they good.

🍺 **Rockbottom Brewpub** [95 A7] 5686 Spring Garden Rd; 📞902 423 2938; rockbottombrewpub. ca; ⏲ 11.30–23.00 Mon–Thu, 11.30–01.00 Fri, 16.00–01.00 Sat, 15.30–22.00 Sun (kitchen closes 30–90mins before bar). Very good beer & generally decent pub food. Located under Your Father's Moustache (below).

🍺 **Your Father's Moustache Pub & Eatery** [95 A7] 5686 Spring Garden Rd; 📞902 423 6766; yourfathersmoustache.ca; ⏲ 10.30–midnight daily. Restaurant, live music, bar & more. Over 15 draft beers. In good weather the rooftop patio overlooking the town is a delight.

Bars

🍷 **Lion & Bright Café Bistro Wine Bar** [100 C2] 2534 Agricola St; 📞902 496 0022; www. lionandbright.com; ⏲ 07.00–01.00 Tue–Sun, 07.00–17.00 Mon. This North End establishment is a good café/bistro during the day, & a bistro/bar (particularly good cocktails) in the evening. Expect to share a long table rather than have your own private space.

🍷 **Obladee, a Wine Bar** [95 E5] 1600 Barrington St; 📞902 405 4505; obladee.ca; ⏲ 16.00–midnight daily (til 01.00 Fri & Sat). Small, relaxed 'modern rustic' wine bar. Carefully chosen charcuterie & cheeses accompany a fantastic selection of wines, more than 30 of which

are available by the glass. Eat & drink alfresco in the summer.

🍷 **Stillwell** [95 E5] 1672 Barrington St; 📞902 421 1672; www.barstillwell.com: ⏲ 16.00–02.00 daily (from noon Sat). Yes, rather tasty snacks are served, but this downtown contemporary 2-floor bar (upstairs generally sedate, downstairs often loud) is all about beer, from Nova Scotia & beyond. Bar staff know their stuff.

🍷 **Stubborn Goat** [95 D6] 1579 Grafton St; 📞902 405 4554; www.stubborngoat.ca; ⏲ 11.30–02.00 daily (from 10.30 Sat & Sun). Downtown gastropub that usually gets the food right. Decent range of beers.

🍷 **Temple Bar** [95 E6] 1533 Barrington St; 📞902 474 4380; templebarhfx.ca; ⏲: 16.00–00.00 Mon–Sat. Chef Craig Flinn (Chives, 2 doors down) is behind this 'artisan cocktails & farm to table small plates appetisers' bar located downtown alongside his other ventures. True purists might not approve, but I like it.

Gay venues

🍷 **Menz & Mollyz** [100 D2] 2182 Gottingen St; 📞902 446 6969; 🇫. Bar with live music, dancing, karaoke, etc. Proudly purveying MENZ Pale Ale, locally brewed & 'Atlantic Canada's first queer beer'. This part of town is known as Halifax's 'gay village'.

Live music

🍷 **Bearly's House of Blues & Ribs** [101 F3] 1269 Barrington St; 📞902 423 2526; www.bearlys. ca. The best of blues both from within the province & further afield.

🍷 **The Carleton** [95 E5] 1685 Argyle St; 📞902 422 6335; www.thecarleton.ca. Great venue showcasing some of the best local & national 'singer-songwriter style' music. Decent food & reasonably priced wine for a live-music venue.

🍷 **The Company House** [100 D2] 2202 Gottingen St; 📞902 404 3050; www.thecoho.ca. The 'gay-friendly but all are welcome' CoHo offers comedy nights, live music (singer-songwriter style), good beer selection, tasty snacks, etc. Between downtown & North End.

🍺 **Gus's Pub & Grill** [100 C2] 2605 Agricola St; 📞902 423 7786; 🇫. Cramped, but a great rock venue (North End). Cheap food, good burgers.

🍺 **Halifax Alehouse** [95 D5] 1717 Brunswick St; 📞902 423 6113; halifaxalehouse.com. Bustling pub near Citadel Hill with live Celtic music.

♀ **The Marquee Ballroom** [94 C1] 2037 Gottingen St; ☏ 902 423 7200; **f**. Almost legendary East Coast venue attracting quite big local, national & international bands.
♀ **The Pavilion** [100 D3] 5816 Cogswell St; **f**. Performances roughly once a week in this brick building near the pool & skate park on Halifax Common.
♀ **The Seahorse Tavern** [94 C1] 2037 Gottingen St; ☏ 902 423 7200; theseahorsetavern.ca. Located below the Marquee Ballroom (see above), this great venue hosts everything from R&B to *klezmer* (Jewish folk/jazz).
📭 **Split Crow Pub** [94 F3] 1855 Granville St; ☏ 902 422 4366; www.splitcrow.com. Good food, beer & regular live music.
📭 **Stayner's Wharf Pub & Grill** [94 G4] 5075 George St; ☏ 902 492 1800; staynerswharf.com. Bustling, waterfront venue. Another popular choice for a drink, a bite, & live music.

Nightclubs
☆ **The Dome** [94 E4] 1726 Argyle St; ☏ 902 422 6907; www.thedome.ca; ⊕ 23.00–03.30 Wed–Sun. Hi-energy nightclub with visiting & resident DJs. Sizeable dance floor but can still get very crowded with those just old enough to drink legally.
☆ **Pacifico** [95 E7] 1505 Barrington St; ☏ 902 422 3633; www.pacifico.ca; ⊕ 21.00–02.00 Fri & Sat. If you're not wearing something bright & shiny you may well feel out of place!
☆ **Reflections** [95 E6] 5187 Salter St; ☏ 902 422 2957; reflectionscabaret.com; ⊕ 22.00–04.00 Thu–Mon. Once known as an exclusively gay venue & still popular with the LGBTQ commuity, now everyone comes here to dance & party.
☆ **Taboo Nightclub** [94 D4] 1739 Grafton St; www.taboonightclub.ca; ⊕ 22.00–03.30 Fri & Sat. Lively, stylish venue.

Theatre and cinema Although we're not talking Shakespeare and Michelin-star cuisine, a fun evening with better than average food can be had by paying one price for a **meal and theatrical production**. If you want a bit of Hollywood, all of the HRM's main **cinemas** are part of the Cineplex (*www.cineplex.com*) group. In addition to the Oxford (below) art-house films might be shown at venues such as the **Rebecca Cohn Auditorium** (below).

Theatre
Neptune Theatre [95 E6] 1593 Argyle St; ☏ 902 429 7070; **tf** 1 800 565 7345; www. neptunetheatre.com. Atlantic Canada's largest professional regional theatre incorporates the main auditorium of the Strand Theatre, built on this site (on the corner of Sackville St) in 1915. Founded in 1962, the theatre group also runs a year-round Theatre School. Normally, the season runs mid Sep–May: 6 mainstream productions are staged in the 485-seat Fountain Hall, whilst the intimate Studio Theatre is home to more innovative productions. Fountain Hall ticket prices tend to be CAN$35–65.
Grafton Street Dinner Theatre [94 D4] 1741 Grafton St; ☏ 902 425 1961; graftonstdinnertheatre.com; ⊕ 18.45 Tue–Sun. A 3-act production & 3-course meal for CAN$54.

Comedy
Yuk Yuks Comedy Club [101 G3] Westin Nova Scotian, 1181 Hollis St; ☏ 902 429 9857; www. yukyuks.com/halifax; ⊕ 20.00 Thu–Sat. Popular stand-up venue with different comedians each week.

Cinemas
Cineplex Cinemas Park Lane [95 B6] Park Lane, 5657 Spring Garden Rd; ☏ 902 423 4598. 8-screen cinema.
Cineplex Cinemas Oxford [100 C4] 6408 Quinpool Rd; ☏ 902 423 7488. Although part of the Cineplex group, this lovely old Art Deco cinema with balcony has yet to be chopped up into a multi-screen. Generally, the programme sticks to art-house films, but sometimes new blockbusters slip in.

Classical music, ballet and opera Symphony Nova Scotia (*symphonynovascotia. ca*), one of Canada's finest chamber orchestras, is renowned for its versatility; it's equally at home performing anything from Baroque to jazz. The orchestra is based at the **Rebecca Cohn Auditorium** [100 D5] (*Dalhousie Arts Centre, 6101 University*

Av; ✆ *902 494 3820;* **tf** *1 800 874 1669; www.dal.ca/dept/arts-centre.html*), which also hosts ballet performances by the likes of the **Atlantic Ballet Theatre** (*www. atlanticballet.ca*), as well as big-name concerts. Opera and ballet are also performed at the Dalhousie University Arts Centre's **Sir James Dunn Theatre** [100 D5] (contacts as Rebecca Cohn Auditorium).

A great place to listen to chamber music is the **Music Room** [100 A2] (*6181 Lady Hammond Rd;* ✆ *902 429 9467; www.themusicroom.ca*), a purpose-built 110-seat venue with superb acoustics.

Casino   Over 19s with money to burn can enjoy table games, slot machines and more at the **Casino Nova Scotia** [94 F1] (*1983 Upper Water St;* ✆ *902 425 7777;* **tf** *1 888 642 6376; casinonovascotia.com;* ⊕ *10.00–04.00 daily*), one of the province's two casinos (the other is in Sydney; page 361). There are a couple of dining options, Trapeze and The Station, and three entertainment venues, the Schooner Showroom, the smaller Harbourfront and the Compass Room. If you don't gamble all your money away, Stay and Play packages (which include meal vouchers, parking and gaming lessons) can be good value.

SHOPPING   **Spring Garden Road** is a good place to start, and now features a number of upmarket shopping arcades (such as City Centre Atlantic [95 B6], Spring Garden Place [95 B7] and Park Lane [95 B6]), housing most of Canada's best-known retail chains – and some good independents. The area also has a great selection of cafés and bistros. There are also boutiques, bars and restaurants in the **Historic Properties** [94 F3] on Upper Water Street, a group of restored warehouses, and the adjoining **Granville Mall** is also worth a wander. **Barrington Place** [94 F3] is a collection of smaller, (generally independent) specialised stores and shops. Down on the waterfront, the upmarket **Piazza** at **Bishop's Landing** [95 F8] houses stylish shops and places to eat and drink.

Away from the centre, the **Hydrostone Market** [100 B1] is a European-style row of boutiques, independents, and mid- to high-range eateries: in contrast, nearby roads such as **Agricola Street** are home to many shops that tread that fine line between antique and junk.

The big shopping malls are outside the downtown area. In Halifax, near the Armdale Rotary, is the **Halifax Shopping Centre** [100 A4] (✆ *902 453 1752; www. halifaxshoppingcentre.com*). Many people head to Dartmouth's (page 128) and Bedford's (pages 133–5) malls, or up to Exit 2A of Highway 102 and the big stores of Bayers Lake's Chain Lake Drive.

Antiques

Finer Things [100 C4] 6438 Quinpool Rd; ✆902 456 1412; finerthingsantiques.com; ⊕ 10.30–17.00 Tue–Sat, noon–16.00 Sun. Antiques & curios.

Plan B Merchants Co-op [100 D2] 2180 Gottingen St; ✆902 406 1254; ▓ PlanBHalifax; ⊕11.00–19.00 daily. Less antiques, more (not-for-profit Co-op-run) disorganised eclectic junk shop.

Arts & crafts

DeSerres [95 E6] 1546 Barrington St; ✆902 425 5566; www.deserres.ca; ⊕ 09.30–19.00 Mon–Fri,

10.00–18.00 Sat, 11.00–17.00 Sun. Wide range of artists' supplies.

Fireworks Gallery [95 E6] 1569 Barrington St; ✆902 420 1735; **tf** 1 800 720 4367; www. fireworksgallery.com; ⊕ 10.00–17.30 Mon–Sat. High-quality jewellery shop selling an extensive range by local & regional artisans.

Jennifer's of Nova Scotia [95 A6] 5635 Spring Garden Rd; ✆902 425 3119; jennifers.ns.ca; ⊕ 09.30–17.30 (or later) Mon–Sat, 11.00–17.00 Sun. A range of quality crafts from all over the province, plus a small selection of the best from other parts of the Maritimes.

Art Gallery of Nova Scotia Shop [95 F5] 1723 Hollis St; ☎ 902 424 5280; www. artgalleryofnovascotia.ca; ⏰ for hours, see main gallery listing, page 117. A fine range of local art, crafts & folk art.

NovaScotian Crystal [94 F4] 5080 George St; ☎ 902 492 0416; **tf** 1 888 977 2797; www. novascotiancrystal.com; ⏰ 09.00–20.00 Mon– Fri, 10.00–17.00 Sat & Sun. North America's only mouth-blown, hand-cut crystal maker. Watch master craftspeople using techniques & tools that haven't changed in centuries.

The Plaid Place [94 E3] 1903 Barrington St; ☎ 902 429 6872; **tf** 1 800 563 1749; www. plaidplace.com; ⏰ 09.30–17.30 Mon–Fri, 10.00– 17.00 Sat. Ideal for kilts, Celtic paraphernalia, & all things Scottish (except perhaps deep-fried Mars bars).

Studio 21 [101 G3] 1273 Hollis St; ☎ 902 420 1852; www.studio21.ca; ⏰ 11.00–18.00 Tue–Fri, 10.00–17.00 Sat. Work from top contemporary artists from all over Canada.

The Vault [95 B7] 5640 Spring Garden Rd; ☎ 902 425 3624; ⏰ 09.30–17.30 Mon–Sat. Created by women for women, it displays designer jewellery collections from all over the world.

Books, magazines, maps, comics & more

Atlantic News 5560 Morris St; ☎ 902 429 5468; www.atlanticnews.ns.ca; ⏰ 08.00–21.30 daily (from 09.00 Sun). Huge selection of magazines & newspapers from around the world.

Binnacle [100 A6] 15 Purcells Cove Rd; ☎ 902 423 6464; **tf** 1 800 224 3937; ca.binnacle.com; ⏰ 09.00–18.00 Mon–Fri, 09.00–17.00 Sat, 10.00–15.00 Sun. Nautical charts.

Bookmark [95 A7] 5686 Spring Garden Rd; ☎ 902 423 0419; bookmarkreads.ca; ⏰ 09.00– 22.00 Mon–Fri, 09.00–18.00 Sat, 11.00–18.00 Sun. Very good independent bookseller.

Chapters [82 B4] Bayers Lake Power Centre, 188 Chain Lake Dr; ☎ 902 450 1023; www. chapters.indigo.ca; ⏰ 09.30–21.00 Mon–Sat, noon–21.00 Sun. Some 17km from downtown, this is Nova Scotia's biggest new book & music retailer.

Maps & More [95 F6] 1601 Lower Water St; ☎ 902 422 7106; www.maps-and-ducks.com; ⏰ 10.00–18.00 Mon–Sat . Should be your first stop for travel books & maps.

Strange Adventures Comic Bookshops [95 D5] 5110 Prince St; ☎ 902 425 2140; www. strangeadventures.com; ⏰ 10.00–18.00 Mon–Fri, 10.00–17.00 Sat, noon–16.00 Sun. An emporium for those who like pictures when they read.

Venus Envy [95 E6] 1598 Barrington St; ☎ 902 422 0004; venusenvy.ca; ⏰ 10.00–18.00 Mon–Sat, noon–17.00 Sun. Erotica shop & adult bookstore for people of (almost) all imaginable kinds of sexual persuasion. Everything from DVDs to dildos – & more. Vegan condoms are a big-seller. No doubt gluten-free ones also do well.

Woozles Children's Bookstore [95 C6] 1533 Birmingham St; ☎ 902 423 7626; www.woozles. com; ⏰: 09.30–17.30 Mon–Sat, 11.00–16.00 Sun. Kids' reads close to Halifax Central Library.

Used books

Dustjacket Books [95 E7] 1505 Barrington St; ☎ 902 492 0666; www.dustjacket.ca; ⏰ 10.00– 17.00 Mon–Fri. Easy to miss, in the Maritime Mall.

The Last Word Bookstore [100 C3] 2160 Windsor St; ☎ 902 423 2932; ⏰ 10.00–17.30 Mon–Sat, noon–17.00 Sun. Tons of used books but not a lot of organisation.

Schooner Books [101 G4] 5378 Inglis St; ☎ 902 423 8419; www.schoonerbooks.com; ⏰ call for hours. South End used-book store.

Trident Booksellers & Café Halifax [101 F3] 1256 Hollis St; ☎ 902 423 7100; ⏰ 08.00–17.30 Mon–Fri, 08.30–17.00 Sat. Another good used-book place, which also dishes up excellent coffee.

Food & wine

Bishop's Cellar [95 F8] 1477 Lower Water St; ☎ 902 490 2675; bishopscellar.com; ⏰ 10.00– 22.00 Mon–Thu, 10.00–midnight Fri, 08.00– midnight Sat, noon–20.00 Sun. Knowledgeable staff & with a huge selection. A top wine store.

Freak Lunchbox [94 E4] 1729 Barrington St; ☎ 902 420 9151; www.freaklunchbox.com; ⏰ 10.00–23.00 daily. Wacky & weird sweets/candy from around the globe.

Halifax Distilling Co [95 F5] 1668 Lower Water St; ☎ 902 431 0505; halifaxdistillingco.ca/; ⏰ 10.00–20.00 daily. New (July 2016) rum distillery. Shop & cocktail bar on site. 'Behind-the-scenes tour (approx 1hr) & tasting CAN$19.95. Run every 30mins until 19.00.

Hooked Halifax [100 C2] 5783 Charles St; ☎ 902 456 9353; www.hookedhalifax.ca;

MARKETS

Halifax is blessed with two excellent farmers' markets: the **Halifax Seaport Farmers' Market** [101 G3] (*1209 Marginal Rd;* ✆ *902 492 6256; www. halifaxfarmersmarket.com;* ⏲ *10.00–17.00 Tue–Fri, 07.00–16.00 Sat, 08.00–16.00 Sun*), which includes food, produce, local crafts and much more; and the **Historic Farmers' Market** [95 F7] (*1496 Lower Water St;* ✆ *902 492 4043; www.historicfarmersmarket.ca;* ⏲ *07.00–13.00 Sat*), which is held in the old Alexander Keith's Brewery.

If flea markets are more your thing, head for the **Halifax Forum** [100 B2] (*2901 Windsor St;* ✆ *902 490 4614*) on a Sunday morning.

⏲ check for hours. New (Oct 2016) fishmonger specialising in small-scale, sustainable seafood from Nova Scotia and all over Canada. Advice on preparation methods/recipes.

Liquid Gold [100 B1] In the Hydrostone, 5525 Young St; ✆ 902 406 8809; www.allthingsolive. ca; ⏲ 10.00–18.00 Mon–Sat (to 17.00 Sat), noon–17.00 Sun. Countless varieties & flavours of premium olive oil & balsamic vinegars, plus olive oil-based cosmetics.

Organic Earth Market [100 B4] 6487 Quinpool Rd; ✆ 902 425 7400; www.organicearthmarket. com; ⏲ 09.00–21.00 Mon–Fri, 09.00–19.00 Sat, 10.00–18.00 Sun. Friendly staff who understand organic/health foods & supplements.

Pete's Fine Foods [95 B6] 1515 Dresden Row; ✆ 902 425 5700; petes.ca; ⏲ 08.00–20.00 Mon–Fri, 08.00–18.00 Sat & Sun. Pete started his business life running a market stall in Nottingham, England. Although primarily a huge, upmarket deli, grocery & greengrocers store (think Waitrose meets the Harrods food hall), there are healthy sandwiches, salads & more to go.

Rum Runners Rum Cake Factory [95 F7] 1479 Lower Water St; ✆ 902 421 6079; tf 1 866 440 7867; www.theuncommongroup.com; ⏲ Jul–Sep 10.00–22.00 daily; Oct–Jun check hours. Delicious rum & whisky cakes that make great gifts.

Sweet Jane's [95 C6] 1300 Queen St; ✆ 902 425 0168; www.sweetjanes.com; ⏲ 09.30–21.00 Mon–

Sat, 10.00–18.00 Sun. More sugarific treats for the sweet-toothed, plus fun stuff for around the house.

Music

Halifax Folklore Centre [95 D6] 1528 Brunswick St; ✆ 902 423 7946; www.halifaxfolklorecentre. com; ⏲ 11.00–17.30 Mon–Wed, 11.00–19.00 Fri, 11.00–17.00 Sat. A good spot for Celtic music & instruments.

Long and Mcquade [100 C3] 6065 Cunard St; ✆ 902 496 6900; www.long-mcquade.com; ⏲ 10.00–18.00 Mon–Thu, 10.00–20.00 Fri, 10.00–17.00 Sat. If hearing all the wonderful Celtic music has inspired you to go & buy yourself an instrument, this is a good place to start.

Taz Records [95 D6] 1521 Grafton St; ✆ 902 422 5976; www.tazrecords.com; ⏲ 10.30–19.00 Mon–Fri, 10.30–18.00 Sat, noon–17.00 Sun. Ideal if you want to try to track down secondhand music (vinyl & CDs).

Outdoor & camping gear

Mountain Equipment Co-op [95 E6] 1550 Granville St; ✆ 902 421 2667; www.mec.ca; ⏲ 09.30–19.00 (or later) Mon–Fri, 09.30–18.00 Sat, 11.00–17.00 Sun. Outdoor gear emporium. Non-members pay a one-off CAN$5 fee when making their first purchase.

Trail Shop [100 C4] 6210 Quinpool Rd; ✆ 902 423 8736; trailshop.com; ⏲ 10.00–18.00 Mon–Sat (til 21.00 Thu & Fri), noon–17.00 Sun.

SPORT For **spectator sports**, head to the Scotiabank Centre to see the Halifax Mooseheads play ice hockey (September–March) and the Halifax Rainmen play basketball (January–March).

Tickets can be purchased from the **Ticket Atlantic Box Office** (✆ *902 451 1221; www.ticketatlantic.com*) at the Scotiabank Centre (*1800 Argyle St*). Prices to see the Mooseheads start from CAN$15, and the Rainmen from CAN$20.

Canoeing and kayaking St Mary's Boat Club [100 C5] (*1641 Fairfield Rd;* ☎ *902 490 4688; www.halifax.ca/smbc*) is located on the Northwest Arm. Canoe rental is free (maximum 1 hour). See also **Kayak Halifax** (page 122).

Diving The water isn't warm, but there are numerous shipwrecks (eg: SS *Havana*, 1906) to keep divers happy, and some good diving companies, both here and in Dartmouth (pages 128–9).

Divers World [82 B4] 11–12 Lakeside Park Dr, Lakeside; ☎ 902 876 0555; www.diversworld.ns.ca. 10mins' drive from Armdale Rotary.
Nautilus Aquatics [100 C4] 6442 Quinpool Rd; ☎ 902 707 9111; www.nautilusaquaticsandhobbies.com

Torpedo Rays Scuba Halifax [100 A5] 7211 Quinpool Rd; ☎ 902 407 0444; www.torpedorays.com

Go karting Head out of the city centre to **Kartbahn Indoor Karting** [82 B4] (*66 Otter Lake Court, Bayers Lake;* ☎ *902 455 5278; www.kartbahn.ca*).

Gaming Videogame lovers should head to the new (October 2016) **Halifax VR Room** [100 B3] (*2363 Oxford St;* ☎ *902 802 7797; www.halifaxvr.com*), a room full of hi-tec virtual reality equipment for gamers to use. 'Until you actually get here and play it, it's really almost indescribable.'

Golf Golfers will find more than a dozen nine- and 18-hole courses within easy reach of Halifax and Dartmouth. Here are five of the best full-length courses open to the public. **Granite Springs Golf Club** (page 139) is another good option.

Eaglequest Grandview Golf & Country Club [82 D4] 431 Crane Hill Rd, Westphal; ☎ 902 435 3767; eaglequestgolf.com. A challenging (particularly the forested back 9) 6,700yd course just outside Dartmouth off Hwy 7. *Green fees CAN$59 Mon–Fri, CAN$69 Sat & Sun.*
Glen Arbour [82 A3] 40 Clubhouse Lane, Hammonds Plains; ☎ 902 835 4653; glenarbour. com. A lovely, well-designed 6,800yd championship course with natural ponds, streams & mature trees. Not cheap in summer, but a great challenge for the serious golfer. Off Hammonds Plains Rd, 1km west of Bedford. *Green fees approx CAN$120.*
Hartlen Point Forces Golf Club [82 D5] Shore Rd; ☎ 902 465 4653; hartlenpoint.blogspot.ca.

This 18-hole 5,862yd, par-71 course has beautiful views overlooking the eastern entrance to Halifax Harbour (& almost constant winds). *Green fees CAN$58.*
The Links at Brunello [82 B4] 120 Brunello Blvd, Timberlea; ☎ 902 876 7649; www. thelinksatbrunello.com. Lovely new (2015) 7,089yd, par-72 course designed by Thomas McBroom. *Green fees approx CAN$115.*
Lost Creek Golf Club [82 B2] 310 Kinsac Rd, Beaver Bank; ☎ 902 865 4653; www.lostcreek.ca. A beautiful, forested lakeside 5,876yd course. Reach it by taking Beaverbank Rd for 9km from Exit 2 of Hwy 101. *Green fees CAN$55.*

Gyms and fitness centres Many of the bigger hotels have some sort of fitness facilities for their guests, ranging from a small room with a few machines to large areas with state-of-the-art equipment. If your accommodation doesn't have suitable facilities, try the following:

Canada Games Centre [82 B4] 26 Thomas Raddall Dr; ☎ 902 490 2400; canadagamescentre.ca; Huge, fab facility outside city centre. Day pass CAN$11.50.

Fitness FX [100 C4] 6330 Quinpool Rd; ☎ 902 422 1431; www.fitnessfx.ca. Day pass CAN$10.

SMUfit [101 F5] Saint Mary's University, The Homburg Centre, 920 Tower Rd; ☎ 902 420 5555; www.smuhuskies.ca. Excellent facilities plus squash courts. Day pass CAN$12.65 (photo ID required).

Horseriding

You'll have to head out of the city centre to saddle up. **Hatfield Farm Adventures** [82 A3] (*840 Hammonds Plains Rd;* ☎ *902 835 5676; www.hatfieldfarm. com*) offer trail rides for all levels, plus some 'dude ranch' type packages.

Spas and tattoos

Spas offer a wide range of services. Expect to pay around CAN$100 for a 60-minute facial. If you're looking for needles and ink rather than pampering, try **Adept Tattoos** (*6265 Quinpool Rd;* ☎ *902 405 4009; www. adepttattoos.com*).

Chrysalis Spa & Skincare Centre [100 B1] In the Hydrostone, 5521 Young St; ☎ 902 446 3929; chrysalisspa.com
Interlude Spa Halifax Marriott Harbourfront Hotel, 1919 Upper Water St; ☎ 902 469 2700; interlude.com

Spirit Spa [95 F6] 5150 Salter St 8200; ☎ 902 431 8100; www.spiritspa.ca
Summit Day Spa [95 C7] 5495 Spring Garden Rd; ☎ 902 423 3888; summitspa.ca

Swimming

Some hotels have pools, and hardy souls may like to brave the sea at one of the region's beaches, eg: Crystal Crescent Beach (page 124). Freshwater swimming is popular – try **Chocolate Lake** [100 A6] (page 123). The Canada Games Centre (page 112) is quite far from downtown but offers various pools and waterslides; much more central is the indoor **Centennial Pool** [94 C1] (*1970 Gottingen St;* ☎ *902 490 7219; www.centennialpool.ca*).

Winter sports and skating

When the snow is on the ground, some of the HRM's walking trails are popular with **cross-country skiers**. The nearest downhill skiing is at Ski Martock (pages 252–3).

You can **ice-skate** indoors year-round in Dartmouth (page 128) and in season (mid October–March) there are several possibilities in Halifax, including the **Halifax Forum** [100 B2] (*2901 Windsor St;* ☎ *902 490 4500; www.halifaxforum.ca*).

Best for outdoor skating is the **Emera Oval** [100 D3] (☎ *902 490 2347; www. halifax.ca/skatehrm*), the largest outdoor, artificially refrigerated ice surface in Atlantic Canada. In the summer this venue offers in-line skating, and gear for both seasons is available to rent on-site.

Several lakes in Halifax are great for skating, including **Chocolate Lake** [100 A6], but you'll rarely find facilities, and skate rental is even harder to come by – it might be worth investing in a secondhand pair.

OTHER PRACTICALITIES

Banks You won't have a problem finding a bank or ABM (ATM) in Halifax or Dartmouth. Many hotels offer currency-exchange services – though the rate may be less competitive – as does the **Casino Nova Scotia** [94 F1] (page 109). The following three are the most central:

$ HSBC [94 F4] 1801 Hollis St; **tf** 1 888 310 4722; www.hsbc.ca; ⊕ 09.00–17.00 Mon–Fri
$ Royal Bank [101 E4] 5855 Spring Garden Rd; ☎ 902 421 8177; ⊕ 09.30–17.00 Mon, Tue & Fri, 09.30–20.00 Wed–Thu, 10.00–15.00 Sat

$ TD Canada Trust [94 E4] 1785 Barrington St; ☎ 902 420 8040; ⊕ 08.00–18.00 Mon–Wed, 08.00–20.00 Thu & Fri, 08.00–16.00 Sat

Health The only medical emergency department in the HRM is located at the **Queen Elizabeth II Health Sciences Centre** [100 D3] (*1799 Robie St; for medical emergencies dial* ☎ *911*). The most central walk-in clinic is the **Family Focus Medical Clinic** [95 A8] (*5991 Spring Garden Rd;* ☎ *902 420 6060;* ⊕ *08.30–21.00 Mon–Fri, 11.00–17.00 Sat & Sun*). **Shoppers Drug Mart** [95 B7] (*5524 Spring Garden Rd;* ☎ *902 429 2400*) has a 24-hour pharmacy.

Internet Public internet access is free at libraries (see below) and more and more places are offering free Wi-Fi access. Internet cafés are something of a dying breed, but **Spring Garden** [95 A7] (*5681 Spring Garden Rd;* ☎ *902 423 0785;* ⊕ *07.00–23.00 Mon–Fri, 08.00–23.00 Sat & Sun*) offers internet for CAN$3.45/30 minutes (packages available).

Laundromats Coin-operated laundries in Halifax include: **Bluenose** [100 C3] (*2198 Windsor St;* ☎ *902 422 7098*); **Murphy's** [100 C2] (*6023 North St;* ☎ *902 454 6294*); and **Olympic** [100 B4] (*6518 Chebucto Rd;* ☎ *902 422 5571*).

Libraries Halifax Public Libraries (*www.halifaxpubliclibraries.ca*) has ten branches close to the downtown area; the largest, most spectacular and most central is the new **Halifax Central Library** [95 C7] (page 118). All libraries offer internet-accessible computers.

Post offices The main post office is at 1680 Bedford Row [95 F5] (**tf** *1 800 267 1177;* ⊕ *08.00–17.00 Mon–Fri*). However, many standard post office services are now offered at a variety of other stores, such as some branches of Shoppers Drug Mart and Lawton Drugs, and these tend to be open on Saturdays and later in the evening.

WHAT TO SEE AND DO Halifax has something of a reputation for being foggy – in an average year, over 100 days will experience fog at some time or other, and mid spring to early summer tends to be particularly bad. Keep your fingers crossed though, because when the sun shines the outdoor attractions, gardens, parks and waterfront are delightful, as is McNabs Island [82 D5].

The unmissables

Halifax Citadel National Historic Site of Canada [94 B3] (*5425 Sackville St;* ☎ *902 426 5080; www.parkscanada.gc.ca/halifaxcitadel;* ⊕ *early May–Oct 09.00–17.00 daily, Jul/Aug til 18.00; grounds open year-round but limited services available Nov–early May; admission free 2017: 2016 rates Jun–mid Sep CAN$11.70, May & Oct CAN$7.80, Nov–Apr free, inc 45–60 min guided tour early May–Oct: fees apply for special programmes*) This is Halifax's main attraction and one of the most visited National Historic Sites in Canada. Officially known as Fort George and built to reduce the threat of a land attack by American forces, the Citadel was one of the largest British fortresses on the American continent, the hilltop setting providing a commanding view of the city and harbour. The first fortifications were constructed on what was then called Signal Hill in 1749. A three-storey octagonal blockhouse was added in 1776, and during the Duke of Kent's time in Halifax (1794–1800) he implemented major changes. In the 1820s, previous fortifications were levelled, and the height of the hill reduced – the earth moved was used to construct ramparts. The huge, star-shaped, Vauban-style Citadel that is seen today was constructed between 1828 and 1856, and it continued its watch over Halifax until the end of

World War II. For today's visitor, from below you get the impression of just a huge grassy mound. But once you've climbed the hill, crossed the plank bridge over the moat and gone through the arched entrance to the inner courtyard, you'll appreciate the full scale of the site. There are good audio-visual presentations, moats, barrack rooms, garrison cells, tunnels and ramparts to explore, and plenty of cannons – one of which is fired daily at noon. Throughout the summer, students dressed in the uniform of the 78th Highland Regiment (MacKenzie tartan kilts and bright-red doublets) enact the drills of 1869, marching to a bagpipe band.

Upstairs in the Cavalier Building is the **Army Museum** (✆ *902 422 5979; www. armymuseumhalifax.ca/; ⊕opening hours as above, admission inc in Citadel fee*), which presents hundreds of artefacts reflecting Atlantic Canada's military heritage and displays on military events in which Canadian forces played a significant role. There's also a café downstairs.

To reach Citadel Hill on foot from the waterfront, follow George Street (which later becomes Carmichael Street) uphill.

Halifax Public Gardens [95 A6] (*Main entrance on the corner of South Park St & Spring Garden Rd;* ✆ *902 490 4000; www.halifaxpublicgardens.ca; ⊕ early May–early Nov 07.00–dusk daily; admission free*) The Nova Scotia Horticultural Society was formed in 1836, and in the early 1840s began to lay out flower beds and vegetable plots. A civic garden opened in 1867 and has evolved into what many consider to be the finest original formal Victorian public garden in North America. In addition to magnificent floral displays (in late May and June, the tulips are stunning), there are beautiful fountains, ponds with ducks and geese, winding pathways, shady benches and an ornate, bronze-roofed bandstand that dates from Queen Victoria's Golden Jubilee and is the site of free Sunday afternoon concerts in July and August. The 7ha park, across Sackville Street from the Citadel grounds, is enclosed by a wrought-iron fence with a magnificent set of ornamental gates at the main entrance. If you need sustenance, there's a nice coffee shop near the bandstand.

Maritime Museum of the Atlantic [95 F5] (*1675 Lower Water St;* ✆ *902 424 7490; maritimemuseum.novascotia.ca; ⊕ Nov–Apr 09.30–20.00 Tue, 09.30–17.00 Wed–Sat, 13.00–17.00 Sun; May & Oct 09.30–17.30 Mon–Sat (til 20.00 Tue), 13.00–17.30 Sun; Jun–Sep 09.30–17.30 daily (til 20.00 Tue); admission May–Oct/ Nov–Apr CAN$9.55/5.15*) Almost everything about Nova Scotia is linked to the sea, and if you visit only one museum in the province, make it Canada's oldest and largest maritime museum.Housed in a well-designed purpose-built c1982 structure which incorporates an early 20th-century chandlery at the heart of the city's waterfront, the museum commemorates Nova Scotia's seafaring heritage, traditions and history. Many visitors come for an excellent collection of *Titanic*-abilia, and are not disappointed with the **Titanic: The Unsinkable Ship and Halifax** gallery . But even more powerful is **Halifax Wrecked**, a gallery that recounts the devastating effects of the 1917 Halifax Explosion (box, page 93). See, too, displays on three centuries of shipwrecks, the Golden Age of Sail and the Steam Age, some fabulous scale models of all manner of sea-going vessels, and much more, too.

In season (⊕ *early Jun–late Oct 10.30–16.30 Thu–Tue, call* ✆ *902 424 7491 to confirm*), the admission charge will also allow you to board the *CSS Acadia*, usually moored on the waterfront by the museum. Built in Newcastle-upon-Tyne, England, in 1913, she was Canada's longest-serving survey vessel, and the only surviving ship to have served the Royal Canadian Navy during both World Wars.

Canadian Museum of Immigration at Pier 21 [101 G4] (*1055 Marginal Rd;* ☏ *902 425 7770; www.pier21.ca;* ⊕ *May–Nov 09.30–17.30 daily (Nov til 17.00); Dec–Mar 10.00–17.00 Wed–Sun; Apr 10.00–17.00 Tue–Sun; admission CAN$11.00*)

Located at the Halifax Seaport, the Canadian Museum of Immigration at Pier 21 is Canada's newest national museum. From 1928–71, one million immigrants and refugees arrived at this gateway to Canada, and during World War II military personnel left for service overseas from Pier 21. Re-opened in 2015 after extensive renovations, the museum is home to interactive exhibits based on first-hand accounts that tell the story of more than 400 years of immigration history from first contact to present day. Displays examine the experiences of journey and arrival and the questions of belonging and impact, and you can explore family roots through immigration records and ship photos. There's also a café and gift shop.

Other museums

Africville Museum [82 C4] (*5795 Africville Rd;* ☏ *902 455 6558; www.africvillemuseum.org;* ⊕ *Jun–Aug 10.00–16.00 Tue–Sun; Sep–May 10.00–16.00 Tue–Fri; admission CAN$4.50*) Housed in a replica of a church destroyed in the 1960s, the museum tells the tragic story of Africville. See box, page 97, for more information.

Discovery Centre [101 F2] (*1217 Lower Water St;* ☏ *902 492 4422; thediscoverycentre.ca;* ⊕*probably year-round 10.00–17.00 Mon–Sat, 13.00–17.00 Sun; admission (was) CAN$10*) This fun, hands-on interactive science centre is a good stop for those with kids. Re-opening in this new, bigger, waterfront location in 2017 – see www.bradtupdates.com/novascotia for updates.

Maritime Command Museum [100 C1] (*Admiralty Hse, 2725 Gottingen St;* ☏*902 721 8250; psphalifax.ca/marcommuseum/;* ⊕ *early Jan–mid Dec 09.00–15.30 Mon–Fri; admission free, photo ID required*) Housed in a stately c1840s Georgian mansion on the grounds of Canadian Forces Base Halifax, this museum focuses on the history and development of the Canadian navy since its inception in 1910: there are also displays on almost two centuries of Royal Navy presence in – and influence on – Halifax.

Museum of Natural History [100 D3] (*1747 Summer St;* ☏ *902 424 7353; naturalhistory.novascotia.ca;* ⊕ *mid-May–Oct 09.00–17.00 daily (til 20.00 Wed); Nov–mid-May 09.00–17.00 Tue–Sun (til 20.00 Wed); admission CAN$6.30*) Enter and you'll find not just the expected – galleries of botanical exhibits, stuffed animals and birds, whale skeletons – but plenty more, too. The Archaeology Gallery tells of 11,000 years of human life, the galleries feature 200- and 300-million-year-old fossils and centuries-old Mi'kmaq craftwork. Live exhibits can be seen in the Marine Gallery's tide tank and the Nature Lab. There's also Science on a Sphere, a high-tech 360° digital experience. A good introduction to the natural wonders of the province.

Other historical sites

Government House [95 E7] (*1451 Barrington St;* ☏ *902 424 7001; www.lt.gov. ns.ca;* ⊕ *by free 30min guided tour Jul–Aug 10.00–16.00 Fri–Mon*). The official office and residence of the Lieutenant-Governor of Nova Scotia was built between 1800 and 1805 for Governor Sir John Wentworth.

Historic Properties [94 F3] (*1869 Upper Water St;* ☎ *902 429 0530; historicproperties.ca*) On the waterfront between the casino and the ferry terminal is a group of Canada's oldest surviving warehouses dating from the early 19th century. Nearly lost to 'urban renewal' in the early 1960s, the solid wood and stone structures – including the c1813 Privateers' Warehouse, built to store the privateers' booty (box, page 19) – were painstakingly restored, pedestrianised, and now house pubs, bars, restaurants and boutiques.

HMCS Sackville: Canada's Naval Memorial [95 G5] (*Sackville Landing;* ☎ *902 429 2132; www.hmcssackville-cnmt.ns.ca;* ⊕ *mid Jun–mid Oct 10.00–17.00 daily; admission CAN$5*) Explore the world's last surviving Flower-class corvette which saw much World War II action escorting convoys across the Atlantic, now restored to 1944 configuration as a memorial to all those who served in the Royal Canadian Navy. Between November and May, the vessel is usually moored in the naval dockyard: ☎ 902 427 2837 for location and opening hours.

Old Town Clock [94 C4] (*Citadel Hill just off Brunswick St*) Sometimes simply called the Town Clock, this three-tiered tower atop a rectangular building, which was originally used as a guard room and residence for the caretaker, is one of Halifax's most famous landmarks. Prince Edward, Duke of Kent, bothered by poor punctuality at the Halifax garrison, commissioned a clock before his return to England in 1800. The original mechanism, crafted in London, England, and wound twice a week, has been going strong since 1803. Unfortunately, when it originally arrived from England, there were no accompanying instructions, and it lay for some time unused and untouched near the (completed) clock building. Finally, a newly arrived soldier who had worked as a clock-maker did the trick.

Galleries and arts centres

Anna Leonowens Gallery [94 F3] (*NSCAD University, 1891 Granville St;* ☎ *902 494 8223; alg.nscad.ca;* ⊕ *early Jan–late Aug & mid Sep–mid Dec 11.00–17.00 Tue–Fri, noon–16.00 Sat; admission free*) In an elegant Italianate building, the gallery displays contemporary art, craft and design: weekly exhibitions focus on the renowned Nova Scotia College of Art and Design (NSCAD) students' work. Occasional shows by visiting artists and curators. See box, page 119, for further information on Anna.

Argyle Fine Art [94 F3] (*1559 Barrington St;* ☎ *902 425 9456; argylefineart.com;* ⊕ *10.00–17.30 Tue–Sat; admission free*) One of Halifax's most progressive galleries, with an exciting range of contemporary art.

Art Gallery of Nova Scotia [95 F5] (*1723 Hollis St;* ☎ *902 424 7542; www. artgalleryofnovascotia.ca;* ⊕ *May–Oct 10.00–17.00 Mon–Sat (til 21.00 Thu), noon–17.00 Sun; Nov–Apr 10.00–17.00 Tue–Sun (til 21.00 Thu); tours are offered at 14.30 & 19.00 Thu; admission CAN$12, free 17.00–21.00 Thu*) Atlantic Canada's largest – and (arguably) – finest art collection is divided between two mid 1860s buildings separated by a cobbled courtyard. The majority has been displayed in the Dominion Building (Gallery North) since 1988: ten years later the collection expanded onto two floors of the Provincial Building. The Permanent Collection includes contemporary and historic provincial, Canadian and international art: there's a wonderful folk-art section which includes the original home of Maud Lewis (box, page 29). To round it off, the gallery has a good shop, and Pavia, a nice café (box, page 103).

Dalhousie Art Gallery [100 D5] (*Dalhousie Arts Centre, 6101 University Av;* ✆ *902 494 2403; artgallery.dal.ca;* ⊕ *year-round 11.00–17.00 Tue–Fri, noon–17.00 Sat&Sun; admission free*) Established in 1953, the oldest public art gallery in Halifax presents changing exhibitions of contemporary and historic art and a programme of lectures, films and artists' presentations. Free guided tours offered.

Halifax Central Library [95 C7] (*5440 Spring Garden Rd;* ✆ *902 490 5706; halifaxcentrallibrary.ca;* ⊕ *09.00–21.00 Mon–Thu, 09.00–18.00 Fri & Sat, noon–18.00 Sun*) This stunning, modern glass building (designed by a Danish architectural firm) opened in December 2014. Books, yes, computers, yes, but also meeting rooms, two cafés (box, page 103) and a roof terrace.

Khyber Institute for Contemporary Arts [95 E6] (*1880 Hollis St;* ✆ *902 422 9668; www.khyber.ca;* ⊕ *by chance or appointment, check website for exhibition hours; admission (usually) free*) Housed in a splendid edifice (leased from NSCAD University), this artist-run centre presents exhibitions, concerts and film.

NSCAD University (Nova Scotia Centre for Craft and Design) [101 G3] (*1061 Marginal Rd;* ✆ *902 492 2522; www.craft-design.ns.ca;* ⊕ *09.00–17.00 Tue–Fri (til 20.00 Thu), 11.00–16.00 Sat; admission free*) Exhibitions of local, national and international fine crafts at the centre's Mary E Black Gallery. Also be sure to visit the centre's Designer Craft Shop (✆ *902 492 2525*) to see (and perhaps buy) students' work. Outside the summer months, the centre offers courses in pottery, jewellery, glass, metal- and woodworking, and textiles.

Brewery tours Nowadays, only **Alexander Keith's** [95 F7] (below) offers tours for individuals, couples or small groups. If there are ten or more of you, **Garrison Brewing** [101 G3] (*1149 Marginal Rd;* ✆ *902 453 5343; www.garrisonbrewing. com*) will run special tours of its brewery for approximately CAN$14 per person. Wacky **Good Robot Brewing Co** [100 B2] (*2736 Robie St; goodrobotbrewing.ca*) will run 60-minute tours for groups of four or more by reservation, costing CAN$20 per person including four samples. Craft beer fans might want to know that a weekend lunchtime Beer Bus is one of the trips offered by **Taste Halifax** (page 99).

Alexander Keith's Nova Scotia Brewery [95 F7] (*1496 Lower Water St;* ✆ *902 455 1474;* tf *1 877 612 1820; keiths.ca;* ⊕ *tours Jun–Oct noon–19.30 Mon–Sat, noon–17.00 Sun; Nov–May 16.00–19.30 Fri, noon–19.30 Sat, noon–17.00 Sun; admission CAN$28*) Theatrical but entertaining 55-minute tours are offered of one of the oldest working breweries in North America, which opened in 1820 in this huge ironstone and granite building. Although most brewing operations were moved elsewhere years ago, the brewery still produces seasonal brews using traditional techniques. Costumed performers, dressed à la 1860s, tell of the brewery's history, often breaking into song (and dance). Fun, slightly camp, and a bit overpriced in my opinion, even with a couple of beers thrown in.

Other sights
Burke-Gaffney Observatory [101 F5] (*Loyola Bldg, Saint Mary's University, Robie St;* ✆ *902 496 8257; www.ap.smu.ca/bgo; free public tours on alternate Fri evenings, in summer every Fri*) Stargazers should hope for cloudless skies when visiting. The largest of the observatory's telescopes is 41cm in diameter.

Halifax City Hall [94 E4] (*1841 Argyle St;* \ *902 490 4000; www.halifax.ca/ facilities/cityhall.php*) This c1888 Second Empire-style building at the opposite end of the Grand Parade from St Paul's Church is the seat of government for the Halifax Regional Municipality. In 1998, one of the clocks on the tower was set permanently to 09.04, the exact time of the Halifax Explosion (box, page 93). Major renovations are ongoing: once these are completed, free guided tours may be offered.

Point Pleasant Park [101 H6] (*Point Pleasant Dr; www.halifax.ca/ PointPleasantPark/index.php;* ⊕ *05.00–midnight daily*) This 75ha park at South End Halifax suffered devastation when Hurricane Juan struck in 2003 (page 92). More than 75% of the 100,000 trees were destroyed: the clean-up closed the park for nine months. Time, Mother Nature (and the park authorities) have done much to repair the damage.

The park is criss-crossed by 39km of walking and biking trails (bikes permitted Monday–Friday only, but not on statutory holidays), and a waterfront trail that is very popular with joggers leads along the Halifax Harbour side to the point, then back along the Northwest Arm shoreline (approx 2km each way). In the park are ruins of several forts and fortifications, including the c1796–97 **Prince of Wales Martello Tower National Historic Site of Canada** (\ *902 426 5080; www.pc.gc.ca/lhn-nhs/ns/prince/ index.aspx; admission free*), built by order of Prince Edward, Duke of Kent, to help protect British gun batteries in Halifax. It was the first of its type in North America.

Occupying such a strategically important position, the park is officially on British territory. In 1866, the (then) city of Halifax agreed to rent the site from the British government for one shilling (five pence, about ten cents Canadian) a year, on a 999-year lease.

Park signage is plentiful but there is a paucity of maps: the only one that I've found is at the Tower Road entrance at Point Pleasant Drive. Smoking is not permitted in the park. To get to the park, take South Park Street south from Sackville Street: South Park becomes Young Avenue, and this leads to Point Pleasant Drive. Tower Road and Marginal Road also lead here. Those using public transport should take bus #9 from Barrington Street.

Province House [94 E4] (*1726 Hollis St;* \ *902 424 4661, 902 424 5982 (tours); nslegislature.ca;* ⊕ *Jul–Aug 09.00–17.00 Mon–Fri, 10.00–16.00 Sat & Sun; Sep–Jun 09.00–16.00 Mon–Fri; admission free*) Opened in 1819 and constructed of Wallace sandstone (page 291), this fine Palladian-style building is the seat of the Nova Scotia government, which was Canada's oldest provincial legislative assembly. Visiting Halifax in 1842, Charles Dickens called it 'a gem of Georgian architecture'. Free guided tours by reservation.

ANNA LEONOWENS

The building at 1740 Argyle Street once housed The Victoria College of Art and Design, founded and run by Anna Leonowens (1831–1915). Her time as governess and tutor to the King of Siam's 67 children was later filmed, first as *Anna and the King of Siam* (1946), then as a musical, *The King and I* (1951), and then again as *Anna and The King* (1999). Leonowens lived in Halifax for 19 years and was an active supporter of education and the arts. Her name and memory live on in an art gallery connected to the school she began (page 117).

Nova Scotia Archives [101 E5] (*6016 University Av;* ✆ *902 424 6060; archives. novascotia.ca;* ⊕ *year-round 08.30–16.30 Mon–Fri (til 21.00 Wed), 09.00–17.00 Sat; admission free*) A splendid resource for genealogists.

Churches and cathedrals

St Paul's Anglican Church [95 E5] (*1749 Argyle St;* ✆ *902 429 2240; www. stpaulshalifax.org;* ⊕ *09.00–16.00 Mon–Sat; tours offered Jun–Aug*) Built in 1750, white, wooden St Paul's is the oldest standing Anglican church in Canada and the oldest surviving building in Halifax. The church – at the edge of the Grand Parade – was modelled on St Peter's, a c1722 church in London, England's Vere Street. the timbers were cut in Boston, Massachusetts, and shipped to Halifax. A number of important colonial figures are buried in the crypt, including Bishop Charles Inglis (1734–1816) who was a driving force towards the construction of many of the province's churches. As a consequence of the Halifax Explosion (box, page 93) a piece of window frame was embedded (and can still be seen) in the interior wall of the narthex (entry lobby area). The blast also damaged one of the windows, creating what looks a bit like the silhouette of a figure: it is said to resemble an early curate, Jean-Baptiste Moreau. The Explosion Window is on the upper level, and is the third from the back of the building.

Cathedral Church of All Saints [101 E4] (*1330 Martello St;* ✆ *902 423 6002; www.cathedralchurchofallsaints.com;* ⊕ *for services, plus year-round 09.00–16.00 Mon–Fri; guided tours early Jul–late Aug Tue–Sat*) Constructed from local stone, the church opened in 1910. There are beautiful stained glass windows, and fine woodcarvings.

Little Dutch (Deutsch) Church [100 D2] (*Brunswick St at Gerrish St;* ✆ *902 423 1059; www.roundchurch.ca;* ⊕ *for services, mid Jun–late Sep, check website for times; tours offered in the summer in conjunction with tours of St George's Round Church; see below*) In 1756, some German Lutheran settlers moved a house to this location and adapted it to be Halifax's second church, after St Paul's. It was consecrated as an Anglican Church in 1761, but held on to its Lutheran roots and was, in practice in many ways, Lutheran until around 1811. Other locals confused 'Deutsch' ('German') with 'Dutch', and the church became known as the Little Dutch Church. Towards the end of the 19th century, the church attracted a growing non-Lutheran congregation – in numbers larger than it could cope with.

St George's Round Church [100 D2] (*2222 Brunswick St;* ✆ *902 423 1059; www.roundchurch.ca;* ⊕ *to visit during services, tours offered in summer*) Built in 1799–1800 to accommodate the growing congregation of the Little Dutch Church (above), this is an excellent example of a circular wooden Palladian church. Founded on a unique combination of German Lutheranism and Anglicanism,

---

I'LL DRINK TO THAT

Born in Caithness, Scotland, Alexander Keith (1795–1873) emigrated to Canada and, having learned the art of brewing before leaving Britain, opened his eponymous brewing company in Halifax in 1820. A Freemason Grand Master, he served three times as mayor of the city. His birthday, 5 October, is not an official holiday, but there are celebrations in his honour on or around that day each year.

St George's became its own Anglican parish in 1827. In 1994, more than a third of the building – including the dome – was destroyed by fire. The church was restored using traditional 19th-century building techniques.

St Mary's Cathedral Basilica [95 E7] (*5521 Spring Garden Rd;* ✆ *902 429 9800; www.halifaxyarmouth.org/cathedral;* ☉ *guided tours by reservation*) The Roman Catholic Church was not permitted to build a house of worship in Nova Scotia until 1784, when a small church was built on this site. Construction on what was to become the second Catholic cathedral in Canada began in 1820 and shipwrights were hired to build the roof. The first mass was celebrated in 1829 and St Peter's Church was renamed St Mary's Cathedral in 1833. Major renovations began in 1860, giving the building a far more Gothic appearance. The cathedral had beautiful stained-glass windows, most of which were destroyed in the Halifax Explosion (box, page 93): these were replaced with equally impressive ones made in Munich, Germany. The title 'Basilica' was bestowed by Pope Pius XII who visited in 1950.

Cemeteries and burial grounds
Fairview Cemetery [100 A3] (*3720 Windsor St;* ✆ *902 490 4883;* ☉ *dawn–dusk daily*) Those fascinated by the story (and film) of the *Titanic* (box, page 92) will want to visit this cemetery, the final resting place of 121 *Titanic* victims. Some graves just have numbers, but where identification was possible, a name accompanies the number.

Ah, the power of Hollywood: the most visited grave is that of J Dawson, 8227. Leonardo DiCaprio played Jack Dawson in the 1997 film. Incidentally, the film's writer and director, James Cameron, said he had thought up the character's name and was not aware that there had been a J Dawson on board.

The cemetery also contains the graves of many victims of the Halifax Explosion (box, page 93). Too far to walk from downtown for most people, to get here take Windsor Street north from Quinpool Road. The cemetery is near the junction with Connaught Avenue. Bus 82 from Water Street will drop you near the entrance.

Old Burying Ground [95 E7] (*Barrington St & Spring Garden Rd;* ✆ *902 429 2240;* ☉ *Jun–Sep 09.00–17.00 daily*) The first burial ground in Halifax was in use from 1749 to 1844. Interpretive signs indicate gravestones of historic significance. Despite the busy surrounds, this graveyard is a tranquil place to wander and reflect.

Camp Hill Cemetery [100 D4] (*Robie & Sackville sts*) In 1844, this cemetery, located to the west of the Public Gardens (page 115), replaced the Old Burying Ground: among provincial big names interred here are statesman Joseph Howe, privateer Enos Collins, Abraham Gesner (inventor of kerosene) and brewer Alexander Keith (box, page 120).

AROUND HALIFAX

MCNABS AND LAWLOR ISLANDS PROVINCIAL PARK Two islands lie at the mouth of Halifax Harbour. The smaller, Lawlor Island, is just off Fishermans Cove (pages 132–3): an important bird nesting site, it is not currently open to the public.

McNabs Island, on the other hand, is not only easy to visit, but one of the HRM's hidden gems. Approximately 5km long and up to 1.5km wide, this 400ha island offers a combination of historical and natural features that will delight hikers, birdwatchers, and those with an interest in (particularly military) history.

Deer, coyote and other animals inhabit the island, and more than 200 bird species, including nesting raptors such as osprey, have been documented here. Walk some of the many trails through the woods and past tidal pools, explore several former military installations and gun batteries, see some of the old residential houses, relax on sandy Mauger's Beach, and enjoy a wonderful view of the mouth of Halifax Harbour. If the weather is kind, this is a great place to spend a few hours or more.

History Evidence, including a 1,500-year-old shell midden, indicates a Mi'kmaq presence on McNabs Island long before the Europeans. The French used the island as a fishing camp during the 1690s, and in 1782, a Peter McNab purchased it. Around the turn of the 19th century, the British Admiralty built a gallows on what became known as Hangman's Beach, and used it to hang deserters. The bodies were left suspended as a warning to other sailors.

Fortifications were added, and in 1866 the island was forced into use as a makeshift quarantine area when a cholera epidemic struck on the *England*, a steamship *en route* from Liverpool to New York. Around 200 of the 1,200 on board are thought to have been buried on the island.

In the 1860s, the British Admiralty established defences including Ives Point Battery, Fort McNab and the Hugonin Battery.

Between the 1870s and 1920s, the island was a popular recreational destination for the people of Halifax and Dartmouth: thousands came to visit the fairgrounds, bath houses and tea rooms and for picnics or socials.

In both World Wars, defences and fortifications were enhanced, and the island anchored one end of a submarine net across the harbour. In 1974, the province began acquiring land for the creation of a provincial park: today, less than 3% of the island is privately owned.

Getting there and away McNabs is a 10-minute boat trip from Eastern Passage (pages 131–2), and **McNabs Island Ferry** (✆ *902 465 4563;* tf *1 800 326 4563; www. mcnabsisland.com; round-trip fare around CAN$20*) departs from Fishermans Cove. **Taylor Made Tours** (✆ *902 448 4982;* f*; round-trip fare approx CAN$20*) also offer trips across from its private wharf at 1425 Eastern Passage Road. Trips by both operators run on an on-demand basis, subject to boat availability. If you fancy getting there by kayak, **Kayak Halifax** (✆ *902 210 7728; kayakhalifax.com*) offer half-day (*approx 5 hours*) guided excursions. These trips cost CAN$138 and run from mid-May to mid-October subject to weather conditions. For other operators – and more details – see the **Friends of McNabs Island Society** website (*www.mcnabsisland. ca*). No services are available on McNabs Island, so remember to bring your own food and water. Be prepared, too, for changeable weather.

DEVILS ISLAND Approximately 12ha in size, Devils Island is situated about 2km southeast of McNabs Island. Originally granted to a Captain John Rous in 1752, the first permanent settlement was in 1830, and in 1900 there were about 20 families living on the island.

There are many explanations of how the island earned its current name. Historians say it was briefly owned and occupied by a man named 'Duval', and that with time his name was corrupted. Others say that some Haligonians visited the island for what was supposed to be a day trip, but – owing to a sudden weather deterioration – were stuck there for several days, describing it on their return as somewhere only the devil would live. There were many reports of shepherds (sheep were pastured on the island after the aforementioned fire) and passing sailors seeing ghosts there.

One of the most unusual stories is from the turn of the 20th century: a man reported that when out fishing, a halibut had popped its head out of the water, announced itself as the Devil, and told him that he would die the next day. On the morrow, the man was found dead in his boat near the spot where he claimed to have seen the satanic halibut: examinations showed that – even though he was found sitting in his boat, hands on oars and bone dry – he had drowned. Members of the dead man's family moved into his house on the island, and their baby died within a day or two with no obvious cause of death. There were also reports of the footsteps of a fisherman's boots walking the corridors.

Some claim that unexplainable lights and fires on the island are still seen from the mainland. A supposedly bottomless pit on the island is said to be either a hiding place for pirate treasure or a gateway to hell.

In 2006, psychic medium Alan Hatfield spent a night on the island with a camera crew filming a two-part television documentary entitled *The Ghosts of Devils Island*. He claims to have recorded several clear and audible spirit voices on audio tape, and an apparition on infra-red video.

Devils Island can be visited, but there are no scheduled boat services (try the McNabs Island operators). Only small vessels can safely navigate into the only landing area, and then only if sea conditions are perfect. If you get there, you'll find it hard to imagine that the island once boasted 18 houses and a small school.

GEORGES ISLAND (902 426 5080; www.pc.gc.ca/eng/lhn-nhs/ns/georges/index.

aspx) For 200 years, Georges Island was the scene of constant military activity, playing an integral role in harbour defence. For the past 45 years or so, however, the island has remained largely undisturbed, although tales of its secret tunnels abound. At this time Parks Canada has reported that the Georges Island NHS will not be developed for public visitation, however the island will continue to be available for special events so it might be worth checking with Parks Canada for the latest news.

THE NORTHWEST ARM, HERRING COVE AND SAMBRO This is a fascinating
excursion of less than 65km in total, especially for those who won't have time to explore much beyond the capital (if you don't have your own transport, you can only do the first part of this trip: York Redoubt is the terminus of bus pages 194–5 which runs hourly along Purcells Cove Road from the terminal in the Halifax Shopping Centre on Mumford Road). It starts at the **Armdale Rotary** [100 A5], at the west end of Quinpool Road. From here, take Herring Cove Road, staying to the right when Purcells Cove Road branches off to the left. Almost immediately, you'll see a sign for **Chocolate Lake Beach**, and a parking area on the right. Walk along a short path to a small, sandy beach, and one of the HRM's favourite swimming lakes.

After your dip, head back towards the roundabout (rotary), but take the first right and right again to join Highway 253, Purcells Cove Road. Look out for the impressive **St George's Greek Orthodox Church** [100 A6] (*38 Purcells Cove Rd;* \ *902 830 3377;* ⊕ *Sun morning for services, otherwise by appointment*): this and the adjacent community centre are the focus for Halifax's Greek community of approximately 400.

Pass the Armdale Yacht Club on Melville Island (formerly the site of a military prison), shortly after which a sign will indicate the turn-off (on the left) to **Deadmans Island Park** [100 B6]. During the war of 1812, thousands of (mainly American) soldiers and sailors were held prisoner close by. Many died in captivity, and almost 200 were buried in unmarked graves on this site. In 2005, the US government erected a plaque to commemorate the men interred here.

You can walk from here to the **Sir Sandford Fleming Park** [100 D7] (*Dingle Rd;* ✆*902 490 4000;* ☉ *08.00–dusk daily*), but it is probably better to continue on Purcells Cove Road, then follow Dingle Road to the car park. This 38ha largely forested park has extensive water frontage with lovely views over the yacht-dotted Northwest Arm, and two main trails. Always popular is the walk along the waterfront, but worthwhile, too, is the trail through the forest to Frog Pond (aka Frog Lake).

The park's distinctive c1912 ten-storey tower, The Dingle, was commissioned by Sir Sandford Fleming (box, page 124) to commemorate 150 years of representative government in Nova Scotia. In theory, the tower is open in summer and early autumn (if it is open, climb the winding staircase for fabulous views) but this seems a bit hit or miss.

Continuing on Purcells Cove Road, you'll pass North America's oldest sailing club, the Royal Nova Scotia Yacht Squadron [101 F7], which dates from 1837.

Originally built in 1793, most of the fortifications you see today at **York Redoubt** [82 C5] (*Purcells Cove Rd;* ✆ *902 426 5080; www.pc.gc.ca/lhn-nhs/ns/york/index. aspx;* ☉*late Jun–early Sep 08.00–20.00 daily; admission free*) date from more recent times, including tunnels, huge muzzle-loading guns, searchlights, and a Martello tower. The site was chosen for its commanding view over the entrance of Halifax Harbour, and has long been a key element in Halifax's defences. Paths lead downhill to the water, and if the weather is kind, the park makes a fine picnic spot.

Next stop is the traditional fishing village of **Herring Cove** [82 C5], built on the rocks around a long narrow inlet. Uncommercialised and souvenir-shop free, places like this and Sambro (below) are far closer to the real Nova Scotia than, for example, Fishermans Cove (pages 132–3). Herring Cove is the terminus for bus 820 which runs every 30 minutes from downtown (Barrington and Duke streets). If you get peckish, stop for a coffee and cookie, or a panini at Pavia Gallery (*995 Herring Cove Rd;* ✆ *902 407 4008; www.paviagallery.com*) or good unpretentious fish and chips/diner fare at Now We're Cookin' (*179 Hebridean Dr;* ✆ *902 479 6666;* **f**).

From Herring Cove, turn left onto Highway 349, Ketch Harbour Road. Look for the sign to the left to **Chebucto Head** and Duncans Cove. A paved, albeit not terribly well-maintained, road leads to a military communications complex at Chebucto Head, and there is a car park right by the c1967 lighthouse. Come here in August and September and you may be able to see whales from this spot high above the ocean. Afterwards, take a quick look at **Duncans Cove** where houses are grouped around a small sandy cove, then return to Highway 359 and turn left.

Just before you reach **Sambro**, take Sandy Cove Road to the left. After 1.4km, stop just before the Agricultural Research Station. This spot offers the best views of Sambro Island and its lighthouse, the oldest standing and operating lighthouse in the Americas, commissioned in 1758.

Photogenic Sambro, at the head of the eponymous harbour, is the largest fishing village on this route. From here, follow signs to **Crystal Crescent Beach**. Short trails lead down from the car parks to three secluded coves with – if the sun's out – turquoise-blue water, white-sand beaches and beautiful natural surroundings. If such things offend you, be aware that the furthest beach is unofficially 'clothing optional'.

A gorgeous trail of approximately 11km return leads south along the shoreline, bending into the woods from time to time, to Pennant Point. Although this area can often be foggy, if it is clear you'll see plentiful seabirds, lovely coastal scenery, perhaps some seals, and views over to Sambro Island.

From here, head back to Sambro from where Highway 306 will whisk you back to Halifax via Harrietsfield.

NEAR THE AIRPORT There are two main attractions within the vicinity of Halifax International. Those with an interest in aviation should head to the **Atlantic Canada Aviation Museum** [82 C1] (*20 Sky Blvd;* \ *902 873 3773; atlanticcanadaaviationmuseum.com;* ⊕ *mid May–end Sep 09.00–17.00 daily; admission free*), where you can see more than two-dozen aircraft, from 'home-builds' to supersonic jets, plus an extensive collection of artefacts and exhibits depicting Atlantic Canada's aviation history. There is also a good gift shop. Car-lovers will enjoy **Scotia Speedworld** [82 C1] (*Bell Blvd;* \ *902 873 2277; www.scotiaspeedworld. ca;* ⊕ *late May–early Sep, races Sat (& some Fri) evenings; tickets CAN$16–40* – watch the motors running at the premiere stock-car racing facility in eastern Canada. Both attractions are on the other side of Highway 102 from the approach road to Halifax International Airport. Take Exit 6 from Highway 102, 38km/24 miles from Halifax.

THE UNIACKE ESTATE [82 A1] (*758 Hwy 1;* \ *902 866 0032; uniacke.novascotia.ca;* ⊕ *Jun–Sep 10.00–17.00 Mon–Sat, 13.00–17.00 Sun; admission CAN$3.90*) Situated on a 930ha estate Uniacke House, a large colonial-style country home, was built between 1813 and 1815 (box, page 127). Now a museum, the house is an all-too-rare example of a 19th-century Georgian estate intact with its original furniture. There are several kilometres of trails to wander – be sure to take the Lake Drumlin Field loop, which offers a fantastic view of the main house. The grounds are open year-round but are not maintained out of season. Uniacke is on Highway 1, approximately 35km/22 miles from Halifax.

DARTMOUTH

Directly opposite downtown Halifax, Dartmouth is a 10-minute ferry ride, or relatively quick drive over a toll bridge, across the harbour. Haligonians love to say that the best thing about Dartmouth is that it offers a great view of Halifax: Halifax may have been founded a year earlier and have the lion's share of attractions, but – views back across the water apart – there are some good (and diverse) reasons to visit this side of the harbour.

While it continues to be a bedroom community for Halifax, Dartmouth also stands on its own feet. It is home to **Burnside,** already the largest industrial/business park north of Boston and east of Montreal, and continuing to expand. Relatively new, too, is the much-loved Dartmouth Crossing shopping mall and entertainment complex. What is to be applauded is that development in the area has shown some sensitivity to the environment: 23 bodies of water were reason enough for Dartmouth to be called the 'City of Lakes'. Although no longer a city (but part of the HRM), Dartmouth is still very popular with nature lovers and outdoor types for its trails, and kayaking, windsurfing, canoeing and swimming in places such as Lake Banook.

SIR SANDFORD FLEMING

Born in Kirkcaldy, Fife, Scotland, Sandford Fleming (1827–1915) came to Canada in 1845. He designed Canada's first postage stamp, proposed, surveyed and engineered Canada's first railway line, and created Standard Time Zones (though these were not fully implemented until many years after his death). He was knighted by Queen Victoria in 1097, and having lived in Halifax for a number of years – deeded his land (now the park that bears his name) to the city in 1908.

Waterfront boardwalks stretch out on both sides of the ferry terminal, providing visitors with excellent views of McNabs and Georges islands, the harbour bridges – oh, and of course the Halifax skyline.

Right by the ferry terminal are the World Peace Pavilion (page 131), and Alderney Landing, home to a Saturday morning farmers' market and a theatre. In easy walking distance are the Dartmouth Heritage Museum, the Quaker House, and the Christ Church.

Further afield are two contrasting don't-miss attractions: the Bedford Institute of Oceanography and the Black Cultural Centre for Nova Scotia (both page 130).

HISTORY Founded in 1750, a year after Halifax, Dartmouth later began to develop as a big whaling town. Many of the whalers were Quakers, originally from New England's Nantucket Island, and by the end of the American Revolution, more than 150 ships were engaged in the whaling business. Whale oil's uses included lighting and lubrication: whale bone – used in the manufacture of items including corsets and umbrellas – brought high prices. For several years, Dartmouth prospered with the profits of the whaling business, before the entire fleet moved to Milford Haven, Wales, in 1792. Soon after, Loyalists moved in and occupied the whalers' old homes.

Vehicle and passenger ferries regularly criss-crossed the water between Dartmouth and Halifax, but it was the opening of the Angus L MacDonald Bridge in 1955 that ushered in an unprecedented development boom in Dartmouth.

GETTING THERE AND AWAY To reach Dartmouth from Halifax, visitors can **drive** over the harbour on either the Angus L MacDonald Bridge [100 C1] or the A Murray MacKay Bridge [off map]. Others may wish to take the longer scenic route around the harbour through Bedford, or – best of all – cross the harbour by **ferry**. For further details, see page 86.

 WHERE TO STAY Dartmouth's accommodation choices tend to be a little cheaper than those in Halifax, but are all outside downtown – meaning that a car or a willingness to use buses and ferries are important.

Dartmouth & around

Best Western Plus Dartmouth Hotel & Suites [129 B4] (121 units) 15 Spectacle Lake Dr; ◝902 463 2000; www.bestwesterndartmouth. com . Decent facilities at this 4-storey property situated away from downtown but close to shopping malls. Good on-site restaurant & wine bar (opposite), indoor pool, fitness centre & business centre. Rooms have fridges, some double whirlpool baths. Hot buffet b/fast inc. **$$**

Comfort Inn Dartmouth [129 A5] (80 rooms) 456 Windmill Rd; ◝902 463 9900; tf 1 800 228 5150; www.choicehotels.ca. Large, well-maintained motel rooms at this 2-storey property near Hwy 111. Good continental b/fast inc. **$$**

Hampton Inn & Suites by Hilton Halifax – Dartmouth [129 C3] (163 rooms) 65 Cromarty Dr; ◝902 406 7700; tf 1 877 406 7701; www. dartmouthhampton.com. Ignore the less than snappy

name – this is a modern, well-run, comfortable 6-storey hotel with spacious rooms & suites. Not downtown but close to Dartmouth Crossing mall & Shubie Park. Rate includes free hot b/fast. **$$**

Blockhouse Hill B&B [129 A1] (2 rooms) 62 Wentworth St; ◝902 463 1811; tf 1 866 873 1699; www.blockhousehillbedandbreakfast.com; ⊕ mid Apr–Oct. The 2 spacious bedrooms share a nice bathroom in this lovely house on a quiet, residential street – but only 5mins' walk to the Halifax ferry. Full b/fast inc. **$**

Braeside Court B&B [129 D5] (1 unit) 34 Braeside Court; ◝902 462 3956; tf 1 866 277 8138; e braeside@ns.sympatico.ca; www. braesidecourtbandb.ca. The spacious, 2-bedroom suite occupies the upstairs of an open-plan, spacious modern townhouse close to a lake & good for hiking trails. Away from downtown. 2 resident cats. Full b/fast inc. **$**

Richard John Uniacke was born in Ireland, in 1753. He spent some time in New York and Nova Scotia before returning to Ireland to study law. He returned to Nova Scotia in 1781 and soon after was appointed solicitor-general for the province. His meteoric rise up the province's legal – and political – ladder continued. He received a 400ha land grant, expanded it and named it Mount Uniacke, and began building a fine house there in 1813. The house was completed two years later. The Uniackes hosted not just Halifax's elite, but international dignitaries too. In the summer, guests could take boat excursions on Lake Martha, named for Uniacke's wife (she died in 1803, having borne 11 children). Uniacke himself died in 1830, 49 of his 77 years having been spent in the public service of Nova Scotia. The oaks that ring the house are the result of a barrel of acorns brought over from Ireland and planted centuries ago.

Further out

⌂ Knightswood B&B & Carriage House [129 D2] (2 units) 453 Waverley Rd; ✆902 435 3969; tf 1 866 363 8797; knightswoodbandb. ca; ⊕ May–Oct. Unusual in that the main house has a 2-bedroom suite (1 with queen bed, the other 2 sgl beds, AC), & the Carriage House (tucked away between trees in the beautifully kept gardens) has AC, a fully-equipped kitchen, foldaway queen bed & 2 smaller sgls in the loft.

Rate (main house) includes full b/fast. Approx 12mins' drive to downtown Dartmouth. **$$**

⛺ Shubie Park Campground (100 sites) [82 C3; 129 D3] Jaybee Dr, off Hwy 318; ✆902 435 8328; tf 1 800 440 8450; www.shubiecampground.com; ⊕ mid May–mid Oct. Open campground with lake access, 3km from Exit 6A north of Hwy 111. Approx 6km to downtown Dartmouth,10km to downtown Halifax. **$**

✗ WHERE TO EAT AND DRINK Whilst not nearly as varied or plentiful as the choice on the Halifax side, you shouldn't find it hard to find a good meal in Dartmouth.

✗ Il Trullo Ristorante [129 C7] 67 King's Wharf Pl; ✆902 461 2030; iltrullodartmouth. wix.com/iltrullo; ⊕ 11.30–22.00 Mon–Sat. Decent waterfront innovative Italian (interesting, tasty take on Caesar salad). Coconut candybar cheesecake may not appear on too many menus in Italy but is worth saving room for. Aim for a table with a view over Halifax rather than Dartmouth. **$$–$$$**

✗ Trendz Café & Wine Bar [129 B4] 15 Spectacle Lake Dr; ✆902 446 3782; www. trendzcafe.ca; ⊕ 07.00–21.30 daily (wine bar til 23.00). Once again a hotel (in this case, the Best Western, page 126) has a surprisingly good restaurant. Start perhaps with ginger carrot soup, then move on to paella or salmon teriyaki. The wine bar also has a good martini & beer selection. **$$**

✗ The Canteen [129 A1] 66 Ochterloney St; ✆902 425 9272; www.thecanteen.ca; ⊕ 10.30–18.00 Mon–Fri; 09.00–15.00 Sat. Bright, open café with ever-changing menu of imaginative gourmet

sandwiches on homemade bread, soup & salad, plus take-home meals. **$–$$**

✗ Mic Mac Bar & Grill [129 D4] 219 Waverley Rd; ✆902 434 7600; micmacbarandgrill.com; ⊕ 10.00–21.00 Mon–Fri, 08.00–21.00 Sat & Sun. Popular, reliable, unpretentious long-established family-run diner. Good value for b/fast, lunch &/or dinner. Approx 4km from downtown Dartmouth. **$–$$**

✗ Humble Pie Kitchen [129 A2] 77 King St; ✆902 431 0444; humblepiekitchen.ca; ⊕ 11.00–18.00 Mon–Fri, 10.00–15.00 Sat. Having discovered how well savoury New Zealand-style pies went down with Dartmouthians, their creators decided to expand. Good quality meats & gravy (with a vegetarian version) encased in flaky pastry. **$**

✗ John's Lunch [129 D7] 352 Pleasant St; ✆902 469 3074; www.johnslunch.com; ⊕ 10.00–21.00 Mon–Sat, 11.00–21.00 Sun. Long-established, unpretentious fish & chip & seafood eatery. Try the haddock tips, or clams. **$**

🖵 **Two if by Sea** [129 B1] 66 Ochterloney St; ☎ 902 469 0721; twoifbyseacafe.ca; ⏰ 07.00–18.00 Mon–Fri, 08.00–17.00 Sat & Sun. Sophisticated but casual coffee shop/bakery/café. $

ENTERTAINMENT AND NIGHTLIFE
Alderney Landing Cultural Convention Centre [129 A3] Ochterloney St; ☎ 902 461 8401; www.alderneylanding.com. Next to the Dartmouth ferry terminal, hosts theatre, concerts & more.

🎭 **Celtic Corner Pub** [129 B2] 69 Alderney Dr; ☎ 902 464 0764; www.celticcorner.ca; ⏰ 11.00–midnight, 11.00–01.00 Fri & Sat. A good Irish pub with splendid rooftop patio, live music & Celtic brunch menu. Kitchen closes 22.00 (23.00 Fri & Sat).

Cineplex Cinemas Dartmouth Crossing [129 C3] 145 Shubie Dr, Dartmouth Crossing; ☎ 902 481 3251; www.cineplex.com. Multi-screen cinema.

DARTMOUTH
For listings, see pages 126–8

⊖ **Where to stay**
1 Best Western Plus Dartmouth
   Hotel & Suites..........................B4
2 Blockhouse Hill B&B................... A1
3 Braeside Court B&B.....................D5
4 Comfort Inn Dartmouth................. A5
5 Hampton Inn & Suites by
   Hilton Halifax – Dartmouth......... C3
6 Knightswood B&B &
   Carriage House........................D2
7 Shubie Park Campground.............D3

✖ **Where to eat and drink**
8   The Canteen................................A1
9   Humble Pie Kitchen.....................A2
10 Il Trullo Ristorante......................C7
11 Mic Mac Bar & Grill.....................D4
    Trendz Café & Wine Bar............(see 1)
12 Two if by Sea..............................B1

Off map
    John's Lunch................................D7

SHOPPING The best **shopping malls** are the **Mic Mac Mall** [129 C5] (☎ *902 466 2056; www.micmacmall.com*) and **Dartmouth Crossing** [129 C4] (☎ *902 445 8883; www.dartmouthcrossing.com*), which is said to be the location for a new IKEA in 2017. For new **books**, magazines and much more, aim for **Chapters** (*Mic Mac Mall;* ☎ *902 466 1640; www.chapters.indigo.ca*), whilst the best bet – and a good one – for the 'previously-owned' variety is John W Doull [129 D6] (*122 Main St;* ☎ *902 429 1652;* **tf** *1 800 317 8613; www.doullbooks.com;* ⏰ *10.00–18.00 Mon–Sat (til 21.00 Thu)*) – the Halifax used-book institution moved across the harbour in 2012 and offers almost 50,000 titles.

The couture-conscious may approve of **Bodega Boutique** [129 B1] (*104 Portland St;* ☎ *902 877 1823; www.bodegaboutique.ca;* ⏰ *11.00–17.00 Tue–Fri (til 18.00 Thu), 10.00–17.00 Sat, noon–15.00 Sun*): in their own words 'Affordable fashion... for pretty things who like pretty things'. **Kept** [129 A2] (*75 King St;* ☎ *902 469 5378; www.keptshop.ca;* ⏰ *10.00–18.00 Mon–Fri, 10.00–17.00 Sat, noon–16.00 Sun*) is an independent boutique selling well-crafted gifts and houseware, and those seeking out CDs or vinyl should find plenty at **Taz Records Dartmouth** [129 B2] (*45 Portland St;* ☎ *902 487 3099; www.tazrecords.com;* ⏰ *07.00–18.00 Mon–Fri, 08.00–17.00 Sat*).

Dartmouth Farmers' Market [129 A2] (*Alderney Landing; www.alderneylanding.com/market;* ⏰ *08.00–13.00 Sat, 11.00–15.00 Sun*) is located in the Alderney Landing complex on the Dartmouth waterfront next to the Ferry Terminal.

SPORTS AND ACTIVITIES For outdoor **ice skating**, Dartmouth maintains groomed surfaces at Lake Charles. There is no charge, but don't expect facilities or skate rental.

Canoeing & kayaking *See also page 131*
KayakNS ☎ 902 222 2432; www.kayakns.ca

Climbing
Ground Zero Climbing Gym [129 B3] Unit 3, Wright Pl, Burnside Industrial Park; ☎ 902 468 8788; www.climbgroundzero.com; ⏰ noon–23.00 Mon–Fri, noon–18.00 Sat & Sun. The largest indoor rock-climbing facility in Atlantic Canada. From CAN$13.80 (day pass). Near the corner of Wright & John Savage aves.

Diving
Torpedo Ray's Scuba Dartmouth [129 A4] 625 Windmill Rd; ☎ 902 481 0444; www.torpedorays.com ⏰ 09.00–18.00 Mon–Thu (til 19.00 Fri), 08.00–

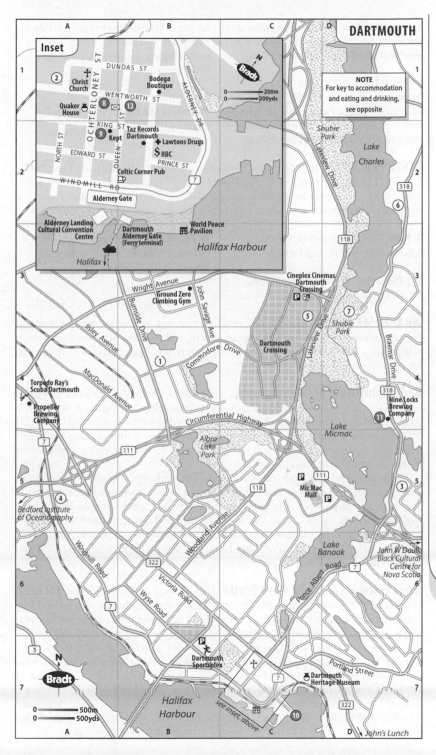

Inset

A B C D

1

Christ Church
Bodega Boutique
DUNDAS ST
OCHTERLONEY ST
WENTWORTH ST
Quaker House
ALDERNEY DR
Taz Records Dartmouth
Kept
KING ST
NORTH ST
QUEEN ST
Lawtons Drugs
EDWARD ST
RBC
PRINCE ST
Celtic Corner Pub
WINDMILL RD
Alderney Gate

0 ————— 200m
0 ————— 200yds

NOTE
For key to accommodation
and eating and drinking,
see opposite

Shubie
Park

Lake
Charles

318

6

Alderney Landing
Cultural Convention
Centre
Dartmouth
Alderney Gate
(Ferry terminal)
World Peace
Pavilion
Halifax Harbour

Halifax

118

2

Cineplex Cinemas
Dartmouth
Crossing

Wright Avenue
Ground Zero
Climbing Gym
John Savage Ave
Burnside Drive
Ilsley Avenue
Commodore Drive
Dartmouth
Crossing
Lakeview Drive
Shubie
Park
Braemar Drive

3

MacDonald Avenue
Torpedo Ray's
Scuba Dartmouth
Propeller
Brewing
Company
Circumferential Highway
Albro
Lake
Park
Lake
Micmac
Nine Locks
Brewing
Company
318

4

7
111
118
Bedford Institute
of Oceanography
Mic Mac
Mall
111
3

5

Windmill Road
322
Victoria Road
Wyse Road
Woodland Avenue
Lake
Banook
Prince Albert Road
John W Doull
Black Cultural
Centre for
Nova Scotia
7

6

7
3
N
Bradt
Dartmouth
Sportsplex
Dartmouth
Heritage Museum
Portland Street
322
John's Lunch

0 ————— 500m
0 ————— 500yds

see inset, above

Halifax
Harbour

7

A B C D

17.00 Sat & Sun. Shore & boat dives from a range of sites around the HRM (PADI Open Water dive courses from CAN$430); full gear rental from CAN$58/day.

Gyms & fitness centres
Dartmouth Sportsplex [129 B7] 110 Wyse Rd; ☎ 902 464 2600; www.dartmouthsportsplex. com; ⊕ 05.30–22.30 Mon–Fri, 06.00–21.00 Sat, 08.00–22.30 Sun. Just by the MacDonald Bridge.

Day pass CAN$12. Facilities include cardio theatre, weight room, lifestyle centre, walking & running track, swimming pool, ice rink & squash courts. Photo ID required.

Swimming
Dartmouth Sportsplex See left. Photo ID required. *CAN$6.25.*

OTHER PRACTICALITIES The most convenient library is the **Alderney Gate Public Library** [129 B2] (*60 Alderney Dr;* ☎ *902 490 5745;* ⊕ *year-round 10.00–21.00 Mon–Thu, 10.00–17.00 Fri & Sat (winter only 14.00–17.00 Sun)),* on the waterfront right by the ferry terminal, which offers internet-accessible computers.

$ Bank [129 B2] RBC Royal Bank, 44 Portland St; ☎ 902 421 8800; ⊕ 09.30–17.00 Mon–Fri (Fri til 18.00)

✉ **Post Office** [129 A1] 53 Queen St; ☎ 902 494 4726; ⊕ 09.00–17.00 Mon–Fri

✚ **Pharmacy** [129 B2] Lawtons Drugs, 46 Portland St; ☎ 902 466 2419; ⊕ 09.00–21.00 Mon–Fri, 09.00–17.00 Sat & Sun

WHAT TO SEE AND DO There is talk of a new museum in Dartmouth: since an old heritage museum closed in 2002, hundreds of objects have been kept in storage waiting for a new home (the existing heritage museum, page 131, is not big enough for many more exhibits.

Bedford Institute of Oceanography [129 A5] (*1 Challenger Dr;* ☎ *902 426 4306; www.bio.gc.ca;* ⊕ *May–Aug Mon–Fri by appointment only, free guided tour available 09.00–16.00 by appointment*) Don't be put off by the uninspiring exterior of this building in the shadow of the A Murray MacKay Bridge: a tour of Canada's largest oceanographic research centre will bring you a new understanding of what goes on in the nooks and crannies of the ocean floor.

Learn about salvage work on the *Titanic*, and techniques used to find aircraft wreckage. Then get up close and personal with marine creatures in the touch tank. There are also displays on Atlantic Canada's sharks and species at risk. To get there from downtown Halifax, take the MacKay Bridge, take the Shannon Park exit immediately after the toll gates, turn right at the 'Stop' sign and then first left. From downtown Dartmouth, take Windmill Road to Shannon Park, or take bus #51 from Dartmouth's Bridge Terminal.

Black Cultural Centre for Nova Scotia [129 D6] (*1149 Main St;* ☎ *902 434 6223;* tf *1 800 465 0767; www.bccns.com;* ⊕ *10.00–16.00 Mon–Fri, plus Jun–Sep noon–15.00 Sat; admission CAN$6*) The first site of its kind in Canada, this museum, cultural and education centre preserves and promotes Nova Scotia's black history and culture. The centre represents black communities across the province and displays tell the story of the black Loyalists who fled the American Revolution, the Maroons who came from Jamaica in 1796, and the American slaves who arrived after the war of 1812. It is a fascinating experience for anyone interested in black and/or Nova Scotia history. Located in Dartmouth's eastern outskirts at the junction of Main Street and Cherry Brook Road, to get there go 6km east along Main Street (Hwy 7) from Exit 6 of Highway 111. Take bus #61 or #68 from Dartmouth's Bridge Terminal.

Dartmouth Heritage Museum [129 C7] (*26 Newcastle St;* ✆ *902 464 2300;* *www.dartmouthheritagemuseum.ns.ca;* ⊕ *year-round 10.00–17.00 Tue–Fri, 10.00–13.00 & 14.00–17.00 Sat (summer also 10.00–13.00 & 14.00–17.00 Sun); admission CAN$5*) This restored c1867 downtown building, also known as Evergreen House, was the home of Dr Helen Creighton, Nova Scotia's best-known folklorist (page 34). A good first stop for those interested in Dartmouth's history.

Quaker House [129 A1] (*57 Ochterloney St;* ✆ *902 464 2300; www.dartmouth heritagemuseum.ns.ca;* ⊕ *Jun–early Sep 10.00–13.00 & 14.00–17.00 Tue–Sun; admission CAN$5*) A charming restored c1785 house furnished in period style – one of the oldest known residences in the area – built by Quaker whalers. Your visit is enhanced by tales told by costumed guides.

Christ Church [129 A1] (*50 Wentworth St;* ✆ *902 466 4270; christchurchdartmouth. weebly.com;* ⊕ *for services & by appointment*) This is the oldest church in Dartmouth. The weather vane atop its steeple depicts Halley's Comet. Close by is **Sullivan Pond** (*Prince Albert Rd*), a great place to see and feed ducks, geese and swans.

World Peace Pavilion [129 B3] (*Ferry Terminal Park;* ⊕ *May–Oct 08.00–dusk daily; admission free*) Opened in 1995 by visiting foreign ministers at the G7 summit, every country that had representation in Canada was asked to contribute something to represent 'our planet and efforts to shape our future'. More than 70 countries responded, and artefacts inside the triangular pavilion include pieces from two walls (the Great one in China, and the old Berlin one), a plaque made from ammunition fragments from Slovakia, and part of a dismantled nuclear missile silo from the USA.

Shubie Park [82 C4] The park takes its name from the Shubie Canal (box, page 132), and trails lead through the woods along the old canal banks. The stretch between Lake Micmac and Lake Charles has been restored, complete with one of the original locks. Many visitors take to the water in canoes and kayaks, paddling from the main day-use area to Lake Charles.

The **Fairbanks Interpretive Centre** (*54 Locks Rd;* ✆ *902 462 1826;* ⊕ *08.30–16.30 Mon–Fri; admission free*) has visitor information and displays on the canal's history. Alongside the centre, **Kaynoe Rentals** (✆ *902 240 3114; shubiecanal.ca;* ⊕ *Jul–Aug 08.00–20.00 Tue–Sun; spring & autumn 08.00–18.00 Sat & Sun*) rents canoes and kayaks from CAN$11/hour. The park is best accessed by taking Braemar Drive north from Exit 6 off Highway 111.

Breweries

Nine Locks Brewing Co [129 D4] 219 Waverley Rd; ✆ 902 434 4471; ninelocksbrewing.ca; ⊕ 11.00–21.00 daily (from 10.00 Sat & Sun). Stop in for a sample, a bottle &/or a look round at this newish craft brewery near the Shubie Canal.

Propeller Brewing Company [129 A4] 617 Windmill Rd; ✆ 902 422 7767; www.drinkpropeller. ca; ⊕ noon–20.00 daily (from 10.00 Sat). Taste (fee), buy, or take a 90min brewery tour (*18.00 & 20.00 daily by reservation, photo ID required, CAN$15*).

AROUND DARTMOUTH

THE EASTERN PASSAGE From downtown Dartmouth, head south down Pleasant Street (Hwy 322): you'll pass big oil refineries just after Woodside. If you continue following Shore Road, you leave the harbour and come to the open sea, with good views out to Devils Island (pages 122–3) before the road dead-ends about 3km from

Soon after Halifax was founded, the idea to use the string of seven lakes and the Shubenacadie River between Dartmouth and Truro as the basis for a canal linking Halifax Harbour and the Bay of Fundy had been discussed. Seemingly endless feasibility studies and surveys were done, and construction began in July 1826. Within five years, the construction company went bust.

Construction started again in 1854, and despite financial problems, the project was completed in 1861. Nine locks and two inclined planes connected the lakes and river. Steam vessels hauled barges laden with goods along the 115km canal system.

Within a few years, problems arose. Gold was discovered at one of the lakes and a dispute arose over the validity of the title of the lands on which the canal was built. Somewhat unhelpfully, fixed bridges (rather than drawbridges or swing-bridges) were built across the canal at a couple of points, meaning that most canal shipping couldn't pass under them. These factors, plus the advantages offered by the newly booming railways put paid to the canal, and it closed in 1870.

Although it fell into disrepair, some parts of the canal have recently been restored for recreational pursuits, and these are best seen at Shubie Park (*shubiecanal.ca*).

Fishermans Cove at Hartlen Point Forces Golf Club (page 112). If you prefer birds to birdies, there are shore and water birds on the beach here year-round, and in spring and autumn Hartlen Point is one of the best areas to see migrants.

Getting there and away Bus #60 leaves Dartmouth's Bridge Terminal roughly every 30 minutes from 06.00 to 21.00 (*CAN$2.50*) and stops near the Aviation Museum and Fishermans Cove.

Where to stay, eat and drink

Eastern Passage B&B [82 D5] (3 rooms) 2148 Shore Rd; 902 465 1637; www. bbcanada.com/easternpassagebb; year-round. Comfortable new house with lovely views over the mouth of Halifax Harbour. Friendly, accommodating hostess. Rate include full b/fast. **$–$$**

Boondocks 200 Government Wharf Rd, Fishermans Cove; 902 465 3474; www. boondocksnovascotia.com; 11.00–20.00 daily. Located at a very popular summer tourist draw with indoor & alfresco dining & a fine view (over the Eastern Passage & McNabs Island), Boondocks

should have a lot going for it. Sometimes, though, the food – &/or service – doesn't always live up to its surroundings. **$$**

Coffee, Tea & Sea 18 Government Wharf Rd, Fishermans Cove; 902 444 3435; ; in season 09.00–18.00 Mon–Fri, 11.00–18.00 Sat, 12.30–19.00 Sun. Just as you'd expect, in a green hut on the boardwalk – coffee, tea, baked treats, fudge & gifts. The surprise is the range of tasty Indonesian dishes (eg: kari ayam – chicken curry). Pass the sambal! **$–$$**

What to see and do

Fishermans Cove (902 465 6093; *www.fishermanscove.ns.ca*; *May–Nov; admission free*) The Eastern Passage's biggest attraction is this restored 200-year-old fishing village set around a picturesque harbour. Although many residents make their living from fishing (primarily haddock, herring, tuna and lobster), the sea is less bountiful than it once was. The present-day version (which opened in 1996)

TALLAHASSEE

In August 1864, during the American Civil War, the badly damaged Confederate blockade-runner, *Tallahassee*, limped into Halifax Harbour (a neutral port) for repairs.

Two enemy (Union) cruisers anchored off Chebucto Head, waiting for her to leave the sanctuary of the harbour. The *Tallahassee*'s captain's only chance of escape was to navigate a route through the Eastern Passage, long considered too shallow, narrow and dangerous a channel for a ship of the *Tallahassee*'s size.

All lights extinguished and with a skiff going ahead to check the depth and best course to follow, the *Tallahassee* set off under cover of darkness. Miraculously, the vessel reached the open seas undetected, and was well on her way to Wilmington before the enemy learnt of her escape.

is primarily a row of craft and gift shops (including pewter, fudge and souvenirs), and a café and restaurant. On my last visit, a number of shops seemed to be closed. Smell the sea air, and be sure to wander the extensive seaside boardwalk. In season, boat trips leave from here for McNabs Island (pages 121–2).

Shearwater Aviation Museum [82 D4] (*34 Bonaventure Av, Shearwater Airport;* \ *902 720 1083; www.shearwateraviationmuseum.ns.ca;* ⊕ *Apr–May & Sep–Nov 10.00–17.00 Tue–Fri, noon–16.00 Sat; Jun–Aug 10.00–17.00 Mon–Fri, noon–16.00 Sat & Sun; Dec–Mar 10.00–17.00 Mon–Fri with reduced services; admission free*) Just off Highway 322 on the site of an active RCAF heliport, the museum chronicles Canadian Maritime military aviation from 1918. Highlights include an airworthy 1943 Fairey Swordfish HS469 biplane, a Beech 18, a full-scale model of a Hawker Hurricane, and a Sikorsky HO4S-3 'Horse' helicopter operational between 1955 and 1970. Always popular is the flight simulator, which allows you to 'fly' one of a variety of aircraft from the Canadian, British and US armed forces. There are also scale models of an aircraft carrier and a helicopter-carrying destroyer, library, and an obligatory gift shop.

BEDFORD

Bedford wraps around the head of Halifax Harbour. It was settled not long after Edward Cornwallis landed in Halifax in 1749. The Mi'kmaq called the Bedford Basin 'Kjipuktuk', which means 'the Great Harbour'. Sawmilling was one of the area's first industries, and Bedford became quite prosperous: in the late 1800s there were a number of upscale hotels here, and these attracted hundreds of Haligonians every summer. These days, sailors gravitate to the Bedford Basin Yacht Club; also on the waterfront, DeWolf Park is pleasant for a wander. A path follows much of the waterfront, and eventually joins an unpaved trail along the Sackville River. Admirals Cove Park at the south end of Shore Drive was popular with rock climbers and hikers, but in recent years it has also become popular with Lyme disease-carrying black-legged ticks, so is best avoided. The major shopping areas are the Sunnyside Mall and the Bedford Place Mall.

GETTING THERE AND AWAY Take the Bedford Highway from Halifax, or Windsor Road and then Dartmouth Road from Dartmouth. By **bus** from Halifax, take #80 from Upper Water Street (*55mins; CAN$2.50*).

Halifax, Dartmouth and Around **BEDFORD**

3

✗ WHERE TO EAT AND DRINK

For something quick, the **Sunnyside Mall** (*1595 Bedford Hwy*) has a food court and a big branch of Pete's (page 111).

✗ Il Mercato Sunnyside Mall, 1595 Bedford Hwy; ☎ 902 832 4531; www.il-mercato.ca; ⏰ 11.00–22.00 Mon–Sat. The food & atmosphere shout 'Italian trattoria' but the décor is contemporary. From the antipasti to the *zucotto* (a dessert that will banish tiramisu from your mind) it is all *molto buono*. A good wine list rounds off the menu. Usually bustling, it might not be the best bet for a quiet evening out. **$$**

✗ Finbar's Irish Pub Sunnyside Mall, 1595 Bedford Hwy; ☎ 902 444 7654; www.finbars.ca; ⏰ 11.00–22.00 Mon–Thu, 11.00–01.00 Fri & Sat, 11.00–21.00 Sun. One of the most authentic Irish menus in the province, a well-chosen bunch of beers, & usually excellent live music. Kitchen closes 21.00 Sun–Tue, 22.00 Wed–Sat. **$–$$**

✗ The Chickenburger 1531 Bedford Hwy; ☎ 902 835 6565; chickenburger.com; ⏰ 09.00– 22.00 daily (til 23.00 Thu–Sat). They tell me that this place hasn't changed all that much since it opened in 1940. They come in droves for fresh, never frozen haddock & chips, burgers, milkshakes & (you guessed it) chicken burgers. Now, if you're expecting the chicken in the eponymous burger to be grilled (or breaded & fried) breast, you're in for a surprise. In the bun are chunks of chicken cooked to a secret recipe (not my cup of tea, but who am I to argue with this diner's popularity?). **$**

✗ Izzy's Bagel Co 1180 Bedford Hwy ☎ 902 832 0028; ▪; ⏰ 07.30–19.00 Mon–Fri, 08.30–17.30 Sat & Sun. Of course you can buy things purporting to be bagels all over, but these are the real thing, made without preservatives, additives, added fat, eggs or dairy. Choose from over 15 types, top with (1 of 10 flavours of) cream cheese, or order a sandwich. Bagel bliss! **$**

WHAT TO SEE AND DO

Park the car and explore **Hemlock Ravine Park** (*Kent Av*; ☎ *902 490 4000*; ⏰ *year-round; admission free*) a wonderful, rugged 75ha tract of dense old-growth forest (box, below), which lies beside the western side of the Bedford Basin between the Bedford Highway and Highway 102. Some of the five

---

MY HEART BELONGS TO JULIE

When Edward, Duke of Kent, arrived in Halifax in 1794 to serve as commander-in-chief of the Halifax Garrison, he was accompanied by his French mistress, Julie de St Laurent. The two lived on Citadel Hill, but Julie was less than impressed with the view – which took in the military gallows in the middle of the parade ground. She demanded a residence with a more pleasant aspect, and Edward had an elaborate estate built, incorporating a magnificent wooden mansion (long gone), the delightful pathways that you see in Hemlock Ravine Park today, and something else that has survived – the heart-shaped Julie's Pond. The only remaining building from the original estate is the Rotunda, a round music room on a knoll overlooking the water. Supposedly one of Julie's favourite places, it is not open to the public. Edward and Julie left Nova Scotia in 1800.

Because of his royal position, Edward was unable to marry his mistress, though rumours persist that the couple had several children together. He tied the knot with a German princess and their only child became Queen Victoria. Julie lived for a while in a Paris convent, before marrying a Russian–Italian nobleman.

Incidentally, the park is said to be haunted by the ghost of the loser of a duel fought in 1795 between a colonel and a naval officer. The two were said to have over-imbibed at a grand reception hosted by Prince Edward. If you want to discuss what went wrong tactically with the colonel's ghost, he is said to (re)appear from time to time at the site of the fatal fight – near the cove south of the Rotunda – most commonly at 02.00.

interconnecting walking trails (see the map by the car park) lead through towering trees to a hemlock-filled ravine, and can be slippery when wet. By the car park is a heart-shaped pond. To reach the park, take the Bedford Highway and turn onto Kent Avenue 1km north of the Kearney Lake Road junction.

Closer to Bedford itself, a turn off the highway the other way (follow the signs) will bring you to **Scott Manor House** (*15 Fort Sackville Rd;* ✎ *902 832 2336; www. scottmanor.ca;* ⊕ *Jul–Aug 10.00–16.00 daily; admission free*), a c1770 gambrel-roofed Dutch Colonial mansion furnished with period antiques. Its simple tea room (⊕ *Jul–Aug 14.00–16.00 daily, cash only*) is a bonus.

UPDATES WEBSITE

You can post your comments and recommendations, and read the latest feedback and updates from other readers online at www.bradtupdates. com/novascotia.

NOVA SCOTIA ONLINE

For additional online content, articles, photos and more on Nova Scotia, why not visit www.bradtguides.com/novascotia.

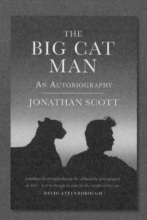

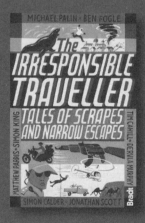
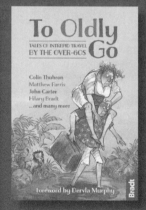

4

South Shore

The province's beautiful South Shore coastline is deeply indented, with many long, narrow bays, once the haunt of privateers and pirates. With lovely sandy beaches, beautiful coastal provincial parks, pretty fishing villages, towns steeped in history and a mysterious treasure island, this region is also well served with plenty of good places to stay. Some of Nova Scotia's best restaurants – and some excellent low-budget eateries – will satisfy your hunger.

You can drive the 300km-length of Highway 103, linking Halifax and Yarmouth, in under 4 hours. Follow this motorway, which cuts across the base of numerous peninsulas, and you'll see a lot of forest, the odd lake, and (occasionally) the sea off in the distance. Getting the most from the South Shore is not about speeding from town to town by the fastest route, but by giving yourself plenty of time to enjoy the historic streetscapes and what lies along – and off – the countless scenic backroads.

With enough time, you can go birding on Cape Sable Island or kayak between hundreds of beautiful islands in Mahone Bay. Sip a coffee and mingle with the yachting crowd in a Chester café. Wander the hilly streets of absorbing Lunenburg, established in 1753 and the best-surviving example of a planned British colonial settlement in North America. Rent a bike to explore the surrounding forested peninsulas and inlets. Join the throngs at Peggys Cove – or other pretty fishing villages that see virtually no visitors. Soak up the sun and breeze on magnificent sandy beaches, particularly around Liverpool, or take a ferry back in time to the Tancook Islands. Experience Acadian life past and present in the Pubnicos, and take to the dance floor at Hubbards' Shore Club. Whereas the majority of the sites and attractions are found on – or close to – the coast, heading inland on Highway 203, just west of Shelburne, leads to the huge expanse of the remote Tobeatic Wilderness Area, a dream come true for experienced back-country explorers.

Now, let's talk about South Shore public transport – or the lack of it. No buses or coaches serve the region, but a daily shuttle service – the **Cloud Nine Shuttle** (902 742 3992; thecloudnineshuttle.com) – connects Halifax with Yarmouth and thereby offers the only transport connection possibilities (taxis apart) for non-drivers. Depending on the driver's schedule for the particular run, door-to-door pick-up may or may not be available. Expect to pay approximately CAN$75, regardless of journey length. If you just want to hop between (say) Liverpool and Bridgewater, a taxi would be a better bet.

TERENCE BAY, LOWER PROSPECT AND PROSPECT

These working fishing villages have very few services and, unlike Peggys Cove (pages 139–44), see very few visitors. Just before you reach Prospect, a right turn, Indian Point Road, offers parking on the left. From the end of this short road, is the High Head Trail, an old Mi'kmaq trail which leads 4km along the coast offering wonderful views.

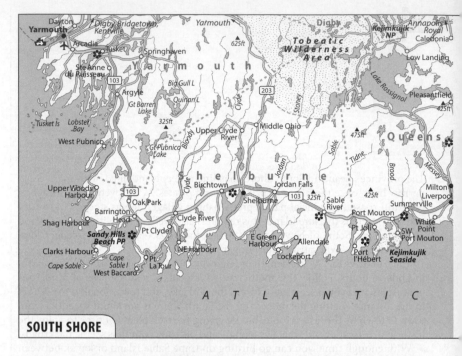

SOUTH SHORE

These communities are off Highway 333 on either side of Prospect Bay, both 32km from Halifax. Terence Bay, to the east, is 17km from Prospect. No public transport serves Terence Bay and the Prospects.

WHAT TO SEE AND DO Set against a beautiful oceanfront backdrop, the **SS** *Atlantic* **Heritage Park and Interpretation Centre** (*180 Sandy Cove Rd, Terence Bay;* ☎ *902 852 1557; www.ssatlantic.com;* ⊕ *(park) year-round (centre) mid May–early Oct 10.00– 17.00; admission free*) mixes the rugged beauty of the local landscape with a tone of solemn remembrance for the lives lost in the SS *Atlantic* tragedy (box, below), and the triumph of the human spirit in the rescue of the survivors. The interpretation centre includes records from the ship and recovered artefacts from the wreck, along with information about those on board, including a passenger list, and information on other local history. In addition to a monument in memory of the victims are picnic tables, a boardwalk and a trail with interpretive panels.

SS ATLANTIC

In 1873, almost 40 years before the RMS *Titanic* disaster, another White Star vessel was involved in what was at that time the greatest loss of life in a single north Atlantic tragedy (and also the White Star Line's first loss at sea). *En route* from Liverpool, England, to New York, the SS *Atlantic* ran aground on Mar's Head, just off Lower Prospect, on 1 April 1873. Although 390 of the 952 people on board survived, all but one (12-year-old John Hindley, from Lancashire) of the 156 women and 189 children on board lost their lives. Of the 562 victims, 277 were interred in a mass grave located on the grounds of the SS *Atlantic* Heritage Park (see above), and another 150 were buried at Lower Prospect.

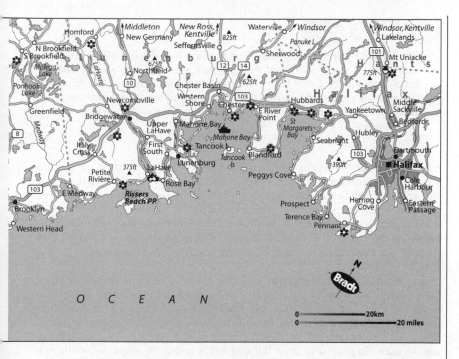

It is well worth a visit to the **Suezan Aikins Studio** (*Prospect Village;* \ *902 852 3154; www.suezan-aikins.com; ⊕ by appointment*) – Suezan's work, including goldleaf/mixed media relief carvings and woodblock prints – is world class. For those interested in getting outdoors, the **East Coast Outfitters** (*2017 Lower Prospect Rd, Lower Prospect;* \ *902 852 2567;* **tf** *1 877 852 2567; www.eastcoastoutfitters.com; ⊕ May–Oct*) gives lessons and offers guided sea kayak trips (*2hrs–multi-day*) to explore the region's beautiful coastline. They can customise a camping or B&B-based trip for you, and also offer kayak, canoe and SUP board rental. Golfers can all enjoy the **Granite Springs Golf Club** (*4441 Prospect Rd, Bayside;* \ *902 852 3419; www.granitespringsgolf.com; green fees CAN$58–69*), a 6,460yd course that winds through mature forest and between granite outcrops.

PEGGYS COVE

Indubitably, Peggys Cove (population: 120) is a very picturesque fishing village with an incredibly photogenic octagonal lighthouse overlooking a perfect little harbour. The white c1914 lighthouse stands atop granite worn smooth by thousands of years of mighty waves. Just below it, weathered fishing shacks on stilts, stacks of lobster pots and piles of fishing nets line the tiny cove where colourful fishing boats bob in the water. Bright green vegetation on the banks above contrasts with the blue of the sea, and the lapping of the waves, rustle of the wind, and squawking seagulls provide the soundtrack.

Incidentally, the lighthouse received a fresh coat of paint in 2012: when the federal and provincial governments couldn't agree on whose responsibility it was to keep the lighthouse looking good, locals bonded together and did the job themselves.

So what's not to like? The problem is that this is no 'off-the-beaten-track' secret. T Morris Longstreth wrote in 1934's *To Nova Scotia*: 'I am afraid that Peggys Cove will meet a tragic end. She will be thrown to the tourists.' In summer the same pleasure you get from thinking how quiet, unspoilt and (relatively) tourist-free the rest of Nova Scotia is can be soured by having to share the beauty of this little village with hordes of other visitors, many of whom arrive by the busload. That doesn't mean that the place is swamped with tacky souvenir shops or rip-off bars, restaurants and hotels: on the contrary, services are limited. There's an interesting gallery, a craft shop or two, a restaurant, a couple of ice cream shops – and two car parks to cater for a lot of visitors.

You might be lucky and find that your visit doesn't coincide with the tour buses, but to escape the worst of the crowds – and perhaps take advantage of the most beautiful light – get here early, or stay late. The busiest times are between about 08.30 and 17.15. This is, of course, easier to do if you're overnighting here or nearby. Take great care if exploring the smooth granite rocks by the sea – even when things appear calm, large waves can strike without warning. It might be worthwhile bringing shoes with a good grip.

GETTING THERE AND AWAY Peggys Cove is approximately 45 minutes (44km/27 miles) **by car** from Halifax. Take Highway 333 (passing the turn-offs for Terence Bay, the Prospects and the Dovers), or Highway 103 to Exit 5, Highway 213 towards Tantallon, and then Highway 333. Better still: combine the two routes to make a loop.

En route to Peggys Cove once you are out of Halifax, Highway 333 is also called Prospect Road. From Peggys Cove to Upper Tantallon the stretch of Highway 333 which runs up the scenic west side of St Margarets Bay is called Peggys Cove Road.

By bus, Murphy's The Cable Wharf (✆ *902 420 1015; www.mtcw.ca*) run a 3½-hour tour daily between June and mid October departing from Halifax at 13.00. Note that you probably won't get more than 90 minutes at the cove. Tickets cost CAN$58.

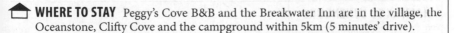

WHERE TO STAY
Peggy's Cove B&B and the Breakwater Inn are in the village, the Oceanstone, Clifty Cove and the campground within 5km (5 minutes' drive).

Breakwater Inn (4 rooms) 130 Peggy's Point Rd; **tf** 1 844 676 2683; www.breakwaterinn. ca; ⏱ year-round. On 3ha of grounds with a rocky ocean shoreline in the heart of the village. Nice, big modern rooms (3 of which sleep up to 4). Credit is given if you don't want b/fast, which is served between 08.30 & 11.00 at the Sou'wester Restaurant (see below). **$$$**

Oceanstone Seaside Resort (25 units) 8650 Peggys Cove Rd, Indian Harbour; ☎ 902 823 2160; **tf** 1 866 823 2160; **e** info@ oceanstoneresort.com; www.oceanstoneresort. com; ⏱ year-round. The resort – with 10 guest/ inn rooms, 7 suites & 8 1-, 2- & 3-bedroom cottages – is located on a private beach. Good, upmarket on-site restaurant (see below). Less than 5mins' drive from Peggys Cove – turn left when leaving the village. **$$–$$$**

Clifty Cove Motel (11 units) 8444 Peggys Cove Rd, Indian Harbour; ☎ 902 823 3178; **tf** 1 888 254 3892; www.cliftycovemotel.com; ⏱ May– Nov. Sgl-storey traditional-style pet-friendly motel with good ocean views, 3km from the village. **$$**

Peggy's Cove B&B (5 rooms) 19 Church Rd; ☎ 902 823 2265; **tf** 1 877 725 8732; www. peggyscovebb.com; ⏱ Apr–Oct. Bearing in mind the fabulous picture-postcard setting, Dan & Sharon's comfortable B&B, housed in a restored fisherman's home once owned by William deGarthe, offers good value. Bedrooms have private decks & all offer views of the lighthouse, cove & ocean. Full b/fast inc. **$$**

King Neptune Campground (65 sites) 8536 Peggys Cove Rd, Indian Harbour; ☎ 902 823 2582; www.kingneptunecampground.ca; ⏱ Jun– Sep. Open hillside campground on waterfront. Serviced & unserviced sites. 5km from Peggys Cove. **$**

WHERE TO EAT AND DRINK
The Sou'wester, Beale's and Dee Dee's are in the village, but within 5km – 5minutes' drive – are other options:

Rhubarb Restaurant 8650 Peggys Cove Rd, Indian Harbour; ☎ 902 821 3013; www. rhubarbrestaurant.ca; ⏱ 11.00–21.00 daily (from 10.00 Sun). Not just rather good creative pizza & burgers, but dinner entrées might also include braised lamb shank or pork tenderloin. Casually sophisticated. **$$–$$$**

Ryer's 5 Ryer's Rd, Indian Harbour; ☎ 902 823 1070; ⏱ Jan–Apr 10.00–17.00 Thu–Sun; May–Dec 10.00–17.00 daily. Not a restaurant or café but somewhere to stop for lobster fresh from the pound. Available live or cooked. Picnic tables outside (for those who choose the 'cooked' option). Forget lobster thermidor, bisque, etc: this is the real deal. **$$**

Sou'wester Restaurant 178 Peggy's Point Rd; ☎ 902 823 2561; ⏱ Jun–Sep 08.30–21.00 daily; Oct–May 10.00–sunset daily. The hordes of tourists need to be fed, & this huge licensed restaurant tries hard to do the job – it can get very busy during the day. The menu features traditional dishes (eg: Solomon Gundy), good pan-fried haddock & an interesting baked beans & fish hash. Dessert fans should try the homemade

gingerbread served warm with ice cream (or go to Dee Dee's!). **$$**

Shaw's Landing 6958 Hwy 333, West Dover; ☎ 902 823 1843; 📘 ; ⏱ mid Apr–mid Oct noon–19.00 daily (til 20.00 in season). Beautifully located seafood restaurant on the waterfront, 4km from Peggys Cove. Authentic local favourite with fresh seafood. Save room for the gingerbread cake. **$–$$**

Espresso on Deck at Beales' Bailiwick 124 Peggy's Point Rd; ☎ 902 823 2099; **tf** 1 800 823 2099; ⏱ in season 09.00– 19.00 daily, o/s weekends only. Good place for a beverage plus snack stop. Decent range of gifts in the shop but perhaps not for the bargain-hunter. **$**

Dee Dee's Ice Cream 110 Peggy's Point Rd; ☎ 902 221 6614; deedees.ca; ⏱ May–Sep noon–18.00 (or later) daily, weather dependent. Delectable ice cream emanates from a window in one of the village's original houses. You pay more than for the mass-produced stuff, but buttered almond, Mexican chocolate, berry berry, & banana cardamom are all superb!

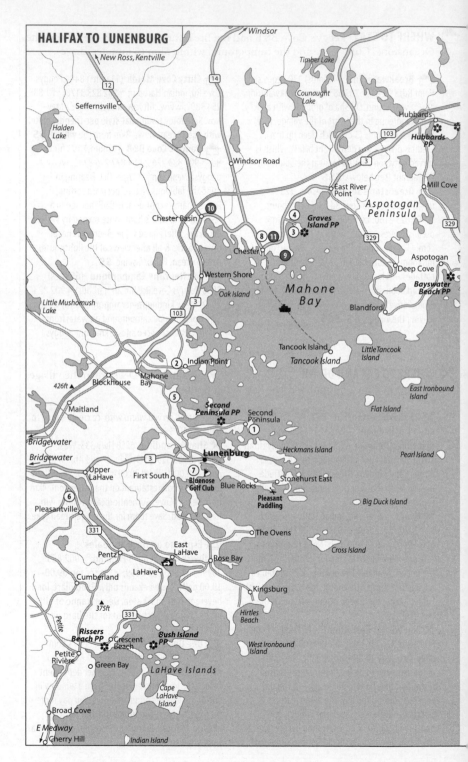

New Ross, Kentville

Windsor

Timber Lake

Seffernsville

Halden
Lake

Counaught
Lake

Hubbards

Hubbards
PP

East River
Point

Mill Cove

Chester Basin

Graves
Island PP

Aspotogan
Peninsula

Chester

Aspotogan

Western Shore

Deep Cove

Bayswater
Beach PP

Little Mushomush
Lake

Oak Island

Mahone
Bay

Blandford

Tancook Island

Little Tancook
Island

Indian Point

Tancook Island

Mahone
Bay

Blockhouse

East Ironbound
Island

Maitland

Second
Peninsula PP

Second
Peninsula

Flat Island

Bridgewater

Bridgewater

Lunenburg

Heckmans Island

Pearl Island

Upper
LaHave

First South

Bluenose
Golf Club

Blue Rocks

Stonehurst East

Pleasant
Paddling

Big Duck Island

Pleasantville

The Ovens

Cross Island

Pentz

East
LaHave

Rose Bay

Cumberland

LaHave

Kingsburg

Hirtles
Beach

Rissers
Beach PP

Crescent
Beach

Bush Island
PP

West Ironbound
Island

Petite
Rivière

Green Bay

LaHave Islands

Cape
LaHave
Island

Broad Cove

E Medway

Cherry Hill

Indian Island

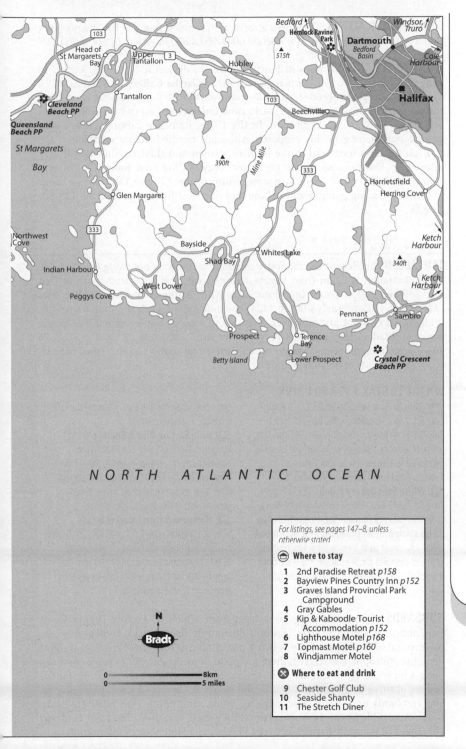

For listings, see pages 147–8, unless otherwise stated

⌂ Where to stay

1 2nd Paradise Retreat *p158*
2 Bayview Pines Country Inn *p152*
3 Graves Island Provincial Park Campground
4 Gray Gables
5 Kip & Kaboodle Tourist Accommodation *p152*
6 Lighthouse Motel *p168*
7 Topmast Motel *p160*
8 Windjammer Motel

✕ Where to eat and drink

9 Chester Golf Club
10 Seaside Shanty
11 The Stretch Diner

OTHER PRACTICALITIES The tourist information centre is found at 109 Peggy's Point Rd (◊ *902 823 2253;* ☺ *early May–Oct 09.00–17.00 daily; Jul–Aug til 19.00 daily).*

WHAT TO SEE AND DO Born in Finland, William deGarthe (1903–83) settled in Peggys Cove in 1955. His former home, the **deGarthe Gallery** (◊ *902 823 2253;* ☺ *mid May–mid Oct 09.00–17.00 daily; admission free),* just across the road from the tourist information office car park, now houses over 60 of his paintings and sculptures, most nautically themed. In the 1970s, he began carving a frieze on a granite outcropping on his property. Although he died before completing the project, the 30m memorial to the local fishermen and their families is still very impressive. You can also take to the water: **Peggy's Cove Boat Tours** (*Government Wharf;* ◊ *902 541 9177; www.peggyscoveboattours.com;* ☺ *May–Oct)* offers a range of tours (including puffin/seal watching and deep-sea fishing) aboard the 42ft *Sea Dog IV.*

SOUTHWEST TOWARDS CHESTER

TANTALLON The last of several pretty communities strung out along Peggys Cove Road, Tantallon is 22km from Peggys Cove **by car,** and is located south of Exit 5 of Highway 103. If stopping, don't miss **ABC: Antiques, Books & Collectibles** (*12723 Peggys Cove Rd;* ◊ *902 826 1128; www.abcantiques.ca*); the shop name says it all. You'll find not just numerous shapes and sizes of bottles varieties of maple syrup at **Acadian Maple** (*13578 Peggys Cove Rd;* ◊ *902 826 2312;* **tf** *1 866 276 2653, acadianmaple.com;* ☺ *year-round 09.00–17.00 daily*) but also jams, biscuits (cookies) and lots of possible gift ideas.

WHERE TO STAY, EAT AND DRINK

🏠 **Rum Hollow Seaside B&B** 13570 Peggys Cove Rd, Upper Tantallon; ◊ 902 826 7683; **tf** 1 866 752 1110; www.rumhollow.com; ☺ Apr–Dec, o/s by reservation. Nice, quiet, waterfront location. Comfortable, elegant rooms with 2-person jacuzzis. Good b/fast inc. Recommended. **$$**

🍴 **White Sails Bakery & Deli** 12930 Peggys Cove Rd; ◊ 902 826 1966; www.whitesailsbakery. com; ☺ 10.00–19.00 Mon–Sat, 10.00–18.00 Sun. Grab a smoked meat deli sandwich, or just a (good) coffee or a sweet treat & enjoy them whilst sitting at one of the café's picnic tables on the waterfront. A word of caution: drivers & cyclists should take extra care when turning into or leaving the café driveway against the traffic. **$**

🍴 **Train Station Bike & Bean** 5401 St Margarets Bay Rd; ◊ 902 820 3400; www. bikeandbean.ca; ☺ year-round 07.00–17.00 Mon–Fri, 08.00–17.00 Sat & Sun. You can rent bikes &/or enjoy sandwiches, wraps, baked goodies, etc, at this bright, friendly café. **$**

🍴 **Mariposa Natural Market & Café** 5229 St Margarets Bay Rd ; ◊ 902 820 3350; www. mariposanaturalmarket.com; ☺ year-round 09.00–17.00 Mon–Sat, noon–17.00 Sun. This large health food store with a café serves light vegetarian lunches/snacks. **$**

HUBBARDS If you're looking for a base from which to explore Peggys Cove, Lunenburg, and even Halifax (about a 50-minute drive away), Hubbards – 'the playground of St Margarets Bay' – isn't a bad choice. Whilst there are no real sights here, the atmosphere is relaxed, there are good (and varied) places to stay and eat, quite a bit going on in summer, and several beaches within easy reach. By far the busiest of these is Queensland Beach: the beach at Cleveland tends to be quieter, and Hubbards itself has a large, popular, white-sand beach with relatively warm water. Accessible **by car,** Hubbards is on Highway 3, less than 2km from Highway 103, Exit 6. It is exactly halfway between Halifax and Lunenburg – 50km from each.

In August 1946, a dance was held to mark the opening of the newly built Shore Club. Was it a success? Well, dances have been held there every summer Saturday night since. Nova Scotia's last dance hall is still going strong, and is a really fun experience. The building is also the location of another Maritime institution, the Lobster Supper (see below).

To get there **by bus**, the Cloud Nine Shuttle (page 137) operates daily both ways between Yarmouth and Halifax.

Shops worth a peek include **Lola's Landing** (*10061 St Margarets Bay Rd;* ❭ *902 858 5652*) for gifts and ladies clothing (in their words 'girly shopping at its best'), and **Mother Hubbards Cupboard** (*30 Main St;* ❭ *902 857 3766; www. motherhubbardscupboard.ca;* ⊕ *May–Dec 10.30–17.00 daily, Jan–Apr 10.30–17.00 Thu–Mon*) offering an eclectic mix of collectibles, antiques and more. The local **farmers' market** (*Hubbards Barn & Community Park, 57 Hwy 3;* ❭ *902 229 1717; hubbardsbarn.org/farmers-market/;* ⊕ *May–late Oct 08.00–noon Sat (Jul–Aug also 10.00–noon Sun)*) is well worth a visit. For a good picnic spot head to Bishop's Park, less than 2km to the east and just off Highway 3.

The **Hooked Rug Museum of North America** (*9849 Hwy 3;* ❭ *902 858 3060; www.hookedrugmuseumnovascotia.org;* ⊕ *check website for opening times; admission CAN$7*) aims to preserve the heritage craft of hand-hooked rugs and their evolution into fine art. There is lots of gallery space exhibiting historic and contemporary rug hooking art and artefacts, and workshops and 'hook ins' where you can sit, hook and chat (registration necessary), plus a fibre-art market.

The town has a few festivals of note, including the **Canada Day Ceilidh on the Cove** at the beginning of July and the beginning of August, where there is music, Irish dancing, a family barbecue and fireworks at dusk. The **World Tuna Flat Races** is held at the end of July/early August; a 'tuna flat' is a cumbersome boat: teams of four rowers compete in the waters of Hubbards Cove to a backdrop of music and barbecues. At **Pumpkinfest** in October, a day of pumpkin-related activities takes place, plus competitions such as pumpkin-seed spitting.

WHERE TO STAY, EAT AND DRINK

Dauphinee Inn (6 rooms) 167 Shore Club Rd; ❭ 902 857 1790; **tf** 1 800 567 1790; www. dauphineeinn.com; ⊕ May–Oct. In a beautiful waterfront setting, away from the main road, offering rooms decorated with period antiques. The licensed **Tuna Blue Bar & Grill** (⊕ *mid Jun–early Oct 16.00–21.00 daily; Jul–Aug 10.00–14.00 Sat & Sun;* $$) has a fab waterside deck, especially for sunset. Continental b/fast inc, full b/fast at extra cost. $$

Hubbards Beach Campground & Cottages (16 units) 226 Shore Club Rd; ❭ 902 857 9460; www.hubbardsbeach.com; ⊕ mid May–Sep. Rustic but comfortable 1- to 3-bedroom cottages (many on the lagoon front). The campground has 129 sites with full-service

motorhome sites & water-only tent sites. All in walking distance of one of the best sandy beaches in the region. There's a laundromat, too. $$
Shore Club Lobster Suppers 250 Shore Club Rd; ❭ 902 857 9555; shoreclub.ca; ⊕ mid May–mid Oct 16.00–20.00 Wed–Sun. Held in the huge, historic Shore Club Dance Hall (see box, above). Choose from 3 sizes of lobster, steak, chicken, vegetarian & children's menu. Price includes salad bar, unlimited mussels, dessert & coffee/tea. Licensed. Complete meal from CAN$38.
Trellis Café 22 Main St (Hwy 3); ❭ 902 857 1188; www.trelliscafe.com; ⊕ year-round 08.00–21.00 daily. The seafood is fresh & very good – whether as chowder, fishcakes or pan-fried haddock – & the mile-high clubhouse sandwich

is also recommended. Baked goods – such as bumbleberry crisp, coconut cream pie, or huge cinnamon buns – & bread are homemade & very tasty. Sit in or out. Licensed; regular live music. $$

OTHER PRACTICALITIES
$ Scotiabank 100 Main Rd; ☏ 902 857 3333; ⊕ 10.00–17.00 Mon–Fri
✉ Post office 10369 St Margarets Bay Rd, Hwy 3; ⊕ 08.30–17.30 Mon–Fri, 08.30–12.30 Sat
JD Shatford Memorial Library 10353 St Margarets Bay Rd, Hwy 3; ☏ 902 857 9176; ⊕ noon–17.00 Tue, 14.00–20.30 Wed & Thu, 10.00–15.00 Fri & Sat

---

HIS ROYAL SAVIOUR

It is said that Prince George – later King George V, and grandfather of the Queen – nearly died in a swimming accident in 1883. Serving on the HMS *Canada*, he took some time off and went angling in Dauphinee Mill Lake, west of Hubbards. After fishing, he fell into the lake and was struggling until rescued by his guide.

ASPOTOGAN PENINSULA Just past Hubbards, consider a detour from Highway 3: Highway 329 takes you around the rugged, beautiful **Aspotogan Peninsula** that separates St Margarets Bay from Mahone Bay. 'Aspotogan' derives from the Mi'kmaq language and means 'Where they block passageways for eels'. The drive around the peninsula is approximately 44km, along which you'll pass fishing villages (**Northwest Cove** is the prettiest), lovely **Bayswater Beach**, another memorial to Swissair Flight 111 (box, page 140), and more wonderful ocean views.

Near **Blandford**, the largest community on the peninsula, and the former home of a whaling station, there are views across to East Ironbound Island (box, page 147). This is home to your best bet for a bite to eat – **The Deck** (*9 Firehall Rd;* ☏ *902 228 2112;* 🄵 *; ⊕ year-round 06.00–21.00 Mon–Fri, 09.00–21.00 Sat & Sun; $–$$*), a general store and licensed café, serving superb coconut cream pie.

CHESTER AND AROUND

On the waterfront at the northern head of beautiful island-dotted Mahone Bay, Chester (population: approx 1,200) enjoys a delightful setting. Whilst specific sights are limited to one museum, it's a great place to take in a performance at the theatre, enjoy the Front Harbour waterfront and browse the trendy upmarket shops, watch the yachts on the beautiful bay, play golf, wander the shady, quiet, tree-lined residential streets past elegant (and particularly expensive) mansions, admire the beautifully kept gardens, or just unwind with a coffee and pastry.

Chester has long been popular with Americans: with all the shiny, sleek yachts replacing the usual rugged fishing boats, it feels more sophisticated – and American – than most of the province's seafront communities. The town's population almost doubles during the summer months.

HISTORY Chester was first settled in 1759, predominantly by New England Planters. A blockhouse – with 20 cannons on the roof – was erected soon after to deter hostile Mi'kmaq from entering the settlement. Two of the original mid 18th-century cannons are now mounted outside the Legion Hall. It is recorded that porcupine and baked beaver were two dishes popular with early settlers.

The village prospered, initially as a result of fishing. Chester's first hotel was built in 1827, and several more followed. In the mid 19th century, John Wister, an American from Philadelphia, stopped here *en route* between Yarmouth and Halifax and fell in love with the place. He built a summer home and a yacht, invited his friends over, and they did the same. From such simple beginnings, Chester became known as the 'American town'.

GETTING THERE AND AWAY Accessible **by car**, Chester is on Highway 3, and about 5km/3 miles from Highway 103, Exit 8. It is 67km/42 miles from Halifax and 31km/19 miles from Lunenburg. The **Cloud Nine Shuttle** (page 137) operates daily between Yarmouth and Halifax.

A **ferry** service connects Chester with the Tancook Islands (page 150).

ROCKBOUND

East Ironbound Island is best known as the setting for a 1928 novel by Frank Parker Day. *Rockbound* gives a wonderfully authentic picture of the lives of those farming and fishing on the island. When published, it has to be said that the islanders were far from happy with the way their lives had been portrayed.

WHERE TO STAY *Map, pages 142–3, unless otherwise stated*

🏠 **Gray Gables** (3 rooms) 19 Graves Island Rd; 📞902 275 2000; www.graygables.ca; ⊕ May–Oct (o/s by reservation). Lovely, spacious house with big veranda on hillside overlooking Mahone Bay.

Outdoor hot tub. Close to the golf course, approx 3.5km from 'downtown' Chester. Rate includes full b/fast (off-season continental b/fast). **$$**

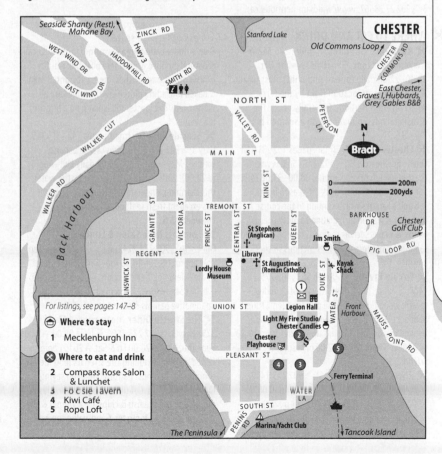

CHESTER

For listings, see pages 147–8

🛏 **Where to stay**
1 Mecklenburgh Inn

✖ **Where to eat and drink**
2 Compass Rose Salon & Lunchet
3 Fo'c'sle Tavern
4 Kiwi Café
5 Rope Loft

South Shore   CHESTER AND AROUND

4

In 1782, three American privateer ships sailed into the harbour and opened fire on the settlement. Shots were exchanged. Knowing that the militia was away from the village and fearing a land attack, something had to be done. The women of the town turned their capes inside out to show their red linings (at the time, the British militia wore red coats), picked up muskets and broomsticks, and marched through the village. Watching from a distance, the privateers were fooled and decided to leave in search of easier pickings, sacking Lunenburg (page 157) the next day.

🏠 **Mecklenburgh Inn** [map, page 147] (4 rooms) 78 Queen St; ☎ 902 275 4638; www. mecklenburghinn.ca; ⊕ May–Dec. A shipwright-built, eclectically decorated c1902 hillside property with fine sea views from covered balconies. Full gourmet b/fast inc (the hostess is a Cordon Bleu chef). **$$**

🏠 **Windjammer Motel** (18 rooms) 4070 Hwy 3; ☎ 902 275 3567; www.windjammermotel.ca; ⊕ year-round. Traditional sgl-storey motel, some rooms have AC, all are spacious & have a small fridge. Camping apart, this is Chester's budget option, so don't expect 5-star frills. **$**

🏕 **Graves Island Provincial Park Campground** (84 sites) Hwy 3; parks.novascotia. ca/content/graves-island; ⊕ late May–early Oct. A pleasant campground with open & wooded sites. **$**

✖ WHERE TO EAT AND DRINK *Map, page 147, unless otherwise stated*

✖ **Rope Loft** 36 Water St; ☎ 902 275 3430; www.ropeloft.com; ⊕ early May–late Oct 11.30–22.00 daily (pub til midnight). Restaurant & pub with great location right by the ferry wharf on Front Harbour. Generally good (the occasional miss) pub food with a seafood bias. **$$–$$$**

✖ **Chester Golf Club** [map, pages 142–3] Golf Course Rd, Prescott Pt; ☎ 902 275 4543; www. chestergolfclub.ca; ⊕ summer 08.00–21.00 Mon–Sat, 08.00–20.00 Sun; check off-season hours. Fab golf apart, it's worth coming to the course for food that is way above par. Good sandwiches & wraps, & mains such as seafood crêpes & poached salmon. Sometimes used for functions so check in advance. **$$**

✖ **Fo'c'sle Tavern** 42 Queen St; ☎ 902 275 1408; ⊕ from 11.00 daily. Nova Scotia's oldest tavern: wood floors, upscale pub food (eg: stuffed haddock), good beer selection (try the Garrison-brewed Fo'c'sle Ale). Closing time varies from 19.30 on a quiet winter day to 02.00 on a summer w/end. **$$**

✖ **Kiwi Café** 19 Pleasant St; ☎ 902 275 1492; www.kiwicafechester.com; ⊕ year-round 08.00–17.00 daily (plus 17.30–21.00 Fri for pizzas). Bright, welcoming, busy, even a bit funky, this friendly licensed café has a fire for cool winter days & an outdoor eating area in warmer months. Local & natural produce used where possible. All-day b/fasts, soups, sandwiches, more substantial meals & baked (including gluten-free) goodies are all worthwhile. The lobster roll (served on a brioche) is a winner. **$$**

✖ **Seaside Shanty** [map, pages 142–3] 5315 Hwy 3; ☎ 902 275 2246; www.seasideshanty. com; ⊕ May–Oct 11.30–20.00 daily (Jul–Aug til 21.00). With a shaded deck right by the water, this charming, understated, licensed restaurant has excellent fresh seafood, & is known for its chowders. **$$**

✖ **Compass Rose Salon & Lunchet** 44-4 Queen St; ☎ 902 273 2242; 🔲 ; ⊕ café May–Sep only approx 08.30–16.30 Tue–Sat. Hairdressers (male & female), beauty salon, & good little café – b/fast sandwiches, homemade baked goods, imaginative paninis & soups, etc. **$–$$**

✖ **The Stretch Diner** [map, pages 142–3] 3758 Hwy 3; ☎ 902 273 7506; 🔲 ; ⊕ 08.00–19.00 Sun–Thu, 08.30–20.00 Fri & Sat. A 2015 *Chronicle-Herald* mention extolling The Stretch's food merely confirmed what most patrons had been saying for some time. Most of the shortish menu doesn't disappoint, but the fish & chips are a winner & the pies worth saving room for. Good-value specials. **$–$$**.

BUTTERBOX BABIES

In the late 1920s, Lila and William Young started up a maternity home in east Chester. Most of those using their services were unwed mothers who paid the Youngs to adopt and care for their babies. The Youngs set up what was effectively a black market for babies: those who could pay thousands of dollars could have their pick of the children in the Youngs' care.

But there was an even more disturbing twist: many babies were deemed 'undesirable', and on these, the Youngs had no desire to waste time or resources. It is thought that hundreds of tiny tragic victims were slowly starved to death and their bodies disposed of in wooden boxes used for packing butter.

OTHER PRACTICALITIES

$ Scotiabank 2 Pleasant St; ✆ 902 275 3540; ⊕ 10.00–17.00 Mon–Fri
✉ Post office 76 Queen St; ⊕ 08.30–17.00 Mon–Fri, 08.00–noon Sat
ℹ Tourist information 20 Smith Rd; ✆ 902 275 4616; ⊕ Jun 10.00–17.00 daily; Jul–Aug 09.00–19.00 daily; Sep 10.00–17.00 daily; Oct–May

11.00–16.00 Thu–Sun. Housed in the old train station just off Hwy 3 on the west side of town.
🚕 South Shore Taxi ✆ 902 277 2727;
f Zoe Valle Library 63 Regent St; ✆ 902 275 2190; zoevallelibrary.wordpress.com; ⊕ hours vary (see website)

WHAT TO SEE AND DO The **Lordly House Museum and Park** (*133 Central St;* ✆ *902 275 3842; www.chester-municipal-heritage-society.ca;* ⊕ *mid Jun–mid Sep 10.00–17.00 Tue–Sat, 13.00–16.00 Sun; admission free*) is a fine, virtually unchanged, restored c1806 Georgian-style house in lovely park grounds. It was home to Charles Lordly, the district's first municipal clerk, and adjacent is a restored cottage, which was – in the late 1800s – Chester's first municipal office. It has survived with many original features intact. In addition to displays on Lordly and family, there is a section on the 'butterbox babies' (box, above), a genealogy research area and a children's playground.

At the **Kayak Shack** (*89 Water St/106 Duke St;* ✆ *902 980 0522; www.kayakshack. ca;* ⊕ *mid May–mid Oct*) are kayaks, canoes, SUP boards and bikes to rent to explore Chester's beautiful waters and coastline. Tours and (possibly) sailing lessons may be offered.

Candle-making studio and gift store, the **Light My Fire Studio/Chester Candles** (*59 Duke St;* ✆ *902 275 5800;* tf *1 866 739 5800; www.chestercandles.com;* ⊕ *Jun–Dec 10.00–17.00 daily, rest of year 10.00–17.00 Thu–Sat, 11.00–16.00 Sun*), holds wax workshops and classes. Also check out the lyrical ceramics at **Jim Smith – Fine Studio Pottery** (*cnr Water & Duke sts;* ✆ *902 275 3272; jimsmithstudio.ca;* ⊕ *Jun–Sep 10.00–18.00 Mon–Sat, noon–18.00 Sun; Oct–May by chance or appointment*).

The **Chester Playhouse** (*22 Pleasant St;* ✆ *902 275 3933;* tf *1 800 363 7529; www. chesterplayhouse.ca*) is a small theatre that hosts a range of music, theatre and more between early spring and late autumn.

Mainland Nova Scotia has many beautiful, scenic golf courses, and the 6,080yd **Chester Golf Course** (*Golf Course Rd, Prescott Pt;* ✆ *902 275 4543; www. chestergolfclub.ca;* ⊕ *May–Oct; green fees CAN$72*) is one of the best – it also has a great restaurant (page 148). When the sun is out, magnificent views of the bay and islands will either inspire your game or make you lose concentration.

A pretty, often breezy park 3km east of Chester, **Graves Island Provincial Park** (*Hwy 3; parks.novascotia.ca/content/graves-island;* ⊕ *late May–early Oct*) can be

South Shore **CHESTER AND AROUND** 4

TEAZER

In 1813, American privateer ships regularly threatened marine traffic off Nova Scotia's shores. One such vessel, *Young Teazer*, was chased into Mahone Bay by a British ship and was trapped. But rather than be captured, one of the crew threw a flaming brand through the magazine hatch. The resulting explosion was felt and seen by hundreds of people around the bay and most on board were killed instantly. Almost 200 years later, there are regular reports of supposed sightings of the ghost of the *Young Teazer* sailing through Mahone Bay before exploding into a ball of fire.

reached by a short causeway – it's a good picnic spot, with a small beach, playground, trails and campground (page 148).

FESTIVALS Under the auspices of the Chester Yacht Club, the big event of the year is the **Chester Race Week** (*www.chesterraceweek.com*), the largest keel-boat regatta in Atlantic Canada, held in mid August. The first documented regatta was held here in 1856 and attracted crowds of over 3,000; these days, the parties and events are every bit as important as the races – a must for sailors and socialites. In Lordly Park on Tuesday evenings in July and August, **Picnic in the Park** (**f** *Picnicintheparkchester*) is popular and fun with live music. **Band concerts** (*www.chesterbrass.com*) are held at the Chester bandstand (*4 Peninsula Rd*) on Friday evenings during July and August.

AROUND CHESTER
Tancook Islands Take a trip back in time to the two Tancook islands at the mouth of Mahone Bay, a 55-minute ferry ride from Chester. Both islands offer walking trails, good birding, and peace and quiet. You can rent bikes 200m from the ferry terminal on the larger island at **Tancook Bicycle Rentals** (*696 Big Tancook Island Rd;* e *tancookbikes@eastlink.ca;* ⊕ *mid May–mid Oct*) or at Carolyn's Restaurant (see below). The passenger ferry makes between one and four crossings a day (⊕ *times vary: they are posted at the ferry terminal or check with the Chester tourist information office; CAN$7 return*). If you're thinking of visiting, www.tancookislandtourism.ca may be of use (if someone updates it).

Where to stay, eat and drink Little Tancook has no services, but the larger Tancook Island (approx 4.5km long and 1.5km wide) offers eat-in or take-out at **Carolyn's Restaurant** (*656 Tancook Island Rd;* ✆ *902 228 2749;* ⊕ *Jun–Oct 11.30–19.00 daily; $–$$*). For overnighters, accommodation choices are limited to wilderness camping or perhaps a private rental (try *airbnb.ca* or *kijiji.ca*).

New Ross New Ross – located approximately 31km inland from Chester – is worth a short detour so you can visit **Ross Farm** (*4568 Hwy 12, New Ross;* **tf** *1 877 689 2210; rossfarm.novascotia.ca;* ⊕ *May–Oct 09.00–17.00 daily; Nov–Apr 09.30–16.30 Wed–Sun; admission CAN$8*). Located on 25ha well inland, this living museum aims to remind people that – in addition to the sea – the land played an important part in shaping Nova Scotia's past. Costumed interpreters demonstrate typical farm activities, heritage skills and crafts common 100–175 years ago. Oxen teams work the fields, there are heritage breeds of farm animals, early 19th-century buildings, a nature trail, several activities and special events throughout the year. Good for children.

New Ross is on Highway 12, between Chester (31km/19 miles) and Kentville (43km/27 miles), and easy to reach **by car**. Take Exit 9 from Highway 103, or Exit 13 from Highway 101.

✗ **Where to eat and drink** Food-wise, **Vittles Café** (*4496 Hwy 12;* ✆ *902 689 2236;* ⊕ *usually 08.00–20.00 daily; $–$$*) is your standard Nova Scotian family diner. More sophisticated is the rather good **Peasant's Pantry & Deli** (*4491 Hwy 12;* ✆ *902 365 5964; www.peasantspantry.ca;* ⊕ *summer 09.00–18.00 Tue–Sun (Thu–Sat til 19.00), winter check; $–$$*) where much is made from scratch and the focus is on fresh, local ingredients (particularly meat). Before you head on, pop in to **Muwin Estates Wines & Bulwark Cider** (*7153 Hwy 12;* ✆ *902 681 1545;* ⓕ; ⊕ *year-round 08.30–16.30*), where you can taste and buy fruit and dessert wines, and the excellent 'hard' cider. Tours may be offered – call to check.

If you are passing through New Ross on a Saturday morning (*Jun–Sep 09.00–noon*) there's a small country **farmers' market** just by Ross Farm.

Western Shore This bayside community has a good low-budget seafood diner, a resort with restaurant and spa, kayak rentals, and one of the world's most storied little islands (box, pages 154–5). Accessible **by car**, Western Shore is on Highway 3, 13km from Chester, 11km from Mahone Bay, and 8–10km from either Exit 9 or 10 from Highway 103.

🏠 **Where to stay, eat and drink**

🏠 **Atlantica Oak Island Resort & Conference Centre** (119 units) 36 Treasure Dr; ✆ 902 627 2600; tf 1 800 565 5075; www. atlanticaoakisland.com; ⊕ year-round. In addition to 103 guestrooms, 13 ocean-front chalets & 3 seaside villas, facilities include indoor & outdoor pools, fitness centre, minigolf, kayaking, tennis & spa. The resort is not on the famous island, but overlooks it. The La Vista restaurant (⊕ *year-round 07.00–10.00, 11.00–14.00 & 17.00–20.00 daily; $$–$$$*) offers ocean views. **$$**

✗ **Island View Family Restaurant** 6301 Hwy 3; ✆ 902 627 2513; ⊕ Mar–Dec daily (winter 11.00–19.00; summer 11.00–20.00). Right on the waterfront, this low-budget favourite known locally as the 'Green Canteen' dishes up good diner-style seafood. The fries aren't great, so pay a bit extra for the sweet potato version. **$–$$**

MAHONE BAY

Apart from Peggys Cove, Mahone Bay's three churches are one of *the* iconic tourist images of Nova Scotia.

But there's far more to do in this charming and prosperous town than take a photo and move on, with several studios and galleries to investigate, a museum to visit, the bay and its islands to explore, and some excellent eateries to try.

Behind the tourist information office is an atmospheric old cemetery, and architecture buffs will find faithfully preserved buildings in a variety of styles including Italianate and Gothic Revival, many of these now housing B&Bs, restaurants and shops. While it may not have the range of accommodation offered in Lunenburg (pages 158–60), it isn't a bad choice for a base from which to explore the region.

In recent decades, the beautiful setting and relaxed way of life have attracted artists, artisans and musicians, and a number of galleries and studios are dotted along Main Street. Worryingly, the first condominiums have begun to spring up and more may be on their way. Hopefully, this 'motel/box store/shopping mall-free' town won't begin to lose its character.

HISTORY Known to the Mi'kmaq as '*Mushamush*' and one of their favourite camping grounds, the town was founded in 1754. The majority of the early settlers were European (specifically German, French, and Swiss) Protestants, enticed by the British government's offer of free land, farm equipment, and a year's provisions. A few decades later there was a large influx of New Englanders; mills were built at the head of the bay, and from 1850 to the early 20th century, shipbuilding thrived along the waterfront. At one time there were 18 different shipyards around Mahone Bay. With over 350 islands offering plenty of hiding places, the area has long been connected with pirates – a *mahone* was a low-lying craft used by buccaneers.

GETTING THERE AND AWAY Mahone Bay is easy to reach **by car**; it is on Highway 3 (take Exit 10 from Hwy 103), 86km/54 miles from Halifax. **By shuttle**, the Cloud Nine Shuttle (page 137) operates daily both ways between Yarmouth and Halifax.

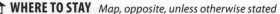 **WHERE TO STAY** *Map, opposite, unless otherwise stated*

Bayview Pines Country Inn [map, pages 142–3] (8 rooms, 2 apts) 678 Oakland Rd, Indian Point; \902 624 9970; tf 1 866 624 9970; www. bayviewpines.com; ⊕ May–Oct; off-season by reservation. An old farmhouse & converted barn on 5.7ha overlooking the bay & islands, approx 6km from town. Most rooms have decks & balconies. Beach access, kayak launch, walking trails. Full b/fast inc in room (but not apt) rates. **$$**

Fairmont House B&B (3 rooms) 654 Main St; \902 624 8089; www.fairmonthouse. com; ⊕ year-round. Built by a shipbuilder, this outstanding c1857 Gothic Revival home still has the original curved staircase – held together with wooden pegs rather than nails or screws – in the entry hall. Cable TV, AC & heat control in rooms; free Wi-Fi. En-suite bathrooms. Full b/fast inc. **$$**

Fisherman's Daughter B&B (4 rooms) 97 Edgewater St; \902 624 0660; www.fishermans-daughter.com; ⊕ May–Nov; off-season by reservation. A heritage-designated home built c1850, once owned by an important shipbuilder & centrally located between 2 of the 3 famous churches. Complimentary snack cupboard. Enhanced 'continental -plus' b/fast inc. **$$**

Kip & Kaboodle Tourist Accommodation [map, pages 142–3] 9466 Hwy 3; \902 531 5494; www.kiwikaboodle.com; ⊕ May–Oct. A small backpacker hostel 3km from the town centre on the road to Lunenburg, with bunk beds in 2 mixed rooms & 1 private dbl room (rooms share 2 bathrooms), communal kitchen, BBQ & common room. Bikes to rent, biking & hiking tours offered. Linen inc. Transfers to/from Halifax can be arranged for those staying 3 nights or more. *Dorm CAN$30, private room CAN$69* **$**

WHERE TO EAT AND DRINK *Map, opposite*

Mateus Bistro 533 Main St; \902 531 3711; www.mateusbistro.com; ⊕ year-round (mid May–mid Oct 11.30–21.00 Thu–Mon, 17.00–21.00 Tue–Wed; mid Oct–mid May 17.00–21.00 Mon, Thu & Fri, 11.30–20.30 Sat & Sun). Bratislava-born Matthew Krizan sources fresh, local produce & prepares it with European flair. Lunch might include 3-cheese fondue or steamed mussels, dinner could be citrus trout with kale. Large deck for alfresco dining. *Lunch* **$$**, *dinner* **$$–$$$**

Biscuit Eater Books & Café 16 Oxford St; \902 624 2665; biscuiteater.ca; ⊕ usually 09.00–16.30 Wed–Mon. Quality soups, salads, sandwiches & much more in this licensed café & new/used book shop. **$$**

Oh My Cod! 567 Main St; \902 531 2600; www.oh-my-cod.ca; ⊕ summer 08.00–21.00 (kitchen til 20.00) daily, reduced hours o/s. Excellent seafood but more too, including good b/fasts. Luckily they've resisted the urge to pepper (ha!) the menu with food puns. **$$**

Rebecca's Restaurant 619 Main St; \902 531 3313; www.rebeccas-restaurant.ca; ⊕ year-round 11.00–20.00 Tue–Sat, 11.00–15.00

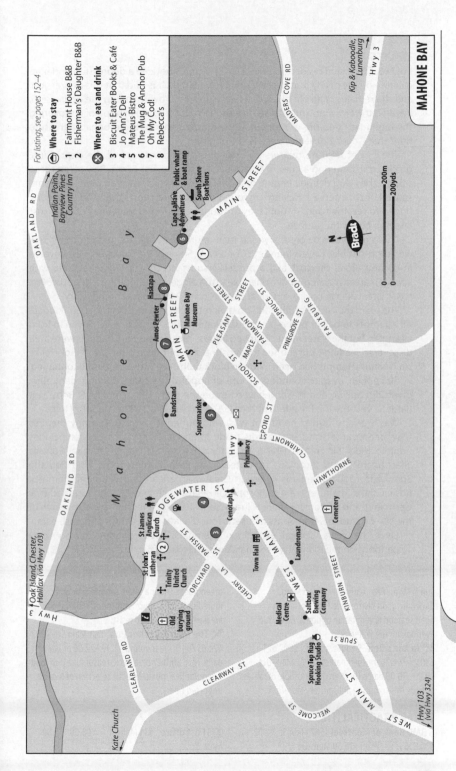

For listings, see pages 152-4

Where to stay
1 Fairmont House B&B
2 Fisherman's Daughter B&B

Where to eat and drink
3 Biscuit Eater Books & Café
4 Jo Ann's Deli
5 Mateus Bistro
6 The Mug & Anchor Pub
7 Oh My Cod!
8 Rebecca's

MAHONE BAY

200m
200yds

In 1795, Oak Island resident Donald Daniel McInnis noticed a depression under an oak tree on the newly purchased land of John Smith. It is said that this depression, and the remains of an old block and tackle on a limb overhanging the depression, inspired the two men and teenager Anthony Vaughn to dig in hope of discovering the legendary treasure of Captain Kidd. In doing so, the three began a treasure hunt that – over 220 years later – is still ongoing.

The trio of treasure hunters dug down in to the soft soil of the depression, quickly encountering a layer of flagstones within the first 60cm. Removing these stones, they dug deeper, finding first one, then another wooden plank platform, spaced in 3m intervals. Having not found the treasure chests they had so eagerly hoped to see, they dug on, until they encountered another thick layer of plank just over 9m below the surface.

It was nine years before the young men returned: at first, the pattern continued, with more oak plank layers found at 3m intervals. Some of the oak layers were covered in coconut fibre, charcoal, and a putty-like substance. A large granite stone with strange, carved markings, indecipherable to the diggers, was found at a depth of 30m. It was later taken to Halifax, and disappeared in 1919 (but that's another story).

The team took a day's break and on their return, found most of the shaft flooded. All attempts to bail or pump out the salt water failed. Tunnels were driven in from all angles, but the water menace proved impossible to conquer. Channels were then discovered leading from the sea towards the site, but even after (what looked like successful) attempts had been made to block them, the water problems continued.

Since then, despite countless groups of hopeful searchers, digging, damming, diverting, drilling and blasting haven't done the trick. Even Franklin D Roosevelt (later to become the President of the USA) was part of a 1909 expedition here.

Was 'treasure' buried here? If it was, who buried it? Almost as many theories have been put forward as attempts made to find it. The list of suspects includes Captain Kidd, Sir Francis Drake, Sir Francis Bacon, Sir Henry Morgan, Edward 'Blackbeard' Teach, Acadians uprooted from their homes, Incas who fled the Spaniards, rogue Spaniards diverting Central American booty, Knights Templar, Rosicrusians (members of a philosophical secret society originating in medieval Germany), and (of course) aliens. Clue-wise, in 1965, an electromagnetic search of the site by students from Massachusetts found a late 16th-century Spanish coin.

Over the years, several expedition members have reported seeing scary apparitions on the island. Two 'regulars' are said to be a man in a red frock coat who

Sun & Mon, (Feb–early May closed Mon). Generally good bistro-style food (including good seafood & vegetarian options), nice patio overlooking the water. $$
✗ **Jo Ann's Deli** 9 Edgewater St; ☏902 624 6305; www.joannsdelimarket.ca; ⊕ May–Oct 09.00–20.00 daily. There are just a couple of tables outside this tempting deli/grocery store/bakery/ greengrocer. Order a salad, sandwich or grab ingredients for a gourmet picnic: the baked goods are particularly hard to resist. $
✗ **The Mug & Anchor Pub** 643 Main St; ☏902 624 6378; ⊕ year-round 11.30–22.00 or later daily. Nice ambience, a deck, reasonable pub food & regular live music. Eclectic selection of local & imported beers. $

OTHER PRACTICALITIES
$ **BMO Bank of Montreal** 562 Main St; ☏902 624 8355; ⊕ 09.30–16.30 Mon–Fri

✉ **Post office** 534 Main St; ⊕ 08.00–17.00 Mon–Fri

leaves no footprints in the sand, and a very large dog with red eyes that appears to stand guard at various sites on the island. More recent searches, studies and excavations suggest that an incredibly sophisticated series of tunnels and cavities connected to the sea lies underground: thus far, modern science and techniques is still losing out to the as yet unidentified engineering genius who designed and constructed it several centuries ago. By 1995, treasure hunters had managed to dig almost 60m underground: the treasure – if there is any – still has not been found.

Well over 220 years have now passed since McInnis made his find: six treasure hunters have lost their lives, including four who died after inhaling noxious fumes on a 1965 expedition. Ironically, regardless of whatever lies buried under Oak Island, literally millions of dollars have been spent trying to find it.

And what of the island in recent times? The greater part of the 58ha island – now connected to the mainland by a causeway – is now owned by Oak Island Tours Incorporated, a group comprised of Dan Blankenship, the Lagina brothers, Craig Tester, and others, who for the last eight years, have carried on the quest to solve the mystery. For the past three years, their efforts have been chronicled in a television show on the History Channel titled 'Curse of Oak Island', giving the general public an unprecedented look into the ongoing treasure hunt. Theories are being examined, evidence cited in the past is being reconfirmed, exploratory holes are being drilled, digging has been carried out, science is being brought to bear, and the island continues to tantalise and fascinate new generations, all while the treasure remains as elusive as ever.

The Oak Island mystery has inspired hundreds of articles, dozens of books and numerous documentaries: in more recent times three good websites (*www.oakislandtreasure.co.uk*, that of the Friends of Oak Island Society; *www.friendsofoakisland.com*, and The Oak Island Compendium, *www. oakislandcompendium.ca*), keep those fascinated by the story up to date. There's a display on Oak Island under the auspices of the Chester Municipal Heritage Society (*www.chester-municipal-heritage-society.ca*) at Chester's old railway station (adjacent to the tourist office; page 149).

The Friends of Oak Island Society offer guided public tours of the island during various weekends in the summer and early autumn. Check the website for details. That apart, there are views of the island from Western Shore's Wild Rose Park, and Crandall Point Road takes you to the beginning of the causeway. For accommodation options, see page 151.

i **Tourist information** 165 Edgewater St; ☎902 624 6151; tf 1 888 624 6151; ✆ Jun–   early Sep 10.00–17.00 Mon–Thu, 10.00–18.00 Fri & Sun

WHAT TO SEE AND DO The classic view of the Mahone Bay skyline – with its three churches reflected in the bay's still water – has become one of the most photographed scenes in Nova Scotia. The white church with a tower on the right is the **Trinity United Church**. The oldest of the three, it dates from 1861 and was formerly Knox Presbyterian. Originally located further back, it was dragged to its present location by teams of oxen in 1885. The middle church is **St John's Lutheran** built in 1869, and the newest church, the high Victorian Gothic Revival-style **St James Anglican Church** sits on the left and was built in 1887. Music at the Three Churches (☎ *902 634 4280; www.threechurches.com*) is a series of classical concerts held fortnightly on Friday evenings between early July and early September. Tickets cost CAN$20.

If you're a fan of arts and crafts, there's plenty to keep you entertained in town. Watch and learn about the pewter-crafting process at **Amos Pewter** (*589 Main St;* ☏ *902 624 9547;* tf *1 800 565 3369; www.amospewter.com;* ⊕ *Jul–Aug 09.00–19.00 Mon–Sat, 10.00–19.00 Sun: check for o/s hours*), or get interactive and finish your own piece (*CAN$5*). Meanwhile, artist **Kate Church** (*60 Old Clearland Rd;* ☏ *902 624 1597; www.katechurch.com;* ⊕ *Jun–Nov by appointment*) is best known for sculptural figures made with wire, cloth and clay. Alternatively, visit the **Spruce Top Rug Hooking Studio** (*255 West Main St;* ☏ *902 624 9312;* tf *1 888 784 4665; www.sprucetoprughookingstudio. com;* ⊕ *year-round 10.00–16.00 Mon & Wed–Sat, noon–16.00 Sun; admission free*), which claims to have the largest collection of hooked rugs in Atlantic Canada. Regular classes are held, and you may be able to see new works being created.

For foodies, **The Saltbox Brewing Company** (*363 Main St;* ☏ *902 624 0653; www. saltboxbrewingcompany.ca;* ⊕ *check hours*) is a new (2016) craft brewery in a historic building. There's a Tap Room for tasting, sampling or just relaxing with a beer. With the meteoric rise of the haskap berry (aka honeyberry), it is no surprise that people want to focus on marketing this 'superfood'. So head in to **Haskapa** (*607 Main St;* ☏ *902 624 8039; haskapa.com;* ⊕ *summer 10.00–18.00 daily, check o/s*) for all things haskap.

For a history of Mahone Bay's shipbuilding industry and the Foreign Protestants who came and settled the area, visit the **Mahone Bay Museum** (*578 Main St;* ☏ *902 624 6263; www.mahonebaymuseum.com;* ⊕ *Jun–Sep 10.00–16.00 daily; admission free*). The story of the family that lived in the (c1847) house is also told.

South Shore Boat Tours (☏ *902 543 5107; www.southshoreboattours.com/tours. html;* ⊕ *Jun–Oct*) runs daily 2-hour tours on a 38ft boat to see dolphins, seabirds, seals, etc, plus 4-hour trips in search of whales and Pearl Island's puffins in season (*CAN$35–50*). If boat tours are for wimps, **Cape LaHave Adventures** (*643 Main St (Mader's Wharf);* ☏ *902 693 2023; www.capelahaveadventures.ca;* ⊕ *May–Oct*) offer SUP and kayaking lessons, rentals and sales – no experience is necessary.

In late September, three days of music, illuminated hand-carved pumpkins, quilting workshops – not to mention scarecrows and antiques – can be enjoyed at the **Scarecrow Festival and Antique Fair**.

LUNENBURG AND AROUND

All in all, Lunenburg – roughly equidistant from Halifax and Shelburne – is one of Nova Scotia's most interesting and appealing towns. Established in 1753, the original town layout has been maintained and many original wooden buildings preserved, with eight dating back to the 18th century. As the best-surviving example of a planned British colonial settlement in North America, Lunenburg's Old Town section was designated a national historic district by the Canadian government, and in 1995 it was declared a cultural UNESCO World Heritage site, one of only eight in the whole of Canada.

The Old Town sits on a steep hillside overlooking the harbour, and as you drive – or better still, walk – through you'll realise just how steep some of the narrow streets are. A guided walking tour should satisfy those wishing to dig deeper, and if walking is not for you, you can even see the sights by horse and carriage. Also within an easy drive or cycle ride are several beautiful small forested peninsulas and two tiny photogenic fishing villages well worth exploring.

Many of the well-preserved brightly painted historical buildings now house inns, cafés, restaurants, shops and a seemingly ever-increasing number of galleries. Long ago, as it prospered and grew, the town spread beyond the original grid. In residential streets a few minutes' walk away are more magnificent homes, this time on much bigger plots of land. Some – with large lawns and beautiful gardens – are now B&Bs or inns. In the Old Town area, most of the shops, museums and services are in the rectangle bounded by the waterfront, Lincoln, Cornwallis and Hopson streets.

Today, the fishing industry may have dried up here, but the marine traditions and its seafaring heritage live on proudly. The Fisheries Museum of the Atlantic (page 163) will help you understand not just Lunenburg, but coastal communities throughout the province. A dory shop on the waterfront has been making small wooden fishing boats since 1895, and traditional methods are still used. The town is the homeport of the *Bluenose II* (box, page 161), and tall ships often grace the picturesque harbour.

Looking down over parts of the town is the imposing black-and-white c1894 academy, **Lunenburg Academy** [159 B1] (*97 Kaulbach St*). Renovations were recently completed, and space has been let out to various tenants, such as the Lunenburg Academy of Music Performance (page 162). There's even talk of a café...

Much of *Haven* (a TV series about a fictional town in Maine, USA, based loosely on a Stephen King novel) was filmed in Lunenburg. The show ran for five seasons until 2015, and visitor numbers have seen an increase as a result.

HISTORY Early in 1753, a fleet of over a dozen ships from Halifax landed on the site of the Mi'kmaq village of *Merligueche* – 'Milky Waters'. The incomers were mostly Protestants from German-speaking parts of Europe. Land was cleared, defences built, and parcels of land dealt out. The settlement was laid out on what had become a standard plan for new coastal towns, in a compact grid with seven north–south streets intersected by nine east–west streets. It was named for King George II, Duke of Brunschweig-Lunenburg.

In the early years, the Mi'kmaq proved a threat to the settlers, several of whom were killed or taken prisoner until peace was agreed between government officials and Mi'kmaq chiefs in 1762. The next threat came from the sea; in 1782, privateer ships arrived without warning and about 100 armed men rushed ashore, plundering and burning at will.

The early settlers were far more familiar with farming than fishing, but many quickly began to take advantage of the seemingly inexhaustible bounty of the sea. As a consequence, they also became skilled shipbuilders. As the years passed, this port – on a splendid harbour protected by long peninsulas – became home to a huge fishing fleet.

At the turn of the 20th century, Lunenburg's schooner fleet sailed the Grand Banks, competing with the fleets of New England to bring home the abundance

4

THE BACK ROAD TO LUNENBURG

From Mahone Bay, the main route to Lunenburg is along Highway 3. A more interesting route – delightful on a sunny day – is to leave Mahone Bay towards Lunenburg on Highway 3 then turn left onto Maders Cove Road. Bear left onto Sunnybrook Road, then turn left onto Hermans Island Road. Bear left onto Princes Inlet Drive. At the fork, either bear right to rejoin Highway 3 (turn left to continue to Lunenburg) or, for another scenic side-trip, bear left along Second Peninsula Road. Go this way and you'll eventually have to turn back and retrace your steps, but you'll have passed some tranquil, delightful waters, and Second Peninsula Provincial Park. If you're doing this route in reverse, from Lunenburg, turn right from Highway 3 onto Second Peninsula Road.

of cod. Fishing – especially in the treacherous seas around Nova Scotia – was a dangerous pursuit, and over the years hundreds lost their lives at sea.

For a comedic and musical version of the area's history, see page 162.

GETTING THERE AND AWAY Lunenburg is on Highway 3 and 14km/9 miles from Highway 103 Exit 11, and easy to reach **by car**. It is 100km/62 miles from Halifax, 19km/12 miles from Bridgewater and 11km/7 miles from Mahone Bay. **By shuttle**, the Cloud Nine Shuttle (page 137) operates daily between Yarmouth and Halifax.

I would recommend staying a night or two at the very least, but if you just want a quick visit from Halifax, Murphy's the Cable Wharf (page 93) runs a 6-hour Lunenburg and Mahone Bay sightseeing tour from June to mid October at 10.00 on Sundays, Tuesdays and Thursdays (*CAN$98*).

 WHERE TO STAY In Lunenburg, it seems as though the wishes of everyone who ever dreamt of owning a centuries-old house and running it as a B&B have come true. There are dozens, many in the Old Town and several in the quiet tree-lined residential streets less than 10 minutes' walk away. Lunenburg is a very popular base for visitors to the South Shore: despite the quantity of places to stay, many only have two or three rooms so it makes sense to book in advance for July and August. The businesses listed below are open year-round unless otherwise stated.

Upmarket

🏠 **2nd Paradise Retreat** [map, pages 142–3] (4 units) Second Peninsula Rd; ✆ 902 634 4099; www.secondparadise.ns.ca. A lovely Second Peninsula location 6km (10mins' drive) from Lunenburg. 2, 2-bedroom cottages, a 6-bedroom farmhouse & loft set on 11ha of protected oceanfront with private beach. Eco-friendly. Reservations required. **$$$**

Mid range

🏠 **Kaulbach House** [159 D3] (6 rooms) 75 Pelham St; ✆ 902 634 8818; **tf** 1 800 568 8818; www.kaulbachhouse.com; ⏰ May–Oct; off-season by reservation. An elegant, c1880 property

---

LUNENBURG BUMP

Not a ghost story or a dance, but a unique architectural feature seen in a number of forms in the Old Town, and occasionally elsewhere in the province, is the Lunenburg bump. Inspired by the five-sided Scottish dormer, the Lunenburg bump is a central dormer extended out and down from the roof, thereby creating an overhang – or 'bump' – above the main entrance. If historical architecture is one of your interests, visit the tourist office and pick up an informative architectural walking tour guide to the town.

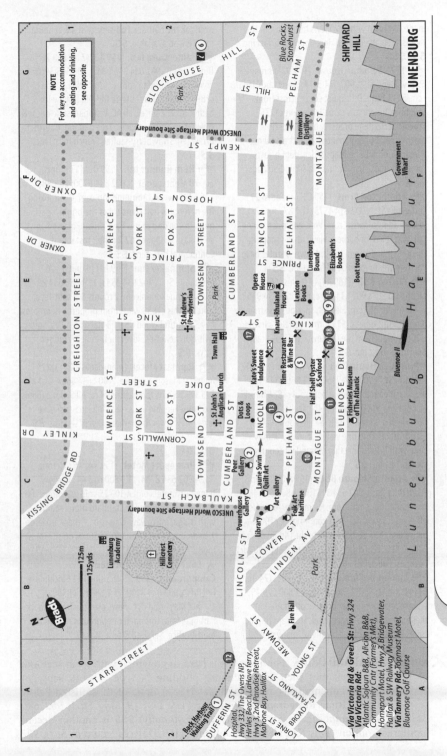

NOTE
For key to accommodation
and eating and drinking,
see opposite

LUNENBURG

in the Old Town with sea views from most of the rooms. Free off-road parking. Gourmet b/fast inc. **$$–$$$**

⌂ **1775 Solomon House** [159 D2] (3 rooms) 69 Townsend St; ✆ 902 634 3477; www.bbcanada.com/5511.html. On a quiet street across from St John's Church, this casually elegant c1775 Provincial Heritage property has one of the most original Georgian interiors in the province. Personalised touring maps & decadent b/fasts (ginger scones, cashew granola & coddled eggs) inc. **$$**

⌂ **Addington Arms** [159 C3] (4 rooms) 27 Cornwallis St; ✆ 902 634 4573; tf 1 877 979 2727; www.addingtonarms.com. Well-equipped suites (all with sea &/or harbour view) above shops in this c1890 building in the Old Town. 3 suites have en-suite steam rooms. Full b/fast inc. **$$**

⌂ **Alicion B&B** [159 A4] (4 rooms) 66 McDonald St; ✆ 902 634 9358; tf 1 877 634 9358; www.alicionbb.com. Elegant, spacious eco-friendly rooms in this quiet c1911 former senator's house a 10min walk from the Old Town. Wi-Fi available. Gourmet b/fast inc. **$$**

⌂ **Ashlea House B&B** [159 A3] (4 rooms) 42 Falkland St; ✆ 902 634 7150; tf 1 866 634 7150; www.ashleahouse.com. A beautiful c1886 house just outside the Old Town with gazebo, 2nd-floor deck & widow's walk (a railed observation platform) offering fine views. There is a family suite with interconnecting rooms. Full country-style b/fast inc. **$$**

⌂ **Atlantic Sojourn B&B** [159 A4] (4 rooms) 56 Victoria Rd; ✆ 902 634 3151; tf 1 800 550 4824; www.atlanticsojourn.com; ◷ mid Apr–mid Nov, off-season by chance. Very comfortable c1904 house less than 10mins' walk to the Old Town. Free 24hr snacks/tea/coffee, off-street parking. Laundry facilities. Full b/fast inc. **$$**

⌂ **Lunenburg Arms Hotel** [159 D3] (24 units) 94 Pelham St; ✆ 902 640 4040; tf 1 800 679 4950; www.eden.travel/lunenburg. Good choice for those who prefer a larger hotel. Standard rooms, suites & 2-level suites, all with AC, many of which

overlook the harbour. Full-service spa & tanning salon is also available. **$$**

⌂ **Lunenburg Inn** [159 A2] (7 rooms) 26 Dufferin St; ✆ 902 634 3963; tf 1 800 565 3963; www.lunenburginn.com; ◷ Apr–Nov. A fine c1893 building just outside the Old Town with 5 bedrooms & 2 suites, all AC. Victorian-style décor & covered veranda, sundeck. Free parking. Gourmet b/fast (eg: strawberry-stuffed French toast) inc. **$$**

⌂ **Rum Runner Inn** [159 D3] (13 rooms) 66–70 Montague St; ✆ 902 634 9200; tf 1 888 778 6786; www.rumrunnerinn.com. Overlooking the harbour & golf course, 4 of the bright, spacious modern-looking rooms have private glassed-in verandas. See page 162 for their restaurant. Continental b/fast inc. **$$**

⌂ **Spinnaker Inn** [159 E4] (4 units) 126 Montague St; ✆ 902 634 4543; tf 1 888 634 8973; www.spinnakerinn.com. 2 rooms & 2 split-level suites in this c1850 waterfront property. Bedrooms have beautiful wood floors & flatscreen TVs. Suites (with kitchenettes) ideal for families & longer stays. **$$**

⌂ **Topmast Motel** [map, pages 142–3] (15 units) 92 Mason Beach Rd; ✆ 902 634 4661; tf 1 877 525 3222; www.topmastmotel.ca. All 9 motel rooms & 6 housekeeping units (with full kitchens) have lovely views over the harbour. Divers' services. **$$**

Budget

⌂ **Homeport Motel** [159 A4] 167 Victoria Rd; ✆ 902 634 8234; tf 1 800 616 4411; www.homeportmotel.com. A 10–15-min walk from the Old Town. In addition to standard motel rooms – with fridge, microwave & toaster – there are large 1-bedroom suites & laundry facilities on site. Most rooms newly renovated. **$**

Å **Lunenburg Board of Trade Campground** [159 G2] (55 sites) 11 Blockhouse Hill Rd; ✆ 902 634 8100; tf 1 888 615 8305; ◷ mid May–mid Oct. Views over the front & back harbours from this open campground next to the tourist office. Serviced & tent sites. **$**

✗ **WHERE TO EAT AND DRINK** Food-wise, it is hard to go wrong with fresh seafood, or try local specialities such as Lunenburg pudding (a type of pork sausage) and sauerkraut. Lunenburg is awash with eateries: if none of those listed below works for you, **Rime Restaurant & Wine Bar** [159 D3] (*9 King St:* ✆ *902 640 3112; rimerestaurant.ca;* ◷ *year-round 17.00–21.00 daily*) **$$$** is another decent 'upmarket' option, as is **Kate's Sweet Indulgence** [159 D3] (*242 Lincoln St;* ✆ *902*

There had long been competition between fishing fleets from Lunenburg and Gloucester, Massachusetts, but so keen was their rivalry that in 1920, the *Halifax Herald* sponsored an annual race for deep-sea fishing schooners from the two fleets. When the Americans won, Canadian pride was hurt: a superior vessel had to be built in time for the next year's competition.

They came up with *Bluenose*, which not only regained the trophy, but won it for 18 years in succession until World War II loomed, and the race was suspended. New steel-hulled trawlers rendered wooden fishing vessels redundant and in 1942, the *Bluenose* was sold to carry freight in the Caribbean. Four years later, she foundered and was lost on a Haitian reef.

For many years, this undefeated champion was featured on the back of the Canadian dime (10-cent piece): she is still remembered on Nova Scotia licence plates.

In 1963, the replica *Bluenose II* was built to the original plans by many of the original workers in the same shipyard as the original. From 1971, she sailed countless thousands of miles as Nova Scotia's floating ambassador.

In the last few years, the vessel has undergone a major repair and restoration programme (which went millions of dollars over budget), and for much of the time has been out of commission.

If you're lucky, the *Bluenose II* will be in port, moored by the Fisheries Museum. Her schedule can be checked – and a 2-hour harbour cruise booked on the website or by phoning (*902 640 3177; bluenose.novascotia.ca*).

640 3399; *www.sweetindulgence.ca;* ⊕ *in season 07.30–18.00 daily (from 08.30 Sat & Sun), off-season until 17.00;* $$–$$$) for coffee, sweet treats and light lunches. New (late summer 2016) but as yet unvisited by your author is **Half Shell Oyster & Seafood** [159 D3] (*108 Montague St;* ✆ *902 634 8503*), next door to – and under the same ownership as – the South Shore Fish Shack (see overleaf).

Luxury

✘ **Fleur de Sel** [159 C3] 53 Montague St; ✆ 902 640 2121; www.fleurdesel.net; ⊕ late May–early Oct 17.00–closing daily; early/late Oct 17.00–closing Wed–Sun; off-season check availability. Housed in a beautiful old sea captain's home with a garden terrace, this award-winning restaurant offers intimate & elegant fine-dining. It was closed in 2016 but is due to re-open in 2017. Try (for example) butter-poached lobster or grilled lamb saddle – or (by advance reservation) the multi-course tasting menu with wine pairings. $$$–$$$$

Upmarket

✘ **Lincoln Street Food** [159 D3] 200 Lincoln St; ✆ 902 640 3002; lincolnstreetfood.ca; ⊕ May–Dec 17.00–closing Wed–Sat, 11.00–14.00 & 17.00–21.00 Sun. Stylish, sleek & modern with a Big City feel. The creative menu changes

daily & favours fresh local produce. A 3-course fixed-price menu is offered (*CAN$45*), or order à la carte (eg seafood bouillabaisse). $$$

Mid range

✘ **Grand Banker Bar & Grill** [159 D4] 82 Montague St; ✆ 902 634 3300; grandbanker. com; ⊕ year-round 11.30–20.30 (or later) daily. Popular pub-style place with great water views, good service, sport on TV & a decent selection of beer (much of which is craft & local). $$

✘ **Magnolia's Grill** [159 E4] 128 Montague St; ✆ 902 634 3287; ⊕ Apr–Nov 11.00–22.00 daily. Laid-back & informal in terms of décor & ambience, but bright & lively in its regularly changing menu. Particular favourites include spicy peanut soup (trust me!), fishcakes & sublime (authentic) key lime pie. The lobster linguine isn't cheap, but is worth pushing the boat out for. Reserve a table on the patio overlooking the waterfront. $$

✖ **Rum Runner Inn** [159 D3] 66–70 Montague St; ✆ 902 634 8778; www.rumrunnerinn.com; ⊕ May–Oct noon–21.00 daily. The inn's licensed restaurant highlights fresh, local ingredients & has a 'Farm-to-Fork' designation. Chef's tasting menu with wine pairings available. Reservations recommended. $$

✖ **Salt Shaker Deli** [159 E4] 124 Montague St; ✆ 902 640 3434; www.saltshakerdeli.com; ⊕ in season 11.00–21.00 daily, o/s 11.00–20.00 Tue–Sat. Nibbles, pizzas, sandwiches, plus more imaginative/eclectic choices such as Thai chickpea curry or pork tacos. Recommended are the seafood chowder & the local mussels (various ways of preparation). Nice deck overlooking the harbour. $$

Budget

🍺 **Knot Pub** [159 A3] 4 Dufferin St; ✆ 902 634 3334; ⊕ noon–21.30 daily (later in season). This dark but lively (& easy-to-miss) pub isn't just a good spot to share a drink with the locals, as the pub grub is pretty good, too. No surprises on the menu – but burgers, club sandwiches, fish & chips & the like are well made & well priced. Can get very busy. $-$$

✖ **The Savvy Sailor** [159 D4] 100 Montague St; ✆ 902 640 7425; www.thesavvysailor.ca; ⊕ summer 07.30–20.30 daily; check for off-season hours. Licensed café (with nice little deck) offering good imaginative b/fasts (til 13.00), soups, salads, sandwiches, scallops, fishcakes, etc. $-$$

🍴 **Shop on the Corner** [159 D3] 263 Lincoln St; ✆ 902 634 3434; ⊕ 08.30–17.00 Mon–Sat, noon–17.00 Sun. A bright corner of this 'gift shop & more' is home to a little café (wraps, bagel sandwiches, etc), which sells & serves local (roasted in the same building) Laughing Whale coffee. $

✖ **South Shore Fish Shack** [159 D4] 108 Montague St; ✆ 902 634 3232; www.southshorefishshack.com; ⊕ mid May–early Oct noon–20.00 daily (til 21.00 Fri & Sat). Excellent beer-battered haddock & chips, plus cod's tongues, lobster, etc. Two patios & usually very busy. $-$$

ENTERTAINMENT AND FESTIVALS For live performances, check the schedules at the **Lunenburg Academy of Music Performance** [159 B1] (*97–101 Kaulbach St;* ✆ *902 634 8667; www.lampns.ca*) or the **Lunenburg Opera House** [159 E3] (*290 Lincoln St;* ✆ *902 640 6500; www.lunenburgoperahouse.com*). **Musique Royale** (✆ *902 634 9994; www.musiqueroyale.com*) is a Lunenburg-based organisation dedicated to promoting traditional and early music in historic venues in town and throughout the province across the year. A musical comedy, **Glimpses** (⊕ *Jul–early Sep, 19.30 Tue & Thu; admission by donation*), based on the history of the town and environs is held at the Fisheries Museum of the Atlantic (opposite): get there early as it is often a sell-out.

This is a town with a full calendar of festivals and events. For more details, see www.lunenburgns.com/festivals-and-events. In June, the **Summer Opera Festival** offers performances by the Maritime Concert Opera, the province's only concert opera company. The excellent four-day **Lunenburg Folk Harbour Festival** (✆ *902 634 3180; www.folkharbour.com*) in August features performances of traditional and contemporary folk and roots music at a variety of venues in the town from pubs to churches, with a main stage in a tent on **Blockhouse Hill** [159 G2]. Also in August, the **Nova Scotia Folk Art Festival** (✆ *902 640 2113; www.nsfolkartfestival. com*) is a colourful event that draws the best proponents of the genre from all over the province: the downside is that – lasting just 4 hours – it gets too busy.

OTHER PRACTICALITIES

$ **BMO Bank of Montreal** [159 E3] 12 King St; ✆ 902 634 8875; ⊕ 10.00–16.00 Mon–Fri

$ **TD Canada Trust** [159 E3] 36 King St; ✆ 902 634 8809; ⊕ 08.00–18.00 Mon–Wed, 08.00–20.00 Thu & Fri, 08.00–16.00 Sat

✚ **Fishermen's Memorial Hospital** 14 High St; ✆ 902 634 8801

✉ **Post office** [159 D3] 242 Lincoln St; ⊕ 08.30–17.00 Mon–Fri

ℹ Tourist information [159 G2] 11 Blockhouse Hill Rd; ☎ 902 634 8100; tf 1 888 615 8305; ☺ May & Oct 09.00–17.00, Jun & Sep 09.00–18.00, Jul–Aug 08.30–19.00

Lunenburg Library [159 C3] 19 Pelham St; ☎ 902 634 8008; ☺ 10.00–17.00 Mon–Wed, Fri & Sat, 10.00–20.00 Thu, noon–16.00 Sun

SHOPPING In the Old Town, **Dots & Loops** [159 D3] (*183 Lincoln St;* ☎ *902 298 5667; dotsandloops.ca;* ☺ *summer 10.00–21.00 Mon–Sat, 10.00–18.00 Sun; check o/s hours*) is a much-loved gift shop. Bookshop fans can find new titles at **Lexicon Books** [159 E3] (*125 Montague St;* ☎ *902 634 4015; lexiconbooks.ca;* ☺ *10.00–17.00 Mon–Sat, 11.00–17.00 Sun*) or used ones at **Lunenburg Bound** [159 E3] (*139 Montague St;* ☎ *902 634 3435; www. lunenburgbound.ca;* ☺ *10.00–18.00 Mon, Tue, Thu & Sat, 10.00–17.00 Wed & Sun, 10.00–20.00 Fri*) or long-established **Elizabeth Books** [159 E4] (*134 Montague St;* ☎ *902 634 8149*). Definitely worth a visit is the **Lunenburg Farmers' Market** [159 A4] (*Community Centre & Arena, 17 Green St; www.lunenburgfarmersmarket.ca;* ☺ *year-round 08.00–noon Thu*), with plants, flowers, fresh produce, baked goods and much more.

WHAT TO SEE AND DO For me, the best introduction to the town is provided by **Lunenburg Walking Tours** (☎ *902 521 6867; www.lunenburgwalkingtours.com;* ☺ *Jun–Sep 3 tours daily, rest of year by reservation; CAN$20*) During the day, 'Essential Lunenburg' is brimming with local history and 18th-century and Victorian architecture, including access to St John's Anglican Church. In the evening, 'Haunted Lunenburg' adds atmospheric tales of hangings and hauntings, superstitions and sightings, all by lantern light. Both last approximately 1 hour, and are informative and entertaining. Or swap horsepower for horse power – you can take a 2km/1.5-mile horse and buggy trip round the Old Town with **Trot in Time** (☎ *902 634 8917; trotintime.ca; CAN$20 for 35 mins; regular departures from the waterfront Sat–Thu*).

Appropriately located on the waterfront, the **Fisheries Museum of the Atlantic** complex [159 D4] (*68 Bluenose Dr;* ☎ *902 634 4794; fisheriesmuseum.novascotia. ca;* ☺ *(in season) mid May–mid Oct 09.00–17.00 daily, Jul–Aug until 19.00 Tue–Sat (admission CAN$12); (off-season) mid Oct–mid May 09.30–16.00 Mon–Fri (admission CAN$4)*) includes two dockside vessels (a restored schooner and a steel-hulled trawler), an aquarium with maritime species and touch-tank, demonstrations of marine-related skills, and three floors of exhibits. Learn about rum-running, traditional Mi'kmaq fishing methods, whales and whaling history, and much more. It's truly absorbing. Cheaper admission is charged in the off-season when parts of the museum complex are closed.

Dating from c1793, the **Knaut-Rhuland House** [159 E3] (*125 Pelham St;* ☎ *902 634 3498; www.lunenburgheritagesociety.ca;* ☺ *early Jun–Aug 11.00–17.00 Mon–Sat, noon–16.00 Sun; Sep noon–16.00 daily; admission by donation*) is one of the best-preserved examples of Georgian architecture in the country, with guides in period costumes. See period furniture and household goods and learn about life in Lunenburg's early years.

Something of a hidden gem and dedicated to preserving the history of the Halifax & Southwestern Railway line on the South Shore, the **Halifax & Southwestern Railway Museum** [159 A4] (*11188 Hwy 3;* ☎ *902 634 3184; www.hswmuseum.ednet.ns.ca;* ☺ *May–Oct 10.00–17.00 Mon–Sat, 13.00–17.00 Sun; off-season by appointment only; admission CAN$7*) situated just outside of town will delight railway buffs and others. See a replica 1940s' stationmaster's office, ever-growing large S-gauge model railway based on the old line, photos of stations, stock and employees, and much more.

Originally built in 1754, the **St John's Anglican Church** [159 D2] (*81 Cumberland St;* ☎ *902 634 4994; www.stjohnslunenburg.org;* ☺ *mid Jun–mid Sep 10.00–17.00 Mon–Sat, noon–19.00 Sun*) is the second-oldest Protestant church in Canada after St

South Shore LUNENBURG AND AROUND

4

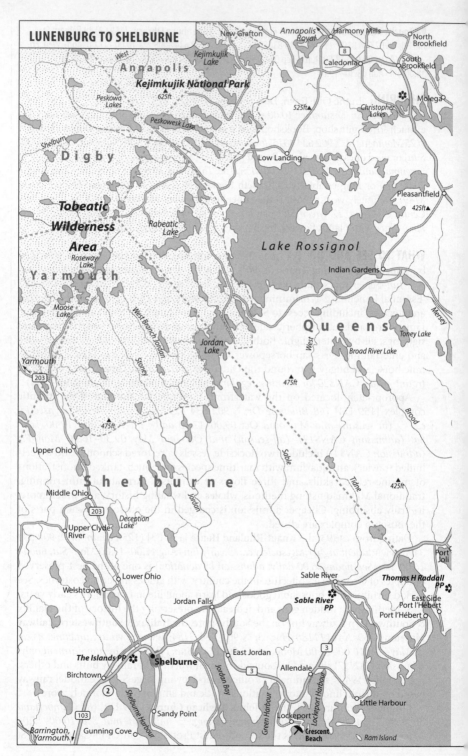

New Grafton

Annapolis Royal

Harmony Mills

North Brookfield

West

8

Caledonia

South Brookfield

A n n a p o l i s

Kejimkujik Lake

Molega

Kejimkujik National Park

Christopher Lakes

Peskowa Lakes

625ft▲

525ft▲

D i g b y

Shelburn

Low Landing

Pleasantfield

Peskowesk Lake

425ft▲

Tobeatic

Rabeatic Lake

Wilderness

Lake Rossignol

Area

Roseway Lake

Y a r m o u t h

Indian Gardens

Mersey

Moose Lake

West Branch Jordan

Q u e e n s

Toney Lake

West

Broad River Lake

Yarmouth

203

Jordan Lake

Stoney

475ft▲

Brood

Sable

475ft▲

Tidne

425ft▲

Upper Ohio

S h e l b u r n e

Middle Ohio

Jordan

203

Deception Lake

Port Joli

Upper Clyde River

Sable River

Thomas H Raddall PP

Lower Ohio

Sable River PP

East Side Port l'Hébert

Welshtown

Jordan Falls

Port l'Hébert

The Islands PP

East Jordan

3

Allendale

Little Harbour

Shelburne

Jordan Bay

3

Birchtown

2

Green Harbour

Lockeport Harbour

Barrington, Yarmouth

103

Shelburne Harbour

Sandy Point

Lockeport

Gunning Cove

Crescent Beach

Ram Island

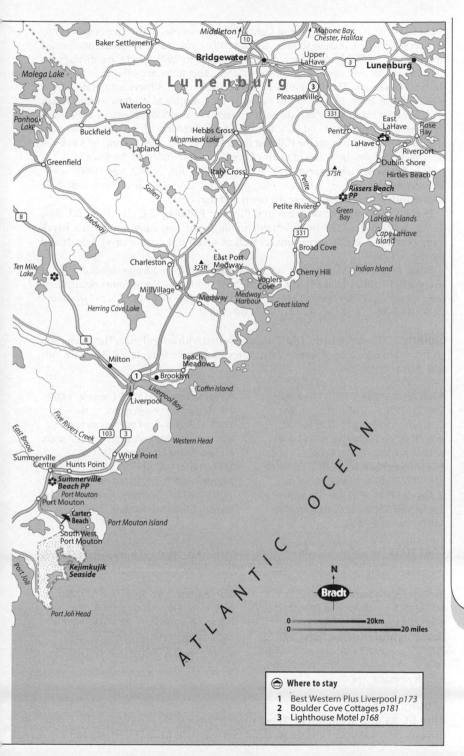

Where to stay

1 Best Western Plus Liverpool *p173*
2 Boulder Cove Cottages *p181*
3 Lighthouse Motel *p168*

Paul's in Halifax (page 120). One of Canada's best examples of the 'carpenter Gothic' architectural style (wherein features traditionally rendered in stone are interpreted in wood), it was faithfully restored and reopened in 2005. There are displays on the history, fire and restoration of the church, and tours are offered in summer. Be sure to see the 'Vinegar Bible', an exceedingly rare 18th-century bible with a typographical error. In addition to St John's look out for **St Andrew's Presbyterian** [159 E2] (*Townsend St*), which dates from 1828 but was 'Gothicised' in 1879. Atop the steeple, a large copper cod indicates the wind's direction. Those who like looking at old tombstones will enjoy the **Hillcrest Cemetery** [159 B2] (*Unity Lane, off Kaulbach St*), which includes the graves of many of the German founders of the town.

The **Bluenose Golf Course** [159 A4] (*18 Cove Rd;* \ *902 634 4260; www. bluenosegolfclub.com;* ⊕ *late Apr–Oct; green fees CAN$36*) is a short nine-hole course with stunning views over the town and harbour.

If you want to get out on the water, **Pleasant Paddling** (*245 The Point Rd, Blue Rocks;* \ *902 541 9233; www.pleasantpaddling.com*) run daily guided sea kayak tours plus other weekly excursions, as well as single and double kayak rentals and shuttle service.

Fruit brandies and liqueurs are hand-distilled in a former blacksmith's at **Ironworks Distillery** [159 F3] (*2 Kempt St;* \ *902 640 2424; www.ironworksdistillery. com;* ⊕ *Jan–mid May noon–17.00 Thu–Sun; mid May–mid Jun & Sep–Dec noon– 17.00 Wed–Mon; mid Jun–Aug 11.00–19.00 daily*).

Galleries
The streets of the Old Town are dotted with art galleries. They come and go, but when one closes it seems two or three more open to replace it. Here are four that stand out for me.

🛇 **Folk Art Maritime** [159 C3] 10 Pelham St; \902 212 2797; www.folkartmaritime.com; ⊕ mid May–mid Oct 10.00–17.00 Tue–Sat, noon–17.00 Sun. Diverse collection of folk art, including paintings, carvings & more.

🛇 **Laurie Swim Quilt Art** [159 C3] 138 Lincoln St; tf 1 877 272 2220; www.laurieswim.com; ⊕ May–Oct 11.00–17.00 Mon–Sat, noon–17.00 Sun. Formerly subtitled 'Art Quilt Gallery of the Atlantic' – which says it all.

🛇 **Peer Gallery** [159 C3] 167 Lincoln St; \902 640 3131; www.peer-gallery.com; ⊕ May–Dec 11.00–17.00 Wed–Sun. Contemporary paintings, Inuit sculpture, historic photography & local artists.

🛇 **Power House Art Gallery** [159 C3] 129 Lincoln St; \902 640 3363; www. powerhouseartists.com; ⊕ year-round 10.00–18.00 Tue–Sat. Nova Scotia & Inuit art, plus jewellery & handmade furniture.

Boat trips
In addition to those on *Bluenose II* (box, page 161), several other boat trips are offered between late spring and early autumn.

Heritage Fishing Tours \902 640 3535; tf 1 877 386 3535; www.boattour.ca. Offers the chance to fish for mackerel in the harbour.

Lunenburg Whale Watching Tours \902 527 7175; www.novascotiawhalewatching.com. Head out in search of whales: dolphins, seals & various seabirds are usually seen.

Star Charters \902 634 3535; tf 1 877 386 3535; www.novascotiasailing.com. A sailing tour on the Eastern Star, a 48ft wooden ketch, is recommended, particularly the Sunset Tour (⊕ Jul–Aug 18.30 daily, check for other months).

AROUND LUNENBURG
Blue Rocks and Stonehurst
These two photogenic fishing villages are a short drive or cycle ride from Lunenburg. Head east from Old Town Lunenburg and you'll

come on to Blue Rocks Road, which you should follow until you reach Blue Rocks (approx 6km/4 miles) and turn right on to Herring Cove Road. Stop in at **The Point General** (*245 The Point Rd;* ☎ *902 880 9663;* ⬛; ⊕ *Jun–late Sep 10.00–17.00 daily;* $) – great coffee, treats and local products in a fascinating old fish shack. From Blue Rocks, take Stonehurst Road and then follow signs to Stonehurst East, parking just before the wooden bridge. Stonehurst is approximately 4km from Blue Rocks.

Hirtles Beach This fine, often wild beach is over 3km long. For a wonderful (sometimes rugged) 7km coastal wilderness hike, walk to the right from the car park towards the end of the beach for approximately 1.5km, follow the path up into the woods, and turn left at the fork. The trail continues to Gaff Point before looping back via the west side of the peninsula. To get there, take Highway 332 from Lunenburg to Rose Bay for approximately 15km, turn left onto Kingsburg Road, then right onto Hirtles Beach Road (approx 8km from Highway 332).

Ovens Natural Park (*Ovens Park Rd;* ☎ *902 766 4621; www.ovenspark.com;* ⊕ *mid May–early Oct 09.00–21.00 daily; admission CAN$11.50*). This privately owned park has a cliffside hiking path giving views of the 'Ovens' – sea caves. The nearby beach was the scene of an 1861 gold rush, and you can rent a pan and try your hand at panning for gold. The park is approximately 17km/11 miles from Lunenburg; to get there, take Feltzen South Road from Highway 332, then Ovens Road.

⌂ ***Where to stay, eat and drink*** There is a 174-site clifftop campground (⊕ *late Jun–early Sep;* **$–$$**) with nine cabins, a swimming pool and a restaurant. The park's owners (the Chapins) had a celebrated sibling, singer/songwriter Harry Chapin (remember 'Cat's in the Cradle' and 'WOLD?'), who was killed in a car crash in 1981. Various family members and local musicians sing and play every evening in July and August.

Lunenburg County Winery (*813 Walburne Rd, nr Newburne;* ☎ *902 644 2415; www.canada-wine.com;* ⊕ *May–Jul & Oct–mid Dec 09.00–17.00 Mon–Fri, Aug–Sep 09.00–18.00 daily*) This winery specialising in fruit (rather than grape) wines is situated on a 40ha blueberry farm and offers tastings and simple tours, both free of charge, plus U-pick (pick-your-own and pay-by-weight) blueberries in season, usually early August to early October. To reach it, from Exit 11 off Highway 103 drive 24km inland to Newburne, then turn right onto Walburne Road.

BRIDGEWATER

Straddling the LaHave River, Bridgewater is the major commercial and service centre between Halifax and Yarmouth. The largest shopping mall on the South Shore sits on the river's eastern bank, and the area's major employer, Michelin, has a plant in the Industrial Park. However, the old downtown area was destroyed by fire in 1899 and isn't particularly attractive. The town has a couple of golf courses and museums and some nice riverside parks: on some tree-lined residential streets stand stately homes which have withstood the test of time. Outdoorsy types shouldn't miss Riverview Park, and the shared-use 8km Centennial Trail following the old rail bed is worth a wander. There has been talk of constructing a municipal marina – watch this space.

Actor Donald Sutherland grew up and went to school in Bridgewater in the late 1940s.

GETTING THERE AND AWAY Located on Highway 3, just off Highway 103 (exits 12 or 13), Bridgewater can be easily reached **by car**. It is 100km/62 miles from Halifax, 20km/12 miles from Lunenburg and 45km/28 miles from Liverpool. By shuttle, the **Cloud Nine Shuttle** (page 137) operates daily both ways between Yarmouth and Halifax .

🏠 **WHERE TO STAY** *Map, opposite, unless otherwise stated*

🏠 **Best Western Plus** (63 units) 527 Hwy 10; ☎ 902 530 0101; www.bestwesternbridgewater. com; ⊕ year-round. Comfortable, functional hotel & convention centre with a choice of rooms or suites. Indoor pool, on-site restaurant/lounge, laundry & business centre. Out of town centre by Exit 12 of Hwy 103. Includes full b/fast. **$$**

🏠 **Lighthouse Motel** [map, pages 164–5] (17 units) Hwy 331, Conquerall Bank; ☎ 902 543 8151; www.lighthousemotel.ca; ⊕ May–mid Oct. 14 pleasant motel rooms, & – directly on the riverside – 3 excellent-value larger units with kitchenettes. A good choice. 10mins' drive from Bridgewater towards LaHave (box, page 172). **$–$$**

✖ **WHERE TO EAT AND DRINK** *Map, opposite*

Look out for **Firkinstein** beer brewed in the, 'burbs of Bridgewater.

✖ **27 South Restaurant** At the Best Western Plus (above); ⊕ year-round lunch Mon–Fri, dinner daily. Decent, reasonably stylish hotel restaurant. A good spot for a business lunch. **$$**

✖ **Lanna Thai Kitchen** 547 King St; ☎ 902 543 4611; www.lannathai.ca; ⊕ year-round 11.30– 14.00 & 16.30–20.00 Wed–Sat, 16.30–20.00 Sun. With good ethnic food hard to track down outside the HRM, this lively, casual, fun licensed eatery is a find. The Pad Gra Prow is popular. **$$**

✖ **Bridgewater Local Public House** 421 LaHave St; ☎ 902 543 1286; bridgewaterlocals.ca: ⊕ year-round 11.30–22.00 Mon–Wed (kitchen til 20.00), 11.30–midnight Thu–Sat (kitchen til 21.00), noon–22.00 Sun (kitchen til 20.00). Casual modern, pub in mall location. Burgers, seafood, etc, plus local brews inc Hell Bay (page 176) & Firkinstein. **$–$$**

✖ **Waves Seafood** Eastside Plaza; ☎ 902 543 2020; wavesseafood.tripod.com; ⊕ year-round

11.00–21.00 daily. Reliable diner specialising in seafood. Lighter options (eg: steamed, herbed haddock & salad) in addition to the standard deep-fried stuff. **$–$$**

🍺 **River Pub** 750 King St; ☎ 902 543 1100; www.riverpub.ca; ⊕ year-round 11.00–23.00 Mon–Sat, noon–closing Sun. The 'house beer' is an eponymous ale brewed by Propeller. Reasonable food, & nice riverside patio. **$–$$**

☕ **Fancy Pants Play Café** 673 King St; ☎ 902 530 2548; fancypantscafe.ca; ⊕ 08.30–16.00 Mon–Sat. Child/young family-friendly café with surprisingly decent food (eg: huevos rancheros or all-day breakfast sandwiches). **$**

☕ **The Interval Café** 807 King St; ☎ 902 543 5681; 🆓. Excellent new coffee/sweet treats café. The management are on a journey (trying different ideas & concepts), so things change often – check Facebook for the latest evolution. **$**

ENTERTAINMENT AND FESTIVALS Catch a film at the **Cineplex Bridgewater** (*349 LaHave St;* ☎ *902 527 4025; www.cineplex.com*), which has a seven-screen cinema complex. There are also great festivals in the area; in May, the **South Shore Colour Festival** (*www.southshorecolourfestival.com*) is a new one-day event inspired by the Hindu festival Holi. The **South Shore Exhibition** (see box, page 170) is held in July, and in August, the **Growing Green Festival** (*www.bridgewater.ca/growinggreenfest*) is a two-day celebration of 'sustainability'. Throughout the year, you'll usually find something of interest going on at **Art Happening Bridgewater** (see page 170 for contact details).

OTHER PRACTICALITIES

$ **Royal Bank** 565 King St; ☎ 902 543 0184; ⊕ 09.30–17.00 Mon–Fri, 09.00–16.00 Sat

$ **Scotiabank** 421 LaHave St; ☎ 902 543 8155; ⊕ 10.00–17.00 Mon–Wed & Fri, 10.00–20.00 Thu, 09.00–13.00 Sat

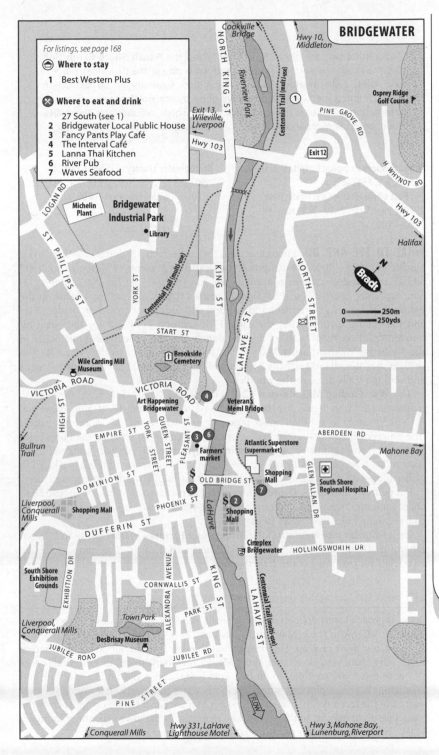

BRIDGEWATER

For listings, see page 168

⬠ **Where to stay**
1 Best Western Plus

✖ **Where to eat and drink**
   27 South (see 1)
2 Bridgewater Local Public House
3 Fancy Pants Play Café
4 The Interval Café
5 Lanna Thai Kitchen
6 River Pub
7 Waves Seafood

Cookville Bridge
Hwy 10, Middleton
Osprey Ridge Golf Course
PINE GROVE RD
Exit 13, Wileville, Liverpool
Exit 12
Hwy 103
H WHYNOT RD
Hwy 103
Halifax
NORTH KING ST
Riverview Park
Centennial Trail (multi-use)

Michelin Plant
Bridgewater Industrial Park
Library
LOGAN RD
ST PHILLIPS ST
YORK ST
KING ST
Centennial Trail (multi-use)
LAHAVE ST
NORTH STREET

Bradt
N
0 ——— 250m
0 ——— 250yds

START ST
Brookside Cemetery
Wile Carding Mill Museum
VICTORIA ROAD
VICTORIA ROAD
Art Happening Bridgewater
Veteran's Meml Bridge
Bullrun Trail
HIGH ST
EMPIRE ST
YORK STREET
QUEEN STREET
PLEASANT ST
3 6
Farmers' market
ABERDEEN RD
Mahone Bay
Atlantic Superstore (supermarket)
DOMINION ST
$
OLD BRIDGE ST
Shopping Mall
7
South Shore Regional Hospital
GLEN ALLAN DR
Liverpool, Conquerall Mills
Shopping Mall
PHOENIX ST
5
$ 2
Shopping Mall
DUFFERIN ST
EXHIBITION DR
LAHAVE ST
Cineplex Bridgewater
HOLLINGSWORTH DR
South Shore Exhibition Grounds
ALEXANDRA AVENUE
CORNWALLIS ST
KING ST
PARK ST
Town Park
Liverpool, Conquerall Mills
DesBrisay Museum
JUBILEE ROAD
JUBILEE RD
PINE STREET
LAHAVE ST
Centennial Trail (multi-use)
FLOW
Conquerall Mills
Hwy 331, LaHave Lighthouse Motel
Hwy 3, Mahone Bay, Lunenburg, Riverport

South Shore BRIDGEWATER

4

Agricultural fairs are big in Nova Scotia, and the **South Shore Exhibition** (✆ *902 543 3341; www.thebigex.com; end Jul*) is one of the province's biggest and best. Held at Bridgewater's Exhibition Grounds at 50 Exhibition Drive, farming methods used in days gone by are not forgotten, with the International Ox-Pull a big draw. The event, which includes arts and crafts, food, entertainment and an amusement park, attracts over 45,000 people.

✚ **South Shore Regional Hospital** 90 Glen Allan Dr; ✆ 902 543 4603
✉ **Post office** Bridgewater Pharmasave, 215 Dominion St; ⊕ 09.00–19.00 Mon–Fri, 09.00–15.00 Sat

Bridgewater Library 135 North Park Stt; ✆ 902 543 9222; ⊕ 10.00–17.00 Mon, Fri & Sat, 10.00–21.00 Tue–Thu, noon–16.00 Sun

WHAT TO SEE AND DO Encompassing the collection of Judge Mather Byles DesBrisay (1828–1900), the exhibits at the **DesBrisay Museum** (*130 Jubilee Rd;* ✆*902 543 4033; www.desbrisaymuseum.ca; ⊕ Jun–Aug 09.00–17.00 Tue–Sat, 13.00–17.00 Sun; Sep–May 13.00–17.00 Wed–Sun; admission CAN$3.50, Sat free*) focus on the natural history, early settlement and cultural and industrial growth of Bridgewater and Lunenburg County from the early 17th century. Look out for the beautiful hooded cradle covered with birch-bark panels and the porcupine quills made in the 1860s by Mi'kmaq artist Mary Christianne Morris. Set in the attractive 8ha Bridgewater Woodland Gardens (with a popular duck pond), there are picnic areas and walking trails through the woods.

The **Wile Carding Mill Museum** (*242 Victoria Rd;* ✆ *902 543 8233; cardingmill. novascotia.ca; ⊕ Jun–mid Sep 09.30–17.30 Mon–Sat, 13.00–17.30 Sun; admission CAN$3.50 adult*) is a c1860 water-powered mill where the wool-carding process (the process where wool is 'combed' – usually by hand – to separate the fibres prior to spinning) was automated. **Art Happening Bridgewater** (*757 King St;* ✆ *902 521 2925; www.arthappeningbridgewater.ca*) is a new community art space for those of all ages to gather and get creative – there are workshops, cultural events, music, activities and more.

For golfing enthusiasts, **Osprey Ridge Golf Course** (*Harold Whynot Rd;* ✆ *902 543 6666; www.ospreyridge.ns.ca; green fees CAN$64*) is a 6,607yd, par-72 championship course: many holes have water in play.

On a Saturday morning, stroll the **Bridgewater Farmers' Market** (*King St, between Empire & Dominion; www.bridgewaterfarmersmarket.ca; ⊕ Jun–mid-Oct 09.00–13.00 Sat*) for fruit, veg, crafts, baked goods, etc.

LIVERPOOL AND AROUND

If you approach Liverpool past shopping malls or heavy industry, don't be too put off. Similarly, when you reach Main Street and see a row of fairly run-of-the-mill shops and services, don't give up. Dig deeper and this town at the mouth of the Mersey River will reward you. Go further along Main Street to the town's most desirable area (if house prices are anything to go by), Fort Point, and you'll find several fine and prestigious homes, a pleasant little park, lovely water frontage, and a wonderful view – albeit of the recently (2012) closed Bowater Mersey Paper Company mill across the river. Eyesore it may be, but the mill was a mainstay of the town's economy for many years, and Liverpool is still adapting to 'life after Bowater Mersey'.

Wander the residential areas behind Main Street and admire the grand houses and their gardens. Enjoy the architecture – on Church Street, for example, the c1854 Court House is one of the province's finest examples of the American Greek Revival movement. There are interesting museums to explore, a Mi'kmaq art gallery, an Old Burial Ground (Main Street at Old Bridge Street) to wander, a couple of good eateries, and, if you're really not in the mood for things urban, wonderful beaches nearby.

Just across the river, **Brooklyn** has a pretty marina and waterfront park which hosts many summer events. The setting is not, however, helped by the monstrous (now closed) paper mill. The area's big supermarkets and box stores are near Exit 19 off Highway 103.

HISTORY When Sieur de Mons arrived in 1604 *en route* to Port-Royal he was surprised to find a French fur trader already here. De Mons named the port after the trader, calling it Port Rossignol: the Mi'kmaq called it Ogumkiqueok, 'a place of departure'. A group of New Englanders, most of whom were said to be direct descendants of the Pilgrim Fathers, founded Liverpool in 1759.

A shipbuilding and shipping industry developed, but during the American Revolution several ships from the port were seized by American privateers. This stung the port's mariners who built new ships and set off to do their own privateering (page 19).

Most of what went on in the town at that time was faithfully recorded by an early settler, Simeon Perkins, who built a fine home on the town's main street – and kept a detailed diary. Perkins records, for instance, that smallpox ravaged Liverpool until the

For listings, see pages 173–4

Where to stay

1 Lanes Privateer Inn

Off map
   Best Western Plus Liverpool
   Gallery Guest House B&B
   Motel Transcotia

Where to eat and drink

2 The Dancing Chicken
3 Liverpool Pizzeria
4 Memories Café & Eatery
5 Paul's German Café,
   Bistro & Restaurant

Hank Snow Hometown Museum,
Beach Meadows, Best Western Plus Liverpool,
Brooklyn Shores, Concrete Creations,
Motel Transcotia, Atlantic Superstore,
Hwy 8, Hwy 103, Brooklyn

BRISTOL AVENUE

RENT RD

Mersey River

MARKET STREET

Fort Point Lighthouse

CORVETTE ST   ELM ST

CARTEN ST   REESE ST

WENTWORTH ST

MAIN STREET

SCHOOL STREET

Perkins House Museum

Queens County Museum

WATER ST

Town Hall Arts & Cultural Centre, Sipuke'l Gallery

JUBILEE

COURT ST

Privateer Park

HENRY ST   HENSEY DR   LEGION ST

Hell Bay Brewing Co

Astor Theatre

GORHAM ST

CHURCH STREET

Old court house

PARK ST

Savage Studio & Gallery, Gallery Guest House B&B, police station, Queens General Hospital

MCLEOD ST   MAIN STREET   WEIR

MACPHERSON ST

Old burial ground

OLD BRIDGE ST

BOEHNER ST

UNION ST

Milton

SUMMER ST

Rossignol Cultural Centre

Thomas H Raddall Library

Liverpool Adventure Outfitters, Hwy 3

LIVERPOOL

South Shore   LIVERPOOL AND AROUND

4

171

From Bridgewater, Highway 331 follows the pretty, west bank of the LaHave River for about 20km to LaHave. This is the western terminus for a car ferry (*CAN$7*), which makes frequent crossings (every 30mins) of the river to East LaHave (on Hwy 332), departing LaHave on the hour and half hour, departing East LaHave on the quarter and three-quarter hour. Just past the ferry dock, a 100-plus year-old former chandlery now houses the **LaHave Crafters Co-op** (⊕ *Jun–Sep 11.00–17.00 daily*), displaying the work of numerous local artists and craftsfolk. The big draw, though, is the justifiably popular **LaHave Bakery** (*Hwy 331;* ☏ *902 688 2908;* ⓕ *; The LaHave-Bakery;* ⊕ *summer 08.30–18.30 daily; winter 08.00–16.00 daily; $*). In addition to baking traditional bread made from additive-free and locally grown ingredients, and tempting cakes and squares, there are sandwiches, good coffee, soup and a couple of hot savoury items (perhaps pizza). There are only a few tables, so if the weather's nice, order 'to go' and – after a stop 150m further on at the waterfront **Westcote Bell Pottery** (*3447 Hwy 331;* ☏ *902 693 2042; www.westcotebellpottery.com*) – walk down for a riverside picnic by the museum where Isaac de Razilly, a French nobleman and explorer, established Fort Ste-Marie-de-Grace in 1632. This was one of the first permanent European settlements in Canada, and – from 1632 to 1636 – the first capital of New France. Razilly died in 1636 and his successor decided to move his headquarters to Port-Royal (page 217). The settlement was destroyed by fire in the early 1650s. On its site, in a former lighthouse-keeper's house, is **Fort Point Museum** (*100 Fort Point Rd;* ☏ *902 688 1632; www.fortpointmuseum.com;* ⊕ *museum & gift shop open Jun–Sep 10.00–17.00; off-season by appointment; park open year-round; admission by donation*), which presents 400 years of local history including the Mi'kmaq, early French settlement and Foreign Protestant settlers. The adjacent cemetery (where Razilly would have been buried) is also worth a wander.

Continuing on Highway 331, in less than 10km from LaHave you'll reach **Crescent Beach** where a causeway shelters a fine, long, sandy beach. Drive or cycle across the causeway to reach the LaHave Islands. **Cape LaHave Adventures** (*90 Bells Cove Rd, LaHave;* ☏ *902 693 2023; www.capelahaveadventures.ca;* ⊕ *May–Oct*) offer half- and full-day (and sunset) guided sea kayak tours in the LaHave Islands archipelago. Paddle and yoga tours and multi-day kayaking and camping expeditions are also possible. On the islands, apart from the **LaHave Islands Marine Museum** (*100 LaHave Islands Rd;* ☏ *902 688 2973; www.lahaveislandsmarinemuseum.ca;* ⊕ *Jun–Sep 10.00–17.00 daily; admission free*) – housed in a former Methodist church – there are no services for the visitor.

people submitted to an ordeal called 'vaccination'. The vaccine was yet to be perfected and Perkins says that as many died of the vaccination as from smallpox.

With the cessation of hostilities, Liverpool settled into a long period of prosperity centred on shipbuilding and lumbering. Many of the downtown buildings were destroyed, however, by a great fire in 1865.

Brooklyn was originally known as Herring Cove, and the ubiquitous Nicolas Denys (box, page 349) had a fishery here in 1634.

GETTING THERE AND AWAY Its location on Highway 3, just off Highway 103, Exit 19 makes Liverpool easy to get to **by car**. It is 147km/92 miles from Halifax and 69km/43 miles from Shelburne. The **Cloud Nine Shuttle** (page 137) operates daily both ways between Yarmouth and Halifax.

Back on Highway 331 it is just 1km to **Rissers Beach Provincial Park** (*Hwy 331; parks.novascotia.ca/content/rissers-beach;* ⊕ *late May–early Oct*). In addition to a long, sand beach, a boardwalk leads across a marsh; when you reach its end, turn left along the bank of the Petite Rivière and walk back along the beach to complete a loop. The park's two camping areas have a total of 93 open and wooded sites, some (not surprisingly the first to be reserved) virtually on the beach.

Again it's about 1km from the park to the village of **Petite Rivière**: cross the bridge and turn left off Highway 331 onto Green Bay Road. The community of **Green Bay** has a couple of lovely (generally sheltered) little beaches, several holiday homes and **Macleod's Canteen** (*542 Green Bay Rd;* ☎ *902 688 2866;* ⊕ *Jul–early Sep 12.00–18.00 daily; $*): eat in or take your fish and chips to the beach across the road.

Retrace your steps to Petite Rivière and, at the crossroads, turn left back onto Highway 331. After about 300m, look out for the **Old Burial Ground** on the left almost opposite the Crousetown turn-off: graves date from the very early 19th century. Back at the crossroads, if you turn onto Petite Rivière Road you'll pass the **Maritime Painted Saltbox Gallery** (*265 Petite Rivière Rd;* ☎ *902 693 1544; www.paintedsaltbox. com;* ⊕ *May–mid Oct 10.00–17.00 daily, otherwise by chance appointment*), a fun and fascinating collection of contemporary fine, fun and folk art, and art furniture. Continue on this road and follow it as it merges onto Italy Crossing Road; after less than 2km (less than 3km from the aforementioned crossroads) you'll find the **Petite Rivière Vineyards** (*1300 Italy Cross Rd;* ☎ *902 693 3033; www.petiterivierevineyards.ca;* ⊕ *May–Oct 11.00–17.00 daily, o/s by chance or appointment*). Free tastings are offered, and at noon, a tour and tastings (reservation required). Turn back on Italy Crossing Road and follow it to rejoin Highway 331. You'll see forest rather than the sea for the next 7km before reaching picturesque **Broad Cove**: on your right, sophisticated but relaxed **Best Coast Coffee Gallery** (*7070 Hwy 331;* ☎ *902 935 2220;* ⊕ *mid May–Sep 09.00–16.00 Tue–Sun; $*) offers not only good coffee, but gourmet sandwiches and tempting baked goodies. Local artists' work is on display.

Five kilometres further on at **Cherry Hill**, it's easy to miss the turn-off to another fine, long, and usually very quiet beach. Coming from Broad Cove on Highway 331, turn left onto Henry Conrad Road by the Fire Department and follow it to its end. Be aware that this beach sometimes attracts biting deer flies.

At **Voglers Cove**, 4km/2.5miles from Cherry Hill, continue along the coast to East Port Medway and on to Highway 103, Exit 17, from where it is 30km to Bridgewater or 17km to Liverpool. You'll have driven approximately 60km from Bridgewater.

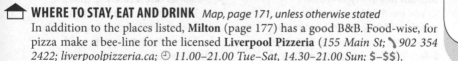

WHERE TO STAY, EAT AND DRINK *Map, page 171, unless otherwise stated*
In addition to the places listed, **Milton** (page 177) has a good B&B. Food-wise, for pizza make a bee-line for the licensed **Liverpool Pizzeria** (*155 Main St;* ☎ *902 354 2422; liverpoolpizzeria.ca;* ⊕ *11.00–21.00 Tue–Sat, 14.30–21.00 Sun; $–$$*).

Best Western Plus Liverpool [map, pages 164–5] (65 rooms) 63 Queens Pl Dr, off Hwy 3 near Exit 19 of Hwy 103; ☎ 902 354 2377; tf reservations 1 888 670 7234; hotelsinliverpo olns.h.bestwestern.com/; ⊕ year-round. Well-equipped hotel with laundry, cocktail lounge, indoor pool & fitness centre. Good choice for those

who like chain hotels. Most rates include hot b/fast. **$$**

Lanes Privateer Inn (26 rooms) 27 Bristol Av; ☎ 902 354 3456; tf 1 800 794 3332; lanesprivateerinn.wordpress.com; ⊕ year-round. A Mersey River waterfront inn. Some guestrooms have balconies. There's a pub, overlooking the river,

Three minutes' drive from Exit 17 off Highway 103 is one of the province's prettiest communities. **Mill Village** – also reached by taking Port Medway Road northwest from Highway 103 between junctions 17 and 18 – boasts a picturesque Medway River setting, numerous beautiful century houses, and a little-known gem. Just by the bridge is the **Riverbank General Store & Café** (*8 Medway River Rd;* ☎ *902 677 2013;* ⓕ; ☉ *08.00–20.00 daily*). The old, beautifully located general store was bought by a 'supported living' association: staff, clients and volunteers worked to transform the space into a combination of craft shop, gift shop, grocery store and riverside café (☉ *May–Nov 11.30–14.30 daily;* $), dishing up a short menu of reasonably priced sandwiches, salads, ice cream etc. Most of the store/café staff are under the wing of the association. Worthy, and worth the detour. Incidentally, if you're heading to Kejimjukik (pages 223–7) or Annapolis Royal (pages 217–23) you can continue along Medway River Road to Greenfield (approx 25km), a lovely, riverside drive along a gravel road, from where it is 6.6km along Chapel Hill Road to Highway 8.

Then again, if instead you take Port Medway Road southeast from Highway 103 and follow it for about 7km, you'll come to **The Port Grocer** (*1615 Port Medway Rd, Port Medway;* ☎ *902 677 2884;* ⓕ; ☉ *year-round 09.00– 19.00 daily (til 20.00 in summer)*). This is a retro, funky, community hub/general store/post office and café (☉ *11.00–14.30 daily;* $) offering good food, such as roast beef panini with caramelised onions and Chipotle sauce, very good seafood chowder, or sweet potato peanut soup), plus Friday night live music 'pub' sessions (☉ *18.00–22.00*). Have a quick look at the c1899 lighthouse, and if you're Liverpool-bound, take Eastern Shore Road for an *en route* stop at beautiful Beach Meadows (page 176).

and a very good restaurant (☉ *07.00–20.00 Mon– Fri, 08.00–20.00 Sat & Sun;* $$) with a varied menu. In particular, the haddock cakes & bread & butter pudding with orange whisky sauce receive many plaudits. On-site book/gift shop. Rates inc good full b/fast. $$

🏠 **Gallery Guest House B&B** (2 rooms) 611 Shore Rd, Mersey Pt; ☎ 902 354 5431; www. bbcanada.com/galleryguesthouse; ☉ year-round. Both guestrooms at this charming oceanfront B&B approx 4km from the town centre on the same premises as the Savage Gallery (page 175) have private entrances & decks overlooking Liverpool Bay. B/fast (cheeses, smoked salmon/cold cuts, warm baguette & more) is brought to your door on a trolley at a pre-arranged time. Recommended. $

🏠 **Motel Transcotia** (22 rooms) 3457 Hwy 3, Brooklyn; ☎ 902 354 3494; ⓕ; ☉ year-round. Step back a decade or 3 at this traditional-style motel. The licensed dining room (☉ *06.00–20.00*

Mon–Fri, 08.00–20.00 Sat & Sun; $–$$) offers simple, good-value home cookin' that packs the locals in. $–$$

✕ **Paul's German Café, Bistro & Restaurant** 343 Main St; ☎ 902 356 3155; ⓕ. Eat in or on the deck. Expect good b/fasts, cakes, sausages, soup & schnitzel cooked in different ways. $$

✕ **Memories Café & Eatery** 28 Water St; ☎ 902 356 3110; www.memoriescafe.ca; ☉ hours vary – check. Decent, bright, friendly coffee & lunch spot. B/fasts, soups (good haddock chowder), sandwiches & paninis. $–$$

✕ **The Dancing Chicken** 279 Main St; ☎ 902 356 2284; www.dancingchicken.ca; ☉ year-round 08.30–16.30 Tue–Sat, 10.00–15.00 Sun. New (2016) café & grocery focusing on fresh local produce. Short, regularly changing menu with b/fasts, soup, salads, sandwiches & baked treats. $

At the end of Main Street just before Fort Point, the building that is now 5 Riverside Drive was built in 1763, and operated as Dexter's Tavern. In the late 18th century, Simeon Perkins (page 176) was a regular patron. It is said to be haunted by a tiny, uniformed, mischievous ghost. Part of another house at the opposite end of Main Street was also an 18th-century tavern and is also supposed to be haunted. Both former taverns are now private residences.

OTHER PRACTICALITIES

$ Royal Bank 209 Main St; ☎ 902 354 5717; ⊕ 10.00–16.00 Mon–Wed, 10.00–17.00 Thu & Fri
$ Scotiabank 183 Main St; ☎ 902 354 3431; ⊕ 10.00–17.00 Mon–Fri
✚ Queens General Hospital 175 School St; ☎ 902 354 3436
✉ Post office 176 Main St; ⊕ 08.30–17.00 Mon–Fri

ℹ Tourist information 32 Henry Hensey Dr; ☎ 902 354 5421; ⊕ mid May–Sep 10.00–18.00 daily
Thomas H Raddall Library 145 Old Bridge St; ☎ 902 354 5270; ⊕ 10.00–17.00 Tue, Wed & Fri, 10.00–20.00 Thu, 10.00–14.00 Sat, noon–16.00 Sun

WHAT TO SEE AND DO Built in 1902 as part of the Town Hall, the **Astor** (*59 Gorham St; ☎ 902 354 5250; www.astortheatre.ns.ca*) staged operas, musicals and town hall meetings, and in 1907, the first film ever shown in Nova Scotia played here. The boom in cinema's popularity was often at the cost of other forms of entertainment, but the late 1970s saw a revival of live theatre/performance and since then the Astor has established itself as a sought-after venue. The rest of this Heritage Trust Property is made up of what is now the **Town Hall Arts and Cultural Centre** (*219 Main St; ☎ 902 354 5741;* ■), the highlight of which is the Acadia First Nation-owned **Sipuke'l Gallery** (*☎ 902 354 5501;* ■; ⊕ *09.00–17.00 Tue–Sat; admission free*) that celebrates 10,000 years of aboriginal existence in the Liverpool area. Check Facebook for regular workshops.

Liverpool's old high school (and grounds) now house an interesting cocktail of exhibits as the **Rossignol Cultural Centre** (*205 Church St; ☎ 902 354 3067;* ■; ⊕ *Jul–Aug 10.00–17.00 Tue–Sun; admission CAN$5*), including a fun outhouse museum, folk art, a large collection of Mi'kmaq artefacts, various mounted birds and animals (you won't see many other polar bears or giraffes in Nova Scotia), a traditional art gallery and the Sherman Hines Museum of Photography. The latter is an extensive collection of photographic equipment, plus displays of work by important past and contemporary Canadian photographers. The exhibits were donated by Liverpool native Sherman Hines, one of Canada's most renowned landscape and portrait photographers.

Art lovers who appreciate land- (and especially sea-)scapes should visit master watercolourist Roger Savage's **Savage Studio and Gallery** (*611 Shore Rd, Mersey Point; ☎ 902 354 5431; www.savagegallery.ca; ⊕ Jul–Aug 10.00–19.00 daily; off-season by chance or appointment*). It's a 5-minute drive from town (on the way to Western Head lighthouse).

It might look much older than it is, but that was the idea when the interesting **Queens County Museum** (*109 Main St; ☎ 902 354 4058; queenscountymuseum.com; ⊕ Jun–mid Oct 09.00–17.00 Mon–Sat, 13.00–17.00 Sun; mid Oct–May 09.00–17.00 Mon–Sat; admission CAN$8 (2016) – includes entry to the Perkins House Museum*) next door to the Perkins House was built in 1980. The interior is jam-packed with a whole variety of things from Mi'kmaq tools to 'privateers and pirates', but pride of place goes to an interactive privateer ship, the *Liverpool Packet*. Genealogists will want to visit the Thomas Raddall Research Centre (fee charged). Next door, interactive 'ghosts' guide you round the c1766 New England-style house that is now the **Perkins House Museum** (⊕ *same contact details & hours*). It was built for Simeon Perkins, a prominent Liverpool citizen best known for his diaries, who lived here until his death in 1812.

Country music legend Clarence Eugene 'Hank' Snow (1914–99), who recorded over 100 albums and sold more than 70 million records, was born in the area – check out the **Hank Snow Home Town Museum** (*148 Bristol Av;* ✆ *902 354 4675;* ✆ *1 888 450 5525; www.hanksnow.com;* ⊕ *mid May–mid Oct 09.00–17.00 Mon–Sat, noon–17.30 Sun; mid Oct–mid May 09.00–16.00 Mon–Fri; admission CAN$3*) and see a wealth of *Yodelling Ranger* material, including his 1947 Cadillac and his stage suits. The centre shares Liverpool's former train station with the Nova Scotia Country Music Hall of Fame.

Across the water in Brooklyn, among the trees and along the paths behind Cosby's Garden Centre, is the delightful and Narnia-like sculpture garden created by Ivan Higgins, **Concrete Creations** (*4122 Hwy 3, Brooklyn;* ✆ *902 354 2133;* ⛶; ⊕ *in season 08.00–20.00 Mon–Sat, 10.00–20.00 Sun; reduced hours o/s*). Wandering amongst the wonderful figures is fun for all ages.

The park on the waterfront at the end of Main Street is said to be the spot where de Mons landed in 1604: today you'll find cannon and an unusually shaped wooden lighthouse, **Fort Point Lighthouse Park** (*21 Fort Point Lane;* ✆ *902 354 5741;* ⊕ *mid May–early Oct; admission free*), constructed in 1855. Shut down in 1989 with talk of demolition, Nova Scotia's fourth-oldest surviving lighthouse was saved and opened as a small museum in 1997. From the old to the new: The **Hell Bay Brewing Co** (*38 Legion St;* ✆ *902 356 3556;* ⛶; ⊕ *brewery noon–17.00 Tue–Fri*) is a craft brewery with a patio beer garden (water views) in summer (serving beer, wine and more). If successful, expect longer hours and/or weekend opening.

Set out on foot, by bike, canoe or kayak with **Liverpool Adventure Outfitters** (*4003 Sandy Cove Rd;* ✆ *902 354 2702; www.liverpooladventureoutfitters.com*), who offer canoe, kayak, SUP, bike and rowing-boat rentals and multi-sport day tours to Kejimkujik National Park (pages 223–7) and other destinations.

Shop for fresh fish, vegetables, fruit, baked goods and more at the **Privateer Farmers' Market** (*Privateer Park* ⛶; ⊕ *summer 08.00–noon Sat*).

FESTIVALS In May, the **International Theatre Festival** (*www.litf.ca*) is a five-day amateur theatre festival held every two years (even years) at the historic Astor Theatre. **Privateer Days** (✆ *902 354 4500; www.privateerdays.ca*), the town's big festival (five days over the first weekend in July) is a lot of fun, with battle re-enactments, town walking tours led by guides in period costume, candlelit graveyard tours, boat races, fireworks and much more. August sees the **Hank Snow Tribute** (contact Hank Snow Hometown Museum, above, for details), a three-day celebration of the Yodelling Ranger. Ukulele concerts and workshops are held every two years (odd years) in October, at the **International Ukulele Ceilidh** (*www.ukuleleceilidh.ca*).

AROUND LIVERPOOL
Beach Meadows This wonderful long, sandy beach approximately 8km east of Liverpool is one of the best on the South Shore. There are two parking areas from which boardwalks lead to it through the sand dunes. There are views of Coffin Island (named after Peleg Coffin, one of the first settlers), with a lighthouse and abandoned fishing shanties.

Milton

Milton Just 4km from Liverpool, either by Highway 8 or by following Main Street away from town, Milton is a pretty village on the Mersey River. There are photogenic churches, good birding and, in late spring, magnificent rhododendrons beneath the white pines at Pine Grove Park (on the left side of Hwy 8 coming from Liverpool, or Exit 19 of Hwy 103). In Milton itself, Tupper Park has a picnic area overlooking the Milton Falls. You can also visit a restored c1903 blacksmith shop (⊕ mid Jun–Sep 10.00–16.00 Mon–Fri; admission CAN$1).

Where to stay, eat and drink

Mersey Lodge (5 rooms & 1 cabin) 2537 River Rd; ✆ 902 354 5547; www.merseylodge.com; ⊕ year-round. This rustic but comfortable lodge is well off the beaten track, approx 13km from Milton mostly on an unpaved road. Fish, swim or canoe on the river. Full b/fast inc. **$$$**

Morton House Inn B&B (7 units) 147 Main St (Hwy 8); ✆ 902 354 2908; **tf** 1 877 354 2908; www.mortonhouseinn.com; ⊕ year-round by reservation. Located in the village, this c1864 Empire-style mansion with 4 B&B rooms & 3 motel-style rooms is just across the road from the river, & beautifully decorated with antiques. Full b/fast inc in B&B rate. **$–$$**

White Point

White Point Off Highway 3, 9–12km from Liverpool, visitors are drawn here for Nova Scotia's only year-round oceanfront beach. In season, many come for the nine-hole **White Point Golf Club** (**tf** 1 866 683 2485; ⊕ mid Apr–early Nov; green fees CAN$35, resort guests CAN$31), set within the **White Point Beach Resort** (see below) on a small peninsula with majestic views. Played as 18 holes (with separate tees for the back nine) the course is 6,200yds long. Ask about packages if staying at the resort. Watersport-wise, the **Rossignol Surf Shop** (✆ 902 683 2350; www.surfnovscotia.com) also at the resort, offers surfboard sales, surfing lessons and clinics, and equipment rentals.

Where to stay, eat and drink
Hunts Point, a couple of kilometres further along Highway 3, has a popular take-away.

White Point Beach Resort White Point; ✆ 902 354 2711; **tf** 1 800 565 5068; www.whitepoint.com; ⊕ year-round. This long-established, popular family resort has a range of recently refurbished accommodation choices from standard rooms to 3-bedroom log cottages, plus a new Main Lodge (opened 2012). There's a spa, golf course (see above), 1km of private beach, indoor & outdoor (seasonal) pools & the usual resort extras – oh, & large friendly rabbits roaming the grounds. At many resorts you're better off dining elsewhere: not so, here. Elliot's (⊕ for b/fast, lunch & dinner year-round; **$$$**), the ocean-side restaurant (with decks & lounge) offers buffet or à la carte dining, an extensive NS wine selection & panoramic sea views: it rarely disappoints. **$$**

Fishermans Cove RV & Campground (22 sites) 6718 Hwy 3, Hunts Point; ✆ 902 683 2772; www.fishermanscoverv.ca; ⊕ mid May–mid Oct. Small store & laundry facilities. **$**

Seaside Seafoods 6943 Hwy 3, Hunts Point; ✆ 902 683 2618; ⊕ late Mar–Oct 11.00–21.00 (summer til 23.00) daily. Simple but much-loved fast-food & seafood eatery. The deep-fried clams are a hit, plus there's the usual selection of fish & chips, burgers & soft ice cream. Picnic tables outside. **$**

Summerville Beach

Summerville Beach This long (over 1km) stretch of whitish sand is one of the best and most accessible of the South Shore beaches. Backed by sand dunes and a salt marsh, it has been designated a Provincial Park. Sunbathe, play beach volleyball, swim in the bracing waters or picnic. The beach is 17km from Liverpool, just off Highway 3, 1.5km from Exit 20 off Highway 103, and therefore easily reached by car.

4

🏠 **Where to stay, eat and drink** At one end of the beach, the **Quarterdeck Beachside Villas and Grill** (*28 units; 7499 Hwy 3, Summerville Centre;* ☎ *902 683 2998;* tf *1 800 565 1119; www.quarterdeck.ca;* ⊕ *year-round;* **$$$**) is well-equipped, with one-bedroom suites, 13 'villas' (two-storey, two-bedroom apartments) each with an oceanfront deck and balcony, two one-bedroom suites with kitchenettes and one three-bedroom cottage. In addition to this, 12 sleek, modern beach lofts on the hillside across the road are due to be ready by the time you read this. Kayak, bike, surfboard rental is available. The new, modern, glassed-in restaurant (⊕ *check hours;* **$$–$$$**) has one of the province's best locations, and a canteen with more casual alfresco dining is also on the cards. Food at the Quartedeck has (traditionally) been good, but – as one might expect – prices are a bit higher because of the location.

SOUTH TOWARDS SHELBURNE

PORT MOUTON This village on the bay of the same name has a couple of places to stay (including a backpackers' hostel) and a restaurant, and is well placed for exploring the region's beautiful parks and beaches. Several uninhabited islands dot the bay. It is located on Highway 3, 19km/12 miles southwest of Liverpool and 48km/30 miles from Shelburne, and is therefore easily accessible **by car**. By shuttle, the **Cloud Nine Shuttle** (page 137) operates daily Yarmouth–Halifax and vice versa. However, a new section of Highway 103 is due to open by early 2017, bypassing the village. Work is ongoing but I'm told the Port Mouton turn-off will be Exit 20.

Port Mouton was named by Champlain in 1604: when his ship was at anchor in the bay, a sheep jumped into the sea. There were a couple of attempts at settlement (by Scots in the 1620s and English around 1770) but the first lasting attempt was made in 1783 by disbanded soldiers who had served under Sir Guy Carleton. Quickly, they built over 200 houses and called their settlement Guy's Borough. The following year a fire destroyed most of their houses. This – combined with the fact that the region's soil wasn't great for farming – caused the settlers to uproot *en masse*. They headed east, and settled in what is now Guysborough (pages 394–7).

Port Mouton makes a good base to explore the **Kejimkujik Seaside** (*St Catherine's Rd;* ☎ *902 682 2772; www.pc.gc.ca/eng/pn-np/ns/kejimkujik/index.aspx;* ⊕ *year-round, although facilities only open May–mid Oct; admission free*), which is, confusingly, a separate part of Kejimkujik National Park (pages 223–7), approximately 100km inland. Kejimkujik Seaside protects 22km² of wilderness on the Port Mouton Peninsula including pristine white-sand beaches, turquoise waters, coastal bogs, an abundance of wild flowers, rich lagoon systems and coastal wildlife. Most easily reached by an 8km unpaved road from Highway 103, this is one of the least disturbed shoreline areas on the south coast of Nova Scotia. No camping is permitted.

From the car park, an easy trail (5.3km return) leads through the trees, on boardwalks over marshy areas, and on to the beach at Harbour Rocks. Here you are likely to see seals basking on the rocks or bobbing about in the water – take binoculars. You can continue along the beach before retracing your steps. A longer (8.8km return from the car park) option is to branch off the first trail and take in Port Joli Head on a coastal loop. Some sections of the beach close between late April and July to protect piping plover nesting sites. Mosquitoes may cause annoyance, even on the beach. Don't forget repellent.

On the way in to town, the **Coastal Queen's Place** (*8100 Hwy 3;* ☎ *902 947 3140;* f; ⊕ *hours vary – best to check*) is worth a stop: backpacker hostel apart, it houses two galleries and a craft shop.

🏠 Where to stay, eat and drink

🏠 **Port Mouton Bay Cottages & Seascape Restaurant** (5 cottages, 1 bungalow) 8403 Hwy 3; ☎ 902 683 2020; tf 1 866 933 2020; www. cottagesinnovascotia.com; ⊕ year-round. Simple, spacious, well-equipped 2-bedroom cottages, plus 1 3-bedroom bungalow. **$$**

🏠 **Port Mouton International Hostel** (30 beds) 8100 Hwy 103; ☎ 902 947 3140; e pmhostel@ eastlink.ca; www.wqccda.com/ PMhostel; ⊕ year-round. Housed in part of a c1961 former school (now called Coastal Queen's Place), this friendly backpackers' hostel has 1 large & 5 small dorms, with most of the beds bunks. There's a big kitchen & common room, & if you don't feel like cooking, the Seascape (see below) is in walking distance. Linen/bedding inc. *Dorm CAN$30.* **$**

✖ **Seascape Restaurant** 8426 Hwy 3; ☎ 902 683 2626; ⊕ early Apr–mid May & Sep–mid Nov 11.00–19.00 Tue–Sun; mid May–Aug 11.00–20.00 daily. Under the same ownership as Port Mouton Bay Cottages & just across the road, this restaurant ain't *haute cuisine* but the fish & chips are very good & you won't go hungry. **$$**

THOMAS RADDALL PROVINCIAL PARK (*East Port l'Hébert Rd, Port Joli;* ☎ *902 683 2664; parks.novascotia.ca/content/thomas-raddall;* ⊕ *late May–early Oct*) This 678ha park is 3km off Highway 103, 9km west of Port Mouton, and has over 11km of trails, some multi-use, as well as an 82-site wooded campground. The best stretches of sand are Camper's Beach and Sandy Bay Beach. The park has a good selection of animal and birdlife.

LOCKEPORT The quaint town of Lockeport is well worth exploring for its lovely old homes and fine beaches (five in all). It was founded in 1755 by settlers from Plymouth, Massachusetts, led by a Jonathan Locke. Several other Planters followed and were joined by British settlers – and a few Icelanders. Although in the early stages of the American Revolution residents were sympathetic to American privateers, sometimes offering them aid and even helping American prisoners who had escaped, that all changed in 1778 when whale boats from Rhode Island arrived

BEACH BEAUTY

At the time of writing, Carters Beach is a prime contender for the 'Most Beautiful Beach in Nova Scotia' title – and, amazingly, it's still a relatively well-kept secret. It's being realistic rather than pessimistic to wonder how long it will stay unspoilt.

When you first see the beaches – there are actually three – and the island-dotted bay, you might think that you're in the Mediterranean, especially if the sun is out. The sand is golden, the crystal-clear water has a slight turquoise hue, and huge, smooth black boulders and sometimes colourful sea kayakers, give the scene depth.

Walk along the first beach and you'll find a stream blocking your way. Depending on the tide and other factors, you may be able to ford it by wading across, or it may be safer to head upstream for about ten minutes and cross there. The second beach is broad and straight, and a good place to look for sand dollars (flat, almost circular, shell-like types of urchin). The third beach is another pretty crescent which ends at high sand dunes well worth climbing for the view.

To reach Carters Beach turn on to Central Port Mouton Road from Highway 3 at Port Mouton. Continue for about 4km until you see a sign to the left to Carters Beach. There's a tiny parking area (painfully inadequate at busy times) but no other facilities, and a short (less than 100m) path through the trees down to the beach.

and raided their homes for food and valuables. Since its founding, Lockeport has been a fishing community, and shipbulding began in the 1880s.

The beautiful 1.5km-long **Crescent Beach**, not to be confused with a beach of the same name near the LaHave Islands (box, pages 172–3), is hard to miss, on the southern edge of the thin strip of land between the 'mainland' and the 'island'. Beach lovers should be aware that there are at least another dozen good beaches in the area: locals will be happy to direct you to their favourite.

Beaches apart, the town also boasts the province's only **Registered Historic Streetscape**. This comprises five houses built by descendants of town founder Jonathan Locke between 1836 and 1876. The houses offer an interesting cross-section of historical architecture with excellent examples of Colonial, Georgian and Victorian styles. A walking-tour guidebook should be available at the tourist office.

Those with children shouldn't miss the excellent marine-themed playground (⊕ *mid May–Oct*) in **Seacaps Memorial Park**, which also hosts a weekly **farmers' market** (⊕ *mid May–early Oct 14.00–18.00 Fri*). In August, there is a weekend fishing tournament, the **Sea Derby** (*lockeportseaderby.ca*).

Accessible **by car**, Lockeport is on Highway 3, 18km from Highway 103, Exit 23, 17km from Highway 103, Exit 24.

 Where to stay, eat and drink

⌂ **Ocean Mist Cottages** (6 cottages) 1 Gull Rock Rd; ✆ 902 656 3200; www. oceanmistcottages.ca; ⊕ year-round. With a fabulous location less than 20m from Crescent Beach, these fully equipped & quiet 2-bedroom cottages are spacious & comfortable. Weekly rentals preferred. **$$$**

⌂ **Lockeport Landing B&B & Café** (4 rooms) 18 Beech St; ✆ 902 656 3333; www. lockeportlanding.ca; ⊕ May–Oct. Bright,

simple rooms with separate entrances, & just a 4min walk to the beach. Rate includes good b/fast (eg: classic bacon & eggs or Montreal bagel with smoked salmon & cream cheese). The cosy, cheery licensed café (⊕ *May–Oct 10.00–14.00 Wed–Mon & 17.00–20.00 Thu–Sun; $*) dishes up tasty, fresh food, such as fab fish cakes, fish tacos, salads & homemade ice cream. Lactose-/gluten-free & vegan options available. Recommended. **$$**

OTHER PRACTICALITIES

$ Royal Bank 25A Beech St; ✆ 902 656 2212; ⊕ 10.00–15.00 Mon–Wed & Fri, 10.00–17.00 Thu

✉ **Post office** 30 Beech St; ⊕ 08.15–17.00 Mon–Fri, 08.30–12.30 Sat

i **Tourist information** 157 Locke St; ✆ 902 656 3123; ⊕ late Jun–mid Sep 10.00–18.00 daily.

At Crescent Beach, adjacent to changing rooms & showers.

Lillian Benham Library 35 North St; ✆ 902 656 2817; ⊕ 14.30–17.00 & 18.00–19.30 Tue & Thu, 10.30–13.00 & 14.00–17.00 Wed, 14.30–17.00 Fri, 10.00–noon Sat

SHELBURNE AND AROUND

The town of Shelburne (population: 1,685) sits at the innermost end of what is said by many to be the third-finest harbour in the world (after Sydney, Australia, and Havana, Cuba). Much of what there is to be seen lies within the area bounded by Water Street (the main street), Dock Street and King Street. Within this area are three museums and over 30 original late 18th-century Loyalist homes, most in good condition.

History aside, the waterfront is a pleasant place for a stroll. Bearing in mind that the choices for both dining and accommodation are limited, if you're visiting at the weekend and/or in peak season, it would be wise to book ahead.

HISTORY In the aftermath of the American War of Independence, the newly formed colonies were not a good place to be for those who had been loyal to the British flag. When offered passage, land under protection of the British flag, provisions and tools, many jumped at the chance. Early in 1783, 18 ships loaded with mostly aristocratic Loyalists and a large number of their black former slaves sailed into Port Roseway (Shelburne's early name).

Trees were felled, land was cleared, streets were laid out and houses were built quickly. The settlement was renamed Shelburne, in honour of Lord Shelburne, Secretary of State for the Colonies. Thousands more Loyalists arrived later in the year, and Shelburne quickly (but only briefly) became the largest urban centre in British North America, having a population of more than 15,000 in 1785.

Then things went sour: the government stopped providing rations and financial assistance. Race riots broke out. Many began to move away, properties were abandoned, houses were torn down for fuel and still more were allowed to fall into ruin and decay. By 1818, the population had dropped to 300.

In time, people began to move back. Shipbuilding started up again, and soon it prospered. New homes were built over the old cellars. The population tripled, and Shelburne became renowned for the building of schooners and brigantines. Late in the 19th century, when steel-hulled steam-powered ships began to replace wooden sailing vessels, Shelburne's economy fell back on fishing. Boatbuilding continued on a much smaller scale and this time yachts were the speciality.

Life continued quietly and without great incident until the 1990s when a couple of Hollywood films were shot here (see box, above). Since then, Shelburne has been used as the backdrop for a number of other films.

> ## HOLLYWOOD HISTORY
>
> Much of *Scarlet Letter*, a 1990s Hollywood flop, was filmed in Shelburne. Wanting to make the location more authentic, the film company built over a dozen 'old' structures. Most were removed after filming, but some remain, including the 'historic' (c1994!) cooperage on the waterfront across from the Cooper's Inn. Other films have been shot here more recently including *Wilby Wonderful* (2004), *Moby Dick* (2010) and six-part mini-series *The Book of Negroes* (2014).

GETTING THERE AND AWAY Shelburne is situated on Highway 3, just off Highway 103, Exit 25 (southbound) or Exit 26 (northbound), and is therefore easy to get to **by car**. It is 210km/130 miles from Halifax, 98km/61 miles from Yarmouth and 67km/47 miles from Liverpool. The **Cloud Nine Shuttle** (page 137) operates daily Yarmouth–Halifax and vice versa.

 WHERE TO STAY *Map, page 182, unless otherwise stated*

Boulder Cove Cottages [map, pages 164–5] (5 cottages) 321 Shore Rd, Churchover; ☏902 875 1542; **tf** 1 866 732 7867; www. bouldercove.com; ☺ year-round. Lovely setting on the Birchtown Bay waterfront a 10min drive from Shelburne. Very comfortable 1- & 2-bedroom cottages. Laundry room, walking trail, bikes & boats for guest use. Within 3km of the Black Loyalist Heritage Centre (page 185). **$$**

Cooper's Inn (8 rooms) 36 Dock St; ☏902 875 4656; **tf** 1 800 688 2011; www.thecoopersinn. com; ☺ Apr–Oct. Historic charm & modern convenience in a restored c1784 Loyalist home with courtyard garden across the road from the waterfront. Check website for packages. Gourmet b/fast inc. **$$**

Inner Harbor Inn (5 units) 1 Dock St; ☏902 875 1131; theseadog.com/inner-harbor-inn;

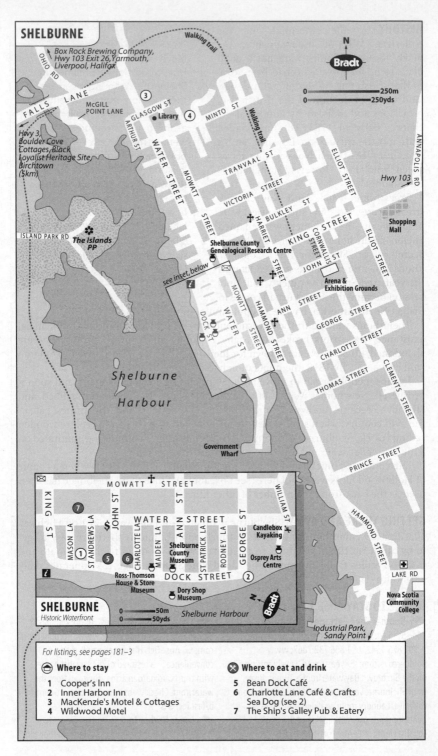

SHELBURNE

Box Rock Brewing Company,
Hwy 103 Exit 26, Yarmouth,
Liverpool, Halifax

Walking trail

OHIO RD

FALLS LANE

McGILL POINT LANE

Hwy 3,
Boulder Cove
Cottages, Black
Loyalist Heritage Site,
Birchtown
(5km)

ISLAND PARK RD

The Islands
PP

GLASGOW ST

Library

MINTO ST

Walking trail

ARTHUR ST

WATER STREET

MOWAT STREET

TRANVAAL ST

VICTORIA STREET

HARRIET STREET

BULKLEY ST

ELLIOT STREET

KING STREET

CORNWALLIS STREET

Hwy 103

ANNAPOLIS RD

Shopping
Mall

Shelburne County
Genealogical Research Centre

JOHN ST

ELLIOT STREET

Arena &
Exhibition Grounds

see inset, below

DOCK ST

WATER STREET

MOWAT ST

HAMMOND STREET

ANN STREET

GEORGE STREET

CHARLOTTE STREET

THOMAS STREET

CLEMENTS STREET

Shelburne Harbour

Government
Wharf

PRINCE STREET

HAMMOND STREET

LAKE RD

Nova Scotia
Community
College

SHELBURNE
Historic Waterfront

0 ____ 50m
0 ____ 50yds

MOWATT STREET

KING STREET

MASON LA

ST ANDREWS LA

JOHN ST

WATER STREET

CHARLOTTE LA

MAIDEN LA

ANN ST

ST PATRICK LA

RODNEY LA

GEORGE ST

WILLIAM ST

Candlebox
Kayaking

Osprey Arts
Centre

Shelburne
County
Museum

DOCK STREET

Ross-Thomson
House & Store
Museum

Dory Shop
Museum

Shelburne Harbour

Industrial Park,
Sandy Point

For listings, see pages 181–3

🛏 **Where to stay**

1 Cooper's Inn
2 Inner Harbor Inn
3 MacKenzie's Motel & Cottages
4 Wildwood Motel

✖ **Where to eat and drink**

5 Bean Dock Café
6 Charlotte Lane Café & Crafts
   Sea Dog (see 2)
7 The Ship's Galley Pub & Eatery

year-round. 3 suites & 2 bedrooms (most with fab water views) in this new, upscale, true harbourfront inn above the Sea Dog Restaurant (but still quiet). Nice modern décor & very comfortable. **$$**

🏠 **MacKenzie's Motel & Cottages, and the Wildwood** (16 & 20 units) 260 Water St & 40 Minto St; 902 875 2842 & 902 875 2964; tf 1 866 875 0740 & 1 800 565 5001; www. mackenzies.ca; both year-round. These 2 properties (with motel rooms, suites (1 with kitchen) & 1- & 2-bedroom cottages) are under the same ownership/management. MacKenzie's has a heated outdoor pool (seasonal). Both are good budget choices. Rate inc continental b/fast. **$**

✕ WHERE TO EAT AND DRINK   *Map, opposite*

✕ **Charlotte Lane Café & Crafts** 13 Charlotte Lane; 902 875 3314; www.charlottelane.ca; early May–mid Dec 11.30–14.30 & 17.00–20.00 Tue–Sat. Discerning locals & visitors travel a long way to enjoy owner-chef Roland Glauser's cooking. The menu is varied & changes seasonally: start, perhaps, with the Bluenose spinach salad. To follow, the lobster & scallop brandy gratin is superb (or try the pork tenderloin Zürich-style), & for dessert the sticky toffee pudding takes some beating. The extensive wine list includes a Nova Scotia section, & a different special cocktail is offered every evening. Although housed in a heritage building, the décor is bright, with funky local artworks. There is a small garden patio. **$$–$$$**

✕ **Sea Dog Restaurant** 1 Dock St; 902 875 1131; theseadog.com; year-round Jun–Nov 11.00–21.00, Dec–May 11.00–20.00 daily. Popular & family-friendly, the large outside deck is a great place for a drink or bite in the sunshine. The fish (haddock) & chips is good, & a glass of Shelburne-brewed Boxing Rock makes a good accompaniment. **$$**

✕ **The Ship's Galley Pub & Eatery** 156 Water St; 902 875 3260; theshipsgalley.com; in season 11.00–20.00 Tue–Thu, 11.00–midnight Fri & Sat, 10.00–15.00 Sun; o/s check hours. Decent pub-style food (eg: good burgers, fish & loads of good fries) with good service. **$$**

☕ **Bean Dock Café** Dock St (cnr with John St); 902 875 1302; summer 08.30–20.00 Mon–Thu, 08.30–17.00 Fri, 10.00–16.00 Sat, 10.00–14.00 Sun; winter 08.30–16.00 Mon–Fri, 10.00–14.00 Sat. Friendly, laidback & a good choice for coffee, light lunches & desserts. **$**

OTHER PRACTICALITIES

$ CIBC 146 Water St; 902 875 2388; 10.00–17.00 Mon–Fri

✚ **Roseway Hospital** 1606 Sandy Point Rd; 902 875 3011

✉ **Post office** 162 Mowatt St; 08.30–17.30 Mon–Fri, 08.30–12.30 Sat

ℹ **Tourist information** 31 Dock St; 902 875 4547; daily Jul–Aug 10.00–19.00; late May–Jun & Sep–late Oct 09.00–17.00

McKay Memorial Library 17 Glasgow St; 902 875 3615; 10.00–17.00 Mon–Wed, Fri & Sat, noon–20.00 Thu

WHAT TO SEE AND DO   Housed in a c1787 Loyalist building, **the Shelburne County Museum** (*20 Dock St;* 902 875 3219; *www.shelburnemuseums.com;* *Jun–mid Oct 09.30–17.30 daily; mid Oct–mid Dec 09.00–13.00 & 14.00–17.00 Mon–Fri; Jan–mid May 09.00–13.00 & 14.00–17.00 Wed–Sat; admission CAN$4, combined ticket CAN$10*) is a good place to get an overview of the town's fascinating history. Be sure to see the Newsham firepumper (one of two early 'fire engines' imported from Boston in 1740) and a good exhibit on black Loyalist history.

There was something of a revolution in the Grand Banks fishing industry when someone came up with the idea of loading a schooner with small, light, stackable wooden boats (dories), sailing out to the fishing grounds, lowering them into the water and then letting fishermen try their luck. Dories made in Shelburne were renowned for their strength. In 1903, the c1000 former dory shop, now the **Dory Shop Museum** (*Dock St;* 902 875 3219; *doryshop.novascotia.ca;* *Jun–mid Oct 09.30–17.30 daily; admission CAN$4, combined ticket CAN$10*) was opened as a museum by Prince Charles and Diana, Princess of Wales.

Amongst the Loyalists who arrived in Port Roseway (Shelburne) in 1783 were over 1,000 blacks, many former slaves who had served the Loyalist cause against the Americans during the War of Independence. For their actions, they were 'rewarded' with land a few kilometres to the west of Shelburne in what became known as Burchtown (and, with time, Birchtown).

For a short while, Birchtown was the largest settlement of free blacks in North America – the population in 1784 was over 1,500 – but this was no paradise. Many blacks had been granted infertile land, there was little or no employment and poverty was commonplace. Those who could find work received about a quarter of the wage received by a white doing the same job. Nova Scotia winters were incredible shocks to systems, particularly as with no money to build houses, many lived in what were effectively roofed-over holes on hillsides. In 1791, things were so bad that an emissary was sent to raise the community's concerns with the Secretary of State in England.

As it happened, in addition to colonising Nova Scotia, the English government had similar plans for West Africa, and came up with an ironic proposal. Any adult male who wished would be given free passage to Sierra Leone where he would receive 20 acres of land (plus ten acres for his wife, and five each for any children). Many agreed to the terms, and in 1792 a fleet of 15 vessels left Halifax for West Africa. On board were over 500 from Birchtown alone.

Many of those who left had led or inspired the community: after their departure there was another exodus from Birchtown, this time to other parts of Nova Scotia. Several sections of Lawrence Hill's 2007 novel *The Book of Negroes* cover this period of history.

Today, fewer than 200 black Nova Scotians live in Shelburne County.

The **Ross-Thomson House and Store Museum** (*9 Charlotte Lane;* \ *902 875 3219; rossthomson.novascotia.ca;* ⊕ *Jun–mid Oct 09.30–17.30 daily; admission CAN$4, combined ticket CAN$10*) is located in a c1785 house that was the workplace of brothers George and Robert Ross, from Aberdeen, Scotland. The highlight is an authentically stocked 18th-century store and chandlery. The garden is laid out and planted in late 18th-century style.

An excellent resource for genealogists, the **Shelburne County Genealogical Research Centre** (*168 Water St;* \ *902 875 4299; nsgna.ednet.ns.ca/shelburne;* ⊕ *summer 09.00–16.30 Mon–Fri (check winter hours); CAN$10/half day*) allows you to trace the roots of Loyalists and Shelburne's other early settlers.

The **Osprey Arts Centre** (*107 Water St;* \ *902 875 2359; www.ospreyartscentre. ca;* ⊕ *year-round; gallery* ⊕ *09.00–16.00 Mon–Fri*) is a performing arts centre featuring music, theatre and film, and also houses the Coastline Gallery, featuring local artists' work.

Sea kayaking is a great way to see the region and the harbour, and single or double kayaks can be rented from the Sea Dog Restaurant (page 183), who will also advise you on suggested routes and waterside attractions. Sea kayak tours and instruction suitable for a variety of skill levels are also offered by **Candlebox Kayaking** (*Shelburne Harbour Yacht Club and Marina, 107 Water St;* \ *902 637 7115; candleboxkayaking. com;* ⊕ *year-round*). If you'd rather someone else did the hard work, **Shelburne Harbour Boat Tours** (\ *902 875 6521; www.shelburneharbourboattours.com;* ⊕ *Jun– Sep*) runs three tours daily around the harbour and beyond from CAN$29.

If all that sea air brings on a thirst, head for the **Boxing Rock Brewing Company** (*78 Ohio Rd; 902 494 9233; boxingrock. ca;* ⊕ *May–Oct noon–18.00 Mon–Fri, Fri & Sat by appointment*), a purpose-built, 1,500m² craft brewery (near Exit 26 of Hwy 103) opened in 2012. Take a tour (CAN$15 including samples, no open-toed footwear) or try a sample.

FESTIVALS June sees the **Shelburne County Lobster Festival**, where you can enjoy crustacean creations at various Shelburne County venues. In July, **Founders' Days** (*www.shelburnefoundersdays. com*) gives the opportunity to look round a Loyalist encampment occupied by volunteers in period military costume. August is busy with the **Songs at Sea Level** music festival at Osprey Arts Centre, the **Kayak Festival** (*www.shelburnekayakfestival. ca*) – three days of instruction, workshops, etc (book well in advance) – and the agricultural-events based **Shelburne County Exhibition** (*shelburneexhibition.ca*). See the waterfront festooned with brightly coloured wind-catching devices at the **Whirligig and Weathervane Festival** (*www.whirligigfestival.com*) in September, and the same month, the **Dock St Uke Camp** (*www.dockstreetukecamp.ca*) is a three-day ukulele instruction camp – book well in advance.

AROUND SHELBURNE
The Islands Provincial Park (*Hwy 3; parks.novascotia.ca/content/islands;* ⊕ *mid Jun–early Oct*) Huge granite boulders – left by melting glaciers 10,000 years ago – dot this pleasant park and open and wooded campground (62 sites) 5km west of Shelburne offering fine views over Shelburne Harbour. The picnic area is joined to the rest of the park by a short causeway, and there's a rocky beach. Take repellent for the wooded areas.

Black Loyalist Heritage Centre (*119 Old Birchtown Rd; Birchtown;* ☏ *902 875 1310; tf 1 888 354 0772; blackloyalist.novascotia.ca;* ⊕ *late May–mid Oct 09.00–17.00 daily; admission CAN$8*) This new centre on a lovely site 9km west of Shelburne tells the story of what was (in the late 18th century) the world's largest 'free' African population outside Africa. Take a guided tour, visit historic buildings and the National Monument commemorating the Black Loyalist Landing in Birchtown in 1783, or take a stroll around the gift shop. See also box, opposite.

The Toby and beyond One of Nova Scotia's few cross-province roads heads north from just west of Shelburne. After passing the Ohios (Lower, Middle and Upper) and crossing and re-crossing the pretty Roseway River, Route 203 skirts one edge of the vast Tobeatic Wilderness Area (box, pages 186–7). The road travels further inland to East Kemptville (nearby is one of the province's few luxury eco-lodges, Trout Point Lodge; page 187), and then meets Route 340 where a left turn will take you towards Yarmouth (pages 194–200) and a right turn towards Weymouth (pages 203–4).

THE FAR SOUTHWEST
BARRINGTON With a lovely setting at the northeast of Barrington Bay, the community of Barrington is one of the oldest on the South Shore, and this area

The pristine Tobeatic Wilderness Area (known as the 'Tobeatic', or just the 'Toby') is vast, covering 120,000ha. Along with adjacent, connected wild spaces including Kejimkujik National Park (38,000ha; pages 223–7), Medway Lakes Wilderness Area (20,000ha), Tidney River Wilderness Area (18,000ha), Silver River Wilderness Area (5,000ha), Lake Rossignol Wilderness Area (4,000ha), and numerous other nature reserves, the area spreads over five counties and represents the largest span of wilderness in the Maritimes at over 175,000ha.

The Tobeatic, at the core of it all, is mostly a rugged landscape best suited for wilderness canoe travel along its many traditional routes in the headwaters of the Shelburne Canadian Heritage, Sissiboo, Roseway, Clyde and Tusket rivers. Barrens (areas of tangled heathland, locally known as 'hardhacks'), bogs, wetlands and remote woodland provide vast areas of diverse wildlife habitat: bear, porcupine, snowshoe hare and beaver are common. The provincially endangered mainland moose inhabits these wild tracts of southwest Nova Scotia. Listen out for the lovely call of the loon from virtually every lake, and the hoot of the barred owl at night. Wild flowers (including rare orchids) are plentiful in late spring and summer along shores and forests, and late summer and early autumn welcome an abundance of blueberries, huckleberries and cranberries. There are several pockets of 400-year-old old-growth forest.

There are no official campsites or officially maintained trails, just those used and kept open by generations of local guides, stewards, and the odd visitor. No motorised travel – including by ATV, motorboat, or float plane – is permitted, and high-clearance access vehicles or transportation by local outfitters is advised in order to reach the Tobeatic's boundaries.

The nearest communities include Bear River to the north, Weymouth to the northwest, Caledonia to the east, and Kemptville to the west, all of which can provide basic supplies.

(including Cape Sable Island) is one of the few parts of Nova Scotia where Quakers settled. Originally from Nantucket, they were whalers. Arriving in 1762, most moved on to Dartmouth (page 126) in 1784 after being harassed repeatedly by American privateers. In more recent times, fishing – particularly for lobster – became the mainstay of the community.

Most services (supermarkets, fast food, etc) are located 8km away at **Barrington Passage**, which is also the gateway to Cape Sable Island (pages 188–9). Barrington itself has a tourist office and the **Barrington Museum complex** (✆ 902 637 2185; www.capesablehistoricalsociety.com; ⊕ Jun–Sep 09.30–17.30 Mon–Sat, 13.00–17.30 Sun; admission fee, typically less than CAN$5/museum), a group of four museums and a genealogical centre (for which a CAN$10 research fee is charged). Most popular is the **Seal Island Light Museum**, a half-height copy of the lighthouse that stood on remote Seal Island. Go to the top for a panoramic view of Barrington Bay and a close up look at a Fresnel Lens. At the c1882 **Barrington Woollen Mill** (powered by a horizontal water wheel), wool was washed, carded, spun, dyed and woven. The **Old Meeting House Museum** was built in 1765 by Planters, and is Canada's oldest nonconformist Protestant house of worship. Behind the building is the region's oldest cemetery. Finally, the **Western Counties Military Museum** houses exhibits ranging from 16th-century cannonballs to coins brought back from the Middle East by Canadian soldiers on peacekeeping

Early spring (around the beginning of May) and autumn are probably the best times to visit: water levels are conveniently higher for wilderness canoeing, there are fewer biting insects, and daytime temperatures are more moderate – but be prepared for extreme weather at any time of year.

This is true, remote wilderness, most of which has no mobile-phone reception: if you overstretch yourself or are unlucky, an exciting adventure could easily turn into disaster. Considerable wilderness experience and advice from local experts and outfitters are essential for a successful trip. Weymouth-based and recommended, **Hinterland Adventures** (m 902 837 4092; tf 1 800 378 8177; www. kayakingnovascotia.com) offers canoe tours and **Ukaliq** (m 902 789 7471; www. ukaliq.com) offers guided customised wilderness tours deep into the Toby.

Don't worry if you aren't a fan of wilderness camping as there are some alternatives, such as the **Trout Point Lodge** (*189 Trout Point Rd, East Kemptville*; m 902 482 8360, 902 761 2142; www.troutpoint.com; ⊕ May–Dec; **$$$**), which is, in my opinion, the province's best upmarket wilderness lodge. The best base for exploring the western part of the Toby, riverside Trout Point Lodge has a wonderful setting right on the edge of the protected wilderness. It offers a variety of accommodation including cottages, a cabin and two lodges. Part of the attraction is the remoteness (the property occupies over 40ha at the convergence of the Tusket and Napier rivers), but this also means that you'll have quite a drive if you choose not to dine on-site. In addition to woodland trails, there is river and lake swimming, canoeing, kayaking, star-gazing, mountain bikes and catch-&-release fishing. The dining room (⊕ *mid May–late Oct; 1 sitting at 19.30; fixed-price dinner CAN$163 per couple*) serves a creative blend of Creole and Mediterranean cuisine, and boasts an extensive wine list. The lodge is somewhat remote, reached by a 3km unpaved road from Highway 203. It is approximately 64km/40 miles from Shelburne, 53km/33 miles from Yarmouth, and 110km/69 miles from Digby.

duty. It shares Barrington's c1843 Old Courthouse with the **Cape Sable Historical Society Centre**.

Also worth visiting in the area are beautiful **Sandy Hills Beach Provincial Park** (*Hwy 309, approx 6km from Barrington*), and the lighthouse at **Baccaro Point** (*Baccaro Rd, off Hwy 309, 18km from Barrington*), a good – if breezy – spot for a picnic, and popular with birdwatchers. In July, the **Nova Scotia Marathon** (*www.barringtonmunicipality.com/festivals-and-events.html*) offers a combination of full and half marathons.

Barrington is located on Highway 103 and is easy to get to **by car**. The town is 40km/25 miles from Shelburne and 67km/42 miles from Yarmouth. The **Cloud Nine Shuttle** (page 137) operates daily both ways between Yarmouth and Halifax.

🏠 **Where to stay, eat and drink** The following establishments are all in Barrington Passage (8km from Barrington), close to the causeway to Cape Sable Island.

🏠 **Horizon Chalets & Motel** (14 units) 3112 Hwy 3; m 902 637 2242; e reservations@ horizonmotels.com; www.horizonmotels.com; ⊕ year-round. 8 motel rooms & 6 larger chalet rooms. **$**

✕ **Capt Kat's Lobster Shack** 3723 Hwy 3; m 902 637 3720; f captkatslobstershack; ⊕ in season 11.00–20.00 daily: check off-season. Popular, nautically themed restaurant offering not just (excellent) lobster – served a variety of ways, such as creamed on toast – but many other good seafood, pasta, poultry & meat choices. Take-away menu available. $$–$$$

✕ **Dan's Ice Cream Shoppe** 3724 Hwy 3; 📞 902 637 3177; ⓕ IceCreamDan; ⊕ Mar–Dec

10.00–22.00 daily. Wraps, smoothies, soup, salads – & quite good ice cream. My daughter likes the chocolate twist covered in multi-coloured sprinkles. Fun place. $

Other practicalities

$ **Royal Bank** 3525 Hwy 3, Barrington Passage; 📞 902 637 2040; ⊕ 09.30–17.00 Mon–Fri

✉ **Post office** 2398 Hwy 3, Barrington; ⊕ 08.00–noon & 13.00–17.00 Mon–Fri

ℹ **Tourist information** 2517 Hwy 3, Barrington; 📞 902 637 2625; ⊕ late May–late Sep 08.30–17.00 daily

Barrington Municipal Library 3588 Hwy 3, Barrington Passage; 📞 902 637 3348; ⊕ 10.00–17.00 Tue, 12.30–17.00 & 18.00–20.00 Wed–Fri, 10.00–14.00 Sat

CAPE SABLE ISLAND Not to be confused with Sable Island (pages 398–401), Cape Sable Island has also seen more than its fair share of shipwrecks in its time. There are few services, but ubiquitous are lobster pots and the smell of the sea. Small communities such as Centreville, Newellton, West Head – and comparatively bustling Clarks Harbour – dot the island. The causeway to the island leads off Highway 3 at Barrington Passage, 8km/5 miles west of Barrington.

The island has four main beaches: seals are sometimes seen at **Stoney** and **South Side** beaches, and **Northeast Point Beach** is popular with sunbathers. The wild expanse of **Hawk Beach** – named for a vessel once shipwrecked here and closest to the c1923 Cape Lighthouse, Nova Scotia's tallest – is great for solitude, proximity to nature and birding.

Named after an early 1760s' settler, the **Archelaus Smith Museum** (*915 Hwy 330*; 📞 *902 745 3361*; ⊕ *late Jun–end Aug 10.30–16.30 Mon–Sat, 11.30–15.30 Sun; admission free*), has displays on local history, island life, lobster fishing and shipbuilding. The most interesting exhibit is a 'wreck chair' made from wooden pieces salvaged from over 20 shipwrecks.

Colourful boats bob in **Clarks Harbour,** a busy little fishing town where the shore is lined with fish plants and boatbuilding yards. There's a petrol station, general store, bank and tourist information centre (*2634 Hwy 330*; 📞 *902 745*

THE SHAG HARBOUR INCIDENT

Around a dozen residents of Shag Harbour (located on Highway 3, 9km west of Barrington Passage), witnessed a mysterious object crashing into the sea on the evening of 4 October 1967. Official investigations were carried out, and books such as *Dark Object: The World's Only Government-Documented UFO Crash* (page 403) were written about what has been described as Canada's version of Roswell (Roswell is a town in New Mexico, USA renowned for what may have been a 'UFO incident' in 1947). The community is now home to the **Shag Harbour Incident Society Museum** (📞 *902 723 0127*; e *shagharbour@gmail. com*; ⓕ *shagharbourUFO*; ⊕ *mid Jun–mid Sep 10.00–17.00 daily, off-season by appointment; admission free, donations welcome*); to find it, look out for a cream-coloured building with a flying saucer on the wall and two alien figures standing outside. The society holds a UFO festival (usually in September). The local post office (*5527 Hwy 3*) has a special UFO cancellation stamp.

2586; ⊕ *early Jun–late Sep 10.00–17.00 Mon–Fri, 10.00–16.00 Sat).* A c1895 edifice constructed by shipbuilders houses the **Seaside Heritage Centre** (*2773 Main St;* ☎ *902 745 0844,* ⊕ *Jun–Sep*). In mid August, the town holds Island Days, a festival of dory races.

🏠 **Where to stay, eat and drink** Self-caterers should stock up on the mainland and – with the exception of West Head – travellers should expect to go to Barrington or beyond to eat out.

🏠 **Mama's By The Sea B&B** (2 rooms) 14 Oscar St, Clarks Harbour; ☎ 902 745 2900; www. mamasbythesea.ca; ⊕ year-round. Friendly B&B with great ocean views. The 2 bedrooms share a bathroom. Rate includes hearty b/fast. Lobster boils on request, boat trips arranged. Good value. **$**

✘ **West Head Takeout** Boundry St, off Hwy 330; ☎ 902 745 1322; ⊕ Apr–late Sep 10.00–20.00 daily. Located just by the wharf at West Head, this well-established take-out is a favourite of the local fishermen – always a good sign. Another take-out (the Route 330 Diner) is almost next door, but this author prefers West Head. **$**

THE PUBNICOS From Barrington, Highway 3 follows the pretty east shore of Pubnico Harbour passing Lower East, Centre East, Middle East and East Pubnico, before reaching Pubnico itself. From here, a turn on to Highway 335 takes you along the Pubnico Peninsula past Upper West, West, Middle West and Lower West Pubnico before fizzling out just before Pubnico Point. The region is well worth exploring by car or bike.

The Pubnico Peninsula is far busier and more prosperous than you might expect, as this is the heart of one of the world's richest and most productive lobster-fishing areas. Rich, too, is the region's Acadian tradition, and you're more likely to hear French spoken than English. While there is no official tourist information office in the Pubnicos, locals will be only too happy to try and help.

Pubnico is situated on Highway 3 and therefore convenient **by car**, just off Exit 31 of Highway 103, 29km/18 miles from Barrington (via Hwy 103), 31km/19 miles from Shag Harbour and 4km/2 miles from West Pubnico. The **Cloud Nine Shuttle** (page 137) operates daily Yarmouth–Halifax and vice versa.

History In 1653, Sieur Philippe D'Entremont was awarded the Baronnie de Pombomcoup, a region covering most of the land between modern-day Shelburne and Yarmouth. Pombomcoup (which became Pubnico) is derived from the Mi'kmaq *Pogomkook* meaning 'land cleared for cultivation'.

D'Entremont built a château here, and when he moved away transferred his title to his eldest son. Fish were plentiful, the land was good, and a prosperous settlement grew.

BIRD ISLAND

Cape Sable Island is the most southerly accessible point in Atlantic Canada, and one of the province's best spring and autumn migration birding sites for waders. The coast around South Side Inlet and south and west of The Hawk are particularly rich viewing areas and tens of thousands of semipalmated sandpipers and short-billed dowitchers can usually be seen. In late winter and early spring, thousands of Brant congregate on the flats of Hawk Channel.

The Pubnico Acadians escaped deportation in 1755, but weren't so lucky three years later. The château and their buildings were destroyed, the surrounding land torched. The Acadians were exiled but eight years later began to return, and unlike those in most other places, were permitted to regain their old lands.

This is the province's oldest Acadian community still inhabited by the descendants of its founder. One 18th-century house still survives, now as a private residence, at the end of Old Church Road in West Pubnico.

🏠 Where to stay, eat and drink

🏠 **Argyle by the Sea B&B** (3 rooms) 848 Argyle Sound Rd, Argyle Sound; ✆ 902 762 2759; e georgegoodwin@hotmail.com; ☉ year-round. Rooms with private or shared bath in this quiet B&B by the ocean. Bookable through www. booking.com . Full b/fast inc. **$**

🏠 **Red Cap Motel & Restaurant** (6 rooms) 1034 Hwy 335, Middle West Pubnico; ✆ 902 762 2112; � Red Cap Restaurant & Motel; ☉ year-round. Attractive-looking traditional motel with in-room fridges, coffee-makers, high-speed internet. Good licensed restaurant (☉ 08.00–21.30 daily; **$$**), where the focus is on fresh local produce. **$**

🏠 **Yesteryear's B&B** (3 rooms) 2775 Hwy 3, Pubnico; ✆ 902 762 2969; www.yesteryears.ca;

☉ year-round; off-season by reservation. A Victorian heritage house with spacious bedrooms – all with en-suite bathrooms – & a good craft shop (items made on the premises). Substantial b/fast inc. **$**

⛺ **La Baronnie Campground** (10 sites) 1207 Hwy 335, Middle West Pubnico; ✆ 902 762 3388; ☉ year-round. Tent sites & 2 serviced sites near the sea, with a laundromat. **$**

✖ **Dennis Point Café** Dennis Point, Lower West Pubnico; ✆ 902 762 1220; www.dennispointcafe. com; ☉ year-round 07.00–20.30 daily. There's an extensive menu at this busy restaurant just across from the wharves where the latest catches are unloaded. They have a deep fryer but fish can also be broiled or pan-fried. The seafood platters are recommended. **$$**

Other practicalities

$ Royal Bank 968 Hwy 335, West Pubnico; ✆ 902 762 2205; ☉ 10.00–16.00 Mon–Fri

✉ **Post office** 15 Church St, Middle West Pubnico; ☉ 10.00–11.30 & 13.00–17.30 Mon–Fri

Pubnico Branch Library 35 Hwy 335, Pubnico; ✆ 902 762 2204; www.westerncounties.ca; ☉ year-round (hours vary)

What to see and do A Day by the Sea Tours (✆ 902 740 0565 novascotiaexperiences. com) offer 5-hour tours (including hands-on experiences such as splicing rope or hauling a lobster trap) of the region's highlights. Several old Acadian buildings have been moved to the pretty 7ha Le Village Historique Acadien (Historic Acadian Village) (Old Church Rd, West Pubnico; ✆ 902 762 2530; tf 1 888 381 8999; levillage. novascotia.ca; ☉ early Jun–mid Sep 09.00–17.00 daily; admission CAN$7), which overlooks Pubnico Harbour. Costumed interpreters demonstrate traditional work methods and tell of Acadian life pre-1920, and there's an on-site café.

Occupying six rooms of a two-storey c1864 homestead furnished in traditional Acadian style and a modern annexe, the collection in the Musée des Acadiens des Pubnicos et Centre de recherche Père Clarence d'Entremont (Museum of the Pubnico Acadians and Father Clarence d'Entremont Research Centre) (898 Hwy 335, West Pubnico; ✆ 902 762 3380; www.museeacadien.ca; ☉ mid May–mid Oct 09.00–17.00 Mon–Sat, 12.30–16.30 Sun; admission CAN$4) displays the history of the Acadians in Pubnico from 1653 to recent times. See a traditional Acadian garden growing plants and vegetables of the type that 17th-century Acadians would have had access to. Bonuses include a collection of more than 300 cameras, and a good research centre for genealogists. The exhibits are labelled in French and English.

CLAW-STOPPERS

The practice of exporting live lobsters, primarily to New England in the USA, began early in the 20th century, however the buyers would only pay if the lobsters reached their destination alive. This posed a problem, as when lobsters are kept together in the same small enclosure, they use their large claws to attack each other, often fatally.

For almost a century, wooden pegs (sometimes called plugs), narrow pine wedges approximately 3cm long, pointed at one end and squared at the other, were inserted under the lobster's claw hinge joint to prevent the claws from opening. The use of pegs had an immediate impact, greatly increasing the survival rate of lobsters during shipping. As the lobster industry boomed, demand for the pegs exploded. The pegs were whittled by hand with a small homemade knife: skilled peg-makers could make a peg using just seven precise cuts. Peg-making, which started off as a cottage industry (making the pegs was a pastime which provided an extra source of money, especially after the Depression when work was scarce) turned into big business.

Finally, machines to automate parts of the peg-making process were designed, and in the late 1970s, the largest lobster-peg factory, located in West Pubnico, was producing over 30 million pegs per year. The community revelled in the title 'lobster plug capital of the world'.

To all intents and purposes, the lobster peg industry came to an end early in the 1980s when strong rubber bands became the standard way to clamp the lobster's claws closed.

The popular, excellent-value 6,052yd par-72 course at **West Pubnico Golf and Country Club** (*Greenwood Rd;* ☏ *902 762 2007; www.pubnicogolf.ca; green fees CAN$25*) has a long playing season, often opening in late March. The 15th hole is the standout.

Turn off Highway 335 towards Dennis Point and follow the road all the way to the wharf area, usually buzzing with fishing boats; not surprising, seeing that this is one of Canada's largest commercial fishing ports. Around 120 boats call it home, over two-thirds of which concentrate on lobster. The others try for haddock, cod, pollock and swordfish.

At the southern end of Highway 335 is the Pubnico Point Wind Farm: the road becomes unpaved but it's worth persevering. Park and follow the Pubnico Point Trail – on your left are timeless sea views, on your right 17 immense turbines, all named after women.

Festival-wise, come early in June to pay homage to *Rheum rhabarbarum* at the **Rhubarb Festival**. A big summer draw is the week-long **Festival Chez-Nous à Pombcoup** in July, celebrating all things Acadian.

THE ROAD NORTH TO YARMOUTH Highway 3 provides a more scenic (and slower) alternative to the motorway (Hwy 103) between Pubnico and Yarmouth. There's some beautiful coastal scenery and a number of little-visited, sleepy, remote peninsulas (with few services) to explore. **By car** on Highway 3, Lower Argyle is 6km/4 miles from Pubnico, Sainte-Anne-du-Ruisseau 23km/14 miles, and Tusket 28km/17 miles from Pubnico and 15km/ 9 miles from Yarmouth.

On Highway 3, 19km from Pubnico, look out for the **Eel Lake Oyster Farm** (*6950 Hwy 3, Lower Eel Brook;* ☏ *902 648 3472; www.ruisseauoysters.com*), where

South Shore **THE FAR SOUTHWEST**

4

Nolan D'Eon and his team raise more than three million oysters. The farm is open to visitors and boat trips to see the oyster habitat are offered for a fee. Call ahead for times, prices, etc. Continue 3km further on Highway 3 to **Sainte-Anne-du-Ruisseau**, home to the magnificent c1900 **Eglise Ste-Anne** (*Church of St Anne; Hwy 3;* \ *902 648 2315;* ⊕ *year-round*), a black-and-white Gothic-style structure with two towers, high, vaulted ceilings featuring beautiful paintings, and ornate stained-glass windows. In July, the **Festival Acadien** is held in the town.

EEL MCMUTTON

In the days of stagecoaches, there were numerous inns between Shag Harbour and Yarmouth. The limited menu at the McDonald Inn in Clyde focused on two of the cheapest foods of that period: mutton and eels.

At **Tusket** you can visit the oldest standing courthouse in Canada, the (c1802) **Argyle Township Court House and Gaol** (*8168 Hwy 3;* \ *902 648 2493; www. argylecourthouse.com;* ⊕ *May–Jun & Sep–Oct 08.30–noon & 13.00–16.30 Mon–Fri; Jul–Aug 09.00–17.00 daily; admission CAN$2*). Recently designated a National Historic Site, on the ground floor you can see the guards' quarters and the cells, whilst upstairs are the courtroom and judge's chambers. There is also a gift shop. The **Argyle Farmers and Artisanal Market** is held in Tusket in the summer (*8168 Hwy 3;* **f** *Argyle Farmers and Artisanal Market;* ⊕ *15.00–19.00 Wed*), but the community's – and region's – culinary highlight is **The Hatfield House** (*8132 Hwy 3;* \ *902 648 1888; www.thehatfieldhouse.ca;* ⊕ *usually May–Dec 16:30–21.00 Wed–Sat; $$$*). Set in a beautifully restored house, this traditional-style restaurant is the place to come for fine dining. Fresh local ingredients including veggies and berries are grown on-site. The creamed lobster sandwich is excellent, as is the filet mignon. Enjoy a cocktail and finish (perhaps) with bread pudding with lemon curd sauce. Check the website for 'Culinary Experiences' – special themed meals prepared by guest chefs. For an interesting authentic, modern lobster fishing-boat experience, head for Wedgeport, approximately 23km south of Tusket via highways 3 and 334, where family-run **Tusket Island Tours** (\ *902 740 2295; tusketislandtours.com*) offer 4-hour trips most days in season (departing at 10.30), including a seafood chowder stop and Acadian/local music *en route*.

 Where to stay, eat and drink Try the comfortable Old English-style lodge right on Lobster Bay, **Ye Olde Argyler Lodge** (*6 rooms; 52 Ye Olde Argyler Rd, Lower Argyle;* \ *902 643 2500;* ☏ *1 866 774 0400; www.argyler.com;* ⊕ *year-round; $$*), which has four rooms with pleasant ocean views. The licensed restaurant (⊕ *year-round 11.00–21.00 daily; $$$*) is housed in a modern lodge-style building and serves up gourmet 'New American' cuisine using local ingredients. Try the root beer baby-back ribs or seared scallops, and for dessert, chocolate rhapsody. There is alfresco dining when the weather permits. Kayak tours and/or a beachside lobster supper can be arranged with at least a day's notice. Room rate includes a full breakfast.

NOVA SCOTIA ONLINE

For additional online content, articles, photos and more on Nova Scotia, why not visit www.bradtguides.com/novascotia.

5

Yarmouth, French Shore and the Annapolis Valley

This region runs from the port of Yarmouth to Windsor, just 66km northwest of Halifax, taking in the Bay of Fundy coast and the fertile Annapolis Valley, which lies between two ridges, the North Mountain and South Mountain. Between Yarmouth and Digby a string of Acadian coastal communities make up the French Shore. Close to Digby, renowned for its scallops and terminus for a year-round car ferry service to Saint John, New Brunswick, the wild and wonderful Digby Neck stretches out into the Bay of Fundy: geologically it is a continuation of the North Mountain ridge. A trip along the narrow peninsula takes you to the departure point for some of North America's best whale-watching experiences.

The Annapolis River empties into the Annapolis Basin: on the basin's north shore is the site of Port-Royal, the first permanent European settlement north of Florida. Close by is the charming historic town of Annapolis Royal, where the streets ooze history. Inland from the south shore of the basin, the funky, pretty artists' community of Bear River is worth a visit.

Highway 8, one of Nova Scotia's cross-province roads, connects Annapolis Royal with Liverpool (pages 170–6), and gives access to Kejimkujik National Park – perhaps the best place to explore the lakes and forests of the interior – while Highway 10 connects Middleton with Bridgewater (pages 167–70). Having good access to the untouched back-country wilderness, and the natural wonders of Kejimkujik National Park and the Bay of Fundy, there is plenty to see, hear and do for lovers of the outdoors.

Although best known for its apple orchards, particularly beautiful when in blossom in late May, the region grows many other crops, and in summer smaller roads parallel to highways 101 and 1 are dotted with U-pick farms where (depending on the time of year) you can pick your own punnets of strawberries, raspberries, blueberries and more.

Towards its northeastern end, the valley becomes busier and more densely populated (relatively speaking). Here you'll find Kentville, the region's commercial centre, and the shopping malls of New Minas. On the Bay of Fundy coast to the north, Capes Split and Blomidon offer high cliffs and magnificent hiking. Also close to Kentville is the lively university town of Wolfville, and just 5km further, the emotive Grand Pré National Historic Site, recently designated a UNESCO World Heritage site.

Digby and Kingston/Greenwood are the major shopping centres between Yarmouth and Kentville. There are backpacker hostels in Digby, at South Milford (between Annapolis Royal and Kejimkujik National Park), and at Caledonia (not far from the Park in the other direction).

Highway 101 is the motorway running between Yarmouth and Halifax, passing close to all the region's major communities. Highway 1 runs through the heart of many of the towns, and parallel roads such as highways 201 and 221 provide pastoral

5

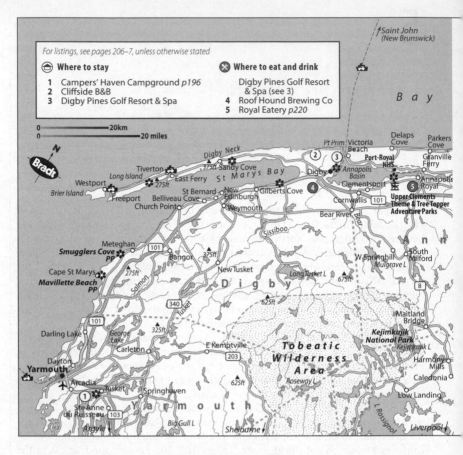

For listings, see pages 206–7, unless otherwise stated

Where to stay
1 Campers' Haven Campground *p196*
2 Cliffside B&B
3 Digby Pines Golf Resort & Spa

Where to eat and drink
Digby Pines Golf Resort & Spa (see 3)
4 Roof Hound Brewing Co
5 Royal Eatery *p220*

0 ——————20km
0 ———————————20 miles

alternatives. Maritime Bus (page 57) connects Kentville with Halifax, and Kings Transit (box, page 204) links communities between Weymouth and Brooklyn.

Many **festivals** occur in the region, and events forming part of an apple-focused celebration are held at the **Apple Blossom Festival** (*appleblossom.com*) in late May/early June at various Annapolis Valley locations including Middleton (pages 231–3), Kentville (pages 234–7) and Berwick (page 234).

YARMOUTH

Located on the eastern side of Yarmouth Harbour, Yarmouth (population: 6,780) is the largest urban centre in western Nova Scotia and has long been one of Nova Scotia's most important ports and communities. The region's largest seaport, long the gateway for ferries to Maine, USA, suffered a huge setback in 2009 when the ferry services were terminated due to funding issues. A (not hugely successful) ferry service ran in 2014 and 2015, and a new operator took over in 2016. The talk is mostly positive, but the first figures released showed passenger numbers well below the target set by the provincial government. Shipping and fishing (especially lobster) are major contributors to present-day Yarmouth's economy, and tourism could be a sizeable contributor if the ferry service lasts for more than a couple of seasons.

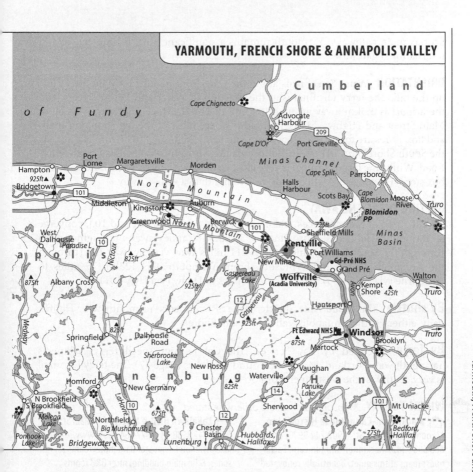

YARMOUTH, FRENCH SHORE & ANNAPOLIS VALLEY

Whilst it is no Lunenburg (pages 156–66) or Annapolis Royal (pages 217–23), there are some good museums, restaurants and places to stay in Yarmouth, plus a restored waterfront with pleasant waterfront park, and many beautiful Victorian mansions – particularly within the **Collins Heritage Conservation District**, which encompasses parts of Alma, Carleton, Clements and Collins streets. It makes a good base from which to explore the lovely peninsulas and quiet backroads – ideal for cycling – to the southwest, as well as the French Shore.

HISTORY The Mi'kmaq called the area *Kespoogwit*, meaning 'the end of the earth': Samuel de Champlain (page 228) landed in 1604, naming it Cap Forchu (or Fourchu) for its two-pronged cape.

After Expulsion, Yarmouth's first families arrived from Cape Cod, Massachusetts, in 1762. There were no roads to connect the site with anywhere else, but wood was plentiful. Boats were needed for fishing, transportation and trade, and so Yarmouth's long history of shipbuilding began.

Peaking in the late 1870s, when Yarmouth ranked as the world's fourth-largest port of registry and possessed more tonnage per capita than any other seaport in the world, shipbuilding then began a rapid decline. From the 1850s, regular steamship services connected Boston and New York with Yarmouth. The railway arrived in the 1880s, increasing the importance of this port as one of Nova

Scotia's main gateways. Yarmouth remains a significant port, fishing centre and international gateway.

ORIENTATION Water Street runs along the waterfront parallel to Main Street just up the hill. The ferry terminal is at the junction of Water and Forest streets, and the airport is 3.5km away at the other end of Forest Street. Highway 1 becomes Main Street and Highway 3 Starrs Road – where most of the big shopping malls and box stores are found – as they come into town: highways 103 (from Halifax via the South Shore) and 101 (from Halifax via the Annapolis Valley) lead on to Starrs Road. Whilst the ferry terminal is very close to the town centre, some hotels and the box stores (see page 67) will be a drive – rather than a walk – away.

GETTING THERE AND AWAY

By car Two of the province's major motorways, highways 101 and 103, converge at Yarmouth. Halifax is approximately 300km/186 miles away via Highway 103 (through the South Shore), and 340km/211 miles away via Highway 101 (through the Annapolis Valley and Windsor). From Yarmouth it is 123km/76 miles to Shelburne (via Hwy 103) and 105km/65 miles to Digby (via Hwy 101).

By shuttle The **Cloud Nine Shuttle** (page 58) connects Yarmouth with Halifax daily, either via the Annapolis Valley or South Shore.

By ferry Operated by Bay Ferries, The Cat (a high-speed ferry) connects Yarmouth with Portland, Maine, in around 5½ hours (page 47). The ferry terminal is very central, at the western end of Forest Street.

 WHERE TO STAY *Map, opposite, unless otherwise stated*

MacKinnon-Cann House Historic Inn (7 rooms) 27 Willow St; ☎ 902 742 9900; tf 1 866 698 3142; mackinnoncanninn.com. Each guest room at this quiet, beautifully renovated c1887 Italianate mansion is decorated in the style of a different 20th-century decade: décor in the public rooms is late 19th-century Victorian. The mix works. A lovely place to stay. Full b/fast inc. **$$$**

Best Western Mermaid Yarmouth (45 rooms) 545 Main St; ☎ 902 742 7821; tf 1 800 772 2774; www.bwmermaid.com. This 2-storey motel-style place has a seasonal heated outdoor pool. Spacious rooms. Rate inc hot b/fast. **$$**

Lakelawn B&B & Motel 641 Main St; ☎ 902 742 3588; tf 1 877 664 0664; www. lakelawnmotel.com. Standard motel rooms & suites, & (in main building) nicer B&B rooms. Not in the heart of downtown but conveniently located. Free parking. **$$**

Campers' Haven Campground [map, pages 194–5] (215 sites) 9700 Hwy 3, Arcadia; ☎ 902 742 4848; tf 1 844 742 4848; www. campershavencampground.com; ⊕ late May–Sep. Large lakeside campground with open & wooded serviced & unserviced sites, 6km from downtown. Heated pool (in season), hot tub, laundromat. **$**

WHERE TO EAT AND DRINK *Map, opposite*

If you're just after a tea/coffee and something to nibble on, **Sip Café** (*357 Main St;* ☎ *902 881 3161;* ⊕ *usually 07.00–20.00 Mon–Fri, 09.00–20.00 Sat, 10.00–17.00 Sun, may close earlier in winter*) is a good bet.

Marco's Grill & Pasta House 624 Main St; ☎ 902 742 7716; www.marcosgrill.com; ⊕ 11.00–21.00 daily (til 22.00 Fri & Sat). Popular place with a varied menu – seafood, pasta, chicken, pizza, etc.

Perhaps not the biggest portions but a good all-rounder. Licensed. **$$**

Rudder's Seafood Restaurant & Brew Pub 96 Water St; ☎ 902 742 7311;

For listings, see pages 196–8

🛏 **Where to stay**

1 Best Western Mermaid Yarmouth
2 Lakelawn B&B & Motel
3 MacKinnon-Cann House Historic Inn

✸ **Where to eat and drink**

4 Marco's Grill & Pasta House
5 Old World Bakery & Deli
6 Rudder's Seafood Restaurant
 & Brew Pub
7 Shanty Café
8 Sip Café

Off map

Bailey's Bakery, Seafood & Grill
Stanley Lobster Pound

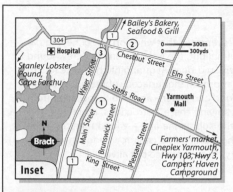

Inset

Bailey's Bakery,
Seafood & Grill

304

✚ Hospital

Chestnut Street

Elm Street

Stanley Lobster Pound, Cape Forchu

Starrs Road

Yarmouth Mall

Water Street

Main Street

Brunswick Street

Pleasant Street

King Street

Farmers' market, Cineplex Yarmouth, Hwy 103, Hwy 3, Campers' Haven Campground

YARMOUTH

Fire-fighters' Museum of Nova Scotia

KING STREET

see continuation north

STORE ST

SOUTH ST

PUBLIC ST

PORTER STREET

W Laurence Sweeney Fisheries Museum

WATER STREET

GRAND STREET

Izaak Walton Killam Memorial Library

GLEBE ST

RYERSON CT

BRUNSWICK STREET

Th'YARC (Performing Arts Venue)

LOVITT ST

FIRST STREET

PARADE STREET

Yarmouth County Museum & Pelton-Fuller House

SECOND STREET

SCHOOL ST

JENKINS ST

COLLINS STREET

Killam Brothers Shipping Office

CENTRAL ST

Art Gallery of Nova Scotia

ALMA STREET

Collins Heritage Conservation District

SEMINARY STREET

WATER STREET

MAIN STREET (Highway 1)

BROWN ST

JOHN STREET

KIRK ST

WILLOW STREET

THURSTON ST

CARLETON ST

HIGH STREET

CLEMENTS STREET

HAWTHORNE ST

CLIFF STREET

CUMBERLAND STREET

PARK ST

ABERDEEN ST

Ferry Terminal

Old World Bakery & Deli

Yarmouth Airport

FOREST STREET

WILLIAM STREET

Maine, USA

ℹ Murray Manor

YARMOUTH

ruddersbrewpub.com; ⊕ 11.00–late daily. Very popular waterfront eatery, pub & microbrewery with wooden floors & beams, & large patio. Good food – start with bacon-wrapped scallops, move on to haddock fishcakes or maritime lobster sandwich, & leave room for the carrot cake or over-the-top chocolate desserts. Wash it down with a Rudder's Red or Yarmouth Town Brown. $$

✖ **Stanley Lobster Pound** 1066 Hwy 304 Yarmouth Bar; ☏ 902 742 8291; stanleylobster. com; ⊕ mid Jun–Sep 15.00–20.00 Wed–Sat. Forget posh restaurants & head here (it's *en route* to Cape Forchu, see page 199). Choose your lobster, then savour it in the characterful dining room on the cobble beach. You can bring your favourite tipple & enjoy your clawed meal with corn on the

In August 1918, *The New York Times* reported that when on one of her regular trips out of Yarmouth in search of halibut, the *Nelson A* and her crew found themselves face to face with a German U-boat. At gunpoint, they were told to load dories with all their fish and approach the surfaced submarine. In return for the fish, the men were given food and water – and told to row away from their boat as fast as possible. Following these instructions, moments later they heard a huge boom: both the submarine and – within minutes – the *Nelson A* disappeared beneath the surface. The crew rowed for shore, and, two days later, arrived back on dry land exhausted but alive.

cob & strawberry shortcake. A fun experience for lobster lovers! **$$**

✖ **Bailey's Bakery, Seafood & Grill** 582 Hwy 1, Hebron; ☎ 902 742 5090; ❤; ⊕ 07.00–19.00 daily. Big portions (diner-style food), low prices, fresh seafood & good desserts/treats. Approx 5km (6min drive) from downtown Yarmouth. **$–$$**

✖ **Shanty Café** 6B Central St; ☎ 902 742 5918; www.shantycafe.ca; ⊕ 07.00–19.00 Mon–Sat (06.00 in summer). Occasionally, worthy ideas work. Enjoy great ethnic (Cuban/Indian/

Spanish; inc tortilla verde, plantain soup, Cuban sandwiches) & local food, good coffee, plus beer/wine, and know that you're supporting a good cause: the café is a project to provide meaningful employment to individuals who face barriers. **$**

🍴 **Old World Bakery & Deli** 232 Main St; ☎ 902 742 2181; ⊕ 07.00–18.00 Tue–Fri, 08.00–16.00 Sat. Excellent sandwiches, dips, soups & baked goods at this popular, family-owned little deli. Great place to grab a lunch on the go. **$**

OTHER PRACTICALITIES

$ Scotiabank 389 Main St; ☎ 902 742 7116; ⊕ 10.00–17.00 Mon–Fri

✚ **Yarmouth Regional Hospital** 60 Vancouver St; ☎ 902 742 3541

✉ **Post office** 15 Willow St; ⊕ 08.00–17.30 Mon–Fri

ℹ **Tourist information** 228 Main St; ☎ 902 742 5033; ⊕ late May–early Oct 09.00–18.00 daily, mid Jul–Aug til 19.00

🚕 **Yarmouth Town Taxi** ☎ 902 742 7801

Cineplex Yarmouth 136 Starrs Rd; ☎ 902 742 7489; www.cineplex.com

Izaak Walton Killam Memorial Library 405 Main St; ☎ 902 742 5040; ⊕ 10.00–20.00 Mon–Thu, 10.00–17.00 Fri, 10.00–16.00 Sat

WHAT TO SEE AND DO With an extensive collection of fire-fighting equipment from days of yore, the **Fire-fighters' Museum of Nova Scotia** (*451 Main St;* ☎ *902 742 5525; firefightersmuseum.novascotia.ca;* ⊕ *Jun & Sep 09.00–18.00 Mon–Sat; Jul–Aug 09.00–21.00 Mon–Sat, 10.00–17.00 Sun; Oct–May 09.00–16.00 Mon–Fri, 13.00–16.00 Sat; admission CAN$4*) is much more interesting than it sounds – and one the kids will enjoy, too. Also worth a visit are the excellent **Yarmouth County Museum and Archives and Pelton-Fuller House** (*22 & 20 Collins St;* ☎ *902 742 5539; www.yarmouthcountymuseum.ca;* ⊕ *Jun–Sep 09.00–17.00 Mon–Sat, 13.00–18.00 Sun; mid Oct–May 14.00–17.00 Tue–Sat; admission CAN$3 each or CAN$5 for both museum & Pelton-Fuller House*); the fantastic museum is housed in a restored granite c1893 church and contains one of Canada's largest collections of ship paintings and one of the province's largest costume collections. Whilst it focuses on Yarmouth's seafaring history and heritage, the complex also includes the largest community archives in Nova Scotia, and another wing with transportation-related exhibits and art galleries. Be sure to see the runic stone (box, opposite), the 1860s' stagecoach and the early lens from the Cape Forchu light (see below). The gift shop is also one of the better ones of the genre. Next door is the antique-packed Italianate (c1895) **Pelton-Fuller House**, once the summer residence of Alfred Fuller who founded the Fuller Brush Company and became known throughout North America as the *Fuller Brush Man*, which has attractive flower gardens.

The **Art Gallery of Nova Scotia** (*Western Branch; 341 Main St;* ✎ *902 749 2248; artgalleryofnovascotia.ca/;* ⊕ *08.30–16.30 Wed–Fri, 11.30–16.30 Sat & Sun*), the only satellite location of Halifax's Art Gallery of Nova Scotia (page 117) is housed in a historical building, once a bank. **Th'YARC** (*76 Parade St;* ✎ *902 742 8150; www.yarcplayhouse.com*), a performing arts complex, includes a 350-seat theatre and art gallery.

Killam Brothers Shipping Office (*90 Water St;* ✎ *902 742 5539; yarmouthcountymuseum.ca;* ⊕ *Jul–Aug 10.00–16.30 Mon–Sat; admission free*) is Canada's oldest shipping office and is housed in a 19th-century building; the Killam family were directly involved with many aspects of shipping for almost two centuries. A scaled-down reproduction (including a coastal freighter) of part of Yarmouth's old working waterfront, the **W Laurence Sweeney Fisheries Museum** (*112 Water St;* ✎ *902 742 3457; sweeneyfisheriesmuseum.ca;* ⊕ *mid May–mid Oct 10.00–18.00 daily; admission CAN$3*) was built using original materials.

Until recently a B&B, the impressive Regency Gothic c1821 **Murray Manor** (*225 Main St;* ✎ *902 742 2632; www.murraymanor.com*) is now an 'Art and Culture House'. Apart from admiring the architecture and (predominantly local) art or attending a workshop, there is also a serving window where (in summer) crêpes, coffee and ice cream can be ordered to enjoy in the garden. A **farmers' market** (*Jul–Sep*) is held on Saturday mornings at the Canadian Tire car park (*120 Starrs Rd*).

Just out of town, adjacent to a lighthouse – one of the highest (23m) and most photogenic in the province – are the original lightkeeper's quarters at **Cape Forchu** (*Hwy 304;* ✎ *902 742 4522; capeforchulight.com;* ⊕ *May–Sep; admission by donation*), which house a small museum and gift shop, but the tea room (good sandwiches and tasty baked goods) was 'closed for renovations' in 2016. Definitely worth the pretty drive. Near the car park, a trail leads down to Leif Ericsson Picnic Park. Take care on the smooth rocks which can be very slippery. To get there, follow Main Street north and turn left at the golden horse fountain onto Vancouver Street. Just past the hospital complex, turn left onto Highway 304 and follow it to its end, approximately 11km from the centre of Yarmouth.

FESTIVALS In July, **Seafest** (*www.seafest.ca*) offers 11 days of parades, pageants and varied events – many marine-related. What started out as an agricultural exhibition has developed into six days of concerts, events and activities for all the family, at the **Western Nova Scotia Exhibition** (*wnse.ca*), held at the end of July/early August. Around the same time is the three-day **Yarmouth Seafood & Wine Extravaganza** (**f** *YarmouthSeafoodWineExtravaganza*), with boat races, dinners and other activities.

THE FRENCH SHORE

Officially part of the Municipality of Clare, those in surrounding areas call this string of more than a dozen adjoining Acadian villages The French Shore, although to most of the residents it is La Ville Française. It's home to the 'longest main street in the world', an interesting alternative to the motorway (Hwy 101).

The Acadian flag (known as the *stella maris*) flies everywhere. Post-Expulsion (page 17), returning Acadians who found their old lands taken over by others kept walking until they found land that no-one else was interested in. Despite the harsh climate and poor quality of the soil, they persevered and, in time, fishing and boatbuilding developed. Mink farms were, and – rightly or wrongly – still are, another money-spinner (box, page 203).

For a fortnight in early August, residents (and many visitors) celebrate the oldest Acadian festival in Canada, the **Festival Acadien de Clare** (*festivalacadiendeclare.ca*), with music, food, parades, competitions and raucous fun.

MAVILLETTE   Reachable in just over 20 minutes from Yarmouth, the main reason for coming here is to visit **Mavillette Beach Provincial Park** (parks.novascotia.ca/content/mavillette-beach; ⊕ year-round), a 2km-wide gently curving stretch of sand backed by marram grass-covered dunes. Behind the dunes, a large salt marsh is home to avian year-rounders and spring and autumn migrators. To reach it from Mavillette, follow Cape St Mary's Road to its end. You might see seals basking on the rocks below, and the coastal views from this point high above the sea are superb.

 Where to stay, eat and drink

↑ Cape View Motel & Cottages (15 units) 124 John Doucette Rd; ☎ 902 645 2258; **tf** 1 888 352 5353; capeviewmotel.ca; ⊕ Jun–Sep. 10 motel rooms & 5 1- & 2-bedroom cottages in a good setting & across the road from the Mavillette Beach Park. Continental b/fast inc. **$**

✕ Le Restaurant Cape View 157 John Doucette Rd; ☎ 902 645 2519; ⊕ end Apr–mid Oct 11.00–20.00 daily. Spacious place with big windows that take advantage of the magnificent setting. The food is usually reliable but the pricing seems to reflect the view & lack of nearby competition. **$$–$$$**

SIGOGNE

Abbé Jean Mande Sigogne (1763–1844), a French priest who fled his homeland for England during the French Revolution, arrived in Nova Scotia in the late 1790s. His mission stations extended from the Pubnicos (pages 189–91) to Annapolis Royal (pages 217–23) and Bear River (pages 214–15). Much loved by his people, the Abbé was a strong influence in the education of the Acadians, and helped inspire them in their farming, fishing and trading. A terrible fire swept through the region in 1820, destroying the St Bernard Church and much else, and again the Abbé was a rock in helping rebuild both the communities' morale and their fire-destroyed buildings. He supervised the construction of many churches in southwest Nova Scotia and died in 1844: his tomb stands outside the university.

SMUGGLERS COVE PROVINCIAL PARK Smugglers Cove is 9km north of Mavillette. Interpretive panels tell of the rum-running past, paths lead to clifftop coastal views, and 110 steep, wooden steps descend through the trees to a sheltered cove with a pebble beach. Apparently, smugglers were attracted by a sea cave 5m high and 18m deep, but –unless the tide is extra-low, in which case take great care – this is only accessible by water.

METEGHAN Meteghan, 3.5km past Smugglers Cove, is the French Shore's largest community, busiest port and commercial hub (though the total population is fewer than 1,000). The port is home to several types of fishing boat and the main wharf is a hive of activity throughout the day. There's also a bank (*8249 Hwy 1;* \ *902 645 2410;* ⊕ *09.30–17.00 Mon–Thu, 09.30–18.00 Fri*) and post office (*8198 Hwy 1;* ⊕ *08.30–noon & 12.30–17.00 Mon–Fri*).

Meteghan River, 4.5km north of Meteghan, is Nova Scotia's largest wooden shipbuilding centre.

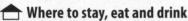
Where to stay, eat and drink

🏠 **L'Auberge au Havre du Capitaine**
(18 rooms) 9118 Hwy 1, Meteghan River; \ 902 769 2001; havreducapitaine.ca. A nice inn with traditional Acadian feel. Rooms have hardwood floors & are decorated with antiques – though bathrooms are modern. **$–$$**

✕ **Around the Bend Restaurant & Café**
8837 Hwy 1, Meteghan River; \ 902 645 3313; ⊕ 05.30–20.00 daily. Prepare for a rural Nova Scotia shock: a diner where the owners have made an effort with the décor! The food is good, too, with the focus on seafood. **$$**

✕ **Sip Café Meteghan** 19 Meteghan Conn Rd; \ 902 645 3333; ◼; ⊕ summer 07.00–21.00 daily (from 09.00 Sun); check o/s hours. Coffee, dozens of varieties of tea, good paninis, salads, baked treats, etc, in a 2-storey wooden building that feels like a sophisticated city place. Recommended. Just off Hwy 1, approx 1km from Smugglers Cove (towards Meteghan) & opposite the Clare Curling Centre. **$**

CHURCH POINT (POINTE DE L'ÉGLISE) A further 15km north, Church Point is the home of **Université Sainte-Anne** – founded in 1891, this is Nova Scotia's only French-language university and is the Acadian cultural centre for the entire Clare region. On the campus is grey-shingled **Église de Sainte-Marie**, the largest wooden church in North America. Constructed between 1903 and 1905, it seats almost 1,800 people.

The **Rendez-vous de la Baie** complex (*23 Lighthouse Rd;* \ *902 769 1234; rendezvousdelabaie.com;* ⊕ *summer 08.00–18.00 Mon–Fri, 09.00–17.00 Sat & Sun; winter check hours*) includes an Acadian Interpretive Centre/museum, gift shop, art gallery, internet café and tourist information centre (\ *902 769 2345;* ⊕ *early May–mid Oct 09.00–17.30 daily*). Just outside is an Acadian Odyssey Monument (page 17), and 5km of easy walking trails through the woods and along the coast, passing a couple of giant wind turbines (see *lepetitbois.ca/en*). Those interested in genealogy won't want to miss the **Acadian Centre Archives** (\ *902 769 2114; centreacadien.usainteanne.ca;* ⊕ *08.30–noon & 13.00–16.00 Mon–Fri; admission free*), a resource at the university.

Where to stay

🏠 **Chateau Sainte Marie B&B** (7 rooms) 959 Hwy 1, Little Brook; \ 902 769 8346; www. chateausaintemarie.ca; ⊕ early Apr–early Nov. Wonderful c1920 Acadian house overlooking

St Marys Bay, rooms individually decorated. Sun room, sitting room & large deck to enjoy lovely sunsets. Plans to include AC in rooms. **$$**

⚑ Belle Baie Park Campground (157 sites)
2135 Hwy 1; ☏ 902 739 3160; www.bellbaiepark.
ca; ⊕ early May–late Sep. Serviced & unserviced
sites at this big St Marys Bay-front campground.
Heated pool (in season), laundromat. **$**

✖ Where to eat and drink *Box, below. In addition…*

✖ 19th Hole Restaurant Clare Golf Club
423 Pf Comeau Rd; ☏ 902 769 0801; claregolf.ca.
This restaurant in Comeauville is another
possibility. **$$**

✖ Beaux Vendredis ☏ 902 769 8618;
beauxvendredis.ca/en. A seafood take on the
Community Supper. Very good-value lobster/
clams/snow-crab dinners are served on Fri

evenings (⊕ Jul–Aug 18.00–21.00) on long,
communal tables at Belliveau Cove Wharf under
the Beaux Vendredis label. Recommended. **$$**

✖ Roadside Grill 3334 Hwy 1, Belliveau Cove;
☏ 902 837 5047. There's usually live Acadian music
(Jul–Sep 17.30–19.30 Tue) to go with the seafood,
plus big portions of clams, fries & rappie pie. The
deep fryer works hard here. **$$**

BELLIVEAU COVE (L'ANSE-DES-BELLIVEAU) Belliveau Cove is 7km north of
Church Point. It has a wharf, with a pretty c1889 lighthouse, and a 5km coastal
interpretive trail. A **farmers' market** (*Parc Joseph et Marie Dugas;* ⊕ *May–Sep
09.00–12.45 Sat*) takes place in the park by the wharf – go for crafts, the freshest
local fruit, vegetables and baked goods. The **Annual Festival Joseph et Marie Dugas**
is a one-day event held in August, which features food, music, games, an arts and
crafts sale and a flea market. If you like the idea of digging for clams with a local
expert, the activity is offered a couple of times a week between the end of June
and end of August (☏ *902 769 2345; baiesaintemarie.ca/en/acadian-experiences;
CAN$10*). For accommodation/dining, see Church Point (pages 201–2).

ST BERNARD St Bernard marks the end of the French Shore. Its **church** (☏ *902 837
5687;* ⊕ *Jun–Sep*) has wonderful acoustics.

J'AI FAIM

There are three good dining choices between Meteghan and Belliveau Cove.
You'll probably want to try Acadian food, but may be tempted by oriental
offerings. Firstly, **Cuisine Robicheau** (*9651 Hwy 1, Saulnierville;* ☏ *902 769
2121; www.lacuisinerobicheau.ca;* ⊕ *May–Dec 08.00–20.00 Tue–Sun; $–$$*)
dishes up simple but tasty Acadian-influenced food – the seafood lasagne
and haddock with creamed lobster stand out. BYOB (no corkage charge).
There's a patio overlooking the sea and live music on Thursday evenings
(⊕ *Jul–Oct*). It's BYOB (no corkage charge), but reservations are a must.

The other two are both at 1008 Highway 1 in Little Brook, in the same
building. Acadian food is king at **Évelina's Râpure** (☏ *902 360 2111; www.
evelinas.ca;* ⊕ *07.00–20.00 Tue–Sun; $*), which serves not just (chicken, beef
or clam) rappie pie – eat in or buy family size ones to heat up at home –
but also chicken fricot, fish cakes, potato pancakes and more. A few feet
away, transport yourself to another continent: **Kizuna Sushi** (☏ *902 774 1153;
www.jfkizuna.com;* ⊕ *11.30–20.00 Wed–Fri, noon–20.00 Sat & Sun; $–$$*)
is surprisingly good and the food would not be out of place at most sushi
restaurants in the western world. All the usual suspects, plus a few surprises,
such as little brook roll, sake, Japanese plum wine and more conventional
beverages. Supposedly it is open year-round but it has been known to close
for a couple of weeks every so often.

WEYMOUTH   This former shipbuilding and lumber centre near the mouth of the Sissiboo River has a few services. Like many coastal communities in the province, today's Weymouth is a much quieter place than it would have been a century ago. Rumour has it that Josephine Leslie, author of the novel *The Ghost and Mrs Muir* (though she used a pseudonym), was inspired to write the book after a visit to the town.

A cultural interpretive centre, the **Sissiboo Landing** (see page 204 for details) tells of the Mi'kmaq, United Empire Loyalists, Black Loyalists, Acadians and the New France settlers who are seen as Weymouth's founders. The excellent company **Hinterland Adventures** (✎ *902 837 4092;* **tf** *1 800 378 8177; kayakingnovascotia.com*) offer a range of canoe tours in the Tobeatic Wilderness Area (box, pages 186–7) and kayak tours along the coast, and also rent equipment.

Weymouth is accessible **by car**, being on Highway 1, just off Highway 101, Exit 28. The town is 4km/2 miles from St Bernard, 76km/47 miles from Yarmouth and 35km/23 miles from Digby. Weymouth is also on the **bus** route to Cornwallis (box, overleaf).

Where to stay, eat and drink

🏠 **Baie Ste-Marie Ocean Front Cottages**   (3 cottages) 5–9 Riverside Rd, New Edinburgh; ✎ 902 769 0797; **tf** 1 866 769 0797; nsoceanfrontcottages.com. 3 themed 2-bedroom cottages in a wonderful setting less than 7km from Weymouth on St Marys Bay at the mouth of the Sissiboo River. Very well equipped (full-size kitchen, BBQ, washer/dryer, etc), making these an excellent base from which to visit southwest Nova Scotia. Min stay 2 nights. **$$$**

🏠 **Goodwin Hotel**   (10 rooms) 4616 Hwy 1; ✎ 902 837 5120; www3.ns.sympatico.ca/ goodwinhotel. Choose between a room with private or shared bath at this simple old-style hotel, an inn since 1890. Food in the licensed dining room (🕐 *summer 07.00–09.00, 11.30–13.30 & 17.00–19.00 Sun–Fri; winter same hours but Mon–Fri;* **$**) is dependable but won't surprise you. **$**

> ### MINK SINKS
>
> Around half of the mink farms in Canada are in Nova Scotia, and over 80% of those are in Digby County, particularly in the Weymouth area (pages 203–4). The number of farms snowballed as pelt prices shot up: in 2015, 2.3 million pelts were produced, and global demand was soaring. As a result, a number of produce farmers switched from raising crops to fur farming.
>
> Those opposing the growth in mink farms complained of cruelty to animals and environmental worries – a 2012 report released by the provincial environment department said that mink farms were the most likely source of water quality problems in nine lakes in western Nova Scotia. The federal and provincial governments poured money into the mink farm industry: rather than tough rules to ensure tight control over waste disposal and welfare of the 'fur coats in the making', toothless 'guidelines' were introduced.
>
> By early 2016, though, things changed. The mink market crashed after demand from China and Russia plummeted. Less than a million (still sounds like quite a lot to me) mink were 'harvested' in 2016, and pelt prices dropped by well over 80% from the previous year's levels. The result was economic disaster for much of southwest Nova Scotia, where the mink industry had become the largest employer.

The area between Weymouth and Wolfville (pages 239–44) is relatively well served by public transport. Five connecting bus lines operated by **Kings Transit** (*902 678 7310;* tf *1 888 546 4442; kingstransit.ns.ca*) stop at most of the major communities along the Annapolis Valley, although buses don't run on Sundays or holiday. Single fare is CAN$3.50, and you can either pay the driver (exact fare only) or buy tickets at one of the outlets listed on the website. If you are connecting on to another bus, ask for a 'transfer'. If you wanted to, you could travel the entire route from Weymouth to Wolfville or vice versa (almost 200km) on one CAN$3.50 ticket! Lines and their major stops are:

Weymouth–Gilberts Cove–Digby–Cornwallis 06.00–18.00 Mon–Fri, 08.00–16.00 Sat; every 2hrs
Cornwallis–Upper Clements–Annapolis Royal–Granville–Bridgetown 07.00–19.00 Mon–Fri, 09.00–15.00 Sat; every 2hrs
Bridgetown–Middleton–Greenwood 06.00–18.00 Mon–Fri, 08.00–16.00 Sat; every 2hrs
Greenwood–Kingston–Aylesford–Berwick–Kentville–New Minas–Wolfville 07.00–19.00 Mon–Fri; 09.00–17.00 Sat; hourly Mon–Fri, every 2hrs on Sat
Kentville–Port Williams–Wolfville–Grand Pre–Hantsport 08.00–18.00 Mon–Fri, 08.00–16.00 Sat; every 2hrs

OTHER PRACTICALITIES

$ Royal Bank Hwy 1; *902 837 5136;* 10.00–15.00 Mon–Fri
Post office 4659 Hwy 1; 08.30–17.00 Mon–Fri, 08.30–12.30 Sat

Tourist information Sissiboo Landing, 4575 Hwy 1; *902 837 4715;* tf *1 800 565 0000;* mid May–mid Oct 10.00–17.00 Mon–Fri
Weymouth Branch Library 4609 Hwy 1; *902 837 4596;* 13.30–16.30 & 18.00–20.00 Tue & Fri, noon–16.30 Wed & Thu, 10.00–13.00 Sat

GILBERTS COVE Situated 1km off Highway 101, 11km/7 miles from Weymouth and 24km from Digby, the site of interest here is the delightfully located **Gilberts Cove Lighthouse** (*Lighthouse Rd;* *902 837 5584; gilbertscovelighthouse.com;* mid Jun–mid Sep 10.00–16.00 Mon–Sat, noon–16.00 Sun; admission free). Reached by a short unpaved road, the c1904 lighthouse now serves as a museum, tea room and craft shop. Climb the tower for wonderful views over the cove, St Marys Bay and Digby Neck. There are picnic tables on the grass above the beach.

DIGBY

This working town (population: 2,150), 5km from the terminal for ferries to and from Saint John, New Brunswick, has a fine setting at the south end of the vast Annapolis Basin. The Mi'kmaq name for Digby is *Weskewinaq*, 'cheerful place'. Since commercial scallop fishing began here late in the 1920s, the mollusc (box, page 207) has been the mainstay of Digby's economy.

A fire in 1899 destroyed more than 40 buildings in the small downtown area. Today, Water Street is lined with a lighthouse, shops, cafés, and restaurants, behind which a boardwalk makes a pleasant place for a wander. It may be a major gateway, but Digby is not awash with too many tacky souvenir shops. One of the province's few resorts – with a top-class golf course – lies between the town and the ferry terminal, and the big box stores and supermarkets stretch out along the road between downtown and Highway 101.

HISTORY The Mi'kmaq name for the area is *Te'Wapskik*, meaning 'flowing between high rocks', a reference to the Digby Gut. Originally called Conway (after a former secretary of state), the current name is in honour of Admiral Robert Digby, who sailed up the Fundy on the *Atalanta* in 1783 and settled the place with 1,500 Loyalists from New England.

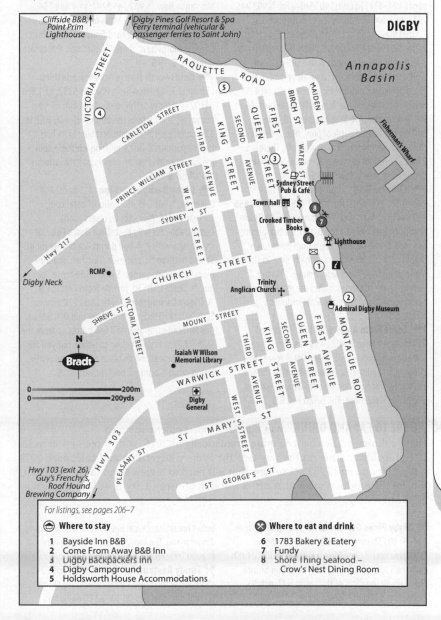

For listings, see pages 206–7

Where to stay
1 Bayside Inn B&B
2 Come From Away B&B Inn
3 Digby Backpackers Inn
4 Digby Campground
5 Holdsworth House Accommodations

Where to eat and drink
6 1783 Bakery & Eatery
7 Fundy
8 Shore Thing Seafood –
   Crow's Nest Dining Room

GETTING THERE AND AROUND **By car,** Digby is just off Highway 101, Exit 26, 105km/65 miles northeast of Yarmouth and 235km/146 miles west of Halifax. Digby is on the Weymouth–Cornwallis **bus** route (box, page 204). The terminus for the **ferry** (page 47) to Saint John, New Brunswick, is 5km from town. Walk there, or take a **taxi** – Digby Cabs (✆ *902 245 6162*) charge CAN$12.

🏠 WHERE TO STAY *Map, page 205, unless otherwise stated*

🏠 **Digby Pines Golf Resort & Spa** [map, pages 194–5] (116 units) 103 Shore Rd; ✆ 902 245 2511; **tf** 1 800 667 4637; www.digbypines.ca; ⏲ mid May–early Oct. With 79 rooms & 6 suites in the c1929 main lodge & 31 well-dispersed 1- to 3-bedroom cottages (each with a sitting room, working stone fireplace, & covered veranda), this casually elegant old-fashioned resort sits on a hillside overlooking the Annapolis Basin outside the town centre. Aveda spa, superb 18-hole golf course, heated outdoor pool, fitness centre, children's playground, & walking trails. There are 2 bars (1 overlooking the golf course), & a main dining room (see below). **$$$**

🏠 **Cliffside B&B** [map, pages 194–5] (4 suites) 1820 Culloden Rd; ✆ 902 245 4285; **tf** 1 855 280 8445; ⏲ May–Oct. Whilst many NS B&Bs are historic houses on leafy roads, this is a big, bright, airy, new house (approx 13km from downtown Digby) with spacious suites virtually on – as the name suggests – a cliff side. 2 suites ('Master' & 'Family') have sea views. Suites are reached by a grand (quite long) staircase. Rate includes b/fast. **$$**

🏠 **Come From Away B&B Inn** (9 rooms) 98 Montague Row; ✆ 902 245 2413; comefromawayinn.ca; ⏲ May–Oct. 3 rooms in a c1904 main building &, tucked behind by the sea, a 2-storey modern addition with 6 more. Garden directly on waterfront. Full b/fast inc. **$$**

🏠 **Bayside Inn B&B** (10 rooms) 115 Montague Row; ✆ 902 245 2247; **tf** 1 888 754 0555; baysideinn.ca; ⏲ May–mid Dec. A c1885 building just across the road from the waterfront. Cheaper rooms have shared bathrooms. Full b/fast included. **$–$$**

🏠 **Holdsworth House Accommodations** (3 rooms) 36 Carleton St; ✆ 902 245 5252; **tf** 1 866 643 1784; holdsworthhousebandb.com; ⏲ year-round (off-season by reservation). Friendly B&B in a beautifully restored, comfortable c1784 house (with 2 parlours & fine views) on a hillside above the town centre. Pets on premises. Rate includes full b/fast. **$–$$**

🏠 **Digby Backpackers Inn** (12 beds) 168 Queen St; ✆ 902 245 4573; digbyhostel.com; ⏲ year-round (Nov–Apr by reservation). Comfortable, friendly hostel in a Dutch Colonial-style house with 2, 4-bed dorms & a private room. Shared bathrooms, communal kitchen, laundry room, sun room, garden & deck. Bike rental for guests. Dorm CAN$30, private room CAN$65 **$**

⛺ **Digby Campground** (49 sites) 230 Victoria St; ✆ 902 245 1985; ⏲ mid May–mid Oct. Sites at this terraced campground a few blocks up from the seafront are a little bit close together, but you are just about in walking distance of the town centre. Laundromat & outdoor pool (seasonal). **$**

✗ WHERE TO EAT AND DRINK *Map, page 205, unless otherwise stated*

Digby's dining scene changed quite dramatically in 2016, with three new arrivals and probably another on the way (see the Sydney Street Pub and café; page 207) – Roof Hound and 1783 are so new that it is hard to review them fairly. Look out, too, for the products of another new local craft brewery, Lazy Bear Brewing (*www.lazybearbrewing.ca*).

✗ **Digby Pines Golf Resort & Spa** [map, pages 194–5] 103 Shore Rd; ✆ 902 245 2511; www.digbypines.ca; ⏲ mid May–early Oct 18.00–21.00 daily; mid Jun–mid Sep 11.00–14.00 Sun brunch. The main dining room of this resort is Churchill's Restaurant & Lounge, which serves a hot/cold buffet breakfast, casual lunch menu & fine-dining dinner menu. The monthly Sun brunch is very popular (reservations required). **$$$**

✗ **Fundy Restaurant** 34 Water St; ✆ 902 245 4950; www.fundyrestaurant.com/fundy.shtml; ⏲ mid Jun–mid Sep 08.30–22.00 daily; mid

DIGBY SCALLOPS

In Nova Scotia the word 'scallops' is almost always preceded by 'Digby': the town is home to the world's largest inshore scallop fleet.

Scallops are marine molluscs, bivalves with two hard, rounded shells with scalloped edges and a soft body. The shells are opened and closed by the adductor muscle. This is the 'meat', the only part of the scallop that is usually eaten. Unlike many other bivalve molluscs, they do not bury themselves in the sand, but live on the soft sea bed.

Scallops are harvested by 'draggers', specially rigged boats that drag huge metal mesh bags along the sea bed. The cages are emptied into the boats, and the scallops opened (or shucked) by hand. The meat is placed in containers and put on ice until the boats return to shore.

Conditions in the sea off Digby (in particular, the year-round, fairly steady cool water temperatures, and nutrient-rich sea) combine to produce scallops that – cooked properly – are a gastronomic treat.

Sep–mid Jun 11.00–21.00 daily. A large, casual restaurant overlooking the wharf. Sit inside in the main dining room, in the large solarium, or out on the deck. Local scallops dominate the menu: have them for breakfast in an omelette, in chowder, with pasta – you get the idea. **$$**

✗ Shore Thing Seafood – Crow's Nest Dining Room 40 Water St; ☏ 902 245 5497; �</br>CrowsNesttoo; ☉ 11.00–19.00 Tue–Sun (from noon Sun). This sister/daughter restaurant of the Crow's Nest at Parkers Cove (page 230) repeats the 'fresh seafood & mounds of fries' formula. This Crow's Nest, however, can add great harbour views. **$$**

✗ Roof Hound Brewing Co [map, pages 194–5] 2580 Ridge Rd; ☏ 902 245 8121; ☐; ☉ 11.00–21.00 or later Tue–Sat, noon–21.00 Sun. New brewpub opened by a (Canadian) *MasterChef* contestant. Approx 6km from Exit 26 of Hwy 101, & 10–12min drive from the Digby waterfront. Creative craft beer (eg: Wasted Days Chocolate Peanut Butter Wheat Beer), plus food (pizzas & sandwiches using fresh local ingredients) & occasional live music. **$–$$**

✗ 1783 Bakery & Eatery 9 Water St; ☏ 902 841 0304/0825/1343. New café for good coffee, home-baked treats, sandwiches, meat pies & more. No deep fryer & (on my recce visit) no seafood in sight. **$**

ENTERTAINMENT, NIGHTLIFE AND FESTIVALS In previous times, nightlife consisted of **Club 98** in the Fundy Restaurant (pages 206–7), or the lounge bar at the **Digby Pines Resort** (☉ *mid May–early Oct 17.00–22.00*). But a new addition – the **Sydney Street Pub and Café** (*14 Sydney St*) – is due to open late in 2016. Expect good pub food, and a range of craft and mainstream beer.

In terms of festivals, celebrate all things 'lobster' – and eat some! – with races, competitions, music and more at the three-day **Lobster Bash** (*www.lobsterbash.ca; usually 30 Jun–2 Jul*). In August, **Digby Scallop Days Festival** (*digbyscallopdays.com*) offers five days of music, races, parades and food – including, of course, Digby scallops! At

DIGBY CHICKEN

The first settlers had very little food – with one exception. Herring were plentiful and consequently were eaten at just about every meal, including on special occasions (when, in New England they would have eaten chicken). Consequently, herring became known as 'Digby chicken'. Even today, locals call herring 'Digby chicks'.

The first **Guy's Frenchy's** opened its doors in Digby in 1972. Specialising in used clothes (but also used books, ornaments and more), there are now almost 20 Guy's Frenchy's (plus some copycat 'Frenchy's') across the province and in to neighbouring New Brunswick. To many Nova Scotians, insulting Frenchy's seems to be akin to how insulting the Royal Family used to be in the UK.

Recently, a couple (who had bought everything that they would need for their wedding at the Digby Guy's Frenchy's) went the whole hog and got married in the store. The bins of used men's shirts, suits, sweaters, etc, were moved to one side making rummaging through them a bit awkward: however, customers continued to burrow into the women's and kids' piles as the couple made their vows.

the end of August/early September, the **Annual Wharf Rat Rally** (*www.wharfratrally. com*), Atlantic Canada's largest motorcycle rally, hits town for five days. Experience the smell of leather, the gleam of chrome, thousands and thousands of bikes, bald men with beards, tattoo and piercing parlours, bandannas, paunches and more.

SHOPPING Crooked Timber Books (*17 Water St;* \ *902 245 1283; crookedtimber. com;* ⊕ *approx May–Nov 10.00–17.00 Mon–Sat*) is a good used bookstore with a special interest in Irish literature. Alternatively, you can rummage through bins of bargain used clothes at the original **Guy's Frenchy's** (*343 Hwy 303, Conway;* \ *902 245 2458; www.guysfrenchys.com; box, above*), between Highway 101 and downtown, and enjoy the view of the Annapolis Basin from the car park.

OTHER PRACTICALITIES

$ Royal Bank 51 Water St; \ 902 245 4771; ⊕ 09.30–17.00 Mon–Fri

✛ Digby General Hospital 75 Warwick St; \ 902 245 2501

✉ Post office 9 Water St; ⊕ 08.30–17.15 Mon–Fri

ℹ Tourist information 110 Montague Row; \ 902 245 5714; **tf** 1 888 463 4429; ⊕ late May–early Oct 09.00–17.00 daily (Jul–early Sep til 18.00)

Isaiah W Wilson Memorial Library 84 Warwick St; \ 902 245 2163; ⊕ 12.30–17.00 & 18.00–20.00 Tue–Thu, 10.00–17.00 Fri, 10.00–14.00 Sat

WHAT TO SEE AND DO Don't miss the c1878 **Trinity Anglican Church** (*Queen St;* \ *902 245 6744; anglicanpdw.ca/church/trinity-anglican-church*), which is both a National Historic Site, and thought to be one of the few churches in Canada built entirely by shipwrights, and the **Admiral Digby Museum** (*95 Montague Row;* \ *902 245 6322; admiraldigbymuseum.ca;* ⊕ *mid Jun–Aug 09.00–17.00 Mon–Sat; check website for rest of year; admission by donation*) housed in a mid 1800s Georgian house, with themed (eg: Marine and Costume) period rooms displaying artefacts in permanent and temporary exhibits. It has an extensive genealogy research facility (fee charged).

Take to the water in a **kayak**: single and double kayaks can be rented by the half or full day from the Fundy Complex (*34 Water St;* \ *902 245 4950; www.fundyrestaurant. com;* ⊕ *spring & summer*). Finish the day looking out across the water at the scallop fleet, watching the action at the wharf, then tuck in to plump, fresh, juicy scallops in one of the restaurants (pages 206–7). Reasonably priced walking (and seafood sampling) tours of Digby are offered by **Gael Tours** (📞 *902 245 4689, 902 247 2146; www.gaeltours.ca*): the company will also customise nature tours in the region (and offer a close-up view of life on the edge of the tide-line).

The **Point Prim Lighthouse** (*1430 Lighthouse Rd*) is worth a short drive at any time, but particularly towards sunset, as it sits on the Bay of Fundy side of **Digby Gut**, the narrow opening through which the huge Bay of Fundy tides pour into the Annapolis Basin. From here, there are fine views across the Gut to the remote wooded coastline north of **Victoria Beach** (page 229). To get there, head towards the ferry terminal but instead of turning on to Shore Road, take the next right on to Lighthouse Road and follow it to the end (about 7.5km). Gael Tours (see above) offers a 2–3-hour 'Plankton, Periwinkles and Predators' tour that neatly complements a whale-watching trip.

For a very challenging **golf** game, head to the 18-hole 6,222yd **Digby Pines** course at the Digby Pines Resort (page 206), which was designed by Stanley Thompson (1894–1953), one of Canada's most celebrated golf course architects. 'Stay and play' packages are popular (*green fees CAN$79*).

DIGBY NECK

Close to Digby, what looks on a map like a thin, skeletal finger (the last two 'bones' are actually islands) stretches for almost 75km and separates the Bay of Fundy from St Marys Bay. Geologically, the Digby Neck, rarely more than 3km wide, is a continuation of North Mountain, which separates the Annapolis River Valley from the Bay of Fundy. Both Brier and Long islands are made up of Jurassic basalt lava – as the lava cooled, it sometimes formed vertical polygonal columns such as Balancing Rock (page 211).

The pace of life in Nova Scotia is generally pretty relaxed, but if you want to slow down even more, enjoy natural splendour, and take a holiday from your holiday, this beautiful area is worth some time. A line of wind turbines is a relatively recent addition to the landscape.

There are few services, but just enough: pretty villages and good hiking, some of the province's best birding opportunities (box, page 9) and what may well be the best whale-watching opportunities along the entire east coast of North America. Although the majority of visitors drive straight to their whale-watching trip and (when it is over) drive back again, try to allow yourself more time to explore this beautiful region.

The wild flowers are out between mid May and late June, mid July brings wild blueberries, and soon after, humpback whales. July and August can be foggy, September and October are usually beautiful, though late October can be windy.

GETTING THERE AND AWAY From Digby, Highway 217 runs down the centre of the peninsula for approximately 50km to East Ferry, from where a 5-minute **car ferry** (*CAN$7 return; at half past the hour westbound*) crosses to Tiverton on Long Island. Highway 217 continues along Long Island for 18km to Freeport, from where another car ferry (*10mins; CAN$7 return*) crosses to Westport on Brier Island. Ferries are timed so that if you're going straight through, you can drive directly from one ferry to the next without too much waiting. When there is too much traffic for the regular schedule, ferries usually make extra trips to clear the backlog.

THE MAINLAND The first dozen kilometres along Highway 217 – a road also labelled the 'Digby Neck and Islands Scenic Drive' – is an unremarkable inland drive, but before too long there are views over St Marys Bay and opportunities to make short side trips – for example, to the Bay of Fundy shore by taking Trout Cove Road from Centreville. Gullivers Cove-based **Fundy Adventures** (*685 Gullivers Cove Rd;* ✆ *902 245 4388; fundyadventures.com*) organises a range of customised experiences such as clam digging, dulse (edible seaweed) harvesting, or lobster fishing for those looking to learn more about the Fundy Shore.

As you continue on Highway 217 along the peninsula, a pretty provincial park on the waterfront at **Lake Midway** offers picnic tables and freshwater swimming. The highlight of this part of Digby Neck is the delightful **Sandy Cove**, one of the province's prettiest communities. The main part of the village is concentrated round the St Marys Bay side of the Neck, but a short drive through the hills along Bay Road leads to a long, quiet, sandy beach on the Fundy shore. This is a lovely beach and a fine spot from which to watch the sun set.

For a magnificent view of Sandy Cove, it is worth heading up nearby **Mount Shubel,** which can be reached by a relatively easy 15–20-minute trail. The trailhead is accessed by turning off Highway 217 a few hundred metres northeast of Sandy Cove on to an unpaved road (turn right if you're coming from the Digby side, left if coming from Sandy Cove itself). There's a small parking area a short distance along the unpaved road. This road isn't named or signed, so ask a local for directions if it is not immediately obvious. Another worthwhile short detour is to turn on to Little River Road at **Little River**, and follow it to the St Marys Bay shore.

The mainland ends at **East Ferry** 46km from Digby, perched atop a cliff overlooking the waters of Petite Passage, and the lighthouse on Long Island.

🏠 Where to stay, eat and drink

🏠 **Graham's Pioneer Retreat** (4 cottages) 8020 Hwy 217, Centreville; tf 1 888 839 2590; www.digbyneck.com; ⏱ May–mid Oct. Come for peace & quiet on this secluded property. These 1- & 2-bedroom cottages – all with wonderful St Marys Bay views – are comfortable with fully equipped kitchens (stock up in Digby), but don't expect TVs or phones. Beach access. **$$–$$$**

🏠 **The Olde Village Inn** (7 units) 387 Church Hill Rd, Sandy Cove; ✆ 902 834 2202, 905 434 5544; theoldevillageinn.com; ⏱ mid May–mid Oct. 6 B&B rooms & 1 5-bedroom vacation home. Impressive c1830 house with sun room, views over St Marys Bay & pool room. An inn since 1890 but seemed in need of a spruce-up on my last visit. Be aware that you might have a long drive to find somewhere to eat... **$$**

⛺ **Whale Cove Campground** (40 sites) 50 Whale Cove Rd, Whale Cove; ✆ 902 834 2025; www.whalecovecampground.com; ⏱ May–Oct. The Neck's only campground is located in Whale Cove, 6km south of Sandy Cove. Some sites at this open campground with laundromat overlooking the Bay of Fundy have electricity & water hook-ups. Take-away food canteen. **$**

JEROME

One evening in 1863, a ship was seen close to the Bay of Fundy shore at Sandy Cove. In the morning, the vessel had gone, but a strange young man sat on the sand. Although well dressed in fine linen, he was very pale: both his legs had recently been amputated above the knees. The only word he would say was 'Jerome', indicating that that was his name. Doctors, police and ministers came to question him, but he was no more loquacious. After a while, the government paid a family in Meteghan (page 201) to take him in: Jerome spent the rest of his long life there, never uttering any other words. He died in 1912 and was buried in Meteghan parish cemetery. His story continues to fascinate.

The warm Gulf Stream water colliding with the cold outflow from the Bay of Fundy, combined with the tremendous tidal influence on the waters in this area, produces some of the most plankton-rich waters in the world. This attracts whales, particularly baleen whales – the largest animals on earth.

Smaller species such as finback and Minke whales and harbour porpoises are plentiful early in the season, and numbers of huge humpback whales increase as June goes on. White-sided dolphins are another possibility, and in August you might see a very rare right whale. Seals are sometimes sighted, and pelagic seabirds abundant.

Most operators offer 2–5-hour boat trips from June to late September or early October for approximately CAN$50–85 (some may offer a 'no whales – try again free' guarantee). It's a good idea to make reservations well in advance, especially between July and early September. Choose between a 'normal' boat and a (more expensive trip in a) small high-speed Zodiac (or Zodiac-like) inflatable boat. The main operators are:

Brier Island Whale and Seabird Cruises Westport; ☎902 839 2995; tf 1 800 656 3660; brierislandwhalewatch.com. Both traditional boats & Zodiacs (or similar)
Freeport Whale and Seabird Tours Freeport; ☎902 839 2177; tf 1 866 866 8797; whalewatchersnovascotia.ca
Mariner Cruises Westport; ☎902 839 2346; tf 1 800 239 2189; www.novascotiawhalewatching.ca
Ocean Explorations Tiverton; ☎902 839 2417; tf 1 877 654 2341; www.oceanexplorations.ca. Zodiac (or similar). Special trips, such as those dedicated to seabirds, on request.
Petit Passage Whale Watch East Ferry; ☎902 834 2226; www.ppww.ca

✘ **Petit Passage Café** 3450 Hwy 217, East Ferry; ☎902 834 2226; ⊕ mid Jun–end Sep 08.30–18.00 daily. A rustic café with deck overlooking Petit Passage. The seafood chowder, soups & scallop rolls are all good, as are the fruit pies. $$

LONG ISLAND
Tiverton A traditional fishing village with a whale-watching company (box, above) and – in high season – the Tiverton Take-out (*Tiverton Wharf;* ☎ *902 839 2060;* f; ⊕ *Jul–mid Sep 11.00–20.00 daily; cash only* $), dishing up fresh seafood and fish and chips. The nearby **Boar's Head Lighthouse** is a great place to gaze out over the Bay of Fundy and try to spot whales. Signs near the lighthouse lead you to the Althouse Look Off Trail – a walk of around 10–15 minutes (each way) rewarded with fine views of the lighthouse, Tiverton, East Ferry and Petit Passage. The **tourist information** centre (*Hwy 217;* ☎ *902 839 2853;* f; ⊕ *Jul–early Sep 09.00–16.00 daily*) is located on the right of the main road as you leave Tiverton,

Approximately 3.5km past Tiverton is the parking area and trailhead to **Balancing Rock**. The first part of the trail is relatively flat, with boardwalks over the wettest parts. You then descend more than 200 steps on wooden staircases (slippery when wet) down to the cliffs from where there is a perfect view of a 9m pinnacle of basalt rock balanced on a seemingly far too narrow base. The route is approximately 1.5km each way.

Freeport Try and allow some time on the way to or way back from Brier Island to explore beautiful Freeport. Although most people stay on Highway 217, there are a couple of worthwhile **detours**. Firstly, before you get to 'town', turn right on to Lovers Lane for a look at Beautiful Cove. Return to the main road, turn right and take the first left after the church (Overcove Road), which eventually leads past the fishing wharves, to the end. Park and follow the trail towards Dartmouth Point. Back on the main road, a lovely trail leads up to a look-out and over the hill from just behind the Freeport Development Office (*243 Hwy 217*).

In town, the c1862 Lent House is now home to the **Islands History Museum and Archives** (*243 Hwy 217;* ✆ *902 839 2034; www.islandshistoricalsociety.com;* ⊕ *Jun–mid Sep 09.00–16.30 Tue–Sat; admission by donation*). The collection focuses on the way Islanders lived and worked in days gone by, both in the home and on the water. In the Marine Room, a working fish shed, many boat models can be seen, as well as fishing gear from the 1930s and 40s. Joshua Slocum (box, above) features prominently, and there are also extensive archives/genealogical records (*CAN$5/half day of research*).

Expect an influx of visitors on the third weekend in August for **Freeport Days**: entertainment, competitions, and (of course) a big parade.

✕ *Where to eat and drink*

✕ **Lavena's Catch Café** 15 Hwy 217; ✆ 902 839 2517; **f**; ⊕ mid May–early Oct 11.30–14.00 & 17.00–20.00 daily, off-season check. Food at my favourite Digby Neck restaurant is freshly made: the lobster dinner, seafood chowder, scallops (pan-seared or baked) & pan-fried haddock are all excellent. The 'chicken' bit of the chicken burger is a grilled breast, & room should be saved for one of Aunt Heather's desserts! Licensed. $–$$

BRIER ISLAND And so to the highlight of Digby Neck. For some, whale watching apart, there will be nothing to do on 6.5km by 2.5km Brier Island. But it won't disappoint those who enjoy the atmosphere of a community little changed by the passing decades, or are just content to watch the swirling sea and pounding waves. If you're in to birdwatching, wild flowers, or even just like walking, cycling or beachcombing, you won't want to leave. Virtually everyone lives in **Westport**: though the village has paved roads, only unpaved roads and walking trails cross the rest of the island.

The squat c1965 **Grand Passage Lighthouse** can be reached via Northern Point Road. A 10–15-minute walk along the coast from the lighthouse's parking area will bring you to **Seal Cove.** Try to time your visit to tie in with low tide and you're likely to see (and hear) a party of grey and harbour seals basking on the offshore rocks. On the island's southwest side is the concrete **Brier Island Lighthouse**, one of the most photogenic in the province. To get there, take Wellington Street from

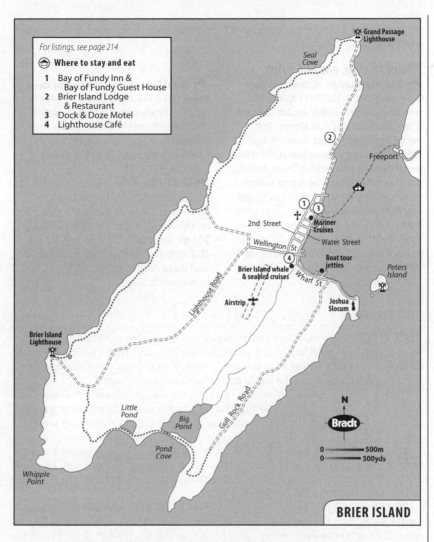

For listings, see page 214

Where to stay and eat

1 Bay of Fundy Inn &
    Bay of Fundy Guest House
2 Brier Island Lodge
    & Restaurant
3 Dock & Doze Motel
4 Lighthouse Café

Grand Passage
Lighthouse

Seal
Cove

Freeport

2nd Street

Mariner
Cruises

Wellington St

Water Street

Brier Island whale
& seabird cruises

Boat tour
jetties

Wharf St

Peters
Island

Airstrip

Joshua
Slocum

Brier Island
Lighthouse

N

Bradt

0   500m
0   500yds

Little
Pond

Big
Pond

Gull Rock Road

Pond
Cove

Whipple
Point

BRIER ISLAND

Westport, then turn left onto Western Light Road. Alternatively, turn left on to Water Street from the ferry and follow the road just a few hundred metres to the end. Park, sit on the rocks and watch seabirds ride the swirling currents, with Peter Island and its 1909 lighthouse as a beautiful backdrop.

Relatively low-lying, the island has far less forest cover than most of the province. This sensitive ecological treasure has sedge and sphagnum bogs, and rare and unusual plants including eastern mountain aven, pitcher plant, dwarf birch, curly-grass fern and several types of orchid. Late spring and summer bring a profusion of wild flowers such as Queen Anne's lace, lady's slipper, blue iris, and many types of wild rose. Even those who couldn't tell an orchid from an Orkin will enjoy the abundance of wild strawberries.

Quite apart from anyone else, the island – on the Atlantic Flyway – is a must-visit for **birdwatchers**. Over 320 species have been noted here, and a wide variety of birds can be seen easily at all times of the year, including many rarities (such as the pied-billed grebe, or Cooper's hawk). Autumn is one of the best times, with the hawk migration a highlight.

🏠 Where to stay, eat and drink *Map, page 213*

🏠 **Brier Island Lodge** (40 rooms) 557 Water St, Westport; ☎ 902 839 2300; **tf** 1 800 662 8355; www.brierisland.com; ⊕ May–mid Oct. 1km north of the village centre in a fine location on a bluff overlooking Westport & Grand Passage. Perhaps 'lodge' suggests more amenities than you'll find here. Most of the rooms are in 2 modern 2-storey buildings, & these are better (& cost more) than the rooms in the main building. The upstairs rooms have the best view! Packages including whale watching are worth looking at. In the licensed dining room (⊕ *May–mid Oct 07.00–10.00 & 18.00–21.30 daily;* **$$**) stick to fresh local seafood. Outside mid Jun–mid Sep the menu is much more limited. **$$–$$$**

🏠 **Bay of Fundy Inn & Bay of Fundy Guest House** 137 & 143 2nd St; ☎ 902 839 2346; **tf** 1 800 239 2189; www.novascotiawhalewatching. ca; ⊕ mid Jun–late Sep. Choose from the inn (4 bedrooms share 2 bathrooms) or rent the 3- to 4-bedroom guest house). Owned by Mariner Cruises (page 211). **$$**

🏠 **Dock & Doze Motel** (3 units) 353 Water St; ☎ 902 839 2601, 902 247 0142; **e** dockanddoze@ hotmail.com; ⊕ May–Sep. Friendly little motel. 1 unit has a full kitchen, the other 2, microwave & fridge. **$**

✕ **Lighthouse Café** 225 Water St; ☎ 902 839 2273; ⊕ end Jun–late Sep 10.00–19.30 daily. Not *haute cuisine* but good burgers, plus fried seafood, sandwiches, etc. **$–$$**

SOUTH OF THE ANNAPOLIS BASIN

BEAR RIVER Don't take too much notice of tourist literature calling it 'The Switzerland of Nova Scotia', but this interesting little laid-back community with an inland riverside setting is well worth a visit. Pretty throughout the year, it is stunning in autumn when the hardwood trees blaze their colours.

Once a major shipbuilding centre, many of the village's riverside buildings are built on stilts – twice a day, those high Bay of Fundy tides make their way into the Annapolis Basin and up the river. Something of a cosmopolitan artists' community, a large Mi'kmaq population (box, page 26) also calls Bear River (and environs) home.

Bear River has long been renowned for its cherries, and hosts a summer cherry festival (page 215). It is said that cherry trees were brought over from England in the 18th century by one William Sutherland (festival cherries, by the way, are usually imported from the northwest USA).

Bear River is 17km/11 miles from Digby, 29km/18 miles from Annapolis Royal and 7km/4 miles from Highway 101, Exit 24. For accommodation, stay in either Digby (page 206) or Annapolis Royal (pages 218–20), or check www.airbnb.ca. Pop in to the tourist information centre (*1884 Clementsvale Rd*; ⨍ *bearriverinformationcentre*) for more info, and there is also an unmanned information kiosk next to the Cherry Brook convenience store (by the junction or River Road and Lansdowne Road).

✕ Where to eat and drink

✕ **Myrtle & Rosie's** 1880 Clementsvale Rd; ☎ 902 467 0176; ⨍; ⊕ summer 07.00–19.00 Tue–Sat, 07.00–15.00 Sun, out of season 07.00– 15.00 Tue–Sun. Friendly café with good diner food – burgers, b/fasts, *teleras* (hot sandwiches in a special bun), & great baked treats. Patio. **$**

✕ **Sissiboo Coffee Roaster** 1886 Clementsvale Rd; ☎ 902 467 0128; ⨍; ⊕ 07.30–16.00 Mon– Sat, 09.00–17.00 Sun. Sophisticated coffee (& tea) shop & gallery. The coffee is roasted on-site. **$**

What to see and do Houses and churches on winding streets peer through the trees on the steep hills on both sides of the river. Be sure to stroll some of these to see Bear River's beautiful old houses and historic churches such as the **United Baptist Church** (*37 Pleasant St*).

Many artists and craftspeople – some very talented – now call the village home, and there are several galleries dotted all over the community including three or four on the short main street. Longest established – and the best – is **The Flight of Fancy** (*1869 Clementsvale Rd;* ✎ *902 467 4171;* **tf** *1 866 467 4171; theflight.ca;* ☼ *May–Oct 10.00–18.00 Mon–Sat, 11.00–17.00 Sun. Nov–Xmas, Apr check for hours. Jan–Mar by appointment*), close to the bridge. It is one of the top craft shops in Atlantic Canada.

Across the road and a few doors up, well-priced secondhand books and a wide variety of nick-nacks and memorabilia are housed in a former bank at **Bear River Bargains & Books** (*1886 Clementsvale Rd;* ✎ *902 467 0334;* ☼ *usually summer 10.00–17.00 Tue–Sun; spring/autumn 11.00–17.00 Tue–Sun; winter 11.00–17.00 Fri–Sun*).

Just off the 'main drag', tucked behind a pretty little garden, is a building that is home to both **Oddacity Designs** and **The Innocent Rose** (✎ *902 467 0268; www. oddacitydesigns.com;* ☼ *mid Jun–mid Sep 10.00–17.00 daily*). Here you'll find 'wearable art', used books, vintage housewares and clothing, and more.

Worth seeing, too, is the atmospheric **Old Baptist/Loyalist cemetery** up the hill on Lansdowne Road near the junction with Riverview Road. The **Bear River Heritage Museum** (*1939 Clementsvale Rd;* ✎ *902 467 0902;* ∎; ☼ *Jul–Aug 10.00–17.00 Mon–Fri; admission by donation*) is a local history museum in the Oakdene Centre, a former school.

Held in early/mid July, the **Cherry Carnival** is a one-day event which includes a parade, flea market, races, competitions – and lots of sweet cherries for sale. In August, the **Digby County Exhibition** is a four-day agricultural show with fairground rides, food and arts and crafts.

Less than 5 minutes' drive from the village, **Annapolis Highland Vineyards** (*2635 Clementsvale Rd, Bear River East;* ✎ *902 467 0363; www.annapolishighlandvineyards. com;* ☼ *Jun–Oct 10.00–18.00 daily*) will be on your left, which offers free tours and tasting.

CORNWALLIS, CLEMENTSPORT AND UPPER CLEMENTS These three communities are on Highway 1 between Exit 23 off Highway 101 and Annapolis Royal, and easy to reach **by car**. Cornwallis is 17km from Digby, 16km from Annapolis Royal and 11km from Bear River (take Chute Road, then Purdy Road from Bear River).

Cornwallis is also the terminus for **buses** (box, page 204) to Weymouth (via Digby), and to Bridgetown (via Clementsport, Upper Clements and Annapolis Royal).

Cornwallis was the site of a big Canadian Forces training base (and is still used as a training facility for international peacekeeping forces and Canadian naval cadets). It is also home to the **Fundy YMCA** (*1043 Hwy 1, Cornwallis;* ✆ *902 638 9622; www.fundyymca.com*), which has a good gym, heated indoor pool and more, and is open to non-members.

Clementsport was once a bustling port with hotels, shops and garages: now, activity centres around the **Moose River Rug Hooking Studio** (*14 Clementsport Rd, Clementsport;* ✆ *902 638 3200; www.mooseriverstudio.com;* ⊕ *10.00–17.00 Mon–Sat*), a bright, welcoming spot, and a good place to be shown how to rug-hook or to buy supplies for the craft. Back on Highway 1 after a studio visit, look out for a former church on your left, now home to **Antiques at the Church** (*1584 Hwy 1;* ✆ *902 526 0137;* ⊕ *mid May–mid Oct 10.00–17.00 Thu–Sat*). The next right (Shawmut Avenue) and then a left will bring you to classy **Clementsport Antiques** (*123 Old Post Rd;* ✆ *902 638 8169; clementsportantiques.com;* ⊕ *most days by chance or appointment*). Whereas some Nova Scotian antique shops walk the fine line between junk and treasures, both of these shops are more 'quality' and less 'flea market'. From here continue along Old Post Road and take the next left to rejoin Highway 1.

As you continue on towards Annapolis Royal, look out for **2697 Highway 1** on your left. The left-hand of the two single-storey buildings (empty and forlorn at the time of writing) was last used as a garden centre. A few decades back, though, it was the Seashell, considered one of the top-ten restaurants in Canada. Patrons included actors Arthur Kennedy and James Cagney: local legend has it that the latter (who apparently 'discovered' the former) often recreated a famous scene from *The Seven Little Foys* (1955) and tap-danced on the tables. Kennedy is commemorated with a room named in his honour at the Annapolis Royal Golf Club, and is buried just south of town.

Still on Highway 1 and heading towards Annapolis Royal, you then come to the area's big draws. On the left is **Upper Clements Amusement Park** (*2931 Hwy 1, Upper Clements;* ✆ *902 532 7557;* ☏ *1 888 248 4567; www.upperclementsparks.com;* ⊕ *mid Jun–early Sep 11.00–18.45 daily; admission free, CAN$5/ride or CAN$34 for unlimited rides*). Disneyland it isn't, but very few come away from the province's largest theme park disappointed. There are more than 30 rides and attractions and live entertainment daily. The park offers something for all ages, from minigolf and pedal go-karts to giant waterslides and Atlantic Canada's only wooden rollercoaster. Great for the kids, but plenty of kid-less adults go and enjoy it, too. There are various food and drink options including a pub Jake's Landing Pub, with decent food and cold beer on tap, or you can bring your own sandwiches and eat on-site.

Just across the road is the **Upper Clements Tree Topper Adventure Park** (⊕ *Jun–Oct 09.00–17.00 daily (weather permitting); admission CAN$34.50*), a giant elevated adventure boasting 14 zip lines, monkey ropes, obstacles and aerial skateboarding.

CLOSE COMBAT TRAINING

A few decades back, when the military training base at Cornwallis was up and running, some obliging local 'girls' – 'Digby Rose', 'Annapolis Polly' and 'Granville Annie' – provided the first insights into carnal pursuits for many raw young male recruits. The mention of these women's names to military men who, many years ago, spent time at the base, usually results in a sheepish smile (unless their wives are in earshot).

above left Nova Scotia's provincial bird, osprey (*Pandion haliaetus*) often make their nests in the most unlikely places (MB) pages 122, 307 & 381

above right Nova Scotia has an abundance of sea birds, such as these semipalmated sandpipers (*Calidris pusilla*) (SS) page 8

below left Canada lynx (*Lynx canadensis*) live in remote areas of Cape Breton Island (SH) page 6

below right American black bears (*Ursus americanus*) are shy but sometimes seen by tourists (TH/FLPA) page 7

bottom right Look out for moose on Cape Breton Island (SS) page 7

above   The new Cabot Cliffs golf course in Inverness is among the best in the world (ES) page 324

left   Tidal-bore rafting on the Shubenacadie River is an unforgettable experience — you will get wet! (TNS) page 261

below   Cyclists along the LaHave River in Lunenburg County, near Riverport (TNS) pages 172–3

above You don't see too many Nova Scotian surfers who don't wear wetsuits – this isn't Hawaii! (TNS) page 73

right With three national – and more than 130 provincial – parks, you'll be sure to find a hiking trail to suit all levels and abilities (TNS) pages 10–11

below The Three Sisters rock formations by the Bay of Fundy are popular excursion sites for sea kayaking (TNS) pages 70–1 & 275

above   **Fifes and drums keep 18th-century military music alive at the Fortress of Louisbourg** (TNS) pages 367–8

below left   **Mi'kmaq dancer at a traditional festival** (Q) page 37

below right   **Scottish heritage lives on in modern-day Nova Scotia** (TNS) pages 30–1 & 318

above Fancy a wee dram? Drop by the Glenora Distillery in Glenville and sample whiskies in their tasting room or tour the whisky warehouse for a sip straight from the barrel (TNS) page 322

left Locally produced maple syrup is a delicious addition to pancakes, waffles and more (ID/TNS) page 66

below left Fruit seller at a farmers' market (TNS) page 67

below right Digby boasts the largest inshore scallop fleet in the world (TNS) page 207

above left Buy a punnet of juicy, ripe blueberries — or better still, pick your own! (TNS) page 67

above right It's not just the lighthouse that is photogenic in the fishing village of **Peggys Cove** (A) pages 139–44

right Nova Scotia lobster — said to be the 'king of seafood' (TNS) page 62

below Most of the province's vineyards are located near the town of Wolfville (VP/S) page 245

above   Philips Harbour, near Queensport, Guysborough County (RC/LSG) page 394

left   The Boar's Head Lighthouse overlooks Petit Passage on Digby Neck (PD/TNS) page 211

below   Carters Beach is unspoilt perfection and a prime contender for the 'Most Beautiful Beach in Nova Scotia' title (DO) page 179

The full course takes 3–4 hours to complete and all participants are escorted by a guide. It is great fun for anyone who is adventure-loving and looking for a challenge. Be aware, though, that there are height, weight, clothing and footwear restrictions. If you don't have time for the whole thing you can just do a three-zip line course and/or take a leap off Canada's highest single tower free-fall.

Both parks are located on Highway 1, 7km from Annapolis Royal. Check the website for park closures if thunderstorms are forecast. You can stay right by the parks at **Upper Clements Cottages** (*3067 Hwy 1, Upper Clements; 7 units;* \ *902 532 0269;* **tf** *1 800 717 6549; www.upperclementscottages.ca;* **$$$**). The two-bedroom cottages are comfortable and well equipped: there's a seasonal pool, sports, and cute bunnies all around the grounds.

ANNAPOLIS ROYAL

It is hard not to like Annapolis Royal. Firstly, it has a delightful setting on the Annapolis Basin shore – and wonderful views across the water to the pretty village of Granville Ferry from a boardwalk with benches, picnic tables and a lighthouse. The town (with a population of approximately 500) has a tree-lined main street, one end of which is dotted with gracious mansions, many of which help make up what is the largest concentration of heritage buildings in Nova Scotia, with more than 120 municipally registered properties, 20 provincial heritage properties and five federally designated properties. Several of these house some of the province's best inns and B&Bs.

You'll find lovely gardens to stroll through and waterside trails to wander, and you can also visit North America's first tidal power-generating plant. There are galleries and a theatre with a good year-round programme. You can visit a historical site dating back four centuries, take a candlelit graveyard tour, wander around a museum housed in a 300-year-old building, or amble through an early 18th-century cemetery. Although all of these can be reached easily on foot, a short drive will take you to the site of one of the earliest permanent European settlements in North America, a good golf course, a beautiful hiking trail to the Bay of Fundy shore, or Nova Scotia's biggest theme park. Despite all this, Annapolis Royal only gets really busy during some of the bigger festivals (and on sunny summer Saturday mornings for the market).

Don't come to 'Canada's birthplace' for the nightlife (though there is a friendly little pub, the evening's best entertainment is a candlelit graveyard walking tour), but do come to soak up the history and unique atmosphere. And note that the town doesn't end at the junction of St George Street and Drury Lane: continue less than a hundred metres further on St George Street to see a couple of interesting shops (one with a café), a nice children's playground, and the O'Dell Museum.

HISTORY   Although the first Port-Royal was destroyed in 1613 (page 16), in the early 1630s, the French built a new version 11km away, this time on the south shore of the Annapolis Basin. Things were relatively calm for a couple of decades but after that the settlement changed hands backwards and forwards between the French and British.

Back under British control in 1710, the town was renamed 'Annapolis Royal' in honour of their queen, and the fort that had seen so much fighting – and had changed hands so many times – renamed 'Fort Anne'. This time – despite almost countless French attacks   the British flag was raised to stay. Annapolis Royal served as Nova Scotia's first capital until 1749 (when it was succeeded by Halifax).

Annapolis Royal prospered and during the Great Age of Sail was a bustling town with several industries and over 3,000 inhabitants. Shipbuilding reached its peak in 1874 and was centred on Hog Island, which now forms part of the causeway crossing the Annapolis River.

Its job done, Fort Anne was abandoned in the 1850s and fell into disrepair. Following a campaign by locals to have the site preserved and maintained, Fort Anne became Canada's first administered National Historic Site in 1917.

In the late 1970s Annapolis Royal was in a state of decline. The population had dwindled and the council had no money to spend on upkeep. However, a citizen-led group formed the Annapolis Royal Development Commission and lobbied both the provincial and federal governments to inject funds to preserve the town's unique heritage. Their efforts paid off, over CAN$2 million was spent on restoration projects, and in 2004, the town was designated the 'World's Most Liveable Small Community'. The following year, the town was listed as one of five Cultural Capitals of Canada.

GETTING THERE AND AROUND If you're coming **by car** on Highway 8, or from Exit 22 of Highway 101, you'll pass through Lequille: shortly after, as it enters town Highway 8 becomes the tree-lined St George Street, which continues past many beautiful houses and the Historic Gardens to a traffic light and crossroads. As you carry on straight, passing the old Courthouse and Fort Anne on your left, St George Street curves downhill to the shopping district and the wharf. If you're coming from Bridgetown on Highway 1, you'll cross the causeway over the Annapolis River, passing the Tidal Generating Station and tourist office on your left, and arrive at the crossroads and traffic light, the junction with St George Street. Annapolis Royal is on the Cornwallis–Bridgetown Kings County **bus** route (box, page 204).

For a **taxi**, try **Annapolis Royal & Bridgetown Taxi** ❨ *902 665 0057;* e *bridgetowntaxi@gmail.com*)

WHERE TO STAY *Map, opposite*
See also Granville Ferry (pages 227–9), less than 2km away. Parkers Cove (page 230) is less than 15 minutes' drive away. All options include a full breakfast.

Queen Anne Inn (14 rooms) 494 St George St; ❨902 532 7850; tf 1 877 536 0403; www. queenanneinn.ns.ca; ⊕ mid Apr–Oct. A striking c1865 grey & white Heritage mansion with a magnificent sweeping mahogany staircase. 10 large bedrooms in main building & 2 2-bedroom suites in Carriage House. Grand, but the atmosphere is relaxed. **$$$**

At the Turret B&B (4 rooms) 372 St George St; ❨902 532 5770; www.attheturret.com. A centrally located (turreted!) c1900s' property with original woodwork, stained glass, & large veranda, across the road from Fort Anne. One of the bedrooms is on the ground floor. **$$**

Bailey House B&B (5 units) 150 St George St; ❨902 532 1285; tf 1 877 532 1285; www. baileyhouse.ca. Directly across a quiet road from the Annapolis Basin, this c1770 Georgian home is the best choice for those who want to be by the water. 4 bedrooms in the main house,

& a 2-bedroom coach house. Large bedrooms, beautifully maintained waterfront & English back gardens. **$$**

Bread & Roses Inn (8 rooms) 82 Victoria St; ❨902 532 5727; tf 1 888 899 0551; www. breadandroses.ns.ca; ⊕ Apr–Nov. One of the town's few old brick buildings in Queen Anne Revival style from c1882 with large bedrooms, superb wood panelling & lovely gardens. **$$**

Garrison House Inn (7 units) 350 St George St; ❨902 532 5750; tf 1 866 532 5750; www.garrisonhouse.ca; ⊕ May–Oct (off-season by reservation). Facing Fort Anne National Historic Site, this c1854 inn has 6 bedrooms, 1 suite (with large jacuzzi), period furniture & whimsical fish folk art. **$$**

Hillsdale House Inn (13 rooms) 519 St George St; ❨902 532 2345; tf 1 877 839 2821; www.hillsdalehouseinn.ca; ⊕ Apr–Oct. Set back from the street on a 5ha estate with manicured

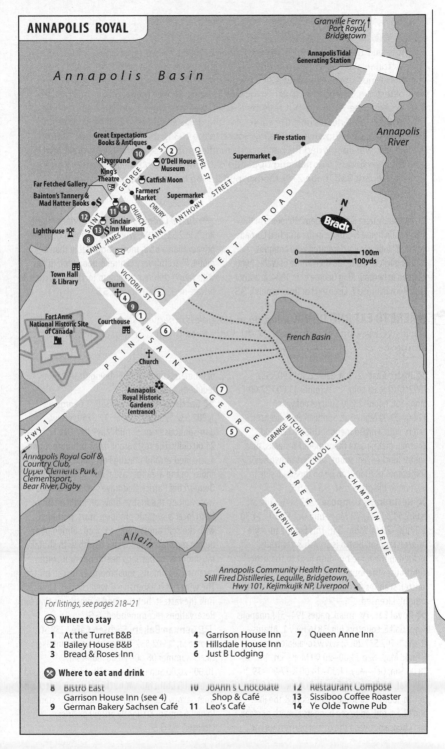

Annapolis Basin

Granville Ferry,
Port Royal,
Bridgetown

Annapolis Tidal
Generating Station

Great Expectations
Books & Antiques

Fire station

Supermarket

Annapolis
River

Playground

O'Dell House
Museum

King's
Theatre

Catfish Moon

Far Fetched Gallery

Farmers'
Market

Supermarket

Bainton's Tannery &
Mad Hatter Books

Sinclair
Inn Museum

Lighthouse

Town Hall
& Library

Church

French Basin

Fort Anne
National Historic Site
of Canada

Courthouse

Church

Annapolis
Royal Historic
Gardens
(entrance)

Hwy 1

Annapolis Royal Golf &
Country Club,
Upper Clements Park,
Clementsport,
Bear River, Digby

Allain

Annapolis Community Health Centre,
Still Fired Distilleries, Lequille, Bridgetown,
Hwy 101, Kejimkujik NP, Liverpool

0   100m
0   100yds

For listings, see pages 218–21

🏠 **Where to stay**

1	At the Turret B&B	4	Garrison House Inn	7	Queen Anne Inn
2	Bailey House B&B	5	Hillsdale House Inn
3	Bread & Roses Inn	6	Just B Lodging

✖ **Where to eat and drink**

8	Bistro East	10	JoAnn's Chocolate	12	Restaurant Compose
	Garrison House Inn (see 4)		Shop & Café	13	Sissiboo Coffee Roaster
9	German Bakery Sachsen Café	11	Leo's Café	14	Ye Olde Towne Pub

lawns, stately trees & fine gardens. 10 rooms in the c1859 main house & 3 more in the attached Carriage House, all individually decorated with antiques. Former guests include the then Prince of Wales (who went on to become King George V) in 1884, & author John Buchan in 1937. Licensed bar (guests only). **$$**

🏠 **Just B Lodging** (1 suite) 92 Prince Albert Rd; ✆ 902 532 2392; www.justblodging.ca. More privacy than a B&B, more comfortable than a motel. Peaceful, very central & good for families with young children (sleeps up to 4). Full kitchen & private deck. B/fast not inc. **$$**

🏠 **WHERE TO EAT AND DRINK** *Map, page 219, unless otherwise stated*
See also Granville Ferry (pages 227–8). Only Restaurant Composé offers waterfront dining.

✖ **Bistro East** 274 St George St; ✆ 902 532 7992; bistroeast.com; 🕐 summer 11.00–22.00 Mon–Sat, noon–18.00 Sun; rest of year 11.00–20.00 Mon–Sat. Sophisticated, licensed eatery with a broad menu including seafood, gourmet pizza, pasta (handmade) & steaks, plus lighter lunches (eg: soups, salads, sandwiches). Sometimes portions can be on the small side in relation to the dish's cost. **$$–$$$**

✖ **Restaurant Composé** 235 St George St; ✆ 902 532 1251; 🕐 May–mid Oct 11.30–14.30 & 17.00–20.00 Mon–Sat. This European-style café/restaurant/bistro is stylish & centrally located in the large building next to the little lighthouse. The food is usually good (schnitzels, lobster, scallops & more) & the waterside deck a delight. Licensed. **$$–$$$**

✖ **Royal Eatery** [map, pages 194–5] Annapolis Royal Golf & Country Club, 3816 Hwy 1, Allains Creek; ✆ 902 532 2064; www.royaleatery.ca; 🕐 mid May–Sep 11.00–20.00 Mon–Sat, 11.00–18.00 Sun; Oct–May 11.00–14.00 & 17.00–19.30 Tue–Sat, 11.00–18.00 Sun. British-owned & run: in addition to scallops, haddock & the like, don't be surprised to see bangers & mash or steak pie. Choose between the casual bar/restaurant

or intimate, candlelit fine-dining (reservations required). Licensed. **$$**

✖ **Garrison House Inn** 350 St George St; ✆ 902 532 5750; tf 1 866 532 5750; www.garrisonhouse.ca; 🕐 mid May–late Oct 17.00–21.00 daily. The restaurant has 3 intimate rooms, a screened veranda facing Fort Anne & is the best choice in the area for casual dining with a heart. Owner/chef Patrick Redgrave's eclectic menus were among the first to draw on high-quality fresh local & organic produce. Start, perhaps, with the cold applewood-smoked salmon plate before moving on to lobster risotto with shiitake mushrooms, or perhaps beef tenderloin with caramelised onions, mushrooms & Tuscan butter. The wine list is extensive & well chosen. Service isn't the fastest, but the food is worth waiting for. Reservations recommended. **$$**

🍺 **German Bakery Sachsen Café** 358 St George St; ✆ 902 532 1990; www.germanbakery.ca; 🕐 summer 08.00–20.00 Mon–Sat, 10.00–20.00 Sun (off-season Thu–Sat only). Good location & authentic name (Heiderose & Dieter are from Saxony). B/fast, lunch & dinner, plus standard (albeit German, & slightly pricey) pastries. Licensed. **$–$$**

JoAnn's Chocolate Shop & Café 165
St George St; ☎ 902 532 0120; www.
joannschocolateshop.com; ⊕ Apr–Dec 10.00–
17.00 Mon–Sat, summer 09.00–18.00. Small café
& chocolate shop featuring exquisite handmade
Belgian chocolate, coffee & espresso, light lunches
& baked goods. Located past the wharf next to
children's playground. $

Leo's Café 222 St George St; ☎ 902 532
7424; ⊕ May–Oct 09.00–16.00 Mon–Sat.
Located in the c1712 Adams-Ritchie House, this
is Annapolis Royal's most popular spot for a light
lunch (salads, soup, wraps, gourmet sandwiches,
etc), fantastic cakes & cinnamon buns. $

Sissiboo Coffee Roaster 262 St George St;
☎ 902 268 3010; ⓕ; ⊕ 07.30–16.00 Mon–Sat,
09.00–17.00 Sun. Friendly, relaxed coffee shop
currently sharing the premises with Dan Froese
Photography. Can be busy at times & there is talk
of a new (nearby) location. $

Ye Olde Towne Pub 9–11 Church St; ☎ 902
532 2244; ⊕ 11.00–23.00 Mon–Fri, 10.00–23.00
Sat, noon–20.00 Sun. This pub in a c1884 former
bank has a popular outside deck. A new owner
took over in summer 2016 & is promising a
welcoming pub with a range of good beer & good-
value upmarket grub. $$

ENTERTAINMENT AND FESTIVALS The c1921 **King's Theatre** (*209 St George St;*
☎ *902 532 7704; www.kingstheatre.ca*) has an art gallery on site, and a varied year-
round programme including theatre, films and live music. **King's Shorts** is a three-
day theatre festival of ten-minute plays, staged in June. In early August, **Natal Days**
is a street parade with community events such as pancake breakfasts, and family
activities in and around town. Later in the month, Paint the Town (*arcac-artsplace.
weebly.com*) is a painting weekend *en plein air* where more than 80 artists set up their
easels at various locations across town. Some of the town's magnificent old houses
(and gardens) are decorated and illuminated for the festive season at **Victorian
Christmas**, in December. There is a parade, craft market, and carol concerts.

SHOPPING **Bainton's Tannery & Mad Hatter Books** (*213 St George St;* ☎ *902 532 2070;*
tf *1 800 565 2070; www.baintons.ca;* ⊕ *daily*) is one of those perfect matches: leather and
new books, with a good selection of Nova Scotia/Maritimes titles. **Great Expectations
Books & Antiques** (*165 St George St;* ☎ *902 532 0120;* ⊕ *Apr–Dec 10.00–17.00 Mon–Sat,
summer 09.00–18.00*) has used (and some new) books, antiques and crafts. It shares a
space with a café and chocolate shop. For all things arty, try **Catfish Moon** (*170 St George
St;* ☎ *902 532 3055; www.catfishmoon.com;* ⊕ *May–Oct Mon–Sat, by chance Sun*) with
whimsical crafts, plus a studio and Nova Scotia folk art gallery, or **Far Fetched** (*218
St George St;* ☎ *902 532 0179; www.shopsmallns.com/listing/far-fetched-antiques-art-
gallery;* ⊕ *May–Oct daily*), which stocks beautifully crafted *objets d'art* from around
the world, especially Asia and the Far East. For both produce and crafts, head to the
farmers' market (⊕ *08.00–13.00 Sat, & Wed afternoons Jul & Aug*). Between mid May
and mid October, the market is held in the town square, and positively bustles. Off-
season it downsizes significantly and moves indoors to the Historic Gardens entrance.

OTHER PRACTICALITIES

$ Royal Bank 248 St George St; ☎ 902 532 2371;
⊕ 10.00–15.00 Mon–Fri

$ Scotiabank 219 St George St; ☎ 902 532 7466;
⊕ 10.00–17.00 Mon–Fri

✚ Annapolis Community Health Centre 821
St George St; ☎ 902 532 2381

✉ Post office 54 Victoria St; ⊕ 08.00–17.00
Mon–Fri, 09.00–noon Sat

✔ Tourist information 236 Prince Albert Rd
(Hwy 1); ☎ 902 532 5454; ⊕ mid/end May–mid
Oct 10.00–18.00 daily. Located in the Annapolis
Royal Visitor Information Centre in the tidal power
plant on the north side of town.

Annapolis Royal Library 285 St George St;
☎ 902 532 2226; ⊕ 14.00–17.00 Mon, 10.00–
17.00 Wed & Fri, 10.00–17.00 & 18.30–20.30 Thu,
10.00–14.00 Sat

WHAT TO SEE AND DO Out-of-season visitors will find many things closed, but the population is less seasonal than in some towns and there's still a little bit of life. The 7ha **Annapolis Royal Historic Gardens** (*441 St George St;* ✆ *902 532 7018; www. historicgardens.com;* ✆ *mid May–Jun & Sep–mid Oct 09.00–17.00 daily; Jul–Aug 09.00–20.00 daily; 2016 admission CAN$14.50*) opened in 1981 and were designed to reflect the various periods of local history through a gardening perspective. The Annapolis Valley climate allows a real diversity of plants to be grown: highlights include a Victorian garden, Governor's garden, innovative garden and rose collection – with around 2,000 bushes of more than 270 cultivars. See, too, the replica of a 1671 Acadian house, complete with thatched roof and traditonal Acadian garden. It is wonderful resource for heritage gardening enthusiasts, and also has an on-site café and shop. Set out for a pleasant, flat walk of approximately 25 minutes on the **French Basin Trail**, which takes you around a pretty pond often brimming with wildlife. Depending on the time of year, you might see muskrats, turtles sunning themselves, Canada geese and a lot more. There are a few access points, for example follow the path from the old railway station (which is almost opposite the entrance to the Historic Gardens), or park in the car park on Highway 1 approximately 250m from the traffic lights in Annapolis Royal heading towards Granville Ferry and the causeway. You're in the right place if you see a small skateboard park.

What is apparently the first legal still to be built in the province is used to produce rums, whiskies, vodkas, gins and 'moonshines' at **Still Fired Distilleries** (*9543 Hwy 8, Lequille;* ✆ *902 471 7083; www.stillfireddistilleries.com;* ✆ *10.00–17.00 Mon–Sat, noon–17.00 Sun*), adjacent to the Lequille Country Store. It is 3 minutes' drive from the Historic Gardens – just head up St George Street towards Highway 101.

Situated on the causeway across the Annapolis River, the **Annapolis Tidal Generating Station** (*236 Prince Albert Rd (Hwy 1);* ✆ *902 532 0502;* ✆ *mid May– mid Oct 10.00–18.00 daily; admission free*) is all about a different kind of liquid, being one of only three tidal power plants in the world, and the only one in the western hemisphere. The plant generates over 30 million kWh of electricity per year, enough to power more than 4,000 homes.

One of Canada's most important historic sites (page 37) is the **Fort Anne National Historic Site of Canada** (*323 St George St;* ✆ *902 532 2397; www.pc.gc.ca/fortanne;* ✆ *late Jun–Aug 09.00–17.30 daily; early–late Jun & Sep 09.00–17.30 Sun–Wed;* ✆ *site & grounds year-round; admission free (2017); CAN$3.90 (2016) museum, grounds free*). Beside the car park and opposite the old parade ground is the distinctive c1797 officers' quarters built by the British (and restored in 1935), which now houses a museum telling the story (through interactive exhibits) of the fort and the Acadians in the area. Be sure to see the 2.4m x 5.5m **Heritage Tapestry**, which depicts four centuries of history and settlement in Annapolis Royal and environs. Over 100 volunteers worked on the project, and even the Queen – on a 1994 state visit to Nova Scotia – chipped in with a few stitches. Outside, see the restored c1708 French gunpowder magazine, and another (1701) gunpowder magazine (the 'black hole') which was later used as a dungeon. The fort's earthworks are the best-surviving example of a Vauban fort in North America: expansive grassy ramparts and grounds overlook the Annapolis Basin and the mouths of the Annapolis and Allain rivers, and lead right down to the water's edge. The location is magnificent: even if you're not interested in history, come for a wander, the views, a picnic, or just to let the kids roll down the slopes.

Part of the site is the **Garrison Cemetery**. Originally the St Jean Baptiste Cemetery and burial grounds for the French military forces here, it later served both the British military and the local parish. The earliest tombstone still in place dates from

1720. Between June and mid October, an entertaining, educational and highly recommended candlelight graveyard tour (*www.tourannapolisroyal.com*) is offered by the local Historical Association at 21.30 several evenings a week.

The c1869 former home and tavern of Corey O'Dell is now the **O'Dell House Museum** (*136 Lower St George St;* ☎ *902 532 7754; www.annapolisheritagesociety. com;* ⊕ *hours vary; admission by donation*). O'Dell was once a rider on the Pony Express run (box, page 229), and the downstairs rooms reflect a house of the 1870–1900 period. Upstairs are temporary exhibits, and the museum offers a genealogical centre and archival research facilities.

One of the most significant buildings in Canada is the **Sinclair Inn Museum** (*232 St George St;* ☎ *902 532 7754; www.annapolisheritagesociety.com;* ⊕ *Jun–Aug 09.00–17.00 Mon–Sat, 12.30–17.00 Sun; Sep–mid Oct 09.00–17.00 Tue–Sat; admission by donation*), the front part of which was built in 1710. It offers a fascinating insight into the construction techniques of the Acadians – where clay and straw were forced into the wall cavities as insulation – to the (relatively) modern. The building and town's history is brought to life by a series of ten projected 'ghosts', each representing a person who lived or worked in the building from its construction through to the 1950s.

Golfing enthusiasts can drop by the **Annapolis Royal Golf and Country Club** (*3816 Hwy 1;* ☎ *902 532 2064; www.annapolisroyalgolf.com;* ⊕ *approx Apr–Oct; green fees CAN$37*), a short 5,417yd course, but worth playing, not least for the wonderful views (and reasonable rates). Aside from weekends, you shouldn't need to book a tee time.

KEJIMKUJIK NATIONAL PARK AND NATIONAL HISTORIC SITE OF CANADA

From Annapolis Royal, Highway 8 running south presents the quickest route to visit Nova Scotia's beautiful Kejimkujik National Park and National Historic Site (*Hwy 8;* ☎ *902 682 2772; www.pc.gc.ca/pn-np/ns/kejimkujik.aspx;* ⊕ *late May–late Oct; admission free (2017), CAN$5.80/day (2016)*). Confusingly, the park comprises two geographically separate sections, the smaller of which, Kejimkujik Seaside, is described on page 178.

Those familiar with some of North America's national parks might not 'get' Keji, at 38,000ha the Maritimes' largest inland national park. Don't come here expecting magnificent sweeping panoramas, soaring mountains, towering waterfalls or vast canyons – this is a place of woodlands, lakes studded with islands, rivers and streams, best viewed not from a car window but on foot, from the saddle of a mountain bike, or, best of all by staying for a few nights, camping and travelling along the waterways by canoe. The modern-day visitor to Kejimkujik's back-country can retrace ancient canoe routes and experience a landscape which is very similar in appearance to that which the Mi'kmaq travelled through for so long.

HISTORY The Mi'kmaq inhabited – or at least regularly passed through – this area for thousands of years, travelling by canoe and on foot, hunting, fishing and camping. Some Mi'kmaq petroglyphs/pictographs dating from the 18th and 19th centuries have survived: these depict scenes of Mi'kmaq family life, hunting and fishing, and scenes inspired by the experience of the Mi'kmaq during the era of European contact. Their locations are closed to public access, but they can be viewed on guided tours led by Parks Canada interpreters.

Europeans settled in the region in the 17th century, logged most of the forests and cleared much of the land for farming. Some (largely unproductive) gold mines

5

were also established within Kejimkujik's boundary. In the 19th and 20th centuries the site contained hunting and fishing lodges which have since been removed. The national park was established in 1967 and the National Historic Site was established in 1995.

GEOGRAPHY AND GEOLOGY The last glaciation, which began approximately 90,000 years ago and ended 11,000 years ago, was responsible for the erratics (glacier-transported rock fragments), eskers (long winding ridges deposited by meltwater from glaciers), drumlins (hills carved by receding glaciers), shallow lakes, streams and rivers seen today.

Although fresh water covers some 14% of the park, hard rock such as slate, granite and quartzite yields precious few natural minerals to the rivers and streams. River, stream and lake water in Kejimkujik is generally a tea-like brown: plants in the many wetlands contain tannin, and this colours the water.

FLORA AND FAUNA Black bears are present throughout the park, though sightings are rare. Beaver lodges and dams can be seen on many waterways, and white-tailed deer, muskrat, racoon and porcupine are common. The coyote was first sighted in the park in 1985, and is still rare, as are the American marten and southern flying squirrel (page 6).

The park is home to five snake species, including the rare Eastern ribbon snake, and three turtles, one of which, the Blanding's turtle, is considered to be an endangered species. The chances of spotting salamanders and frogs are very good.

Six species of woodpecker, including the pileated woodpecker and the rare black-backed woodpecker, and 20 species of warbler contribute to the park's 200 or so bird species. Most common of the owls is the great barred owl, and the call of the common loon delights many campers after dark. Rarities include the scarlet tanager, great crested flycatcher and the wood thrush.

Kejimkujik's vascular plant count is close to 550 including 90 species of woody plants, more than 20 ferns, 15 orchids, and almost 40 aquatic species. Wild flowers are at their best between late May and the end of June.

The park's forest cover is representative of the Atlantic Coast Plain region, including a mix of coniferous and deciduous species. Whilst most areas have been logged over the centuries, some stands of old growth Eastern hemlock and sugar maple-yellow birch can still be found.

The park is considered to be home to one of the healthiest populations of brook trout in Nova Scotia and possibly in all of Atlantic Canada. Kejimkujik is also home to 11 other species of fish including white and yellow perch, brown bullhead (one of the catfish family), and the American eel, which due to declining populations is now listed as a 'species of special concern'.

THE ROAD TO KEJI

Highway 8 leads south from Annapolis Royal, under Exit 22 off Highway 101 and on to Kejimkujik National Park 47km away, and then on to Liverpool (pages 170–6) 115km away. Just off Highway 8, 27km from Annapolis Royal, the **Raven Haven South Milford HI-Hostel** (*4 beds; Virginia Rd, West Springhill;* ☏ *902 532 7320;* ⏰ *mid–Jun–Aug;* **$**) is on the shore of Sandy Bottom Lake. It has 4- or 5-bed male or female rooms. There's a supervised swimming beach, canoe rentals and a canteen, and it is open to non-guests.

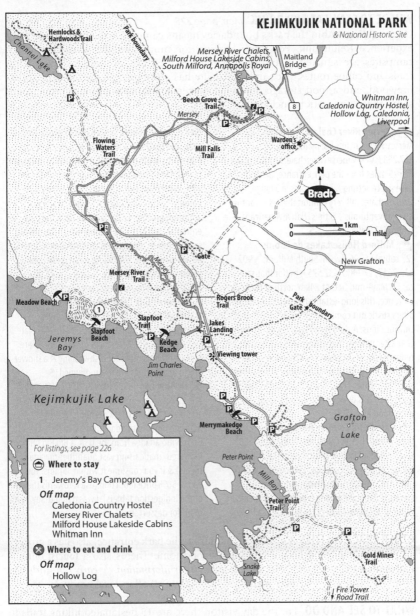

KEJIMKUJIK NATIONAL PARK
& *National Historic Site*

Hemlocks &
Hardwoods Trail

Channel Lake

Park boundary

Mersey River Chalets,
Milford House Lakeside Cabins,
South Milford, Annapolis Royal

Maitland
Bridge

Whitman Inn,
Caledonia Country Hostel,
Hollow Log, Caledonia,
Liverpool

Beech Grove
Trail

Mersey

Flowing
Waters
Trail

Mill Falls
Trail

Warden's
office

Bradt

N

0 _____ 1km
0 _____ 1 mile

Gate

New Grafton

Mersey River
Trail

Mersey

Rogers Brook
Trail

Park
boundary

Meadow Beach

Gate

Jeremys
Bay

1

Slapfoot
Beach

Slapfoot
Trail

Kedge
Beach

Jakes
Landing

Viewing tower

*Jim Charles
Point*

Kejimkujik Lake

Merrymakedge
Beach

*Grafton
Lake*

Peter Point

For listings, see page 226

🛏 **Where to stay**

1   Jeremy's Bay Campground

Off map
    Caledonia Country Hostel
    Mersey River Chalets
    Milford House Lakeside Cabins
    Whitman Inn

✕ **Where to eat and drink**

Off map
    Hollow Log

Mill Bay

Peter Point
Trail

Gold Mines
Trail

*Snake
Lake*

Fire Tower
Road Trail

GETTING THERE AND AWAY The park's entrance is off Highway 8, which connects
Liverpool – and Highway 103 Exit 19 – with Annapolis Royal and Highway 101,
Exit 22. It is approximately 70km/43 miles from Liverpool and 48km/30 miles
from Annapolis Royal. If you're **driving** from anywhere between Halifax and
Lunenburg, your quickest route is to take Highway 103 to Exit 13, then follow the
signs. It is a drive of around 165km/103 miles from Halifax. **Liverpool Adventure
Outfitters** (page 176) offer hike, bike, kayak and canoe day tours to the park from
Liverpool.

5

🏠 WHERE TO STAY, EAT AND DRINK *Map, page 225*

Overnighting within the park's boundaries means camping – the best way to truly experience Kejimkujik. For those looking for more solitude, 46 back-country campsites are situated in beautiful wilderness settings, scattered along hiking trails and canoe routes. Each individual site has a fire box, picnic table, pit toilet, firewood, and a food storage device. However, for those wanting a proper bed, some alternative options include:

🏠 **Mersey River Chalets** (16 units) 315 Mersey River Chalets Rd, Maitland Bridge; **tf** 1 877 667 2583; www.merseyriverchalets.com. Approx 8km/5 miles from the park entrance, these chalets have a nice setting & offer rooms in a lodge, 2 sizes of chalet (all very comfortable), & – for the more adventurous – 3 tipis (Native American-style tents), & 2 walled tents. **$$**

🏠 **Milford House Lakeside Cabins** (27 cabins) 5296 Hwy 8, South Milford; ✆902 532 2617; **tf** 1 877 532 5751; milfordhouse. ca; ⊕ May–mid Oct. At 24km north of the park entrance, this long-established accommodation offers rustic but comfortable cabins in wooded surroundings. A number of families return here year after year. Activities include lake swimming, tennis, croquet, horseshoes, canoe rentals & fishing. The licensed dining room (⊕ *May–mid Oct high season 17.30–20.00; $$*) dishes up good food & is open to non-guests: reservations are a good idea. **$$**

🏠 **Caledonia Country Hostel** (2 rooms & dorm) 9960 Hwy 8, Caledonia; ✆902 682 3266; www.caledoniacountryhostel.com. This friendly budget option in Caledonia, 15km from the park entrance, offers a 6-bed dorm, twin room & private dbl room. Bedding is provided, & there's a communal kitchen & deck (with BBQ), & a lounge.

Bike rentals & shuttle service (inc to airport) are available for those without their own transport. Rates inc simple b/fast. *Dorm CAN$30; twin/private room CAN$65 (discounts for longer stays).* **$**

🏠 **Whitman Inn** (8 units) 12389 Hwy 8, Kempt; ✆902 682 2226; **tf** 1 800 830 3855; whitmaninn.com. Less than 4km from the park entrance road is this c1912 inn, which has simple smaller rooms, larger ones, a 'honeymoon suite' & an apt sleeping 4. The dining room is open for b/fast (⊕ *08.00–09.30*) & dinner (⊕ *18.00– 20.00 Oct–Jun by reservation only); $$*). **$**

🏕 **Jeremy's Bay Campground, Kejimkujik National Park;** **tf** 1 877 737 3783; www. reservation.parkscanada.gc.ca; ⊕ late May–late Oct. Over 350 sites (electric & unserviced). There are washrooms, sinks for dishwashing & a shower block: reservations are recommended. **$**

✕ **Hollow Log** 9902 Hwy 8; ✆902 682 2086; 🅵; ⊕ late May–mid Oct 09.00–19.00 Mon–Sat, 10.00–19.00 Sun: check o/s hours. A simple roadside diner with good burgers, milkshakes, etc. Borrowing an idea from the USA, a Big Rig burger is offered (made using vast quantities of various meats) & if you consume it within 15mins, you earn a 50% price reduction (use it towards the cost of the indigestion tablets). I was going to say 'save room for dessert', but… **$**

OTHER PRACTICALITIES Caledonia (15km from the park entrance) also has a grocery shop, liquor store (off-licence), and a fast-food joint. There's also a **tourist office – Caledonia VIC** (✆ *902 682 2470;* 🅵 *caledoniavisitorinformation;* ⊕ *early Jun–early Oct 10.00–17.00 daily*). A **farmers' market** (⊕ *May–Oct Sat*) offers local produce.

WHAT TO SEE AND DO For the day visitor, there are 15 designated **hiking trails** to explore, ranging from a 300m loop to a 3.5km each-way riverside wander. The trails are generally pretty flat, so hiking here is more about enjoying the forest, waterways, and animal, bird and plant life than gazing out over far-reaching panoramas. They might not be the giant redwoods of California, but the 300-year-old stand of towering hemlock is pretty impressive: view these and other hardwoods on the aptly named 6km **Hemlocks and Hardwoods loop**. **Mill Falls** is an easy, short (2km return) riverside wander starting at the visitor centre. The **Rogers Brook Trail** is even shorter (at just 1km), but nevertheless enjoyable. The 3km return **Gold Mines**

Trail leads – as you might have guessed – to an old gold mine. For a good overview of woodlands and riverside, I would recommend combining the **Mersey River Trail** (3.5km one-way) with the 3.2km **Slapfoot Trail**.

Mountain bikers will want to try the 3km **Peter Point Trail** and the 19.5km **Fire Tower Road Trail**. Bikes can be hired at **Whynot Adventure – The Keji Outfitters** at Jake's Landing (✆ *902 682 2282; www.whynotadventure.ca;* ⊕ *late May–late Oct*): this is also the place to rent canoes and kayaks (*from CAN$12/hour*).

Canoeing has always been the best way to explore Kejimkujik. There are spectacular routes for a wilderness camping trip or even just a day paddle: at very least rent a canoe for an hour or two. The dark, warm waters are also great for the swimming. The fishing season (special licence is required) runs from April to August. A range of guided experiences and adventures are organised within the park (free with park admission), including canoe events, hikes, children's activities, concerts, dark-sky viewing, campfire programmes and guided tours of the **Mi'kmaq petroglyphs**.

AROUND ANNAPOLIS ROYAL

GRANVILLE FERRY Granville Ferry is a village of two parts. Coming from Annapolis Royal, turn left after crossing the causeway and you'll find fine views across the water to Annapolis Royal, especially in the afternoon (when the sun is further west). The community, which in the 1920s attracted several upper-class British families who had been living the good life in India, boasts several elegant old houses and a couple of fine B&Bs.

If (instead of turning off) you continue along Highway 1, the other part of Granville Ferry has a campground and café, two petrol stations, and a little further on, a good budget-priced B&B. As it's just across the causeway from Annapolis Royal, it makes a pleasant walk or easy cycle ride if the weather's clement (though Croft House – overleaf – is too far out to walk for most).

Granville Ferry is on Highway 1 and therefore convenient **by car**, just 1km/0.6 miles from Annapolis Royal and 22km/14 miles from Bridgetown, 9km/6 miles from Exit 22 off Highway 101. It is also on the Cornwallis–Bridgetown **bus** route (box, page 204).

🏠 **Where to stay, eat and drink** The following are all within 2km of Annapolis Royal – less than 3 minutes' drive.

🏠 **Grand Oak Manor B&B** (3 units) 5345 Granville Rd; ✆ 902 308 1592; grandoakbnb. ca. 2 bedrooms (1 with en-suite, 1 with private bathroom) plus a 2-bedroom suite in this lovely c1800 Regency-style former tavern. Art & Martha love to chat with their guests. Rate includes b/fast (with broccoli quiche or topped homemade waffles). **$$**

🏠 **A Seafaring Maiden** (3 rooms) 5287 Granville Rd; ✆ 902 532 0379; **tf** 1 888 532 0379; www.aseafaringmaiden.com. An award-winning, beautifully decorated c1881 home with wonderful views across the water to Annapolis Royal, Fort Anne & the Annapolis River Basin. A real treat. Full gourmet b/fast inc. **$$**

🏠 **Croft House** (2 rooms) 51 Riverview Lane; 📞 902 532 0584; tf 1 866 532 0584; www. crofthouse.ca. Comfortable traditional-style B&B in old farmhouse on quiet side road less than 5mins' drive from Annapolis Royal. Asparagus fields, large wildlife-attracting pond. The 2 spacious bedrooms share a bathroom making this an ideal choice for families. Rate includes wholesome organic b/fast. Pets on premises. Excellent value. **$**

⚑ **Dunromin Waterfront Campground** (207 sites) 4618 Hwy 1; 📞 902 532 2808; www. dunromincampsite.com; ⊕ May–mid Oct. Open & wooded sites, serviced & unserviced, on the bank of the Annapolis River. Laundry, grocery store, café, pool, activities including boat rental & kayak lessons/trips. **$**

✗ **Stone Horse Café** 4616 Hwy 1; 📞 902 532 5554; ⊕ May–mid Oct 08.00–14.00 Thu–Tue. Situated in the Dunromin Campground, & with no deep fryer in sight – just good healthy, tasty homemade food at this simple unpretentious café. Soups, salads & sandwiches at lunch, & all-day b/ fasts. Garden patio for warmer weather. **$**

What to see and do Having crossed the causeway, take the first left on to Granville Road toward the **North Hills Museum** (*5065 Granville Rd;* 📞 *902 532 2168; www.annapolisheritagesociety.com;* ⊕ *Jun–mid Oct 09.30–17.30 Mon–Sat, 15.00–17.30 Sun; admission by donation*). The museum is on the right, 4km past the centre of the village. Housed in a charming, superbly restored c1764 salt box-style farmhouse with Georgian décor, it has a wonderful collection of antiques including 18th-century paintings, furniture, ceramics and glassware. The museum hosts several summer events, usually on Sunday afternoons.

The **Port-Royal National Historic Site** (*Granville Rd;* 📞 *902 532 2898; www.pc.gc.ca/portroyal;* ⊕ *late May–late Jun & Sep–mid Oct 09.00–17.30 Tue– Sat; late Jun–Aug 09.00–17.30 daily; admission free (2017), CAN$3.90 (2016)*) offers a fascinating look in to the life of early French settlers in this region, and is one of the most historically important sites in not just Canada, but the whole of North America. Learn more about it in the refurbished Boulay Room and sit in the dining room and try to imagine the chatter and laughter from over four centuries ago. Accessible toilets and a picnic area are located by the car park. The site is 10km/6 miles from Granville Ferry and 12km/7 miles from Annapolis Royal.

In 1605, Sieur de Mons and Samuel de Champlain (from France) established a permanent camp, naming it 'Port-Royal': their habitation was the first permanent European settlement north of St Augustine, Florida. To keep morale high, in 1606, de Champlain set up North America's first European social club, *L'Ordre de Bon Temps* (usually translated as the 'Order of Good Cheer'). Fine food and drink helped keep the men healthy and well fed, and distracted the settlers from the hardships of life in this remote outpost.

De Champlain established fine gardens with reservoirs and canals, and he built a summer house among trees. The gardens are marked clearly on his 1607 map, the original of which is at the Congress Library in Washington, DC.

The French settlers got on very well with the area's indigenous people, the Mi'kmaq, and when Sieur de Mons's monopoly was revoked in 1607, the habitation was left in the care of Mi'kmaq chief Membertou. The Mi'kmaq chief did a fine job, and when the French returned in 1610, De Mons's successor, Jean de Poutrincourt encouraged Membertou and the Mi'kmaq to convert to Catholicism. A force commissioned to expel all Frenchmen from territory claimed by England, led by Samuel Argall from Virginia, arrived in 1613 whilst the inhabitants were away up the river. The habitation was looted and destroyed.

Between 1939 and 1940, the Canadian government built a reconstruction of the c1605 French fur-trading post based on de Champlain's drawings, using 17th-century construction techniques where possible. The buildings form a rectangle around a courtyard and are fortified by a stockade, with two cannon platforms at the southerly corners. A well representing one dug by Champlain is in the centre of the courtyard, and the site contains a blacksmith's shop, kitchen, communal dining room, guardroom and artisans' quarters. Costumed interpreters are on hand to provide more details.

If you feel like getting out on the water, **kayaking** introduction and tours (*2–8 hours*) exploring the Annapolis Basin are offered by Dunromin Waterfront Campground (page 228).

VICTORIA BEACH   Rather than turning back after visiting Port-Royal (page 228), if time allows consider making a side trip to Victoria Beach. Shortly after the Port-Royal site, the c1885 **Shafner's Point Lighthouse** makes a pleasant picnic spot. As you drive, there are fine views over the Annapolis Basin, and you'll pass some beautiful heritage homes in different architectural styles. As you near Victoria Beach, look out at the narrow, turbulent currents and whirlpools of the **Digby Gut**. Victoria Beach doesn't have a beach to speak of, or much to see other than a large wharf, a colourful collection of boats and a small lighthouse. It does, however, have a storied past and numerous ghost stories emanate from the community. Tales of the sounds of vessels docking but no visible signs of ships, of men dressed in clothes from bygone days who greet people on the path and then disappear into thin air, of a sailor who had died at sea returning each night to stand on the doorstep of his house leaving a puddle of seawater and seaweed, of several sightings of the Grey Lady (page 379), and even a sea serpent with a huge head and eyes which reared up out of the water.

In the 1940s, the village was the home of historical novelist Evelyn Eaton, best known for *Quietly My Captain Waits*.

Victoria Beach is at the western end of Granville Road, 25km/16 miles from Granville Ferry and 27km/17 miles from Annapolis Royal. The road ends in uninhabited coastline at this point and you will have to go back along Granville Road to return to Port-Royal or head north towards Delaps Cove.

DELAPS COVE   Other than to stay at the Fundy Trail Campground & Cottages (*7 cottages; 62 Delaps Cove Rd;* ✆ *902 532 7711; www.fundytrail.com;* ⊕ *mid*

PONY EXPRESS

Early in 1849, six American news organisations clubbed together to finance a pony express. A steamer arrived in Halifax from England bringing newspapers from Europe. These were transported by a relay team of horseback couriers from Halifax to Digby Gut, whence they were shipped to the telegraph station at Saint John, New Brunswick. From there, the news items were relayed by telegraph to the press of the American seaboard cities. The Halifax Express covered the 232km in an average time of eight hours. Riders were changed at Kentville, but horses (not ponies) were changed every 19km. As the rider passed through Annapolis Royal, a cannon was fired to signal a steamship waiting at Victoria Beach to prepare to depart. Operating between February and November 1849, this successful system was superseded by the extension of the telegraph to Halifax. A monument to the Pony Express is found on the seaward side of the road a little before you get to the Victoria Beach wharf area.

May–mid Oct; camping **$**, cottages **$–$$**), which has one-bedroom cottages and a variety of campsites, the only reason to head out to this remote area is to hike the **Delaps Cove Wilderness Trail**.

The better (of what are actually two) trail is the 2.2km Bohaker Loop, which leads from the trailhead car park through softwoods and hardwoods to the rocky Bay of Fundy shore, on to a fascinating rock cove jammed with driftwood, flotsam and a wrecked boat. The sure-footed can descend to the cove via a steep, sometimes slippery, path (watch out for the incoming tide). On the other side of the cove, Bohaker's Brook drops over the cliff edge as a 12m waterfall. There's a look-out right by the top of the cascade, from where a short extension to the trail is worth a quick look. Retrace your steps back across the bridge to rejoin the trail which follows the brook upstream before curving back to the parking area. There's a rustic loo at the trailhead parking area, but no other services.

To reach Delaps Cove **by car**, either take Parkers Mountain Road from Highway 1, just east of Granville Ferry, or (a bit quicker) take the unpaved Hollow Mountain Road from Granville Road just east of Port-Royal. Either way, turn left at the T-junction and follow Shore Road West – look for a sign on the left to Delaps Cove Wilderness Trail. It's approximately 17km from Granville Ferry by the shorter route.

PARKERS COVE On the Bay of Fundy shore over North Mountain from Granville Ferry, less than 10km from Granville Ferry and Annapolis Royal, Parkers Cove is a working fishing village with a lobster pound where the crustacean can be purchased live or cooked. The cove can be reached **by car** by taking Parkers Mountain Road from Highway 1 just east of Granville Ferry; it is less than 15 minutes' drive from Annapolis Royal.

 Where to stay, eat and drink

Mountain Top Cottages & Campground (17 units & 21 sites) 888 Parker Mountain Rd; ☎902 532 2564; **tf** 1 877 885 1185; www.mountaintopcottages.com; ☺ May–Oct. Simple 1- & 2-bedroom cottages (the latter sleeps up to 6) set in the woods overlooking a lake on an 80ha property. All cottages have a fridge, microwave & stove. Heated outdoor pool (seasonal), hiking & biking trails & watercraft for use on the lake. The wooded, semi-private sites have 2- or 3-way hookups. Camping **$**, cottages **$$**
✖ **Nautical Seafoods Market** 4336 Shore Rd; ☎902 532 2212; **f**; ☺ summer 11.00–20.00

daily. Almost opposite the wharf, this sells (not surprisingly) seafood, & offers a tasty but very limited menu inc seafood chowder & good lobster rolls to take away or eat at a picnic table on the deck. **$–$$**
✖ **Shore Road Seafood/Crow's Nest Dining Room** 3931 Shore Rd W, Hillsburn; ☎902 532 0155; www.shoreroadseafood.com; ☺ year-round 11.00–19.00 daily. Less than 3mins' drive from here & only 15mins from Annapolis Royal, this place turns out good fresh seafood & mounds of fries. It is very popular & reservations are advised. It is less than 15 minutes' drive from Annapolis Royal. **$–$$**

EAST TOWARDS KENTVILLE

BRIDGETOWN This pretty riverside town (*population: 970*) of wide tree-lined streets and grand heritage homes makes a nice wander. Pick up a **Cyprus Walk** leaflet from the tourist office (*232 Granville St West;* ☎ *902 665 5150;* ☺ *mid Jun–Sep 09.00–17.00 Mon–Fri*), or download it from www.bridgetownnovascotia.com.

Bridgetown is on Highway 1 and just off Highway 101 (exits 20 and 21), 26km from Annapolis Royal and 23km from Middleton. It is easy to reach **by car**, but

Bridgetown is the terminus for **bus** routes west to Cornwallis and east to Greenwood (box, page 204). For **taxis**, try **Annapolis Royal & Bridgetown Taxi** (❀ *902 665 0057;* e *bridgetowntaxi@gmail.com*).

🏠 Where to stay, eat and drink

🏠 **Bridgetown Motor Inn** (28 rooms) 396 Granville St East; ❀ 902 665 4403; **tf** 1 888 424 4664; www.bridgetownmotorinn.ca. Dependable – if somewhat outdated – motel with spacious rooms & laundry facilities. B/fast available at extra cost. **$**

🏠 **Harrington House B&B** (2 rooms) 325 Granville St; ❀ 902 665 4938; www. harringtonhouse.ca; ⊕ year-round (by reservation only Nov–May). A c1896 house with large gardens. 1 room has en-suite, the other a private bathroom. B/fast inc. **$**

🏕 **Annapolis River Campground** (75 sites) 56 Queen St; ❀ 902 665 2801; www. annapolisrivercampground.ca; ⊕ May–mid Oct. Seniors' park & adults only: serviced & unserviced riverside sites; laundry service & canoe rentals. **$**

🏕 **Valleyview Provincial Park Campground** (30 sites) 960 Hampton Rd; ❀ 902

665 2559; parks.novascotia.ca/content/valleyview; ⊕ mid Jun–early Sep. Hillside park 6km from town offering wooded sites, panoramic views over the Annapolis Valley & the province's remote forested interior. Take Hampton Mountain Rd from Granville St to get there. **$**

✖ **End of the Line Pub** 73 Queen St; ❀ 902 665 5277; www.endofthelinepub.com; ⊕ 09.00–20.00 Mon–Wed, 09.00–21.00 Thu–Sun (kitchen 11.00–20.00 or earlier). In the former train station across the road from the bookshop (see below), this pub offers over 20 types of beer & food usually a bit brighter than its lighting. **$–$$**

✖ **The Mason Jar at the Firefly Makery** 29 Queen St; ❀ 902 665 2454; 🔲; ⊕ 08.00–14.00 Tue–Thu, 08.00–20.00 Fri. Only a few tables but good, creative soups, salads, sandwiches, coffee & baked treats. **$**

What to see and do Just over the bridge, **Endless Shores Books** (*67 Queen St;* ❀ *902 665 2029; www.endlessshoresbooks.com;* ⊕ *call or check website for hours*) is a friendly, used bookshop well worth browsing. The **Firefly Makery** (*29 Queen St;* ❀ *902 665 2454; fireflymakery.com;* ⊕ *10.00–16.00 Tue–Sat*) is a bright, airy spot for crafts and craft supplies. Swot up on community history at the c1835 **James House Museum** (*12 Queen St;* ❀ *902 825 1287;* ⊕ *Jun–Aug 09.30–16.30 Mon–Fri, off-season by appointment; admission free*), and the pleasant **Jubilee Park** is on the Annapolis River with a good kids' playground.

MIDDLETON The self-labelled 'Heart of the Valley', Middleton has a couple of contrasting museums, and a fascinating mix of architecture, especially on Main, School and Commercial streets and Gates Avenue. One of this part of Nova Scotia's few cross-province roads, Highway 10, connects Middleton with Liverpool (pages 170–6).

To get here **by car**, the town is on highways 1 and 10, and just off Highway 101, Exit 18. Middleton is also on the Bridgetown–Greenwood **bus** route (box, page 204).

🏠 Where to stay, eat and drink

🏠 **Middleton Motel & Suites** (46 units) 121 Main St; ❀ 902 825 3433; **tf** 1 855 825 3433; www.middletonmotel.ca. One of the area's largest accommodations with rooms laid out in traditional motel drive-up style. Standard & deluxe rooms, & 1- & 2-bedroom suites. Outdoor pool (seasonal) **$–$$**

> ### SAUPON
>
> In days of yore, one Bridgetown hotel – now long gone – was renowned for its signature dish, *saupon*. Cornmeal was boiled in milk for several hours on an even heat. By dinner time, it had thickened, and was served with sugar.

⌂ Orchard Queen Motel & RV Park (8 units & 64 sites) 425 Main St; ☎902 825 4801; **tf** 1 855 825 4801; ⊕ mid Apr–Oct. Spacious, good-value motel rooms (2 with kitchenettes) & mostly full-service campsites (with a few for tents). Seasonal outdoor pool. **$**

✗ Pasta Jax 300 Main St; ☎902 825 6099; www.TheRestaurantPastaJax.com; ⊕ 11.30–14.00 & 16.30–19.30 Mon–Fri, 17.00–20.00 Sat. Don't take too much notice of the name, this is actually an upscale Italian-style steakhouse – & a very good one at that. Most ingredients are local & almost everything made to order from scratch. Start, perhaps, with crispy ravioli, & if you have room after your steak (or lobster risotto or seafood pasta), both the panna cotta & tiramisu are sublime. Another plus is an extensive wine & single malt Scotch list. Reservations encouraged for dinner. **$$**

Other practicalities

$ Scotiabank 293–301 Main St; ☎902 825 4894; ⊕ 10.00–17.00 Mon–Fri

✚ Soldiers Memorial Hospital 462 Main St; ☎902 825 341

✉ Post office 275 Main St; ⊕ 08.00–18.00 Mon–Fri, 09.00–17.00 Sat

ℹ Tourist information 8 Bridge St; ☎902 825 4100; ⊕ mid May–Jun 09.00–17.00 Thu–Mon; Sep 10.00–17.00 Thu–Mon; Jul–Aug 08.30–18.00 daily

Rosa M Harvey Middleton and Area Library 45 Gates Av; ☎902 825 4835; ⊕ 10.00–17.00 & 18.30–20.30 Tue & Fri, 10.00–17.00 Wed & Thu, 14.00–17.00 & 18.30–20.30 Fri, 10.00–14.00 Sat

---

WINDMILLS OF YOUR MIND

One point if – when asked who sang the Academy Award-winning *The Windmills of Your Mind* for the 1968 film *The Thomas Crown Affair* – you say 'Noel Harrison'. A second point if you knew that Noel (who passed away in 2013) was a former Olympic skier, and the son of actor Sir Rex Harrison. Ten bonus points if you know that Harrison Jnr also recorded 'The Middleton Fire Brigade', dedicated to Middleton's finest who came to the rescue when Harrison's house (located between Middleton and the Bay of Fundy) caught fire in the 1970s.

What to see and do On Commercial Street, by the Church Street junction next to the Town Hall, see North America's first water-run **town clock**. At dusk throughout the summer months, watch out for hundreds of swifts entering the big chimney of the Middleton Regional High School at 18 Gates Avenue. One of only five remaining Loyalist churches in North America, **Old Holy Trinity Church** (*49 Main St;* ☎ *902 825 5500;* ⊕ *Jul–Aug or by appointment*) was consecrated in 1791.

The grand **Annapolis Valley Macdonald Museum** (*21 School St;* ☎ *902 825 6116; macdonaldmuseum.ca;* ⊕ *mid Jun–mid Oct 09.00–16.30 Mon–Sat; mid Oct–mid Dec & early Apr–mid Jun 10.30–16.30 Mon–Fri; modest admission fee*) is housed in a big red-brick building from c1903 which was the first consolidated school in Canada. Varied exhibits include an old schoolroom, a recreation of a 1930s' general store, the Nova Scotia Museum's clock and watch collection, and much more.

For railway enthusiasts, the **Memory Lane Railway Museum** (*61 School St;* ☎ *902 825 6062; memorylanerailwaymuseum.org;* ⊕ *May–Sep 09.00–17.00 Mon–Fri, 10.00–14.30 Sat; admission by donation*), close to the Macdonald Museum, is a complete contrast to its neighbour but is every bit as interesting. Housed in the old railway station (in use 1917–90) is an eclectic collection of bits and pieces from days gone by. Trains are the focus and there are both indoor and outdoor working model train tracks.

Bookworms should seek out **Blue Griffin Books** (*68 Commercial St;* ☎ *902 363 2665; www.bluegriffinbooks.com;* ⊕ *09.00–18.00 Mon–Fri, 09.00–17.00 Sat*). It has a good selection of used books – but not necessarily for those who like things well organised!

A BREATH OF SEA AIR

If you feel like a stroll along the Fundy shore, or just seeing a couple of pretty coastal villages, two good choices are Margaretsville and Hampton. Both have lighthouses, little harbours, and pleasant beaches (much more cobble and pebble than sand). There's a little more going on at the former, with a tiny gallery by the wharf, a wonderful live music venue in a former church, the **Evergreen Theatre** (*1941 Stronach Mountain Rd, East Margaretsville;* \ *902 825 6834; evergreentheatre.ca*), and a waterfall a couple of hundred metres along the beach. Hampton was once a busy resort with a very popular, cavernous dance hall near the wharf. Today's visitor will find a **lighthouse**, a clifftop walk and a long stretch of beach (which is one of the best places to collect beach pebbles). For Margaretsville, take Stronach Mountain Road from Kingston. In Bridgetown, following Church Street – which becomes Hampton Mountain Road – will take you over the North Mountain to Hampton.

EAST TOWARDS WOLFVILLE

KINGSTON AND GREENWOOD The main attractions of these two communities for visitors are a tourist office (*510 Main St (Hwy 1);* \ *902 765 6678;* ⊕ *mid/end May–early Oct 10.00–17.00 daily*) – and an Atlantic Superstore very close by – in Kingston and box stores, a huge enclosed shopping mall and the largest air force base on Canada's east coast (with museum) in Greenwood.

The **Greenwood Military Aviation Museum** (*Canex Mall, Ward Rd;* \ *902 765 1494 ext 5955; gmam.ca;* ⊕ *Jun–Aug 10.00–17.00 daily; Sep–May 10.00–16.00 Tue–Sat; admission free*) tells the story of the World War II RAF station that went on to become Atlantic Canada's largest air base. Several aircraft are on display, and there is a gift shop and café. The mall hosts a little **farmers' market** (⊕ *noon–16.00 Thu*), and just across from the mall, **The Inside Story** (*1016 Central Av, Greenwood;* \ *902 765 6116;* tf *1 800 565 6116; theinsidestory.ca;* ⊕ *09.30–21.00 Mon–Fri, 09.30–18.00 Sat, noon–17.00 Sun*) is well-stocked with magazines and new books. Self-caterers should also bear in mind that there are no other big supermarkets in the 125km between here and Digby (pages 204–9).

Kingston is on Highway 1, 11km/7 miles east of Middleton and 40km/25 miles west of Kentville. Greenwood is 3km from Kingston: **by car**, take Bridge Street then turn left at the traffic lights. At the next lights, go straight on for the museum, or turn right for the mall. Greenwood, 2.5km from Kingston, is the terminus of **bus** routes west to Bridgetown and east to Wolfville, and Kingston is on the Greenwood–Wolfville bus route (box, page 204).

🏠 Where to stay, eat and drink

🏠 **Best Western Aurora Inn** (23 units) 831 Main St, Kingston; \ 902 765 3306; bestwesternatlantic.com. Sgl-storey motel-style hotel with spacious, well-equipped rooms. Most rates inc b/fast. **$$**

🏠 **Creekside B&B** (3 rooms) 140 Hwy 221, North Kingston; \ 902 765 0346; www. creeksidebedandbreakfast.ca; ⊕ May–mid Oct. Large rooms in a c1892 house on a quiet rural minor road. Library, sun room & deck overlooking vineyard. Less than 5mins' drive to Kingston. Full b/fast (eg: salmon omelette or gingerbread waffles) inc. **$–$$**

✕ **Oaken Barrel Pub** 944 Pickering Lane, Greenwood; \ 902 765 8933; f; ⊕ 11.00–23.00 Mon–Thu, 11.00–01.00 Fri & Sat, 11.00–22.00 Sun. Somewhat unprepossessing exterior, but decent, well-priced pub food & drink. Behind the mall. **$–$$**

Other practicalites

$ CIBC 655 Main St, Kingston; ☎902 765 3355; ⊕ 10.00–17.00 Mon–Fri

$ Scotiabank 963 Central Av, Greenwood; ☎902 765 6383; ⊕ 10.00–17.00 Mon–Fri

Kingston Library 671 Main St, Kingston; ☎902 765 3631; www.valleylibrary.ca; ⊕ 14.00–17.00 & 18.30–20.30 Tue, 10.00–17.00 & 18.30–20.00 Thu, 18.30–20.30 Fri, 10.00–14.00 Sat

BERWICK This busy town calls itself the 'Apple Capital of Nova Scotia' – the reason for the giant apple perched outside the recently rebuilt Town Hall – as apple orchards occupy swathes of the surrounding countryside. Commercial Street – which links Highway 101 and Highway 1 – is where you'll find the majority of the shops and services. Berwick is just off Highway 101, Exit 15, 20km/12 miles west of Kentville and 21km/13 miles east of Kingston.

 Where to stay, eat and drink

🏠 **Candle Inn the Window** (4 rooms) 156 Brown St; ☎902 532 0698; **tf** 1 866 338 0698; www.candleinnbandb.com; ⊕ mid Apr–early Mar. All of the bedrooms (all AC) at Polly & Bill's lovely Georgian house on a quiet side street have private bathrooms; 3 of these are en suite (with whirlpool tubs). Recommended. Full b/fast inc. **$$**

✖ **Kellock's** 160 Commercial St; ☎902 538 5525; **f**; ⊕ 11.30–14.30 & 16.30–closing Mon–Fri, 09.00–14.30 & 16.30–closing Sat. Located in a 135-year-old Victorian home ringed by towering elms, with stained-glass windows, tin ceilings & hardwood floors, this popular restaurant offers relaxed dining. Try the applewood-smoked chicken. **$$**

✖ **Union Street Café & The Wick Pub** 183 Commercial St; ☎902 538 7787; www. unionstreetcafe.ca; ⊕ 11.00–20.00 Sun–Thu, 11.00–22.00 Fri & Sat. Cosy, colourful & inviting café-restaurant with an eclectic menu. The chicken & roasted vegetable focaccia is a lunchtime favourite; in the evening try bacon-wrapped pork tenderloin with apple-butter sauce, followed by chocolate truffle tart. Live music (often high-quality) in the adjoining pub on Fri & Sat evenings. **$$**

✖ **Driftwood Restaurant** 229 Commercial St; ☎902 538 8393; www.driftwoodrestaurant. ca; ⊕ 08.00–20.00 daily (Sun from 09.00). Now housed in former fire station after it outgrew its far-smaller previous location. Much loved by fans of standard diner fare. **$–$$**

☕ **North Mountain Coffee** 210 Commercial St; www.northmountaincoffee.com; ⊕ 07.00–16.00 Mon–Fri, 08.00–16.00 Sat. It's not always easy to get a seat in this cosy, friendly coffee shop. Excellent lattes, espresso & freshly brewed coffees, & baked goods to go with them. **$**

KENTVILLE AND AROUND

The largest community in – and commercial hub of – the Annapolis Valley, Kentville (population: 6,094) has some lovely old homes, a good museum in the old courthouse, and some pleasant walking trails both by the riverside and on the bed of old railway tracks. The town is home to the Valley's major hospital, plus medical,

LIGHTS! CAMERA! APPLES!

When local writer Graig Benton's story (about a community, Bigfoot Town, suffering because its mill closed down) was picked up by Netflix, he decided to film the feature-length movie in Berwick. Shooting began in 2016, using predominantly local actors and actresses. So if the cashier at Bargain Harley's or the person in front of you in the ice-cream line at Mum's Bake Shoppe looks familiar... There are hopes that a series will be commissioned if the pilot show is well received.

legal and financial offices. The grounds of the **Kentville Agricultural Centre** (page 236) are beautiful in late spring.

GETTING THERE AND AWAY Kentville is accessible **by car**, being on highways 1 and 12, the latter of which crosses the province down to Chester (pages 146–50), and off Highway 101, exits 12–14, 11km/7 miles from Wolfville, 74km/46 miles from Chester and 105km/66 miles from Annapolis Royal. Kentville is also on the Greenwood–Wolfville **bus** route (box, page 204) and is the terminus of the Maritime Bus route to Halifax (page 57).

WHERE TO STAY

Allen's Motel (12 rooms) 384 Park St; 902 678 2683; tf 1 877 678 2683; e allensmotel@ns.sympatico.ca; www.allensmotel.ns.ca; Apr–Nov. What was a traditional motel set on a 1.2ha property has had renovations & additions, including 2 upstairs rooms & an accessible deluxe suite. Coin laundry. Good-value set b/fast available (extra cost). **$**

Grand Street Inn (4 units) 160 Main St; 902 679 1991; tf 1 877 245 4744; grandstreetinn.com. 2 nice rooms in lovely, quiet c1870 Queen Anne Revival home, plus 2 2-bedroom carriage houses, all on spacious grounds. Outdoor pool (seasonal) & hot tub. Full b/fast inc. **$**

South Mountain Park Family Camping Resort (240 sites) 3022 Hwy 12, South Alton; 902 678 0152; tf 1 866 860 6092; southmountainparkcampground.com; mid May–mid Oct. A facility-packed 44ha campground 9km south of Exit 13 of Hwy 101. Open & wooded serviced & tent sites. Family activities. **$**

WHERE TO EAT AND DRINK

King's Arms Pub 390 Main St; 902 678 0066; kingsarmspub.ca; 11.00–21.00 Sun–Wed, 11.00–midnight Thu–Sat. An Irish-influenced pub with relaxing atmosphere & decent well-priced food (served til 20.00 Sun–Wed, 21.00 Thu–Sat). In summer, the patio is pleasant. **$–$$**

Paddy's Brew Pub & Rosie's Restaurant 42 Aberdeen St; 902 678 3199; www.paddyspub.ca. For details, see page 242. **$–$$**

Half Acre Café 395 Main St; 902 678 2273; ; 07.00–17.00 daily, from 08.00 Sun. New (Aug 2016) large, spacious city-like café with good coffee & a selection of imaginative sandwiches/paninis/wraps. Buzzy & usually busy. **$**

T.A.N. Coffee 431 Main St; 902 678 1225; www.tancoffee.ca; 07.00–18.00 Mon–Fri, 08.00–18.00 Sat, 09.00–17.00 Sun. Good micro-roasted Fair Trade coffee & a wide selection of snacks, sandwiches, tray bakes, etc. **$**

FRENCH CROSS

When the Expulsion began in 1755, many Acadians living in the valley received word of what was happening further east and 50–300 community members decided to try and escape, intending to get to the coast, cross the sea and head for safety. They crossed the North Mountain but when they reached what is now Morden, they found that the winter weather had beaten them: crossing the sea would be impossible until the spring. Living mainly on shellfish – and anything the Mi'kmaq could bring them – few survived the winter. Pitifully few Acadians survived long enough to cross the water. A cross in a memorial park marks the spot: some of the shells discarded by the Acadians were used to pave the park's entrance. In good weather, this is one of the area's best coastal picnic spots. To get there, from Highway 1 at Auburn, follow Morden Road north for 12km, 14km from Highway 101, Exit 16.

OTHER PRACTICALITIES

$ Royal Bank 63 Webster St; ☎902 679 3850;
⊕ 09.30–17.00 Mon–Fri
$ Scotiabank 47 Aberdeen St; ☎902 678 2181;
⊕ 10.00–17.00 Mon–Fri
✚ Valley Regional Hospital 150 Exhibition St;
☎902 678 7381
✉ Post office 495 Main St; ⊕ 08.00–17.00
Mon–Fri

ℹ Tourist information 66 Cornwallis St; ☎902
678 4634; ⊕ 09.00–15.00 Mon–Fri, plus summer
weekends.
Kentville Library 440 Main St; ☎902 679 2544;
www.valleylibrary.ca; ⊕ hours change with
seasons

WHAT TO SEE AND DO Drop by the community **CentreStage Theatre** (*61 River St;* ☎ *902 678 3502; www.centrestagetheatre.ca*) for a show or head to the beaches to search for semi-precious stones with **Rob's Rocks** (*677 West Main St;* ☎ *902 678 3194;* ℹ/*Robs-Nova-Scotia-Rock-Mineral-Custom-Jewelry-Shop-127786399389;* ⊕ *by appointment*).

The huge (well over 200ha) grounds of the **Kentville Agricultural Centre** (*32 Main St;* ☎ *902 365 8555;* ⊕ *grounds year-round; admission free*) are a government facility, and one of the most modern and sophisticated research centres in Canada. Planted with crops and orchards, it also offers a magnificent rhododendron garden. The **Kentville Ravine Trail** leads from the car park along a river and through old growth forest, or take a shorter wander at **Miner's Marsh** – accessible from the parking area behind the County of Kings Municipal building on Cornwallis St, this is a wetland area popular with birds with 1.7km of maintained trail.

Housed in the three-storey former c1904 courthouse – with the original courtroom on the top floor (a must-see!) – the **Kings County Museum** (*37 Cornwallis St;* ☎ *902 678 6237; www.kingscountymuseum.ca;* ⊕ *Apr–mid Dec 09.00–16.00 Mon–Fri, plus Jun–Aug 09.00–16.00 Sat; admission by donation*) has good displays on Founding Cultures, Nova Scotia glass and natural history, plus seasonal exhibitions. Archives for genealogical research (*CAN$5 fee*).

The 6,300yd **Ken-Wo Golf Course** (*9514 Commercial St;* ☎ *902 681 5388; ken-wo. com; green fees CAN$65*) might sound pseudo-Japanese, but got its name because it lies halfway between Kentville and Wolfville. Course-wise, the last five holes are the toughest.

THE NEW MINAS FLY OVER

New Minas was the location for what was probably the first reported sighting of UFOs over North America. An entry in the diary of Simeon Perkins (pages 171–2) for 12 October 1796, reads:

> A strange story comes from the Bay of Fundy that ships have been seen in the air … they were said to be seen at New Mines … by a girl about sunrise. The girl cried out and two men who were in the house came out and saw them. There were 15 ships and a man forward with his hand stretched out. They made to the eastward. They were so near people saw their sides and ports.

In our age of aircraft and space travel, UFOs are likened to flying saucers and spacecraft: in the Age of Sail more than 200 years before planes were invented, UFOs looked like ships. Maybe human technology and alien technology are advancing at roughly the same rate.

FESTIVALS The **Canaan Country Music Festival** (*www.canaancountrymusicfest. com*) is a new (2016) one-day event held in July in Canaan, just off Exit 12 of Hwy 101, less than 10km from Kentville, while the **Harvest Festival** in October offers wagon rides, music, food – and people dressed as pumpkins!

AROUND KENTVILLE

New Minas The main reasons for going to **New Minas** (population: 5,035), less than 3km east from Kentville along Highway 1, are side-by-side box stores and shopping malls, fast-food outlets and petrol stations. A redeeming feature is – at the Kentville end of town – a decent licensed eatery, **McGill's Restaurant & Café** (*18 Kentucky Ct;* ✆ *902 681 3225; mcgillsrestaurant.com;* ⊕ *year-round 09.00–15.00 Mon–Wed, 09.00–20.30 Thu–Sat;* **$$–$$$**), which serves good fish and chips, especially if they have halibut.

Halls Harbour This pretty working fishing village is named after Captain Samuel Hall, an early 19th-century American privateer who terrorised those living in the region with frequent raids to pillage and plunder. Locals say that every seven years in winter, a phantom ship's lights are seen going up the Bay of Fundy.

Above the harbour, steep cliffs are capped with groves of hardwoods and softwoods: the cobble beach is popular for rockhounding (when the tide's out), and there's a 2km forest and river-view eco-trail. Several artists have studios in the village.

Halls Harbour is on Highway 359, 18km/11 miles from Kentville. A rustic restaurant (*1157 West Halls Harbour Rd;* ✆ *902 679 5299;* ⊕ *mid May–Jun & Sep–mid Oct noon–19.00 daily; Jul–Aug 11.30–20.30 daily;* **$$**) is attached to the **Halls Harbour Lobster Pound** and has become a very popular eating spot – choose your clawed lunch and eat it at a wharf-front table. Dining here can be a great experience – if it doesn't become a tourist trap.

Cape Split and Cape Blomidon At almost 8km each way, the trail to **Cape Split** can be a long walk for the inexperienced hiker, but is well worth the effort. The trailhead is at the end of Scots Bay Road, approximately 30km from Exit 11 of Highway 101. Once you're on your way, you'll have to decide whether to take the more difficult coastal trail (which stays close to the clifftops and is not for those who don't like heights) or the more straightforward inland route that initially leads through mixed forest and is easier going. Later on the trail, the forest is more deciduous: ferns cover much of the forest floor, and lichens and mosses cling to the trees. As you near the end of the cape, the trees end and you arrive at a grassy area high above the water, with the sea on three sides. If it is not misty or foggy, the views are fantastic.

Take particular care here close to the cliff edges. Either way, allow a minimum of 3½ hours for the return hike.

There are more spectacular views – and a network of over 14km of hiking trails – on the other (eastern) side of the peninsula at **Blomidon Provincial Park** (*Pereaux Rd;* ☏ *902 582 7319; parks.novascotia.ca/content/blomidon;* ⊕ *mid May– early Sep*). This 759ha park, the entrance of which is 25km from Highway 101, Exit 11, is largely forested with sugar maple, beech, white spruce and yellow birch, and includes 180m-tall red sandstone cliffs and looks out over the Bay of Fundy. At low tide, wander the beaches where you might be lucky enough to find amethysts or agates. There are four official interconnecting walking trails, from the 1.6km **Look-off Trail** to the spectacular 6km **Jodrey Trail**. The **Woodland Trail** is 2.5km, and the 3.5km **Borden Brook Trail** leads through white spruce forest to

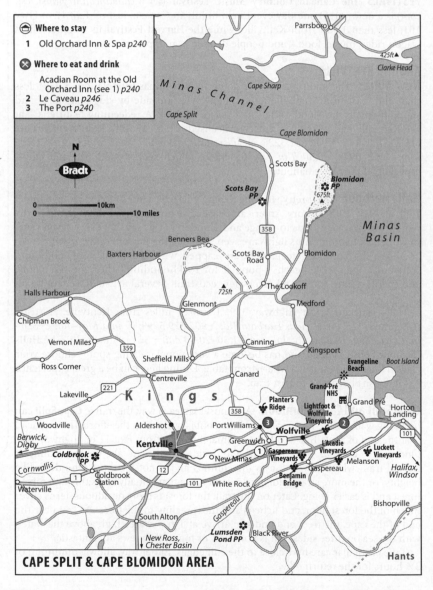

Where to stay

1 Old Orchard Inn & Spa *p240*

Where to eat and drink

   Acadian Room at the Old
   Orchard Inn (see 1) *p240*
2 Le Caveau *p246*
3 The Port *p240*

CAPE SPLIT & CAPE BLOMIDON AREA

a series of waterfalls. The park has a 70-site **campground** (⊕ *mid May–early Sep*) with open and wooded sites.

As the home of their demi-god Glooscap, the Cape Blomidon area has great spiritual significance for the Mi'kmaq.

WOLFVILLE

With a prosperous feel and a pleasant climate, Wolfville may not have the history of, say, Annapolis Royal (pages 217–23), but this charming town has a popular and highly regarded university, several excellent restaurants, and no shortage of beautiful heritage homes or interesting historic architecture. I mention the university because it brings a clear vitality to the town: in general, the large student population is well mannered and enhances the atmosphere, rather than overpowering it.

Highway 1 runs through town as Main Street, and (as you'd expect) this is where most shops, eateries and accommodations are found. To the east of the town centre, Main Street is lined with majestic trees. Although not immediately obvious, Wolfville does have a waterfront, and its appropriately named Waterfront Park (which opened in 2000) hosts several outdoor events and offers fine views of Cape Blomidon. The park at the junction of Front Street and Harbourside Drive (which is the extension of Gaspereau Avenue) offers totally different views at high and low tide: interpretive panels tell of the area's history of shipping and shipbuilding. The old railway station now houses the town's library.

The land reclaimed by the 17th-century Acadian dykes is a good spot for a walk or cycle ride: hillier, the scenic hiking trail through the 12ha Reservoir Park is also a good choice. If you have a car, pop over to the pretty Gaspereau Valley for wineries, pretty riverside vistas, and more.

HISTORY Originally known to the Mi'kmaq as '*mtaban*' ('muddy catfish-catching place'), European settlement began with Acadians in the mid to late 17th century (some of their dykes can still be seen). After the Expulsion, New England Planters settled here, naming it 'Mud Creek' – a small harbour was connected to the Cornwallis River by a narrow, twisting stretch of water, virtually impassable at low tide. Despite problems with navigation caused by the tide and sandbars, a busy little port was established, and ships were built here.

One of the community's most important residents was Judge Elisha DeWolf (1756–1837) and it was in his honour that the town was renamed.

In 1911, Wolfville became the first town in Nova Scotia with a paved main street.

GETTING THERE AND AWAY Wolfville is easy to get to by car – it is on Highway 1 and between exits 10 and 11 of Highway 101, 90km/56 miles from Halifax, 27km/17 miles from Windsor and 117km/73 miles from Annapolis Royal. It is also on the **bus** route to Greenwood, the route between Kentville and Hantsport and the

Kentville–Halifax Maritime Bus route (page 57).

WHERE TO STAY *Map, opposite, unless otherwise stated*

 Blomidon Inn (29 rooms) 195 Main St; ☎ 902 542 2291; **tf** 1 800 565 2291; www.blomidon.ns.ca. The main building is a beautifully restored c1882 shipbuilder's mansion, with magnificent interior dark wood features & Italian marble fireplaces: each guest room is individually decorated. It is worth choosing a 'Superior' or above (note that not all rooms are in the original building). Paths lead through landscaped themed gardens, & there are tennis courts. The top-notch dining room is open to non-guests (see below). Various packages are available. Continental b/fast & afternoon tea inc. **$$**

Old Orchard Inn & Spa [map, page 238] (130 units) 153 Greenwich Rd; Greenwich; ☎ 902 542 5751; **tf** 1 800 561 8090; www.oldorchardinn. com; ⊕ year-round (cabins May–Oct). Located 5km from Wolfville, just off Hwy 101 Exit 11 with 100+ well-maintained rooms & 29 cabins. Indoor pool, sauna, hot tub, spa & tennis court. Includes the excellent Acadian Room Restaurant (see below). **$$**

Stella Rose B&B (3 rooms) 611 Main St; ☎ 902 697 2368; **tf** 1 855 533 2368; www. thestellarose.com. Delightful very well-equipped rooms each with comfortable seating. Over-12s

only. Recommended. Rate includes welcome refreshments & full b/fast. **$$**

Victoria's Historic Inn B&B (16 units) 600 Main St; ☎ 902 542 5744; **tf** 1 800 556 5744; www.victoriashistoricinn.com. The c1893 3-storey main building contains 4 rooms & 5 suites (with jacuzzi & fireplace); 7 rooms are in the adjacent Carriage House. All are well equipped. Beautifully restored, the property blends Victorian character & modern comforts. Full b/fast inc. **$$**

Garden House B&B (3 rooms) 220 Main St; ☎ 902 542 1703; e gardenhouse@ns.sympatico.ca; www.gardenhouse.ca. Cosy, friendly, good value B&B in a c1830 house a short walk from the town centre; rooms with shared or private bathroom & views out over the dykes. B/fast inc. **$**

> ## WOLFVILLE
> *For listings, see pages 240–2*
>
> ⊕ **Where to stay**
> 1 Blomidon Inn
> 2 Garden House B&B
> 3 Victoria's Historic Inn B&B
> *Off map*
>   Stella Rose B&B
>
> ⊗ **Where to eat and drink**
>   Blomidon Inn (see 1)
> 4 Just Us
> 5 The Naked Crepe Bistro
> 6 Paddy's Brew Pub & Rosie's Restaurant
> 7 The Rolled Oat Café
> 8 Slow Dough Pastries & Café
> 9 Troy
> *Off map*
>   The Noodle Guy

WHERE TO EAT AND DRINK *Map, opposite, unless otherwise stated*

Fine-dining options are the Blomidon Inn (below), and – just a few minutes' drive away – Le Caveau (page 246).

Blomidon Inn 195 Main St; ☎ 902 542 2291; **tf** 1 800 565 2291; www.blomidon.ns.ca; ⊕ 11.30–14.00 & 17.00–21.30 daily. The Blomidon's restaurant is renowned, & reservations are therefore strongly recommended. The lobster linguini is a speciality, & filet mignon & game feature, too. The wine list is superb. W/end brunch is another treat. **$$$**

Acadian Room at the Old Orchard Inn [map, page 238] 153 Greenwich Rd; Greenwich; ☎ 902 542 5751; **tf** 1 800 561 8090; www.oldorchardinn.com; ⊕ 07.00–14.00 & 17.00–21.00 daily. Another fine licensed restaurant, the Acadian Room has wide windows overlooking Cape Blomidon, & a large stone

fireplace. To start, the mussels & seafood chowder are both very good, followed by sautéed Digby scallops or Bay of Fundy lobster. Local poultry & pork also feature. To follow, warm apple crumble pie is a winner. *Lunch* **$$**, *dinner* **$$$**

The Port [map, page 238] 980 Terry's Creek Rd, Port Williams; ☎ 902 542 5555; www. theportpub.com; ⊕ 11.00–21.00 Sun–Wed, 11.00–22.00 Thu–Sat. This stylish gastropub less than 7km from Wolfville has a beautiful deck overlooking the Cornwallis River. The lobster club & Starr's Point burger are both very popular. Sip a Planters Pale beer or a glass of one of the carefully selected wines. **$$**

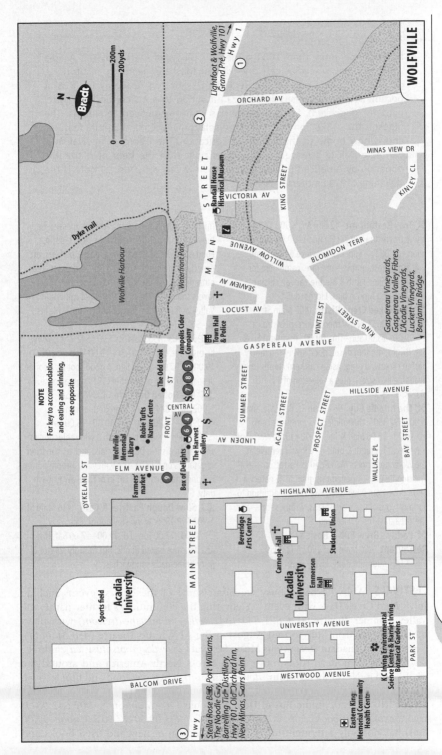

WOLFVILLE

Hwy 1

Lightfoot & Wolfville,
Grand Pré, Hwy 101

ORCHARD AV

MINAS VIEW DR

KINLEY CL

M A I N S T R E E T

Randall House
Historical Museum

VICTORIA AV

KING STREET

WILLOW AVENUE

BLOMIDON TERR

Dyke Trail

Wolfville Harbour

Waterfront Park

SEAVIEW AV

LOCUST AV

WINTER ST

KING STREET

Gaspereau Vineyards,
Gaspereau Valley Fibres,
L'Acadie Vineyards,
Luckett Vineyards,
Benjamin Bridge

GASPEREAU AVENUE

Annapolis Cider
Company

The Odd Book

FRONT ST

5 8 7

Town Hall
& Police

SUMMER STREET

ACADIA STREET

HILLSIDE AVENUE

PROSPECT STREET

NOTE
For key to accommodation
and eating and drinking,
see opposite

Robie Tufts
Nature Centre

Wolfville
Memorial
Library

CENTRAL AV

6 4 3

The Harvest
Gallery

LINDEN AV

WALLACE PL

BAY STREET

Box of Delights

Farmers'
market

9

ELM AVENUE

DYKELAND ST

HIGHLAND AVENUE

Beveridge
Arts Centre

Carnegie Hall

Students' Union

Emmerson
Hall

M A I N S T R E E T

Acadia
University

Sports field

Acadia
University

UNIVERSITY AVENUE

K C Irving Environmental
Science Centre & Harriet Irving
Botanical Gardens

PARK ST

WESTWOOD AVENUE

BALCOM DRIVE

Eastern King
Memorial Community
Health Centre

Hwy 1

Stella Rose B&B, Port Williams,
The Noodle Guy,
Barrelling Tide Distillery,
Hwy 101, Old Orchard Inn,
New Minas, Scarrs Point

N

Bradt

0   200m
0   200yds

In term-time, more than 3,000 students – plus staff – at Wolfville's Acadia University (www.acadiau.ca), one of Canada's top learning institutions, double the town's population. Beginning as Horton Academy in 1828, it became Acadia University in 1891. In addition to a gallery and botanical gardens (page 243), the university has some magnificent buildings. The oldest is the c1878 Seminary, which displays many Second Empire features and is now home to the School of Education. The Georgian Revival-style Carnegie Hall (a science building) was built with the help of a sizeable donation by American philanthropist Andrew Carnegie. Also of note is the Italianate c1913 Emmerson Hall.

✕ **Troy Restaurant** 12 Elm Av; ☎ 902 542 4425; www.troyrestaurant.ca; ⏰ noon–20.00 Sun–Thu, noon–21.00 Fri–Sun. In a province where lamb – & ethnic restaurants – are rare, come here for delicious grilled lamb & Mediterranean cuisine with a strong Turkish bias. Licensed. $$

✕ **The Naked Crepe Bistro** 402 Main St; ☎ 902 542 0653; www.thenakedcrepebistro.ca; ⏰ 09.00–23.00 Sun–Thu, 09.00–midnight Fri & Sat. Bright, modern décor, good sweet (eg: berry parfait) & savoury (eg: Asian chicken) crêpes (many available in 2 sizes), plus a selection of 11-inch pizzas. $–$$

✕ **The Noodle Guy** 964 Main St, Port Williams; ☎ 902 697 3906; thenoodleguy.wordpress.com; ⏰ 10.00–18.00 Mon & Tue, 10.00–19.00 Wed–Sat. Having cut his teeth & built up a loyal clientele at the Wolfville Farmers Market, Ross Patterson – aka The Noodle Guy – opened this great little eatery a 5min drive from downtown Wolfville. In addition to various types of pasta are salads, wraps, soup – and the 'Breakfast Thing'. Licensed. $

✕ **Paddy's Brew Pub & Rosie's Restaurant** 460 Main St; ☎ 902 542 0059; ⏰ 11.00–midnight daily. Lively pub, microbrewery & restaurant. Atrium, glassed-in brewery, cosy booths, hardwood floors, patio. Food is good – seafood, pizza, pasta, burgers, etc, especially the home-smoked ribs, & desserts (eg: outrageous Irish Cream Bash Cheesecake). Beer lovers should try the house-brewed Annapolis Valley or Raven ales. Frequent live music nights. $–$$

☐ **Just Us** 450 Main St; ☎ 902 542 7731; www.justuscoffee.com; ⏰ 07.30–19.00 Mon–Fri, 08.00–19.00 Fri, 09.00–18.00 Sun. A good spot for a coffee or snack in lobby of a former c1911 opera house. $

☐ **The Rolled Oat Café** 420 Main St; ☎ 902 542 9884; www.therolledoat.com; ⏰ 09.00–15.00 Mon–Fri, 10.00–15.00 Sat. Funky, friendly little café with a wide selection of vegetarian dishes. Daily specials, such as stir-fried vegetables on quinoa. The Valley Mushroom panini is a personal favourite. Eat in or take-away. Cash only. $

☐ **Slow Dough Pastries & Café** 416 Main St; ☎ 902 698 1856; www.slowdough.ca; ⏰ 10.00–17.00 Tue–Fri, 11.00–17.00 Sat. Not just delicious baked goods, but friendly service & tasty homemade sandwiches. $

FESTIVALS Wolfville has a busy calendar: some of the biggest events include July's **Mud Creek Days** with events celebrating the community's former name; the **Valley Summer Theatre** (tf *1 877 845 1341; valleysummertheatre.com*) with plays most evenings from July to mid August at the Al Whittle Theatre (*450 Main St*); September's **Canadian Deep Roots Music Festival** (*www.deeprootsmusic.ca*), a three-day festival of modern roots music from across North America and around the world; and in November, **Devour** (*devourfest.com*), a five-day food and film festival.

SHOPPING Eclectic, indie **Box of Delights Books** (*466 Main St;* ☎ *902 542 9511; www.boxofdelightsbooks.com;* ⏰ *10.00–18.00 Mon–Fri, 09.00–17.00 Sat, noon–17.00 Sun*) has not only a thoughtfully curated collection of new and used books and large selection of cards (featuring many local artists), but it also hosts free weekly readings and other literary events – 2016 marked its 40th anniversary. Also worth a visit for quality used books is **The Odd Book** (*112 Front St;* ☎ *902 542 9491; www. theoddbook.ca;* ⏲ *09.30–18.00 Mon–Fri (til 21.00 Fri), 09.00–17.00 Sat, noon–16.00 Sun*), situated a couple of blocks along and one behind. Although it specialises in out-of-print literature and academic works, the selection is varied.

Less than 10 minutes' drive from downtown Wolfville, **Gaspereau Valley Fibres** (*830 Gaspereau River Rd;* ☎ *902 542 2656;* tf *1 877 634 2737; www. gaspereauvalleyfibres.ca;* ⏲ *10.00–21.00 Tue, 10.00–17.00 Wed–Fri, 11.00–16.00 Sat & Sun*) sells home-produced and 'imported' yarn, wool and wool products in a pastoral Gaspereau Valley setting.

OTHER PRACTICALITIES

$ Bank of Montreal 424 Main St; ☎ 902 542 2214; ⏲ 10.00–17.00 Mon–Fri

$ Royal Bank 437 Main St; ☎ 902 542 2221; ⏲ 10.00–17.00 Mon, 09.30–17.00 Tue–Fri, 09.00–16.00 Sat

✚ Eastern Kings Memorial Community Health Centre 23 Earnscliffe Av; ☎ 902 542 2266

✉ Post office Shoppers Drugmart, 433 Main St; ⏲ 10.00–20.00 Mon–Fri, 10.00–15.00 Sat

ℹ Tourist information 11 Willow St; ☎ 902 542 7000; tf 1 877 999 7117; ⏲ early May–late Oct 10.00–18.00 daily

Wolfville Memorial Library 21 Elm Av; ☎ 902 542 5760; ⏲ hours vary with seasons

WHAT TO SEE AND DO On the main street, a c1800s former farmhouse, the **Randall House Historical Museum** (*259 Main St;* ☎ *902 542 9775; www.wolfvillehs.ednet.ns.ca;* ⏲ *Jun–mid Sep 10.00–17.00 Tue–Sat, 13.30–17.00 Sun; admission by donation*) houses displays and collections on the community's history. The **Acadia University Art Gallery** (*Beveridge Arts Centre, cnr of Highland Av & Main St;* ☎ *902 585 1373; gallery. acadiau.ca/Acadia_Art_Gallery/;* ⏲ *noon–16.00 Tue–Sun; admission free*) has a year-round exhibition programme of contemporary and historical work, and the **Harvest Gallery** (*462 Main St;* ☎ *902 542 7093; harvestgallery.ca;* ⏲ *10.00–17.00 Tue–Sun (Jul-Oct also Mon)*) offers an interesting selection of local arts and crafts.

Despite the grand title – named for a renowned ornithologist and Wolfville resident – the **Robie Tufts Nature Centre** (*Front St*) is a roofed shelter supporting a high stack that is home to numerous chimney swifts. Around dusk on summer evenings, watch as the birds swoop down through the chimney top for the night. Nature lovers will also enjoy the **K.C. Irving Environmental Science Centre and Harriet Irving Botanical Gardens** (*32 University Av;* ☎ *902 585 5242; botanicalgardens. acadiau.ca;* ⏲ *dusk–dawn daily; admission free*), 2.5ha of gardens showcasing flora from the Acadian Forest Region. See nine native habitats including: a bog and marsh; a formal Walled Garden and Herbaceous Bank using only indigenous plants; and a Medicinal and Food garden. Even for non-botanists, these gardens make a pleasant wander, and there's a café (with fireplace in winter) which is open daily. Or pick up a picnic from the **farmers' market** (*DeWolfe Bldg, 24 Elm Av;* ☎ *902 697 3344; www.wolfvillefarmersmarket.com;* ⏲ *year-round 08.30–13.00 Sat, mid Jun–Dec 16.00–19.00 Wed*), which takes place in a converted former apple warehouse. In my opinion, on busy Saturdays, it can get too overcrowded and is not for the claustrophobic, but it's definitely still well worth a visit, with food, produce, crafts, live music and more.

Although this is wine country, those who favour hops and apples over grapes don't need to miss out. On the town's main street, at the **Annapolis Cider Company** (*388 Main St;* ☎ *902 697 2707; drinkannapolis.ca;* ⏲ *10.00–19.00 daily*) juice from locally grown apples is fermented to produce 'hard' (ie: alcoholic) cider, and tastings and free tours are offered. Also within a tankard's throw of each other in Port Williams are **The Sea Level Brewing Company** (*980 Terry's Creek Rd;* ☏ *902 542 5544; www.sealevelbrewing. com;* ⊕ *10.00–17.00 daily, Sun from noon*), which shares premises with The Port Pub (page 240), and the new **Wayfarers' Ale** (*1116 Kars St; wayfarersale.ca;* ⊕ *noon–20.00 Mon–Sat; tours (check price for groups of 4 or more) by appointment*) brewery, which offers free tasting to those looking to buy. Close by (take Starr Point Rd, then right onto Parkway Dr) is the (also new) **Barrelling Tide Distillery** (*1164 Parkway Dr;* ☏ *902 542 1627; www.barrellingtidedistillery.com;* ⊕ *11.00–17.00 Tue–Sun*), where gin, vodka and fruit liqueurs are made from local produce. Free tastings are offered.

Situated 10km from Wolfville, **Prescott House** (*1633 Starr's Point Rd, Starr's Point;* ☏ *902 542 3984; prescotthouse.novascotia.ca;* ⊕ *Jun–Oct 10.00–17.00 Mon–Sat, 13.00–17.00 Sun; admission CAN\$3.90*) is one of the province's best-surviving examples of Georgian architecture and was completed in 1814 by Charles Ramage Prescott, a businessman and horticulturist. In addition to period furnishings, see Prescott's granddaughter's collections of oriental rugs and hand-stitched samplers.

Paths atop the **Acadian Dykes** in and around Wolfville can be ideal for a stroll, bike ride, or long hike along the waterfront. Easiest access is either from the lower part of Gaspereau Avenue, or from the car park across from the junction of Main Street and Willow Avenue.

GRAND PRÉ

Grand Pré's pastoral landscape, dyked lands, and air of tranquillity, broken only by a steady stream of tour buses, give little clue as to its part in one of the most heart-rending events in Canadian history (page 17). It is situated just off highways 1 and 101, 1.5km/1 mile east of Wolfville, or Exit 10 from Highway 101, 21km/13 miles from Windsor.

HISTORY Grand Pré (French for 'great meadow') was first settled in the early 1680s by a couple of Acadian families from Port-Royal (page 228). More came to join

WOFLVILLE'S WINERIES

The Wolfville area, including the Gaspereau Valley just over the hill and Port Williams just across the river, is home to a growing number of wineries. Most are open to the public (at least in the form of a shop selling their products), and at the other end of the scale, some have dining options, rides, tours, etc. Four of the wineries listed are in the Gaspereau Valley, easily reached by taking Gaspereau Avenue from Wolfville's Main Street up and over the hill (approx 5km). See also Domaine de Grand Pré (page 247).

On Thursdays, Fridays, Saturdays and Sundays between June and mid October, the **Wolfville Magic Winery Bus** (♦ 902 *542 5767; www. wolfvillemagicwinerybus.ca; fare CAN$25–CAN$30*) goes on loop run to several of the region's wineries allowing you to hop on and off.

L'Acadie Vineyards 310 Slayter Rd, Gaspereau; ♦ 902 542 8463; www.lacadievineyards.ca; ⊕ May–Oct 11.00–17.00 daily. Nova Scotia's top producer of sparkling wines was also the province's first certified organic winery & vineyard. The Prestige Brut is highly regarded. The winery is 6km from Wolfville, follow Gaspereau Av to Slayter Rd.

Benjamin Bridge White Rock Rd, Gaspereau; ♦ 902 452 1560; www.benjaminbridge.com; BB's marketing makes it clear that the operation is not looking to attract riff-raff or casual sightseers. No road signage leads you here, & 'exclusive & intimate' tastings & tours are 'private & by appointment only'. Oenophiles can choose from 3 experiences, 2 inc food.

Gaspereau Vineyards 2239 White Rock Rd, Gaspereau; ♦ 902 542 1455; www.devoniancoast. ca; ⊕ mid May–late Dec 10.00–18.00 daily; tours noon & 15.00. 14ha of vineyards overlooking the Gaspereau Valley 3km from Wolfville on a former apple orchard. Specialising in fruit forward whites & easy drinking reds. Tasting bar available, licensed patio with light food service.

Lightfoot & Wolfville Vineyards 11197 Hwy 1; lightfootandwolfvillewines.com. This poultry farm has successfully developed another string to its bow. A retail outlet is due to open on-site in 2017.

Luckett Vineyards 1293 Grand Pré Rd, Gaspereau; ♦ 902 542 2600; luckettvineyards.com; ⊕ May 10.00–17.00 daily; Jun–Oct 10.00–18.00 daily. Beautifully located vineyards & farm with fabulous views over the rows of vines to Cape Blomidon & beyond, offering tours, tastings, etc. The bistro patio (⊕ May–Oct 11.00–16.00 daily; $) has good deli sandwiches, soups & salads; it is usually open Fri & Sat evenings in summer.

Planters Ridge 1441 Church St, Port Williams; ♦ 902 542 2711; www.plantersridge.ca; ⊕ May–late Dec 10.30–17.30 Mon–Sat, noon–17.00 Sun; Jan–Apr noon–17.00 Fri–Sun. Tours by appointment: 3 flight tastings CAN$5.

them, and through hard work and clever use of dykes to reclaim tidal marshlands, created rich farmland. Life was not problem-free: in 1704, for example, the settlement was attacked by New Englanders who broke dykes and burned crops. But the real battle occurred in the winter of 1746–47 when a French force surprised almost 500 soldiers from New England, who had arrived to establish a blockhouse at Grand Pré, and killed more than 70 before a ceasefire was agreed.

By the 1750s, Grand Pré had become the largest of all the Acadian communities around the Bay of Fundy. In 1755, when the Acadians refused to sign an oath of allegiance to the British Crown, the governor ordered them to be deported (page 16) and Grand Pré was one of the first communities selected. On 5 September 1755, a Colonel Winslow gathered the men of Grand Pré in the church and informed them that they and their families were to be deported and their lands confiscated.

245

The village buildings were burnt to the ground, and on 29 October a fleet of a dozen ships sailed away with 2,921 Acadians on board.

In late June 2012, the Grand Pré National Historic Site and environs were designated as a UNESCO World Heritage site.

🏠 WHERE TO STAY, EAT AND DRINK

🏠 **Evangeline Inn & Motel** (23 rooms) 11668 Hwy 1; ☎902 542 2703; tf 1 888 542 2703; www. evangeline.ns.ca; ⊕ May–late Oct. The 5-room inn is housed in the boyhood home of Sir Robert Borden, Prime Minister of Canada 1911–20. The 18-room motel was built in the 1950s (with a 2004 addition): rooms are spacious & pleasant, & there is an indoor pool. Evangeline's Café (⊕ early May– late Oct 07.00–19.00; $–$$) has a simple menu of b/fasts, salads, sandwiches, burgers & tasty pies. Inn rates includes b/fast. **$**

🏕 **Land of Evangeline Family Camping Resort** (230 sites) 84 Evangeline Beach Rd; ☎902 542 5309; evangelinecampground. wordpress.com; ⊕ May–Sep. Open & wooded sites, serviced & unserviced, with laundromat. Located near the beach with fine views. **$**

🍽 **Le Caveau Restaurant at Domaine de Grand Pré Winery** [map, page 238] 11611 Hwy 1; ☎902 542 7177; www.grandprewines.com/restaurant; ⊕ May–Oct 11.30–14.00 & 17.00–21.00 daily; Nov–Dec 17.00–21.00 Tue–Sat. Bright, stylish, excellent winery restaurant with arched windows, textured walls & rich use of wood. Chef Jason Lynch uses the best seasonal local produce & cooks with a global flair. The menu changes regularly, but might include stuffed lamb shoulder with farro, shallots, and seasoned with pumpkin seed oil, or blue salmon smoked with L'Acadie vines, with horseradish pearls, sumac granola and micro greens. Accompanied of course by award-winning wines, this is a great dining experience. **$$–$$$**

🍵 **Just Us** 11865 Hwy 1; ☎902 542 7474; ⊕ 07.00–17.00 Mon–Fri, 08.00–17.00 Sat, 09.00–17.00 Sun. Not just a coffee shop, there's also a chocolate factory & Fair Trade museum. Bright, airy & relaxed. Close to Exit 10 of Hwy 102. **$**

WHAT TO SEE AND DO The **Tangled Garden** (*11827 Hwy 1; ☎ 902 542 9811; tangledgardenherbs.ca;* ⊕ *Apr–late Dec 10.00–18.00 daily*) sells delicious homemade jams, chutneys, liqueurs, herb jellies and more (including homemade herb ice cream in season), and its beautiful spiritually inspired herb and sculpture gardens are also worth exploring (*admission CAN$5*). You don't need to descend to muddy **Evangeline Beach** to enjoy stunning views across the sea to Cape Blomidon. In the summer, this has long been one of the best spots to watch tens of thousands of migrating shorebirds – particularly the semipalmated sandpiper (*Calidris pusilla*), which come to gorge themselves on mud shrimp. In recent times, in addition to nature lovers, this area has also come to the notice of a number of peregrine falcons who are bigger, stronger and almost as hungry as the mud shrimp-eaters. Consequently, the sandpipers are more dispersed. It is still quite a sight, though: come a couple of hours before or an hour after high tide and you shouldn't be disappointed.

A UNESCO World Heritage site, the **Grand Pré National Historic Site of Canada** (*2205 Grand Pré Rd;* ☎ *902 542 3631; tf 1 866 542 3631; www.pc.gc.ca/eng/lhn-nhs/ns/ grandpre/index.aspx, www.visitgrandpre.ca;* ⊕ *mid May–mid Oct 09.00–18.00 daily, grounds accessible year-round – no charge; admission free (2017), CAN$10.80 (2016)*) is located in what was the centre of the Acadian village (page 245), and this 5.7ha park commemorates the deportation of the Acadians in 1755. Paths lead from the modern interpretive centre (with display panels, a model of Grand Pré in Acadian times, multimedia theatre and gallery) to landscaped Victorian gardens and a bronze statue of Evangeline, fictional heroine of Longfellow's poem (box, opposite), and the c1922 Saint Charles Memorial church. Inside, the church paintings and stained-glass windows depict the story of the Acadians. Be aware that other than an Acadian well, nearby dykes and a row of old willow trees, nothing physical remains from the

Acadian days, but there are expansive grounds to wander, plus vegetable gardens, a blacksmith shop, orchard, and a look-out over dyked farmland. The money to buy the land for the park – and to build the church – came from the Dominion Atlantic Railway (DAR) in 1917. Taking a lead from steamship companies connecting Yarmouth with Boston and New York, the DAR marketed its Yarmouth–Halifax line as 'The Land of Evangeline Route'.

Approximately 3km away from the Historic Site, a cross by the sea marks the point from which the fleet carrying the expelled Acadians departed. Ironically, very close by, a monument at Horton Landing commemorates the 8,000-plus New England Planters who came in the 1760s to replace the deported Acadians.

The current owners of **Domaine de Grand Pré** (*11611 Hwy 1;* ✆ *902 542 1753;* tf *1 866 479 4637; www.grandprewines.ns.ca;* ⊕ *Jan–mid May 11.00–17.00 Sat; mid May–mid Oct 10.00–18.00 Mon–Sat, 11.00–18.00 Sun; mid Oct–Dec 11.00–17.00 Wed–Sat; 45min winery tours mid May–Oct 3 times daily for CAN$10*), originally from Switzerland, bought this winery (located on former Acadian farmland) in 1994 and have transformed it completely with great success – not only has it produced several award-winning wines (such as Nova Scotia's signature wine, Tidal Bay), but it is a delightful place to visit. To round things off, there's an excellent restaurant, too (page 246).

Set on a nearby hill, the **Covenanters' Church** (*1989 Grand Pré Rd*), constructed between 1804 and 1811 to replace an earlier log structure, is a pretty church built in the style of a New England Meeting House. The tower and steeple were 1818 additions. If you find it open, seize the chance: I've been by loads of times and the doors have always been locked.

WINDSOR

People are beginning to realise that Windsor (population: 3,700) is well located, on the Avon River, close to Wolfville and an easy run on Highway 101 to Halifax (or Hwy 14 to Chester and the South Shore). Several beautiful heritage homes are dotted about (though not in the slightly bland downtown area), efforts have been made to regenerate the waterfront, and new restaurants and a hotel have opened. Although there were plans to develop the huge old Nova Scotia Textiles building just outside town into flats, galleries, shops, eateries and more, the project went bust, and Windsor remains somewhere that could be up and coming. More important for some, Windsor claims to be the birthplace of (ice) hockey. there are plans to build a new arena and ice rink in the town, most likely near King's-Edgehill School. In addition, the town is home to Canada's oldest private school, **King's-Edgehill School** (*kes.ns.ca*), and the Mermaid Theatre of Nova Scotia, renowned for children's theatre.

HISTORY Situated at the confluence of the Avon and St Croix rivers, Windsor was known to the Mi'kmaq as '*Piziquid*' (or '*Pesaquid*'), meaning 'the meeting of the waters'. The French began to settle in significant numbers from about 1685. They ploughed fields, planted orchards and built grist mills. By 1748, well over 2,000 Acadians lived in the area. When Halifax was founded in 1749, the decision was made to fortify Piziquid, and a blockhouse was constructed. In 1750, Fort Edward (page 252) was built. Much of the planning for the Expulsion of the Acadians (page 16) was done here, and many Acadians were held in the fort to await deportation.

After the Expulsion, new settlers began to arrive to replace the Acadians, settling on both sides of the river and renaming it the 'Avon'. In 1764, they named their settlement on the east bank 'Windsor'.

The University of King's College and its secondary school, King's Collegiate School, were founded in 1788–89 by United Empire Loyalists as Anglican academic institutions.

Shipping and shipbuilding prospered here, particularly in the second half of the 19th century. The huge Windsor Cotton Mill opened in the early 1880s, and later became Nova Scotia Textiles.

Huge fires in 1897 and 1924 accounted for much of the downtown, and a 1920 blaze destroyed the university which reopened in Halifax two years later.

With water transport made almost redundant by road and rail travel, a causeway was built across the Avon River in 1970, putting an end to shipping for Windsor.

GETTING THERE AND AWAY Windsor is easy to get to **by car** – the town is 26km/16 miles from Wolfville, 66km/41 miles from Halifax (both via hwys 101 or 1), and 134km/83 miles from Truro (via hwys 14 and 102). The closest **Maritime Bus** (page 57) stop (the Kentville–Halifax route) will probably be at Falmouth's Circle K/Irving Mainway petrol station (*2113 Hwy 1*), a 10-minute walk from Windsor's downtown.

 WHERE TO STAY *Map, opposite*

Clockmaker's Inn (8 units) 1399 King St; ☏ 902 792 2573; tf 1 866 778 3600; www. theclockmakersinn.com. A beautifully restored c1894 Victorian mansion with 4 rooms & 4 suites.

Original woodwork, antique furniture, stained-glass windows. Full b/fast inc. **$$**

Phoenix Hollow B&B (2 rooms) 65 Chestnut St; tf 1 866 900 6910; phoenixhollow.

BLUE BEACH FOSSILS

Although fossil tracks were discovered at Blue Beach more than 150 years ago, this site is yet to receive the recognition of (say) Joggins (pages 279–80) or Arisaig (page 312). Local residents Sonja Wood and Chris Mansky have long been trying to change that, and have poured their own money and time into the **Blue Beach Fossil Museum** (*127 Blue Beach Rd, Hantsport;* ☏ *902 790 9541; www.bluebeachfossilmuseum.com;* ⊕ *mid Apr–Oct 09.30–17.00 daily; admission free, donations very welcome*), which claims the largest collection of fossil bones and tracks in eastern Canada. Both museum and beach are a must for fossil fans. To get there from Wolfville or Grand Pré, take Exit 9 off Highway 101, and at the roundabout turn first on to Oak Island Road, then right on to Bluff Road. After about 3.5km, turn left on to Blue Beach Road. From Windsor, take Highway 1 through Hantsport, and shortly after bear right on to Bluff Road – Blue Beach Road will be on the right after approximately 4km.

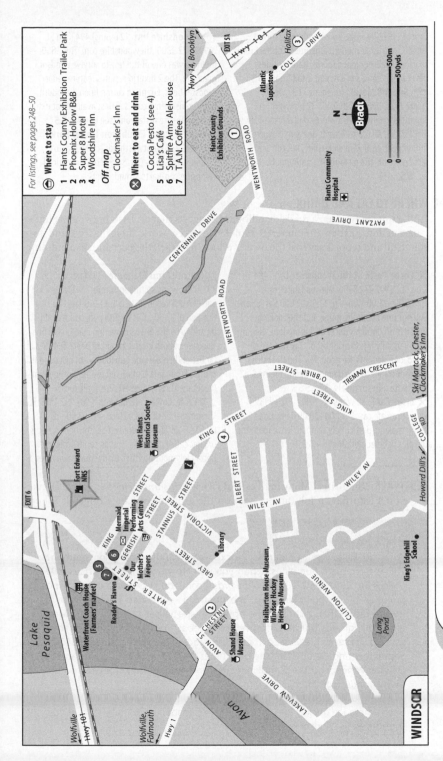

WINDSOR

5

For listings, see pages 248–50

Where to stay
1 Hants County Exhibition Trailer Park
2 Phoenix Hollow B&B
3 Super 8 Motel
4 Woodshire Inn

Off map
Clockmaker's Inn

Where to eat and drink
Cocoa Pesto (see 4)
5 Lisa's Café
6 Spitfire Arms Alehouse
7 T.A.N. Coffee

com. A c1873 Heritage house with magnificent curved staircase & modern amenities. Comfortable, spacious, well-equipped rooms. Rate includes beverages & snacks in evening & full b/fast. **$$**

🏠 **Super 8 Motel** (66 rooms) 63 Cole Dr; 📞902 792 8888; tf 1 800 454 3213; www.super8windsorns.com. 3-storey motel just off Hwy 101 Exit 5A. All rooms have fridge & microwave. Indoor pool, with 25m waterslide, hot tub & a jacuzzi. No on-site restaurant. Continental b/fast inc. **$$**

🏠 **Woodshire Inn** (2 rooms) 494 King St; 📞902 472 3300; thewoodshire.com. This 1850s' building was one of the few to survive Windsor's great fire. The 2 luxurious suites feature cedar 4-poster beds, Egyptian cotton linen & modern bathrooms with jacuzzis. B/fast available at extra charge. On-site restaurant (see below). **$$**

⋏ **Hants County Exhibition Trailer Park** (25 sites) 237 Wentworth Rd; 📞902 798 1615; ⏲ mid May–early Oct. Serviced & unserviced campsites, go-karts & minigolf. **$**

✕ WHERE TO EAT AND DRINK *Map, page 249*

At the time of writing, a roadside billboard suggests that an Irish brewpub is under construction next to the Super 8 Motel. However, work there has ground to a standstill and reports say that the owner is looking to sell the part-finished building.

✕ **Cocoa Pesto at the Woodshire Inn** 494 King St; 📞902 472 3300; thewoodshire.com; ⏲ 16.00–21.00 Mon–Fri, 11.30–21.00 Sat & Sun. Still not sure about the name, but the cooking (using fresh, local produce) at this modern, elegant eatery usually hits the right spot. The ribs are a stand-out, desserts are good, too. The closest Windsor comes to fine dining. 3 dining rooms & a terrace for alfresco meals. **$$–$$$**

✕ **Lisa's Café** 30 Water St; 📞902 792 1986; www.lisascafe.ca; ⏲ 11.00–20.00 daily. Good home cooking, particularly seafood; leave room for the pies or bread pudding! **$–$$**

🍺 **Spitfire Arms Alehouse** 29 Water St; 📞902 792 1460; www.spitfirearms.com; ⏲ 11.00–23.00 Sun–Wed (kitchen til 21.00), 11.00–late Thu–Sat (kitchen til 22.00). This English pub, which could be said to be the town's gathering place, has a fine selection of both local & imported beers, & dishes up far better than average pub food – not just good fish & chips & bangers & mash but even a Birmingham (vegetarian) curry! Desserts are good, too. **$–$$**

☕ **T.A.N. Coffee** 42 Water St 📞902 792 1518; f; ⏲ summer 07.00–18.00 Mon–Fri, 08.00–18.00 Sat, 09.00–17.00 Sun (reduced off-season hours). Good organic coffee plus baked goods, sandwiches, etc. Décor feels more 'city' than many small town cafés. **$**

FESTIVALS The **British Motoring Festival** (*www.britishmotoringfestival.com*) takes place on a Saturday in July, and is held on the grounds of Kings-Edgehill School.

GREAT GOURD ALMIGHTY

What do Halloween, Cinderella, hockey and Windsor have in common? The answer: giant pumpkins. When you visit **Howard Dill Enterprises** (*400 College Rd;* 📞 *902 798 2728; www.howarddill.com*), don't expect a café serving pumpkin pie or pumpkin soup: the pumpkins cultivated here are grown for size rather than taste and the operation specialises not only in growing enormous gourds but also in developing seeds for others to do the same. One of Dill's seeds grew into a (then) world-record pumpkin weighing 656kg. September and October are the best times to see the field of giants and in October Windsor hosts a pumpkin festival and other pumpkin-related events (*www.worldsbiggestpumpkins.com*).

I mentioned hockey: an iced-over pond on Dill's land is said to have been where ice hockey was first played in Canada. Incidentally, cricket was introduced to Windsor in 1840 but didn't catch on.

Come to see more than 150 vintage British-made cars. **Avon River Days** (*www. avonriverdays.com*) is a three-day event in August, which includes waterside activities, theatre workshops, games, parades, concerts and fireworks.

The **Hants County Exhibition** (*hantscountyex.com*) is the oldest continuously run agricultural fair in North America, established in 1765. It takes place in September, with a variety of agricultural and family events – and some surprises. The **Pumpkin Festival and Regatta** (*worldsbiggestpumpkins.com*), Windsor's Pumpkin Festival, takes place in October and includes a weigh-in to find the region's heaviest gourd, plus the excitement of the Pumpkin Regatta, where teams race to paddle hollowed-out and decorated giant pumpkins across a lake.

SHOPPING Reader's Haven (*40 Water St;* ☎ *902 798 0133;* ⏰ *09.00–17.00 Mon–Fri, 10.00–16.00 Sat*) is a friendly used bookshop, while close by in the Victoria Hotel building, **Our Mother's Keepers** (*85 Water St;* ☎ *902 472 8733;* ◻) offers local and imported goods 'for the soul and planet'.

OTHER PRACTICALITIES

WHAT TO SEE AND DO A c1830s elegant wooden villa on 10ha owned by 19th-century author, humourist, and historian Thomas Haliburton (box, overleaf), the **Haliburton House Museum** (*414 Clifton Av;* ☎ *902 798 2915; haliburtonhouse. novascotia.ca;* ⏰ *Jun–Sep 10.00–17.00 Mon–Sat, 13.00–17.00 Sun; admission CAN$3.90*) is much altered since Haliburton's time (he lived here 1836–56), but still worth a visit. The museum is furnished with period antiques, including Haliburton's desk. It is said that if you run around Piper's Pond within the grounds near the Clifton Gate House 13 (some say 20) times in an anti-clockwise direction, the ghost of a piper will rise up from the water and play his bagpipes. I haven't tried it.

Outlining Windsor's claim to be the birthplace of **ice hockey** (called *hockey* in Canada), the **Windsor Hockey Heritage Centre** (*Haliburton House Museum;* ☎ *902 798 1800; www.birthplaceofhockey.com;* ⏰ *summer hours as Haliburton House, check for mid Oct–May hours; admission free, donations welcome*) contains displays including old photos of players and teams, and some of the earliest ice-hockey equipment, as well as ice-hockey souvenirs. Note that this museum may well move to the new arena/ice rink (page 247) when that is completed: if so, hours are likely to change.

Still known to locals as the Imperial Theatre, the **Mermaid Imperial Performing Arts Centre** (*132 Gerrish St; www.mermaidtheatre.ns.ca*) contains a 400-seat auditorium and intimate 60-seat studio used by the Mermaid Theatre and a variety of other types of entertainment.

A fine c1890 Queen Anne-style mansion built on a hill above the Avon River for a newlywed couple, the **Shand House Museum** (*389 Avon St;* ☎ *902 798 2915; shandhouse.novascotia.ca;* ⏰ *Jun–Sep by appointment; admission CAN$3.90*) is beautifully furnished with wonderful interior woodwork. It was one of the first houses in the area fitted with electric lighting and indoor plumbing. There's a good view from the tower, and fascinating bike-related memorabilia – the bridegroom, Clifford Shand, was a champion cyclist (on a penny-farthing). Unfortunately, in recent times the provincial government hasn't made funds available to open the museum with regular hours.

The **West Hants Historical Society Museum** (*281 King St;* ☏ *902 798 4706; westhantshistoricalsociety.ca;* ⊕ *summer 09.00–17.00 Tue–Sat; admission by donation*) offers displays on Hants County history and a genealogy library in a former Methodist Church.

Built in 1750 to protect the land route from Halifax to the Annapolis Valley, the **Fort Edward National Historic Site** (*Fort Edward St;* ☏ *902 532 2321; www. parkscanada.gc.ca/fortedward;* ⊕ *grounds year-round, blockhouse late Jun–early Sep 09.00–17.00 Tue–Sat; admission free*) includes the oldest-surviving wooden blockhouse in Canada. In 1755, the fort served as a base of operations for the deportation of approximately 1,000 Acadians from the area, and it saw service during the American Revolution and War of 1812. The officers' quarters and barracks survived until 1897 when they were destroyed by fire. Between 1903 and 1973 the site was a golf course: the blockhouse offers impressive views of the Avon and St Croix rivers, and a 1km trail leads around the site's perimeter.

Some downtown walls are home to **large historical murals** (seven in total): five are by Ken Spearing, a local artist, one is by Mi'kmaq artist Alan Syliboy and the other (Acadian-themed) by Kosovo-born Nova Scotia resident Zeqirja Rexhepi.

After a morning of sightseeing, head to the Windsor **farmers' market** (*Waterfront Coach Hse;* **f**; ⊕ *Jun–Dec 09.00–13.00 Sat*) for organic fruit and veg, baked goods, crafts and buskers – the farmers' market at Wolfville (page 243) incidentally, is much bigger.

In winter, go downhill skiing near Windsor (and within an hour's drive of Halifax) at **Ski Martock** (*370 Martock Rd;* ☏ *902 798 9501; www.martock.com;* ⊕ *in season 09.00–21.00 Sun–Wed, 09.00–22.00 Thu–Sat; 1-day lift pass CAN$40*), off Highway 14, approximately 9km from Windsor and 71km from Halifax (take Exit 5 from Hwy 101). A quad chair and T-bar rise 183m, and it's good for beginners and families. Next door to the ski area, the **OnTree at Ski Martock** (✆ *902 798 8855; www.ontreepark.com;* ⊕ *Apr–Jun & Sep–Nov 10.00–18.00 daily; Jul–Aug 09.00–19.00 daily; admission CAN$39*) is an outdoor attraction involving climbing, high-rope tracks, obstacles and ziplining. You'll need to sign a waiver, and must arrive at least 3 hours before closing.

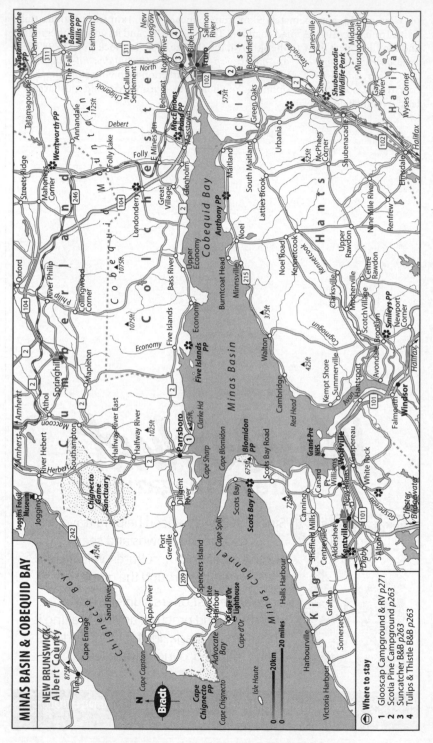

MINAS BASIN & COBEQUID BAY

NEW BRUNSWICK
Albert County

N

Bradt

0   20km
0   20 miles

6

Minas Basin and Cobequid Bay

Twice a day, the massive tides of the Bay of Fundy pour through the Minas Channel to the Minas Basin, the eastern part of which is Cobequid Bay. Two large rivers, the Shubenacadie (pronounced 'shuben-ACK-addee') and the Salmon, empty into this bay.

In the late 1600s, Acadians settled along these shores, constructing extensive dykes to turn the tidal marshlands into fertile fields. After the deportation of the Acadians, the land was resettled, primarily by New England Planters (page 17).

For well over a century, shipbuilding was the mainstay of the economy for just about every coastal community in this region. Particularly between 1850 and 1890, many of today's tiny, sleepy communities were bustling and prosperous, and home to a couple of shipyards. Very few traces remain.

This region divides into three main parts. One road, the 125km-long Highway 215, runs along the bay's southern shore (usually called Hants Shore) to – and along – the Shubenacadie River. From the town of Shubenacadie, one of the province's major arteries, Highway 102 (which originates in Halifax), runs north to Truro, the third-largest town in Nova Scotia, set on the bank of the Salmon River. From Truro, Highway 2 runs west along the northern shore of Cobequid Bay and the Minas Basin to Parrsboro, from which Highway 209 continues west along the coast to Capes d'Or and Chignecto, before turning north along Chignecto Bay towards Amherst.

Whilst busy Truro has no shortage of services or places to stay and eat, the same cannot be said of the two shorelines, particularly the southern, where there is little tourist infrastructure.

The Hants Shore is for those looking to unwind and enjoy a quiet, relaxing drive with lovely views past green fields to the red-sand shores and the water. This is the road less travelled – except perhaps by our feathered friends: it is part of the Western Hemisphere Shorebird Reserve and serves as a critical feeding and roosting area for huge flocks of migrating shorebirds. You can visit a couple of old lighthouses, one of which – Burntcoat Head – marks the spot of the world's highest tides. The region's fascinating shipbuilding history and a high concentration of wonderful heritage buildings can be seen in Maitland. By contrast, a few kilometres away are the thrills and spills of a rather unusual pastime – tidal-bore rafting.

Shubenacadie has the province's biggest wildlife park, and Truro one of the best city parks, plus rare (for Nova Scotia) urban treats such as a seven-screen cinema. There are also huge supermarkets where you can stock up for your onward journey.

The northern shore starts off with a couple of pleasant communities, but as you head west the coastal scenery becomes more dramatic. The Five Islands area is interesting and photogenic, the town of Parrsboro has a fine geological museum and is making a name for itself as a centre for artists, and you can stay or eat in a lightkeeper's cottage at Cape d'Or. Talking of food, Advocate Harbour has one of the province's best rural restaurants. This is a region of soaring cliffs, and the provincial park at Cape Chignecto is nirvana for hikers and photographers when the weather is clement. The fossil-packed cliffs at Joggins have been designated a UNESCO World Heritage site.

You'll find a few more places to stay and eat on this side of the water, but overdeveloped it isn't. Come not for cinemas and supermarkets, but for solitude and scenery.

While you can enjoy *haute cuisine* on the ocean floor (box, page 258) or join a race across the sea bed at low tide (box, page 270), a word of caution: the tide changes quietly but quickly, and activities such as digging for clams or fossil/gemstone hunting can make you forget to keep an eye out. It is easy to get trapped with the only escape route blocked by sheer cliffs. Ignore the tides and you could pay dearly.

AROUND WINDSOR

BROOKLYN With Windsor close by, apart from the nearby provincial park and farm/brewery, there is little reason to stop in Brooklyn. Accessible **by car**, it is just off Highway 14, 14km/9 miles east of Windsor; take Exit 5 from Highway 101 (or Exit 4 if coming from the Halifax side).

On the Meander River, **Smileys Provincial Park** (*109 Clayton MacKay Rd;* ✆ *902 757 3131; parks.novascotia.ca/content/smileys;* ⊕ *mid Jun–mid Sep*) takes in forest, farmland and white gypsum cliffs. It is a good picnic spot – and you can cool off with a dip in the river. There's a quiet, pleasant 86-site campground (*reservations* **tf** *1 888 544 3434; www.novascotiaparks.ca;* **$**) with sites in both forest and on farmland. Grab something for a picnic at **The Bread Gallery** (*7778 Hwy 14;* ✆ *902 757 3377;* **f**; ⊕ *08.00–17.00 Tue–Sat, 10.00–16.00 Sun;* **$**), which has not just good bread and tasty baked treats, but also soup, sandwiches and coffee, and art.

Less than 4km from the park (take McKay Road), the **Meander River Farm & Brewery** (*906 Woodville Rd, Ashdale; 902 757 3484; www.meanderriverfarm.ca;* ⊕ *check website for opening times; admission free*) is a 75ha farm specialising in hops, lavender and livestock. The on-site brewery produces several types of beer and cider, and visitors are welcome.

AVONDALE Once home to two thriving shipyards, this tiny, quiet community on the Avon River now has a nice museum and an award-winning winery, both serving food. Accessible by car, it is 12km/7 miles off Highway 14 (the Mantua turn-off).

Be sure to stop at the **Avondale Sky Winery** (*80 Avondale Cross Rd;* ✆ *902 253 2047; www.avondalesky.com;* ⊕ *May–Oct 11.00–18.00 daily; o/s usually w/ends only*). The vines have been here for years, but the vineyard's main building – a former church – was floated here from Walton (see opposite) in 2011. The winery produces sparkling wine, whites, reds and rosés, and the on-site **D'Vine Morsels Restaurant** (⊕ *in season 11.00–16.30 daily;* **$$**) offers delicious, beautifully presented food to enjoy with the wine. In September, an annual **Garlic Festival** (*www.avondalegarlicfest.com*) is held – expect art, music, demonstrations by chefs, and, of course, garlic products. The nearby **Avon River Heritage Society Museum** (*15–17 Belmont Rd;* ✆ *902 757 1718; www.avonriverheritage.com;* ⊕ *May & Sep–Oct 10.00–17.00 Sat & Sun, Jun–Aug 10.00–17.00 Wed–Sun*) has exhibits on the Age of Sail and traditional shipbuilding skills, and displays on the New England Planters. It's also home to the Hants County Arts Council and their Artists Landing Studio & Gallery. There's a (surprisingly good) licensed tea room/café (check for opening hours), too, with an outdoor deck overlooking the Avon River. Rural artists don't always find it easy to come up with

Kempt Shore, 5km from Summerville, is home to July's Acoustic Maritime Music Festival and a three-day August festival where the theme might be bluegrass, country or dance: both are held at the 8ha Peterson's Festival Campground (*6055 Hwy 215;* \ *902 633 2229; www.novascotiabluegrass.com*). The 29-site open campground (⊕ *Jun–Sep*) has 300m of beach frontage and offers views over the Avon River mouth and the Minas Basin.

'windows' for their work, but both professionals and novices display and sell their recent creations every Saturday and Sunday at May's annual **Great Little Art Show**, and open-mic nights are held at 19.00 on Fridays from May to October.

SUMMERVILLE Between 1880 and 1937, Summerville was the terminus for a ferry service to Windsor, and the pretty community once had a thriving shipbuilding industry. Nowadays (since 2014) the village is home to an excellent restaurant/inn. Situated on Highway 215, 18km/11 miles from Brooklyn, it is easily accessible **by car**.

Most people stopping in Summerville these days do so to visit the **Flying Apron Inn & Cookery** 'complex' (*5 rooms; 3 Summerville Wharf Rd;* \ *902 633 2300;* tf *1 844 633 2300; flyingaproncookery.com; inn **$$***, *restaurant **$$***), home to a top-notch cookery school, art gallery, food and gift shop, and used book store. The charming inn has a TV room, common room and private inn entrances, and a hot breakfast is included in the rate. The menu in the stylishly casual restaurant (check website for hours) is based on the best local produce and changes frequently. Whether you're looking for a light lunch or gourmet dinner, Chef Chris Velden and his team won't disappoint. Patio seating overlooks the gardens, and reservations recommended, particularly for Sunday brunch. See also box, overleaf.

ALONG COBEQUID BAY

WALTON What – at the time – was the world's largest-known barytes deposit was discovered in the area in 1941. The mineral – the main source of barium, used in industry and for X-ray imaging – was mined until 1978 when flooding halted operations. At one stage the mine accounted for 90% of Canada's barytes production. Concrete silos are the only obvious reminder that not so long ago this sleepy little harbour buzzed with cargo ships. Inside the c1873 three-storey tower of the **Walton Lighthouse** (*Weir Rd;* \ *902 528 2411; waltonns.wordpress.com;* ⊕ *mid May–mid Oct 08.00–19.00 daily*) are display panels on the area's history, and a telescope. Outside, picnic tables and a short loop trail through the woods to a coastal look-out.

Walton is on Highway 215, 46km/29 miles from Brooklyn and 44km/27 miles from Maitland, and convenient **by car**. The only accommodation in the area is at **Whale Creek Campsite** (*50 open & wooded sites; Hwy 215;* \ *902 528 2063 or 902 757 3489;* ⊕ *late May–Sep; **$***), at the mouth of the Walton River. In town, the **Walton Pub** (*39 Shore Rd;* \ *902 528 2670; www.waltonpub.ca;* ⊕ *11.00–20.00 Mon–Wed, 11.00–21.00ish Thu–Sat, noon–20.00 Sun; **$***) serves reliable pub food at sensible prices, with daily specials, and has a patio overlooking the water.

BURNTCOAT HEAD Many places claim the record, but most scientists – and the *Guinness Book of World Records* – concur with the claim of the Burntcoat (or is it

Burncoat – the debate is ongoing) area as the actual site of the world's highest tides. The maximum tidal range (the difference between high and low tides) recorded here is an astounding 16.8m.

Set in a pretty park, the **Burntcoat Head Park Lighthouse** (*611 Burntcoat Rd;* ☏ *902 369 2478; www.burntcoatheadpark.ca;* ⊕ *park open year-round, mid May– mid-Oct Thu–Mon 10.00–17.00)* The lighthouse is a replica of the 1913 version and now serves as an interpretive centre. There is a panoramic view from the tower, and a short walking trail leads to the beach, which is well worth a visit when the tide is out. Walk on the ocean floor between unique flower-pot-red sandstone formations topped by trees.

Burntcoat Head is easy to reach **by car**, being just off Highway 215, 60km/37 miles from Windsor, 100km/62 miles from Halifax and 50km/31 miles from Truro. If you fancy stopping over, Nany and Blake's **Shangri-la Cottages** (*3 cottages; 619 Burntcoat Rd;* ☏ *902 369 2050;* tf *1 866 977 3977; www.shangri-lacottages.com;* ⊕ *Apr–Nov;* **$$**) are spacious, quiet, well equipped and comfortable, with 1- and 2-bedroom options overlooking Cobequid Bay. They are just a stone's throw from the lighthouse park and make a good base from which to explore the region.

TOWARDS MAITLAND Housed in a beautifully decorated c1865 former Presbyterian church 9km west of Maitland along Highway 215, the **Lower Selma Museum & Heritage Cemetery** (*Hwy 215, Lower Selma;* ☏ *902 890 7804; www.ehhs. weebly.com;* ⊕ *Jun–Sep 10.00–17.00 daily; admission free*) has local family and community history but few surprises (except perhaps a small *Titanic* display).

A pretty picnic park 9km west of Maitland along Highway 215 and overlooking Cobequid Bay, **Anthony Provincial Park** (*Hwy 215, Lower Selma; open: mid May– mid Oct*) has wharf-side interpretive displays on the area's history and beach access at low tide.

Gallery 215 (*8247 Hwy 215, Selma;* ☏ *902 261 2151; www.artgallery215.com;* ⊕ *late Jun–early Oct*), a former c1868 schoolhouse 2km west of Maitland along Highway 215, was built by shipbuilding carpenters and reopened in 2006 as a gallery/community centre. The work of around 40 local artists and craftspeople is displayed.

MAITLAND With a lovely location on Cobequid Bay at the mouth of the Shubenacadie River, Maitland (known to the Mi'kmaq as '*twitnook*' – 'the tide runs out fast') was a very important shipbuilding centre in the second half of the 19th century. It was here in 1874 that Canada's largest wooden ship was built by William D Lawrence. Somewhat unimaginatively, he called it the *William D Lawrence* – its nickname, 'the Great Ship', didn't show much originality either. The vessel was more than twice the size of the usual ocean-going ships of the time.

While no traces of the shipyards remain, the village was designated Nova Scotia's first Heritage Conservation District for its many well-preserved 19th-century homes: styles include Second Empire, Classical Revival and Greek Revival. See, for example,

NOT YOUR AVERAGE BEACH PICNIC

On certain dates between late July and early September you can combine guided foraging for edible plants on the shore, walking on the sea bed, gourmet dining at a table on the ocean floor (the tide is out), some of the best local beer and wine, and a campfire on the tidal flats. Advance reservations are a necessity. Contact the **Flying Apron Inn & Cookery** (page 257).

the c1870 Victorian Gothic **Springhurst** (*8557 Hwy 215*), once the home of Alfred Putnam, one of Maitland's most prominent shipbuilders. Pick up a booklet with a self-guided Historic Homes walking tour at the **Lawrence House Museum** (*8660 Hwy 215;* ✆ *902 261 2628; lawrencehouse.novascotia.ca;* ⊕ *Jun–Sep 10.00–17.00 Mon–Sat, 13.00–17.00 Sun; admission CAN$3.90*), the home of aforementioned William D Lawrence. Located in an elegant c1870 Classical Revival-style building, it is here, on a hill overlooking the site of his shipyard, that he drew up the plans for construction of Canada's largest wooden ship. Most of the furnishings are original, including furniture and exotic souvenirs collected from around the globe. Not just for those interested in the history of shipbuilding, Lawrence House also opens a window on Victorian life in the area. The **Launch Day Festival**, held on a Saturday in late September, commemorates the launch of the *William D Lawrence* – expect a non-motorised procession, a launch re-enactment and a whisky barrel race.

Maitland also offers a waterfront day-use park with an Acadian dyke and a reconstructed wharf. There are a few **shops** here – antiques and bric-a-brac – a c1839 general store with an uninspiring take-out on the north side of Highway 215, the main street, and a post office (*8829 Hwy 215;* ⊕ *07.30–12.30 & 13.30–16.30 Mon–Fri, 09.00–noon Sat*). There is also a **Christmas Festival**, held in November, which includes a craft fair, Gentlemen's Tea and Christmas Tree Stroll. Incidentally, local town planners recently renamed a couple of Maitland's roads and re-numbered the houses thereon.

Accessible **by car**, Maitland is on Highway 215, 9km/6 miles from Lower Selma, 30km from Shubenacadie and 79km/49 miles from Windsor.

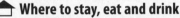

Where to stay, eat and drink

Cresthaven by the Sea B&B (3 rooms) 19 Ferry Lane; ✆ 902 261 2001; **tf** 1 866 870 2001; www.cresthavenbythesea.com. Lovely, luxurious B&B in a c1859 former shipbuilder's house with magnificent setting. Rate includes excellent b/fast. **$$**

Tidal Life Guesthouse (3 rooms) 78 Cedar Rd; ✆ 902 957 1524; **e** thetidallife@gmail.com; www.thetidallife.ca; ⊕ May–Oct. A 170-year-old heritage c1870 home in more than 5ha of grounds.

Rooms with private & shared bathroom. Decks, walking trails & herb gardens. Guest lounges. Friendly, good value, & nice b/fast inc. **$**

✗ BING'S Eatery & Socialhouse 8913 Hwy 215; ✆ 902 261 3287; www.bingseatery.com; ⊕ summer for dinner Tue–Fri, lunch & dinner Sat & Sun; check for off-season hours. Part art gallery, part stylish but casual licensed 'farm-to-table' café/bistro, part live music venue. Good views. Recommended. **$–$$**

SOUTH MAITLAND Water is the focus of this small community on the Shubenacadie River, which offers rafting, wetlands birdwatching, and a good opportunity to learn about the Bay of Fundy tides. The **Fundy Tidal Interpretive Centre** (*9865 Hwy 236;* ✆ *902 261 2250;* ⊕ *mid May–early Oct 10.00–17.00 daily; admission free*) explains the Fundy tides and the tidal bore; it's also home to a tourist information centre. Behind this, an observation deck high above the Shubenacadie is a good place to watch the watery action, and the rafters (box, page 261): time your visit to coincide with the bore arrival. Very close by, **Ducks Unlimited** maintains ponds that are home to a variety of waterfowl. Easy walking trails and interpretive boards enhance the birdwatching experience. The lush, green vegetation contrasts with the chocolate-brown river banks, with a backdrop of the decrepit old railway bridge.

South Maitland can be reached **by car** on Highways 215 and 236, 8km/5 miles from Maitland and 22km/14 miles from Shubenacadie. Accommodation options include the comfortable 1-, 2- and 5-bedrooms cabins and chalets at **Rafters Ridge Cottages** (*14 units; 12215 Hwy 215, Urbania;* ✆ *902 758 8433; www.raftingcanada.*

The Bay of Fundy sees the world's highest recorded tides. Twice daily, one hundred billion tonnes of seawater flows into the funnel-shaped bay. At the end of the bay furthest from its mouth, rivers (such as the Shubenacadie and Salmon) empty into it. The immense force and volume of the incoming tide not only halts these rivers' flows, but reverses them and sends them several kilometres backwards. The first wave caused by the incoming tide reversing the rivers' flows is called the 'tidal bore'.

The highest bores occur around the full and new moons: and although it can move at speeds over 10km/hour, sound travels a lot faster, and you're likely to hear the rush of water before you see it.

But don't be taken in by tourist brochure hype. Many see the tidal bore for the first time and say 'Is that it?' If you expect a huge tsunami-type wave, you will be very disappointed: what you are likely to see – and hear – is a wave of approximately 25cm moving steadily upriver.

In this area, South Maitland and the nearby Tidal Bore Rafting Park are excellent spots from which to view the phenomenon.

Times for the bore's arrival (generally, pretty accurate) can be found on the Rafting Resort website (box, opposite), or obtained from local newspapers, accommodations, or tourist offices. Try to arrive at your chosen vantage point a good ten minutes early as nature doesn't always observe the timetable strictly.

On the Shubenacadie, following behind the bore are a series of rapids. These rapids are a vital factor in one of the province's most exciting water-based activities.

ca; ⊕ *year-round; off-season by reservation;* **$$–$$$**), set between trees on a hillside overlooking the Shubenacadie River. Discounts are available for those rafting with Tidal Bore Rafting Resort (box, opposite). Even if you're not rafting, this is a pleasant place to stay, with a seasonal outdoor pool and walking trails. Alternatively, the **Wild Open Wilderness Family Campground** (*218 sites; 11129 Hwy 215, Urbania;* ☏ *902 261 2228;* tf *1 866 811 2267; www.wowcamping.com;* ⊕ *mid May–Sep;* **$**), a popular big open and wooded campground with serviced and unserviced sites. To eat, head back to Maitland.

SHUBENACADIE AND AROUND

SHUBENACADIE The word 'Shubenacadie' comes from the Mi'kmaq '*Segubunakade*' meaning 'place where the ground nuts grow'. These ground nuts should not be confused with peanuts – often called 'ground nuts' – but *Apios americana*, a climbing vine and member of the pea family and distantly related to the soya bean.

The major attraction here is the **Shubenacadie Wildlife Park** (*149 Creighton Rd;* ☏ *902 758 2040; wildlifepark.gov.ns.ca;* ⊕ *mid May–mid Oct 09.00–18.30 daily; mid Oct–mid May 09.00–15.00 Sat & Sun; admission CAN$4.75 summer, CAN$3.25 winter*), where 2km of largely shaded paths lead through 40ha home to more than 25 species of mammals and 45 bird species (most native to Nova Scotia). Species include black bear, moose, Sable Island horses, skunks, groundhogs, beavers and bald eagles. To see the animals out in the open, choose a cooler day or come early in the morning or in the late afternoon.

For those seeking soaking thrills and spills, Nova Scotia offers its own unique version of white-water rafting. Things usually start with a gentle boat trip on the Shubenacadie River on which you may see bald eagles. Near its mouth, rather than a rocky bottom, the river has several sandbars. As the incoming tide rushes up the river, big – but temporary – tidal rapid waves are created over each sandbar. These rapids dissipate after ten to 15 minutes.

Skilled and experienced guides are out to thrill, and pilot motorised inflatable (zodiac-type) boats to hit the waves head-on, lifting the craft and its occupants into the air and crashing them back onto the water. Apart from the splashing and rushing water, expect shrieks and screams of laughter from your fellow passengers. The boats ride the rapid and have time to turn and do it again two or three times at each sandbar.

Some operators include a break for lunch before you return to the boats for a much calmer trip exploring upriver. Some also throw in the opportunity to slide over and through slippery, chocolate-brown mud as a (voluntary) free extra.

The rafting season runs from May to October: the moon and tides determine the expected intensity of the experience (the rafting companies' websites have tide charts to help you choose your level). Each company offers three levels of trip depending on whether regular, high or extremely high tides are expected. During lower tides, more time is spent on nature observation.

Wear old, dark clothes that you don't mind getting wet and dirty. Take a towel and extra set of clothes. Tidal-bore rafting is very popular, especially around the highest tides, so book early. Operators include:

Shubenacadie River Adventure Tours 10061 Hwy 215, South Maitland; **tf** 1 888 878 8687; www.shubie.com; ⊕ Jun–Sep. 90mins CAN$75, 3hr trips CAN$98 inc all-you-can-eat burger/hot-dog BBQ. Mud sliding offered.
Shubenacadie River Runners 8681 Hwy 215, Maitland; \ 1 800 856 5061; www.tidalborerafting.com; ⊕ May–Sep. Based in Maitland at the river's mouth, it offers longer trips: half day (from CAN$69) or full day (from CAN$92 inc snacks).
Tidal Bore Rafting Resort 12215 Hwy 215, Urbania; \ 902 758 8433; **tf** 1 800 565 7238; www.raftingcanada.ca; ⊕ May–Oct). 2hr (from CAN$69) & 4hr (from CAN$98) trips. Mud sliding offered.

Also worth a visit is the **Tinsmith Shop Museum** (*2854 Main St; \ 902 758 2013; ⊕ mid May–mid Oct 10.00–17.00 daily; off-season by appointment admission free, donations welcome*) which was built in the 1890s and initially produced tin cans for milk, later branching out to sell all kinds of hardware. The original machinery – installed in 1896 – can still be seen. There's a craft shop and pretty garden.

To get to Shubenacadie **by car**, the town is on Highway 2, and just off Exit 10 of Highway 102, 66km/41 miles from Halifax and 35km/22 miles from Truro. There is also a bank in town (*2824 Main St; \ 902 758 2295; ⊕ 09.30–17.00 Mon–Fri*) and a post office just south on Highway 2 (⊕ *08.00–17.00 Mon–Fri*).

 Where to stay, eat and drink
ʎ **Wild Nature Camping Ground** (445 sites) 20961 Hwy 2; \ 902 758 1631; ⊕ late May–Sep.
Open & wooded serviced & unserviced sites, 1km from Shubenacadie Wildlife Park. **$**

✗Shubie Pizza 2842 Main St; ✆ 902 758 3535; **f** ShubiePizzeria; ⊕ 11.00–22.00 daily (Fri & Sat til 24.00). Fish & chips and other deep-fried food, but stick to the pizzas, individual pitta pizzas, or – if you must – *panzerotti* (fried folded pizza). **$**

STEWIACKE Said to be exactly halfway between the North Pole and the Equator – though some claim that the real midpoint is about 15km to the south – Stewiacke (the name comes from the Mi'kmaq meaning 'flowing out in small streams') is home to a somewhat un-Nova Scotian (more US-style) commercial attraction. The **Winding River Gallery and Complex** (*Hwy 102, Exit 11;* ✆ *902 639 2345; www. mastodonridge.com;* ⊕ *late May/Jun & Sep/mid Oct 10.00–17.00 daily; Jul–Aug 09.00–19.00 daily*) is not easy to miss – a life-size replica of an 89,000-year-old mastodon, whose bones were unearthed in 1991 in a nearby gypsum quarry, stands outside in full view of Highway 102. Here (at what used to be called 'Mastodon Ridge'), you'll find a slightly eclectic mix of a gallery featuring local artists, and in high season a souvenir/ice cream shop and 18 holes of minigolf. Another (adjacent) 'attraction' (depending on your point of view) is the biggest KFC in Atlantic Canada.

Stewiacke is about half an hour **by car** from Halifax International Airport on Highway 2, and just off Exit 11 on Highway 102, 68km/42 miles from Halifax, 30km/19 miles from Truro and 7km/4 miles north of Shubenacadie. **Maritime Bus** (page 57) stops here *en route* between Halifax and Truro.

 Where to stay, eat and drink

⌂ Nelson House B&B (3 rooms) 138 Main St East; ✆ 902 639 1380; **tf** 1 866 331 1380; www.thenelsonhousebb.com. A stately c1905 house with a lovely veranda built for the then mayor of Stewiacke. Full b/fast inc (eg: eggs Benedict with Hollandaise sauce, homemade granola with yoghurt & fresh fruit or Belgian waffles with local maple syrup). **$$**

✗Whistler's Pub 285 George St; ✆ 902 639 9221; ⊕ 11.00–22.00 daily (food til 20.00 Sun–Wed, til 21.00 Thu–Sat). The portions are generous & the pub food cheap, standard & not too greasy. **$**

Other practicalities

✉ **Post office** 55 Riverside Av; ⊕ 08.30–17.00 Mon–Fri
Stewiacke Branch Library 295 George St; ✆ 902 639 2481; ⊕ 13.00–17.00 & 18.00–20.00 Tue, 10.00–noon, 13.00–17.00 & 18.00–20.00 Thu, 10.00–noon & 13.00–17.00 Fri, 13.00–17.00 Sat

TRURO AND AROUND

Centrally located, situated at the convergence of two of the province's major expressways, on two coach routes and served by VIA Rail, Truro has long been known as the 'Hub of Nova Scotia', and was once known for its tall, beautiful elm trees, but sadly these were ravaged by Dutch elm disease in the 1970s. It is the province's third-largest town, with an economy based on shipping, dairy products and manufacturing. Neighbouring Bible Hill was home to the Nova Scotia Agricultural College (Canada's third-oldest agricultural college) for more than a century, but in 2012 this became the Dalhousie Faculty of Agriculture.

Many of those planning a trip to Nova Scotia get out a map and look for a base from which to make day trips to see all of the province's highlights. Many choose Truro. However, compared with much of the rest of the province, Truro is busy, lacks charm, and doesn't really have the same laid-back small-town feel. Railway level crossings often cause long traffic jams. But if you're happy to do a lot of driving and want somewhere with shopping, services, a good choice of accommodation and eateries from which to visit the capital, the Minas Basin shore, and perhaps the western half of the Northumberland Strait shore, then maybe Truro's for you.

HISTORY The Mi'kmaq named Truro '*Cobequid*' meaning 'the end of the water's flow' or 'place of rushing water' – a sure sign the tidal bore (box, page 260) isn't a new phenomenon. Pre-Expulsion, Acadian families farmed and traded in this area. A small group of New Englanders made their homes here in 1759, and in the following years, were joined by a number of Irish who Colonel McNutt (page 18) had brought over. They dreaded the 'savage' Mi'kmaq and built a stockaded fort, retiring into it every evening. After some time passed and the Mi'kmaq had failed to display any hostility, the fort was abandoned.

GETTING THERE AND AROUND Truro is on Highway 2, very close to the junction of Highway 104 (the Trans Canada Hwy, Exit 15) and Highway 102, Exit 14, and easy to reach **by car**. It is 117km/73 miles from Amherst, 91km/57 miles from Parrsboro and 100km/62 miles from Halifax. Two **Maritime Bus** coach routes stop here (*280 Willow St*): one connects Amherst (and New Brunswick) with Halifax, and the other, Sydney with Halifax (page 57). Three days a week, one **train** (page 58) in each direction connects Truro with Halifax, and Amherst (and Montreal). The **VIA Rail** (tf *1 888 842 7245; www.viarail.ca*) journey between Halifax and Truro takes approximately 90 minutes. Tickets start at CAN$23 for a single.

Taxis are available from **Layton's** (\ *902 895 4471*) and **Truro** (\ *902 893 4999*).

 WHERE TO STAY   *Map, page 264, unless otherwise stated*
Truro is a major hub and offers a number of accommodation choices in addition to those listed here. For example, in terms of hotel chains, Holiday Inn, Best Western, Comfort Inn and Super 8 are all in or around town. However, when looking for a larger property, I still prefer the independent Willow Bend Motel (below).

Baker's Chest B&B (4 rooms) 53 Farnham Rd; \ 902 893 4824; tf 1 877 822 5655; e info@ bakerschest.ca; www.bakerschest.ca. Century home with lovely gardens, a large indoor jacuzzi, outdoor pool (seasonal) & a fitness room. Full b/fast inc. **$$**

Belgravia B&B (3 rooms) 5 Broad St; \ 902 893 7100; tf 1 866 877 9900; www. belgravia.ca. A fine c1904 house with many period features & within easy walking distance of the town centre. Hearty full b/fast inc (eg: focaccia with scrambled eggs & smoked salmon, or homemade waffles with fresh blueberry sauce & vanilla yoghurt). **$$**

Suncatcher B&B [map, page 254] (2 rooms) 25 Wile Crest Av, North River; \ 902 893 7169; tf 1 877 203 6032; e suncatcherbnb@gmail. com, www.suncatcherbnb.com. A comfortable c1970s' B&B about 5km from the town centre . Host Ruth is friendly & knowledgeable about the area. Full b/fast & evening snack inc. **$$**

Tulips & Thistle B&B [map, page 254] (4 rooms) 913 Pictou Rd; \ 902 895 6141; tf 1 866 724 7796; www.tulipsandthistlebedandbreakfast. com. Very friendly & comfortable; nice deck, sun room, pleasant garden. A 9km drive outside town, off Hwy 104, Exit 17. Full gourmet b/fast inc. **$$**

Willow Bend Motel (28 units) 277 Willow St; \ 902 895 5325; tf 1 888 594 5569; www. willowbendmotel.com. With 15 standard rooms, 6 (larger) deluxe rooms & 7 suites. All have microwaves & fridges. Seasonal outdoor (heated) pool. 'Deluxe' continental b/fast inc. **$$**

Eagle's Landing B&B (3 rooms) 401 Robie St; \ 902 893 2346; tf 1 866 893 2346; www.bbcanada.com/10009.html. Comfortable & friendly with garden & nice balcony/deck & an easy walk to the town centre. Gourmet full b/fast & evening snacks inc. **$ $$**

Scotia Pine Campground [map, page 254] (210 sites) Hwy 2, Hilden; \ 902 893 3666; tf 1 877 893 3666; www.scotiapinecampground.

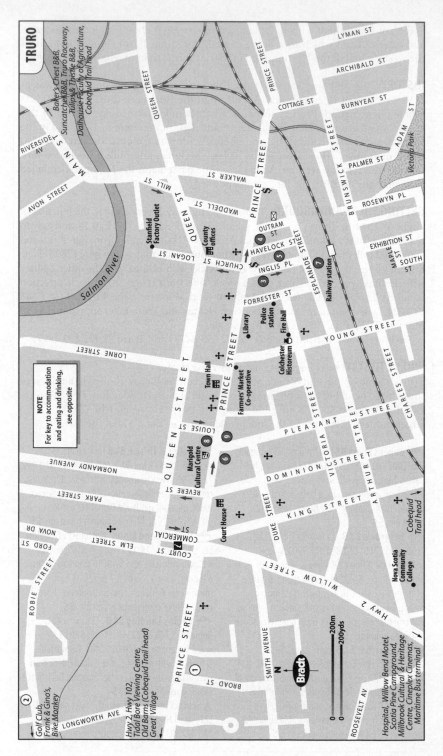

TRURO

Baker's Chest B&B,
Suncatcher B&B, Truro Raceway,
Tulips & Thistle B&B,
Dalhousie Faculty of Agriculture,
Cobequid Trail head

RIVERSIDE AV

MAIN

AVON STREET

QUEEN STREET

Salmon River

Stanfield
Factory Outlet

County
offices

LOGAN ST

QUEEN ST

MILL ST

WADDELL ST

WALKER ST

PRINCE STREET

COTTAGE ST

LYMAN ST

ARCHIBALD ST

BURNYEAT ST

PALMER ST

BRUNSWICK STREET

ADAM ST

Victoria Park

ROSEWYN PL

EXHIBITION ST

MAPLE ST

SOUTH ST

OUTRAM ST

CHURCH ST

HAVELOCK STREET

INGLIS PL

ESPLANADE STREET

4

5

3

7

Railway station

FORRESTER ST

Library

Police
station

Fire Hall

Colchester
Historeum

YOUNG STREET

CHARLES STREET

LORNE STREET

NOTE
For key to accommodation
and eating and drinking,
see opposite

QUEEN STREET

PRINCE STREET

Town Hall

Farmers' Market
Co-operative

8

9

6

Marigold
Cultural Centre

LOUISE ST

REVERE ST

PLEASANT STREET

VICTORIA STREET

DOMINION STREET

KING STREET

ARTHUR STREET

NORMANDY AVENUE

PARK STREET

NOVA DR

Court House

COMMERCIAL ST

ELM STREET

COURT ST

FORD ST

ROBIE STREET

DUKE STREET

WILLOW STREET

Cobequid
Trail head

Nova Scotia
Community
College

Hwy 2,
Tidal Bore Viewing Centre,
Old Barns (Cobequid Trail head)
Great Village

Golf Club,
Frank & Gino's,
Bike Monkey

2

LONGWORTH AVE

PRINCE STREET

BROAD ST

SMITH AVENUE

ROOSEVELT AV

1

Bradt

N

0   200m
0   200yds

Hospital, Willow Bend Motel,
Scotia Pine Campground,
Millbrook Cultural & Heritage
Centre, Cineplex Cinemas,
Maritime Bus terminal

Hwy 2

com; ⊕ Jun–mid Oct. Large campground between Truro & Brookfield (take exit 12 or 13 from Hwy 102); serviced sites for motorhomes, open & wooded tent sites. Pool (in season), sauna & laundromat. **$**

✖ WHERE TO EAT AND DRINK *Map, opposite*

Those looking for fast-food chains will find the usual suspects on Highway 2 (Robie Street) near Exit 14 of Highway 102. In addition to the 'independents' listed below, a walk along Prince Street will offer other possibilities.

✖ **Bistro 22** 16 Inglis Pl; ✆ 902 843 4123; www.bistro22.ca; ⊕ 11.00–14.00 Tue & Wed, 11.00–14.00 & 17.00–20.30 Thu–Sat. Lunches at this casual but upmarket restaurant are good salads, pizzas, gourmet sandwiches & paninis; the dinner menu might include roasted halibut, or pork chop stuffed with Gouda & spinach. *Lunch* **$–$$**, *dinner* **$$–$$$**

✖ **Lokal Resto & Food Market** 604 Prince St; ✆ 902 896 8678; ⚹; ⊕ 11.30–14.00 Tue&Wed, 11.30–14.00 & 17.00–21.00 Thu–Sat, 17.00–21.00 Sun. This comfortable rustic-style licensed eatery (think fresh locally sourced food, homemade pasta) shares the building with a good food store. **$$**

✖ **The Nook & Cranny Brew Pub** 627 Prince St; ✆ 902 895 0779; thenookandcranny. ca; ⊕ 11.00–22.00 Mon, 11.00–23.00 Tue–Fri, 11.00–00.30 Sat, 11.00–21.00 Sun. Not just a restaurant & brew pub – this ever-popular venue also offers a wide range of draft beers & ciders. The eating area is in 2 parts – the room with the brew tanks feels quieter & a bit more upmarket. Good food (eg: Baja fish tacos & the Club sandwich). **$$**

✖ **Fireside Tea Room at the Nova Scotian Emporium** 880 Prince St; ✆ 902 893 8285; ⊕ 08.00–15.30 Mon–Thu & Sat, 08.00–18.00 Fri. Not just tea but very good light meals (salads, soups, etc), plus tempting & tasty baked treats. **$–$$**

✖ **Frank & Gino's** 286 Robie St; ✆ 902 895 2165; www.frankandginos.com; ⊕ 11.00–22.00 Mon–Thu & Sun, 11.00–23.00 Fri & Sat. Popular family-style restaurant that covers the bases (eg: grill, pasta, pizza, burgers, Mexican, etc). *Lunch* **$**, *dinner* **$–$$**

✖ **Murphy's Fish & Chips** 88 The Esplanade; ✆ 902 895 1275; murphysfishandchips.ca; ⊕ 11.00–19.00 Mon–Sat (til 20.00 Fri), noon–19.00 Sun. An uninspiring location in a little shopping mall, but this family-friendly eatery offers well-cooked, well-priced seafood. **$**

🍴 **Jimolly's Bakery Café** 41 Inglis Pl; ✆ 902 843 3385; ⚹; ⊕ 08.00–17.30 Mon–Fri, 09.00–15.00 Sat. Fun, funky café & bakery – named after Jim & Molly, the owners' Basset hounds – with good sandwiches (eg: nutty ham & apple), quiche & salad bar. **$**

🍴 **NovelTea Bookstore Café** 622 Prince St; ✆ 902 895 8329; ⊕ 08.30–18.00 Mon–Fri, 09.30–17.30 Sat. Large selection of good used & collectible books, & decent speciality drinks & desserts. Try the 'James Joyce' (Irish Cream latte macchiato) or recharge with an 'Energy Bomb' (centre of seeds, honey & nuts, topped with chocolate). **$**

FESTIVALS April's chill is warmed up by the **Truro Music Festival:** the Provincial Exhibition Grounds in nearby Bible Hill are the new home of the **Nova Scotia Bluegrass & Oldtime Music Festival** (*www.downeastgrass.com*), a three-day event held in July. In August, drumming, dancing, Mi'kmaq food and crafts are to be seen and sampled at the four-day **Mi'kmaq PowWow**. Also in August is the six-day **Nova Scotia Provincial Exhibition** (nspe.ca), the province's premier agricultural and industrial fair with crafts, farm animal competitions, concerts and much more.

OTHER PRACTICALITIES

$ Royal Bank 940 Prince St; ☏902 893 4343; ⊕ 09.30–17.00 Mon, Tue & Fri, 09.30–20.00 Wed–Thu, 09.00–16.00 Sat

$ Scotiabank 7 Inglis Pl; ☏902 895 0591; ⊕ 09.30–17.00 Mon, Tue & Fri, 09.30–19.00 Wed & Thu, 09.00–15.00 Sat

✚ Colchester Regional Hospital 207 Willow St; ☏902 893 4321

✉ Post office Esplanade PO, Pharmasave, 179 Esplanade St ⊕ 09.00–21.00 Mon–Fri, 10.00–17.00 Sat, noon–16.00 Sun

ℹ Tourist information Victoria Sq, Court St; ☏902 893 2922; ⊕ mid-May–Jun & Sep–mid Oct 09.00–17.00 daily; Jul–Aug 08.30–19.30 daily; Truro Tidal Bore Viewing Visitor Information Centre; Tidal Bore Rd, Lower Truro ☏902 897 6255; ⊕ late May–late Jun & early Sep–mid Oct 09.00–17.00 daily, late Jun–early Sep 09.00–18.00 daily

Truro Branch Library 754 Prince St; ☏902 895 4183; ⊕ 10.00–20.00 Tue–Thu, 10.00–18.00 Fri, 10.00–17.00 Sat

WHAT TO SEE AND DO In and around the downtown area is some fine Victorian and vernacular architecture: Truro has three designated Heritage Conservation Districts (see *www.truro.ca/heritage-conservationdistricts.html*). Golf lovers can head to the **Truro Golf Club** (*86 Golf St;* ☏ *902 893 4650; www.trurogolfclub.com;* ⊕ *approx May–Oct; green fees CAN$64*) and there are several other courses within a few minutes' drive of town.

The town's *pièce de résistance*, though, is the wonderful **Victoria Park** (*Brunswick St & Park Rd;* ⊕ *Apr–Nov; admission free*). Occupying over 160ha, this is one of the most beautiful natural parks in eastern Canada offering an unusually wide variety of geographical features. The grassy day-use area at the main entrance can get busy on sunny weekends, but from there, you can choose from numerous walking and cycling trails through the woods of red and white spruce, ancient hemlock, and white pine. Head along a deep Triassic gorge, taking in two picturesque waterfalls on Lepper's Brook, and climb Jacob's Ladder, a 175-step wooden staircase up the side of the gorge. For a fabulous view over the surrounding area and the Cobequid Basin, take the trail to the look-out at the top of Wood Street (there is also road access to Wood Street). Download a park trail map from www.truro.ca/vic-park.html.

For more exercise, the **Cobequid Trail** offers 17km of walking/cycling trails (*www.colchester.ca/cobequid-trail*). The westerly terminus is on Shore Road just off Highway 236 in Old Barns: follow the old railway track for 11km to downtown Truro. An additional 6km section is in and around Bible Hill. You can rent bikes by the day (or longer) from **Bike Monkey** (*109 Robie St, Lower Truro;* ☏ *902 843 7111; www.bikemonkey.ca*), or explore Truro by Segway (a two-wheeled, self-balancing type of scooter), available from **Cobequid Segway** (☏ *902 893 4588 or 902 305 8758; cobequidsegway.wix. com/cobequidsegway*). After a 30-minute training session, the latter will take you for a 90-minute tour (over 13s only, weight restrictions apply) of Victoria Park and other town highlights.

> ### ICH BIN EIN BERLINER
>
> A local Truro businessman has loaned the town six sections of the Berlin Wall. These are on display at the grounds of the Dalhousie Faculty of Agriculture. They can be seen from the Bible Hill section of the Cobequid Trail.

Truro's Salmon River is one of the most accessible places to watch the **tidal bore**, the incoming tide forcing the Salmon River back the wrong way and filling the riverbed. Tidal-bore (box, page 260) times are listed in the *Truro Daily News* and at the tourist information office. A good place to bore-watch is at the new (2016) **Truro Tidal Bore Viewing Visitor Information Centre** (*Tidal Bore Rd, Lower Truro*), close to Exit 14 of Highway 102. There is floodlighting for nocturnal visitors.

Housed in a c1900 brick building, the **Colchester Historeum** (*29 Young St;* ✆ *902 895 6284; colchesterhistoreum.ca/www.genealogynet.com/colchester;* ⊕ *Jun–Aug 10.00–17.00 Mon–Fri, 10.00–16.00 Sat; Sep–May 10.00–noon & 13.00–16.00 Tue–Fri; admission CAN$5*) has displays on the town and region's heritage and natural history; its bookshop has a good selection of titles on Truro and the surrounding province.

The **Marigold Cultural Centre** (*605 Prince St;* ✆ *902 897 4004; www.marigoldcentre. ca*) is a performing arts centre with small art gallery and 206-seat auditorium. It has a good year-round theatre and live music schedule.

The UK has Marks & Spencer's, but for Nova Scotia and much of Canada, Truro's Stanfield's – established well over a century ago – is the company most associated with underwear – if you're keen for a browse, head over to the **Stanfield Factory Outlet** (*1 Logan St;* ✆ *902 895 5406; www.stanfields.com;* ⊕ *09.00–17.00 Tue–Sat*). The Saturday Truro **Farmers' Market Co-operative** (*Old Fire Hall, 15 Young St;* ✆ *902 843 4004; www.trurofarmersmarket.org;* ⊕ *Mar–mid Dec 08.00–13.00*) has more than 45 stalls (there are plans to open year-round).

AROUND TRURO

AROUND TRURO To find out what harness racing is all about, head out on a Sunday afternoon to the **Truro Raceway** (*Bible Hill Exhibition Grounds, Ryland Av, Bible Hill;* ✆ *902 893 8075; www.truroraceway.ca*), the largest of the province's three harness-racing tracks.

Just off the motorway (4km from Truro at Exit 13A off Hwy 102) and guarded by a 13m statue of Glooscap, the **Millbrook Cultural and Heritage Centre** (*65 Treaty Trail, Millbrook;* ✆ *902 843 34937; millbrookheritagecentre.ca;* ⊕ *mid May–Sep 09.00–17.00 daily; Oct 08.30–18.30 Mon–Fri, 08.30–16.30 Sat & Sun; mid Oct–mid May 08.30–16.30 Mon–Fri; admission CAN$6*) is the best of the province's few museums/centres devoted to the Mi'kmaq. In 2016 it was still finding its feet after major changes, but expect a multimedia presentation on Mi'kmaq heritage and Glooscap legends, and displays of traditional Mi'kmaq porcupine quillwork, beadwork and clothing. There are regular workshops (charges may apply, advance registration may be required). Ask about a couple of short walking trails nearby.

Catch a film at the multi-screen **Cineplex Cinemas Truro** (*20 Treaty Trail, Millbrook;* ✆ *902 895 8022; www.cineplex.com*), right by the Millbrook Cultural Centre.

Great Village

Great Village This pretty community is associated with Pulitzer Prize-winner Elizabeth Bishop (box, page 268). Many large Victorian homes are still standing. Great Village was a major shipbuilding area: the first four-masted vessel ever built in Canada, the *John M Blaikie*, was constructed here in the 1880s.

As well as offering three antique shops, the village has several galleries nearby. Contemporary art fans will want to pop into **Joy Laking Studio Gallery** (*6730 Hwy 2, Portaupique;* ✆ *902 890 8450 or 902 890 8730;* **tf** *1 800 565 5899; www. joylakinggallery.com;* ⊕ *Jun–Sep 10.00–17.00 Mon–Sat, 13.00–17.00 Sun, or by appointment; admission free*), 10km west of Great Village, to see watercolours, oils and acrylics that capture the beauty of Nova Scotia and the world beyond, and serigraphs – including works in progress – made by one of the province's top contemporary painters. Stop by **heather lawson** (*5759 Hwy 2, Bass River;* ✆ *902 647*

6

2287; *www.heatherlawson.ca;* ⊕ *mid Jun–early Sep 08.00–18.00 Thu–Sat, otherwise by chance or appointment*) to see this gifted stone carver (and capital-letter disliker) at work – and perhaps pat a goat! She is based approximately 16km from Great Village towards Economy.

St James United Church (*cnr of Hwy 2 & Lornevale Rd*) dates from 1845 but was rebuilt by shipbuilders in 1883 after a fire the previous year: the ceiling resembles an inverted ship's keel. A **farmers' market** is held here on Saturday mornings (*Jun–mid Sep*).

Great Village is on Highway 2, 27km/17 miles from Truro and 62km/39 miles from Parrsboro.

Where to stay, eat and drink

Willie Ed's B&B (2 rooms) 64 Station Rd; ☎ 902 668 2373; willieedsbandb.com; ⊕ Apr–Oct. Second Empire-style house (once owned by a Mrs Willie Ed Spencer) surrounded by ample, well-tended gardens. Spacious rooms with en-suite bathrooms (baths – there is also access to a shared bathroom with shower). Robes & slippers provided. Rate include b/fast (eg: special house French toast with NS maple syrup). **$$**

Ⱥ Hidden Hilltop Family Campground (148 sites) 2600 Hwy 4, Glenholme; ☎ 902 662 3391;

tf 1 866 662 3391; www.hiddenhilltop.com; ⊕ mid May–mid Oct. 6km from Great Village, the majority of sites here are serviced, many surrounding a large, open grassy play area. Lots of summer activities, store, decent-sized outdoor pool (seasonal) & a laundromat. **$**

⌨ In the Village Café 8729 Hwy 2; ☎ 902 668 2659; f; ⊕ Wed–Sun in season, check o/s hours. The basement of a former church is now home to this friendly spot dishing up soups, salads, sandwiches & a hot special. **$**

EN ROUTE TO PARRSBORO

ECONOMY AND AROUND There are few services in the village or environs, but great natural beauty. Worth a visit is **Thomas's Cove Coastal Preserve** off Economy Point Road, an almost completely enclosed tidal estuary. Hike the three trails (the longest is 4km), explore tidal mud flats (watch out for the incoming tide) and see the effects of the Bay of Fundy tides on the sandstone coastal landscape. Look out, too, for blue heron, cormorants, raptors and belted kingfisher.

Several wonderful hiking trails run along and around the **Economy River**, from less than 1km (Economy Falls) to a spectacular 18km hike (Kenomee Canyon), much of it in wilderness. To reach the trailheads, turn inland from Highway 2 onto

River Phillip Road. Even if you're not hiking, it's worth a drive along this road for the views from the roadside look-out.

If you are here in August, indulge at the **Clam Festival**, which celebrates the bivalve mollusc over three days. Epicures will also love the shop at **That Dutchman's Cheese Farm, Animal & Nature Park** (*4595 Hwy82, Upper Economy;* ✆ *902 647 2751; www. thatdutchmansfarm.com;* ⊕ *09.00–17.00 daily but Dec–Apr ring ahead to check; admission free*), a traditional Dutch-style farm making a variety of cheeses, located off Highway 2. Gouda, both natural and flavoured, is popular, but look out, too, for the award-winning Dragon's Breath. There is also a park with gardens, ponds, trails and farm animals to pet.

The **Cobequid Interpretive Centre** (*3246 Hwy 2;* ✆ *902 647 2600;* ⊕ *Jun–Sep 09.00–17.00 daily, admission free*) is well worth a stop for its displays, videos and more on the geology, history and culture of this stretch of Cobequid Bay coastline. You can pick up information on local wilderness hiking trails here, too. A climb up the steep stairs of the adjacent World War II coastal observation tower will reward you with fine views of the bay and further afield. There's also a large picnic area in the grounds.

Economy is accessible **by car**, on Highway 2, 52km/32 miles from Truro and 36km/22 miles from Parrsboro. If you want to stay in the area, **Four Seasons Retreat** (*10 cottages; 320 Cove Rd, Upper Economy;* ✆ *902 647 2628;* tf *1 888 373 0339; www.fourseasonsretreat.ns.ca;* **$$**) has comfortable, well-equipped 1-, 2-, and 3-bedroom cottages spread out and tucked between the trees, plus fine views over Cobequid Bay. There's beach access, a seasonal outdoor heated pool and a hot tub. There's also a post office just north of town (*2676 Hwy 2;* ⊕ *08.00–noon Mon/Wed/ Fri, 13.00–17.00 Tue/Thu*).

FIVE ISLANDS Mi'kmaq legend has it that Glooscap (page 33) created the Five Islands when he threw pebbles at Beaver (who had built a dam and flooded Glooscap's medicine garden). More recent tales tell of ghosts and buried treasure, though no-one has yet reported finding anything. The power of the water has worn a sea arch or tunnel through Long Island, the third in the chain.

The main attraction in this area is the **Five Islands Provincial Park** (*Bentley Branch Rd, off Hwy 2;* ✆ *902 254 2980; parks.novascotia.ca/contentfive-islands;* ⊕ *mid Jun– early Oct*), on the side of Economy Mountain – it's a must for hikers, fossil hunters, beachcombers, geologists and those who enjoy magnificent coastal scenery. The 637ha park lies on red sandstone deposited more than 225 million years ago. Much of the sandstone and basalt was removed by erosion over the next 180 million years. When the Ice Age ended, flooding rapidly eroded more of the remaining sandstone, creating the 90m cliffs. The sea stack known as the Old Wife, and the protective caps of the five islands themselves, are examples of basalt, more resistant to erosion than the soft sandstone. Keep your eyes open on the beach (not just for the incoming tide): not only are agate, amethyst, jasper and stilbite sometimes found, but also fossils. In July 2016, a hiker found a 200-million-year-old three-toed dinosaur footprint on the beach: the footprint can be viewed at the Fundy Geological Museum (page 273).

Hikers can enjoy the 4km **Estuary Trail** along the shore of East River's tidal estuary, the 5km **Economy Mountain Trail**, which follows an old logging road, passing through stands of maple, birch, beech and white spruce, and the (recently modified due to erosion but still worthwhile) 2.2km each-way **Red Head Trail**. Although it is the most difficult – with a few ups and downs and a long uphill section – of the park's trails, it gives access to look-outs, some of which are spectacular. Look out over the magnificent sandstone cliffs, rock formations and sea stacks such as the Old Wife – and, of course, the five islands. The trail can be walked in an hour or two, but allow a lot more time to enjoy the look-out side-trips.

The park has a pleasant campground and two picnic areas.

Five Islands is on Highway 2, 24km/15 miles from Parrsboro and 67km/42 miles from Truro, convenient to reach **by car**.

🏠 Where to stay, eat and drink

🏠 **Gemstow B&B** (2 rooms) 463 Hwy 2; \ 902 254 2924; f; ⏶ year-round; off-season by reservation. Comfortable B&B in century house with fine views. Judy, Gerry & their pets are very welcoming. Rate includes full b/fast with homemade bread & preserves. **$–$$**

⅄ **Five Islands Ocean Resort & Campground** (105 sites) 482 Hwy 2, Lower Five Islands; \ 902 254 2824; tf 1 877 454 2824; www.fiveislands.ca; ⏶ mid May–mid Oct. New owner & management (May 2016). Lovely coastal views, sea-view outdoor pool, laundromat, canteen, playgrounds. **$**

⅄ **Five Islands Provincial Park Campground** (87 sites) For contact details, see page 269. Open & wooded sites. A beautiful location. **$**

✕ **Mo's Family Restaurant, Accommodations & Tackle Shop** (2 'suites') 951 Hwy 2; \ 902 728 2075; www.mosrestaurantandaccom.ca. 2 large rooms (both sleep 3 or more **$$**). Restaurant offers diner food plus wood-fired pizzas & more – regular Kitchen Parties (music jam sessions with food & drink). **$–$$**

✕ **Diane's Restaurant** 874 Hwy 2; \ 902 254 3190; ⏶ May & Oct 11.00–20.00 Fri–Sun; Jun–Sep 11.00–21.00 daily. Linked to a clam factory, so those molluscs are a good choice. So too are fishburgers, seafood chowder & more. If you're here in blueberry season, save room for dessert. B/fast served from 08.00–11.00 Sat & Sun. Licensed. **$**

✕ **Granny's** 1193 Hwy 2; \ 902 728 3311; ⏶ early May–mid Sep 11.00–20.00 daily. Another good (although again high cholesterol) choice. Generous portions of fish & chips or clams & chips; ice cream also available. Ask about the charity 'fish & buoy wall'. **$**

NOT SINCE MOSES

Experience a rare opportunity to run along the ocean floor. Once a year when the Bay of Fundy's tides recede low enough, more than 1,000 competitors come from all over the world to participate in a 10km run or 5km run/walk across the bottom of the ocean in Five Islands. Established in 2007, this summer event has made quite a splash. For more, see www.notsincemoses.com.

PARRSBORO

Thanks to its population (1,400), Parrsboro is easily the largest community along the north shore of the Minas Basin. Named in 1784 after Lieutenant-Colonel John Parr, Governor of Nova Scotia, from the late 18th to the early 20th centuries, Parrsboro was a busy mercantile centre, an important transport hub, and the focus of a vast shipbuilding region. The town leapt into the limelight – at least for those interested in palaeontology – in the mid 1980s when two Americans unearthed one of the biggest and most important fossil finds in North America at nearby **Wasson's Bluff**. The cliffs yielded more than 100,000 fossilised bone fragments, all dating from shortly after the mass extinction some 200 million years ago that marked the end of the Triassic period and the beginning of the Jurassic.

Since then, Parrsboro has become a base for fossickers and rockhounds, and every August the town hosts the **Gem and Mineral Show** (previously called the 'Rock Hound Roundup'). But don't come expecting fossil-themed commercialisation – this is Nova Scotia! Rockhounding is nothing new in this area, however; Samuel de Champlain (page 228) was the first recorded European visitor in 1607, collecting amethysts from the beach.

Located at the head of a tidal river, the town has some services, a couple of modest supermarkets and some magnificent old houses – some of which are now inns – built by those who prospered during Parrsboro's glory days. In addition, there's an excellent museum, an interesting (summer) theatre, some browse-worthy shops, and a golf course. Recently, Parrsboro has also decided to turn itself into a hub for artists. It is an obvious base from which to explore the region.

In the past few years, feasibility and environmental impact studies have been carried out with regard to constructing the province's second tidal power project (the first is at Annapolis Royal; page 222). The test site is in the sea approximately 10km west of Parrsboro, but you can learn more about the site – and tidal energy in general – at the FORCE visitor centre (page 274).

Situated on Highway 2 and Highway 209, Parrsboro is easy to get to **by car** – it's 65km/40 miles from Amherst, 97km/120 miles from Truro and 193km/160 miles from Halifax. **Tourist information** can be found at the Fundy Geological Museum (page 273).

🏠 **WHERE TO STAY** *Map, page 272, unless otherwise stated*

🏠 **Gillespie House Inn** (7 rooms) 358 Main St; ☎ 902 254 3196; **tf** 1 877 901 3196; www. gillespiehouseinn.com; ⊕ year-round; off-season by reservation. Conveniently located & housed in a gracious c1890 eco-friendly home. Peaceful, charming & tastefully decorated. Yoga studio available. Wholesome full b/fast inc. Various packages (such as kayaking, theatre, dining) offered – check website for details. **$$**

🏠 **Maple Inn** (8 rooms) 2358 Western Av; ☎ 902 254 3735; **tf** 1 877 627 5346; www.mapleinn.ca; ⊕ May–mid Oct. 2 adjacent c1893 Victorian Italianate-style properties were converted to create this B&B. 6 comfortable rooms, a 1- & 2-bedroom suite & a honeymoon suite. Full b/fast & afternoon refreshments inc. **$$**

🏠 **Riverview Cottages** (18 cabins) 3575 Eastern Av; ☎ 902 254 2388; **tf** 1 877 254 2388; www.riverviewcottages.ca; ⊕ May–mid Oct. Clean cabins in a peaceful setting on the Farrell River Aboiteau. Most cabins have simple kitchenettes but don't expect TVs, in-room phones or Wi-Fi. **$**

🏠 **Mad Hatter Hostel** 16 Prince St; 902 254 3167; e madhatterhostel@hotmail.com; madhatterhostel.webs.com. Small, friendly, centrally located hostel offering sgl, dbl, family & dorm rooms. Kitchen, library, common room, laundry facilities & free parking. *Dorm CAN$23.* **$**

🏕 **Glooscap Campground & RV** [map, page 254] (73 sites) 1300 Two Islands Rd; ☎ 902 254 2529; www.town.parrsboro.ns.ca; ⊕ late May–Sep. 6km from the town centre, with sea views, sandy beach & open & wooded sites. **$**

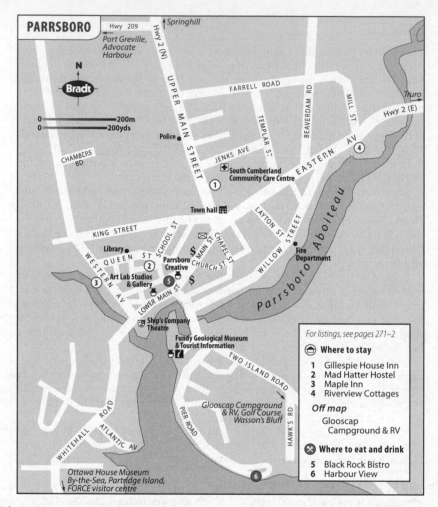

For listings, see pages 271–2

Where to stay

1 Gillespie House Inn
2 Mad Hatter Hostel
3 Maple Inn
4 Riverview Cottages

Off map

Glooscap
Campground & RV

Where to eat and drink

5 Black Rock Bistro
6 Harbour View

✗ WHERE TO EAT AND DRINK *Map, above*

✗ **Black Rock Bistro** 151 Main St; 902 728
3006; www.blackrockbistro.ca; ⊕ May–late Oct.
Opened in 2013 by David Beattie & Lori Lynch
(who own & run the Gillespie House Inn), the
menu features fresh locally sourced vegetables,
seafood, meats & cheeses with a selection of Nova
Scotia wines & craft beers. The seafood chowder is
good, also blackened haddock, Advocate Harbour
scallops, & homemade pasta. Finish off with
flourless chocolate cake. *Lunch $–$$, dinner*
$$–$$$

✗ **Harbour View Restaurant** 476 Pier Rd; ✆902
254 3507; ⊕ mid May–mid Oct 07.00–20.00 daily.
Popular seafood restaurant by the water. The usual
suspects (scallops, clams, lobster, seafood chowder,
haddock), plus flounder. Deep-fried is the norm, but
grilling or pan-frying may be available on request.
Reasonable prices, generous portions. $$

ENTERTAINMENT AND FESTIVALS The repertoire of the highly acclaimed and
innovative **Ship's Company Theatre** (*18 Lower Main St;* ✆ *902 254 2003;* **tf** *1 800 565
7469; www.shipscompany.com;* ⊕ *Jul–Sep, main stage performances 20.00 Tue–Sun
& 14.00 Sun; tickets CAN$28, Sun eve CAN$18.50*) focuses on new works from
Atlantic Canadian playwrights. The company staged its first production aboard the

shell of a disused 1924 ferry; when a new theatre was built in 2004, the remains of the vessel were incorporated into the lobby. Now, each year the theatre puts on more than 75 performances, six concerts, a tribute show, three drama camps and more, including a Monday Night Concert series in summer.

Held in June, **Classics by the Bay** stages three days of classical music performances. In August, the **Nova Scotia Gem and Mineral Show** is a three-day festival celebrating the province's rich mineral and fossil heritage. Art festival **10 Days in October** is organised by the Parrsboro Creative (*www.parrsborocreative.com*) and in the same month the **Parrsboro Film Festival** (*www.parrsborofilmfestival.com*) features Atlantic Canadian and Canadian films.

OTHER PRACTICALITIES

$ CIBC 209 Main St; ☏ 902 254 2066; ⊕ 10.00–17.00 Mon–Fri.
$ Royal Bank 188 Main St; ☏ 902 254 2051; ⊕ 09.30–17.00 Mon–Fri
✚ South Cumberland Community Care Centre 50 Jenks Av; ☏ 902 254 2540

✉ Post office 247 Main St; ⊕ 08.30–17.00 Mon–Fri, 09.00–12.30 Sat
Parrsboro Library 91 Queen St; ☏ 902 254 2046; ⊕ 13.00–16.00 & 18.00–20.00 Tue & Wed, 10.00–13.00, 14.00–17.00 Thu & Fri, 10.00–15.00 Sat

WHAT TO SEE AND DO If you enjoy art and galleries, have a look at two relatively recent additions to Parrsboro. First, **Art Lab Studios & Gallery** (*121 Main St;* ☏ *902 254 2972; www.artlabstudios.ca;* ⊕ *early May–late Dec – check website for days/ hours*) is a co-operative gallery and studios where you can watch professional artists working in a variety of styles and media including paint, ink, clay, stone, photography, fabric, and more. Second, **Parrsboro Creative** (*151 Main St;* ☏ *902 728 2007; www.parrsborocreative.com*) offers professional art studios, a rich variety of fine arts, and artisan courses in painting, stone carving, blacksmithing, basketry, writing, photography, music and more.

Those with an interest in fossils and geology – or just more beautiful coastal scenery – should drive along **Two Islands Road**. There are magnificent views of the rugged coastline, and about 6km from town you'll reach a car park where interpretive panels describe the area's unique geology, and the fossil discoveries made here. A trail leads down to the beach and to **Wasson's Bluff**, an area protected by law, where no fossil collecting is allowed, except by permit (page 38). At the excellent award-winning **Fundy Geological Museum** (*162 Two Islands Rd;* ☏ *902 254 3814;* **tf** *1 866 856 3466; fundygeological.novascotia.ca;* ⊕ *Jun–mid Oct 10.00–17.00 daily; mid Oct–May 08.30–16.30 Mon–Fri; admission CAN$8.25*), see locally found minerals, semi-precious stones, fossils, and some of the oldest dinosaur bones ever found in Canada. Guided geological tours of the nearby beaches are offered in July and August: there's a year-round calendar of events.

FOSSIL FINDER

Eldon George was born in Parrsboro around 1930 and began collecting minerals and fossils when he was eight. A year later he put a 'Rocks For Sale' sign in the window of the family house. In 1984, he discovered the world's smallest dinosaur footprints as he sheltered from a hailstorm whilst fossicking at Wasson's Bluff. Most of Eldon's legacy is now on display at the **Fundy Geological Museum** (see above).

Interpretive displays and interactive exhibits abound in the Fundy Ocean Research Center for Energy (FORCE's) **visitor centre** (*1156 West Bay Rd;* ☎ *902 254 2510; fundyforce.ca/visit;* ⊕ *Jun–Sep daily 10.00–17.00, May & Oct see website; admission free),* all overlooking the tidal energy test site.

Beautifully located by the Partridge Island causeway, the **Ottawa House Museum By-the-Sea** (*1155 Whitehall Rd;* ☎ *902 254 2376; www. parrsboroughshorehistoricalsociety.ca/the-ottawa-house-museum;* ⊕ *late May–mid Sep 10.00–18.00 daily; admission by donation*) – 3km from the town centre and used as a summer home for more than 30 years in the late 1800s by Sir Charles Tupper, Canada's sixth prime minister – has parts that date back to 1765. On display are artefacts and exhibits highlighting the region's shipbuilding and commercial history, including rum running. Special events are held in summer. The museum is also a genealogical research centre.

Mi'kmaq legend has it that Glooscap created **Partridge Island** (a sandy natural causeway appeared in 1869 after freak weather, connecting it to the mainland) from a disobedient partridge. The island is also revered as Glooscap's grandmother's traditional campsite. Archaeological evidence points to Mi'kmaq occupation 10,000 years ago. Various trails start from the end of the causeway, most rewarding of which is the **Look-Off Trail**, which climbs to a look-out offering panoramic views in all directions. Reach the causeway by continuing on Whitehall Road past Ottawa House (see above). The island is less than 5km from Parrsboro.

Just southeast of the town centre, **Parrsboro Golf Course** (*Two Island Rd;* ☎ *902 254 2733; www.parrsborogolf.ca;* ⊕ *mid May–mid Oct; green fees CAN$25 for 9 holes, CAN$35 for 18 holes*) offers a nine-hole 2,343yd cliff-top course with above-par views over Minas Basin. I like the seventh, where there is an apple tree on the green.

WEST TOWARDS CAPE CHIGNECTO

PORT GREVILLE Considering Nova Scotia's worldwide importance during the 'Age of Sail', there are precious few signs left of such an important part of the province's history. This is another example of a pleasant little community that would now show few indications of its ship building glory days, were it not for the fascinating **Age of Sail Heritage Centre** (*Hwy 209;* ☎ *902 348 2030; www.ageofsailmuseum.ca;* ⊕ *Jun & Sep–mid Oct 10.00–18.00 Thu–Mon, Jul–Aug daily; admission CAN$5*). Housed in a former c1854 Methodist church are audio-visual and panel displays, and thousands of artefacts which bring life to the history of shipbuilding along this shore. The centre comprises a two-storey main building, newer hull-shaped wind and wave display building with research and archive area, blacksmith shop, band-saw shed and a c1907 lighthouse. Take a guided tour to truly appreciate the centre. There is a gift shop, play area and a good café (⊕ *early Jun & Sep 10.00–18.00, Thu–Mon & Jul/Aug daily;* $) serving light lunches (eg: lobster rolls), soup or chowder, sandwiches and desserts (the carrot cake is a stand-out). The food is good and the prices very reasonable.

Port Greville is 22km/14 miles from Parrsboro and 82km/51 miles from Joggins.

SPENCERS ISLAND At the western end of Greville Bay, this isn't actually an island but takes its name from a real one just off nearby Cape Spencer. That island is said to have been formed by mythical Mi'kmaq hero Glooscap when he upturned his large stone cooking pot.

The community became another important shipbuilding centre in the second half of the 19th century: the first large vessel to be launched was the *Amazon*, built in 1861 (box, overleaf). In summer, the c1904 beachfront **lighthouse** is sometimes open to the public: beside it is a picnic park.

Spencers Island is 1.2km from Highway 209, 40km/25 miles from Parrsboro.

Where to stay, eat and drink

Spencers Island B&B (3 rooms) 789 Spencer's Beach Rd; ☎ 902 392 2721; e spencebb@ yahoo.ca; ⊕ Jun–Sep. Close to the beach & well located for exploring the region: pity the season is so short. 3 guest rooms share 2 bathrooms. Full b/fast inc. **$**

Å Old Shipyard Beach Campground (24 sites) 774 Spencer's Beach Rd; ☎ 902 392 2487; www.oldshipyardbeachcampground.com;

⊕ Jun–Sep. Open serviced & unserviced beachfront sites. Camp store, laundromat & bike rentals. **$**

✗ Spencers Island Beach Café 769 Spencers Island Beach Rd; ☎ 902 392 2390; f; ⊕ late May–early Oct 08.00–20.00 daily (hrs/days may reduce early/late in the season). Beachfront café offering b/fast, chowder, lobster rolls, burgers & homemade desserts, plus ice cream. **$–$$**

ADVOCATE HARBOUR AND CAPE D'OR Many people rush through in a hurry to get to nearby Cape Chignecto Provincial Park, but try to make time to explore this beautiful area on Advocate Bay, tucked between the towering cliffs of Cape d'Or and Cape Chignecto, and backed by forested mountains.

A 5km-long natural barrier pebble beach – always piled high with driftwood – almost closes off the harbour entrance, especially when the tide is out. Grey seals are sometimes seen (their rookery is 20km out to sea, on Isle Haute; box, page 278). The easiest beach access is from West Advocate. Dykes built centuries ago by the Acadians to reclaim farmland from the sea are still visible, and make for pleasant walks, and the sunsets are magnificent.

If you fancy some sea kayaking, **NovaShores Adventures** (☎ 902 392 2222; tf 1 866 638 4118; e seakayak@novashores.com; www.novashores.com) offer tours from 6 hours to three days. It's a great way to explore the region's natural splendour – such as the Three Sisters, one of the province's most iconic rock formations – and highly recommended. Prices start at CAN$114. Alternatively, **Advocate Boat Tours** (☎ 902 392 2222; tf 1 866 638 4118; advocateboattours.com) offer 2-hour small boat adventures combining scenic highlights with wildlife viewing to Cape Split, Isle Haute (box, page 278) or Three Sisters. Prices from CAN$79.

Once known only to nature lovers, sea kayakers and those looking for unusual accommodation, Advocate Harbour also has one of the top 'rural' restaurants in the province.

THE MYSTERY SHIP

When the first vessel was built at Spencers Island, few would have believed that 150 years later, she would still fascinate the world at large. Around 1860, Joshua Dewis built a brigantine designed to carry lumber as her main cargo, and named her *Amazon*.

On her maiden voyage, the captain died of a heart attack within 24 hours of setting sail. Other bumps and tangles included the *Amazon* grounding in the English Channel. After suffering severe damage in a storm off the coast of Cape Breton Island, she was sent to a New York marine scrapyard. Sold at auction and made seaworthy again, she was relaunched and renamed *Mary Celeste*. On 5 November 1872, she departed New York, bound for Genoa, Italy, with a hold full of alcohol. On board were a well-respected captain, his wife and two-year-old daughter, and a crew of seven.

A month later, she was spotted by another ship's crew floating aimlessly near the Azores. Their calls unanswered, they boarded the silent vessel finding it fully provisioned with the sails set and nothing out of place. There were hints that those on board had left in a hurry – the single lifeboat was gone, the child's toys strewn on deck. None of those who had been on board the *Mary Celeste* were ever seen again.

A board of inquiry concluded that piracy or foul play was unlikely, and, while her true fate will never be known, theories abound as to why the captain and crew abandoned ship. The most plausible of these suggests that, although very experienced, the captain had never carried crude alcohol on any of his ships. When the alcohol casks began to leak, he may have feared that the vapour might ignite and explode, and may have ordered a hasty evacuation. Their lifeboat could have drifted for days before perhaps being capsized by a big wave and sending its passengers to a watery grave.

After the inquiry she continued sailing for years, but, beset by more troubles, was sold and resold 17 times. In 1884, the *Mary Celeste* was finally scuttled off Haiti for insurance reasons and rediscovered by a team of Canadian divers in 2001.

During the late 1800s, crewless ships left to founder were not unheard of, and rarely attracted media attention. But in 1884, a budding writer penned a short story closely based on the *Mary Celeste* mystery. The author – who changed the name of the ship to the *Marie Celeste*, and added a few other bits of fiction – was Arthur Conan Doyle.

At East Advocate, signs lead you towards **Cape d'Or**, where the road soon becomes unpaved. One Samuel de Champlain named the cape in 1604, but the metal he saw glittering in the sunlight wasn't gold – it was copper. At **Horseshoe Cove**, located down a left turn about 4.5km after the crest of the hill, a copper-mining community thrived during the late 19th century, and to this day pure copper nuggets are sometimes found on the beach, as too are agates and other semi-precious stones.

Cape d'Or provides the only opportunity in Nova Scotia to stay in a lightkeeper's cottage. The c1965 **Cape d'Or Lighthouse**, manned until 1989, is now automated, but the cottages – built late in the 1950s – now house (another) excellent restaurant and a guesthouse. The lighthouse and foghorn warn those at sea of the **Dory Rips**, or riptides: three separate tides converge, resulting in incredibly treacherous, turbulent waters. If the mist starts to roll in during your visit, prepare yourself: the modern-day foghorn – which sounds every 60 seconds – will make you jump.

The main unpaved road continues to a car park with interpretive boards and a replica lighthouse (rumours in 2016 were that the replica lighthouse might be moved elsewhere...). Trails lead along the cliffs to spectacular viewpoints, or down to the (real) lighthouse. Going down is fine but not everyone enjoys the steep, steady 1km trek back up.

Both Cape d'Or and Advocate Harbour can be reached **by car**. Cape d'Or is off Highway 209, 44km/27 miles from Parrsboro and 59km/37 miles from Joggins. Advocate Harbour is on Highway 209, approximately 2km from the Cape d'Or turn-off at East Advocate.

Where to stay, eat and drink

Driftwood Park Retreat (6 units) 49 Driftwood Lane, Advocate Harbour; 902 392 2008; tf 1 866 810 0110; www.driftwoodparkretreat.com; ⊕ Apr–Oct. Choose from 4 2-bedroom chalets, a studio & a 1-bedroom chalet with loft. All are fully equipped, comfortable & very close to the seafront. A great get-away-from-it-all spot within a couple of kilometres of the entrance to the provincial park. **$–$$**

Lightkeeper's Kitchen & Guest House (4 rooms) Cape d'Or; 902 670 0534; www.capedor.ca; ⊕ May–mid Oct. A rare opportunity to stay in a lightkeeper's cottage in Nova Scotia. It has a spectacular setting with the pounding tides on one side & basalt cliffs behind. Rooms are with en-suite, private or shared bathroom & there are fabulous views & a common room. Note that the lighthouse's foghorn is an important navigation aid: if the fog rolls in, the horn is called into action – regardless of whether or not guests might be sleeping. The attached licensed restaurant (⊕ May–mid-Oct for lunch & dinner Thu–Tue; **$$**) has similar panoramas. Reservations are recommended & payment accepted only in cash. Light lunches (eg: salads, sandwiches, fishcakes, seafood chowder) & imaginative evening meals are served, using fresh local ingredients where possible. During lobster season (May–Jul) fresh lobster boils

are offered (⊕ 18.00–20.00, by reservation only). The guesthouse & restaurant are a few mins' walk downhill from the car park. Make the effort – it's worth it! **$**

Reid's Tourist Home (4 units) 1391 West Advocate Rd, West Advocate; 902 392 2592; reidstouristhome.ca; ⊕ Jun–late Sep. 3 motel-style guest rooms & 1 2-bedroom cottage on a working cattle farm. **$**

Wild Caraway Restaurant & Café 3721 Hwy 209, Advocate Harbour; 902 392 2889; wildcaraway.com; ⊕ summer 11.00–21.00 Mon, Thu–Sat, 11.00–21.00 Sun; check off-season hrs. A real foodie's delight, Andrew Aitken & Sarah Griebel's restaurant focuses on locally sourced products: the eponymous wild caraway, for example, the seeds of which are used in their Caesar salad dressing, grows just outside the building; and the *ceviche* is prepared using locally caught flounder. The décor is contemporary, the service very professional, & the wonderful food is matched by an equally good wine list. Lovely views are a bonus! Accommodation is also available in 2 pleasant rooms, with shared bathroom. Rate inc hearty gourmet b/fast, such as herb scrambled eggs with homemade sourdough bread & local bacon (⊕ approx May–Oct; **$**). **$$**

Other practicalities

✉ **Post office** 3727 Hwy 209; ⊕ 08.30–15.30 Mon–Fri, 09.00–13.00 Sat

Advocate Harbour Library 93 Mills Rd; 902 392 2214; ⊕ 10.00–noon & 13.00–16.00 Wed & Fri, 14.00–20.00 Thu, 09.00–13.00 Sat

CAPE CHIGNECTO PROVINCIAL PARK (*West Advocate Rd;* 902 392 2085; *parks.novascotia.ca/content/cape-chignecto;* ⊕ *mid May–early Oct*) Covering a vast area of 4,200ha, Cape Chignecto is Nova Scotia's largest provincial park and should certainly not be missed by lovers of the wild outdoors. It is located on an arrow-shaped headland pointing in to the Bay of Fundy, flanked by Chignecto Bay and the Minas Basin. Although encompassing 29km of pristine coastline, much of the park sits high above the huge tides, with some cliffs reaching 185m. In the water below, nature has created a range of natural sculptures, such as the Three Sisters, huge misshapen sea stacks.

The park has no roads, and to stay within its boundaries you'll have to camp. Partly for these reasons – and the somewhat 'out-of-the-way' location – Cape Chignecto is still something of a hidden gem.

Ten **marked trails** give access to the natural highlights. These range from quick jaunts to the beach from the Red Rocks visitor centre, or the Three Sisters look-out from Eatonville Beach , to challenging all-day hikes that should only be attempted by experienced hikers, such as the spectacular Red Rocks visitor centre–Refugee Cove trail. The big one is a multi-day circuit of the Cape (box, below). The longer hikes are all likely to involve climbing steep slopes and following vertiginous cliffside paths, but the wonderful nature, magnificent scenery and spectacular views are a just reward.

Expect to see yellow birch, American beech, Eastern hemlock, balsam fir, sugar maple and white and red spruce. For much of the summer, you'll also see wild flowers. Whilst the peninsula is home to bobcats, moose and black bear, these are very rarely encountered; far more common are whitetail deer, rabbit and hare. Grey seals can often be seen in late summer, basking on rocks in the coves.

Hiking apart, the park's stunning shoreline, secluded coves and beaches are a wonderful area for **sea kayaking** (page 275).

There are two entrances to the park: the long-established entrance very close to Advocate Harbour, and the newer entrance at Eatonville, accessed via the West Apple River Road. Near both entrances are picnic tables.

Access to the park **by car** is via West Advocate Road from the village of West Advocate on Highway 209, 46km/29 miles from Parrsboro, or by West Apple River Road 13km/8 miles further northwest along Highway 209.

🏠 **Where to stay, eat and drink** The park has 31 well-spread walk-in **campsites** between 75m and 300m from the car park, and almost 60 beautifully located back-

ISLE HAUTE

Approx 8km out to sea from Cape Chignecto is mysterious, deserted Isle Haute. The Mi'kmaq, lighthouse and pirates are long gone but the 100m basalt cliffs, seal and bird colonies still thrive. A permit is required to land, but Advocate Boat Tours (page 275) will get you a pretty good view.

CAPE CIRCUIT

The 49km circumnavigation of Cape Chignecto is one of Nova Scotia's – and eastern North America's – great coastal hikes. Although it can be hiked in two to three days, this is not a hike to be rushed. Accommodation is a choice of remote hike-in campsites, and two wilderness cabins near Arch Gulch and Eatonville: reservations are required. Sections of the trail are strenuous with steep ascents and descents. This is a fantastic trail, but should only be attempted by self-sufficient, experienced hikers – who have a good head for heights.

country hike-in sites. The New Yarmouth campground can be reached by dirt road, but doesn't have great views and can be rather insect. There are also a couple of wilderness cabins. Reservations (**tf** *1 888 544 3434; www.novascotiaparks.ca*) are required for hike-in campsites and cabins, and recommended for walk-in campsites.

THE NORTHWEST COAST AND INTERIOR

JOGGINS Although noted for its coal mining – there are records of coal from Joggins being sold in Boston as early as 1720 – what gives Joggins a prominent position on the 21st-century map goes back much further. At the head of the bay, Joggins's 15- to 30m-high sea cliffs stretch for 15km and – twice daily – feel the force of the Bay of Fundy's huge tides. Over time this has eroded the cliff face to reveal thousands of fossils. The exposed alternating grey and reddish-brown cliff faces date from the Carboniferous period.

These fossil cliffs were first brought to public attention in 1852 when geologists found tiny fossilised bones of *Hylonomous lyelli*, one of the world's first reptiles. This was the first evidence that land animals had lived during the Coal Age.

Since then, the cliffs – labelled the 'Coal Age Galapagos' – have revealed a wealth of other important discoveries and are recognised as a world-class palaeontology site, with many experts believing that they preserve the most complete record of life in the Pennsylvanian Period (341 million to 289 million years ago) anywhere in the world. This was declared a UNESCO World Heritage site in the summer of 2008.

Although you can access the beach below the cliffs from several points, you will gain far more from your experience if you precede your exploration with a visit to the purpose-built and environmentally friendly **Joggins Fossil Centre** (*100 Main St;* *902 251 2727;* **tf** *1 888 932 9766; www.jogginsfossilcliffs.net;* ⊕ *late Apr–May & Sep–Oct 10.00–16.00 daily; Jun–Aug 09.30–17.30 daily; off-season by appointment; admission CAN$10.50 inc 30min beach tour, or CAN$25 inc 90–120min guided tour*), which includes interpretive displays of 300-million-year-old fossils of insects, amphibians, plants and trees. Guided tours of Joggins Fossil Cliffs can be booked through the centre (phone or see website for schedule), and it also contains the tourist information centre, a gift shop and a café (⊕ *Jun–Aug 10.00–16.00 daily;* $) serving fair-trade, organic coffee and tea, as well as wholesome, homemade salads, sandwiches, cakes and cookies.

You can wander the rock strewn beach at the cliff base and search for fossils which have fallen from the cliff face, but can't take any fossils away with you without a permit (page 38). The cliff site has picnic tables and interpretive signage. Most of the rocks on the beach have fallen from the cliff face, so proceed with caution – and pay attention to the tides, which come in very quickly.

TINY TOES

In September 2012, Gloria Melanson was walking along Joggins Beach when something caught her eye. Across the corner of a piece of rock (which measured about 10cm by 10cm) were tiny tracks. It transpired that Gloria had found the world's smallest known fossil vertebrate footprints, tiny tracks left by a fossil specimen of the ichnogenus *Batrachichnus salamandroides* approximately 315 million years ago. Gloria must have good eyes. the salamander-like creature which left the tracks was probably only about 8mm from snout to tail, and the whole trackway measures less than 5cm.

In 1891, an underground mine explosion claimed 125 lives, including more than a dozen boys. In 1956, several railcars broke loose from a mine train and rolled backwards down into the mine, derailing and then hitting a power line. The resulting blast killed 39 miners. Rescuers with no breathing equipment were able to rescue 88 survivors.

Less than two years later, an underground earthquake (or 'bump') occurred in a mine, killing many miners instantly and trapping numerous others underground with no food and water and a dwindling air supply. Mine officials, workers, volunteers and local doctors risked their lives and rescued 104 trapped miners: 74 others were not so lucky. The dead are remembered in the Miners' Memorial Park on Main Street.

Incidentally, the disaster had been predicted by Mother Coo, a fortune teller from Pictou, who also gave advance notice of other mining tragedies including the disasters at Westville's Drummond Mine (59 dead) and Stellarton's Foord Pit (50 dead) in 1873 and 1880 respectively.

Rather than being seen as a human early-warning system, Mother Coo was regarded as a pariah and driven from the area.

To get there **by car**, Joggins is on Highway 242, 55km/34 miles from Advocate Harbour, 35km/22 miles from Amherst and 45km/28 miles from Parrsboro.

SPRINGHILL   Not the prettiest community in the province, Springhill is a coal-mining town. The mines – which brought happiness, prosperity and tragedy – are long closed, but still benefit the community. Since they were shut down, the shafts filled with water that has been heated by the surrounding earth to an average temperature of 18°C. Since the1980s, technology has allowed businesses in Springhill's industrial park to use the heated water to reduce their winter heating bills substantially. The town is home to the province's largest 'correctional facility'. Other than visiting inmates, there are two contrasting attractions.

Two years after the Syndicate Mine closed in 1970, the **Springhill Miners' Museum** (*145 Black River Rd;* ✆ *902 597 3449;* ⏱ *mid May–mid Oct 09.00–17.00 daily; admission CAN$7*) opened on the site. Mining artefacts, the miners' washhouse and their lamp cabin are quite interesting but the highlight is the mine tour: don overalls, hard hats and rubber boots and descend 100m underground (most guides are former coal miners). Note that the tour is not for the claustrophobic nor those not keen on the dark.

Anne Murray was born in Springhill in 1945. Some 25 years later, she released a song called *Snowbird* that went on to become one of North America's most played songs of 1970. Over the years, she has racked up more gold and platinum albums, Grammy awards and country music awards than any other Canadian and sold more than 55 million albums. Exhibits at the **Anne Murray Centre** (*36 Main St;* ✆ *902 597 8614; www.annemurraycentre.com;* ⏱ *mid–May–mid-Oct 09.00–17.00 daily; admission CAN$6*) range from a lock of hair from her first haircut to glittering stage costumes and her plentiful gold/platinum albums. Buy Murray-memorabilia in the gift shop, or record a duet with Anne in the centre's mini recording studio. All together now, 'Spread your tiny wings and fly away...'

Springhill is accessible **by car**, on Highway 2, 7km from Exit 5 of the Trans Canada Highway (Hwy 104), 25km/16 miles from Amherst and 50km/31 miles from Parrsboro. If you're here in June, the three-day **Irish Festival** is a celebration of Irish music, with food, dancing and a street parade.

 Where to stay, eat and drink It's fair to say that Springhill doesn't have a reputation as a gourmet's paradise. Probably the best choice is the **Rollways Motel & Restaurant** (*12 rooms; 9 Church St;* ☎ *902 597 3713;* **$**), which has spacious if old-fashioned style rooms above a restaurant and shop, with friendly management. The restaurant (**$**) dishes out decent diner-style food.

Other practicalities

$ CIBC 41 Main St; ☎ 902 597 3741; ⏲ 10.00–17.00 Mon–Fri

✚ All Saints Springhill Hospital 10 Princess St; ☎ 902 597 3773

✉ Post office 68 Main St; ⏲ 08.30–17.00 Mon–Fri

ℹ Tourist information Anne Murray Centre, 36 Main St; ⏲ Jul–Aug 09.00–17.00 daily

Springhill Library 75 Main St; ☎ 902 597 2211; ⏲ 11.00–13.00 & 14.00–20.00 Tue & Fri, 10.00–13.00 & 14.00–18.00 Wed & Thu, 10.00–15.00 Sat

NOVA SCOTIA ONLINE

For additional online content, articles, photos and more on Nova Scotia, why not visit www.bradtguides.com/novascotia.

SEND US YOUR SNAPS!

We'd love to follow your adventures using our *Nova Scotia* guide – why not send us your photos and stories via Twitter (*@BradtGuides*) and Instagram (*@bradtguides*) using the hashtag #novascotia. Alternatively, you can upload your photos directly to the gallery on the Nova Scotia destination page via our website (*www.bradtguides.com/novascotia*).

7

Northumberland Shore

Mainland Nova Scotia's north shore fronts the Northumberland Strait and stretches from the provincial border with New Brunswick to the west, to Aulds Cove, from where the Canso Causeway leads to Cape Breton Island to the east. The shortest and quickest way to get between the two points is on Highway 104, the Trans Canada Highway (TCH), a drive of 265km. However, Highway 104 runs well inland, and just about everything of interest in the region is away from the motorway, on or within a few kilometres of the waterfront. So once again it is best not to rush things, but to take the smaller, quieter, far more scenic roads through quaint communities such as Pugwash, Oxford and Tatamagouche.

Paddle the coastal inlets in a sea kayak, enjoy a scenic round of golf, or hike beautiful trails high above Antigonish Harbour. Or go for a dip: this region of rolling hills and pastoral landscapes is renowned for its beaches, most of which are within provincial parks, and summer swimming is a pleasure – the slogan 'warmest water north of the Carolinas' is oft heard. The average sea temperature between July and late September is over 22°C. To the west, the tide recedes from the red sand beaches to expose vast mud flats, and further to the east the stretches of sand at Melmerby and Pomquet beaches are not to be missed.

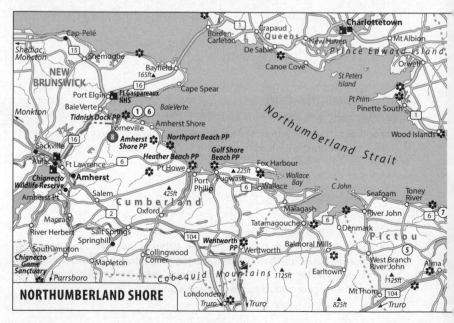

NORTHUMBERLAND SHORE

Scottish Heritage is a big draw for many – from 1773, Pictou was the gateway to Nova Scotia for thousands of Scottish Highlanders, and their history and culture lives on through much of the region.

Those who enjoy things urban should like the pleasant towns of Amherst, Pictou and Antigonish (home to the St Francis Xavier University) but as Amherst, the biggest of the three, has a population of just under 10,000, we're not talking about vast built-up sprawl. Stellarton's vast and impressive Museum of Industry is an ideal rainy-day choice.

NORTHUMBERLAND SHORE

⊜ Where to stay

1 Amherst Shore Country Inn *p286*
2 Azelia Farmhouse B&B *p308*
3 Blue Tin Roof B&B *p309*
4 Pictou Lodge Beach Resort *p300*
5 Smith Rock Chalets *p300*
6 Stuart House by the Bay B&B *p286*
7 Waterview Rooms *p300*

✖ Where to eat and drink

Amherst Shore Country Inn
  (see 1) *p287*
Pictou Lodge Beach Resort (see 4) *p301*
8 Riverside *p287*

AMHERST AND AROUND

On higher ground than the surrounding marshland and overlooking the Bay of Fundy, Amherst (population: 9,700) is the land gateway between Nova Scotia and all points west, and the largest town in Cumberland County. The historic downtown – with many magnificent well-preserved sandstone buildings and beautiful old homes on Victoria Street East – is relaxing and pleasing on the eye. Large, colourful murals bring the community's heritage to life, and more continue to be added. One of the most impressive is the **Signature Mural** on the corner of Havelock Street and Victoria Street East, depicting the downtown area during a big parade in 1910.

Sadly, you've missed the chance to shop at a real old-fashioned department store: Dayle's (which opened in 1906 as 'The Two Barkers') closed its doors in 2016.

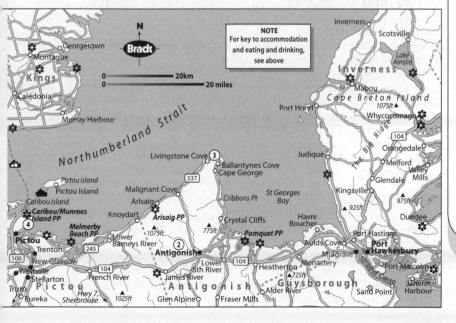

In 1916, socialist Leon Trotsky was deported to the USA. The following year, when revolution overthrew Tsar Nicholas II, the door was open for him to return to Russia, and he departed New York on the SS *Kristianiafjord*. The ship docked in Halifax, where Canadian and British naval personnel arrested Trotsky, and took his wife and young sons into custody. After a short time at the Citadel in Halifax, Trotsky was transferred to an internment camp in Amherst, which contained around 800 German prisoners, many of them sailors from submarines, where he stayed for almost a month. He aired his political views to the inmates at every opportunity, and it is said that when he left, it was to the sound of the international Socialism anthem *Internationale* being sung by cheering German prisoners. The Trotsky family left Nova Scotia from Halifax a few days later, *en route* to Copenhagen.

HISTORY The town of Amherst was founded in 1764 near the site of a British fort destroyed in 1755. It was named after General Jeffrey Amherst, one of the leaders in the victory over the French at Louisbourg in 1758. Many of the early settlers originated in Yorkshire, England.

Centrally located on the only land route between Nova Scotia and the 'mainland', Amherst prospered between the mid 1800s and the early 20th century. The town became renowned for its diverse and active economy, including mining and manufacturing, and was labelled 'Busy Amherst'. Textiles, footwear and even pianos were just some of the items produced here, and in 1908, no other town in the Maritimes had a higher industrial manufacturing output. It was during this period that many of the town's largest and most impressive buildings and homes – many of which still stand – were built.

GETTING THERE AND AROUND Amherst is just off Highway 104 (TCH), via exits 2–4, and therefore very convenient to reach **by car**. It is 4km/2 miles from the New Brunswick border, 117km/73 miles from Truro, 207km/129 miles from Halifax, 183km/114 miles from Pictou and 231km/144 miles from Antigonish. Amherst is on the **Maritime Bus** coach (page 57) line between Moncton (New Brunswick) and Halifax; there is also a service to Charlottetown, Prince Edward Island. Buses stop at the Esso 'gas station' at the junction of Victoria Street West and Highway 104, 2km from downtown. Amherst is also accessible **by train**, being on the VIA Rail line (page 46) between Montreal and Halifax. Three days a week, one train a day in each direction stops *en route* at Amherst's impressive century-old sandstone station at Station Street. The journey to or from Halifax takes around 3 hours 10 minutes, and just under 19 hours to or from Montreal. **Taxis** are available from **Amherst Taxi** (📞 *902 667 8690*).

 WHERE TO STAY Rather than overnight in Amherst, some people prefer to stay in Lorneville on the Northumberland Strait shore (the region is known locally as the 'Amherst shore area'), where you can also camp at the Amherst Shore Provincial Park (page 288).

Amherst *Map, opposite*
📱 **Apothic Inn** (3 rooms) 169 Victoria St East; 📞 902 661 8654; www.apothicinn.ca. Beautiful,

comfortable, newly renovated old (c1870) house furnished with antiques. 2 nice ground-floor rooms, 1 (perhaps even nicer) upstairs.

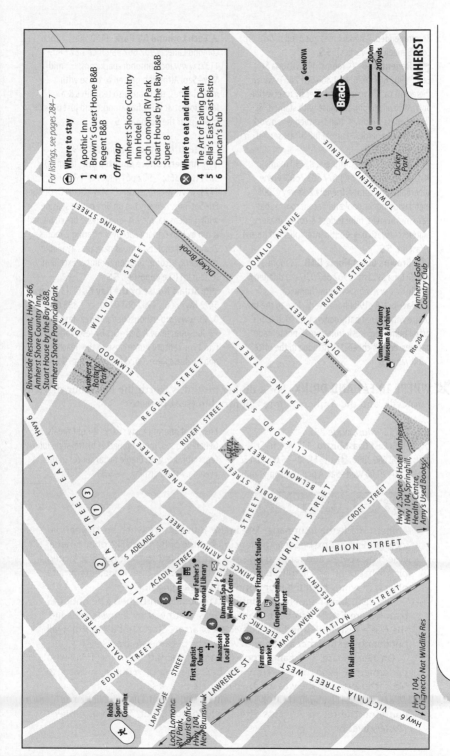

AMHERST

Bradt

N

0   200m
0   200yds

For listings, see pages 284–7

Where to stay
1 Apothic Inn
2 Brown's Guest Home B&B
3 Regent B&B

Off map
Amherst Shore Country
   Inn Hotel
Loch Lomond RV Park
Stuart House by the Bay B&B
Super 8

Where to eat and drink
4 The Art of Eating Deli
5 Bella's East Coast Bistro
6 Duncan's Pub

Dickey Park

TOWNSHEND AVENUE

• GeoNOVA

SPRING STREET

WILLOW STREET

DONALD AVENUE

Dickey Brook

Riverside Restaurant, Hwy 366,
Amherst Shore Country Inn,
Stuart House by the Bay B&B,
Amherst Shore Provincial Park

Hwy 6

ELMWOOD DRIVE

Amherst
Rotary
Park

REGENT STREET

RUPERT STREET

SPRING STREET

RUPERT STREET

DICKEY STREET

Cumberland County
Museum & Archives

Amherst Golf &
Country Club

Rte 204

AGNEW STREET

CLIFFORD STREET

City
Park

BELMONT STREET

ROBIE STREET

CROFT STREET

Hwy 2, Super 8 Hotel Amherst,
Hwy 104, Springhill,
Health Centre,
Amy's Used Books

VICTORIA STREET EAST

3
1

2

ADELAIDE ST

ACADIA STREET

ARTHUR STREET

CHURCH STREET

ALBION STREET

DALE STREET

EDDY STREET

5 Town hall

Four Father's
Memorial Library

Damaris Spa &
Wellness Centre

4

Manasseh
Local Food

First Baptist
Church

6

Farmers'
market

PRINCE STREET

HAVELOCK ST

ELECTRIC ST

Deanne Fitzpatrick studio

Cineplex Cinemas
Amherst

CRESCENT AV

MAPLE AVENUE

STATION STREET

Robb Sport
Complex

Loch Lomond
RV Park,
Tourist office,
Hwy 104,
New Brunswick

LAPLANCHE STREET

LAWRENCE ST

VIA Rail station

Hwy 6,
Hwy 104,
Chignecto Nat Wildlife Res

VICTORIA STREET WEST

Recommended. Rate includes good full b/fast (eg: eggs Benedict or waffles). **$$**

🏠 **Regent B&B** (4 rooms) 175 Victoria St East; ☎ 902 667 7676; **tf** 1 866 661 2861; www.theregent.ca; ⊕ year-round (Dec by reservation only). A lovely Georgian house with stained- & leaded-glass windows, hand-carved woodwork & sun deck in garden. Formal full b/fast served on fine china inc. **$$**

🏠 **Super 8 Hotel** Amherst 8 (50 rooms) 40 Lord Amherst Dr; **tf** 1 877 503 7666; www.super8amherst.com. A friendly 2-storey c2005 motel with indoor pool and decent rooms that have microwaves, mini fridges & coffee makers. Motorcycle wash bay. Continental (plus hot items) b/fast inc. **$$**

🏠 **Brown's Guest Home B&B** (3 rooms) 158 Victoria St East; ☎ 902 667 9769; **e** dnallen@eastlink.ca; www.brownsguesthome.ca; ⊕ May–Oct. A c1904 house very close to the town centre with shared bathrooms. A 'no fried foods' b/fast buffet (eg: fresh fruit, cereal, homemade pastries, eggs & cheese) is included in the price. Good value. **$**

🏕 **Loch Lomond RV Park** (150 sites) 1 Loch Lomond Lane; ☎ 902 667 3890; **tf** 1 877 809 1137; www.lochlomondrvpark.com; ⊕ mid May–Sep. Although geared to those with motorhomes, there are also tent sites & a laundromat at this 6ha campground just outside town (near the hospital). **$**

Lorneville   *Map, pages 282–3*

🏠 **Amherst Shore Country Inn** (8 units) 5091 Hwy 366; ☎ 902 661 4800; **tf** 1 800 661 2724; www.ascinn.ns.ca; ⊕ May–Oct & Dec–Apr Fri&Sat only. A lovely inn on 8ha by the seaside with gardens, lawns & a long private beach owned & run by Rob & Mary Laceby & offering 2 rooms, 2 suites & 4 chalets. Various packages available combining accommodation & dining. Excellent restaurant (see opposite). **$$**

🏠 **Stuart House by the Bay B&B** (3 rooms) 5472 Hwy 366; ☎ 902 661 0750; **tf** 1 888 661 0750; www.stuarthousebedandbreakfast.com; ⊕ Jun–Aug (May & Sep–Oct by reservation). This late 19th-century home close to the beach is a good-value choice. Good full b/fast inc. **$**

✕ WHERE TO EAT AND DRINK   For a dining treat, it is worth the half-hour drive to Lorneville and the Amherst Shore Country Inn (see opposite).

Amherst   *Map, page 285*

✕ **Bella's East Coast Bistro** 117 Victoria St East; ☎ 902 660 3090; 🅵; ⊕ 11.00–16.00 Mon & Tue, 11.00–20.00 Wed–Sat. A popular, sometimes busy, spot offering tasty snacks & light meals. Generally good, more upmarket bistro-style food (eg: crabcakes with Creole tartar sauce) in the evening. Art on display. **$–$$**

THE AMHERST MYSTERY

Amherst made the front pages late in the 19th century when an 18-year-old local girl, Esther Cox, began experiencing strange poltergeist-like phenomena: little fires, voices, and rapping noises. Doctors called to treat her also noted bizarre happenings: inexplicable movements under the bedclothes, inanimate objects moving about the room, and sudden banging noises.

The disturbing happenings continued unabated, and when a neighbour's barn (where Esther had been working) was destroyed by a mysterious fire, she was arrested, charged and convicted of arson. She spent a month in jail but during her trial met a man with whom she became smitten.

On her release, her fiancé took her to a Mi'kmaq medicine man who performed a type of exorcism on her. The happy couple moved to Massachusetts and she was troubled no more by evil spirits.

In 1888, a best-selling book was written about Esther's experiences. Her house on the town's Princess Street is long gone, but *The Great Amherst Mystery* lives on.

✖ The Art of Eating Deli 85 East Victoria St; 902 660 9105; ⨍; ⊕ usually 08.30–17.00 Mon–Fri, plus 11.00–15.00 Sat in summer. Friendly service & well-priced wraps, homemade goodies, daily specials, smoothies, toasties, salads – often with an international twist. $

⊟ Duncan's Pub 49 Victoria St West; 902 660 3111; ⨍; ⊕ kitchen 11.00–22.00 Mon–Sat, noon–22.00 Sun (bar open later Thu–Sun). The town's best pub has a relaxed atmosphere, a good selection of drinks (including cocktails) & live entertainment Thu & Fri evenings. The food's good, too: scallop-stuffed mushroom caps & seafood chowder stand out – & that's just for starters. Save room for the cheesecake or - if you're lucky - *tiramisu*. Book in advance if you're dining. $$

Lorneville and around
Map, pages 282–3

✖ Amherst Shore Country Inn See opposite for contact details; ⊕ *May–Oct for dinner daily; Dec–Apr Fri & Sat only (reservation only), dinner served at 19.30*. The fixed-price menu comprises a soup, a salad, a choice of 2 entrées & choice of 2 desserts. Dinner at the inn has long been considered one of the province's gastronomic treats. It has wonderful sea views. *Set meal CAN$49.50.*

✖ Riverside Restaurant 3636 Hwy 366, Tidnish Bridge; 902 661 2521; ⊕ end May–early Sep 11.00–19.00 Wed–Fri, 09.00–19.15 Sat & Sun. Good diner-style fare: fish & chips, pan-fried haddock, club sandwiches, etc. 24km from Amherst *en route* to Lorneville. $–$$

ENTERTAINMENT AND FESTIVALS Whilst not nearly on the scale of Digby's Wharf Rat Rally (page 208), the three-day **Bordertown Biker Bash** (*www. bordertownbikerbash.ca*) is hoping to become an alliterative July biker calendar fixture. In October, the **Nova Scotia Fibre Arts Festival** (*www.fibreartsfestival.com*) is a five-day event celebrating rug hooking, knitting, quilting, sewing and more. The multi-screen cinema – here the Cineplex Cinemas Amherst – is located on Church St (902 667 3456; *www.cineplex.com*).

SHOPPING For a huge selection of books – more than 500,000, including many rare and out-of-print editions – with a particularly good maritime history section, stop by **Amy's Used Books** (*51 South Albion St;* 902 667 7927; ⊕ 10.00–18.00 *Mon–Thu,* 10.00–21.00 *Fri,* 10.00–17.00 *Sat*). The provincial government's only 'bricks and mortar' map shop is in Amherst: to reach **GeoNOVA** (*160 Willow St;* 902 667 7231, ☏ 1 800 798 0706; *geonova.novascotia.ca;* ⊕ *year-round 08.30– 16.00 Mon–Fri*) take Townshend Avenue from Highway 204. Nourishment-wise, **Manasseh Local Food** (*85 East Victoria St;* 902 660 3663; *www.manasseh.ca;* ⊕ *08.30–20.00 Mon–Fri, 09.00–17.00 Sat, noon–17.00 Sun*) offers a range of local and organic products, and the local **farmers' market** (*Maple Av & Electric St;* ⊕ *May–Dec 10.00–14.00 Fri*) also offers a variety of fresh produce.

OTHER PRACTICALITIES In the main, the many practicalities (services, department stores, supermarkets and shopping malls) are out of the centre along uninspiring South Albion Street.

$ CIBC 32 Church St; 902 667 3376; ⊕ 10.00– 17.00 Mon–Fri

$ Royal Bank 103 Victoria St East; 902 667 7275; ⊕ 09.30–17.00 Mon–Fri

✚ Cumberland Regional Health Care Centre 19428 Hwy 2, 902 667 3361. Just outside town in Upper Nappan.

✉ Post office 38 Havelock St; ⊕ 08.30–17.00 Mon–Fri

ℹ Tourist information Provincial Welcome Centre; Exit 1, Hwy 104 (TCH); 902 667 8429; ⊕ mid Oct–Apr 09.00–16.30 daily; May–mid Oct 08.30–17.00 daily (or later, eg: 21.00 in Jul–Aug)

Four Fathers Memorial Library 21 Acadia St; 902 667 2549, ⊕ 10.00–17.00 Mon, Fri & Sat, 10.00–20.00 Tue–Thu

WHAT TO SEE AND DO Those interested in rug hooking shouldn't miss the **Deanne Fitzpatrick Studio** (*33 Church St*; ✆ *902 667 0560*; ℡ *1 800 328 7756*; *www.hookingrugs.com*; ⏲ *09.00–17.00 Mon–Sat*) – Deanne may well be the best contemporary exponent of the genre in the province.

South of Amherst's main historic district, the **Cumberland County Museum and Archives** (*150 Church St*; ✆ *902 667 2561*; *www.cumberlandcountymuseum.com*; ⏲ *Feb–mid Dec 09.00–17.00 Tue–Fri, noon–17.00 Sat; admission CAN$3*) is housed in the c1838 Grove Cottage, home of Father of Confederation, Robert B Dickey (box, page 21). See articles and documents relating to Trotsky's time in Amherst (box, page 284), a player piano, a wonderful Victorian c1870 staircase and art gallery, plus beautiful gardens. It also has a well-stocked research library and archives.

For some relaxation, the AVEDA **Damaris Spa and Wellness Centre** (*16 Church St*; ✆ *902 660 3030*; *www.damarisspa.com*) offers various feel-good treatments, and you can feed your soul at the red sandstone **First Baptist Church** (*66 Victoria St East*; ✆ *902 667 2001*; ⏲ *09.00–16.00 daily*), built in Queen Anne Revival style in 1846.

AROUND AMHERST Spend a night at the woodland campground in **Amherst Shore Provincial Park** (*42 sites; Hwy 366; parks.novascotia.ca/content/amherst-shore*; ⏲ *mid Jun–early Oct*; **$**), close to a lovely beach (box, opposite) or go green at **Amherst Golf and Country Club** (*John Black Rd*; ✆ *902 667 1911; www.amherstgolfclub.com*; ⏲ *mid May–late Oct; green fees CAN$56*), a 6,347yd course to the east of town, with lush fairways, fast greens, and, more often than not, strong winds to contend with.

Chignecto National Wildlife Reserve (*Southampton Rd*; ⏲ *year-round 24hrs; admission free*) This 1,670ha reserve encompasses the Amherst Point Migratory Bird Sanctuary and is best known for its variety of waterfowl, both breeding and migratory; the wetlands are among the best waterfowl-breeding grounds in the

---

TRAINS AND BOATS

Ships travelling between the Gulf of St Lawrence and New England had to make a long and arduous journey around Nova Scotia. To save well over 1,000km of sailing, the construction of a canal across the 27km Isthmus of Chignecto (which separates the Northumberland Strait from the Bay of Fundy) had long been suggested. In 1881, Henry Ketchum, a Scottish-born engineer, proposed the Chignecto Marine Transport Railway. His plan was for hydraulic lifts to be built to raise ships onto 'cradles' which would then be pulled by locomotives along a special railway track. The line was to run between Fort Lawrence on the Bay of Fundy coast and Tidnish Dock on the Northumberland Strait. After years of negotiations and feasibility studies, Canada's federal government agreed to subsidise the railway's construction in 1888 – subject to the railway's completion within an agreed timescale.

The timescale was too tight, especially considering the marshy nature of much of the land, and in 1892, when the line wasn't completed by the deadline agreed, the government withdrew its financial support.

At Tidnish Dock Provincial Park (*Hwy 366*) a few remains can still be seen, such as the railbed, a stone culvert over the Tidnish River, and remnants of the dock. The park, 25km from Amherst, has interpretive panels and a short walking trail alongside the old rail track.

Along Highway 366, three provincial parks – Amherst Shore, Northport Beach and Heather Beach – offer beach access and more. The beaches are visually striking, with lush green vegetation contrasting with both the red sandstone cliffs (over 10m high in many places) and the blue of the sea. At low tide, the tidal flats often extend well over 1km. The park at Amherst Shore, 36km from Amherst and 27km from Pugwash, has a campground (page 288) and walking trails; at Northport Beach, 42km from Amherst and 21km from Pugwash, sandbars keep the sea shallow and the water even warmer; whilst Heather Beach, 50km from Amherst and 14km from Pugwash, is usually the busiest of the three.

province. Some 8km of trails wind through a diverse landscape of woodlands, fields, ponds and marshes, offering several bird-viewing sites. To get there follow Victoria Street West to the southwest, cross Highway 104, then continue for 3km.

Oxford The Oxford region produces over half of the country's total blueberry harvest each year, earning the town the title of 'Wild Blueberry Capital of Canada' – approach from Highway 104 and you'll be greeted by a giant smiling blueberry. The town is also a centre for products made from the sap of the region's thousands of maple trees. Oxford's rivers are popular with anglers trying for salmon and trout, and for those with canoes. The surrounding forests are home to abundant wildlife – this attracts hunters in the autumn, so wear something bright if you're out leaf-peeping.

In town, the **Capitol Theatre** (*5220 Main St;* ☎ *902 447 2068; www.town.oxford. ns.ca*) is a c1923 Art Deco-style 163-seat theatre, which hosts films, music jam sessions, etc. The **Cumberland County Exhibition and Wild Blueberry Harvest Festival** (*cumberlandcountyexhibition.canadianwebs.com*) is a six-day agricultural festival held at the end of August/early September, which includes dances, concerts, kids' events and craft displays.

Situated 1.5km off Highway 104, Exit 6, Oxford is easy to get to **by car**. If you're approaching from Highway 6, take Highway 301 south for 16km/10 miles from Port Howe. The road follows the wooded banks of the River Philip and passes through verdant farmland for 16km/10 miles to Oxford. To return to Highway 6, cross the river and follow Highway 321 north. This circuit is beautiful when the autumn colours are blazing. Oxford is also on the **Maritime Bus** coach line between Amherst and Halifax (page 57).

If you want to stay over, the **Parkview Family Restaurant and Inn** (*4670 Main St;* ☎ *902 447 2258;* ☉ *07.00–19.30 Mon–Fri, 08.00–19.30 Sat & Sun;* $) is an old-fashioned motel with restaurant ($) offering functional rooms and dishing up generous portions of diner food, such as liver and onions or fish and chips. Other practicalities in town include a tourist information centre (*105 Lower Main St;* ☎ *902 447 2908; www.town.oxford.ns.ca;* ☉ *May–Jun & Sep–Oct 09.00–16.30 Mon–Fri; Jul–Aug 09.00–16.30 daily*) housed in a former bank, and a post office (*5152 Main St;* ☉ *08.00–17.15 Mon–Fri, 08.00–noon Sat*).

ALONG HIGHWAY 6 TO PICTOU

PUGWASH This quaint community is located on a pretty harbour at the mouth of the Pugwash River. Across the river from downtown, Pugwash's **salt mine** isn't easy to miss – each year, the mine produces over one million tonnes of salt. No tours are offered, but you can watch vast quantities of sodium chloride being loaded on to cargo ships. Whilst this operation spoils an otherwise idyllic riverside, it brings a much-needed boost to the local economy.

Scottish heritage is strong here, and street signs are in both Gaelic and English. Durham Street, part of Highway 311, is the main street: the waterfront walkway in Eaton Park makes for a pleasant wander. Over the 1 July Canada Day holiday, Pugwash hosts the **Gathering of the Clans Highland Festival**, with Highland games, traditional music and dancing. There is also a Saturday **farmers' market** (*10222 Durham St; ⊕ May–Oct 08.30–13.00 Sat*), and **Seagull Pewter** (*9926 Durham St; ✆ 902 243 3850; tf 1 888 955 5551; www.seagullpewter.com; ⊕ May–Dec 10.00–17.00 Mon–Sat, noon–17.00 Sun; Jan–Apr 10.00–17.00 Thu–Sat*) is a long-established operation creating, designing and handcrafting pewter. Tours are offered in season.

Just 4km north of town, the **Gulf Shore Provincial Park** (below) has picnic areas and a nice red sand beach. A very scenic 6,160yd links course, **Northumberland Links** (*1776 Gulf Shore Rd; ✆ 902 243 2808; tf 1 800 882 9661; www.northumberlandlinks.com; ⊕ approx late Jun–mid Oct; green fees CAN$75*) is 9km from Pugwash.

Pugwash is on Highway 6, 50km/31 miles east of Amherst and 37km/23 miles west of Tatamagouche, convenient **by car**.

🏠 Where to stay, eat and drink

🏠 **Hillcrest View Inn** (6 rooms) 11054 Hwy 6; ✆ 902 243 2727; www.hillcrestview.ca. Standard traditional roadside motel. **$$**

🏠 **Inn the Elms** (4 rooms) 10340 Durham St; ✆ 902 243 2885; www.inntheelms.com. Furnished with antiques, this lovely old house has 3 rooms with en-suite bathroom, & 1 with a shared bathroom. The 30-seat restaurant (⊕ *usually year-round 11.00–14.00 Wed & Thu, 11.00–14.00 & 17.00–20.00 Fri, 09.00–14.00 Sun; $–$$*) offers nicely presented, tasty, good-value food. Reservations recommended. Rate includes full b/fast. **$**

⚐ **Gulf Shore Provincial Park** (50 sites) 2367 Gulf Shore Rd; ✆ 902 243 2389; www.

gulfshorecampingpark.com; ⊕ mid Jun–mid Sep. In the provincial park. A grassy, open campground on the seafront. **$**

✕ **Sandpiper Restaurant** 8244 Hwy 6, Port Philip; ✆ 902 243 2859; www.sandpiperrestaurant.ca; ⊕ Apr–Nov 11.00–19.00 daily (summer til 20.00). A licensed, good-value place, approx 8km west of Pugwash, specialising in seafood & 'East Coast home-style' cooking. **$–$$**

✕ **Sheryl's Bakery & Café** 10480 Durham St; ✆ 902 243 2156; f; ⊕ summer 07.00–16.30 Mon–Fri, 07.00–15.00 Sat; winter same but closed Mon. Tasty bread, baked goods, soups & salads. Renowned for its cinnamon rolls. **$**

CAPTAIN PUGWASH

The name 'Pugwash' comes from the Mi'kmaq word 'pagweak', meaning 'deep water'. Incidentally, this Pugwash did not provide the inspiration for the surname of one of the UK's favourite cartoon characters. The late John Ryan created Captain Horatio Pugwash in 1950 when he was an art teacher in Middlesex, England. Seven years later, he was surprised to hear that a gathering of great minds (box, opposite) was being held in a previously virtually unknown Nova Scotia town which happened to his captain's name.

THE BRAIN GAME

In 1955, Albert Einstein called for a conference to discuss the dangers of a nuclear war. Pugwash-born millionaire, Cyrus Eaton, offered to sponsor the event in town. Part of his sales pitch was that the beauty of the Pugwash area would produce clarity of thought. And so in 1957, 13 nuclear scientists, including three from the Soviet Union, met on the Pugwash foreshore at Eaton's large but otherwise unremarkable residence (which became known as the Thinkers' Lodge).

It was the first of many such gatherings, now known as the Pugwash Conferences on Science and World Affairs (*www.pugwash.org*), which take place annually or biennially in some of the world's greatest metropolises, London, Washington, Rome, Tokyo – and, as recently as 2003 – Pugwash.

Although the lodge (*249 Water St; thinkerslodge.org;* ⊕ *Jun–Aug 10.00– 17.00 Tue–Sun or by appointment, guided tours available*) was designated a National Historic Site (NHS) in 2008, unlike most such sites is not under Parks Canada's jurisdiction: the lodge is owned and managed instead by the Pugwash Parks Commission.

Other practicalities

$ Scotiabank Water St; ☎ 902 243 2541; ⊕ 10.00–17.00 Mon–Fri
✉ Post office 10154 Durham St; ⊕ 08.00– 17.00 Mon–Fri

Pugwash Library 10222 Durham St; ☎ 902 243 3331; ⊕ hours vary: phone or check website

WALLACE For almost two centuries, this community on the shore of beautiful Wallace Bay has been renowned for its sandstone, which exists as a result of geological activity 300 million years ago. The first quarry opened in 1811, and several others followed. Wallace sandstone was used in the construction of many important buildings both in and outside Nova Scotia: these include the Nova Scotia Legislature in Halifax, the Peace Tower of the Canadian Parliament buildings in Ottawa and the Montreal Stock Exchange.

The stone is still quarried here, but this picturesque seaside village now depends primarily on fishing, farming and lumbering for its livelihood. The bay's salt marshes and tidal inlets attract a whole range of birdlife, and Wallace's public wharf is a popular spot from which to watch the sun rise and set. Accessible **by car**, the town is located on highways 6 and 307, 19km/12 miles from Tatamagouche and 17km/11 miles from Pugwash.

Where to stay, eat and drink

🏠 Fox Harb'r Golf Resort & Spa (72 suites) 1337 Fox Harbour Rd; ☎ 902 257 1801; **tf** 1 866 257 1801; www.foxharbr.com; ⊕ May–Oct. Approx 9km from Wallace, each of the 12 modern 'guesthouses' contains 6 deluxe suites. The resort has its own marina & private airstrip, & incorporates a private gated community, full facility spa & wellness centre, golf academy & seaside tennis courts. Other activities include clay-pigeon shooting & sea kayaking. Formal dining in the Cape Cliff Dining Room (**$$$$**), or more casual at The Willard **$$–$$$**. Golfing guests

STAR FROM WALLACE

One of the world's greatest astronomers, Simon Newcomb (1835–1909) was born (and grew up) in Wallace.

can take a swing at the fabulous Graham Cooke-designed private 7,253yd par-72 course. **$$$$**

🏠 **Jubilee Cottage Inn** (3 rooms) 13769 Hwy 6; ☎ 902 257 2432; **tf** 1 800 481 9915; jubileecottage.ca. Comfortable inn in a tastefully restored c1912 home with several period features. Set on 1.2ha on Wallace Bay – kayaks available for guest use. The Qi Sera Restaurant (🕐 *10.30–14.00 Sun brunch, dinner 18.30–21.30 daily; reservations required; 4-course dinner CAN$51*) offers a good set-menu Sun brunch & an innovative themed set-menu dinner (which might include such things as butternut & coconut soup, & pan-seared maple trout with turnip-apple compote): first to book chooses that evening's culinary theme (which could be eg: Caribbean, or south east Asian). Local organic ingredients used where possible. You can bring your own wine (corkage CAN$5 per bottle). Gourmet b/fast inc. **$$**

▲ **D&D Bayview Campground** (15 sites) 3323 South Shore Rd, Malagash Centre; ☎ 902 257 2209; 🕐 mid May–mid Oct. Delightful views over Tatamagouche Bay from the open campsites: 6km off Hwy 6. Canteen (take-out). **$**

Festivals In May, the **Dandelion Festival** (*www.wallacebythesea.ca/ListEvents.php*) includes crafts stalls, yard sales, community supper and more. Nearby Malagash's Jost Vineyards (see below) play host to a couple of festivals: the **Summer Festival** in July, a Saturday afternoon of food, music and winery tours; a celebration of all things blueberry during the **Malagash Blueberry Festival**; and the unusual **Jost Vineyards Grape Stomp** in September, where teams of four stomp grapes for charity. Also in August, spend a Saturday afternoon enjoying music, food and displays of work by local artists at the **Art & Jazz Festival**.

Shopping and other practicalities At **Collector Canes** (*659 Ferry Rd;* ☎ *902 257 2817;* **e** *zperry@ns.sympatico.ca;* 🕐 *by appointment*), Doug and Zella Perry handcarve each cane from Nova Scotia hardwoods. Walking sticks, hiking sticks and shepherd's crooks can be customised. The post office is found just south of town on Highway 307 (*3872 Hwy 307;* 🕐 *08.00–17.00 Mon–Fri*).

What to see and do The 585ha **Wallace Bay National Wildlife Area** (*Aboiteau Rd;* 🕐 *year-round 24hrs; admission free*) is a reserve just west of Wallace, encompassing a large marsh and small forest at the head of Wallace Bay. Although primarily of interest to birdwatchers – this is an important migration and breeding habitat for waterfowl – a 4km loop trail along a raised dyke makes a pleasant and easy wander. Housed in the restored c1840 home of a local shipbuilder, the **Wallace and Area Museum** (*13440 Hwy 6;* ☎ *902 257 2191; www.wallaceandareamuseum.com;* 🕐 *Jun–Sep 09.00–17.00 Mon–Sat, 13.00–16.00 Sun; May 09.00–17.00 Mon–Fri; Oct 09.00–16.00 Mon–Fri; off-season 10.00–14.00 Mon & Thu; admission free*) offers local history and changing themed displays, plsu 4km of walking trails on the museum grounds.

Around Wallace

Malagash Peninsula Wallace is a good base for a visit to the **Malagash Peninsula**, where lush green farmlands roll down to the red sandy shore. Three sites are well worth a visit. **Bay Enterprises** (*2642 Malagash Rd;* ☎ *902 257 2690; bayent.wix.com/ shellfish*) run a boat tour (for up to four people) to learn about the oyster production process. The opportunity to dig up your own quahogs (hard clams) is also offered. **Jost Vineyards** (☎ *902 257 2636;* **tf** *1 800 565 4567; devoniancoast.ca;* 🕐 *Mar–Christmas 10.00–17.00 daily (until 18.00 mid Jun–mid Sep); free tours mid Jun–mid Sep noon & 15.00*) was created by the Jost family from Germany's Rhine Valley – the first vines actually came from the agricultural research station at Kentville (page 236). The most common grapes grown are French and German varieties (Marechal Foch, Vidal, Muscat, Baco Noir and L'Acadie). Smaller quantities of other grapes are grown on a more experimental basis, and most harvesting takes place in September and October. Pair the vineyard's produce with tasty fare at its licensed **Seagrape Café** (◷ *11.00–16.00 daily; $$*), or put a picnic together at the Devonian Deli Bar. You can also rent a bike and ride the vineyard's (and surrounding) trails.

Canada's – and the British Commonwealth's – first salt mine operated at the **Malagash Salt Miner's Museum** (*1926 North Shore Rd;* ☏ *902 257 2407;* ◷ *mid Jun–mid Sep 10.00–17.00 Tue–Sat, noon–17.00 Sun; admission CAN$2*) between 1918 and 1959. The salt was particularly pure owing to long slow crystallisation, and despite a large amount of unmined salt, the mine was closed as the harbour here was too shallow for larger shipping. Operations moved to Pugwash (pages 289–91), which has a deeper harbour.

Wentworth If you feel like an inland excursion, the Wentworth Valley is a good choice. Although best known as the largest of the province's few downhill-skiing destinations, Wentworth and the Wentworth Valley are popular year-round with lovers of the outdoors – when the snow has gone, the hilly region is ideal for hiking and biking. In autumn, the high proportion of maple trees contribute to a fine display of colours. If you're here on Canadian Thanksgiving weekend in October, take a ski-lift up a mountain to see the autumn colours in all their glory at the **Fall Colours Festival**.

Ski Wentworth (*14595 Hwy 4;* ☏ *902 548 2089; skiwentworth.ca*) has the highest vertical in the province at 250m and the largest area of downhill skiable terrain in the Maritimes. A quad-chair, T-bar and 'magic carpet' get you to the top of the 20 trails, three of which are open for skiing after dark. There are numerous packages and offers, but a basic one-day lift pass is CAN$42, and learn-to-ski or snowboard schools are offered. There is also a rental shop, cafeteria, and for *pendant-, après-,* and *en place de-ski*, visit **Ducky's Pub & Restaurant** (☏ *902 548 2404;* ◷ *hours vary; $$*) in the main lodge. Snowmobilers can purchase a trail pass to explore more than 170km of groomed trails.

There is a network of over 25km of hiking trails all centred on the Wentworth Hostel and nearby **Wentworth Provincial Park**, which lies about 4km off Highway 4, just past the entrance to Ski Wentworth if you're coming from Truro or Halifax. Tough but not too long – and very rewarding if it is clear – is the 2km **Look-off Trail** from the hostel. In addition, an easy, short (400m return) trail starts 0.5km south of the Wentworth Valley Inn and leads to the picturesque Wentworth Falls.

Easily accessible **by car,** Wentworth is on Highway 4, 24km/15 miles from Exit 7 of Highway 104, 28km/17 miles from Exit 11 of Highway 104 and 22km/14 miles from Wallace (via Hwy 307).

NICE ICE WINE

Grapes are hand-picked before dawn in December or January, when the night-time temperature drops below −8°C. At these temperatures virtually all of the liquid in each grape is frozen, leaving just a tiny amount of intensely flavoured juice. Before the grapes can thaw, they are pressed to release these drops. The resulting juice then undergoes many weeks of fermentation and ageing before the final flavour-packed product emerges. It has to be said that thick, amber, sweet ice wine is not everyone's cup of tea (and isn't cheap).

Where to stay, eat and drink If you're staying at the hostel, you can buy some supplies at **Wentworth Market** (*13415 Hwy 4, Wentworth Centre*) a combined petrol station, convenience store and 'liquor' store. Otherwise, there's **Patsy's Diner** (*13353 Hwy 4, Wentworth Centre;* ☎ *902 548 2237;* 🅕; ⏰ *07.00–21.00 daily;* **$**), perhaps not the greatest diner in the world, but if you're hungry and don't fancy driving any further…

🏠 **HI-Wentworth International Hostel & Lodge** (2 family rooms & 2 dorms) 249 Wentworth Station Rd; ☎ 902 548 2379; e wentworth@hihostels.ca; www.hihostels.ca. A former c1870s' farmhouse with fully equipped kitchen, shared bathrooms, common room & large patio deck. 25km of trails for human-powered activities including hiking, trail running, mountain biking, snow-shoeing & cross-country skiing. Snowshoes & cross-country skis to rent. *Dorm from CAN$30; private room from CAN$50, family room from CAN$55* **$**

TATAMAGOUCHE This pretty community at the confluence of the French and Waugh rivers has become a popular stop for visitors. Its name evolved from the Mi'kmaq '*takamegoochk*', meaning 'meeting of the waters'. Some fine Victorian homes still stand and you'll also find a couple of museums (one housed in the old railway station), and interesting dining and accommodation choices.

The **Trans Canada Trail** offers a great opportunity for hiking or biking along the coast, and the old railway bed passing through the village has been converted to a trail popular with hikers, cyclists and cross-country skiers in winter. You can park on Creamery Road (off Main Street): the trail stretches from Nelson Park over the French River and along the shores of the Waugh River. Explore on foot or rent a 'buggie' (canopied multi-person bike; box, opposite).

Tatamagouche is accessible **by car**, 84km/52 miles from Amherst and 49km/30 miles from Pictou.

🏠 **Where to stay** As well as the options listed, you can also camp at Brule Point's Sunset Watch Family Campground (*Peninsula Point Rd;* ☎ *902 657 0009; www. sunsetwatchfamilycampground.com;* **$**) approximately 15km from Tatamagouche.

🏠 **Balmoral Motel** (18 rooms) 131 Main St; ☎ 902 657 2000; tf 1 888 383 9357; e stay@ balmoralmotel.ca; www.balmoralmotel.ca; ⏰ Apr–Oct. A traditional motel overlooking Tatamagouche Bay comprising 2 sgl-storey buildings. Hot b/fast, Wi-Fi, most phone calls & guest laundry all inc. **$$**

🏠 **Train Station Inn** (10 rooms & suites) 21 Station Rd; ☎ 902 657 3222; tf 1 888 724 5233; www.trainstation.ca; ⏰ mid May–mid-Oct. See box, below, for further information. The licensed restaurant (*reservations recommended; lunch* **$–$$**, *dinner* **$$**) is open daily. Full b/fast available for a surcharge. **$$**

TATAMAGOUCHE CHOO-CHOO

The c1887 railway station was scheduled for demolition in the 1970s but was acquired by an enterprising teenager, Jimmie LeFresne. At first he used it to house a farmers' market, but later purchased seven (1911–78) railway carriages and converted them into comfortable suites. A 1928 dining car became the restaurant (soups, salads, sandwiches at lunch, salmon, pasta and steak for dinner). His ambition created a unique, character-packed fun place to stay and eat (see Train Station Inn, above).

PICNICS, PEDALS, PASTA AND POLLINATION

The **Insect Recovery Project** (*IRP; www.insectrecovery.org*) was established in January 2013 in response to the seeming lack of global concern about the sudden disappearance of common insects. The project uses social media to educate the public about the ecological importance of insects and about their recent precipitous numerical decline worldwide. Based in Tatamagouche (opposite Big Al's and just up from the Train Station Inn), **Remember Adventures** (*365 Main St;* ☎ *902 293 1533; rememberadventures. ca;* ⏰ *08.30–20.00 Wed–Sun*) has been set up to help fund the IRP, and their core business is renting out canopied four-wheel pedal-powered bikes ('buggies') to allow couples or families (each buggie can hold two adults plus a teenager and two small kids) to explore some delightful bayside parts of the Trans Canada Trail (access to which is less than 300m away). Among other things (eg: excellent breakfasts, various pastas and yummy desserts) the on-site Caper Café offers great value picnics (including basket, cutlery and napkins) for buggie renters. Enjoy healthy exercise, bucolic scenery, tasty food – and make an insect smile.

✕ Where to eat and drink In town, the **Caper Café** (box, above) is another recommended eatery: and see also the **Train Station Inn** (opposite).

✕ Big Al's Acadian Restaurant & Lounge 9 Station Rd; ☎ 902 657 3341; www.big-als.ca; ⏰ noon–20.00 Mon–Wed, noon–21.00 Thu–Sat, 11.00–20.00 Sun (kitchen closes at 20.00 Mon–Wed & Sun, at 21.00 Thu–Sat). Good portions of pub-style seafood (eg: breaded scallops). A 'Tata' institution for over a quarter of a century. Licensed. $–$$

✕ Chowder House on Main 265 Main St; ☎ 902 657 2223; ⓕ; ⏰ summer 07.00–21.00 daily; rest of year 08.00–19.00 daily. A family-style restaurant offering usually good seafood (decent chowder), plus burgers, etc. Licensed. $–$$

▱ The Tipperary Bakery & Café & Meeting Waters Coffee Roastery 259 Main St; ☎ 902 657 3388 or 902 890 2091; ⓕ; ⏰ summer 08.00–18.00 daily, check off-season. Not just a rather good café and bakery (the butter tarts are among the stand-outs) but also home to a coffee roastery. $

Festivals In July, the **Lavender Festival** (Seafoam Lavender Farm; contact details on page 297) is a newish two-day aromatic fest celebrating all things lavender – lavender oat cakes, lavender ice cream … you get the picture.

Over the last weekend in September, Tatamagouche also hosts eastern Canada's largest **Oktoberfest** (☎ *902 305 3153; www.nsoktoberfest.ca*), attracting over 3,000 revellers. Think beer garden, dances, polkas and oom-pah music. Food is a mix of Canadian and German, with lobster rolls, sausages and schnitzels. German and local beers are served, and there's a schnapps bar.

Shopping Inside the Tipperary Bakery, **Appleton Chocolates** (☎ *902 548 2323;* tf *1 844 403 2323; appletonchocolates.ca*) is a purveyor of hand-dipped chocolates that are 'a celebration of the flavours of Nova Scotia'. For a different type of handcrafted work, **Sara Bonnyman Pottery** (*326 Maple Av;* ☎ *902 657 3215; www. sarabonnymanpottery.com;* ⏰ *Jul–Aug 10.00–16.00 Mon–Sat; off-season by appointment*) has a range of pottery – including unique Moss scuttles (types of jugs used in shaving) – and hooked rugs. For crafts of the hops kind, the **Tatamagouche Brewing Co** (*235 Main St;* ☎ *902 657 4000; tatabrew.com;* ⏰ *10.00–18.00 Sun–Thu,*

10.00–20.00 *Fri & Sat*), Tata's new (2016) open-concept brewery, is already a hit. There are free sips (tasting flights CAN$2), a tasting room, and you can see the brewing operation in what was previously a butcher's shop.

Other practicalities

$ **Scotiabank** 243 Main St; ✆ 902 657 2440; ⊕ 10.00–17.00 Mon–Fri

✉ **Post office** 236 Main St; ⊕ 08.00–17.00 Mon–Fri, 09.00–13.00 Sat

ℹ **Tourist information** The Fraser Cultural Centre; 362 Main St; ✆ 902 657 3285; ⊕ Jul–mid Sep 10.00–17.00 Mon–Fri, 10.00–16.00 Sat,

noon–16.00 Sun. This c1889 former Canadian Red Cross building also houses an art gallery.

Tatamagouche Branch Library 237 Main St; ✆ 902 657 3064; ⊕ 11.00–17.00 & 18.00–20.00 Tue & Thu, 10.00–14.00 Wed, 13.00–17.00 Fri, 10.00–13.00 Sat

What to see and do There are a number of attractions within the **Creamery Square** complex (*Creamery Rd;* ✆ *902 657 3500; www.creamerysquare.ca*), such as the Saturday-morning **farmers' market** (⊕ *Feb–late Dec*), which is (deservedly) one of the most popular in the region. The **Margaret Fawcett Norrie Heritage Centre** (⊕ *mid May–mid Oct 14.00–17.00 Sun–Fri (Jul–Aug from 10.00), 09.00–16.00 Sat; admission free*) is a former c1925 creamery that now houses a fascinating interactive museum with a varied collection including exhibits on Acadian, Mi'kmaq and European settlement, butter production, and Anna Swan (box, below). You can also see the Brule Fossils, discovered nearby in 1994, and the only example of a 29-million-year-old fossilised Walchia (primitive conifer) forest found in its original growth position. There are also local genealogical and historical archives.

The **Senator's Stage** is an open-air venue with frequent live performances in season (and views over the Waugh River estuary). You may be able to see work on the reconstruction of an 18th-century wooden boat underway in the boatshop. The **Grace Jollymore Joyce Arts Centre** houses the Ice House Art Gallery along with a performing arts theatre. Upcoming events and exhibits are on the Creamery Square website.

Elsewhere, the 23m wooden structure that is now the focus of the **Tatamagouche Grain Elevator Village** (*44 Creamery Rd;* ✆ *902 657 1040; www.tatagrainelevator. com;* ⊕ *Jun–Sep, check for hours; admission free*) was built in 1957 and is said to

BIG SWAN

The third of 13 children of (average-height) Scottish immigrants, Anna Swan was born near Tatamagouche in 1846. She was healthy at birth, but tipped the scales at 8.18kg, and measured 69cm long. By the age of seven she had outgrown her mother. When in her teens, she was offered a position at Barnum's American Museum in New York. She married in 1871 (her husband was well over 2m tall) at London's St-Martin-in-the-Fields Church, after first being introduced to Queen Victoria. The couple had two children: a daughter (stillborn) weighing over 8kg, and a son who – at the time – was the largest newborn ever recorded, at 10.6kg and 71cm tall. Sadly, he died within 24 hours. Anna died of tuberculosis in 1888, aged 41. At her height she was 2.36m tall and weighed 179kg.

Big Al's Restaurant (page 295) has life-size wooden statues of Anna and her husband.

I TAWT I TAW A DINOSAUR

Patrick Keating was walking his dog on a beach near Tatamagouche in summer 2012 when something sticking out of the mud attracted his attention. What he saw turned out to be a sizeable fossilised part of a sail-back reptile, 300 million years old and the only one ever found in Nova Scotia (previously footsteps believed to have been made by this type of creature had been found at nearby Brule). A week later, Keating and his family returned to the beach: his wife found the reptile's head, and his son another portion of the rib cage. The sail-back creature is classified as a reptile, not a dinosaur. The specimen the Keatings found is believed to have been a juvenile, approximately 1m from head to tail. Adult sail-back reptiles are thought to have been four- or five-times larger.

be the only prairie-style grain elevator east of the Canadian province of Manitoba. Attached warehouses are home to gift/arts and crafts shops - (an eatery is planned for 2017) – and the venue hosts a variety of entertainment.

Around Tatamagouche Around 10km from Tatamagouche off Highway 311, the **Balmoral Grist Mill** (*660 Matheson Brook Rd;* ✆ *902 657 3016; balmoralgristmill. novascotia.ca;* ⊕ *Jun–Sep 10.00–17.00 Mon–Sat, 13.00–17.00 Sun; admission CAN$3.90*) is a photogenic three-storey c1874 mill in a delightful riverside setting. Although originally a water mill, electricity now supplies the power. That apart, wheat, oats and barley are still ground using 19th-century methods.

Wander the beautiful lavender fields overlooking the sea at the **Seafoam Lavender Farm** (*3768 Hwy 6, Seafoam;* ✆ *902 657 1094; lavendercanada.com;* ⊕ *Jun–Sep 10.00–18.00 daily*), located 31km from Tatamagouche, 25km from Pictou, then purchase all sorts of lavender goodies from cosmetics to brownies.

The **Sugar Moon Farm** (*Alex MacDonald Rd, Earltown;* ✆ *902 657 3348;* tf *1 866 816 2753; www.sugarmoon.ca;* ⊕ *Sep–Jun 09.00–16.00 Sat & Sun; Jul–Aug 09.00–16.00 daily; admission free*) is a working sugar maple farm just off Highway 311, approximately 35km from Tatamagouche. Learn all about maple syrup production and taste the results. Buttermilk pancakes with lashings of maple syrup are served in the pancake house and maple products are available in the gift shop. It also has accessible hiking trails and snowshoe rentals in winter. The regular Chef's Nights featuring top guest chefs from around the province are very popular.

On Highway 326, 17km from Tatamagouche, see the workings of a c1894 lumber mill at the **Sutherland Steam Mill** (*Hwy 326; Denmark;* ✆ *902 657 3016; sutherlandsteammill.novascotia.ca;* ⊕ *Jun–Oct 10.00–17.00 Mon–Sat, 13.00–17.00 Sun; admission CAN$3.90*), powered by steam generated from a huge boiler. Learn how wagon wheels, windows and architectural trim were manufactured before automated assembly lines, and observe many examples of resourcefulness throughout the mill. Rain barrels on the roof provided fire protection, a copper bathtub was used for soaking shingles, and a recycled cream separator was converted into a band-saw.

Some 21km from Tata along Highway 6 is the community of **River John**: here, if you're lucky (hours are irregular), you can tuck in to relatively authentic southern USA-style barbecue fare (eg: ribs, pulled pork, chicken, brisket) at **Jo Dearings Southern Smoke BBQ and Grill** (*1837 Hwy 6, River John;* ✆ *902 351 2922;* **$$**). When it is open, it has an 'open until we sell out' policy. So be sure to call

7

ahead. Nearby, **Caldera Distilling** (*65 River John Rd;* \ *902 351 2035; caldera.ca;* ☉ *mid-May–mid-Oct*) produces whisky and is named after one of the biggest ships ever built at River John – tours and tastings are offered. Based 8km away at Cape John, **Coastal Spirit Expeditions** (\ *902 351 2283; www.coastalspiritexpeditions. com*), offers half- and full-day guided sea kayaking trips, instruction and rentals.

PICTOU

The harbour town of Pictou (population: 3,400) is one of the largest communities on the Northumberland Shore. Although just 8km from the terminal of the car ferry service (to and from Prince Edward Island), it is largely bypassed by the provincial highway system.

Only in the last 15–20 years has Pictou – derived from the Mi'kmaq name for the area, Piwktook ('exploding gas') – become a popular destination for visitors. The redevelopment of the waterfront, and, in particular, construction of a replica of an 18th-century ship, have been instrumental in putting the town firmly on the tourist map. The principal attractions, main museum, restaurants, and historic accommodations are found on or close to the waterfront, but there are also some lovely old houses in the residential streets further back. Granite was imported from Scotland and used to build several town edifices; you'll see fine examples of Scottish vernacular, New England Colonial, Gothic and Second Empire styles.

The local paper mill, which has been known to waft unpleasant odours over the water, shipbuilding, and one of tyre-manufacturer Michelin's three factories in Nova Scotia are major employers (though tough times at the paper mill have meant many job cuts), and there's lobster fishing.

HISTORY In an effort to boost Nova Scotia's population, in 1773 an agent named John Ross was sent to Scotland to try to attract disgruntled Highlanders (page 18). Ross placed a notice in the *Edinburgh Advertiser*, promising any family prepared to move to Nova Scotia (which he portrayed as a rich paradise with the most fertile of soil) free passage, their own farm land, and one year's provisions. In total, 189 Highlanders, including 71 children under eight, took up the offer.

Ross had chartered an old Dutch cargo ship, the *Hector* (said to be in poor condition), and she set sail from Loch Broom, Ross-Shire, in July 1773. It took the *Hector* 11 weeks to cross the ocean – 18 of the passengers died *en route*, most from smallpox. When she limped in to Brown's Point in Pictou Harbour on 15 September, the land didn't seem to live up to the promises. Those on board were greeted by miles and miles of thick, unbroken forest right down to the shoreline and the nearest settlement several days' travel away. But the industrious new arrivals – 33 families and 25 single men – pulled together, set to work, felled trees and began to build a town on the site of an old Mi'kmaq village.

The almost ubiquitous stands of pine were put to good use, and less than a year after the *Hector*'s arrival, a ship laden with lumber sailed for England. This business boomed, and before too long shipbuilding also became established.

BURNING QUESTION

If you look out across the Northumberland Strait after dark, you might be able to add yourself to the list of those who have seen a three- (some say four-) masted ship ablaze. The spectral burning vessel has also been seen from Prince Edward Island.

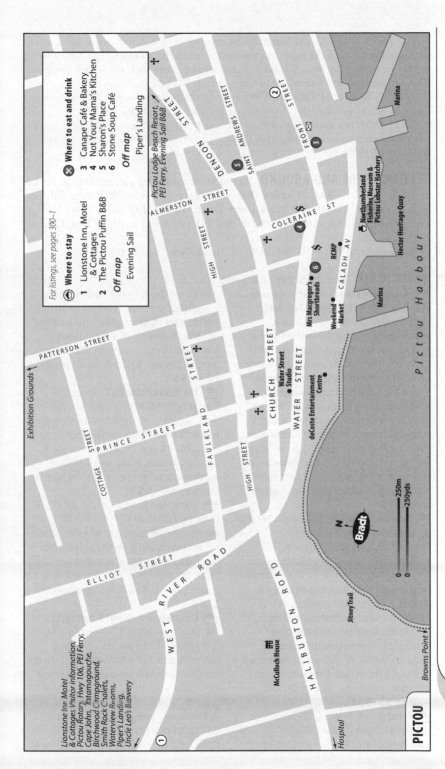

PICTOU

Key map labels:

PATTERSON STREET

COTTAGE STREET

PRINCE STREET

FAULKLAND STREET

HIGH STREET

CHURCH STREET

WATER STREET

ELLIOT STREET

WEST RIVER ROAD

HALIBURTON ROAD

ALMERSTON STREET

HIGH STREET

DENOON STREET

SAINT ANDREWS STREET

FRONT STREET

COLERAINE ST

CALADH AV

Pictou Harbour

Exhibition Grounds

Hospital

Browns Point

Jitney Trail

McCulloch House

deCoste Entertainment Centre

Water Street Studio

Mrs Macgregor's Shortbreads

Weekend Market

RCMP

Northumberland Fisheries Museum & Pictou Lobster Hatchery

Hector Heritage Quay

Marina

Pictou Lodge Beach Resort, PEI Ferry, Evening Sail B&B

Lionstone Inn, Motel & Cottages Visitor information, Pictou Rotary, Hwy 106, PEI Ferry, Cape John, Entamagouche, Birchwood Campground, Smith Rock Chalets, Waterview Rooms, Piper's Landing, Uncle Leo's Brewery

N

Bradt

250m
250yds
0
0

For listings, see pages 300–1

Where to stay
1 Lionstone Inn, Motel & Cottages
2 The Pictou Puffin B&B

Off map
Evening Sail

Where to eat and drink
3 Canape Café & Bakery
4 Not Your Mama's Kitchen
5 Sharon's Place
6 Stone Soup Café

Off map
Piper's Landing

The *Hector*'s voyage marking the beginning of a massive wave of Scottish immigration through the port over the next century, Pictou quickly became known as the 'birthplace of New Scotland'. Many of the Scots then dispersed along the Northumberland Strait shore, or to Cape Breton Island.

In 1817, Thomas McCulloch, a Presbyterian minister who was a great believer in equal access to education, established the Pictou Academy. For many decades it was said that any eastern American university worth its salt would have at least one professor who had graduated at Pictou. The original Pictou Academy was torn down in the 1930s.

GETTING THERE AND AROUND Pictou is accessible **by car**, situated at Exit 3 of Highway 106, 10km/6 miles from the ferry terminus to Prince Edward Island (page 47), 75km/47 miles from Truro, 169km/105 miles from Halifax and 183km/105 miles from Amherst, and 14km/9 miles north of Exit 22 from Highway 104.

For **taxis**, try **Alf's** (✆ *902 485 5025*) or **Dime's** (✆ *902 485 6089*).

 WHERE TO STAY *Map, page 299, unless otherwise stated*

🏠 **Pictou Lodge Beach Resort** [map, pages 282–3] (102 units) 172 Lodge Rd, Braeshore; ✆902 485 4322; **tf** 1 800 495 6343; www. pictoulodge.com; ⊕ mid May–mid Oct. Set in a quiet location overlooking the calm waters of the Northumberland Strait, the lodge's main building was built using logs in the 1920s; for 3 decades this was a Canadian National Railways resort, welcoming royalty & Hollywood stars. There is a wide range of accommodation, from standard & motel-style rooms to 3-bedroom executive chalets. There's a restaurant (see opposite), private beach with loungers, & on-site activities include free use of canoes, kayaks & paddleboats, heated outdoor pool (seasonal) & outdoor games area. Bikes are available. **$$$**

🏠 **Smith Rock Chalets** [map, pages 282–3] (22 units) 310 Fitzpatrick Mountain Rd, Scotsburn; ✆902 485 4799; www. smithrockchalets.com. A lovely hilltop retreat overlooking Pictou County & the Northumberland Strait approx 15mins' drive from Pictou & the PEI ferry. Accommodation comprises 10 1- to 3-bedroom chalets (full kitchens) & 12 rooms (kitchenettes & whirlpool baths) in a new building (drive-up entrances, private decks). Access to scenic hiking /biking trails, heated pool (seasonal) & fitness room with sauna. Nearest restaurants are in Pictou. Continental b/fast available. **$$–$$$**

🏠 **Evening Sail** (6 rooms) 279 Denoon St; ✆902 485 5069; **tf** 1 866 214 2669; www.eveningsail.ca; ⊕ year-round (o/s by

reservation). This delightful, comfortable B&B is a real treat: the 3 suites have private decks, & 2 of the other 3 bedrooms have small balconies (the other bedroom is small but has a large bathroom). Free Wi-Fi. Excellent b/fast inc (eg: pumpkin pancakes, fresh fruit, freshly ground coffee). **$$**

🏠 **The Pictou Puffin B&B** (4 rooms) 90 Front St; ✆902 982 4986; **tf** 1 800 970 1791; thepictoupuffin.com. Alex & Lorie have lovingly restored & decorated this splendid c1855 house with both old & new. 3 rooms have en-suite, 1 a private bathroom, all have king beds (2 can accommodate an extra person). Rate inc full b/fast. Cats on premises. **$$**

🏠 **Waterview Rooms** [map, pages 282–3] (2 rooms) 1338 Shore Rd; ✆902 982-3023; www.waterview-rooms.com. Very nice Austrian-run accommodation in a pretty hamlet. Large new (2010) rooms. 5mins away from nice, sandy beach, less than 10mins from the PEI ferry & approx 15mins (18km) from downtown Pictou. **$–$$**

🏠 **Lionstone Inn, Motel & Cottages** (14 rooms & 14 cottages) 241 West River Rd; ✆902 485 4157; **tf** 1 866 785 4157; www. lionstoneinn.ca. Better than you'd expect for the price, this is a decent low-budget choice. Near Pictou Rotary but within walking distance of town. **$**

🏕 **Birchwood Campground & Cottages** (55 sites & 3 cottages) 2521 Hwy 376, Lyons Brook; ✆902 485 8565; **tf** 1 888 485 8565; www.

birchwoodcampground.ca; ⊕ mid May–Sep. Open & wooded serviced & unserviced sites (plus self-catering cottages) 3.5km from Pictou Rotary. Heated outdoor pool. $

✖ WHERE TO EAT AND DRINK *Map, page 299, unless otherwise stated*

Food fans might also want to enjoy a day with a top chef (box, below).

✖ **Pictou Lodge Beach Resort** [map, pages 282–3] 172 Lodge Rd, Braeshore; ☎ 902 485 4322; **tf** 1 800 495 6343; www.pictoulodge. com; ⊕ mid May–mid Oct for b/fast, lunch & dinner. The resort's Dine Oceanside offers chef-inspired local cuisine best enjoyed with a great sunset view over the Northumberland Strait. The Fireside Lounge has great local craft beers, extensive wine list, live entertainment & pub menu. *Dine Oceanside* $$$, *Fireside Lounge* $$

✖ **Piper's Landing** 2656 Hwy 376, Lyons Brook; ☎ 902 485 1200; www. piperslandingrestaurant.com; ⊕ year-round (weather-dependent) from 17.00 daily by reservation only. Imaginative, modern, country cooking in this elegant restaurant, 8km from downtown Pictou with a magnificent riverside setting. Start perhaps with mushroom caps stuffed with *escargots*, & continue with seafood casserole or strip-loin steak. Last reservations 20.00. $$$

✖ **Not Your Mama's Kitchen** 2 Water St; ☎ 902 484 7950; ▪; ⊕ 17.00–21.00 Tue, 11.30–14.30 & 17.00–21.00 Wed–Sat, 11.30–19.00

Sun. Good new (2015) 'farm-to-table' restaurant using fresh local ingredients to tasty effect. Menu changes frequently but might include smoked haddock chowder or pan-fried flounder with lemon-butter sauce. Licensed & recommended. $$–$$$

✖ **Sharon's Place** 12 Front St; ☎ 902 485 4669; ⊕ 10.00–19.00 Mon–Fri, 09.00–18.00 Sat & Sun. Breakfast, burger and fish & chip diner popular with the locals. The deep fryer dominates but pan-fried options, too. Big portions. $–$$

✖ **Stone Soup Café** 41 Water St; ☎ 902 485 4949 ▪; ⊕ 07.00–15.00 daily (from 08.00 Sun). Not just good soups but imaginative & tasty breakfasts & lunches (eg: wild pacific salmon burger, falafel on pita, Thai chicken wrap). Good coffee & water views. $–$$

☕ **Canape Café & Bakery** 31 Front St; ☎ 902 382 3002; ⊕ 08.00–15.00 Mon–Wed, 08.00–16.00 Thu & Fri. Bakery, yes, but nice salads, sandwiches, soups etc make the little Canape worth seeking out as a Pictou lunch stop. $

OTHER PRACTICALITIES

$ **Royal Bank** 25 Water St; ☎ 902 485 4352; ⊕ 10.00–17.00 Mon–Fri

$ **Scotiabank** 70 Coleraine St; ☎ 902 485 4378; ⊕ 10.00–17.00 Mon–Fri

✚ **Sutherland Harris Memorial Hospital** 222 Haliburton Rd; ☎ 902 485 4324

✉ **Post office** 49 Front St; ⊕ 08.30–17.00 Mon–Fri

ℹ **Tourist information** 350 West River Rd; ☎ 902 485 8540; ⊕ Jun–early Oct 09.30–18.30. Just off the Pictou Rotary, where Hwys 106 & 6 meet.

Pictou Library 40 Water St; ☎ 902 485 5021; ⊕ 10.00–21.00 Tue & Thu, 10.00–17.00 Wed, Fri & Sat

---

LOOK UP THE KILTED CHEF

Foodies with a few dollars to spare may wish to get up close and personal with highly experienced, award-winning Alain Bosse – aka the 'Kilted Chef' (*kiltedchef.ca*). You can sign up for a Pictou-area culinary adventure experience, which includes going with chef to a seafood plant, abattoir or farm to source ingredients before cooking and dining together. Reservations are a must as dates (between May and October) fill fast.

WHAT TO SEE AND DO To most of the hundreds of thousands of Canadians of Scottish descent, the *Hector*'s arrival in Pictou (page 298) was every bit as important as the Pilgrim Fathers' arrival in New England on the *Mayflower* over 150 years earlier. The story of the *Hector* is told in the three-storey interpretive centre, **Hector Heritage Quay** (*33 Caladh Av;* ☏ *902 485 7371; www.shiphector. com;* ⊕ *spring–autumn 10.00–16.00 (or later) daily; guided tours offered; admission CAN$8*), which was designed to resemble an 18th-century Scottish warehouse. Costumed interpreters answer questions or tell stories to a background of bagpipe music. Rigging, blacksmithing and carpentry demonstrations relate to shipbuilding in the 18th century. But the highlight is the chance to explore the replica of the three-masted *Hector*. Go below deck and try to imagine what the voyage to a new life might have been like in the middle of the Atlantic for all those on board. The combination of the absorbing centre and the *Hector* replica – and the story they tell – make this one of Nova Scotia's most important heritage attractions.

If you feel like a wander, the 3km each way **Jitney Trail** starts at the Hector Heritage Quay and follows the abandoned rail line west along the shoreline around Norway Point and under the causeway to Browns Point.

At the c1805 brick and stone **McCulloch House** (*100 Old Haliburton Rd;* ☏ *902 485 4563; museum.gov.ns.ca/mch;* ⊕ *Jun–mid Oct 09.00–17.00 Mon–Fri; admission CAN$5*), built for Thomas McCulloch (page 300), learn how one man's passion launched him on a journey to create public education in the province. Exhibits of his writings give a picture of early 19th-century Pictou life, and also include local newspapers from the period. For some Scottish flavour, pop in to **Mrs Macgregor's Shortbreads** (*59 Water St;* ☏ *902 382 1878; www.mrsmacgregors.com;* ⊕ *year-round 10.00–17.00 Mon–Sat, noon–16.00 Sun*) for some traditional and/or gourmet shortbread – the sticky toffee cake is also scrumptious.

On the waterfront, the Lobster Stock Enhancement Research Facility, an operating lobster hatchery, is probably the part of the three-section **Northumberland Fisheries Museum & Pictou Lobster Hatchery** (*21 Caladh Av;* ☏ *902 485 8925;* ⨏; ⊕ *Jun & Sep 09.00–17.00 Mon–Fri; Jul–Aug 09.00– 17.00 daily; adult CAN$8*) that visitors find most interesting. The main museum has over 2,000 exhibits on the heritage and culture of the fishing and boatbuilding industries along the Northumberland Strait; next door is a replica 1908-style lighthouse with information on the lighthouses of the province and Maritimes.

The **deCoste Entertainment Centre** (*85 Water St;* ☏ *902 485 8848;* tf *1 800 353 5338; www.decostecentre.ca;* ⊕ *Mar–Dec*) is the regional performing arts centre, housed in an excellent modern venue with a calendar of generally high-class events. In July and August on Tuesday–Thursday evenings, the centre hosts informal ceilidhs (page 30) and other entertainment under the 'Festival of Summer Sounds' label.

Craft beer fans should check out **Uncle Leo's Brewery** (*2623 Hwy 376, Lyon's Brook;* ☎ *902 382 2739; www.uncleleosbrewery. ca;* ⊕ *year-round 10.00–18.00 Tue–Sat*). Approximately 2km from Pictou Rotary,

SCOTLAND THE BRAVE

In the 18th century, the Mi'kmaq who lived in the Pictou area had a particularly hostile reputation and were said to be fearless. However, they fled in terror at the sound of bagpipes.

this successful new (2013) craft brewery makes three ales on a weekly basis, plus others seasonally, which you can sample and buy. Offering crafts, fruit and vegetables, other food and much more, the **Weekend Market** (*New Caledonia Curling Club, Waterfront;* ☎ *902 485 6329; www.pictouweekendmarket.com;* ⊕ *late Jun–mid Sep 10.00–17.00 Sat & Sun*) is perfect for a stroll, whilst the **Water Street Studio** (*110 Water St;* ☎ *902 485 8398; waterstreetstudio.weebly.com;* ⊕ *10.00–17.00 Mon–Sat (o/s Thu–Sat only)*) displays and sells a range of predominantly Maritimes-produced crafts in a c1820 former artists' co-operative.

If you're here in July, the **Lobster Carnival** (*www.pictoulobstercarnival.ca*) has music, parades, antique cars, races, a beer garden and many other activities to mark the end of the lobster-fishing season. In August, expect parades, buskers, yacht races and more at **Natal Day**.

AROUND PICTOU From the **Caribou/Munroes Island Provincial Park** entrance (*2119 Three Brooks Rd;* ☎ *902 485 6134; parks.novascotia.ca/content/caribou-munroes-island;* ⊕ *mid Jun–early Oct*), 11km north of the junctions of highways 6, 106 and 376 and 4km east of the Caribou–Wood Islands ferry terminal (page 47), a trail leads for 2km along the Little Caribou Spit to a traffic-free 100ha island. Here you'll find saltwater lagoons, salt marshes, small, secluded barrier beaches and wooded areas, good for birding, swimming and hiking. The park's campground (**$**) offers 95 wooded or open sites on a hillside overlooking the sea.

NEW GLASGOW, TRENTON, WESTVILLE AND STELLARTON

Across the harbour from Pictou the towns of New Glasgow, Trenton, Westville and Stellarton make up 'Industrial Pictou County'. Coal mining has been an integral part of this area's history since the first commercial mine opened in Stellarton in 1807, and since then, industry has continued to dominate. As with most of the world's industrial areas, unspoilt natural beauty is not abundant in these communities. There is one major attraction for the visitor – Atlantic Canada's biggest museum – but otherwise I would recommend sticking to the coastal corridor. New Glasgow (population: 9,550) is the region's largest community.

All listings are in New Glasgow and open year-round unless stated otherwise. However, the **tourist information centre** is in Westville (*Cowan St Rest Area, 2500 Old Truro Rd;* ☎ *902 396 2800;* ⊕ *mid Jun–Aug 09.30–17.30 daily*).

GETTING THERE AND AWAY New Glasgow is convenient to reach **by car**. It is just off Highway 104, exits 24–25, 2km/1.2 miles from Trenton, 4km/2.3 miles from Stellarton, 8km/5 miles from Westville, 22km/14 miles from Pictou, 69km/43 miles from Truro and 165km/103 miles from Halifax. A **taxi** to Pictou will cost

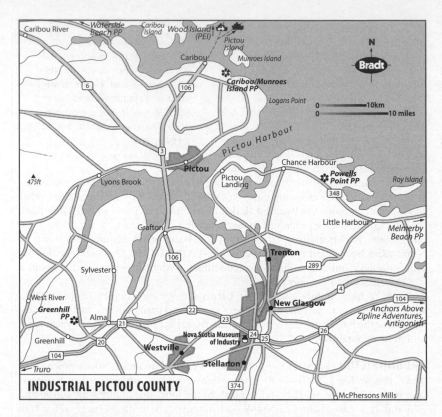

INDUSTRIAL PICTOU COUNTY

approximately CAN$26: try **Central Cabs** (\ *902 755 6074)* or **Metro-Midtown Taxi** (**tf** *1 855 633 5976*). **By bus**, New Glasgow is on the **Maritime Bus** coach line between Halifax and Sydney (page 57).

 WHERE TO STAY

Travelodge Suites New Glasgow
(65 units) 700 Westville Rd; \ 902 928 1333;
tf 1 800 5787878; www.travelodge.ca. An early 1990s 3-storey motel with decent standard rooms & 1-bedroom suites. All rooms have mini fridges; suites also have microwaves. Hot buffet b/fast inc. **$$**

Tara Inn Motel (33 rooms) 917 East River Rd; \ 902 752 8458; **tf** 1 800 565 4312;

www.taramotel.com. 32 (drive-up) rooms & a 2-bedroom suite with kitchenette. Clean, comfortable & good value. Continental b/fast inc. **$**

Ⱥ Trenton Park Campground (43 sites) Park Rd, Trenton; \ 902 752 1019; ⊕ mid Jun–early Sep. Wooded & open serviced sites: pool, minigolf, fishing & laundromat. 4km from New Glasgow. **$**

✗ WHERE TO EAT AND DRINK

✗ Hebel's Restaurant 71 Stellarton Rd;
\ 902 695 5955; www.hebelsrestaurant.ca;
⊕ 17.00–20.30 Tue–Sat. Housed in a mid 19th-century sea captain's house & former inn, Peter Hebel's restaurant attracts discerning foodies in the area with good use of the best local ingredients. Start, perhaps, with almond-breaded baked brie

or half-a-dozen oysters, continue with seafood Creole or braised lamb shank, & round off with the 3-coloured Belgian chocolate mousse. **$$$**

✗ The Bistro 216 Archimedes St; \ 902 752 4988; www.thebistronewglasgow.com;
⊕ 17.00–closing Tue–Sat. Favouring fresh, organic & locally sourced produce, this backstreet

Stellarton hit the national news early in 2016 when the Euphoria B&B was closed down because it had been operating without a permit. It transpired that the B&B – on a leafy suburban street – catered primarily to (what is known as) the BDSM (bondage and discipline, sadism and masochism) market. Whilst many people said that they had no problem with what consenting adults did behind closed doors, some local parents pointed out that they felt uneasy about a neighbourhood business that advertised on websites aimed (for example) at men interested in women who are of legal age but look and act younger. The Town Planner was quoted as saying that having worked with Stellarton for almost 14 years, he couldn't recall any other S&M-related businesses setting up shop. Or B&B.

bistro (work by local artists adorns the walls) has a nice atmosphere, good service, & decent food. $$–$$$

🍺 **The Dock Food Spirits & Ales** 130 George St; ☏ 902 752 0884; ⊕ 11.30–late Mon–Sat (kitchen to 21.00). Friendly well-established Irish pub with good atmosphere & (generally) good food. Rooftop patio in summer. $$

🍴 **The Appleseed Modern Diner** 33 MacGregor Av; ☏ 902 695 7333; www. theappleseed.ca; ⊕ 10.00–20.00 daily. Fun & funky 'modern diner' with great fries & onion rings.

Lots of good choices including (beer-battered) fish & chips, the Appleseed burger, & Thanksgiving On a Bun (roast turkey, apple stuffing, gravy & cranberry mayo). Licensed. $–$$

🍴 **BaKED Food Café** 209 Provost St; ☏ 902 755 3107; 𝐟; ⊕ 08.00–17.00 Tue–Sat. Great licensed bakery/café turning out not just artisan bread but good soups, sandwiches, paninis, coffee & more. $

☕ **Coffee Bean Kitchen** 168 Archimedes St; ☏ 902 755 1919; 𝐟; ⊕ 07.00–16.00 Mon–Fri. This little place (which therefore can be crowded) serves good coffee, fresh baked goods & more. $

ENTERTAINMENT AND FESTIVALS New Glasgow is home to a **cinema** (*612 East River Rd;* ☏ *902 928 0550; www.cineplex.com*), and the **Glasgow Square Theatre** (*155 Glasgow St;* ☏ *902 752 4800;* ☏ *1 800 486 1377; www.glasgowsquare.com*), situated on the river, hosts a varied year-round programme of indoor and outdoor entertainment.

In summer, Westville holds what is said to be the largest **Canada Day celebration** in Atlantic Canada. Although Canada Day is 1 July, this birthday party lasts at least five days, with parades, games, barbecues, community suppers and more, climaxing in a huge firework display. In August in New Glasgow is the **Festival of the Tartans & Highland Games** (*www.festivalofthetartans.ca*), a four-day celebration including a kilted golf tournament, pipe bands, ceilidhs and – you may have guessed – Highland games.

WHAT TO SEE AND DO The huge **Nova Scotia Museum of Industry** (*147 North Foord St, Stellarton;* ☏ *902 755 5425; museumofindustry.novascotia.ca;* ⊕ *Nov–May 09.00–17.00 Mon–Fri; Jun–Oct 09.00–17.00 Mon–Sat, 10.00–17.00 Sun; admission CAN$8.90*) is amongst the biggest in Atlantic Canada and sits just off Exit 24 off Highway 104. It is far more interesting than the name might suggest: there are tens of thousands of artefacts that take you from the Industrial Revolution to 21st-century hi-tech. Highlights include the *Samson* (Canada's oldest steam locomotive), the *Victorian* (the first petrol-powered car built in the Maritimes), a display of much-prized Trenton glass, and there's an abundance of interactive stuff to keep kids happy.

The c1880 Victorian **Carmichael-Stewart House Museum** (*86 Temperance St, New Glasgow;* ☏ *902 752 5583;* ⊕ *Jun–early Sep 09.30–16.30 Mon–Sat; admission free*)

The dangers of life underground are well known to miners and their families. On 9 May 1992, after only five months in operation, the Westray Mine in nearby Plymouth was destroyed by a huge gas explosion. All 26 men working underground at the time were killed, the youngest just 22. Fifteen bodies were recovered, but 11 remain underground. A memorial – 26 rays of light emitting from a miner's lamp, each bearing the name and age of one of the miners lost – was erected a year later at what is now the Westray Miners Memorial Park. Interpretive panels give details of the tragedy. The memorial is at the east end of Park Street, New Glasgow.

also takes you back in time, with original hardwood floors and beautiful stained-glass windows, and was formerly owned by the Carmichael family, prominent New Glasgow shipbuilders. There are lovely grounds (including a Victorian garden). In addition to local history – particularly relating to shipbuilding – the collection includes old Trenton glassware and clothing from the late 1800s to the 1920s, including wedding gowns worn by some of New Glasgow's high society. After all the time spent in the past, jump back to the present at the **New Glasgow Farmers Market** (*261 Glasgow St;* \ *902 301 9087; ngfarmmarket.com;* ⊕ *09.00–13.00 Sat*), a good, generally lively market.

AROUND NEW GLASGOW Nova Scotia's first zipline park, **Anchors Above Zipline Adventures** (*464 McGrath Mountain Rd, French River;* \ *902 922 3265; www.anchorsabovezipline.ca;* ⊕ *10.00–17.00 daily; from CAN$30*) boasts two lines: the first is 335m long and 73m above the ground and the second is 275m long and 58m with a drop equivalent to a ten-storey building. There's a 15-minute hike to the first line and you'll need to sign a waiver. It is best to call a day (or more) in advance to book, especially off-season. The park is 23km (*15–20 minutes*) from New Glasgow: turn off Highway 104 at Exit 27, go through French River, and follow the signs.

Called 'The Merb', **Melmerby Beach Provincial Park** (*Little Harbour Rd;* ⊕ *late May–early Oct*) near Little Harbour, 14km from Highway 104, Exit 27A, 16km northeast of Exit 25 from Highway 104, is a popular 1.7km beach on an isthmus. The left side (as you first walk along the beach) is more sheltered, the right is open ocean. In late summer, the water can be quite warm. Changing rooms are available.

ANTIGONISH AND AROUND

With a concentration of supermarkets, shopping malls, fast-food outlets, petrol stations and light industry along Highway 104 and (to a lesser degree) along the approaches to the town centre from exits 31–34, Antigonish (population: 4,000) is yet another town where you could be put off if approaching from this direction. However, it is worth persevering to the downtown area of this bustling university town, where you'll find a range of good places to stay and eat, and some fine architecture. The Greek Revival-style c1855 **County Court House** (*168 Main St*), for example, survived a serious fire in the 1940s and still houses the county's Supreme Court – and the local jail.

About 20 sculptures (carved from dying elm trees) of life-size figures – including a piper and a highland dancer – dot the town. Antigonish has a strong Scottish heritage and has been home to the popular **Antigonish Highland Games** (page 310)

In Montgomery, Alabama, USA in December 1955, Rosa Parks refused to surrender her bus seat to a white passenger. She was arrested and convicted of violating the laws of segregation. The incident triggered a wave of protest that swept through the country, and led to Mrs Parks being called the 'mother of the modern day civil rights movement' in America.

Nine years earlier, in New Glasgow, Nova Scotia, Viola Desmond decided to go and see a film while she was waiting for her car to be repaired. The Roseland Theatre maintained a segregated seating policy with the stalls (ground floor) reserved for 'whites only'. Ms Desmond had weak eyesight, and did not want to sit in the balcony: she took a seat in the stalls. She was forcibly removed from the cinema, arrested and thrown in jail overnight. She was not allowed counsel at her trial or to cross-examine the witnesses testifying against her. Ms Desmond was eventually found guilty of trying to avoid paying the difference between the tax on a balcony ticket and the tax on a ticket from the cinema's main floor. The amount in question? One cent. She was sentenced to 30 days in jail and was ordered to pay a total of CAN$26 in fines. Viola moved to Montreal, and died in New York in 1965 aged 50.

In 2010, 64 years after the incident, Ms Desmond was pardoned posthumously by the then Nova Scotia lieutenant-governor, Mayann Francis. Ms Desmond's niece was reported as saying of her aunt, 'She would have laughed and said, "Pardon me for what? I didn't do anything wrong".

The Roseland Theatre at 188 Provost Street, New Glasgow, later became the Roseland Cabaret. Closed since late 2011, it has since been converted to offices.

for over 150 years (expect the town – especially accommodation and eateries – to be packed whilst the games are on). The town also hosts an excellent summer theatre festival (page 310).

In addition to the urban attractions, the town has a range of good beaches and hiking trails close by: its harbour borders a large tidal marsh where ospreys and bald eagles are commonly seen. Having said all that, first and foremost this is a working regional centre, with tourism further down the list.

For **Arisaig**, 29km/18 miles northeast of Antigonish via Hwy 245, see page 312.

HISTORY The name Antigonish probably derives from the Mi'kmaq '*n'alegihooneech*', meaning 'where branches are torn off' – a reference to a place where bears came to forage for beechnuts.

Post-Expulsion settlement is said to date from 1784 when Irish Loyalists, led by Captain Timothy Hierlihy, took up a large land grant surrounding Antigonish Harbour. The majority of settlers who followed were Scots from the Highlands, who were predominantly Catholic, so whereas Pictou County's churches are mainly Presbyterian, in Antigonish County the churches tend to be Roman Catholic.

GETTING THERE AND AWAY By car, Antigonish is just off Highway 104 by exits 31–34, 55km/34 miles to the Canso Causeway, 74km/46 miles from Pictou, 123km/76 miles from Truro, 218km/135 miles from Halifax and 231km/144 miles from Amherst. It is also on the **Maritime Bus** coach line between Halifax and Sydney (page 57).

Northumberland Shore   ANTIGONISH AND AROUND

7

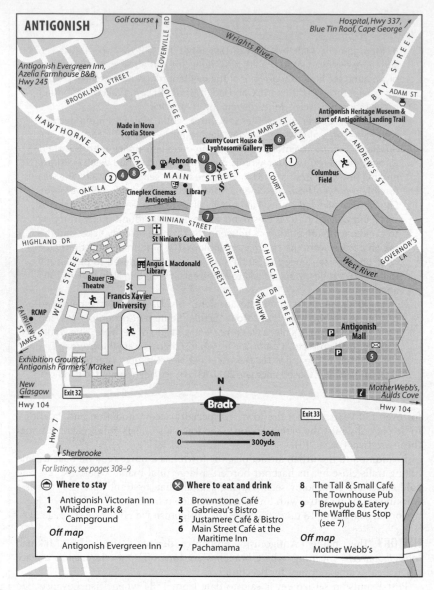

ANTIGONISH

Golf course

CLOVERVILLE RD

Wrights River

Hospital, Hwy 337,
Blue Tin Roof, Cape George

BAY STREET

ADAM ST

Antigonish Evergreen Inn,
Azelia Farmhouse B&B,
Hwy 245

BROOKLAND STREET

COLLEGE ST

HAWTHORNE ST

ACADIA ST

Made in Nova
Scotia Store

ST MARY'S ST

ELM ST

ST ANDREW'S ST

Antigonish Heritage Museum &
start of Antigonish Landing Trail

County Court House &
Lyghtesome Gallery

6

9

Aphrodite

3 **$**

2 **4** **8**

M A I N   S T R E E T

1

Columbus
Field

OAK LA

Cineplex Cinemas
Antigonish

Library

$

COURT ST

7

ST NINIAN STREET

HIGHLAND DR

WEST STREET

St Ninian's Cathedral

KIRK ST

CHURCH STREET

GOVERNOR'S LA

West River

Angus L Macdonald
Library

HILLCREST ST

Bauer
Theatre

St
Francis Xavier
University

MARINER DR

FAIRVIEW ST

RCMP

JAMES ST

P

P

Antigonish
Mall

5

Exhibition Grounds,
Antigonish Farmers' Market

New
Glasgow

Exit 32

N

Bradt

Exit 33

MotherWebb's,
Aulds Cove

Hwy 104

Hwy 104

Sherbrooke

0 ————— 300m
0 ————— 300yds

For listings, see pages 308–9

Where to stay
1 Antigonish Victorian Inn
2 Whidden Park &
   Campground

Off map
   Antigonish Evergreen Inn

Where to eat and drink
3 Brownstone Café
4 Gabrieau's Bistro
5 Justamere Café & Bistro
6 Main Street Café at the
   Maritime Inn
7 Pachamama

8 The Tall & Small Café
   The Townhouse Pub
   Brewpub & Eatery
9 The Waffle Bus Stop
   (see 7)

Off map
   Mother Webb's

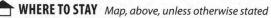

WHERE TO STAY   *Map, above, unless otherwise stated*

Antigonish Victorian Inn (13 units) 149
Main St; ☎ 902 863 1103; **tf** 1 800 706 5558;
www.antigonishvictorianinn.ca. In the past, this
fine (c1904) house with 10 rooms, 2 apts & a
modern suite (in annex) was a hospital & a bishop's
residence. Set on 2ha & conveniently located; a
good blend of old & new. Full b/fast inc. **$$–$$$**

Antigonish Evergreen Inn (8 rooms) 295
Hawthorne St; ☎ 902 863 0830; **tf** 1 888 821 5566;

www.antigonishevergreeninn.ca. A highly regarded
(particularly for service & value), pleasant, quiet
sgl-storey motel less than 2km from downtown.
All rooms have fireplaces. Continental b/fast (with
home-baked items) inc. **$$**

Azelia Farmhouse B&B [map, pages
282–3] (2 rooms) 309 Connors Rd; ☎ 902 863
4262; **tf** 1 866 309 0474; www.bbcanada.
com/7409.html. Quiet & rural but just 6.5km

from Antigonish, this turn-of-the-20th-century renovated farmhouse is surrounded by ash & sugar maple trees. Lovely, panoramic view from the veranda. B/fast is a highlight – perhaps buckwheat pancakes with hazelnuts & maple cream, or asparagus & crab meat omelette. **$$**

🏠 **Blue Tin Roof B&B** [map, pages 282–3] (4 rooms) 7957 Hwy 337, Livingstone Cove; ✆902 867 3560; www.bluetinroof.com. Nice B&B – albeit somewhat isolated. Approx 30mins' drive from downtown Antigonish. Some rooms aren't huge, but overall a good choice. Free use of kayaks. No shoes indoors & no under 11s. Full b/fast inc. **$$**

🏠 **June's B&B by the Sea** (2 rooms/1 suite) 10700 Hwy 337, Malignant Cove; ✆902 863 2115;

www.junesbb.ca; ◷ May–Oct. A lovely, relaxing spot 20mins' drive from Antigonish. 2 comfortable rooms, or rent both for a family suite sleeping 5. Good full b/fast inc. **$$**

⚊ **Whidden Park & Campground** (6 units & 154 campsites) 11 Hawthorne St; ✆902 863 3736; www.whiddens.com; ◷ mid May–mid Oct. These 2-bedroom well-equipped mini homes might not be for aesthetes, but provide good value for those requiring more than 1 bedroom. 2 fully equipped (exc bed linen) camper trailers, serviced & unserviced campsites. Outdoor pools (seasonal), games & laundromat. Within walking distance of the town centre. **$$**

✖ WHERE TO EAT AND DRINK *Map, opposite*

If a waffle – topped with any of a huge variety of fillings, sweet and/or savoury – will do the job, join the crowds at **The Waffle Bus Stop** (*18 College St;* ✆ *902 735 2406;* �; ◷ *09.00–17.00 Tue–Sat, 10.00–16.00 Sun; $*).

✖ **Gabrieau's Bistro** 350 Main St; ✆902 863 1925; www.gabrieaus.com; ◷ 10.00–21.00 Mon–Fri, 16.00–21.30 Sat. Stylish bistro with outdoor eating area. An extensive, imaginative menu & wine list (the chef is also a certified sommelier). Lunch features gourmet sandwiches & flatbread; in the evening the chef specialises in 'anything seafood' - look out for fab crab cakes or wonderful lobster & scallop risotto. *Lunch* **$$**, *dinner* **$$$**

✖ **Justamere Café & Bistro** 137 Church St; ✆902 735 3353; justamere.ca; ◷ 07.00–21.00 Mon–Sat (from 08.00 Sat), 08.00–15.00 Sun. Don't be put off by the corner-of-a-mall location: good atmosphere, music & art on the walls. Fresh, tasty diner-style food including good seafood chowder, all-day b/fast (eggs Benedict is a hit) & more. Patio. **$$–$$$**

✖ **Main Street Café at the Maritime Inn** 158 Main St; ✆902 863 4001; www. maritimeinns.com; ◷ 07.00–21.00 daily (from 08.00 Sat & Sun). Tasty, well-cooked dishes (although some portions can be a bit on the small side) such as maple-roasted salmon salad, panko-coated haddock, or caramelised apple almond crisp (served in a 'mason' jar). **$$–$$$**

✖ **Brownstone Café** 244 Main St; ✆902 735 3225; �; ◷ 11.00–21.00 Mon–Sat. Tasty, decadent – sometimes Mediterranean-inspired – pub & comfort food (eg: chicken souvlaki, mussels, sticky toffee pudding) & a good drinks selection. **$$**

✖ **Mother Webb's** Hwy 104; ✆902 863 3809; www.motherwebbs.com; ◷ 11.00–22.00 daily. You'll see billboard advertising for this American roadhouse-style restaurant long before you get near to Antigonish. Hearty portions of usually reliable (if not gourmet) burgers, steaks & ribs (though the 'sides' sometimes fall flat). Very quick service & reasonable prices (if you don't add too many extras). Near Exit 35, approx 6km east of the town centre. **$$**

✖ **The Townhouse Pub Brewpub & Eatery** 76 College St; ✆902 863 2248; �; ◷ daily 16.30–23.30 (til 22.30 Sun); kitchen to 21.00 except Fri&Sat to 22.00. Good food, decent beer, great staff & friendly atmosphere – not surprisingly a popular pub! **$$**

☕ **Pachamama** 18 College St; ✆902 308 3104; www.pacha-mama.ca; ◷ 09.00–17.00 Mon–Sat. It's a tea shop, a homemade chocolate shop, a whole foods deli & a good vegan lunch spot – what could be better (apart from Arsenal, Creedence, *Homicide: Life on the Street*...). **$**

☕ **The Tall & Small Café** 342 Main St; ✆902 863 4682; �; ◷ 07.00–18.00 Mon–Fri, 08.00–16.00 Sat. Friendly student/bohemian atmosphere, very good sandwiches, soups & coffee, & far better than usual vegetarian options. Can be very busy at lunch but you don't usually have to wait too long. Recommended. **$**

When they arrived in their new Nova Scotia home, the Hadhads, the first Syrian refugee family to settle in Antigonish, used their kitchen to try to continue to make chocolates as they had back at their (30-employee) factory in Damascus, which were sold at the weekly farmers' market. When monstrous wildfires destroyed much of Fort McMurray (in the western Canadian province of Alberta) the Hadhads donated some of their chocolate sales profits to the Canadian Red Cross's relief efforts for the stricken community. In August 2016, a small Antigonish shed became the new Peace by Chocolate factory.

ENTERTAINMENT AND FESTIVALS The **Antigonish Highland Games** (◌ *902 863 4275; www.antigonishhighlandgames.ca*), a hit since 1863 and said to be the longest-running Highland Games outside Scotland, are held in the second week of July. Expect to see dancing, bagpipes and caber-tossing. In July, **Music on Main** (◨ *MusicOnMainAntigonish*) stages free Wednesday evening concerts. Established in 1988, **Festival Antigonish** (*festivalantigonish.com*) is one of the province's biggest and best summer theatre programmes, with performances from early July to late August at the wonderful **Bauer Theatre** on the St Francis Xavier University campus. Held over five days at the end of August/early September, the **Eastern Nova Scotia Exhibition** (*ense.ca*) has tug-of-wars, prize farm animals aplenty, live entertainment and much more. Antigonish's **cinema** (◌ *902 863 4646; www.cineplex.com*) is found on Main Street.

SHOPPING Antigonish Mall, the town's major shopping mall, is out of the centre on Church Street by Exit 33 of Highway 104. The downtown area also has a couple of shops worth a quick browse, including **Aphrodite** (*292 Main St;* ◌ *902 863 0606; aphroditeartandfashion.com;* ◔ *10.00–17.00 Mon–Sat, noon–17.00 Sun*), an interesting blend of women's fashion and jewellery, and **The Made in Nova Scotia Store** (*324 Main St;* ◌ *902 867 2642; www.themadeinnovascotiastore.com;* ◔ *11.00– 17.00 Mon, 10.00–17.00 Tue, Wed & Sat, 10.00–20.00 Fri, noon–16.00 Sun*), with no prizes for guessing where the crafts, preserves, cosmetics, etc, sold here were made.

OTHER PRACTICALITIES

$ Royal Bank 236 Main St; ◌ 902 863 4411; ◔ 09.30–17.00 Mon–Fri

$ Scotiabank 255 Main St; ◌ 902 863 4800; ◔ 10.00–17.00 Mon–Fri

✚ St Martha's Regional Hospital 25 Bay St; ◌ 902 863 2830

✉ Post office 133 Church St; ◔ 09.00–17.00 Mon–Fri

ℹ Tourist information Antigonish Mall complex, Church St; ◌ 902 863 4921; ◔ Jun & Sep 10.00–16.00 daily, Jul–Aug 09.00–18.00 daily. The mall is just by Exit 33 of Hwy 104. The tourist office isn't in the main mall buildings, but in a small building right by the highway.

Antigonish Library College St; ◌ 902 863 4276; ◔ 09.00–17.00 Mon & Sat, 09.00–21.00 Tue–Fri 10.00–21.00

WHAT TO SEE AND DO The bells of the c1870s' **St Ninian's Cathedral** (*120 St Ninian St;* ◌ *902 863 2338; www.saintninian.ca*) were cast in Dublin, Ireland, and slate for the roof tiles was imported from Scotland. High on the cathedral's façade you can see the words '*Tigh Dhe*' – Gaelic for 'House of God'.

St Francis Xavier University (*University Av*), commonly known as 'St FX' or just 'X', was founded as a college by Roman Catholics in the 1850s, and gained university status in 1866. Other than for prospective students, no tours are offered, but the landscaped grounds make for a pleasant wander.

Containing one of the most significant collections of Celtic culture in North America, the **Hall of the Clans** (*Angus L Macdonald Library, St Francis Xavier University;* \ *902 867 2267; sites.stfx.ca/library;* ☉ *hours vary; admission free*) comprises over 10,000 items including Scottish Gaelic-, Welsh- and Irish-language resources and Celtic literature, folklore and music. Fifty coats of arms of Scottish clans adorn the walls.

Housed in the restored former c1908 railway station, the **Antigonish Heritage Museum** (*20 East Main St;* \ *902 863 6160; www.heritageantigonish.ca;* ☉ *10.00–noon & 13.00–17.00 Mon–Fri (& Sat Jul–Aug); admission free*) has two display rooms of photos and artefacts – including Mi'kmaq baskets – depicting the early

MINI CABOT TRAIL?

Lovers of lighthouses, magnificent coastal scenery and hiking should include this detour (or side trip from Antigonish) in their itineraries. The **'Cape George Scenic Drive'** also gets labelled the 'mini Cabot Trail' (for the real Cabot Trail, one of the world's great scenic drives, see pages 325–30 and 333–48); that's going a bit far, but this is still a delightful and scenic little diversion. The drive begins at **Malignant Cove** on Highway 245, 8km east of Arisaig (if you are starting in Antigonish, take Highway 245 north for approx 21km). Here, June's B&B (page 309) is a good accommodation option. Turn on to Highway 337, and you'll pass through **Livingstone Cove**, which also has an excellent B&B, the Blue Tin Roof (page 309), and in less than 20km you'll reach Cape George Point. As you round the cape, watch for Lighthouse Road, a left turn on to a 1km unpaved road to the **lighthouse** (*www.parl.ns.ca/lighthouse;* ☉ *May–Nov hours vary*). *En route*, you'll pass **Cape George Day Park** with picnic areas and a parking area for trailheads. From this lofty setting, Prince Edward Island (over 50km away) and the highlands of Cape Breton are often clearly visible. The **Cape George Hiking Trail**, accessible from the park, comprises over 30km of loops and point-to-point trails, some reaching over 180m above sea level.

Back on the road, just past Cape George, there is a striking view of a line of cliffs, which head off in to the distance towards Antigonish, with the brightly painted homes of the pretty and predominantly tuna-fishing community of **Ballantynes Cove** directly below. Learn about bluefin tuna fishing past and present at the cove's **Tuna Interpretive Centre** (☉ *mid Jun–mid Sep 10.00–19.00 daily; admission free*). With indoor dining and a deck overlooking St Georges Bay, **Boyd's Seafood Galley** (*Cribbons Point Wharf;* \ *902 863 0279;* ☉ *mid Jun–early Sep 11.00–19.30 daily; $–$$*) is the obvious lunch spot.

You'll then pass the **Crystal Cliffs**, named for their whitish appearance (a result of their high gypsum content), and will then have a view of the narrow entrance to Antigonish Harbour. A left turn on to Mahoney's Beach Road will lead you to a pleasant 1.8km beach trail: art aficionados will want to visit **Anna Syperek's home/studio** (*Mahoney's Beach Rd;* \ *902 863 1394; annasyperek.ca;* ☉ *by appointment only*). Working with oils and watercolour, drawing and etching, Syperek is one of the province's top artists.

Just past **Mahoney Beach** on Highway 337, several more hiking trails ranging from 3km to 13km allow you to explore beautiful Fairmont Ridge, which overlooks the harbour. From here it is just 9km to Antigonish.

days of the town and Antigonish County. There is also a genealogical resource room. The well-maintained 4.8km **Antigonish Landing Trail** leads from the museum along part of the harbour and river estuary. It's very popular with birdwatchers but just as enjoyable for walkers, joggers and cyclists. You don't have to walk the whole way – just retrace your steps when you feel like turning round.

For those looking to bring home a piece of Antigonish, the interesting **Lyghtesome Gallery** (*166 Main St;* \ *902 863 5804; www.lyghtesome.ns.ca;* ⊕ *Jan–May 10.00– 17.00 Tue–Sat; Jun–Dec 10.00–17.00 Mon–Sat; admission free*) is worth a visit for a range of works by artists from Nova Scotia and the Maritimes, plus historic Scottish prints, Celtic art and more. If you're in town on a Saturday morning, pop along to the **Antigonish Farmers' Market** (*304-H barn behind the arena on James St;* \ *902 867 7479; www.antigonishfarmersmarket.org;* ⊕ *early May–mid Dec 08.30–13.00 Sat*).

AROUND ANTIGONISH
Arisaig Provincial Park (*5704 Hwy 245;* \ *902 863 4513; parks.novascotia.ca/ content/arisaig;* ⊕ *late May–early Oct*) Around 400 million-plus years ago, this area was covered by the sea, and as the layers of sediment built up on the sea bed, various creatures were buried. Within the boundaries of the park, the erosion of shale cliffs has exposed a continuous record of conditions here from the late Ordovician period (448 million years ago) through the entire Silurian to Early Devonian (401 million years ago) periods. This is one of the only places in the world where such a long period of time is exposed in a single layered cliff line. Fossils of brachiopods (shellfish), nautiloids (a type of shelled squid), trilobites (extinct spider or crab-like arthropods), snail-like gastropods, and crinoids (plant-like filter feeders) are among those that have been found and continue to be unearthed here.

In addition, experts can see differences in the geology of northern and southern Nova Scotia here with a major geological fault dividing the park. Cliffs on the east side expose dark grey shale layers, but very few fossils; on the west side, the shale layers are thinner, have more sandstone and contain abundant fossils. An interpretive kiosk explains fossil formation. There is a picnic area, and 3km of trails, one of which leads down past observation platforms to the beach and cliffs. You're not permitted to disturb fossils embedded in the cliffs without a permit (page 38).

The provincial park is the main reason to visit, but in recent years enterprising Arisaig residents have come up with other attractions/distractions. The **Arisaig Lighthouse** is a (2007) replica of the original Arisaig Point Lighthouse, which burned in the early 1930s – interpretive panels tell the story of the historic fishing community of Arisaig. Close by, a **Lobster Interpretive Centre** (⊕ *Jul–Aug 11.00– 19.00 daily*) displays information on the local lobster fishery, and also hosts the **Dockside Café** ($) offering fishcakes, fish chowder and brunch (served *10.00–noon Sun*). Ice cream and drinks are also sold at the lighthouse during July and August. Talking of drinks, vodka is produced at the **Steinhart Distillery** (*5963 Hwy 245;* \ *902 863 5530; steinhartdistillery.com*), where tours and tastings are available, and also two-bedroom chalets (*sleeping up to 6;* **$$$–$$$$**) for those wanting to stay overnight.

Pomquet You'll see many houses flying the Acadian flag in this village, established in 1774 by five families originally from St Malo, France. It's less than 20km from Antigonish – take Taylor Road (between exits 34 and 35) from Highway 104. At **Pomquet Beach Provincial Park** (*parks.novascotia.ca/content/pomquet-beach;* ⊕ *mid May–early Oct*), the eponymous beach is backed by a series of 13 dunes stretching almost 4km. Boardwalks protect the dunes, while woods and both salt-

En route back to France from America in 1815, Father Vincent De Paul Merle of the Trappist Order was stranded in Halifax. He was given charge of three parishes and in 1826 his house became the Monastery of Petit du Clairvaux, North America's first Trappist monastery. He died in 1854, but the monastery continued to blossom and was 'upgraded' to an abbey by Pope Pius IX in 1876.

It later suffered a couple of devastating fires and was abandoned until 1938, when the current owners, the Order of St Augustine, purchased and rebuilt the monastery. Late in 2007, the complex – now called Our Lady of Grace Monastery (*www.ourladyofgracemonastery.com*) became home to a group of Augustinian Contemplative Nuns. To reach the monastery, take Exit 37 off Highway 104. Turn south onto Highway 16 and then right onto Monastery Road.

and freshwater marshes attract a variety of wildlife; birdwatching is good, too. The park has changing rooms, loos, and interpretive panels explaining the dune formation.

If you wish to stay nearby, **Pomquet Beach Cottages** (*5 cottages; 198 Pomquet Beach Rd;* ☏ *902 971 0314;* **tf** *1 855 240 2487; www.pomquetbeachcottages.com;* **$$$**) offer four two-bedroom and one (wheelchair-accessible) one-bedroom comfortable, pet-friendly, fully equipped cottages (each with barbecue on deck) adjacent to the beach provincial park.

Aulds Cove This community is on the mainland side of the **Canso Causeway** (box, page 315). Other than seeing some larger-than-life models – dotted about town are a big iceberg, a giant puffin, and a huge lobster in an even bigger lobster trap – and, if necessary filling up with petrol, eating and/or sleeping, there isn't much to delay you. You can choose from 18 rooms at the reliable **Cove Motel** (*30 units;* ☏ *902 747 2700; www.covemotel.com;* ☉ *May–Oct;* **$$**), set in a nice location on a small peninsula jutting out in to the Strait of Canso. The large licensed restaurant (☉ *May–Jun 11.00–20.00 daily; Jul–Oct 08.00–20.00 daily;* **$$**) can be busy with coach tours, but has a glassed-in patio with water views, and the extensive menu serves good food including lobster.

Aulds Cove is on highways 104, 4 and 344, 5km/3 miles from Mulgrave, 10km/6 miles from Port Hawkesbury and 55km/34 miles from Antigonish **by car**.

UPDATES WEBSITE

You can post your comments and recommendations, and read the latest feedback and updates from other readers online at www.bradtupdates.com/novascotia.

8

Cape Breton Island

Joined to the mainland since 1955 by the 2km-long Canso Causeway that crosses the narrow Strait of Canso, Cape Breton Island has a population of just under 150,000. Approximately 175km long and 135km wide, it covers 10,300km². At the island's core is the vast 260km² saltwater Bras d'Or Lake, to the northeast two natural passages connect the lake to the open sea, and in the southwest a short canal constructed in the 1850s and 1860s performs the same purpose. Cape Breton Island has the province's largest bald eagle population, many of which nest along the lake's shoreline.

Rugged highlands occupy much of the northern portion of Cape Breton Island: here you'll find the Cape Breton Highlands National Park, a region of deep, forested canyons, and magnificent coastal cliffs – and the best place in the province to see moose in the wild. This area of natural wonders is accessed by one of the world's great scenic drives, the 300km Cabot Trail. But don't just see it all through your car window – get out of your vehicle to hike, bike, kayak, play one of the superb golf courses, take a whale-watching trip or just relax on one of the beautiful beaches. Take a detour to remote Meat Cove, or wander the streets of the Trail's de facto capital, lakeside Baddeck, where Alexander Graham Bell was a summer resident for more than 35 years.

Set on a magnificent harbour on the east coast, the port of Sydney is by far the biggest urban area: with the surrounding communities it makes up what is still called Industrial Cape Breton, a region largely built on coal mining and steel manufacturing which is home to over 70% of the island's population.

The island's major manmade attraction is in the southeast, a wonderful reconstruction of the Fortress of Louisbourg which played a major part in Nova Scotia's Anglo-French conflicts in the mid 18th century. In the southwest soak up the sleepy pastoral beauty and pretty backroads of Isle Madame.

But man has contributed another particular highlight of any visit to Cape Breton Island, part of the legacy left by the 50,000 Highland Scots who came here and settled in the late 18th and early 19th centuries – joyous Celtic music and dancing. Be sure to go to a ceilidh (page 30) whilst in Cape Breton Island – or better still, try to time your visit to coincide with the Celtic Colours International Festival (box, page 318), a fantastic blend of traditional music, dancing and nature's splendour.

A century ago, Alexander Graham Bell said: 'I have travelled the globe. I have seen the Canadian and American Rockies, the Andes and the Alps and the Highlands of Scotland: But for simple beauty, Cape Breton outrivals them all.' He still has a case.

THE WEST COAST

This section covers the region between Port Hastings (on the Cape Breton Island side of the Canso Causeway) and the village of Margaree Harbour 110km away on the Cabot Trail.

Scots first settled in this area in the 1770s, and their traditions are still strong. This part of Cape Breton Island seems to have produced a disproportionately high number of good dancers and musicians – Natalie MacMaster and her uncle Buddy, Ashley MacIsaac and the Rankins are amongst those who hail from the region. You get the feeling that a ceilidh is held in one community or another almost every evening. Music and dancing apart, there are some good beaches, the province's first – and best-known – whisky distillery, and some of Nova Scotia's greatest hiking.

PORT HASTINGS Port Hawkesbury (pages 373–4), 6km away, has accommodation and restaurants, so the only reasons to stop in this community at the Cape Breton end of the Canso Causeway are the well-stocked **tourist office** (*96 Hwy 4;* ✆ *902 625 4201;* ⊕ *high season 09.00–19.00 daily, off-season 09.00–17.00 daily*) and the local **Port Hastings Museum** (*24 Hwy 19;* ✆ *902 625 1295;* ⓕ *;* ⊕ *mid Jun–mid Oct 09.00–17.00 Mon–Fri, noon–16.00 Sat & Sun; admission CAN$3*), which was once Canada's largest sweet shop. As a welcome to Cape Breton Island, the collection focuses on life before, during and after construction of the causeway. Check local genealogy and look out, too, for a collection of model ships by local craftsman Mark Boudreau.

Port Hastings is accessible **by car**, 51km/32 miles from Antigonish, 132km/82 miles from Chéticamp, 85km/53 miles from Baddeck and 171km/106 miles from Sydney.

JUDIQUE Most visitors come here for the **Celtic Music Interpretive Centre (CMIC)** (*5471 Hwy 19;* ✆ *902 787 2708; www.celticmusiccentre.com;* ⊕ *09.00–17.00 Mon– Fri, 10.00–17.00 Sat & Sun*), which collects, preserves and promotes Celtic music with emphasis on Cape Breton-style. Music demonstrations are CAN$7, a self-guided tour of the Exhibit Room is CAN$8, and Gaelic lessons are CAN$5 – ask about reduced price combos. The centre's **Ceilidh Pub** (⊕ *mid Jun–mid Oct 11.30–15.00 Mon–Sat, 14.00–17.00 Sun*) has a licensed bar and combines good food and traditional live music. In town, keep an eye out, too, for Judique's fine stone **St Andrew's Church**. Special events are held year-round – particularly during October's **Celtic Colours International Festival** (box, page 318). In August, the town holds the **Kintyre Farm Scottish Concert**, an outdoor afternoon celebration of local music and dance.

Judique is on Highway 19, 27km/17 miles from Port Hastings and 18km/11 miles from Port Hood, convenient **by car**.

CANSO CAUSEWAY

The Canso Causeway connects Cape Breton with the mainland. Construction began in 1952: engineers blasted solid rock and fill from Cape Porcupine on the mainland side and dumped it into the water. Slowly the roadway-to-be began to elongate. Locks were constructed on the Cape Breton side to allow shipping to pass through the barrier. Completed in 1955, the causeway is 1.37km long with a surface width of 24m. Ten million tonnes of rock fill were used in the construction, piled to a depth of 66m. On the Cape Breton side, a 94m swing bridge allows larger vessels to pass through the locks. The causeway's construction created one of the finest ice-free harbours in the world.

Fishermen say that this wall across the strait has killed off tuna fishing in the area. On the other hand, they say lobsters are much easier to catch as the crustaceans crawl back and forth under the sea looking for a way through.

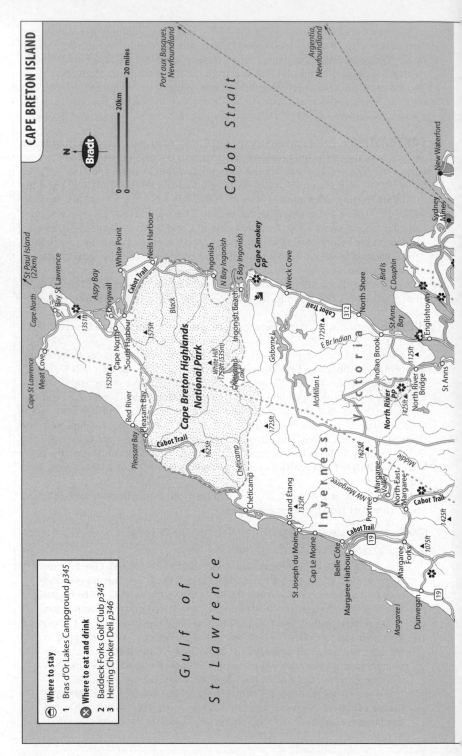

CAPE BRETON ISLAND

N

Bradt

0 _____ 20km
0 _____ 20 miles

Where to stay
1 Bras d'Or Lakes Campground *p345*

Where to eat and drink
2 Baddeck Forks Golf Club *p345*
3 Herring Choker Deli *p346*

*Gulf of
St Lawrence*

Cabot Strait

*Port aux Basques,
Newfoundland*

*Argentia,
Newfoundland*

*St Paul Island
(22km)*

Cape St Lawrence
Cape North
Meat Cove
Bay St Lawrence
1351ft
Aspy Bay
Dingwall
White Point
Neils Harbour

1525ft
Red River
Pleasant Bay
Cape North
South Harbour
Cabot Trail
575ft
Black

**Cape Breton Highlands
National Park**
White Hill
1758ft (535m)
Cheticamp
Lake
1725ft

1625ft
Cheticamp
1325ft
Grand Étang
St Joseph du Moine
Cap Le Moine
Belle Côte

Ingonish
(N Bay) Ingonish
Ingonish Beach
(S Bay) Ingonish
**Cape Smokey
PP**
Wreck Cove
Gisborne L

McKillan L
E Br Indian
1725ft
Cabot Trail
North Shore
312

Victoria

St Anns
Bay
Bird Is
C Dauphin
St Anns
Indian Brook
1125ft
**North River
PP**
1425ft
North River
Bridge
St Anns

1625ft
Margaree
Valley
NW Margaree
North-East
Margaree
Margaree
Middle
Cabot Trail

Inverness

Portree
19
Margaree Harbour
Margaree
Forks
1075ft
1425ft

Dunvegan
Margaree I
19

Englishtown

Sydney
Mines
New Waterford

316

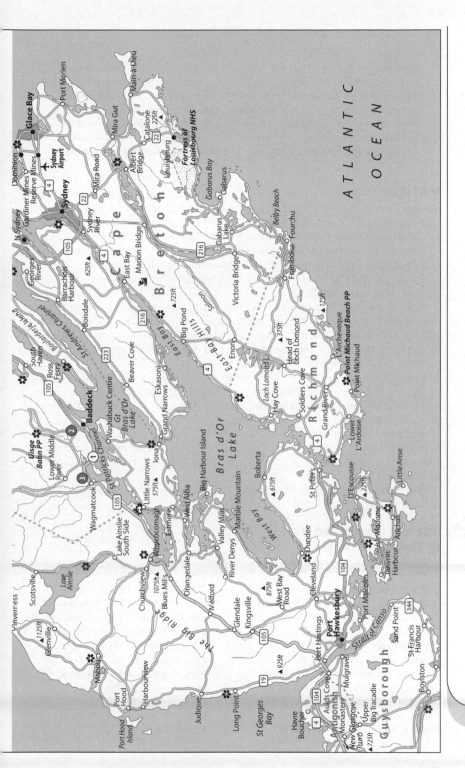

PORT HOOD This pretty community – the self-proclaimed 'step-dancing capital of Cape Breton' – is the second largest on this route. For the non-terpsichoreal, step-dancing is a fast-paced dance that involves a lot of quick, intricate footwork, but little hand or arm movement, usually performed to traditional fiddle music.

There are fine views over **Port Hood Island** and if the weather is behaving, a few nice beaches to enjoy. The sea is very shallow, allowing the water to heat up early in the season and stay warm. There are days when the 'warmest water in eastern Canada' claim seems justified.

What is now Port Hood Island was connected to Cape Breton Island until the turn of the 20th century when the effects of severe winter storms cut across the isthmus and created an island. Once one of the region's most important lobster-fishing bases, the brightly coloured houses amid meadows and high bluffs are now occupied only by those who come for the summer.

Named Just-au-Corps by the French (after a garment popular at the time), much of the stone used to construct the Fortress of Louisbourg (pages 367–8) came from here. With time, Just-au-Corps became Chestico (this name lives on as the name of the local museum and summer festival (see opposite).

Settling in the late 18th century, Catholic Highland Scots and New England Loyalists produced the Port Hood of today. It became an important port in the mid 19th century, and coal mining which began in the 1890s helped the town prosper over the next few decades.

Port Hood is on Highway 19, 45km/28 miles from Port Hastings and 35km/22 miles from Inverness and easily reached **by car**.

Where to stay, eat and drink

🏠 The Fiddle & the Sea B&B
(4 rooms) 109 High Rd; 📞 902 631 5980; www.thefiddleandthesea.com. Denise & Alain are great hosts & their attractive, purpose-built house overlooking the water is very comfortable. Owners also speak French & Spanish. Good b/fast (inc). **$$**

🏠 Haus Treuburg Country Inn & Cottages
(7 units) 175 Main St; 📞 902 787 2116; www.haustreuburg.com; ⊕ May–Dec. 2 rooms & a suite are in the main house, but it's worth splashing out for 1 of the 4 cottages (the 2-bedroom cottage is up the hill). Private beach. The dining room (⊕ Jun–Oct 18.00–22.00 daily) offers a set 4-course dinner for CAN$45–51

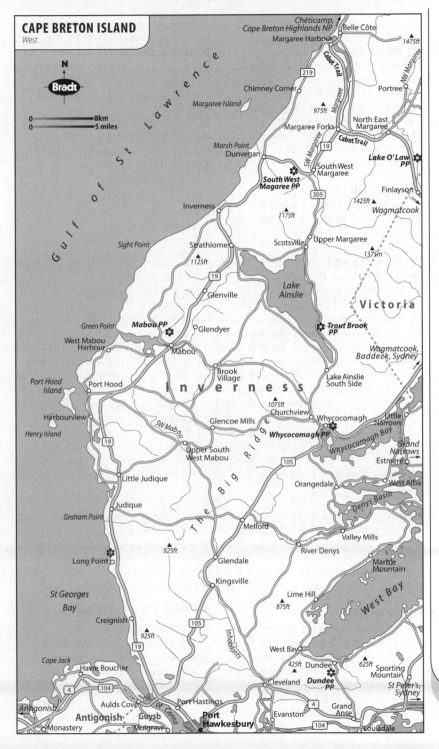

CAPE BRETON ISLAND

West

N

Bradt

0 — 8km
0 — 5 miles

Gulf of St Lawrence

Chéticamp,
Cape Breton Highlands NP
Margaree Harbour
Belle Côte
1475ft

Cabot Trail

219

Chimney Corner

Portree

Margaree Island

975ft

North East
Margaree

Margaree Forks

Cabot Trail

19

Lake O'Law
PP

Marsh Point
Dunvegan

SW Margaree

South West
Margaree

**South West
Magaree PP**

Finlayson

1425ft

Wagmatcook

Inverness

305

1175ft

Scotsville

Upper Margaree

1375m

Sight Point

Strathlorne

1125ft

Lake
Ainslie

Victoria

19

Glenville

Green Point

Mabou PP

Glendyer

**Trout Brook
PP**

*Wagmatcook,
Baddeck, Sydney*

West Mabou
Harbour

Mabou

Port Hood
Island

Port Hood

Brook
Village

Lake Ainslie
South Side

I n v e r n e s s

1075ft

Churchview

Whycocomagh

Little
Narrows

Harbourview

Glencoe Mills

Whycocomagh PP

Whycocomagh Bay

*Grand
Narrows*

Henry Island

SW Mabou

Estmere

19

Upper South
West Mabou

105

Orangedale

West Alba

Little Judique

Denys Basin

Judique

Melford

Valley Mills

Graham Point

The Big Ridge

925ft

River Denys

**Marble
Mountain**

Long Point

Glendale

West Bay

*St Georges
Bay*

Kingsville

Lime Hill

875ft

Creignish

105

925ft

19

Inhabitants

West Bay

425ft

Dundee

625ft

Sporting
Mountain

Cape Jack

Havre Boucher

Cleveland

**Dundee
PP**

*St Peter's,
Sydney*

4

104

Antigonish

Aulds Cove

Port Hastings

4

Grand
Anse

8

Antigonish

Guysb

Evanston

104

Monastery

Mulgrave

**Port
Hawkesbury**

Louisdale

Strait of Canso

(seafood, European & traditional German dishes); reservations recommended. B/fast not inc. **$$**

🏠 **Hillcrest Hall Country Inn** (11 rooms) 24 Main St; ☎ 902 787 2211; **tf** 1 888 434 4255; www.hillcresthall.com; ⊕ mid Jun–mid Oct. Magnificent c1910 Queen Anne Revival building. 1 accessible unit, 2 suites. Fine views of harbour & beyond. Rate includes continental b/fast. **$$**

✖ **Clove Hitch Bar & Bistro** 8790 Hwy 19; ☎ 902 787 3030; www.clovehitch.ca; ⊕ 11.30–21.00 daily. Nice, modern décor, friendly service, &

a varied menu that is well executed - particularly seafood. Food served until 21.00. **$$**

✖ **Sandeannies Bakery & Tea Room** 8263 Hwy 19; ☎ 902 787 2558; www.sandeannies. com; ⊕ 07.30–15.00 daily. A good stop for bread & treats, sandwiches, all-day b/fast & lunch. **$–$$**

✖ **The Admiral Lounge & Dining Room** 148 Main St; ☎ 902 787 3494; ◼; ⊕ 11.00–23.00 Mon–Sat, 13.00–23.00 Sun. Burgers, wraps, pizzas, etc. Food served until 21.00. **$**

Other practicalities

$ **East Coast Credit Union** 138 Main St; ☎ 902 787 3246; ⊕ 09.30–16.30 Mon–Wed, 09.30–18.00 Thu

What to see and do

For a bit of culture, the **Chestico Museum and Historical Society** (*8095 Hwy 19, Harbourview;* ☎ *902 787 2244; chesticoplace.com;* ⊕ *Jun–Oct 09.00–17.00 Mon–Fri, Jul–Aug also noon–16.00 Sat; admission CAN$2.50*) is a local history museum 2km south of Port Hood. Peruse artefacts and historical/genealogical records related to the area's early settlers, or join in one of the Thursday ceilidhs (*Jul–Aug at 19.00*). Shop-wise, **Galloping Cows Fine Foods** (*59 Justin Rd;* ☎ *902 787 3484; www.gallopingcows.com;* ⊕ *summer 10.00–17.00 Mon–Thu, 10.00–20.00 Fri&Sat, noon–17.00 Sun; winter check hours*) offers gourmet spreads, jams and pepper jellies. Excellent pizza is served Friday and Saturday from 15.00. At **Four Mermaids** (*8790 Hwy 19;* ☎ *902 787 3030; www.fourmermaids.ca;* ⊕ *10.00–18.00 Thu–Sat, noon–17.00 Sun, 10.00–15.00 Wed*) check out the gifts and 'treasures' made from and inspired by some of the bounty collected by local beachcombing. Meanwhile, a 2-hour tour with Captain Danny Gillis of **Gillis Lobster & Port Hood Island Tours** (*Port Hood Government Wharf, Wharf Rd;* **tf** *1 844 610 2669; www.gltc.ca;* ⊕ *Jul daily, Aug most days; from CAN$48*) gives you the chance to catch a lobster or maybe a mackerel, and learn about how fishing has shaped the region and its people. Port Hood Island tours are also offered.

MABOU

One of the most attractive villages on Cape Breton Island's west coast, Mabou (population: 410) is the province's centre of Gaelic education (the language is taught in the local school). The beautiful surrounding area offers wonderful hiking, too.

Easy to get to **by car**, Mabou is on Highway 19, 60km/37 miles from Port Hastings, 86km/53 miles from Chéticamp and 66km/41 miles from Baddeck.

🏠 **Where to stay**

🏠 **Duncreigan Country Inn** (8 rooms) 11409 Hwy 19; ☎ 902 945 2207; **tf** 1 800 840 2207; e duncreigan@ns.aliantzinc.ca; www.duncreigan. ca. A lovely, comfortable c1990 harbourside inn, with a blend of traditional & modern features. 4 rooms in the main house & 4 rooms in the 1996 adjacent Spring House. Full buffet b/fast inc. **$$–$$$**

POSSIBLE DETOUR

For a pleasant scenic break from Highway 19, take the Colindale Road from the north end of town: unpaved for much of the way, it rejoins Highway 19 just south of Mabou.

Mabou's celebrated Red Shoe Pub (see below) was named for a well-known fiddle reel. When the pub opened, the new owners were presented with a pair of red (ladies) wooden high-heeled shoes. One of these shoes disappeared without trace within the year, but the other – as prized as Cinderella's glass slipper – became the pub's emblem, and featured in the photos of many a pub patron. When not being used as a prop for souvenir snapshots, the shoe was kept on a sill in the middle of the front left-hand window. What a time we live in: after midnight one Friday night in September 2012, someone (as yet unidentified) grabbed the shoe and left the pub. A waitress gave chase, but could only watch as a car sped off. This same shoe had been purloined once before, but that time the culprit rang the pub within a day to say that he was at Halifax Airport and was couriering the stolen shoe back to Mabou. At the time of writing, no similar phone calls or ransom notes have been received.

Ceilidh Cottages & Camping Park (5 units, 12 sites) 1425 New Rocky Ridge Rd, West Mabou; ☎902 945 2992; www.ceilidhcottages.ca; ⊕ Jun–mid Oct. 5 2-bedroom cottages with fireplace & deck, & a 12-site campground with tent & serviced motorhome sites. Facilities include laundromat, tennis court & heated pool (in season). **$$**

Mabou River Inn (10 units) 19 South West Ridge Rd; ☎902 945 2356; tf 1 888 627 9744; mabouriverinn.com; ⊕ year-round, off-season by reservation. Choose from 7 inn rooms, or 3 2-bedroom units with full kitchen. Good source of information & advice on fishing. Sea kayaks & mountain bikes. Rate includes deluxe continental b/fast. **$$**

✕ Where to eat and drink

✕ The Mull Café 11630 Hwy 19; ☎902 945 2244; www.duncreigan.ca; ⊕ late Jun–mid Oct 11.00–20.00 daily; mid Oct–late Jun 11.00–19.00 Sun–Thu, 11.00–20.00 Fri & Sat. Popular, unpretentious licensed restaurant with extensive menu. Eat inside or on the all-weather deck. *Lunch* **$-$$**, *dinner* **$$**

✕ Red Shoe Pub 11573 Hwy 19; ☎902 945 2996; www.redshoepub.com; ⊕ Jun–mid Oct 11.30–23.00 Mon–Wed, 11.30–02.00 Thu–Sat, noon–23.00 Sun. Owned since 2005 by members of local singing favourites the Rankin Family

& looking like a big-city coffee house. Offers sophisticated pub food & regular (& occasional spontaneous) live music performances; you're probably paying a dollar or 2 extra for the celebrity connections (box, above). Food served until 21.00. **$$**

Shining Waters Bakery 11497 Main St; ☎902 945 2867; ⊕ usually May–Nov for b/fast & lunch, call for hours. Locals value good, simple food & low prices more highly than fancy décor – they love this small place. Come for excellent sandwiches, homemade bread & baked goods. **$**

Other practicalities

$ East Coast Credit Union 11627 Hwy 19; ☎902 945 2003; ⊕ 09.30–16.30 Mon–Wed & Fri, 09.30–18.00 Thu

✉ Post office 11541 Main St; ⊕ 09.00–11.30 & noon–17.00 Mon–Fri

What to see and do In summer, the town resonates to the sound of Celtic music with a Tuesday-evening ceilidh at Mabou Community Hall, the four-day **Mabou Ceilidh** in July, and music at the **Red Shoe Pub** and **Strathspey Place** (*11156 Hwy 19;* ☎ *902 945 5300; www.strathspeyplace.com*), a modern 500-seat theatre with excellent acoustics that offers a varied programme.

Cape Breton Island   THE WEST COAST

8

MABOU HIKING

The Mabou area offers enough excellent trails to fill a book. More than a dozen well-marked trails through the beautiful highlands have been developed (and are maintained) by the Cape Mabou Trail Club, which produces an invaluable map, sold in various places in Mabou, including the general store.

If you'd rather stay on more level ground, one of several possibilities is to walk the Rail Trail from Mabou (near the bridge over the Mabou River) to Glendyer Station, approximately 4km each way. Old railway line it may be, but the views are stunning. West Mabou Beach Provincial Park (see below) also has good trails.

A shrine, **Mother of Sorrows Shrine** (*45 Southwest Ridge Rd;* ↘ *902 945 2221;* ⊕ *daily; admission free*) is dedicated to Our Lady of Seven Sorrows and the pioneers of the Mabou area, and enclosed in a miniature pioneer church. Housed in a c1874 former general store, **An Drochaid (The Bridge Museum)** (*11513 Hwy 19;* ↘ *945 2311;* ⊕*Jul–Aug 19.00–16.00 Wed–Fri, 10.00–17.00 Sat & Sun, noon–16.00 Tue; admission free*) focuses on traditional Cape Breton music and local history, and special events are held year-round. Also worth a visit is the buzzy **Mabou Farmers' Market** (*Mabou Athletic Centre, 186 Mabou Harbour Rd; 902 787 2323; www. maboufarmersmarket.ca; Jun–mid Oct 11.00–14.00 Sun*). Look out for local oysters, plus a whole lot more.

A (usually quiet) park, **West Mabou Beach Provincial Park** (*1757 Little Mabou Rd*) has a picnic area, good birding, ponds, sand dunes, old farm fields and marshes, and a beautiful 2km sandy beach. For walkers, the Old Ferry Road and Acarsaid (Harbour) trails are both worthwhile. To reach the park from Highway 19, take Colindale Road at Port Hood, or the West Mabou Road just before you get to Mabou Station.

GLENVILLE   Although green hillsides flank this village on Highway 19, it was once known as Black Glen. These days, most people stop here for one reason: since 1990, Glenville has been home to **The Glenora Inn and Distillery** (*13727 Hwy 19;* ↘*902 258 2662;* ☏ *1 800 839 0491; www.glenoradistillery.com;* ⊕ *early May–late Oct;* see also box, opposite). Standard (25min) guided distillery tours (including sample) run on the hour daily (⊕ *09.00–17.00; CAN$7*); private tours (which include a visit to the whisky warehouse where you will draw and taste a barrel sample, followed by a tutored tasting in the pub), are available by advance reservation, and you can buy whisky-related souvenirs and more at the gift shop. At the inn (**$$$**), choose from 14 spacious rooms or six hillside chalets, with a lovely brookside setting and delightful flowered courtyard. The highly regarded restaurant (*lunch* **$$**, *dinner* **$$$–$$$$**) focuses on local ingredients prepared with modern flair – try, for example, the lobster and scallop fettuccini or the coffee-rubbed rib-eye steak – and the pub (**$$**) has free live Celtic music sessions twice daily. Many people choose to stay and eat here rather than in Mabou or Inverness.

Glenville is approximately 9km north of Mabou and 10km from Inverness and easily reachable **by car**.

INVERNESS   Visitors have long been attracted to the largest community (population: 1,800) along Highway 19 not by the town's mining history (coal was mined commercially here from 1890 to 1958), but by a huge, long sandy beach. An

THE BATTLE OF THE GLEN

Many have likened the straths, glens and lochs in this region to the land that lies to the north of England. One of the highlights of a holiday in bonnie Scotland is the abundance of wonderful whisky distilleries to visit. As you tour Cape Breton Island, make a stop between Mabou and Inverness at Glenville. Here you'll be rewarded with a good place to stay, eat, tap your feet – and to sample a wee dram or two. And like the province itself, the precious liquid produced at the Glenora Distillery (which opened in 1990) has a story to tell.

In 2001, the Edinburgh-based Scotch Whisky Association (SWA) filed a suit against the Glenora Distillery, arguing that the use of the word 'Glen' in the distillery's main product (Glen Breton Rare Single Malt Whisky) misled consumers to believe the spirit was a 'Scotch', a designation that can only be used for whiskies made in Scotland. Although Glenora Distillery made (and makes) no references to 'Scotch' anywhere in its marketing, in 2008, the Federal Court of Canada ruled that the company could not register a trademark including the word 'Glen' in the name of its whisky. Glenora appealed the decision, compiling 4,000 pages of documentation. A panel of three judges from the Federal Court of Appeal found in favour of the distillers.

Still the SWA would not accept defeat. It may have lost that battle, but the war was not yet over. Its last chance was to take the matter to the highest court in the land (even though there was no evidence of even one whisky-drinker being misled by the nomenclature).

In June 2009, the Supreme Court of Canada dismissed the SWA's final appeal and awarded court costs to the distillers. More than eight years of litigation finally ended, and the distillery registered the Glen Breton trademark.

In 2010, the good folk of Glenora celebrated their victory and the first anniversary of the trademark registration by releasing a 15-year-old Single Malt, appropriately named the 'Battle of the Glen™'. It is not a Scotch.

---

extensive boardwalk runs alongside it, and – compared with many other beaches further south – the sea can be quite warm. In the last few years, new big draws have been added – two fabulous golf courses, Cabot Links and Cabot Cliffs. It's amazing what you can do on the site of an old coal mine. On the downside, locals claim that they are losing access to some of the town's public beaches. At the wharf, depending on the season, watch fishermen unload lobster, crab or tuna.

Incidentally, Inverness is home to acclaimed author Alistair MacLeod, whose work includes the Cape Breton Island-set *No Great Mischief*.

To reach Inverness **by car**, the town is on Highway 19, 80km from Port Hastings, 57km/35 miles from Chéticamp and 153km/95 miles from Sydney.

⌂ Where to stay, eat and drink

⌂ **Cabot Links Lodge** (86 units) 15933 Central Av; ☎ 902 258 4653; **tf** 1 855 652 2268; www.cabotlinks.com; ⊕ May–Oct. The well-appointed guest rooms at this fabulous resort have floor-to-ceiling windows with panoramic golf course & sea views. Design is contemporary, & the lodge lives up to its 'low-key luxury' billing. See overleaf for details of the golf courses. The

Panorama Restaurant (⊕ May–Oct 17.00–22.00 daily, reservations recommended; $$$–$$$$) offers wonderful views, unpretentious fine dining & a good wine list. At dinner, try, for example, the lobster-stuffed chive ravioli, followed by pan-seared local rainbow trout. You can also choose snacks & more substantial fare at the well-stocked Cabot Bar (⊕ May–Oct 07.00–22.00 daily; $$)

8

adjacent to the 18th green, which also has a nice patio. There's also a pub offering local craft beers & food. All are open to non-guests. **$$$–$$$$**

🏠 **Inverness Beach Village** (41 cottages) 50 Beach Village Rd; 📞902 258 2653; www.macleods. com; ⊕ Jun–mid Oct. The 1- & 2-bedroom cottages are OK, but what keeps people coming back here is the magnificent beach location. There's an open & wooded 50-site campground (serviced & unserviced) on the same site, plus laundry facilities & tennis court. **$$–$$$**

✗ **Coal Miners Café** 15832 Central Av; 📞902 258 3413; ⊕ 07.00–21.30 daily. This friendly eatery offers quite a sophisticated menu, though on occasions can't quite cope with it. Live entertainment Jul–Aug Thu evenings. **$$**

✗ **Village Grill Restaurant & Reel Pizza** 15862 Central Av; 📞902 258 3666; 🟦 ; ⊕ VGR: 11.00–20.00 daily; RP 16.00–20.00 Thu–Sun. Nothing too fancy, but good diner food & friendly service. **$–$$**

☕ **Downstreet Coffee Company** 15844 Central Av; 📞902 258 3477; www. downstreetcoffeecompany.com; ⊕ 07.00–18.00 daily. This stylish café – not just good coffee but baked goods, b/fasts (until noon), sandwiches & soups – is owned by the people behind the golf resort. **$–$$**

Other practicalities

$ Royal Bank 15794 Central Av; 📞902 258 2776; ⊕ 10.00–17.00 Mon– Fri

✚ **Inverness Consolidated Memorial Hospital** 39 James St; 📞902 258 2100

✉ **Post office** 16 Railway St; ⊕ 08.45–17.15 Mon–Wed & Fri, 08.45–18.00 Thu

What to see and do Housed in the former c1901 railway station, the **Inverness Miners' Museum** (*62 Lower Railway St;* 📞*902 258 3822;* ⊕ *mid Jun–Sep 09.00–17.00 Mon–Fri, noon–17.00 Sat & Sun; admission CAN$2*) was saved from demolition by a noble citizen, and contains information on the region's mining history. The **Inverness County Centre for the Arts** (*16080 Hwy 19;* 📞*902 258 2533; nvernessarts. com;* ⊕ *check for hours; admission free*) exhibition centre features a good gallery including local and international artists, and also hosts occasional live music performances. There's also a gift shop. You can watch horse-harness racing on Sunday afternoons at the **Inverness Raceway** (*Forrest St*) from May to October (*Jul–Aug Wed evenings*).

The active will want to stop in at **Eagle Eye Outfitters** (*15860 Central Av;* 📞*902 258 5893; www.eagleeyeoutfitters.ca*), where you can rent sea kayaks, mountain bikes or paddleboards, take a guided tour, or sign up for a bit of deep-sea or fly-fishing. Try your hand at the famous **Cabot Links and Cabot Cliffs golf courses** (see page 323 for contact details; ⊕ *May–Oct, depending on weather; green fees (2016): resort guests CAN$213, non-guests CAN$247*). The former (which opened in 2012) is a challenging, 6,803yd par-70 links seaside course (five holes play adjacent to the beach), designed by Rod Whitman, and has already established a wonderful reputation. Six yardages are offered (the shortest, 3,733yds). Designed by Bill Coore and Ben Crenshaw – and already hailed by golf experts as more impressive – Cabot Cliffs opened officially in 2016. Before then it had already been called 'Best New Course' by *Golf Digest*, and the same magazine listed it as the19th best course in the world.

The **Broad Cove Scottish Concert**, at Broad Cove, near Inverness is the largest outdoor Scottish concert on Cape Breton Island and is held on the last Sunday in July. In summer, there's a weekly ceilidh at Inverness Fire Hall on Thursday evenings.

MARGAREE HARBOUR This quaint village with a cluster of shingle and clapboard houses wraps around a once-bustling harbour flanked by two c1900 lighthouses. The busy old-fashioned general store is the hub of village life.

By car, Margaree Harbour is at the junction of Highway 219 and the Cabot Trail, 112km/70 miles from Port Hastings, 27km/17 miles from Chéticamp and 60km/37 miles from Baddeck. Just a short walk from the village, the **Duck Cove Inn** (*24 rooms; 10289 Cabot Trail;* ✆ *902 235 2658;* tf *1 800 565 9993; www.duckcoveinn. com;* ☉ *Jun–late Oct;* **$$**) is situated on a hillside overlooking the Margaree River. Rooms are clean but perhaps a bit dated for the price. The licensed dining room (☉ *Jun–late Oct 07.30–10.00 & 17.30–20.00 daily;* **$$**) offers good-value family dining, and there are laundry facilities.

THE CABOT TRAIL: WEST

The Cabot Trail is the official name for a road that loops around northern Cape Breton Island. This region is justly renowned for its stunning unspoilt beauty and regularly features high on lists of the world's best scenic drives.

The most spectacular stretch of the approximately 300km trail is the 115km between Chéticamp and Ingonish Beach, much of which passes through the Cape Breton Highlands National Park. From early summer well into autumn, pilot, minke, fin and humpback whales come to feed in the Gulf of St Lawrence and off the northern tip of Cape Breton Island. Whale-watching tours depart from Chéticamp, Pleasant Bay, Bay St Lawrence and the Ingonishes.

The national park apart, there are many other beautiful sections of the Cabot Trail, such as the drive through the Margaree Valley. There are also some pretty side trips such as the one from Cape North to Meat Cove.

This is not a drive to be rushed: plan to stay a couple of nights (ideally more) *en route* to have time to walk some trails, appreciate the look-outs, take a side trip or two, look round Baddeck, try your hand at sea kayaking, go whale watching, cycling, or just relax on the beach.

As no public transport operates here, you'll need your own vehicle or to join a tour. One-day Cabot Trail tours are offered by **Blackwood Tours** (✆ *902 862 3791;* e *donblackwood@seascape.ns.ca*), based in New Waterford (near Syndey), and Baddeck-based **Bannockburn Discovery Tours** (page 347).

Guided and self-guided bike tours of the entire Cabot Trail are offered by **Pedal and Sea Adventures** (page 87), **Freewheeling Adventures** (page 87) and **Cabot Trail Adventures** (page 335). There are several strenuous climbs, and some sections have no paved hard shoulders: not for the novice! Cabot Trail Adventures, in my opinion, offer the best activity tours of the northern Cabot Trail and vicinity – including possibilities to cycle some of the best sections of the Cabot Trail via shuttled day trips from accommodations based at the 'Top of the Island'. For other tour operators, see pages 39–41.

BELLE CÔTE Just north of the Margaree River, the wharf at the fishing village of Belle Côte tends to be busy with fishermen returning with their catches in the middle of the day between spring and autumn. Wander the beach on the other side of the breakwater, and, in season, buy a fresh-

A WORD OF WARNING

The first time I drove this route it was through thick fog and although I suspected that I was passing magnificent scenery, I could just make out the trees by the side of the road. I tried to make the best of it, and did a couple of 'atmospheric' forest trails, but felt quite down. Luckily, the fog lifted on the second morning, and I saw what all the fuss was about. Keep your fingers crossed!

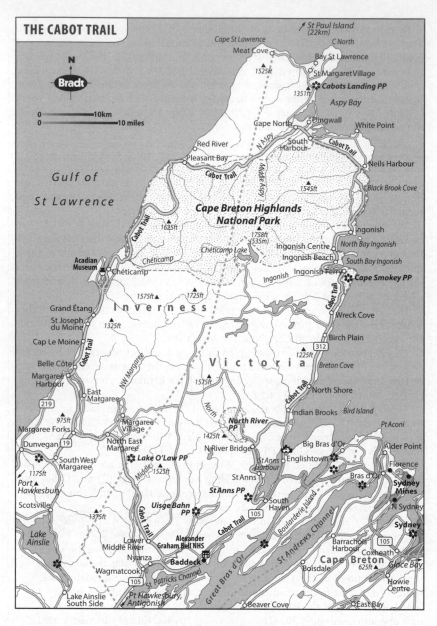

cooked lobster at the pound. Held in July, **Belle Côte Days** festival includes five days of concerts, dances, barbecues and competitions, as well as a golf tournament.

Belle Côte is just off the Cabot Trail, less than 4km/2 miles from Margaree Harbour and 23km/14 miles from Chéticamp.

 Where to stay, eat and drink

 Island Sunset Resort (18 units) 19 Beach Cove Rd; ☎ 902 235 2669; **tf** 1 866 515 2900; www.

islandsunset.com; ⏱ mid Jun–mid Oct . The very comfortable, well-decorated cottages overlook the beach, with wonderful sea views. The licensed restaurant (☺ *mid Jun–mid Oct plus mid May–mid Jun & mid Sep–mid Oct 16.00–21.00 w/knds;* $$$) serves good, fresh food: start perhaps with Cape North mussels, whilst the prime rib & snow crab are both delicious. The resort also has its own lobster pound, & the Lobster Pound Bistro (☎ 902 235 1614; ☺ *mid Jun–mid Sep 11.00–18.00 daily;* $$) offers a more casual shellfish dining experience. $$$

⌂ **Ocean Haven & Acres & Ocean** (3 units) 49 Old Belle Côte Rd; ☎ 902 235 2329; **tf** 1 888 280 0885; www.oceanhaven.ca; ☺ Jun–mid Oct. Choose a room with en-suite or private bathroom at this restored farmhouse B&B on 40ha overlooking the ocean. Or rent Acres & Ocean, the 2-bedroom self-catering cottage with full kitchen (3-night minimum rental). Full b/fast inc (B&B only). $$

CHÉTICAMP (Chéticamp – the largest Acadian village in North America with a population of 1,000 – is a busy fishing village set along a protected waterway that opens to the Gulf of St Lawrence. Just 5km from the western entrance to the **Cape Breton Highlands National Park**, the community has long been regarded as a centre for the craft of **rug hooking**. It is also a departure point for **whale-watching** cruises to the Gulf of St Lawrence (one company even offers the chance to snorkel with the whales), and home to a good golf course overlooking the harbour. Virtually all attractions, services and places to stay and eat are strung along the main road through town, the Cabot Trail.

Chéticamp is easy to get to **by car**: it is 88km/55 miles from Baddeck and 115km/71 miles from Ingonish Beach. If you continue more than a few kilometres past Chéticamp, the Cabot Trail passes through the national park , and – even if you have no intention of stopping or using facilities – park entry fees are payable (though free park entry applies in 2017; page 10).

History The history of Chéticamp was strongly influenced by fishermen from Jersey, Channel Islands, particularly the Robin Company which came to Chéticamp in the late 1760s to exploit the fisheries. Two families settled permanently in 1782, and they were joined by 14 Acadians from St Johns Island (as Prince Edward Island was then known) who became affectionately known as 'Les Quatorze Vieux', and many other Acadians who had spent the post-Expulsion years looking for somewhere new to put down roots. Formerly called Eastern Harbour, following the influx of impecunious Acadians the community was labelled *cheti camp*, or 'poor camp'.

Construction of the imposing Romanesque-style c1892 Église St-Pierre was a team effort: parishioners donated a day's work per month, and blocks of stone

---

MASKS

In the Middle Ages, the French took a one-day respite from the rigours of Lent to enjoy themselves. Disguised from head to toe, locals went from house to house getting people to try to guess their identity: they were known as *mi-carêmes*. They then removed their masks and were offered treats. This tradition has largely died out in most French and Acadian regions but remains strong here and in Chéticamp. Festivities take place in the third week of Lent (usually March) and last a week. The celebration has led to the revival of carnival mask-making as a folk art. A purpose-built Centre de la Mi-Carême (*51 Harbour Rd, Grand Étang;* ☎ *902 224 1016; www.micareme.ca;* ☺ *mid Jun–late Oct 10.00–16.00 daily, admission CAN$5*) opened in the summer of 2009, displaying more than 100 masks crafted locally for the annual festival. There's also a gift shop and small café.

donated by the Robin Company were dragged across the ice from Chéticamp Island by horses. In addition to man-hours, the parishioners also donated all the lumber. The Baroque-style interior – redecorated in the late 1980s – is spectacular, with four plaster columns looking remarkably like marble: the 1904 Casavant organ is still in excellent working order.

Where to stay

Maison Fiset House (8 units) 15050 Cabot Trail; ☎902 224 1794; **tf** 1 855 292 1794; www. maisonfisethouse.com. Friendly, new, modern inn/B&B with good views. 6 rooms & 2 suites with whirlpool baths. All have balconies, & there's a nice patio. Rate includes full b/fast. **$$–$$$**

L'Auberge Doucet Inn (11 rooms, 2 suites) 14758 Cabot Trail; ☎902 224 3438; **tf** 1 800 646 8668; www.aubergedoucetinn.com; ⏲ May–mid Nov. In pleasant grounds, the rooms feel a bit more 'motel' than 'inn', but are clean & quite spacious. Full b/fast inc. **$$**

Cornerstone Motel (17 units) 16537 Cabot Trail; ☎902 224 3232; **tf** 1 844 224 3232; cornerstonemotel.com; ⏲ May–mid Oct. 3 room types in this comfortable motel on 4ha, all with fridges. Walking trails on property, plus facilities for motor bikers. **$–$$**

Chéticamp Outfitters Inn B&B [map, page 332] (6 rooms) 13938 Cabot Trail, Point Cross; ☎902 224 2776; chéticampoutfitters.com; ⏲ May–Nov. Wonderful views from this modern cedar home set on a hillside 3km south of Chéticamp. Rooms with private or (cheaper) shared bathroom. The Acadian hosts know the area very well. Full b/fast inc. **$**

Merry's Motel & B&B (10 units) 15356 Cabot Trail; ☎902 224 2456; www.merrysmotel. com; ⏲ mid May–mid Oct. 2 rooms in the main house (shared bath), 7 traditional motel units (private bath) & a 1-bedroom apt with full kitchen. Clean, friendly & good value. Light b/fast inc. **$**

Ⅹ Chéticamp Campground [map, page 332] (122 sites) Cape Breton Highlands National Park western entrance, Cabot Trail; **tf** 1 877 737 3783 (reservations); www.pccamping.ca; ⏲ May–Oct; sites can be reserved for late Jun–early Sep. Open & wooded campground with flush toilets, showers & kitchen shelters, oTENTiks (page 61), serviced & unserviced sites. Note: national park entrance fee payable (page 331). **$**

Ⅹ Plage St-Pierre Beach & Campground [map, page 332] (94 sites & 50 seasonal) 635 Chéticamp Island Rd; ☎902 224 2112; www.plagestpierrebeachandcampground. com; ⏲ mid May–mid Oct. Open & wooded serviced & tent sites, laundromat & canteen. On Chéticamp Island, with a long stretch of beach frontage. **$**

Where to eat and drink

Le Gabriel 15424 Cabot Trail; ☎902 224 3685; www.legabriel.com; ⏲ early May–late Oct 11.00–22.00 daily, rest of year 11.30–20.00. This large licensed restaurant/sports bar (incorporating a mock lighthouse) is about as upmarket as things get in Chéticamp. The seafood (eg: shrimp & scallop kebabs, broiled fillet of haddock, or sole stuffed with scallops & crab) is good. Lounge, billiard table & a regular programme of live Acadian/Celtic music. **$$**

All Aboard Restaurant 14925 Cabot Trail; ☎902 224 2288; ▮; ⏲ 11.00–21.00 daily. Good-value, licensed Acadian family restaurant with decent food (strong on seafood – eg: steamed crab – but carnivore options, too) & regular live music. Not huge so can get very busy (worth making a reservation in high season). **$–$$**

Seafood Stop 14803 Cabot Trail; ☎902 224 1717; www.chéticamp.ca/seafoodstop; ⏲ May–mid Oct 11.00–20.00 daily. Not just an unpretentious seafood restaurant (several pan-fried options), but also a lobster pound & fish market (good for self-caterers or barbecuers). **$–$$**

Restaurant Evangeline 15150 Cabot Trail; ☎902 224 2044; ▮; ⏲ 06.30–21.00 daily. A simple, unsophisticated diner dishing up hearty b/fasts, reliable fish & chips, pizzas & the like. **$**

Aucoin Bakery Rue Lapointe 14, Petit Étang; ☎902 224 3220; aucoinbakery.com; ⏲ 07.00–17.00 Mon–Fri (plus May–early Oct Sat until late). Take-away energy-boosting (albeit calorific) treats between Chéticamp & the national park. **$**

Shopping A stop that seems to be on every coach-tour itinerary is **Flora's** (*14208 Cabot Trail;* ✆ *902 224 3139; www.floras.com;* ⊕ *May–Oct 08.30–18.00 daily*), but this big, often-busy craft and souvenir shop isn't a tourist trap; whilst there are few real bargains, in general, prices are fair. Well worth a visit for gift-seekers and crafters is **Proud To Be Hookers** (*aka Jean's Gift Shop; 10 Prairie Rd, Petit- Étang;* ✆ *902 224 2758;* �; ⊕ *approx mid May–mid Oct 09.00–17.00 Mon–Sat, 10.00–17.00 Sun*) between Chéticamp and the national park. There's also a Saturday-morning **farmers' market** (*15118 Cabot Trail;* ⊕ *late Jun–Oct 10.00–13.00*).

Other practicalities

$ Royal Bank 15374 Cabot Trail; ✆ 902 224 2040; ⊕ 10.00–17.00 Mon–Fri

➕ Sacred Heart Community Health Centre 15102 Cabot Trail; ✆ 902 224 1500

✉ Post office 15240 Cabot Trail; ⊕ 08.30–17.30 Mon–Thu, 08.30–18.00 Fri

ℹ Tourist information Les Trois Pignons Museum, 15584 Cabot Trail; ✆ 902 224 2642; ⊕ mid May–mid Oct 08.00–19.00 daily

What to see and do For hooked-rug enthusiasts, Chéticamp is the perfect stop. Head to **Les Trois Pignons Museum of the Hooked Rug and Home Life** (*15584 Cabot Trail;* ✆ *902 224 2642; www.lestroispignons.com;* ⊕ *mid May–mid Oct 08.30–17.00 daily; Jul–Aug to 18.30; admission CAN$57*, whose collection links Chéticamp's history with the development of rug hooking. The museum's **Elizabeth LeFort Gallery** has a unique collection of hooked rug masterpieces by Ms LeFort, Chéticamp's most famous daughter, and, some would say, the country's best rug hooker – her works have graced walls in Buckingham Palace, the White House and the Vatican.

In July and August, the **Festival de l'Escaouette** (*www.chéticamp.ca/en*) celebrates Acadian culture and heritage through food, music, dancing and more.

Relax on the green at **Le Portage Golf Club** (*15580 Cabot Trail;* ✆ *902 224 3338;* tf *1 888 618 5558; www.leportagegolfclub.com; green fees CAN$92*), a 6,751yd par-72 course. Not quite up there with Cape Breton Island's very best courses, but still well worth a round.

A road along a sandbar leads to **Chéticamp Island**, where you can walk (or drive) to the Enragee Point Lighthouse. The island's large cow population probably accounts for the large number of flies.

Whale watching Local operators offering 2½–3-hour boat trips two or three times a day for approximately CAN$55 include:

Captain Zodiac Whale Cruise tf 1 877 232 2522; www.novascotiawhales.com; ⊕ tours early Jun–mid Oct. Not just regular tours by Zodiac, but also 'Snorkel with Whales' trips. In theory the latter are offered up to twice daily in summer, but this is dependent on suitable (ie: calm) water conditions

& co-operative whales. These trips cost from CAN$95.Book in advance & try to allow a 2–3 day 'window' for the best chance of success.
Love Boat Seaside Whale Cruises ✆ 902 224 2899; tf 1 877 880 2899; www. loveboatwhalecruises.ca;. ⊕ tours mid Jun–mid Oct.

PLEASANT BAY The Cabot Trail leaves the park just before Pleasant Bay, a working fishing village that bills itself 'Whale Watching Capital of Cape Breton Island' and 'The Jewel of the Cabot Trail'. Whales come closer to Pleasant Bay than they do to Chéticamp, so tours from here tend to be shorter. There are beautiful sunsets from the beach and hikers should be sure to take the **Roberts Mountain Trail**: not all that long, but steep. If it is clear, you'll be rewarded with a magnificent 360° view.

Pleasant Bay is on the Cabot Trail, accessible **by car**. The village is 42km/26 miles from Chéticamp and 73km/45 miles from Ingonish Beach.

🏠 Where to stay, eat and drink

🏠 **Highland Breeze & Gulf Breeze Accommodations** (3 rooms & 3 apts) 42 Harbour Rd & 23329 Cabot Trail; ✆ 902 224 2974; **tf** 1 877 224 2974; www.highlandbreeze.com. Moose are often seen from the deck of Highland Breeze, a modern chalet-style 3-bedroom B&B with outdoor hot tub & seasonal pool. Just over 1km away (15–20mins' walk) Gulf Breeze is a 3-apt house with a games room & outdoor hot tub. All rooms have en-suite baths, many with jacuzzis. Rate includes country b/fast (served for both properties at Highland Breeze), & evening dessert (🕐 20.00–21.30) at the Highland Breeze Bistro. Both **$$$**

🏠 **Midtrail Motel & Restaurant** (20 rooms) 23475 Cabot Trail; ✆ 902 224 2529; **tf** 1 800 215 0411; www.midtrail.com; 🕐 mid May–mid Oct. Recently renovated motel rooms at this pink complex with wonderful views on 12ha on the waterfront. The licensed restaurant (🕐 *mid May– mid Oct 08.00–20.00 daily;* **$$**) isn't bad, & the seafood is recommended. **$$**

🏠 **The Poplar B&B** (2 rooms) 23606 Cabot Trail; ✆ 902 224 3176; **tf** 1 877 224 3176; www. bbcanada.com/thepoplarbnb; 🕐 mid May–mid Oct. Simple, pleasant, centrally located B&B. Rate includes self-serve continental b/fast. **$**

🏠 **HI-Cabot Trail Hostel** 23349 Cabot Trail; ✆ 902 224 1976; **e** cabottrailhostel@hotmail.com; 🕐 May–Oct. A clean & friendly backpackers' hostel with a 10-bed co-ed dorm & 3 private rooms.

OMM

Turn off the Cabot Trail on to Pleasant Bay Road, and within 5 minutes you'll come to the remote community of Red River. As you'd expect, there are weathered houses and fishermen's shacks; less predictable are quite a few new, expensive homes – and a Shambhala Buddhist Monastery. If you wish to look round **Gampo Abbey** (✆ 902 224 2752; gampoabbey.org; 🕐 tours are generally offered Jul– Aug 13.30 & 14.30 Mon–Fri), it's best to ring ahead to check.

Shared bathrooms, 2 kitchens. Bike friendly. *Dorm CAN$33; private room CAN$665 (discounts offered for HI members)* **$**

✗ **Rusty Anchor Restaurant** 23197 Cabot Trail; ✆ 902 224 1313; therustyanchorrestaurant. com; 🕐 May–Oct 11.00–22.00 daily. Set on a hill with a fabulous view & a deck overlooking Pleasant Bay, this is a great spot. The menu is a bit more creative than many, & once again fresh seafood the best choice. Save room for dessert, too. **$$**

✗ **Highland Breeze Bistro** 23582 Cabot Trail; ✆ 902 224 3663; **tf** 1 877 224 2974; 🕐 in season only. This new place (under the same management as the 2 'Breezes'; see above) is a bit more cafeteria than bistro. Sandwiches, lobster burgers, soups & chowders, plus baked goods. **$**

What to see and do The **Whale Interpretive Centre** (*104 Harbour Rd;* ✆ *902 224 1411;* **e** *whaleintcentre@gmail.com;* 🕐 *Jun–mid Oct 09.00–17.00 daily; admission CAN$5*) is the ideal place to learn more about whales before a whale-watching trip – and you can see a life-size model of a pilot whale.

Whale watching It's worth booking in advance for July and August trips. Operators include:

Captain Mark's ✆ 902 224 1316; **tf** 1 888 754 5112; www.whaleandsealcruise.com. Both conventional boats (*CAN$45*) & Zodiac-type (*CAN$55*) offered.

Guaranteed Whales ✆ 902 224 1919; **tf** 1 855 942 5315; guaranteedwhales.com. Conventional boat (*CAN$49*), maritime music.
Pleasant Bay Zodiac ✆ 902 2242174; **tf** 1 844 224 2101; www.cabottrail.com/ PleasantBayZodiacTours. Zodiac-type (*CAN$49*).

CAPE BRETON HIGHLANDS NATIONAL PARK

Established in 1936, the Cape Breton Highlands National Park (CBHNP) (📞 *902 224 2306; www.pc.gc.ca/pn-np/ns/cbreton;* ⊕ *May–Oct; admission CAN$7.80 (2016), free in 2017*) was the first national park in the Maritime Provinces. The largest protected wilderness area in the province, it encompasses 950km² of the Maritime Acadian Highlands, one of the 39 natural regions of Canada. In addition to the magnificent forested highlands and deep river canyons, large sections of northern Cape Breton Island's stunning coastal wilderness fall within the park's boundaries. Wildlife is plentiful, with moose top of most visitors' 'want to see' lists. If you drive the western part of the Trail in late afternoon or early evening, you're very likely to see moose standing in the roadside ditches: drive slowly and carefully. From the Trail's look-outs, you might see whales just offshore.

The Cabot Trail is the only road through the park: along the road are two-dozen scenic roadside look-outs, many with interpretive panels, and if the weather is clear, enjoy magnificent breathtaking views of the Highlands, the Gulf of St Lawrence, and, on the eastern side, the Atlantic. Pass soaring cliffs, rocky shorelines, fabulous beaches – and one of the world's top golf courses. Although I strongly advise you to get out of your vehicle as often as possible to walk a few trails, enjoy a picnic with an awesome view, or just wander a deserted beach, this is a park that *can* be enjoyed by those much happier doing their sightseeing without having to undo their seat belts.

With all this and sandy beaches, mountain trails, old-growth forests, waterfalls and highland barrens carpeted in rare wild flowers, this national park is one of the finest in Canada – and that's saying something.

The Cabot Trail dips in and out of the park: this means that those who do not wish to camp can stay very close to all the natural beauty, albeit just outside the park's boundaries.

From mid June to mid September Parks Canada offer visitors a variety of guided hikes, and there's a wide array of diverse interpretive programming offered daily in July August. Many programmes are free: for others (eg: Lantern Walk through Time, or How to Hook a Mackerel), fees are payable. Held at various Cabot Trail communities, the **Hike the Highlands Festival** (*www.hikethehighlandsfestival.com*) in **September** includes guided hikes in the Highlands of Cape Breton Island.

GEOGRAPHY AND GEOLOGY The CBHNP protects a spectacular portion of the largest remaining wild area of the Maritime Acadian Highlands. The dominant feature is the forested high plateau, which encompasses White Hill, the province's highest point at 535m. Extensive bog systems on the plateau are drained by numerous streams, stained the colour of tea by tannins leeching from the vegetation. After heavy rain, or during the spring snow melt, these in turn feed plunging waterfalls. There are also deep, forested canyons, and magnificent coastal cliffs which tend to be steeper to the west and more gently sloping on the park's eastern side.

A unique mix of Acadian, Boreal and Taiga forest regions co-exists as a result of the rugged topography and cool maritime climate.

The park's plateau is part of the worn-down Appalachian mountain chain which stretches from Georgia to Newfoundland. Part of the park belongs to the Blair River inlier (an area, or formation of, older rocks completely surrounded by a more recent formation), formed 1,500 to 1,000 million years ago, and the oldest rocks in the Maritime Provinces.

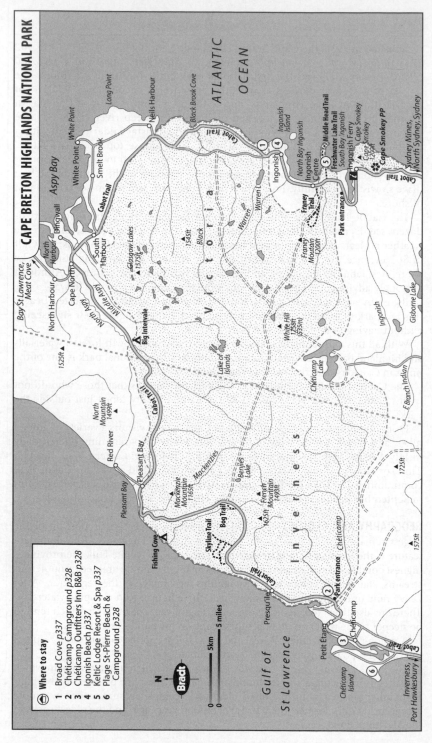

CAPE BRETON HIGHLANDS NATIONAL PARK

Where to stay
1 Broad Cove p337
2 Chéticamp Campground p328
3 Chéticamp Outfitters Inn B&B p328
4 Ingonish Beach p337
5 Keltic Lodge Resort & Spa p337
6 Plage St-Pierre Beach & Campground p328

Bradt

N

0   5km
0   5 miles

ATLANTIC OCEAN

Gulf of St Lawrence

FLORA AND FAUNA The most common tree species include balsam fir, white and yellow birch, white and black spruce and sugar maple – there are more than 750 vascular plant species, the vast majority native. These include Arctic–Alpine species such as dwarf birch (*Betula nana*) and southern temperate plants such as Dutchman's breeches (*Dicentra cucullaria*).

The park is also home to white-tailed deer, moose, black bear, beaver, mink, red fox, snow-shoe hare, Gaspe shrew, rock vole and lynx, and more than 200 bird species, including eagles and red-tailed hawks. Wildlife can be seen offshore too, with pilot and minke whales, and grey seal the most commonly seen marine mammals. Humpback whales and harbour seals are spotted less frequently.

TRAILS Walkers and hikers can choose from 26 trails which range from 10 minutes to 6 hours. A short summary of each trail is given on the park map obtainable at the visitor centres, or on the website (page 331). Mountain biking is permitted on seven of the trails.

Suggestions include the 10–15-minute **Bog Trail**, where a boardwalk – with interpretive boards – leads through a highland plateau bog; flora includes pitcher plants and wild orchids. Or try the well-hiked (and well-liked) 9km **Skyline Trail**, which despite its name, doesn't involve a huge amount of climbing: it leads to a headland clifftop high above the sea. On this trail, look carefully for moose that often lie down in the undergrowth very close to the path; the majority of walkers pass them by without noticing them. Many people visiting the park stay at the Ingonishes (pages 336–8), and that area has some good and understandably popular trails, such as the 2km wander around Freshwater Lake by Ingonish Beach (look for beavers towards dusk). Very hard work but worth it for the view is the 7.5km **Franey Trail**, which involves an ascent of over 300m. And despite starting behind a resort, the 4km **Middle Head Trail** is very enjoyable, with fine coastal views, and the possibility of seeing whales from the end of the peninsula. It is definitely worth talking to the visitor centre staff and listening to their hiking suggestions.

TOURIST INFORMATION The park has visitor centres (⊕ *May–Oct 09.00–17.00 daily; Jul–Aug until 19.00*) at both entrances: **Chéticamp** (✎ *902 224 2306*), and **Ingonish** (✎ *902 285 2691*). Off-season, ask for information at the park office at the Chéticamp entrance, which is by far the larger of the two centres, and in addition to exhibits on natural history, sightseeing and hiking opportunities, also houses a well-stocked bookshop, **Les Amis du Plein Air** (✎ *902 224 3814*).

 WHERE TO STAY The park has seven **campgrounds** [map, opposite], six accessible by road (and ranging from 10 to 202 sites), and one hike-in. Reservations are only accepted at three: Chéticamp (page 328), Broad Cove (page 337) and Ingonish Beach (page 337) (**tf** *1 877 737 3783 to reserve*). Suggestions for non-campers are shown under the appropriate area.

THE CABOT TRAIL: NORTH

The Cabot Trail community of Cape North is the launching point for a beautiful side-trip to explore some of Nova Scotia's most stunning scenery and remote communities.

CAPE NORTH The small community of Cape North is about 30km from the eponymous geographic feature – which, as the name might suggest, is Nova Scotia's most northerly point.

Consider a beautiful, scenic side-trip from Cape North to Bay St Lawrence and Meat Cove, the province's most northerly community.

Follow Bay St Lawrence Road along the lovely Aspy Bay shore to **Cabot Landing Provincial Park**. This picnic park has a long red sand beach – tinged white in places by naturally occurring gypsum – facing Aspy Bay, and a cairn commemorating the supposed landfall of John Cabot in 1497 (page 16). If the weather is clear, you'll have a good view of St Paul Island (page 335). For those who feel like burning off some calories in return for amazing views, the park is also the starting point for a hike up the 442m **Sugar Loaf Mountain**.

St Margaret's Village has a lovely setting, and a right turn leads to **Bay St Lawrence**, another pretty fishing village (crab is a speciality). Whale-watching and other boat trips depart from the wharf with some of the province's most remote and stunning coastal scenery as a backdrop. Fin whales – the second-largest whale species after the blue whale – are often seen. Local operators include the excellent **Oshan Whale Watch** (tf *1 877 383 2883; www.oshan. ca;* ⏰ *Jul–Oct*), who can also arrange birdwatching boat trips, deep-sea fishing charters, and (with notice) trips to St Paul Island. There's also **Captain Cox's Whale Watch** (✆ *902 383 2981;* tf *1 888 346 5556; www.whalewatching-novascotia.com;* ⏰ *mid Jun–Oct*). Very fresh seafood can be purchased at the village's Victoria Co-op Fisheries, or stock up with groceries at the store. Other eating options include The Hut, a decent take-out, and a simple café in the Community Centre, and there's also an ATM.

Continue to **Capstick**, and then on a 7km unpaved road: virtually all the way, you will enjoy spectacular views from high above the sea. Whilst drivers will want to concentrate on the road, passengers can look out for pods of whales in the bays below. The road descends to (and ends at) remote **Meat Cove**. Here, you'll find a **Welcome Centre** (⏰ *Jun–early Oct 09.30–16.30 Mon–Fri*), which houses a tea room and a couple of simple places to stay – the rustic **Meat Cove Lodge** (✆ *902 383 2970;* 🔲; ⏰ *Jun–mid Sep;* **$**), the **Hines Ocean View Lodge** (✆ *902 383 2512, 902 383 2562; hinesoceanviewlodge.ca;* ⏰ *May–early Sep; off-season by request;* **$**), and the amazingly located clifftop 26-site **Meat Cove Campground** (✆ *902 383 2379; meatcovecampground.ca;* ⏰ *mid Jun–mid Oct;* **$**), which offers a 'chowder hut' and also rents kayaks. There are some very good hikes and Meat Cove is a place for those who appreciate nature and the great coastal outdoors: ironically, this is also a popular moose-hunting area in the hunting season. For trail suggestions – and more on Meat Cove – see the campground's website.

It is on the Cabot Trail, 71km/44 miles from Chéticamp and 44km/27 miles from Ingonish Beach, and is easily reached **by car**.

Where to stay, eat and drink

🏠 **The Markland Coastal Beach Cottages** (20 units) 802 Dingwall Rd; ✆ 902 383 2246; tf 1 855 872 6048; e info@themarkland. com; www.themarkland.com; ⏰ May–mid Oct. Close to the quaint fishing village of Dingwall, 5km from Cape North, the Markland offers rustic log rooms & 1- & 2-bedroom chalets. A simple place (no TVs in rooms) to stay & enjoy the outdoors. Heated outdoor pool (seasonal), & private beach in a magnificent, scenic location. Its restaurant (**$$$**) menu is good (fresh, local ingredients, seafood, organic vegetables, etc), if limited, but not cheap. Rate includes 'continental plus' b/fast. **$$$**

Ặ Hideaway Campground, Cabins & Oyster Market (7 cabins, 37 campsites) 401 Shore Rd, South Harbour; ☎ 902 383 2116; www. campingcapebreton.com; ⊕ mid May–mid Oct. Rustic camping cabins & well-spread open & wooded sites approx 5km from Cape North, overlooking Aspy Bay, with laundromat. Canoe & kayak rentals, & boat launch. Oysters sold. Recommended for campers. *Cabins CAN$55.* **$**

✕ Angie's Family Restaurant 29329 Cabot Trail, Cape North; ☎ 902 383 2531; ⊕ in season 14.00–20.00 daily; check off-season hours. The diner fare tends to be standard at best, but the fresh seafood stands out. **$–$$**

⊑ Danena's Café & Bakery 30001 Cabot Trail, South Harbour; ☎ 902 383 2408; **f**; ⊕ in season 08.00–20.00 daily. Good, imaginative pizzas & specials (eg: ginger pork & rice or Classic chilli with garlic cheese bread), b/fasts, decent coffee, & delish desserts. Service can be slow. **$–$$**

What to see and do The North Highlands Community Museum (*29243 Cabot Trail;* ☎ *902 383 2579; www.northhighlandsmuseum.ca;* ⊕ *mid Jun–mid Oct 09.00–17.00 daily; admission CAN$2*) houses displays that tell of pioneer days in the Cape Breton Highlands, and more recent history. See, too, artefacts from the *Auguste*, a ship wrecked in Aspy Bay in 1761 *en route* from Quebec to France. Of the 121 on board, only seven reached the shore alive. Traditional skills – for example, net mending, weaving, ropemaking and quilting – are demonstrated in July and August. There is also a settlers' garden, operational forge and culture centre that hosts a summer concert and presentation series.

Some 2km west of Cape North village, **Arts North** (*28571 Cabot Trail;* ☎ *902 383 2982; www.arts-north.com;* ⊕ *Jun–Oct 09.00–19.00 daily*) displays the work of more than two-dozen surprisingly gifted resident artisans, including handmade pottery, native-wood cutting boards, jewellery, prints, driftwood carvings, quilting and basketry. Meanwhile, the **St Paul Island Museum** (*Dingwall Rd, Dingwall;* ⊕ *mid Jun–mid Oct 10.00–17.00 daily*) tells the story of St Paul Island (see below). Alongside is a well-travelled **lighthouse**; originally the St Paul Island Southwest Lighthouse, it arrived in Dingwall in 2012 by way of Dartmouth.

For the active, **Cabot Trail Adventures** (*299 Shore Rd, South Harbour;* ☎ *902 383 2732; www.cabottrailoutdooradventures.com;* ⊕ *year-round, hours vary*) offers a wealth of local knowledge, cycle hire and a range of guided and self-guided tours from hiking, cycling, sea kayaking and trail running in summer to snow-shoeing, cross-country and back-country skiing in winter.

Winter visitors may be tempted to don cross-country skis – the **North Highlands Nordic Ski Club** (*nhn.xcski.ca*) is based here and offers equipment rentals.

ST PAUL ISLAND The rocky shores of St Paul Island – 22km offshore between the tip of Cape North and the Ingonishes – have accounted for more than 350 recorded shipwrecks. The **Graveyard of the Gulf** lies directly in the path of marine travel to and from the Gulf of St Lawrence, and in an area prone to thick fog in the spring and early summer and squalls and snowstorms in the autumn and winter.

In the early days, each year, when fishermen came to St Paul in spring, they would find the frozen bodies of shipwreck survivors who had managed to scale the island's cliffs only to perish from exposure and starvation.

For decades, demands were made for a lighthouse: in just one stormy 1835 night, four ships were wrecked on the island's shores. Finally in 1837, construction of two lighthouses, one at each end of the island, began. A building was also put up to house shipwreck victims. Subsequently there were still occasional tragedies, but far less loss of life.

Very hilly, the 4.5km by 1.5km island is covered with stunted spruce. Two lakes feed several streams. In season, there are abundant wild flowers but no animal life. The only relatively safe landing areas are Atlantic Cove, and Trinity Cove on the island's opposite side. Visits to the island can be arranged through Oshan Whale Watch (box, page 334) – you'll need a permit from the federal government if you want to go ashore..

The island's shipwreck-dotted waters are popular with **divers** – if you'd like to join them, Terry Dwyer (e *shipwrecked@ns.sympatico.ca; www.wreckhunter.ca*) may be able to help.

THE CABOT TRAIL: EAST

Beautiful though the Cabot Trail is, at the start of the next section of the Trail, a simple detour will yield rich rewards. Further south is a popular resort area known collectively as 'The Ingonishes' at the southeastern boundary of the Cape Breton Highlands National Park. Just a few kilometres further on is magnificent Cape Smokey before the scenery eases down a gear or two from the highs further north.

For a spectacular alternative to the next stretch of the Cabot Trail, turn off at Effies Brook and follow White Point Road.

Along this road you'll pass high cliffs and a photogenic sheltered lagoon before a long descent to the picturesque and beautifully situated village of **White Point**. See the colourful fishing boats protected by the little harbour, and be sure to wander down the track towards the point (the site of the village during the Age of Sail). Watch for whales, sit in the meadow and tuck into a picnic, or just soak up the coastal scenery. Climb back up the hill and continue through the fishing villages of New Haven and Neils Harbour to rejoin the Cabot Trail.

NEILS HARBOUR This busy working fishing community has a sandy beach bordered by high cliffs. On a hillock is a pyramid-shaped white wooden lighthouse with a square base, topped by a red light. In the summer the lighthouse is home to an ice-cream shop.

Neils Harbour is just off the Cabot Trail, 28km/17 miles north of Ingonish Beach. There are two simple, unpretentious seafood-focused diner/take-outs within approximately 500m of each other: **Chowder House** (❀ *902 336 2463; ⊕ May–Sep 11.00–20.00 daily; $*), on the point near the lighthouse; and my preferred option, **Sea Breeze** (❀ *902 336 2450; ⊕ mid Apr–mid Sep 11.30–18.00 daily; $*) offering good, simple, fresh home-cooking in a converted old house overlooking the beach.

THE INGONISHES On the shores of two lovely large bays (North and South), separated by the ruggedly beautiful Middle Head Peninsula, are the communities of (from north to south) Ingonish, Ingonish Centre, Ingonish Beach, Ingonish Harbour and (16km from Ingonish) Ingonish Ferry. Offshore is Ingonish Island.

Ingonish Beach is the eastern gateway to the Cape Breton Highlands National Park: within this region are a range of fine accommodations, excellent eateries, beautiful beaches (offering swimming in both fresh and salt water), and a relaxed resort atmosphere. Many will be drawn by the chance to play one of the world's best golf courses, others for the hiking. You can camp here, but it is also a good base from which non-campers can explore the national park and Cape North area.

Dotted about the Ingonishes are a couple of convenience stores, a liquor store, a bank and a laundromat.

Many people come and stay for a week or more – even if you're on a tight itinerary try to give yourself a couple of nights at least. Demand for accommodation can exceed supply in July and August, so book well ahead.

The Ingonishes are on the Cabot Trail, 110km/68 miles east of Chéticamp and 100km/62 miles north of Baddeck.

🏠 Where to stay

🏠 **Keltic Lodge Resort & Spa** [map, page 332] (105 units) Middle Head Peninsula, Ingonish Beach; ☎ 902 285 2880; **tf** 1 800 565 0444; kelticlodge.ca; ⊕ mid May–mid Oct. This Ingonish institution is in a magnificent setting on the peninsula dividing North & South bays. There are 3 types of accommodation: guest rooms, 2-bedroom suites & cottages (2- & 4-bedroom). Facilities include 3 restaurants, a bar, outdoor heated pool, tennis courts & Aveda spa, but the *pièce de résistance* is the golf course (page 338). Standards rise & fall: Ontario-based GolfNorth Properties took over the property in 2015 and over CAN$4m has already been spent in upgrades, but there is still work to be done both on the property & in staff training. In my opinion, at these prices overall guest satisfaction should be a touch higher. Various packages are offered. **$$$$**

🏠 **Seascape Coastal Retreat** (10 cabins) 36083 Cabot Trail, Ingonish; ☎ 902 285 3003; **tf** 1 866 385 3003; www.seascapecoastalretreat. com; ⊕ May–Oct. The comfortable 1-bedroom cottages with kitchenettes in a wonderful location are 'adults only'. Picnic lunches available & the rather good restaurant (retreat guests only) is open for dinner. Use of kayaks & mountain bikes. Recommended. Full b/fast & welcome snack inc. **$$$**

🏠 **Castle Rock Country Inn** (17 rooms) 39339 Cabot Trail, Ingonish Ferry; ☎ 902 285 2700; **tf** 1 888 884 7625; www.castlerockcountryinn. com. A modern Georgian-style inn on a cliffside high above the Ingonishes with magnificent views. Rooms are on 3 levels (basement rooms are smaller but still have ocean views). For the on-site Avalon Restaurant, see below. B/fast buffet inc Apr–Dec. **$$–$$$**

🏠 **The Point Cottages by the Sea** (6 cottages) 2 Point Cottages Lane, Ingonish; ☎ 902 285 2804; www.thepointcottages.com; ⊕ Jun–mid Oct. 3 1-bedroom, 2 2-bedroom & 1 3-bedroom cottage in a group of 12 in a great location virtually on the beach. A 1-week min rental applies Jul–Aug. **$$–$$$**

Å **Broad Cove** [map, page 332] (202 sites) **tf** 1 877 737 3783 (reservations); www. pccamping.ca; ⊕ late May–mid Oct. A large open & wooded campground with serviced & unserviced sites, flush toilets, oTENTiks (page 61), showers & kitchen shelters. Only a short walk to the sea, approx 5km north of Ingonish. **$**

Å **Ingonish Beach** [map, page 332] (60 sites) Ingonish Beach; ⊕ May–Oct. Open campground, unserviced sites, flush toilets, showers & kitchen shelters. 10mins' walk to the lake or beach. **$**

✕ Where to eat and drink
If you're just after a pizza, **Andrew's Pizzeria** (*37092 Cabot Trail;* ☎ *902 285 2475;* 📘; $–$$) should keep you happy.

✕ **Keltic Lodge Resort & Spa** Middle Head Peninsula, Ingonish Beach; ☎ 902 285 2880; **tf** 1 800 565 0444; **e** keltic@signatureresorts. com; www.kelticlodge.ca. Keltic offers 3 dining options: the hotel lounge-like **Highland Sitting Room** ($$) serves light fare & desserts (patio if weather permits); the high-ceilinged, spacious, airy **Arduaine Restaurant** (⊕ *early Jun–mid Sep 11.00–20.00 daily;* $$), offering casual family-style upmarket pub food (alfresco possibilities); & the fine-dining gourmet **Purple Thistle** (⊕ *mid May–mid Oct 18.00–21.00 daily;* $$$$) with wonderful views. Reservations recommended; dress code (smart casual) applies.

✕ **Avalon Restaurant at Castle Rock Country Inn** 39339 Cabot Trail, Ingonish Ferry; ☎ 902 285 2700; **tf** 1 888 884 7625; www.castlerockcountryinn.com; ⊕ year-round 17.00–20.00 daily (Nov–Jun by reservation only). The on-site licensed restaurant shares the inn's views & offers alfresco dining when the weather permits. In 2016, the Avalon's menu offered Asian–Cape Breton fusion cuisine & this may change in the future. It is unlikely that standards will drop suddenly. Considering the panorama & food quality, prices are reasonable. **$$–$$$**

✕ **Coastal Restaurant & Pub** 36404 Cabot Trail, Ingonish; ☎ 902 285 2526; ⊕ May–Oct

08.00–22.00 daily. Good, dependable family dining with the emphasis on seafood. If you prefer red meat, you won't have much room for pudding after the Coastal's signature 'ringer burger'. Patio. Live music Thu eve Jul–Aug. Licensed. $$

✕ **Main Street Restaurant & Bakery** 37764 Cabot Trail, Ingonish Beach; ☏ 902 285 2225; ⊕ Sep–Jun 07.00–20.00 Thu–Tue; Jul–Aug 11.00–21.00 Thu–Tue. Good-sized portions, well-cooked food & friendly service. Another place that does superb seafood chowder – & a lot more. Licensed. $$

✕ **Seagull Restaurant** 35963 Cabot Trail, Ingonish; ☏ 902 285 2851; **f**; ⊕ end May–early Oct noon–19.30 Wed–Mon. The Seagull doesn't claim to do haute cuisine: here, the deep fryer is king. Big portions of diner food, low prices & fabulous views from the outdoor (covered) patio. Easy to miss – look out for a sgl-storey white building on the waterfront. $

☕ **Bean Barn Café** 36741 Cabot Trail; ☏ 902 285 2767; **f**; ⊕ mid May–late Oct; check hours. Good, homey, casual, family-friendly café dishing up mainly homemade food, such as all-day breakfasts, seafood chowder, tasty cheesecakes & more. $

Other practicalities

$ **Scotiabank** 37787 Cabot Trail, Ingonish Beach; ☏ 902 285 2555; ⊕ 10.00–17.00 Mon–Fri

✉ **Post office** 37813 Cabot Trail, Ingonish Beach; ⊕ 08.00–17.00 Mon–Wed & Fri, 09.00–18.00 Thu

Victoria North Regional Library 36243 Cabot Trail; ☏ 902 285 2544; ⊕ noon–17.00 & 18.00–20.00 Tue–Thu, 09.00–noon & 13.00–17.00 Fri, 10.00–noon & 13.00–17.00 Sat

What to see and do Ingonish whale-watching tour operators seem to come and go, but options include **Ingonish Whale Watching** (☏ 902 285 1053; **f** Ingonish-Whale-Watching-111655125592530; ⊕ Jun–late Oct; 2–4 tours per day; CAN$40) and **Keltic Express Zodiac Adventures** (tf 1 866 688 2424; www.capebretonwhaletours.com; ⊕ mid May–mid Oct) runs a 90-minute to 2-hour tour costing CAN$55. If golf is your thing, **Highland Links Ingonish Beach** (☏ 902 285 2600; tf 1 800 441 1118; kelticlodge.ca/golf; green fees CAN$113–144) is one of Canada's top courses. Featuring on most 'World's 100 Best Courses' lists, this 6,592yd par-72 course was designed by Stanley Thompson, who was also responsible for the Digby Pines course (page 209) – the setting is truly magnificent. Note that there are walks of up to 500m between holes.

CAPE SMOKEY From Ingonish Ferry, the Cabot Trail climbs steadily to the crest of 360m Cape Smokey, named for the white cloud that often sits atop the red granite promontory. You're no longer within the national park, but nature is just as stunning here.

A turn-off leads to the **Cape Smokey Provincial Park** (parks.novascotia.ca/content/cape-smokey; ⊕ late May–early Oct), which provides magnificent vistas of the mountainous coastline. There are several picnic areas, and a moderate to difficult 10km return trail leads past several look-outs to the very tip of the Cape. Bald eagles and hawks can often be seen soaring the updrafts and moose are plentiful in this area; on my last visit I saw three by the roadside between the Cabot Trail and the parking area. From the top of old Smokey, the steep and twisting road descends, offering views of the offshore Bird Islands (page 342).

Cape Smokey is on the Cabot Trail, 13km/8 miles south of Ingonish Beach, and 87km/54 miles from Baddeck.

WRECK COVE TO INDIAN BROOK The Cabot Trail continues along the coastal plain passing little fishing communities, a handful of studios/craft shops, and a couple of beaches. If you would like a glimpse of local handiwork, stop by **Leather Works**

by Jolene (*45808 Cabot Trail, Indian Brook;* ✆ *902 929 2414; www.leather-works. ca;* ⊕ *May–Oct; off-season by chance or appointment*) to see a variety of handmade beautiful leather goods including belts, bags and ice buckets. Also visit Barbara Longva's shop/studio **Sew Inclined** (*41819 Cabot Trail, Wreck Cove;* ✆ *902 929 2050;* m *902 304 0123; www.sewinclined.ca;* ⊕ *May–Oct 09.00–17.00 daily*) for unique hats and historic clothing. There are several other crafters and artisans based along the 22km/14 miles between Wreck Cove and Indian Brook – and between Indian Brook and St Anns Bay. For details, see www.glassartisans.ca/artisan-loop.

🏠 **Where to stay** The Dancing Moose (see below) offers 'The Sleeping Moose', a two-bedroom fully equipped cottage (**$$**), or four comfortable 'Zzzz Moose Camping Cabins' – very comfortable, deluxe wood 'tents' (**$**).

🏠 **Cabot Shores Wilderness Resort**
(9 units) 30 Buchanan Dr, Indian Brook; tf 1 866 929 2584; www.cabotshores.com. 5 rooms in the old farmhouse, & 4 2-bedroom chalets on a 22ha lake & ocean-front property. On-site bistro (open to non-guests, caters to vegetarians/vegans; **$$–$$$**) & licensed bar (check opening times), live music. Canoes, kayaks, bikes, plus meditation, yoga, etc. Pet friendly. Also offers various camping options including Mongolian yurts, a cedar yurt & geodesic domes. **$$**

🏠 **English Country Garden B&B**
(5 rooms) 45478 Cabot Trail, Indian Brook; tf 1 866 929 2721; e ipgreen@ns.sympatico. ca; www.capebretongarden.com. Penny & Ian have created a luxurious B&B on 15ha of lakeside

grounds. There are 4 beautifully decorated themed suites in the main house, & an open-plan private B&B cottage down the path. A 3-course set menu is offered for CAN$63 in the (reservation only) dining room (⊕ *Oct–Apr 19.00 Thu–Sat; year-round Thu–Sat by advance reservation for guests*); the main course might be maple-baked salmon, or perhaps *filet mignon* with hunter sauce. Full b/fast inc. **$$**

🏠 **Wreck Cove Wilderness Cabins** (2 cabins) 42314 Cabot Trail, Wreck Cove; ✆ 902 929 2800; tf 1 877 929 2800; www.capebretonsnaturecoast. com. Cosy, fully equipped, good-value 2-bedroom cabins ideal for lovers of the outdoors, just 5mins' walk from the sea & close to highland walking trails. **$$**

✗ **Where to eat and drink**

🍴 **Clucking Hen Café & Bakery** 45073 Cabot Trail, North Shore; ✆ 902 929 2501; ⊕ May 08.00–18.00; Jun & Sep–mid Oct 07.00–19.00 daily; Jul–Aug 07.00–19.30 daily. A friendly, laidback licensed eatery. The fish chowder is very good, & the pan-fried haddock dinner recommended. Outdoor eating area. For a calorific treat, grab a cinnamon roll, blondie or wedge of homemade pie. Gluten-free options. *Lunch* **$**, *dinner* **$–$$**

🍴 **The Dancing Moose Café, Cottage & Camping Cabins** 42691 Cabot Trail, Birch Plain; ✆ 902 929 2523; www.thedancingmoosecafe.

com; ⊕ in-season 07.00–16.00 daily; check for off-season times. Good accommodation/dining choice offering Belgian waffles, Dutch pancakes, lobster rolls, coffee, baked goods – & a wonderful sea view. **$–$$**

🍴 **Wreck Cove General Store** 42470 Cabot Trail, Wreck Cove; ✆ 902 929 2900; www. wreckcovegeneralstore.com; ⊕ daily. This well-stocked old-fashioned store is worth a stop: excellent lobster or crab sandwiches in season, pizza by the slice, oatcakes, & in summer, ice cream. **$**

NORTH RIVER Shortly after Indian Brook, the Cabot Trail turns inland before reaching North River. With beautiful provincial parks nearby, several artisans' shops and galleries to visit, and a good kayaking company just up the road, this is worth considering as a base from which to explore the Cabot Trail and the Bras d'Or Lake area. It also has an excellent place to stay and eat: the 'green' **Chanterelle Country Inn** (*12 units; 48678 Cabot Trail;* ✆ *902 929 2263; tf 1 866 277 0577; www. chanterelleinn.com;* ⊕ *May–Oct;* **$$**) is set on 60ha overlooking the North River estuary, with nine very comfortable guest rooms (imaginative buffet breakfast included) and three well-equipped nearby cottages, although don't expect TVs or air conditioning. The menu in the rather good licensed dining room (⊕ *May–Oct 18.00– 20.00; \$\$\$*) uses locally sourced ingredients, changes nightly and always includes a vegetarian, non-vegetarian and seafood main course and freshly baked artisan bread.

Popular with anglers and hikers, **North River Provincial Park** is a small riverside picnic park that gives access to the North River Wilderness Area. A moderate–difficult (9km each-way) trail leads to the 31m North River Falls. Take up a paddle with **North River Kayak** (✆ *902 929 2628;* tf *1 888 865 2925; www.northriverkayak.com;* ⊕ *mid May–mid Oct*), a good, award-winning, long-established operator offering kayak rentals, lessons, courses, and guided half-, full- and multi-day trips around the region's lovely waters. There's even a 'kayak and learn songwriting' trip. There are plans to offer accommodation in 'bird house wilderness cabins with river views' from 2017. Winter visitors looking to do some wilderness Telemark skiing should check out **Ski Tuonela** (✆ *902 295 7694; skituonela.com*), between North River and St Anns.

North River is on the Cabot Trail, 20km/12 miles from Exit 11 of Highway 105, 55km/22 miles from Ingonish Beach and 36km/22 miles from Baddeck.

ST ANNS At 17km further along the Cabot Trail from North River is St Anns, a community considered to be the centre of Cape Breton's Gaelic culture. It's home to the **Gaelic College of Celtic Arts and Crafts** (*Colaside Na Gàidhlig; 51779 Cabot Trail;* ✆ *902 295 3441; www.gaeliccollege.edu*), the only institution of its kind in North America. The college was first established in 1938 in a log cabin to encourage the study and preservation of the Gaelic language, arts and culture. Primarily an

RELOCATION, RELOCATION, RELOCATION

The Reverend Norman McLeod (or MacLeod), originally from Scotland, arrived in Pictou (page 298) in 1817 and quickly established and ran a church there. Having earned a good reputation, he was offered a church in Ohio (USA) to minister to other Highland Scots who had settled there. He accepted on the condition that all the members of his congregation who wished to join him could come too.

McLeod and his flock sailed out from Pictou in the Ark, bound for America. As luck would have it, before the ship had lost sight of Nova Scotia's shore, the Ark was caught in (not a flood but) a big storm, and – in darkness – the ship's captain took refuge in the nearest safe water, St Anns Bay.

When the new day dawned, the passengers cast their eyes on a landscape very similar to their old Scottish homeland, and decided that they'd done more than enough travelling. They dispensed with all thoughts of Ohio and made their new homes here. They were rewarded with severe winters and crop failures.

McLeod's son sailed off to take cargo to Glasgow, but was not heard from for eight years. Finally, word came from him in Australia, suggesting that his father (and, of course, the entire congregation) come to join him. By now, there were too many parishioners for one ship, and so between 1851 and 1858 seven shiploads of McLeod's followers sailed almost halfway across the planet.

Incidentally, McLeod was less enamoured with Australia than his son had been, and led his followers across the Tasman Sea to New Zealand instead. It was from there – in his late eighties – that he went to meet his maker.

Angus MacAskill was one of 14 children and as a baby was so small that few thought he would survive. He was six when the family came to Nova Scotia from the island of Harris in the Scottish Hebrides, and 14 before anyone began to notice his unusual size and strength. He grew to be 2.36m tall and weighed 193kg and became known in Gaelic as *Gille Mòr St Anns* ('The St Ann's Big Boy'). An entrepreneurial tradesman met him by chance and took him on tour to show off his size and strength. He often performed with a tiny midget, who, it is said, would dance in the palm of MacAskill's huge hand. Like all good giants from Nova Scotia, he went to England to meet Queen Victoria. Her majesty is said to have commented that he was the tallest, strongest and stoutest man ever to have entered her palace, and the *Guinness Book of World Records* listed him as 'the tallest true (non-pathological) giant'. When he tired of showbiz, he returned to a simple life as a St Anns storekeeper, and passed away in 1863 aged 38. He is buried in the local cemetery. Learn more at the Giant MacAskill Museum (see below).

educational institution, it offers year-round programming in the study of the Cape Breton Gaelic language, music, dance, arts, and crafts that came with the first Scottish settlers to the area. Several musical and cultural events take place during the summer, including the two-day **Festival of Cape Breton Fiddling** (*www.capebretonfiddlers.com*) with concerts and workshops, which takes place in August. The **Great Hall of the Clans** (⊕ *09.00–17.00 daily; admission CAN$8*) features interactive exhibits portraying the cultural and linguistic evolution of the Gaels of Cape Breton Island, Nova Scotia and Canada. There is a craft shop with a wide range of Celtic gifts, Gaelic-language books, and music books and supplies. An art gallery tells the Reverend McLeod saga (box, opposite), and there are daily demonstrations in kiltmaking, music, dance, weaving and language, and a Gaelic film presentation (July–August).

Nearby, **St Anns Provincial Park** has a picnic area and a short walking trail that leads to a vantage point overlooking the beautiful harbour.

St Anns is on the Cabot Trail and just off Highway 105, Exit 11, 74km/46 miles south of Ingonish Beach and 17km/11 miles between Baddeck and North River.

🏠 Where to stay, eat and drink

🏠 **St Ann's Motel** (8 rooms & 1 housekeeping unit) 51947 Cabot Trail; ☏ 902 295 2876; stannsmotel.com; ⊕ mid May–Oct. A traditional-style motel right on the waterfront with wonderful views. Rooms are simple but perfectly comfortable. Housekeeping unit (weekly rentals preferred) has 2 queen beds & kitchen. **$$**

✕ **Lobster Galley** 51943 Cabot Trail, South Haven; ☏ 902 295 3100; ⨍; ⊕ late May–late Oct 08.00–21.30 daily. Start with lobster-stuffed mushrooms & move on to sautéed Digby scallops. Fab water views & deck. Licensed. Next door to St Ann's Motel. **$$**

ENGLISHTOWN In addition to taking a boat to the Bird Islands (page 342), you can visit a museum commemorating another of Nova Scotia's larger-than-life characters – the **Giant MacAskill Museum** (*Hwy 312;* ☏ *902 929 2875;* ⊕ *Jul–Aug 09.00–17.00 daily (May & Jun by appointment); admission CAN$4;* box, above). Incidentally, there's also a Giant MacAskill Museum at Dunvegan on the Scottish Isle of Skye.

Englishtown is on Highway 312, 10km/6 miles from St Anns. In town, the **Englishtown Ridge Campground** (*73 sites; 938 Englishtown Rd;* ☏ *902 929 2598;*

www.englishtown-ridge.com; ⊕ *late May–mid Oct;* **$**), overlooking St Anns Bay and Harbour, offers good facilities, serviced and tent sites.

THE BIRD ISLANDS Birdwatchers (and others) will want to take a boat trip around Hertford and Ciboux islands, much more commonly known as the Bird Islands. You won't land on either island, but the boat goes close enough to get a good view, though binoculars and/or telephoto lenses will enhance the experience of the thousands of seabirds that nest here. Depending on the time of year (June and July are probably best), expect to see black guillemots, razorbills, black-legged kittiwakes, great cormorants and Atlantic puffins. Grey seals and bald eagles are also often seen. Contact **Donelda's Puffin Boat Tours** (*1099 Hwy 312, Englishtown;* ❧ *902 929 2563;* **tf** *1 877 278 3346; www.puffinboattours.ca;* ⊕ *mid May–mid Sep; 2½–3hr boat trip CAN$35–40*). En route are good views of Cape Dauphin: according to Mi'kmaq legend, somewhere at the cape (the exact location is kept secret to protect the site) is Glooscap's Cave – sometimes called Fairy Hole – where the man-god was supposed to have lived for several winters.

THE CABOT TRAIL: SOUTH

BADDECK With a beautiful setting on the shores of the sparkling **Bras d'Or Lake** and well located on the Cabot Trail but in relatively easy reach of many of Cape Breton Island's highlights, Baddeck (population: 1,100) is understandably popular. There are numerous activities, ranging from ceilidhs to kayaking, within walking distance for the visitor, and one must-see museum.

While here, be sure to get out on to the water (Baddeck's yacht club is the sailing centre of the Bras d'Or Lake) – take a trip on a sail boat, rent a kayak, or, in summer, have a swim in the lake from an island beach. There's also a top golf course and beautiful waterfall hike within easy driving distance.

If you are coming **by car**, Baddeck is just off Highway 105, exits 8 or 9, 85km/53 miles from Port Hastings, 77km/46 miles from Sydney and 111km/69 miles from Louisbourg. It is also on the **Maritime Bus** coach route between Halifax and Sydney (page 57).

History The name Baddeck derives from the Mi'kmaq '*abadak*', 'place near an island' – referring to what is now called Kidston Island (page 347). European settlement began late in the 1830s when an Irish and a Scottish family made their homes here. Within 50 years, Baddeck was home to several hotels, a post office, a library, three newspapers and numerous other services. A well-known celebrity, Alexander Graham Bell, arrived to settle with his family (box, below).

In 1908, Baddeck was struck by an outbreak of cholera that claimed more than 30 lives, and there was more tragedy in 1926 when fire destroyed almost two dozen buildings along Main Street.

Where to stay *Map, page 344, unless otherwise stated*
If you're looking for somewhere quiet and off the beaten track (but accessible by car in 15 minutes from Baddeck), **Big Hill Retreat** (*Rear Big Hill Rd;* \ *902 295 2726;* tf *1 888 356 0303; www.bighillretreat.com;* **$$**) offers three secluded getaway cabins.

LET'S HEAR IT FOR THE BELLS

Alexander Graham Bell (AGB) was born in Edinburgh, Scotland in 1847. By 1885, he had already invented the telephone and was living with his American wife in the USA. Travelling via Nova Scotia to Newfoundland, the Bells passed through and fell in love with this area. In 1885, AGB bought land across the inlet from Baddeck and had a summer home built (Beinn Bhreagh).

Although best known for inventing the phone, Bell's major interests were flight and aerodynamics. Financed by his wife, he formed the Aerial Experiment Association. Experiments with man-carrying kites led to the creation of the *Silver Dart*, and this craft, piloted by Baddeck native Douglas McCurdy, took off from iced-up Baddeck Bay on 23 February 1909. Flying 9m in the air for a distance of about 1.4km, this was the first heavier-than-air flight in the British Empire.

In 1919, AGB (aged 72), his wife and his estate manager invented a prototype hydrofoil: the *HD-4* smashed the then world water-speed record, travelling at 114km/h.

Bell had many other interests – including the pastoral. For example, he experimented on raising multi-nippled sheep for 30 years. In addition to providing financial support and input for her husband's work, Mabel Bell was instrumental in the development of one of Cape Breton Island's traditional crafts. Rug hooking had always been popular, but Mrs Bell hired a teacher of the art to come over from Washington, and this revolutionised the colours and designs that the rug hookers used.

AGB died in 1922, and his wife the following year: both are buried at Beinn Bhreagh. Still owned by the family, the estate is not open to the public.

The couple – and their life in Baddeck – are now the subjects of an opera: written by staff at the University of Toronto, *The Bells of Baddeck* premiered in 2016.

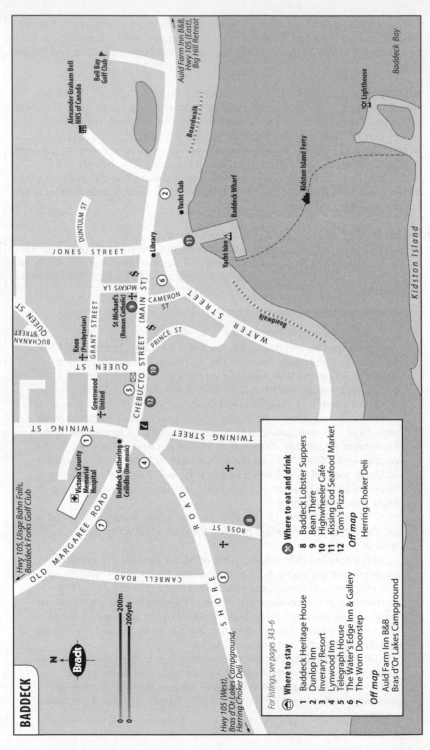

BADDECK

N
Bradt

0 200m
0 200yds

*Hwy 105 (West),
Bras d'Or Lakes Campground,
Herring Choker Deli*

OLD MARGAREE ROAD

CAMBELL ROAD

SHORE ROAD

ROSS ST

TWINING STREET

TWINING ST

QUEEN ST

BUCHANAN QUEEN STREET

QUEEN STREET

GRANT STREET

DUNTUM ST

JONES STREET

CHEBUCTO STREET

PRINCE ST

CAMERON ST

McKAYS LA

WATER STREET

Boardwalk

JONES STREET

*Hwy 105, Uisge Bahn Falls,
Baddeck Forks Golf Club*

Victoria County
Memorial Hospital

Baddeck Gathering
Ceilidhs (live music)

Knox
(Presbyterian)

Greenwood
United

St Michael's
(Roman Catholic)

Library

Yacht Club

Yacht hire

Baddeck Wharf

Kidston Island Ferry

Lighthouse

Boardwalk

*Auld Farm Inn B&B,
Hwy 105 (East),
Big Hill Retreat*

Alexander Graham Bell
NHS of Canada

Bell Bay
Golf Club

Baddeck Bay

Kidston Island

For listings, see pages 343–6

Where to stay
1 Baddeck Heritage House
2 Dunlop Inn
3 Inverary Resort
4 Lynwood Inn
5 Telegraph House
6 The Water's Edge Inn & Gallery
7 The Worn Doorstep
Off map
Auld Farm Inn B&B
Bras d'Or Lakes Campground

Where to eat and drink
8 Baddeck Lobster Suppers
9 Bean There
10 Highwheeler Café
11 Kissing Cod Seafood Market
12 Tom's Pizza
Off map
Herring Choker Deli

🏠 **Inverary Resort** 368 Shore Rd; 📞 902 295 3500; **tf** 1 800 565 5660; www.inveraryresort.com; ⊕ May–mid Oct. This lakeside resort on over 4ha offers an on-site spa, Adventure Centre (various activities) & several types of accommodation. As you'd expect, the higher-cost rooms & units are better, less popular rooms cheaper. The resort's licensed Thistledown Restaurant, Pub & Patio (⊕ *mid Jun–mid Oct b/fast & dinner daily; $$*) has live music every evening in season. **$$–$$$**

🏠 **Baddeck Heritage House** (4 rooms) 121 Twining St; 📞 902 295 3219; **tf** 1 877 223 1112; ⊕ mid May–Oct. Liz & Dick's welcoming & charming late 19th-century house makes a great Baddeck & area base. Nice deck, excellent b/fast (inc). (Friendly) cat on premises. **$$**

🏠 **Dunlop Inn** (5 rooms) 552 Chebucto St; 📞 902 295 3355; **tf** 1 888 290 1988; www. dunlopinn.com; ⊕ May–Oct. A very comfortable centrally located Victorian inn with individually decorated rooms right by the water. 2 waterside decks, sun room & private beach. Continental b/fast inc. **$$**

🏠 **Lynwood Inn** (32 suites) 441 Shore Rd; 📞 902 295 1995; **tf** 1 877 666 1995; www. lynwoodinn.com; ⊕ year-round; off-season by reservation. 3 rooms in this c1868 original house, 29 suites (some with balconies) in the 2002 addition. The elegant licensed Victorian-style restaurant (⊕ *mid Jun–mid Oct 07.00–21.00 daily; $$*) has a casual atmosphere & is one of the better ones in Baddeck. Fresh, local ingredients are used where possible, the lobster platter is good value, & the desserts very good. Live local entertainment most evenings. **$$**

🏠 **Telegraph House** (39 units) 479 Chebucto St; 📞 902 295 1100; **tf** 1 888 263 9840; www. baddeckhotel.com. In addition to rooms (some up a couple of flights of stairs) in the grand c1861 main building – a former telegraph office – there is also a modern motel section & 4 cabins. Alexander Graham Bell (box, page 343) stayed here several times in the 1880s (Room 1). The dining room (⊕ for dinner daily; *$$*) is good without being outstanding. **$$**

🏠 **The Water's Edge Inn & Gallery** (7 units) 18–22 Water St; 📞 902 295 3600; www. thewatersedgeinn.com. Tastefully decorated, stylish & comfortable rooms – most with stunning lake views – are on the 1st or 2nd floor, above a rather good gallery of unique Maritime original arts & crafts. **$$**

🏠 **The Worn Doorstep** (4 suites) 43 Old Margaret Rd; 📞 902 295 1997; worndoorstep. baddeck.com; ⊕ mid May–late Oct. Spacious, comfortable suites (all with private entrances) in friendly guesthouse. Highly recommended. **$$**

🏠 **Auld Farm Inn B&B** (8 rooms) 1817 Bay Rd, Hwy 205, Baddeck Bay; 📞 902 295 1977; www. auldfarminn.ca; ⊕ May–Oct. Nice, characterful renovated farmhouse 7km east of Baddeck with en-suite or private bathrooms. Veranda. Rate includes full b/fast. **$**

⛺ **Bras d'Or Lakes Campground** [map, pages 316–17] (95 sites) 8885 Hwy 105, between exits 7 & 8; 📞 902 295 2329; www. brasdorlakescampground.com; ⊕ mid Jun–Sep. 5km from Baddeck, with open serviced & unserviced sites, set back from over 100m of lakeshore. Pool, store & laundromat. **$**

🍴 **Where to eat and drink** *Map, opposite, unless otherwise stated*
Seafood-loving self-caterers should check out the Kissing Cod. Another dining option is the **Baddeck Forks Golf Club** [map, pages 316–17] (page 347).

🍴 **Baddeck Lobster Suppers** Ross St; 📞 902 295 3307; www.baddecklobstersuppers. ca; ⊕ Jun–mid Oct 16.00–21.00 daily. The lunch menu is short & simple; dinners are the big draw. Not a good choice for an intimate, romantic meal, but fun & reasonable value. Most come for lobster served with all-you-can-eat mussels, seafood chowder, etc, but salmon or steak are possible substitutes. Price includes beverage, dessert & tea/coffee. *Set dinner CAN$44.* **$$$**

🍴 **Kissing Cod Seafood Market** 1 Jones St; 📞 902 929 2289; 🟦; ⊕ Jun–Aug 11.00–18.00 Mon–Sat. Down by the wharf, this is primarily a fresh seafood market, but also serves simple lunches including excellent lobster or crab rolls & mussels. **$$**

🍴 **Tom's Pizza** 464 Chebucto St; 📞 902 295 1510; visitbaddeck.com/toms pizza, ⊕ usually 11.00–23.00 daily. Not much in the way of décor, but decent, handmade pizza & friendly service. **$–$$**

Herring Choker Deli [map, pages 316–17] 10158 Hwy 105, Nyanza; 902 295 2275; herringchokerdeli.com; mid Apr–late Oct 09.00–18.00 daily. Good café/deli/bakery 10km west of Baddeck with deck overlooking the lake offering a range of freshly made wraps, paninis, soups, salads, sandwiches & baked goods. An ideal spot for b/fast or a light lunch. In case you're wondering, the name comes from the slang term for someone from New Brunswick. $–$$

Bean There 503 Chebucto St; 902 295 1634; Bean There Café; 06.30–16.00 Mon– Sat, 07.00–16.00 Sun. In case you hadn't guessed the speciality from the first part of the name, the 'subtitle' is Coffee Café. So, coffee, plus baked goods, bagels, paninis, etc. Tables inside (not many) or out, & can get busy. $

Highwheeler Café 486 Chebucto St; 902 295 3006; Highwheeler Café and Bakery; May–mid Oct 06.00–18.00 Tue–Sun. Superb coffee, friendly service, great sandwiches, snacks & baked goods, all made on site. Also does a good-value packed lunch to take away. Patio deck. $

Festivals Not only are events held in town during the Celtic Colours International Festival (box, page 318), but you can enjoy Cape Breton fiddle music and dancing every evening in July and August as part of the **Baddeck Gathering Ceilidhs** (*St Michael's Parish Hall, 6 Margaree Rd;* 902 295 0971; www.baddeckgathering.com; admission CAN$10). The first full week of August sees seven days of races at the **Bras d'Or Yacht Club Regatta**. The Bell Bay golf course (page 347) hosts the PGA Tour Canada's **Celtic Classic golf tournament** in September.

Other practicalities

$ Royal Bank 496 Chebucto St; 902 295 2224; 10.00–17.00 Mon–Fri

Victoria County Memorial Hospital 30 Old Margaree Rd; 902 295 2112

Post office 485 Chebucto St; 08.00–17.00 Mon–Fri, 08.00–noon Sat

Tourist information 454 Chebucto St; 902 295 1911; Jun–Oct 10.00–16.00 daily (Jul–Aug to 18.00)

Baddeck Public Library 526 Chebucto St; 902 295 2055; noon–17.00 & 18.00–20.00 Tue–Thu, 10.00–17.00 Fri&Sat

What to see and do An absorbing museum dedicated to Baddeck's most famous resident, on a 10ha site with lovely views of the Bras d'Or Lake, **Alexander Graham Bell National Historic Site** (*559 Chebucto St;* 902 295 2069; www.pc.gc.ca/lhn-nhs/ns/grahambell.aspx; late May–late Oct 09.00–17.00 daily; admission free (2017),

---

HIGHLAND VILLAGE/BAILE NAN GAIDHEAL

On a 17ha hillside site with a magnificent view of the Bras d'Or Lake and surrounding countryside, the **Highland Village Museum** (*4119 Hwy 223, Iona;* 902 725 2272; tf 1 866 442 3542; highlandvillage.novascotia.ca; Jun–mid Oct 10.00–17.00 daily; admission CAN$11) is North America's only living-history museum for Gaelic language and culture. The museum is 24km east of Highway 105, Exit 6, via the Little Narrows ferry (CAN$7), and 61km from Sydney. The complex includes a visitor centre and 11 historic buildings (some original, some replicas). Costumed staff, activity demonstrations, language, stories, music and song bring to life the culture and lifestyle of the Gaels who settled in Nova Scotia from the Highlands and Islands of Scotland in the late 1700s and early 1800s. Be prepared for a lot of walking. If you want to stay nearby, the best choice is The Iona Heights Inn (*4115 Hwy 223, Iona;* 902 622 2190; tf 1 844 733 4662; www.ionaheightsinn.com; $–$$), home to the well-liked Frolic & Folk Pub & Grill (daily; $$).

There's a Little Narrows and a Grand Narrows but more famous than both is **Big Narrows**, the town where Dave – protagonist of raconteur **Stuart McLean's** highly entertaining and long-running *Vinyl Café* stories – grew up. Though Dave moved to Toronto, the occasional story (usually broadcast a couple of times per week on CBC Radio) is set back in Big Narrows, but you won't find it on the map. There are many small towns like it all over the Maritimes, but this one is a creation of McLean's fertile imagination.

CAN$7.80 (2016)) contains working models, photographs and multimedia exhibits on flight and much more, including programmes for adults and kids. There is also a full-sized replica of the *HD-4* hydrofoil, and the award-winning behind-the-scenes 'White Glove' tour (*CAN$12.27 extra*), allows you to touch and feel some of AGB's personal mementos. Maybe some of his magic will rub off on you (through the gloves). Adventurous pottery fans may wish to visit the pottery studio – and/or stay – at **Big Hill Retreat** (page 343). Experienced potter and pottery teacher Linda Wright experiments with new glazes and techniques.

Just 200m across the water from Baddeck, wooded **Kidston Island** has short walking trails, a beach with supervised swimming, and a lighthouse dating from 1875. Reach it by a free ferry every 20 minutes in July and August only (⊕ *10.00–18.00 Mon–Fri, noon–18.00 Sat & Sun*). Those keen on walking should get in touch with **Bannockburn Discovery Tours** (☏ *902 295 3310;* tf *1 888 577 4747; bannockburntours. com*), who run 6–8-hour Cabot Trail tours to and from Baddeck from CAN$109.

Approximately 16km from Baddeck, **Uisge Bahn Falls Provincial Park** has a 1.5km (each way) trail to its namesake photogenic falls ('*Uisge Bahn*' is Gaelic for 'white water'). To reach the park, take Margaree Road from Baddeck, or Exit 9 of Highway 105, to Baddeck Bridge, then turn right towards Big Baddeck and Baddeck Forks. After 6.5km, turn left on to North Branch Road.

Just 14km from Baddeck, the scenic nine-hole 3,000yd par-36 riverside **Baddeck Forks Golf Course** (*12 Extension, Baddeck Forks;* ☏ *902 295 2174; www.baddeckforksgolf. com;* ⊕ *May–late Oct; green fees CAN$25*) has a pro-shop and decent licensed dining (⊕ *May–Oct 11.00–20.00 Mon–Fri, 08.00–20.00 Sat & Sun;* **$$**) – call or see website for directions. Elsewhere, the 7,037yd par-72 course at **Bell Bay Golf Club** (*761 Hwy 205;* ☏ *902 295 1333;* tf *1 800 565 3077; www.bellbaygolfclub.com; green fees CAN$104*) is one of Cape Breton Island's best, with excellent facilities and fabulous views over the Bras d'Or Lake. Ask about play-and-stay packages (*May, Jun & mid Sep–Oct*).

MARGAREE RIVER VALLEY The Margaree River is divided into two main channels: the Northeast Margaree, which rises on the plateau of the highlands, and the Southwest Margaree. The two branches tumble over rapids and waterfalls, through deep salmon pools and verdant forested floodplains before merging at Margaree Forks and then flowing into the Gulf of St Lawrence at Margaree Harbour. The valley is peaceful, pastoral and beautiful in any season, though at its most spectacular when ablaze with autumn colours.

From Margaree Forks, choose the road on either bank of the river to reach Margaree Harbour (pages 324–5) or Belle Côte (pages 325–7). The official Cabot Trail follows the west bank, but East Margaree Road also offers wonderful river views.

The Margaree River is renowned for its **fishing**, particularly salmon and trout, and the valley offers good **hiking**. Angling, salmon fishing and local history are all housed in a former schoolhouse, now **The Margaree Salmon Museum** (*60 East Big Intervale Rd, Northeast Margaree;* ☎ *902 248 2848;* ⊕ *mid Jun–mid Oct 09.00–17.00 daily; admission CAN$2*).

The Margaree Valley is easily reached **by car** from Inverness via Highway 19, or from Highway 104 via the Cabot Trail. Margaree Forks is 27km/17 miles from Inverness, and 50km/31 miles from Baddeck. Margaree Forks is home to a **tourist information centre** (*7972 Cabot Trail;* ☎ *902 248 2356;* ⊕ *mid Jun–mid Oct 09.00–17.00 daily (Jul–Aug to 19.00)*).

Where to stay, eat and drink

🏠 **Old Miller Trout Farm Guest House**
(1 cottage) 408 Doyles Rd, Margaree Forks; ☎ 902 248 2080; tf 1 800 479 0220; www.oldmiller.com; ⊕ mid May–Oct. A fully equipped, *gîte*-like quiet 2-bedroom cottage (can sleep 6) by a pond on a working trout farm: U-fish (rainbow & speckled trout). Approx 2km off the Cabot Trail. 2-night min stay. **$$$**

🏠 **Normaway Inn** (29 units) 691 Egypt Rd, Margaree Valley; ☎ 902 248 2987; tf 1 800 565 9463; www.thenormawayinn.com; ⊕ mid Jun–mid Oct. 9 inn rooms, 3 1-bedroom & 3 2-bedroom suites in an old-fashioned c1928 main lodge 3km off the Cabot Trail, & 17 1- & 2-bedroom rustic

cabins spread out over a peaceful 100ha estate. Guided fishing trips can be arranged. Food in the dining room (⊕ *mid Jun–mid Oct 07.30–10.00 & 18.00–21.00 daily;* **$$$**) is generally good & there's live entertainment in the evenings (eg: dances & ceilidhs in The Barn). **$$**

🍴 **Dancing Goat** 6289 Cabot Trail, Margaree Valley; ☎ 902 248 2727; 🅵 The Dancing Goat Café and Bakery; ⊕ 07.00–17.00 Mon–Sat, 08.00–17.00 Sun. The Goat closed for quite a while but loyal locals helped its rebirth in the new location. Excellent coffees, sandwiches & wonderful desserts. Try the cranberry almond scones. Long live the Goat! **$**

AROUND BRAS D'OR LAKE

In addition to Baddeck (pages 342–7) and apart from the ever-changing views of the beautiful bays, islands and yachts and pleasure boats on the tidal waters, the lake shores offer several other points of interest. A scenic drive (look out for signs with a bald eagle motif – the shore and surrounding areas are a major nesting area for hundreds of these majestic birds) runs all the way around the shore of this vast lake, but most people just choose a section depending on their interests and itinerary.

WHYCOCOMAGH Located just east of the Skye River, Whycocomagh's name comes from the Mi'kmaq '*We'koqma'q*', meaning 'head of the waters'. Wrapped in mountains on three sides, the community's 'open' side fronts the Bras d'Or Lake. Its main claims to fame are the fact that Alexander Graham Bell once described it as 'the Rio de Janeiro of North America', and the view from trails in its eponymous provincial park (page opposite).

To reach Whycocomagh **by car**, it is on Highway 105, 50km/31 miles from the Canso Causeway, 30km/19 miles from Baddeck and 115km/71 miles from Sydney. Whycocomagh is on the **Maritime Bus** coach route between Halifax and Sydney (page 57).

🏠 Where to stay

🏠 **Cape Breton Cottage B&B** (2 units) Portage Rd, South Side Whycocomagh Bay; ☎ 902 756 2865, www.capebretoncottage.com; ⊕ May–Oct; off-season by reservation. With a ground-floor B&B room with private entrance in a

modern house, or a well-equipped, comfortable 1-bedroom cottage close by. Bald eagles often nest on this 12ha beautifully landscaped forested lakeshore property. B&B rate includes full b/fast. **$–$$**

Born in Tours, France, in approximately 1598, Nicolas Denys's name crops up throughout Nova Scotia and Atlantic Canada's early history. Denys first came to Nova Scotia as part of an expedition led by Isaac de Razilly in 1632. He settled on the LaHave River (page 172), and after a spell in France returned to these shores as Governor of Canso and Ile Royale (what is now Cape Breton Island). He established various settlements, including one here at Saint Pierre (St Peter's) in 1650. Trading extensively with the Mi'kmaq and other settlers at that time, he constructed a track on the isthmus between the sea and the lake to allow teams of oxen to haul boats onto skids and across the portage.

In 1654, Denys obtained a concession from Louis XIV to work all the island's minerals in return for a 10% royalty.

In the years that followed, he ran many businesses here (eg: fishing, lumber, and farming) but in 1669, his home and business were destroyed by fire. In financial ruin, he moved to Nipisiguit (now Bathurst, New Brunswick) and began writing about the lands he had lived in and visited, and their peoples. Denys wrote the first guidebook to Cape Breton, published in 1672: copies (in English and French) can be viewed at his eponymous museum (page 352). He died in 1688 and legend has it that he is buried near what is now the 15th hole of Bathurst's Gowan Brae Golf Course.

🏠 **Bear on the Lake Guest House** 10705 Hwy 105, Aberdeen; ☎902 756 2750; **tf** 1 866 718 5253; www.bearonthelake.com; ⊕ mid May–Oct. 7km east of Whycocomagh. 4-bed dorms & private rooms, lounge, deck overlooking the lake, fully equipped kitchen, laundry facilities, bike rentals, free Wi-Fi & more for backpackers & low-budget travellers. *Dorm CAN$32; private room CAN$78 (discount for HI members).* **$**

🏠 **Fair Isle Motel** (20 units) 9557 Hwy 105; ☎902 756 2291; **tf** 1 877 238 8950; www. fairislemotel.com; ⊕ mid May–Oct. A traditional-style motel on the hill above the main road overlooking the lake, offering standard rooms, a couple of suites & some larger rooms (all recently renovated & all with kitchenettes). Laundry facilities. **$**

⛺ **Whycocomagh Provincial Park** (37 sites, 3 yurts) **tf** 1 888 544 3434 (reservations); ⊕ mid Jun–mid Oct. Serviced & unserviced sites on grassy slopes or tucked into the forest on a hillside less than 500m east of town. 3 yurts (outfitted with beds, solar lighting, outdoor decks & propane BBQs). 3 short but steep & challenging trails lead up Salt Mountain, 240m above sea level. If it is clear, views from the mountaintop are sensational. **$**

✗ Where to eat and drink

✗ **Auld Brass Door Restaurant & Bar** 9814 Hwy 105; ☎902 756 3284; www.auldbrassdoor. com; ⊕ 11.00–late daily. Decent pub menu with a few surprises (eg: bison burger) & friendly service. 'We serve Cape Breton fare with an international flair!' **$$**

✗ **Charlene's Bayside Restaurant & Café** 9657 Hwy 105; ☎902 756 8004; ⊕ 11.00–19.00 Mon–Thu, 08.00–20.00 Fri–Sun. Come not for the décor but for the justifiably renowned seafood-packed chowder. The other options are diner style & tend to be more hit than miss. Desserts will please those with a sweet tooth. **$$**

✗ **Vi's Restaurant** 9381 Hwy 105; ☎902 756 2338; ⊕ 07.00–20.00 Mon–Sat, 08.00–20.00 Sun. This institution recently celebrated its 50th birthday. Nothing fancy or pretentious, just reliable home cooking. **$**

Other practicalities

$ **Royal Bank** 72 Village Rd; ☎902 756 2600; ⊕ 10.00–16.00 Mon–Wed, 10.00–17.00 Thu & Fri

✉ **Post office** 115 Main St; ⊕ 08.30–17.00 Mon–Fri

ORANGEDALE This little community is worth a short stop for those with an interest in railway history – the **Orangedale Railway Museum** (*1428 Main St;* \ *902 756 3384;* ☺ *Jul–late Aug 10.00–18.00 daily; off-season by appointment* (\ *902 756 3412)*), housed in the restored c1886 station that was in operation until 1990, has a number of good displays, several pieces of rolling stock, and an interpretive centre in a replica freight shed. Passenger trains haven't stopped here for more than two decades, but the memory lives on in 'Orangedale Whistle', a song by The Rankins (page 30).

Just off Orangedale Road, Orangedale is 7km/4 miles south of Highway 105, Exit 4.

DUNDEE On West Bay on the southern shore of Bras d'Or Lake, Dundee has a small provincial park with a sandy beach, and a resort with one of Cape Breton Island's highly regarded 18-hole golf courses. Located in a stunning setting, **The Dundee Resort Championship Golf Course** (\ *902 345 0420;* tf *1 800 565 5660; www.dundeegolfclub. com;* ☺ *May–Oct; green fees CAN$86*) is absolutely beautiful, but you'll really need to concentrate and play hard, particularly on the front nine. Expect a lot of hills and long par-fours! Various stay-and-play packages are available, and the course is open to non-resort guests. Buy the resort (see below) and this course comes free. At **Roberta**, 12km along the shore, you can rent kayaks to explore this part of the lake.

To reach Dundee **by car**, it is 51km/32 miles from Orangedale and 24km/ 15 miles from St Peter's.

🏠 Where to stay, eat and drink

🏠 **Dundee Resort & Golf Club** (98 units) 2750 West Bay Hwy; \ 902 345 2649; tf 1 800 565 5660; capebretonresorts.com/our-resorts/dundee; ☺ mid May–Oct. With 60 hotel rooms & 38 1- & 2-bedroom cottages. The potential is there, and (when offered) facilities include tennis, indoor & outdoor (seasonal) pools, spa, hiking, canoe & pedal-boat rental. But this resort has been looking rather worn in recent years & was offered for sale early in 2016. The restaurant serves b/fast, lunch & dinner, & there's a pub on site. You can also eat in the golf clubhouse. Various packages are offered. **$$$**

🏠 **Kayak Cape Breton & Cottages** (2 cottages) 5385 Dundee Rd, Roberta; \ 902 535 3060; www.kayakcapebreton.com; ☺ May–late Oct. 2 well-equipped 2-bedroom cedar-log cottages are tucked between the trees by the lakeside. Min stay applies: 2 nights May/Jun & Sep/ Oct; 3 nights Jul/Aug. Kayak lessons, guided trips & rentals are all offered. 12km from the Dundee Resort & 16km from St Peter's. **$**

ST PETER'S One of Nova Scotia's oldest communities, pleasant St Peter's is situated on a narrow strip of land separating the Atlantic Ocean and the Bras d'Or Lake. The largest community on the southern part of the lake shore (population: 735) and the service centre for Richmond County can almost be described as bustling in summer. The eponymous canal is one of two access points for boats entering Bras d'Or Lake and there are picnic areas on the canal's grassy banks.

Founded by Nicolas Denys (box, page 349) as Saint Pierre in 1650, the French later built a fort on this strategically important portage between the Atlantic and the Bras d'Or Lake. They seriously considered establishing their capital here, but that honour went to Louisbourg (page 363). In 1745, the British attacked the fort and torched the buildings, and in 1793, built Fort Grenville on the site.

Work on the construction of an 800m canal, now the **St Peter's Canal National Historic Site** (\ *902 733 2280; www.pc.gc.ca/lhn-nhs/ns/stpeters.aspx ;* ☺ *mid May– mid Sep 08.00–16.00 daily; admission free*), began in 1854 and was completed in 1869. Its opening saved over 120km of sailing for vessels wishing to enter or leave the southwest of the Bras d'Or Lakes. The lock system operates on some summer days – call to check dates/times.

The Potlotek First Nation Reserve (PFN) is sometimes described as the Mi'kmaq 'capital'. The PFN encompasses Chapel Island itself ('Mniku' to the Mi'kmaq), and a strip of land from the lakeshore back across Highway 4 which was granted to the Mi'kmaq in the 1830s. The first missionary priest to visit this region lived among the Mi'kmaq and settled with them on Chapel Island in the 1740s: he built a church here in 1754. This is the longest continuous mission in Canada.

Held over the weekend starting on the third Friday in July, the Potlotek Pow Wow is an important social, cultural and spiritual event for the Mi'kmaq and gives an opportunity for them to share their culture and heritage with others. In addition to daily feasting, there are dancing demonstrations, story telling, traditional games, and masses. Authentic arts and crafts are sold.

There isn't a huge amount for the casual visitor to see but the island still holds great spiritual significance for the Mi'kmaq. To visit the island, turn from Highway 4 onto Chapel Island Road (10km east of St Peter's) or onto Mountain Road (1km further east along Hwy 4). Ask around near the shore, and someone will probably take you across by boat (make sure that they wait around to take you back) for a few dollars.

There is also a Mi'kmaq-owned-and-operated eatery, the Bistro (*12012 Hwy 4; $*), but don't expect any traditional Mi'kmaq cuisine.

The PFN is approx 10km/6 miles east of St Peter's via Highway 4.

St Peter's is accessible **by car**, being on Highway 4, 55km/34 miles from Port Hastings, 24km/15 miles from Isle Madame, 38km/24 miles from Big Pond and 87km/54 miles from Sydney. **By shuttle**, MacLeod's Shuttle Service (page 58) passes through *en route* between Halifax and Sydney.

Where to stay, eat and drink

Bras d'Or Lakes Inn (19 rooms) 10095 Grenville St; ✆ 902 535 2200; tf 1 800 818 5885; e info@brasdorlakesinn.com; www. brasdorlakesinn.com. A red cedar-log building in a lovely lakefront location. Rooms are comfortable & well equipped. Wood features strongly in the décor of the licensed restaurant & lounge (⏰ *May–Dec 07.30–20.00 daily; $$$*) & large picture windows look out over the lake. The restaurant offers Canadian cuisine with a French influence: try scallops provencal or cedar-planked salmon. Dinner reservations recommended. There is a lounge with live entertainment most nights (ceilidh on Thu), a patio, exercise room & private dock. Kayaks, paddleboat, canoe & bicycles for rent. **$$$**

Joyce's Motel & Cottages (24 units) 10354 Grenville St; ✆ 902 535 2404; www. joycesmotel.com; ⏰ Jun–Oct. 6 simple motel rooms, 6 small basic cabins & 12 large 2-bedroom units with kitchenettes. Across the main road from the lake. Laundromat, park & outdoor pool. **$**

Diddles Café & Bakery 9969 Grenville St; ✆ 902 785 3020; ⏰ summer 08.00–20.00 daily; check hours off-season. New café with friendly service & home-cooked food. Good b/fasts (eg: banana bread French toast, waffles, etc), lunches, baked goods. Hope they continue as they've started. **$**

Festivals At **Nicolas Denys Days** at the end of July/early August, events include auctions, a parade, ceilidhs, and chowder lunches. St Peter's is the starting-off point for a major sailing event, July's five-leg week-long **Race the Cape** (*www.racethecape. ca*). September brings **Paddlefest** (*www.capebretonpaddlefest.org*), with clinics and

Big Pond, on Highway 4, halfway between St Peter's and Sydney, is best known as the home of the late Rita MacNeil, acclaimed singer, songwriter and recording artist. Her fans, and other hungry travellers, will want to stop at **Rita's Tea Room** (*8077 Hwy 4;* \ *902 828 2667; www.ritamacneil.com;* ⊕ *Jul–mid Oct 10.00–17.00 daily; $–$$*) to see – and buy – a collection of Rita memorabilia, and to tuck in to soup, salads, sandwiches, sweet things and more. It is good stuff, but prices seem a few celebrity connection dollars higher than the norm.

events for kayakers and SUPers, and then aaargh me hearties, it be **Pirate Days**, celebrating International Talk Like a Pirate Day (September 19 every year – has the world gone mad?). Live Celtic music comes to the fore at October's **KitchenRackets** (*www.kitchenrackets.org*); then get festive in November with a display of decorated Christmas trees at the **Festival of Trees**.

Other practicalities

$ Royal Bank 9955 Grenville St; \ 902 535 2001; ⊕ 10.00–17.00 Mon–Fri

✉ **Post office** 9981 Grenville St; ⊕ 09.00–17.00 Mon–Fri, 09.00–13.00 Sat

Ⓩ Tourist information 10259 Grenville St; \ 902 535 2185; ⊕ early Jun–mid Oct 09.00–18.00 daily

What to see and do Walking trails in **Battery Provincial Park** (\ *902 535 3094; parks.novascotia.ca/content/battery;* ⊕ *mid June–early Sep; admission free*) lead to the c1883 Jerome Point Lighthouse, and a short but steep section to the site of Fort Grenville (page 350). Both of these offer lovely views.

The town also has the world's only museum, the **Nicolas Denys Museum** (*46 Denys St;* \ *902 535 2379;* ⊕ *mid Jun–Sep 09.00–17.00 daily*), dedicated to this important historical figure (box, page 349). The **Wallace MacAskill Museum** (*7 MacAskill Dr;* \ *902 535 2531;* ⊕ *mid Jun–Aug 09.30–17.30 daily; Sep–Oct by appointment; admission free*) is also well worth a visit: this c1850s' house with period furnishings is the restored birthplace and childhood home of perhaps the world's best marine photographer, Wallace MacAskill (1890–1956). In addition to a good collection of his works – many in their original frames – there is a display of vintage cameras. Photography walking tours are offered, and there's a nautically themed gift shop.

If you've ever wondered what to do with old or unwanted musical instrument strings, visit **Encore Jewellery** (*10101 Grenville St;* \ *902 631 0223; www.encorejewel. com*), where owner Dawn makes 'beautiful things from recycled strings'. **MacIsaac Kiltmakers** (*4 MacAskill Dr;* \ *902 535 4000;* tf *1 866 343 4000*) will look after your Scottish apparel needs, but more practical clothing should be worn when you join Captain Greg on a half-, full-, or multi-day hands-on sailing experience with **Cape Breton Sailing Charters** (\ *902 631 5050; capebretonsailing.com*): highly recommended!

EAST BAY East Bay offers the chance to play golf between spring and late autumn, and to hit the slopes when the snow comes down. A newish (2009) Graham Cooke-designed 6,973yd par-72 course, **The Lakes** (*Hwy 4;* \ *902 828 4653; www. thelakesgolfclub.ca; green fees CAN$91*) offers fabulous views and dramatic elevation changes. In winter, take to the scenic slopes of **Ski Ben Eoin** (*Hwy 4;* \ *902 828 2222; www.skibeneoin.com*), overlooking the lake (snowshoe rentals also available). The 75-berth **Ben Eoin Yacht Club and Marina** (*4950 East Bay Hwy;* \ *902 828 1099;*

Less than 4km northeast along Highway 4 from East Bay, Highway 216 leads 26km west to the Eskasoni (the name comes from the Mi'kmaq for 'still waters') First Nation, the biggest Mi'kmaq reserve in the province (in fact, in the world). The setting is scenic, and the people of Eskasoni are becoming aware of how important their culture and history is to the visitors. **Eskasoni Cultural Journeys** (902 322 2279; www.eskasoniculturaljourneys. ca) has been developed to showcase the way of life of the Mi'kmaq and teach visitors traditions including dance, drumming, language, hunting and fishing, smudging and basket making. Over 19s can gamble at the **Eskasoni Gaming Centre** (4716 Shore Rd; 902 379 1451; www.eskasoni.ca), which boasts 60 video lottery terminals (VLTs). Eskasoni is also home to the **Unama'ki Institute of Natural Resources** (902 379 2163; www.uinr.ca), which represents Cape Breton's Mi'kmaq voice on natural resources and environmental concerns.

www.beneoinmarina.com) opened in 2012. The largest marina on the lakes has a full-service clubhouse. Bald eagles are also often seen in this area.

East Bay is on Highway 4, 27km/17 miles from Sydney and 54km/34 miles from St Peter's.

 Where to stay, eat and drink

Birches at Ben Eoin Country Inn (12 units) 5153 Hwy 4; 902 828 2277; **tf** 1 866 244 8862; www.thebirchescountryinn. ca; Feb–Dec. Welcoming, comfortable 2-storey inn – very close to golf course & marina – with 10 spacious, luxurious modern rooms & 2 suites. Outdoor jacuzzi. Bike friendly. Rate includes deluxe continental b/fast. **$$**

Malcolm's May–mid Jun 17.00–21.00 Tue–Sat; mid Jun–Oct 17.00–21.00 daily. The Country Inn's licensed restaurant offers fine dining in elegant & intimate surroundings. The menu changes with the seasons (most ingredients are local) & might include lobster, halibut, steak, or lamb. **$$$**

SYDNEY AND AROUND

With a past in which the words 'steel' and 'coal mining' feature prominently, not to mention years of bad press about its 'tar ponds' (box, overleaf), those who are not industrial historians could be forgiven for wondering if they should include Nova Scotia's second (and Cape Breton Island's) largest urban centre in their itineraries. In fact, Sydney is no longer a city, but since 1995 has been part of the Cape Breton Regional Municipality (population: 104,000), which also includes communities such as North Sydney, Sydney Mines and Glace Bay.

Like Halifax (and its namesake in Australia), Sydney lies on a magnificent harbour, and the downtown area occupies part of a peninsula jutting out into the water. Despite the setting, with the exception of a pleasant historic district and a nice waterfront boardwalk, it isn't the most attractive of places. Some visitors say that, once you've walked along both the **Esplanade** and parallel **Charlotte Street** (just one block inland) between Townsend and Amelia streets, you've done Sydney. But the historic 'North End' – home to (among other things) the Cossit House and Jost Heritage House (page 360) is worth a wander, and **Wentworth Park** (established in 1785) just south of downtown has benefited from major redevelopment and is once again an attractive green space – with duck ponds, walking paths and picnic areas.

There are, of course, some other attractions, including a good art gallery at **Cape Breton University** and a **casino**, and for those who like an urban base, Sydney is well placed for day trips to Louisbourg and many of the Bras d'Or Lake communities. It is blessed with good accommodation choices, and – where they once feared to tread – foodies are now spoilt for choice.

Sydney's 3km waterfront boardwalk buzzes with activity on nice summer days. Around the harbour, **North Sydney**'s former railway station, now housing offices, at 1 Station Street, is worth a look for its fine Victorian architecture. Neighbouring **Sydney Mines** is more attractive: its red sandstone c1904 Gothic-style former post office is now used as the **Town Hall**, and the c1905 railway station now houses a heritage museum. It's also one of the province's important fossil sites, particularly for plant fossils.

HISTORY Previously known as Spanish Bay, Sydney was founded in 1785 by Colonel DesBarres, a Swiss-born Huguenot. It was first settled by Loyalists from New York State: a garrison, in use until 1854, was constructed. The settlement was named for Lord Sydney, the British Home Secretary. Immigrants from the Scottish Highlands began to arrive in the early 1800s. For 35 years, until the island was reunited with mainland Nova Scotia in 1820, Sydney was the capital of the colony of Cape Breton. As industrial development increased, so did the population. Sydney became home to the largest self-contained steel plant in North America, fed by the area's numerous coal mines. One pit – Princess Colliery in Sydney Mines – operated continuously from 1875 to 1975.

COKE IS BAD FOR YOU

Being a huge steel, coal and coke producer had its downsides for Sydney. An unwanted consequence of almost a century of coke-making was massive-scale pollution caused by waste run-off. Most of the estimated 700,000 metric tonnes of hazardous, contaminated sludge collected in two ponds, an area of approximately 31ha. In 1986, the federal and provincial governments decided it was time to think about cleaning up the Sydney Tar Ponds, and drew up a plan to try to achieve this. Coke production didn't stop until 1988. By 1994, it was clear that the intended cure for the clean-up was not going to work, and the project was abandoned a year later. The years passed with a lot of hot air and little action, the sludge sloshing about virtually untouched at Canada's most contaminated industrial site.

In 2004, a CAN$400 million ten-year clean-up plan was announced which involved incinerating almost four metric tonnes of carcinogenic toxicants, stabilising contaminated sediments by mixing them with cement, and using friendly bacteria to decontaminate soil. The area would then be covered with special materials, and later landscaped.

At the time of writing, the pungent stench common in previous decades has gone. Areas of the site now look green and lush: a stream with clear, clean water bubbles along. Industrial machinery is still at work elsewhere on the site, but you feel (and hope) that the end is in sight. The reclaimed land (which is very close to downtown Sydney) is now called the Open Hearth Park, and is a wonderful addition to Sydney. There are walking paths, bike trails, a dog park, concession stand, and children's play park, and it has already been used as a major concert venue.

Sydney ranked as Canada's third-largest steel producer through World War II, a time when its harbour was an important staging point for Europe-bound shipping convoys. Post-war came decades of economic decline, not least for Sydney's iconic mainstays: both the coal and steel industries had completely dried up by the end of 2001.

GETTING THERE AND AWAY

By air Sydney Airport (*IATA code YQY; www.sydneyairport.ca*) is 14km/9 miles northeast of the city centre. A **taxi** from outside the arrivals area to downtown Sydney costs CAN$15; try **City-wide Taxi** (♦ *902 564 5432*). For flights within Nova Scotia, see page 54, for flights further afield, page 44, and car hire, page 56.

By road Highway 105 connects North Sydney with Port Hastings and the Canso Causeway; Highway 125 links North Sydney, Sydney River and Sydney. Highway 22 heads from Sydney to Louisbourg, and Highway 4 to Glace Bay. Sydney is some 400km/249 miles from Halifax, a drive of about 5 hours (without stops). **Maritime Bus** coach services connect Sydney with Halifax (page 57): the coach terminal is at 565 George Street (the Irving/Circle K petrol station). A stop is also made in North Sydney (13 Blower St). Several shuttle services (page 58) also make the run.

By sea For those travelling to and from Newfoundland (page 47), the **Sydney Marine Terminal** is on the North Sydney waterfront (which is also home to a tourist office and what is said to be the world's biggest violin – the fiddle is of course a vital part of Celtic music).

GETTING AROUND Transit Cape Breton (♦ *902 539 8124; www.cbrm.ns.ca/transit.html*) offers limited **bus** services (*Mon–Sat only*) between Sydney and nearby communities, including North Sydney, Sydney Mines and Glace Bay. There is also an accessible **Handi-Trans service** (♦ *902 539 4336*) that provides transportation for those unable to use the normal buses, but note that pre-registration (by phone) is required to use the service.

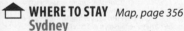

WHERE TO STAY *Map, page 356*
Sydney

🏠 **Cambridge Suites Hotel** (145 units) 380 Esplanade; ♦ 902 562 6500; **tf** 1 800 565 9466; www.cambridgesuitessydney.com. Fine downtown Esplanade location, with a rooftop patio & fitness centre. These clean & comfortable modern suites are a good choice for families & those who like spacious accommodation. Overnight parking CAN$7. The hotel's restaurant, Trio (page 357), is reliable. Rate includes hot buffet b/fast. **$$$**

🏠 **Colby House B&B** (4 rooms & 4 full-service suites) 10 Park St; ♦ 902 539 4095; **tf** 1 855 539 4055; www.colbyhousebb.com. Beautiful c1904 home on a tree-lined street in walking distance of downtown. Tastefully furnished with many original features including grand staircase. Comfortable, well-equipped rooms with en-suite or private bathrooms. Lovely veranda. Rate includes full b/fast. **$$**

🏠 **Spanish Bay Inn – Premiere Executive Suites** (13 suites) 10 Pitt St; ♦ 902 562 5747; **tf** 1 866 259 6673; www.spanishbayinn.ca. Successful mix of B&B, hotel & suites, including well-equipped apt-like suites (with kitchenette or full kitchen) in historic downtown waterfront building. Free parking & free laundry facilities. Rate includes deluxe continental b/fast. **$$**

🏠 **Hampton Inn by Hilton Sydney** (128 units) 60 Maillard St, Membertou; ♦ 902 564 6555; hamptoninn3.hilton.com/en/index.html. Excellent new 6-storey hotel connected to the Membertou Trade & Convention Centre via a pedestrian walkway. 2–3km from the downtown area but easily reachable by cab or foot (approx 25mins). Rate includes hot b/fast. **$$**

🏠 **Weary Gardener B&B** (2 suites) 40 Richardson Av; ♦ 902 270 2987; www.

8

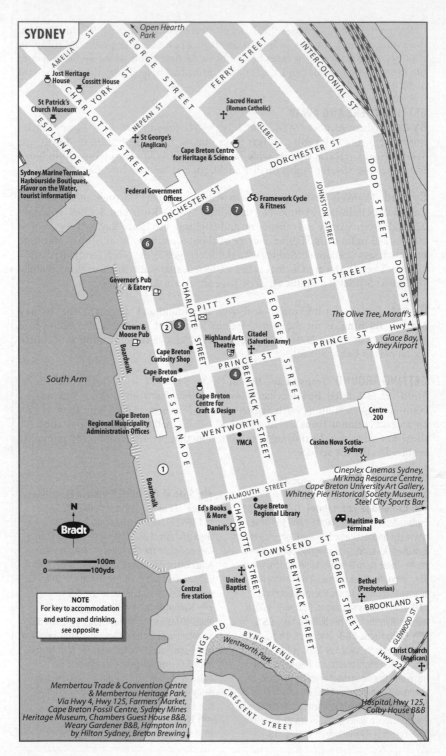

SYDNEY

Open Hearth Park

AMELIA ST

GEORGE STREET

FERRY STREET

INTERCOLONIAL ST

Jost Heritage House

Cossitt House

St Patrick's Church Museum

YORK STREET

CHARLOTTE STREET

ESPLANADE

NEPEAN ST

St George's (Anglican)

Sacred Heart (Roman Catholic)

GLEBE ST

Cape Breton Centre for Heritage & Science

DORCHESTER STREET

DODD STREET

Sydney Marine Terminal, Harbourside Boutiques, Flavor on the Water, tourist information

Federal Government Offices

DORCHESTER ST

3 **7** 🚲 Framework Cycle & Fitness

JOHNSTON STREET

6

Governor's Pub & Eatery

CHARLOTTE STREET

PITT ST

PITT STREET

GEORGE STREET

DODD ST

Boardwalk

Crown & Moose Pub

2 **5**

Cape Breton Curiosity Shop

Highland Arts Theatre

Citadel (Salvation Army)

PRINCE ST

The Olive Tree, Moraff's

Hwy 4

Glace Bay, Sydney Airport

South Arm

Cape Breton Fudge Co

PRINCE ST

4

BENTINCK ST

Cape Breton Centre for Craft & Design

Cape Breton Regional Municipality Administration Offices

ESPLANADE

WENTWORTH ST

YMCA

BENTINCK STREET

Centre 200

Casino Nova Scotia-Sydney

Boardwalk

1

FALMOUTH STREET

Cineplex Cinemas Sydney, Mi'kmaq Resource Centre, Cape Breton University Art Gallery, Whitney Pier Historical Society Museum, Steel City Sports Bar

Ed's Books & More

Cape Breton Regional Library

Daniel's

CHARLOTTE STREET

🚌 Maritime Bus terminal

N

Bradt

0 ____ 100m
0 ____ 100yds

Central fire station

United Baptist

STREET

TOWNSEND ST

BENTINCK STREET

GEORGE STREET

Bethel (Presbyterian)

BROOKLAND ST

GLENWOOD ST

NOTE
For key to accommodation and eating and drinking, see opposite

KINGS RD

BYNG AVENUE

Wentworth Park

Christ Church (Anglican)

Hwy 22

Membertou Trade & Convention Centre & Membertou Heritage Park, Via Hwy 4, Hwy 125, Farmers' Market, Cape Breton Fossil Centre, Sydney Mines Heritage Museum, Chambers Guest House B&B, Weary Gardener B&B, Hampton Inn by Hilton Sydney, Breton Brewing ↓

CRESCENT STREET

Hospital, Hwy 125, Colby House B&B

wearygardenerbedandbreakfast.com. Another lovely old house, beautifully furnished. Delightful gardens, nice library/common area. Rate includes full b/fast. **$$**

North Sydney

🏠 **Chambers' Guest House B&B** (4 rooms) 64 King St, North Sydney; ☏ 902 794 7301; **tf** 1 866 496 9453; www.bbcapebretonisland.com; 🕐 May–Oct. A lovely c1880 former sea captain's house with shared or en-suite bathrooms & a veranda, & pleasant garden. Full b/fast inc. **$**

✗ WHERE TO EAT AND DRINK
Map, opposite
Sydney

✗ **Flavor on the Water** 60 Esplanade; ☏ 902 567 1043; cbflavor.com/flavor; 🕐 11.00–20.00 Mon–Fri, 10.00–20.00 Sat & Sun. A sister of Flavor Downtown adds harbour views (especially if you can secure a sought-after window table) to the winning formula. Seafood & contemporary comfort food. In the Joan Harriss Cruise Pavilion next to the 'Big Fiddle'. **$$$**

✗ **Flavor Downtown** 16 Pitt St; ☏ 902 562 6611; cbflavor.com/downtown; 🕐 08.30–20.30 Mon–Sat, 10.00–15.00 Sun. Modern, bistro-style eatery serving all-day b/fast, gourmet sandwiches & wraps, plus more substantial fare (eg: seafood, pasta, beef tenderloin). Imaginative & tasty food. *Lunch* **$–$$**, *dinner* **$$–$$$**

✗ **Trio at the Cambridge Suites** 180 Esplanade; ☏ 902 563 7009; www. cambridgesuitessydney.com; 🕐 07.00–10.30 & 11.30–22.00 Mon–Sat, 07.00–10.30 & 17.00–22.00 Sun. One of the better hotel eateries. Start with crab cakes à la Louisbourg & move on to seafood hot pot or beef tenderloin. Good choice of wine & cocktails. **$$–$$$**

✗ **A Bite of Asia** 76–80 Dorchester St; ☏ 902 270 7777; ⬛ A Bite of Asia Restaurant; 🕐 11.00–20.00 Tue–Fri, noon–20.30 Sat, 16.00–20.30 Sun. New (2016) eatery dishing up hearty portions of (predominantly) Chinese/Thai food. Good atmosphere, pleasant décor. **$$**

✗ **The Lebanese Flower** 14 Dorchester St; ☏ 902 562 3412; ⬛; 🕐 11.00–22.30 daily. Friendly service, generous portions of tasty, fairly authentic Lebanese food (this is Sydney, NS, not Beirut or the Bekaa Valley). Not fine dining but a decent ethnic eatery. **$$**

SYDNEY
For listings, see pages 355–8

🛏 **Where to stay**
1 Cambridge Suites
2 Spanish Bay Inn
Off map
Chambers' Guest House B&B
Colby House B&B
Hampton Inn by Hilton Sydney
Weary Gardener B&B

✗ **Where to eat and drink**
3 A Bite of Asia
4 Doktor Luke's
5 Flavor Downtown
6 The Lebanese Flower
7 No Quarter Deli & Market
  Trio at the Cambridge Suites (see 1)
Off map
Black Spoon Bistro
Commercial Street Deli
The Lobster Pound & Moore
The Olive Tree

✗ **The Olive Tree** 137 Victoria Rd; ☏ 902 539 1553; ⬛; 🕐 11.00–20.00 Mon–Sat. Friendly, licensed pizzeria/bistro. Very good pizzas (light, thin crust) & tasty Mediterranean-style cuisine (eg: Greek-style shrimp & scallop fettucine with tomato & ouzo sauce). Good-value lunch specials. **$–$$**

🍽 **No Quarter Deli & Market** 270 George St; ☏ 902 270 3886; ⬛; 🕐 11.00–18.30 Mon–Fri, 11.00–17.00 Sat. New Italian-style deli serving excellent gourmet sandwiches, soup, salads, etc. **$–$$**

🍽 **Doktor Luke's** 54 Prince St; ☏ 902 270 5800; www.doktorlukes.com; 🕐 08.00–17.00 Mon–Sat. Good downtown espresso bar (plus tea, hot apple cider, hot chocolate, etc) plus munchies. Despite some good roasteries in the province, the owners get theirs from a New Brunswick company. **$**

North Sydney

✗ **Black Spoon Bistro** 320 Commercial St, North Sydney; ☏ 902 241 3300; www. blackspoonbistro.com; 🕐 11.00–20.00 Mon–Sat (til 21.00 Fri & Sat). Lunch at this great bistro includes gourmet paninis (try the chipotle chicken), soups, & salads (eg: grilled vegetable). In the evening, try the pan-fried halibut or hazelnut-crusted salmon. Save room for bananas Foster. **$$–$$$**

✗ **The Lobster Pound & Moore** 161 Queen St, North Sydney; ☏ 902 794 2992; ⬛; 🕐 noon–

8

15.00 & 17.00–20.00 Wed–Fri, 16.00–20.00 Sat & Sun. Great lobster & seafood, good service & atmosphere at chef Richard Moore's (justifiably) popular restaurant. Meat/poultry dishes are tasty, too. Recommended – reservations advised! $$–$$$

⌨ Commercial Street Deli 194 Commercial St; ☎ 902 794 3354; **f**; ◷ 07.00–15.00 Mon–Fri, 08.00–14.00 Sat & Sun. Good b/fasts (eg: banana bread French toast), fab salads & deli sandwiches (meat is prepared in-house), plus smoothies, etc. $–$$

ENTERTAINMENT AND NIGHTLIFE
Music & theatre
Centre 200 481 George St; ☎ 902 564 2200; www.centre200.ca. Home to the Cape Breton Screaming Eagles ice-hockey team from mid Sep to mid Mar, this large modern facility (6,500 capacity as an arena, 3,000 in theatre-mode) & exhibition centre hosts big-name concerts.

Cineplex Cinemas Sydney 325 Prince St; ☎ 902 539 9050; www.cineplex.com. The cinema offers 10 film choices.

Membertou Trade and Convention Centre 50 Maillard St; ☎ 902 539 2300; www. membertoutcc.com. Concerts, performances, comedy shows & more.

CAUGHT IN THE WEB

Born in 1935 in New Brunswick, Melissa Friedrich was convicted of killing her husband in 1991: on a deserted road near Halifax, she ran him over twice with a car. She had drugged him heavily to encourage him to lie down in the road. Sentenced to six years in jail for manslaughter, she was released after serving two.

Shortly after her release, she went to Florida and met a man at a Christian retreat. The two married in Dartmouth, Nova Scotia in 2000, but a year later his family members noticed his health seemed to be deteriorating rapidly: there were unexplained fainting spells, his speech was often slurred, and he had to have frequent hospital stays. His family claimed that his money was disappearing far more rapidly than one might expect. He died of cardiac arrest in 2002: no post mortem was carried out and there were no charges over his death.

Melissa found her next husband – a divorcee in his 70s – on an internet dating site, and met him in Florida. Having enjoyed relatively good health up until the wedding, his fortune changed post nuptials. After eight hospital visits in as many weeks, he was told that he had an unwelcome drug in his system. He also discovered that his bank balance had plummeted to zero. Melissa was sentenced to five years in a Florida prison: she was released in 2009 and deported back to Canada, settling in New Glasgow.

Melissa married again in September 2012: she and her 75-year old husband Fred (it is rumoured that she met him via the internet) honeymooned in Newfoundland before stopping for the night in North Sydney. Hours later, Fred was taken ill, and rushed to hospital. After a few days, Melissa was arrested for attempted murder. Fred was released from hospital and Melissa – labelled the 'Internet Black Widow' by the media – was convicted of attempted murder. She served almost three years of a 3½-year sentence and was released in March 2016 on various conditions. One of these was that she should not access the internet: however, just a month later she was caught doing just that in the new Halifax Central Library. On 4 August, her lawyer entered a 'not guilty' plea: her next trial has been set for 1 February 2017.

Highland Arts Theatre 40 Bentinck St; ☎902 565 3637; www.highlandartstheatre.com. The HAT has taken over the c1911 former St Andrew's Church as an already popular 650-seat venue.

Pubs & bars

🍺 **Crown & Moose Pub** 300 Esplanade; ☎902 567 7014; ⏰ 11.00–midnight daily (til 01.00 Fri & Sat). This British-style pub is a popular spot for locals & hotel guests. Live music Fri & Sat evenings; patio in summer.

🍺 **Governor's Pub & Eatery** 233 Esplanade; ☎902 562 7646; governorseatery.com; ⏰ 11.00–midnight or later Tue–Sat,16.00–midnight Sun&Mon. An upmarket restaurant downstairs, & 1 floor up a rather good Celtic gastro pub (⏰ 11.00–02.00 daily) with nice patio & regular live music.

🍷 **Daniel's Restaurant & Bar** 456 Charlotte St; ☎902 562 8586; ⏰ 10.00–02.00 Mon–Sat, noon–02.00 Sun. Generally good food, nice atmosphere, live entertainment most Thu–Sat eves.

🍷 **Steel City Sports Bar** 252 Townsend St; ☎902 562 4501. Almost legendary Sydney venue. Pub, restaurant, sports bar, dancing & live music.

FESTIVALS Held in May, **PierScape** is a week-long eclectic arts and food festival. The rejuvenated Wentworth Park is home to free concerts on Thursday evenings in July under the **Makin' Waves Music Festival** label (*www.cbrm.ns.ca*). At the end of the month, Membertou is the base for the four-day **Cape Breton Bike Rally** (*capebretonbikerally. com*) – and we're talking motor- rather than leg-powered bikes. In August, **Action Week** (*www.actionweek.com*) includes concerts, a Busker festival, a Caribbean festival and more. The terminus for ferries to and from Newfoundland (page 47) is around the harbour in North Sydney, where horse shows and events – the biggest of which is the **Cape Breton County Exhibition** festival – are held in the summer at the Exhibition Grounds on Regent Street. In September, Lumière (*lumierecb.com*) is a three-night 'art-after-dark' festival that takes over the core of downtown Sydney.

SHOPPING Aimed at cruise-ship passengers, and therefore only open when cruise ships are visiting Sydney in high season, the **Harbourside Boutiques** (*Joan Harriss Cruise Pavilion, 74 Esplanade*) is like a 'best of' for what's on offer in Sydney and the island in general. For other versions of most-things-under-one-roof, head for the **Sydney Shopping Mall** (*272 Prince St*).

In addition to the stores mentioned below, be sure to visit the shop at the **Centre for Craft and Design** (page 361). **Cape Breton Curiosity Shop** (*296 Charlotte St;* ☎ *902 564 4660*) is one of the better gift/souvenir shops with helpful, friendly staff. Craft beer lovers should head for **Breton Brewing** (*364 Keltic Dr;* ☎ *902 270 4677; bretonbrewing. ca;* ⏰ *10.00–20.00 Mon–Sat, noon–17.00 Sun*), and the sweet-toothed to the **Cape Breton Fudge Co** (*331 Charlotte St;* ☎ *902 539 9930; www.capebretonfudgeco.com;* ⏰ *10.00–17.00 Mon–Sat*), which has loads of flavours of fudge, all made on site. The cat-loving and knowledgeable owner at **Ed's Books & More** (*446 Charlotte St;* ☎ *902 564 2665;* 🛈) should be able to find a suitable used book for you, and **Moraff's Yarns & Crafts** (*752 Victoria Rd;* ☎ *902 564 8339;* 🛈) is an old-fashioned shop with old-fashioned service, selling all you need for knitting, sewing and more.

On your way in or out of town? Drop by **Cape Breton Farmers' Market** (*340 Keltic Dr, Sydney River;* ☎ *902 564 9948;* 🛈 *CBFarmersMarket ;* ⏰ *08.30–13.00 Sat*) – it's well worth a visit between late spring and the end of autumn.

OTHER PRACTICALITIES

$ **CIBC** 15 Dorchester St; ☎902 562 6420; ⏰ 10.00–17.00 Mon–Fri

$ **RBC Royal Bank** 404 Charlotte St; ☎902 567 8750; ⏰ 09.30–17.00 Mon–Fri, 09.00–16.00 Sat

➕ **Cape Breton Regional Hospital** 1482 George St; ☎902 567 8000

✉ **Post office** 269 Charlotte St; ⏰ 08.00–17.00 Mon–Fri

In 2002, a British couple, both 19, booked their flights on the internet and flew here via Halifax. Before too long, they realised that although there was a big harbour and the name was the same, this wasn't the Sydney they were expecting. They didn't get to climb the Harbour Bridge, sunbathe on Bondi Beach or have a drink in a Paddington bar, but a kind and sympathetic Air Canada employee took them under her wing. She drove them to see many of Cape Breton Island's delights, and invited them home for dinner. The couple were particularly impressed with the friendliness of the local people. Sydney (Nova Scotia) airport staff said that although on occasion the odd bag turned up here instead of Australia, this was the first time it had happened to humans.

ℹ️ Tourist information Marine Terminal, 74 Esplanade; ☎902 539 9876; ⊕ Jun–mid Oct 08.30–16.30 daily.
Framework Cycle and Fitness 333 George St; ☎902 567 1909; **tf** 1 866 567 1909; frameworkfitness.com; ⊕ 10.00–17.00 Mon–Fri, 09.00–13.00 Sat. Bike hire; daily or weekly rentals.

James McConnell Memorial Library 50 Falmouth St; ☎902 562 3161; ⊕ 10.00–21.00 Tue–Fri, 10.00–17.30 Sat
YMCA Gym 399 Charlotte St; ☎902 562 9622; capebreton.ymca.ca. Day pass (pool & gym access) CAN$10.50.

WHAT TO SEE AND DO There are two beautiful churches worth visiting in Sydney. **St Patrick's Church Museum** (*87 Esplanade;* ☎ *902 562 8237;* ⊕ *Jun–Aug 09.00–17.00 daily (from 13.00 Sun); admission CAN$2*) is a small c1828 Pioneer Gothic-style building and Cape Breton Island's oldest standing Roman Catholic church and displays focus on the city's history. Some stone used in the building's construction came from the ruins of Louisbourg (pages 363–4). Much has been added to **St George's Anglican Church** (*119 Charlotte St*) since its construction (1785–91) as a garrison chapel – this was the first Anglican church on Cape Breton Island. The adjoining graveyard has several interesting sandstone and limestone grave markers.

Also on Charlotte Street, **Cossit House** (*75 Charlotte St;* ☎ *902 539 7973; cossithouse.novascotia.ca;* ⊕ *Jun–mid Oct 09.00–17.00 Tue–Sat; admission CAN$2*) proudly bills itself as Sydney's oldest house: the c1787 manse was home to the town's first Anglican minister, a Rev Ranna Cossit. The house has been restored almost to its original condition, and several rooms have been furnished based on an 1815 inventory of Cossit's estate. Costumed guides give tours. Nearby, **Jost Heritage House** (*54 Charlotte St;* ☎ *902 539 0366;* ⊕ *Jun–Aug 09.00–17.00 daily; Sep–Oct 10.00–16.00 daily; admission CAN$4.75*) is another historical house; parts of this building also date from 1787, but unlike the Cossit House, there have since been additions in several different architectural styles. Each part of the house has been furnished in keeping with the era in which it was built.

On the ground floor of a c1904 Colonial Revival-style former theatre, **The Cape Breton Centre for Heritage and Science** (*225 George St;* ☎ *902 539 1572; www.oldsydney. com;* ⊕ *Jun–Aug 09.00–17.00 Mon–Fri; Sep–May 10.00–16.00 Tue–Fri; admission by donation*) has displays focusing on the social and natural history of eastern Cape Breton.

Just south of town, the 2ha **Membertou Heritage Park** (*35 Su'n Awti, Membertou;* ☎ *902 567 5333; www.membertouheritagepark.com;* ⊕ *09.00–16.30 Mon–Sat (Nov–May closed Sat); admission CAN$8*) honours the spirituality and strength of the

Membertou people by sharing and preserving Mi'kmaq culture and heritage. In theory one can have a guided tour but guides aren't always available. Luckily, there are informative videos and indoor/outdoor exhibits to help. A worthwhile excursion, particularly for those wishing to learn more about the Mi'kmaq.

At the University, you can find a repository of documents relating to the Mi'kmaq at the **Mi'kmaq Resource Centre** (*Beaton Institute, Cape Breton University, 1250 Grand Lake Rd;* ☏ *902 563 1660; www.cbu.ca/indigenous-affairs/unamaki-college;* ⊕ *09.00–16.30 Tue–Fri; Mon by appointment; admission free*). While you're there, stop by Cape Breton Island's first (and only) full-time public art gallery, the **Cape Breton University Art Gallery** (*1250 Grand Lake Rd;* ☏ *902 563 1342; www.cbu.ca/campus/art-gallery;* ⊕ *10.00–16.00 Mon–Fri; admission free*), which has a diverse permanent collection of historical and contemporary Canadian and international artwork. Also for art-lovers, **The Cape Breton Centre for Craft and Design** (*322 Charlotte St;* ☏ *902 270 7491; www.capebretoncraft.com;* ⊕ *10.00–16.00 (or later) Mon–Sat; admission free*) has an overview of the work of some of Cape Breton Island's best artisans and an excellent gallery shop.

Get two (actually three) museums for the price of one at the **Cape Breton Fossil Centre and Sydney Mines Heritage Museum** (*159 Legatto St, Sydney Mines;* ☏ *902 544 992; sydneymineheritage.ca;* ⊕ *Jun–mid Sep 09.00–17.00 Tue–Sat; off-season by appointment; admission CAN$9.20*). Numerous 300-million-year-old fossils have been found over the years in the area's coalfields: fossil hikes are also offered three or more times weekly for an extra CAN$17.25. In the adjacent former railway station is a museum telling the story of the community of Sydney Mines – with emphasis of course on coal mining and steel manufacture. A recent addition is a local sport museum.

Staffed by enthusiastic volunteers and housed in a former synagogue, **Whitney Pier Historical Society Museum** (*88 Mt Pleasant St;* ☏ *902 564 9819; whitneypiermuseum.org;* ⊕ *Jun–Aug 09.00–noon & 13.00–16.30 Mon–Fri; off-season by appointment; admission by donation*) is an unusual hands-on museum that illustrates the multi-cultural (in close proximity are the Holy Ghost Ukrainian Church, Polish St Mary's Parish Church and St Phillips, the only African Orthodox Church in Canada) community that developed around the steel plant and coal piers.

If you're keen to try your luck at the tables, head over to the **Casino Nova Scotia-Sydney** (*525 George St;* ☏ *902 563 7777; sydney.casinonovascotia.com;* ⊕ *11.00–03.00 daily*). You'll find the typical assortment of slot machines and table games (*17.00–02.00 Wed–Sun*). For 19s and over only.

AROUND SYDNEY

Glace Bay Glace Bay is the former heart of Cape Breton Island's once-flourishing coal industry. Maybe it will be again: as I write, work is underway to re-open the Donkin mine, possibly before the end of 2016. Mining apart, the town has another claim to fame as the place from which in 1902, the first west-to-east transatlantic wireless message was sent by **Guglielmo Marconi.**

Despite the death of the mining, Glace Bay is very much alive. For the visitor, in addition to the excellent **mining museum** (more interesting than it sounds!), there's a very good **heritage museum**, the beautifully renovated c1920s' **Savoy Theatre** (*116 Commercial St;* ☏ *902 842 1577; www.savoytheatre.com*) – a wonderful live-music venue – and the Marconi site. There's a decent restaurant in the miners' museum, or try **TALO Café Bar** (*195 Commercial St;* ☏ *902 842 2195; talocafebar.com;* ⊕ *11.30–20.00 Tue–Sun (Fri & Sat til 23.00);* $$), an excellent coffee shop, bar and licensed restaurant.

Accessible **by car**, Glace Bay is on highways 4 and 28, 21km/13 miles northeast of Sydney. An hourly **bus** – #1 *(Mon–Sat; CAN$3.25)* – connects Glace Bay with downtown Sydney.

What to see and do Displays on the history of coal mining both in Cape Breton and internationally can be found at the **Cape Breton Miners' Museum** (*17 Museum St;* \ *902 849 4522; www.minersmuseum.com;* ⊕ *Jun–late Oct 10.00–18.00 daily; Nov–May by appointment; admission CAN$7.50)*; also check out the recreation of a mining village between 1850 and 1900, with a miner's home and company store. Well worth the extra admission is the guided tour of the **Ocean Deeps Colliery** (extra *CAN$7.50*), over which the museum has been built. Don a hard hat and cape to be guided deep underground by a retired miner to where the coal was extracted manually. A summer bonus is weekly concerts by the Men of the Deeps, a choir of working and retired Cape Breton Island miners (*late Jun–late Aug 20.00 most Tue; book in advance*). The museum is also home to the licensed Miners' Village Restaurant (⊕ *early May–late Sep 11.00–20.00 daily; $$*), offering a varied menu at reasonable prices. Try the seafood chowders or Atlantic halibut – and save room for old-fashioned dessert. At the time of writing, the museum is having problems with major roof leaks, and is appealing for government funding for repairs needed to avoid closure...

The interesting **Glace Bay Heritage Museum** (*14 McKeen St;* \ *902 842 5345;* ⊕ *Mar–Jun & Sep–Dec 14.00–16.00 Tue, Thu & Sat; Jul–Aug 10.00–17.00 Tue–Sat, 13.00–18.00 Sun; admission free*) occupies two storeys of the restored c1903 former town hall. A large mural depicts both mining and another pursuit popular in Glace Bay in days gone by, sword fishing. See also the old court room (tea and oat cakes are served here) and council chambers. There's also a gift shop with a good selection of books on Cape Breton Island, and a well-priced secondhand bookstore.

On the site of the **Marconi National Historic Site** (*Timmerman St;* \ *902 842 2530; www.pc.gc.ca/eng/lhn-nhs/ns/marconi/index.aspx;* ⊕ *Jul–early Sep 10.00–18.00 daily; admission free*) in 1902, with use of a 400-wire antenna suspended from four 61m wooden towers, Guglielmo Marconi sent the first west-to-east transatlantic wireless message. In addition to displays on Marconi's life on Cape Breton Island and his experiments and achievements, there's a model of the original radio station, and the foundations of the huge transmitting towers are visible outside.

THE SOUTH

By far the biggest attraction in the southeast of Cape Breton Island is the reconstruction of the fortress at Louisbourg. Much of the island's south coast is rugged, remote and sparsely populated, even by Nova Scotia standards. You won't see many people, or many (if any) shops, eateries and places to stay. Somewhat harsh – even bleak – for much of the year, it is best enjoyed in good weather by those who like pottering along on quiet roads, taking side-trips to pretty fishing villages, and soaking up an atmosphere of days gone by.

Highlights of this comparatively little-travelled trail include an opportunity to explore the gorgeous beaches at Belfry and Point Michaud, and the delightful Isle Madame.

PORT MORIEN This pleasant, quiet little seaside lobster-fishing village has a wide sandy barrier beach and a migratory bird sanctuary. It's not a bad choice for those who want a quiet base from which to explore the larger old industrial urban centres, and Louisbourg, a 45-minute drive away. The local eatery closed a couple of years

In 1937, Human Rights activist Marcus Garvey started a speech in Glace Bay thus: 'We are going to emancipate ourselves from mental slavery because whilst others might free the body, none but ourselves can free the mind.' Reggae legend Bob Marley's (c1980) 'Redemption Song' begins 'Emancipate yourself from mental slavery / None but ourselves can free our minds.'

ago, so Glace Bay is your best dining option. Housed in a c1885 former Anglican Church rectory, the only accommodation option is the **Port Morien Rectory B&B** (*2 rooms; 2652 Hwy 255;* ✆ *902 737 1453;* tf *1 888 737 1453;* e *pmrectorybb@seaside. ns.ca; www.bbcanada.com/pmrectorybb;* **$$**), offering guestrooms with ocean views (full breakfast included).

To reach Port Morien **by car**, the village is on Highway 255, 10km/6 miles from Glace Bay, 30km/19 miles from Sydney and 50km/31 miles from Louisbourg.

MAIN-À-DIEU The name Main-à-Dieu is a French corruption of the region's Mi'kmaq name, *Menadou*. This is the largest fishing village on the coast between Port Morien and Louisbourg (population: 235). As you enter the village, look out for the tiny roadside **St James Cemetery**, dating from 1768. Stop off first at the **Coastal Discovery Centre** (*2886 Louisbourg–Main-à-Dieu Rd;* ✆ *902 733 2258; www. coastaldiscoverycentre.ca;* ⊕ *Jul–Aug 10.00–16.00 daily; Sep–Jun 09.00–17.00 daily, admission free*), which houses the Fishermen's Museum, a seasonal café (⊕ *Tue–Fri but call ahead to check*) and a public library (✆ *902 733 5708*), before wandering the sandy beach or the boardwalk just behind. A short but worthwhile shoreline hike is the 3km return **Moque Head Trail**.

To reach Main-à-Dieu from Port Morien **by car**, continue south on Highway 255 then turn left onto Main-à-Dieu Road, a total distance of approximately 28km /17 miles. The village is 17km from Louisbourg, via Main-à-Dieu Road.

LOUISBOURG Although best known for its wonderfully impressive reconstructed historic site, the small fishing town of Louisbourg (population: 1,250) has a few other attractions, too. These include a lighthouse with a spectacular setting, shipwrecks in the harbour for divers to explore, a railway museum, an Elizabethan-style theatre and some good beaches a short 10-minute drive away along the unpaved Kennington Cove Road. You will see both English (Louisburg) and French (Louisbourg) spellings used, with the latter much more common.

Louisbourg is on the coast in the southeast corner of Cape Breton Island, 32km/20 miles from Sydney via Highway 22. It is 111km/69 miles from Baddeck and 207km/129 miles from the Canso Causeway. The town can only be reached **by car**, as no scheduled public transport comes this way.

History Around 1719, the French began a huge project to construct what was not to be just a military fort, but a fortified town that would be a prestigious centre for commerce, culture and government, the capital of Ile Royale (as Cape Breton Island was then known). Home to 2,000–5,000 French soldiers, fishermen, merchants and their families and children, it was just about ready when New Englanders attacked by land in 1745, supported by a large British naval force. The fortress fell in seven weeks.

The victors' success was tempered by the reality of the severe winters here: food (particularly fresh food) was scarce, shelter limited – owing to damage

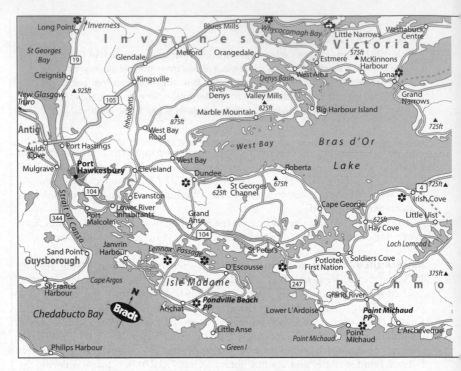

caused by the assault – and sanitary conditions awful. Ten times more New Englanders died of the cold, disease or starvation than had been killed in the fighting.

In 1748, the Treaty of Aix-la-Chapelle returned the fortress to France, and back under French control, it thrived again. Fortifications were repaired, strengthened and added to. But the second assault came in 1758, when a huge British force led by Major-General Geoffrey Amherst once again took the 'impregnable' fortress after a six-week siege.

In 1760, the British totally demolished the fortifications and outer works: in later years some of the stones were recycled and used in the construction of new buildings such as Halifax's Government House (1800), and Sydney's St George (1785) and St Patrick's (1828) churches.

As mines boomed in the Sydney area, the need for transport to connect that area with an ice-free port, so that coal could be shipped year-round, grew. As a result, the Sydney and Louisburg Railway was constructed in 1895.

Two centuries after the British had laid Louisbourg to waste, the Canadian government approved a plan to rebuild a section of the fortifications and parts of the historic town to show how they would have looked in the 1740s. Where possible, traditional French construction methods – and many of the original stones – were used in the painstaking reconstruction.

Where to stay   *See also pages 368–9*

Campers may also consider staying at Mira River Provincial Park (*parks.novascotia. ca/content/mira-river*) approximately 20 minutes' drive from Louisbourg.

DIB DIB DIB

The first Boy Scout troop in North America was established in Port Morien in 1908.

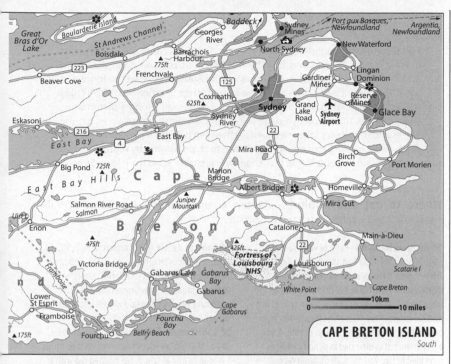

CAPE BRETON ISLAND
South

🏠 **Cranberry Cove Inn** (7 rooms) 12 Wolfe St; ✆ 902 733 2171; **tf** 1 800 929 0222; www. cranberrycoveinn.com; ☼ mid May–Oct. A fine, comfortable inn with individually themed guestrooms. Rate includes full b/fast. **$$**

🏠 **Louisbourg Heritage House B&B** (6 rooms) 7544 Main St; ✆ 902 733 3222; **tf** 1 888 888 8466; www.louisbourgheritagehouse.com; ☼ mid May–mid Oct. Each of the rooms in this centrally located c1886 former rectory have lovely wood floors & private balcony. Full b/fast inc. **$$**

🏠 **Louisbourg Harbour Inn B&B** (4 rooms) 9 Lower Warren St; ✆ 902 733 3222; **tf** 1 888 888 8466; www.louisbourgharbourinn.com; ☼ mid May–mid Oct. Sister property of Louisbourg Heritage House. Another lovely old house, formerly a sea captain's, with a grand staircase & tasteful 2nd- & 3rd-floor rooms. Rate includes full b/fast. **$$**

🏠 **Point of View Suites** (16 units) 15 Commercial St Ext; ✆ 902 733 2080; **tf** 1 888 374 8439; www.louisbourgpointofview.com; ☼ Jun– mid Oct. Bright, modern, well-designed deluxe suites & apts – many with kitchen facilities – in a great location on a 1.6ha peninsula with private beach & fortress views. **$$**

🏠 **Wolvespack Cottage** (2 rooms) 157 West Shore Rd; ✆ 902 733 2062; **e** wolvespackcottage@ ns.sympatico.ca; ☼ Jun–Oct. Choose from a room with private or en-suite bathroom at this quiet, relaxing modern oceanfront home approx 5km from the historical site. Borrow a bike or kayak to work off the excellent b/fast (inc in the room rate). **$$**

🏠 **The Stacey House B&B** (4 rooms) 7438 Main St; ✆ 902 733 2317; **tf** 1 866 924 2242; www. bbcanada.com/thestaceyhouse; ☼ mid Jun–mid Oct. Well-located Victorian house with views over the harbour & very friendly hosts. Rooms with en-suite or shared bathrooms. Good b/fast (inc) & good value. **$**

⛺ **Lakeview Treasures Campground & RV Park** (75 sites) 5785 Louisbourg Hwy; ✆ 902 733 2058; **tf** 1 866 233 2267; www. louisbourgcampground.com; ☼ Jun–mid Oct. Open & shaded campground 10km from the fortress with lake frontage & motorhome & serviced sites. Pool (in season), small store & take-out. **$**

The second-oldest lighthouse on the North American continent, and the first in what is now Canada, was built by the French at Louisbourg in the 1730s, and destroyed (though later rebuilt) when the British besieged the fortress in 1758. The current version, on a volcanic rock outcrop, was first lit in 1924: enjoy the views! The Lighthouse Trail is a 2 km (1.2 mile) walk along a picturesque, coastal trail with interpretive panels and benches. Rest and relax; watch the waves and the lobster fishermen hauling their catch. Enjoy a panoramic view of the fortress, looking much as it would have to ships passing by more than two centuries or more ago. To get there, follow Havenside Road from Main Street.

✗ Where to eat and drink
In addition to the listings below, there are also restaurants and a café inside the historic site.

✗ Beggars Banquet Point of View Suites, page 365; ⊕ Jul–Aug 1 sitting at 18.00 daily. Not just dinner (soup, salad bar, choose from lobster, snow crab, halibut & chicken – plus all the trimmings – then ginger cake & tea or coffee) but musical entertainment, too. The idea comes from banquets held for the poor in days of yore, & you are encouraged to dine clad in period costumes (provided before you are seated). Reservations strongly recommended. Fixed price *CAN$46*.

✗ Grubstake Restaurant 7499 Main St; ☏902 733 2308; www.grubstake.ca; ⊕ late Jun–mid Oct noon–20.15. Long established, & often just about the only place open in town. The varied menu includes seafood & other interesting choices: steaks aren't bad, the BBQ pork has countless fans, but I'm partial to the shrimp/scallop flambée. **$$**

✗ Lobster Kettle 41 Commercial St; ☏902 733 2723; www.lobsterkettle.com; ⊕ Jul–Sep noon–20.00 Mon–Sat. With a wonderful waterfront setting & fantastic views, generally, this licensed restaurant tends to do seafood well (especially lobster & snow crab). **$$**

✗ Louisburger Chip Wagon Minto St; ☏902 304 7358; ⊕ May–Oct (hours vary). Not so much a wagon as an old school bus painted red with a few picnic tables outside. It churns out surprisingly good fries (plus hot dogs, onion rings) & – of course – the Louisburger! Located behind the Louisbourg General Store, next to the Fire Hall and near the waterfront. **$**

Entertainment and festivals
Based on London, England's (Elizabethan) Globe Theatre, Louisbourg's version, the Louisbourg Playhouse (*11 Aberdeen St;* ☏ *902 733 2996; www.louisbourgplayhouse.com;* ⊕ *late Jun–mid Oct*), opened in 1994. The programme focuses on live theatre and Cape Breton music. In June, the **Roots to Boots Festival** (*www.rootstobootsfestival.ca*) is an Acadian celebration with storytelling, music, food and more. July sees a three-day 1700s-style multicultural **Culture Fête** at the fortress. Then don your plastic bib for the end of July/early August **Louisbourg Crabfest** (*louisbourgcrabfest.ca*) when thousands turn up to eat crab (and mussels) and be entertained. Later in August, the **Feast of St Louis** is a recreation of an 18th-century celebration honouring French monarch Louis IX, with cannon salutes, musket firings, dancing, children's games and music.

Other practicalities
$ Royal Bank 7509 Main St; ☏902 733 2012; ⊕ 10.00–16.00 Mon–Wed, 10.00–17.00 Thu & Fri
✉ **Post office** 7529 Main St; ⊕ 08.00–17.30 Mon–Fri, 09.30–13.30 Sat

🛈 Tourist information 7495 Main St; ☏902 733 2720; ⊕ early Jun–early Oct 09.00–17.00 daily (Jul–Aug to 19.00)

18.00–20.00 Tue & Thu, 14.00–17.00 Wed & Sat,
10.00–11.30 & 14.00–17.30 Fri

What to see and do Appropriately housed in the former c1895 Sydney and Louisburg railway station, the **Sydney and Louisburg Railway Museum** (*Main St;* ☎ *902 733 2720;* ⏰ *Jun & Sep 09.00–17.00 Mon–Fri; Jul–Aug 10.00–19.00 daily; admission free*) has exhibits for train fans, including two passenger carriages from 1881 and 1914 and a working model of the line in an original freight shed.

If you're keen to get out and explore the island from above or below the water, there are a couple of tour operators you can contact. **Louisbourg Scuba Services** (☎ *902 578 1497; www.louisbourgscuba.com*) offer a range of services, including courses and charters to dive wrecks such as the *Celebre*, which sank in 1758. Based 8km north of Louisbourg, **Paradise Kayaks** (*200 Byrnes Lane, Catalone;* ☎ *902 733 3244; www. paradisekayaks.com*). Paradise offer half-, full-, multi-day & night guided kayak tours.

Fortress of Louisbourg [map, below] (☎ *902 733 3552; www.pc.gc.ca/louisbourg;* ⏰ *late May–early Oct 09.30–17.00 daily (limited services except Jul–early Sep); early Oct–late May 09.30–16.00 Mon–Fri when buildings closed but grounds open; admission CAN$7.30; Jul–early Sep CAN$17.60*) You can't miss Louisbourg's *pièce de résistance*: the **Fortress of Louisbourg National Historic Site of Canada**. To say that this site is the largest historical reconstruction in North America doesn't really begin to give an idea of the scale of the 6,700ha site.

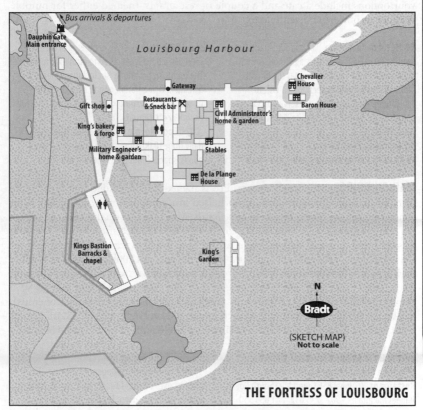

THE FORTRESS OF LOUISBOURG

Park directly on site via Entrance 2 between mid September and mid June, or park (for free) at the visitor centre at other times, buy your ticket and take the 7-minute bus ride to the fortress area. The reconstructed area alone sprawls across some 10ha, with dozens of buildings to visit and numerous activities to entertain you.

Theme centres and exhibits abound, each of which offers insight into a different part of the history and everyday life of the fortress in the 1740s. Whereas in many other living museums you'll see a few interpreters demonstrating a few traditional techniques, when everything is up and running Louisbourg seems alive with men, women and children in costume, only too prepared to interact – in character – with visitors. Strikingly obvious is the class difference at the time, with both fine houses for the gentry, and simple spartan dwellings for the have-nots.

See building techniques demonstrated, nail making, open-hearth cooking and lace making. Observe military exercises and in July and August fire a cannon (*extra CAN$55.20*) or a real musket (*extra CAN$36.80*) whilst in period costume. Herbs and vegetables are tended in tidy back gardens.

Join a guided walking tour or one of the various programmes, including the story and tasting of rum (check in advance for tour times), or use the site map to explore on your own. Be prepared for windy and/or wet weather, and a lot of walking. Allow far more time than you usually would for a 'standard' historical site or living museum. Get in the mood, and go back more than three centuries!

✕ Where to eat and drink If you work up an appetite whilst exploring the site, your options include a café and a couple of restaurants, themed either for humble soldiers, or officers and gentlemen.

✕ Hotel de la Marine ⊕ mid Jun–early Oct from 11.00 daily. This 'upper class' (more formal) dining experience represents what the higher-ranks of society could expect upon a visit to Louisbourg. Your finer dining is served on Chinese porcelain – & you also get a knife & fork. Licensed. **$$–$$$**

✕ Grandchamp's Tavern ⊕ Jul–Aug from 10.30 daily. You are given a spoon with which

to eat 18th-century-style rustic French cuisine served in a bowl & prepared to authentic recipes. The menu isn't overlong but includes at least 1 fish, meat & vegetarian option each day. With period décor & waiting staff in costume, it is a fun experience. Licensed. **$$**

▭ L'Epee Royale Café ⊕ mid May–early Oct daily from 10.00. Offers period desserts, baked goods, snacks & hot & cold beverages. **$**

MARION BRIDGE This small community is named for the bridge that crosses the Mira River, both of which were immortalised in a composition by Glace Bay-born songwriter Allister MacGillivray. In *Song for the Mira* (aka Out on the Mira) he writes, 'I'll trade you ten of your cities for Marion Bridge. And the pleasure it brings'. The song was the inspiration for *Marion Bridge*, a 2002 film. Just 8km west of Marion Bridge at the confluence of the Salmon and Mira rivers, the peaceful 200ha **Two Rivers Wildlife Park** (*Grand Mira North Rd;* ☏ *902 727 2483; www.tworiverspark.ca;* ⊕ *mid Oct–mid May 10.00–16.00 daily; mid May–mid Oct 10.00–19.00 daily; admission CAN$7*) displays wildlife native to the Maritimes (with a couple of exotic extras such as emus).

Marion Bridge is convenient to reach **by car**; it is on Highway 327, 15km/9 miles from Sydney, 31km/19 miles from Louisbourg and 25km/16 miles from Gabarus.

🏠 Where to stay, eat and drink

🏠 Mira River Cottages & Riverbank Restaurant (6 units) 856 Grand Mira South Rd, Juniper Mountain; ☏ 902 727 2012; **tf** 1 866 550

5824; www.mirarivercottages.de; ⊕ May–Oct. 4 comfortable cottages (3-night min stay) & 2 guest rooms. German spoken. The licensed restaurant

(☺ *summer 16.00–20.30 Wed–Sun; $$*), serving Swiss-German & Canadian specialities, good seafood chowder & desserts, is good value. To get there, turn on to Grand Mira South Rd from Hwy 327 approx 800m after crossing the Mira River (heading south): the complex is around 5km from the junction. **$$**

GABARUS This is a truly picturesque fishing village. Before you reach the breakwater, turn left on to Harbour Point Road past the **Harbour Cemetery,** which has lost several graves to the sea, to reach the c1950s' **lighthouse**. It is a pity that there is nowhere to stay or eat. If you feel like a **coastal hike,** at the breakwater turn right on to Gull Cove Road, and follow it to its end. The walking trail (6km each way) leads to what was the fishing community of **Gull Cove**. After about 1km you'll reach **Harris Beach**, and have a wonderful view over Gabarus Bay.

Gabarus is on Highway 327, 45km/28 miles from Sydney, 56km/35 miles from Louisbourg and 88km/55 miles from St Peter's.

BELFRY BEACH Don't be surprised to have this magnificent long stretch of sand – backed by Belfry Lake – to yourself. This is a remote and very sparsely populated corner of Cape Breton Island, and the beach itself is easily missed by the casual tourist. Long may it stay that way! Enjoy the solitude and natural splendour, and wander for miles. You might see harbour or grey seals in June and July, you'll definitely see a range of seabirds, and – in spring and summer in particular – migratory shorebirds.

To reach Belfry Beach **by car**, it is located at the end of Belfry Road, off Fourchu Road approximately 8.5km/5 miles south of the tiny community of Gabarus Lake.

POINT MICHAUD A fine beach justifies Point Michaud's inclusion in this book. There's not a lot else going on. Encompassing a glorious 3km curve of sand backed by marram grass-covered dunes, **Point Michaud Beach Provincial Park** makes for a stunning stop. The beach is popular (perhaps that is the wrong word to use – it rarely gets at all busy) with surfers, windsurfers and birdwatchers.

Point Michaud is 21km/13 miles from St Peter's and 67km/42 miles from Gabarus.

ISLE MADAME

Despite the name, this is actually a cluster (measuring approx 16km x 11km) of islands separated from Cape Breton Island by the narrow Lennox Passage. **Arichat** is the most significant of the main communities, and several tiny hamlets such as picturesque **Little Anse** and **Samsons Cove** fringe secluded inlets and coves. Acadian heritage is still strong here, and you will often hear French being spoken.

Once again, specific sites are few, the attraction being beautiful coastal scenery, genuinely friendly people, and a very relaxed atmosphere. With a wooded interior, relatively gentle terrain, virtually no heavy traffic, a lovely beach, a fine hiking trail and a few good places to stay and eat, this is a delightful area to motor (or better still, cycle) around, especially when the sun is out.

On the Lennox Passage waterfront, **Martinique** has a picnic park, the c1884 Grandique Point Lighthouse and a small beach, but the best beaches are on **Janvrin Island** and at **Pondville**, where the sandy 1km-long strand is backed by dunes and a lagoon.

You'll see them on many menus, in tanks in restaurants and supermarkets, and the contraptions used to capture them in a multitude of fishing villages.

A lobster has a long body and five sets of legs, including two large front claws, one of which is large and flat while the other is thinner and smaller. The body, tail and claws are protected by a hard shell. Lobsters grow by moulting, or shedding their shell. After a moult (typically in summer), the lobster is soft-shelled and filled with the sea water it has absorbed in the process. Up to two months pass before the absorbed sea water is replaced by new flesh. The shell hardens again in the cold sea before the cycle repeats.

Although live lobsters range in colour from brownish-rust to greenish-brown, all lobster shells turn bright orangey-red when cooked – traditionally by being immersed in a pot of salted water that has been heated to a rolling boil. Lobsters die within moments when immersed in boiling water. They have very primitive nervous systems, and the jury is out on whether they experience anything similar to the concept of pain. Often called the 'King of Seafood', though it can be messy to extract (especially for novices), the lobster's white flesh is firm and dense with a rich flavour.

Lobster fishers use small boats to fish with baited, wooden-frame or plastic-coated steel-mesh traps which are weighted and lowered to the sea bottom. The traps are hauled by ropes attached to buoys which mark their location.

Atlantic Canada's waters are divided into specific fishing areas, each with its own season, varying in length from eight weeks to eight months. These are staggered to protect summer moults.

If you're wondering how fresh lobster manages to appear on menus year-round, the answer is lobster pounds. In the past, these were large, fenced areas of the ocean where captive lobsters lived until required, new technology has meant huge dry-land holding facilities being built. One of the biggest of these is owned by Clearwater Seafoods, and is on Isle Madame at Presqu'Ile Cove.

Here, around one million lobsters usually reside in individual containers stacked over 30 levels high. Their environment makes the crustaceans lose all inclination to moult. Lobsters caught all over the Maritime provinces are brought here, and, when required, shipped all over the world.

Although no scheduled tours are offered, in the past staff at the pound have been happy to show visitors around. If you'd like to see the facility, it might be worth phoning ahead. For various reasons, you may choose not to eat it during your time in Nova Scotia, but be prepared to be offered lobster frequently (and, more often than not, for the offerer to be surprised if you decline).

Cape Breton lobster has been called the best in the world by Dorothy Cann Hamilton, founder and CEO of the USA's International Culinary Center.

Probably the best of Isle Madame's numerous trails is the **Cape Auguet Eco Trail,** which begins near Boudreauville, offering a short trail (Lake Loop, signed blue, approx 2.5km) and a lovely longer Main Trail (signed yellow, approx 9km round-trip) to Mackerel Cove.

Accessible **by car**, the bridge across to Isle Madame is 5km/3 miles from Exit 46 of Highway 104, 35km/22 miles from Port Hastings, 24km/15 miles from St Peter's, and 109km/68 miles from Sydney.

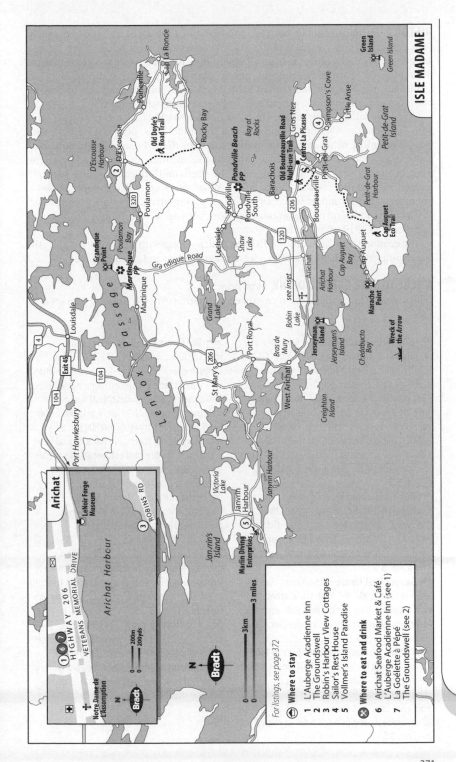

ISLE MADAME

Arichat

Notre Dame de l'Assomption

LeNoir Forge Museum

HIGHWAY 206

VETERANS MEMORIAL DRIVE

ROBINS RD

Arichat Harbour

0   200m
0   200yds

N

Bradt

For listings, see page 372

Where to stay

1 L'Auberge Acadienne Inn
2 The Groundswell
3 Robin's Harbour View Cottages
4 Sailor's Rest House
5 Vollmer's Island Paradise

Where to eat and drink

6 Arichat Seafood Market & Café
   L'Auberge Acadienne Inn (see 1)
7 La Goélette à Pépé
   The Groundswell (see 2)

0   3km
0   3 miles

N

Bradt

Port Hawkesbury

Port Hebert

Louisdale

Exit 45

St Mary's

West Arichat

Creighton Island

Victoria Lake

Janvrin Harbour

Janvrin's Island

Marin Diving Enterprise

Janvrin Harbour

Bras de Mury

Port Royal

Grand Lake

Martinique

Grandique Point

Martinique PP

Grandique Road

Poulamon

Poulamon Bay

D'Escousse

D'Escousse Harbour

Poinerville

Cap La Ronce

Rocky Bay

Old Doyle's Road Trail

Shaw Lake

Lochside

Pondville South

Pondville

Pondville Beach

Pondville PP

Bay of Rocks

Barachois

Old Boudreauville Road
Multi-use Trail

Gros Nez

Sampson's Cove

Centre La Picasse

Boudreauville

Petit-de-Grat

Little Anse

Petit-de-Grat Island

Petit-de-Grat Harbour

Green Island

Green Island

Arichat

see inset

Arichat Harbour

Cap Auguet

Cap Auguet

Cap Auguet Eco Trail

Marache Point

Chedabucto Bay

Wreck of the Arrow

Bobin Lake

Jerseyman Island

Jerseyman's Island

Lennox Passage

HISTORY European contact with Isle Madame goes at least as far back as the early 16th century, when Basque and Portuguese fishermen took refuge from storms at Petit-de-Grat, the oldest fishing village in the area. The name is a combination of French and Spanish/Basque and means 'little fishing place (station)'.

Initially, Isle Madame was named Sante Marie. The name change was in honour of Madame de Maintenon, second wife of French monarch Louis XIV.

One of the oldest communities in Nova Scotia, Arichat had strong business ties with Jersey in the Channel Islands during the mid 1700s, not least because that was where most of its early inhabitants, many of them French Huguenots, had come from. The red-petalled Jersey lilies visible in many of the island's gardens were brought over three centuries ago. In the late 18th century, the harbour teemed with commerce and shipbuilding. When tall ships ruled the seas, it was a booming Atlantic seaport with 17 consular representatives. Previously connected to Cape Breton Island only by water transport, a bridge across Lennox Passage was completed in 1919.

The economy was built around fishing, which, along with fish processing, is still hugely important. Shellfish and to a lesser degree, mackerel, predominate now.

WHERE TO STAY, EAT AND DRINK *Map, page 371*

Self-caterers can purchase fresh or frozen seafood at Arichat Seafood Market and Café.

L'Auberge Acadienne Inn (17 rooms) 2375 Hwy 206, Arichat; ✆902 226 2200; **tf** 1 877 787 2200; e inn@acadienne.com; www. acadienne.com. Friendly, comfortable, modern – but traditional Acadian-style – country inn. There are 9 rooms in the main building & 8 roomy drive-up motel-style units. Laundry facilities. The licensed dining room (⊕ *mid Jun–mid Oct daily, off-season 18.00–21.00 Wed–Sun;* **$$**) specialises in Acadian dishes & seafood & is good. **$$**

Robin's Harbour View Cottages (3 cottages) Robin's Rd, Arichat; ✆902 226 9515; www.robinscottages.ca; ⊕ May–Oct. Overlooking the harbour, these well-equipped 2-bedroom cottages are good for those wanting extra space. **$$**

Sailor's Rest House 83 Sampsons Cove Rd, Sampson Cove; ✆902 704 0604; www.airbnb.ca/ rooms/9886007. Nice, comfortable, well-equipped 3-bedroom rental property on Petit-de-Grat island. 3-night min stay. **$$**

Vollmer's Island Paradise (6 units) 1489 Janvrin's Harbour Rd; ✆902 226 1507; www. vipilodge.com; ⊕ May–Oct. Hand-built log cabins on lovely Janvrin Island really allow you to get away from it all. Canoes, kayaks, bikes & SUPs available, boat trips & scuba diving offered (*Jul–Sep*). **$$**

The Groundswell (4 rooms) 3281 Hwy 320, D'Escousse; ✆902 777 7777; www. thegroundswell.ca; ⊕ May–Oct. Accommodation (spacious if sparsely furnished rooms named after Beatles' songs; rate includes b/fast), an English-style pub (⊕ noon–21.00 Tue–Fri, 10.00–21.00 Sat & Sun: bar til midnight Fri, 01.00 Sat; **$$**) with cocktails, craft beers, live music & good fresh & local food, & a bunch of outdoor activity rentals (kayaks, SUPs, surfboards & cycles) make The Groundswell a hub of youthful activity. **$**

Arichat Seafood Market & Café 2392 Hwy 206, Arichat; ✆902 226 0091; www. premiumseafoods.ns.ca/market.html; ⊕ 06.30–18.00 Mon–Fri, 09.00–16.00 Sat. Though the café focuses on fresh seafood, there are always land-lubber options. Service is friendly & helpful. Plus a range of ocean treats to cook/ enjoy elsewhere. Don't miss. May open on summer Fri eves. **$–$$**

La Goélette à Pépé 2393 Hwy 206, Arichat; ✆902 631 4051; www.lagoeletteapepe. ca; ⊕ 06.30–19.00 Mon–Sat, 09.30–16.00 Sun. Excellent locally roasted coffee & a range of loose-leaf teas, plus tasty home-baked goodies. Not your usual petrol station café. **$**

OTHER PRACTICALITIES

$ St Joseph's Credit Union 3552 Hwy 206, Petit de Grat; ✆ 902 226 2288; ⏰ 09.00–16.00 Mon–Fri (til 19.00 Thu)

✉ **Post office** 2451 High Rd, Arichat; ⏰ 08.00–17.00 Mon–Fri, 10.00–13.00 Sat

Petit-de-Grat Branch Library 3435 Hwy 206; ✆ 902 226 3534; ⏰ 14.00–20.00 Mon, Tue & Thu, 10.00–16.00 Wed, 10.00–16.00 Sat

WHAT TO SEE AND DO Overlooking the harbour is the large, wooden cathedral of **Notre Dame de L'Assomption (Our Lady of the Assumption)** dating from c1837. In 1858, the then bishop imported a pipe organ – now considered to be one of very few of its kind in North America – from Philadelphia, USA. Just by the cathedral, **Cannon Look-Off** offers fine views and has interpretive displays detailing the region's history. The islands' strong Acadian presence is recognised by a francophone/Acadian cultural community centre, **Centre La Picasse** (*3435 Hwy 206, Petit-de-Grat;* ✆ *902 226 0149; www.lapicasse.ca;* ⏰ *09.00–17.00 Mon–Fri*) with French library, archives and gift shop.

The LeNoir Landing Site hosts a Saturday-morning **Farmers' Market** (*alternate Sats, mid Jun–Aug*) and **live music** (*alternate Thu evenings, mid Jun–Aug*). This is also where you'll find the **LeNoir Forge Museum** (*Lower Rd;* ✆ *902 226 9364;* ⏰ *early Jun–Aug 10.00–17.00 daily; admission free*) The c1789 forge down on the waterfront was built in the French Regime style. It was used more recently as an ice house, and in 1967, restored as a working forge museum. Beacon fans won't want to miss the **Guiding Lights of Isle Madame Tour** (*by reservation* e *info@islemadamelighthouses. ca; www.islemadamelighthouses.ca/tours;* ⏰ *Jun–mid Oct 09.00–15.00*), a driving and walking tour of the island's lighthouses. The **Acadian Festival** at Petit-de-Grat is a five-day event celebrating Acadian culture and heritage, which takes place in August.

Certificated **divers** can check out packages offered by **Marlin Diving Enterprises** (*contacts as Vollmer's Island Paradise; see page 372*).

PORT HAWKESBURY

A short drive from Port Hastings, Port Hawkesbury is a major commercial and industrial centre on the Strait of Canso. As at Mulgrave across the water, construction of the nearby Canso Causeway has created an ice-free deep-water port capable of accommodating the largest ships in the world. Tough economic times have meant much uncertainty: many depend on neighbouring Port Tupper's industries for work and when a huge paper mill closed in 2011, it took over CAN$160m of provincial government sweeteners to get it going again. Worrying signs returned in June 2016, when many mill staff were laid off for a week to slow down production.

If you feel like stretching your legs, some nice walking trails head off into the woods around town.

Port Hawkesbury is easy to get to **by car**. The town is situated on Highway 4, 6km/4 miles from Port Hastings and 7km/4.3 miles to the Canso Causeway. It is 43km/27 miles from St Peter's and 165km/103 miles from Sydney. Port Hawkesbury is on the **Maritime Bus** coach route between Halifax and Sydney (page 57).

🏠 WHERE TO STAY

🏠 **Maritime Inn Port Hawkesbury** (73 rooms) 717 Reeves St; ✆ 902 625 0320; tf 1 888 662 7484; www.maritimeinns.com. A comfortable mid-range hotel with indoor pool & a fitness centre. See overleaf for Millers Tap & Grill restaurant. **$$**

🏠 **Gagnon House** (3 rooms) 24 Philpott St; ✆ 902 625 1146; ⏰ Apr–Dec. Conveniently located Cape Cod-style house. Rooms with en-suite or shared bathroom. Warm & knowledgeable hosts. Front & back decks, Strait of Canso views. Full b/fast inc. **$**

WHEN THE CIRCUS CAME TO TOWN

It was the summer of 1870. A local man was short-changed as he bought a ticket for the circus, and when one of the circus staff struck the indignant chap, all hell broke loose. One man was killed, several were badly injured, and most of the circus animals escaped. When order was finally restored, the show was cancelled and the circus limped out of town, battered and bruised – and missing two monkeys. The primates enjoyed a few days of swinging around Port Hawkesbury and frightening the townsfolk before they were shot.

🏠 **Harbourview B&B & Motel** (9 units) 209 Granville St; ✆902 625 3224; **tf** 1 877 676 6886; www.harbourviewbb.com. There are 3 rooms in the c1880 main house (built for a ferry captain), & 6 motel rooms with fridge & microwave. Guest laundry, Wi-Fi, satellite TV & free off-street parking. Watch the modern-day water traffic from the glass-enclosed patio. Full b/fast inc. **$**

✕ WHERE TO EAT AND DRINK

✕ **Millers Tap & Grill** 717 Reeves St; ⊕ 06.30–23.00 Mon–Fri, 07.00–23.00 Sat & Sun; food served until 21.00 (Jul–Sep until 22.00). Maritime Inn Port Hawkesbury's on-site restaurant is licensed. The food – the closest you'll come to fine dining in these parts – is good value. *Lunch* **$$**, *dinner* **$$–$$$**

✕ **BaRyKin Bistro** 3 Water St; ✆902 625 5570; **f**; ⊕ 11.00–21.00 Mon–Sat. Newish café-style eatery right on the waterfront. Good, sophisticated, tasty food, much of it sourced locally. **$$–$$$**

✕ **Fleur-de-Lis Tea Room & Dining Room** 634 Reeves St; ✆902 625 2566; fleurdelistearoom. com; ⊕ 07.00–19.00 Mon–Sat, 10.00–14.00 Sun. An easy-to-miss little gem tucked away in the Causeway shopping mall. There's no deep fryer, & very few processed ingredients are used. All-day b/fast, seafood, Scottish & Acadian cuisine & more. Start with maple nut salad, then go for Acadian fishcakes or the grilled haddock dinner. Desserts are homemade & usually very good. Recommended. **$$**

✕ **The New Shindigs Pub & Steakhouse** 510 Granville St; ✆902 625 0263; ⊕ 11.00–late daily (from 15.00 Sat & Sun). Waterfront pub with good atmosphere. Regular live music (which tends to be a better reason to visit than the hit or miss food). **$$**

🍺 **Haven Coffeebar** 47 Paint St; ✆902 302 0735; **f**. Coffee, baked goods, bread, creative salads & sandwiches & artistic pastries. In the Port Hawkesbury Shopping Centre mall. **$**

OTHER PRACTICALITIES

$ BMO Bank of Montreal 634 Reeves St; ✆902 625 1250; ⊕ 10.00–16.00 Mon–Fri

➕ **The Strait Richmond Hospital** 138 Hospital Rd, Evanston; ✆902 625 3100. 11km east of Port Hawkesbury at Exit 45 of Hwy 104.

✉ **Post office** 25 Pitt St; ⊕ 08.30–17.00 Mon–Fri, 08.30–12.30 Sat

Port Hawkesbury Branch Library 304 Pitt St; ✆902 625 2729; ⊕ 10.00–18.00 Mon & Tue, 10.00–15.30 Wed–Fri; closed 11.30–noon daily

WHAT TO SEE AND DO The **Port Hawkesbury Civic Centre** (*606 Reeves St;* ✆*902 625 2591; www.phcivic.com*) is a fine modern facility, housing an arena, performance space, YMCA fitness centre and art gallery. There are weekly ceilidhs (*Jul–late Aug Tue*), and a community market (*late May–early Oct 14.00–18.00 Thu*). In October, the opening ceremony of the Cape Breton-wide **Celtic Colours International Music Festival** (box, page 318) is held here.

Summer evenings bring free outdoor concerts on Sundays at **Granville Green** (*Granville St;* ✆*625 2591; www.granvillegreen.ca*). A four-day festival in July, **Festival of the Strait** (*festivalofthestrait.ca*) hosts a variety of activities including sailing, canoe races, outdoor concerts and dances.

9

Eastern Shore

Stretching for almost 350km from Lawrencetown to the Canso Causeway, this is the least visited of any of the mainland tourist regions of Nova Scotia.

Ask those who live in other parts of the province about the Eastern Shore and 'always foggy' or 'no infrastructure' will probably be the most common answers. They have a point in terms of infrastructure. There are no sizeable towns, and accommodation, shopping and services are limited and public transport non-existent.

So why come here? This region offers some of Nova Scotia's wildest and most scenic coastal landscapes. Along the length of much of the coast, dozens of forested finger-like peninsulas protrude out into the Atlantic. The so-called main highway – in reality, for all but the first 35km of its length just a quiet two-lane road – cuts across the base of the peninsulas but from time to time be sure to turn off onto one of the side roads to get to a small fishing village, beautiful beach or wild rocky headland with a view of a lighthouse on a nearby island.

Much of the region is forest-covered, with spruce, fir, birch, larch and maple predominant. This is also one of the province's most rewarding destinations for viewing the beauty of the autumn colours.

There aren't any luxury hotels, but the relatively few – but delightful – B&Bs and inns, a handful of motels, some lovely campsites and one 'nature lover's' resort do the job.

The restaurants are also widely spaced, but although you may have to drive for a while there are some excellent dining opportunities, especially for lovers of seafood.

The sea is cold but the beaches are uncrowded and beautiful with the province's best surfing and windsurfing, and the hundreds of uninhabited, forested islands, many of which contain ruins of long-abandoned dwellings or fishing camps, and inlets make for ideal sea kayaking.

Birdwatchers will be in their element, and in addition, there is some wonderful riverside, forest and coastal hiking, and a history of gold mining. There's also an abundance of folklore, with seafaring traditions and legends still very much alive, and a very popular annual music festival.

There are, of course, foggy days, but wandering along a beautiful deserted beach, watching the sea mist roll in, and hearing the moan of a faraway foghorn can be very atmospheric.

Here, perhaps more than anywhere else in Nova Scotia, you'll feel like a traveller rather than a tourist. Come and enjoy the slow pace of life and the proximity to virtually untouched nature. It is no surprise that most of the Eastern Shore's manmade attractions celebrate days gone by, a life pre-electricity and pre-modern technology.

Having said that, what is probably the world's only combined brewery, distillery and golf course (box, page 396) has just opened just outside remote Guysborough,

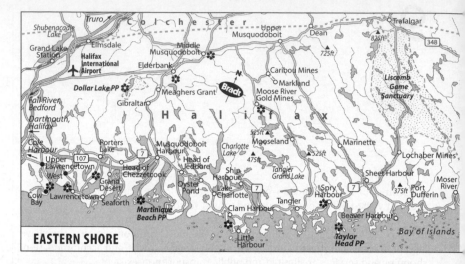

and in the same remote but beautiful area a huge annual cycle extravaganza (box, page 395) has just been inaugurated.

If you headed out to sea for approximately 170km from Tor Bay, you would reach intriguing Sable Island National Park Reserve (pages 398–401) – though virtually all of the limited number of people who visit this long, narrow, storied strip of sand fly from Halifax Airport.

LAWRENCETOWN TO SHEET HARBOUR

LAWRENCETOWN AND SEAFORTH Lawrencetown has an interesting – albeit short – list of attractions, but little to offer service-wise – **MacDonald House**, the building on the right at the top of the hill, has a gallery, antique shop, a tea room and a basement surf shop. Just as you'd expect in a surfing haven in the Maritimes (??), the **Atlantic Dutch Shop** (*94 Horseshoe Turn, East Lawrencetown;* \ *902 827 3654;* ⊕ *10.00–18.00 daily*) offers Dutch food specialities and giftware imported from the Netherlands. Soused herring and *stroopwaffels*, anyone?

However, many visitors come for another reason – to surf (box, page 378) at **Lawrencetown Beach Provincial Park.** For those who merely want to watch, the beach is well worth a (breezy) stop, look and stroll. Lifeguards are on duty in season, and the park has changing rooms, showers and toilets. Far quieter, and usually surfer-free, is **Conrad Beach**, at the end of Conrad Road, 6km east of Lawrencetown. Here your only companions are likely to be birds – and birdwatchers. Boardwalks connect the small parking area with the (especially at low tide) huge, fine-sand beach. The first September weekend (with favourable conditions) sees the **September Storm Classic** (*www.surfns.com*), a surfing competition.

Before, after, or instead of surfing, visit the **Hope for Wildlife Society** in nearby Seaforth (*5909 Hwy 207;* \ *902 407 9453; www.hopeforwildlife.net*), which specialises in the care, treatment and rehabilitation of injured or orphaned native mammals and birds.

Both Lawrencetown and Seaforth are accessible **by car**. Lawrencetown is on Highway 207, 18km/11 miles from Dartmouth, 20km/12 miles from Halifax and 24km/15 miles from Musquodoboit Harbour. Seaforth is also on Highway 207, 9km/6 miles east of Lawrencetown, 27km/17 miles from Dartmouth and

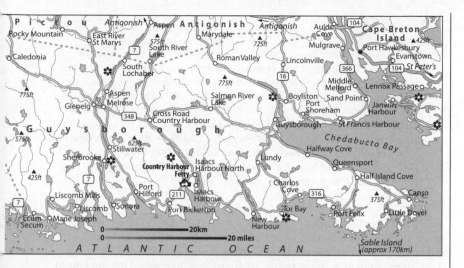

15km/9 miles from Musquodoboit Harbour. **By shuttle,** E.A.S.T. Shuttle (📞 902 877 7433; www.eastshuttle.com) charges CAN$35 per person (minimum three passengers) between Halifax/Dartmouth and Lawrencetown.

Where to stay, eat and drink

Moonlight Beach Suites (4 units) 2 Wyndenfog Lane; 📞 902 827 2712; www. moonlightbeachinn.com. In a magnificent location virtually on Lawrencetown Beach, each guest suite has a sitting area, fireplace, fully equipped kitchenette, dining nook, private entrance & a deck overlooking the ocean. Complimentary bikes, BBQs & lobster cookers available. Reductions may be offered out of season. **$$**

Å Porter's Lake Provincial Park Campground (81 sites) 1160 West Porter's Lake Rd; 📞 902 827 2250; parks.novascotia.ca/content/ porters-lake; ⊕ late May–early Oct. Beautifully located & virtually surrounded by water, 10km from Lawrencetown. RV, unserviced & walk-in sites. **$**

✗ Heron's Nest Tea Room 4144 Lawrencetown Rd; 📞 902 434 7895; ⊕ Jun–Nov 11.00–17.00 Tue–Sun, Dec–May 11.00–16.00 Wed–Sun. Salads, soups, chilli & sandwiches & an enticing array of baked goods. **$**

THE CHEZZETCOOKS West and East Chezzetcook are pretty villages dotted along the Chezzetcook Inlet's shores. On the eastern side of the inlet a road offering more

---

NOT JUST FOR TWITCHERS

En route between the city and Lawrencetown, nature lovers may wish to make a detour. First get to Cole Harbour. Either follow Portland Street (Hwy 207) for 7km from Dartmouth, or if you're on Highway 107, turn on to the Forest Hills Parkway (5km past Exit 14) and follow it for about 3km to Cole Harbour Road (Hwy 207). Turn onto Bissett Road and after 3km you'll see the parking area and trailhead for the Salt Marsh Trail. In a few minutes you'll reach the harbour itself, and this tends to be a particularly rewarding area for watching autumn shorebirds. This is actually part of the Trans Canada Trail, and a number of footbridges lead out across the water. You don't have to do the whole 6.5km each way – just head out for a while then make your way back.

Lawrencetown Beach Provincial Park is renowned for offering the province's best and most consistent wave breaks. The waves are best for surfing in the autumn and winter, in particular between September and May, but whatever time of the year people surf, wetsuits are a must – this isn't Hawaii. And the closest you'll get to a pina colada is a coke from the (summer-only) canteen. Various outfits cater to cater for aficionados of the activity including long-established **Kannon Beach** (*4144 Hwy 207;* ☎ *902 434 3040; kannonbeach. com*). Other options are **East Coast Surf School** (*4348 Hwy 207;* ☎ *902 449 9488; www.ecsurfschool.com*) and **Happy Dudes Surf Emporium** (*4891 Hwy 207;* ☎ *902 827 4962; happydudes.wordpress.com*).

lovely harbour views leads to East Chezzetcook. Ask local residents the best things about their community and most will mention the Acadian roots and heritage, fishing history, wild Misener's Head (further down the road), and Chad Doucette. East Chezzetcook is home to young Mr Doucette who reached the top four in the 2006 series of reality pop talent contest *Canadian Idol*.

The neighbouring communities of Grand Desert, Gaetz Brook and Porter's Lake offer more accommodation and dining choices.

Situated on Highway 7, and between exits 20 and 21 of Highway 107, the Chezzetcooks are convenient to reach **by car**. They are some 23km/14 miles from Dartmouth, and 14km/9 miles from Musquodoboit Harbour.

History '*Chezzetcook*' is a Mi'kmaq word for 'running waters divided into many channels'. The first permanent Acadian settlers arrived in 1764, who befriended the local Mi'kmaq and joined them in harvesting clams and fishing. Dykes were built to enable farming of the marshland. In the 1870s, Chezzetcook was Nova Scotia's biggest oyster producer. West Chezzetcook's Saint Anselm Church was founded in 1740, but the current (brick) version was built in 1894. Each local family was asked to pay for 400 bricks to help meet construction costs. The church remains the major focus of the area's communities.

🏠 Where to stay

🏠 **Changing Tides B&B** (2 rooms) 6627 Hwy 207, Grand Desert; ☎ 902 827 5134; www. changingtides.ca. A spacious, modern house 3km from West Chezzetcook with magnificent views of the ocean, wetlands & islands. Fireplace in lounge; deck & sun room. Full b/fast inc. **$$**

🏠 **The IN House Musical B&B** (1 room) 5315 Hwy 7, Porter's Lake; ☎ 902 827 2532; f arthur.m.zilkowsky; ⏰ year-round by reservation. A Victorian-style country house less than 3km from Head of Chezzetcook, decorated with the hostess's art work. Enjoy live original music performed by the hosts (one of whom delights in his alter-ego soubriquet, *The Cosmic Surfer*). Sauna, gallery, library & healing circle. Continental b/fast inc. **$**

🍴 Where to eat and drink   See also **Acadian House Museum** (page 379).

🍴 **Cicero's on the Water** 122 Post Office Rd, Porter's Lake; ☎ 902 827 3287; www.ciceros.co; ⏰ 17.00–20.00 Wed, Thu & Sun, 17.00–22.00 Fri & Sat. Italian & Canadian cuisine in a great waterside location. Start with flash-fried chilli-infused calamari, & follow with one of the many good pasta choices. Lovely large deck. Adjacent is the restaurant's Water's Edge Grill (fish & chips, burgers, etc; ⏰ Jun–Sep hours as above). Licensed. **$$**

GREY LADY

Although not exclusive to this region – you hear such tales throughout the Maritimes – many of those on the Eastern Shore will tell stories about the Grey Lady, a mysterious forerunner (box, page 33) seen by seafarers seemingly as a warning of impending danger.

Over the centuries (and that includes the 21st), there have been numerous sightings of a female apparition (some say veiled, some say headless) who appears to be floating on top of the water, enshrouded by a grey fog: some speculate that she is the spirit of a victim of one of the region's hundreds of shipwrecks. The vision is said to appear to those who may be heading into danger as if to warn them of the proximity of a reef, or a sudden approaching storm. The Grey Lady is not something to be scared by, but a wake-up call: see her, sharpen your senses and you could avoid danger.

Tin Roof Mercantile & Café 6321 Hwy 7, Head of Chezzetcook; 902 827 5313; f; summer 11.00–16.00 Wed–Sat, 11.00–15.00 Sun; winter 11.30–14.00 Thu–Sat, noon–14.30 Sun. Sit by the big open fire & tuck into good home cooking. Organic, local ingredients used where possible. Popular with Halifax/Dartmouth residents for w/end lunches. **$$**

Porter's Lake Pub 5228 Hwy 7, Porter's Lake; 902 827 3097; www.porterslakepub.ca; 10.00–22.00 daily (kitchen til 21.00). Don't be put off by the mall location – this relaxed & popular pub offers good pub food, quick service & entertainment Thu evenings. **$–$$**

Rose & Rooster 6502 Hwy 207, Grand Desert; 902 827 1042; roseandrooster.com; check website for hours. Great (licensed) stop for breakfast (eg: orange spice French toast), lunch (soups, sandwiches, salads, fishcakes) & weekend brunch (eg: chorizo burrito). Good coffee. Patios for alfresco dining. Recommended. **$–$$**

Other practicalities

$ Royal Bank 5228 Hwy 7, Porter's Lake; 902 827 2930; 09.30–17.00 Mon–Wed & Fri, 09.30–20.00 Thu, Sat 09.00–16.00

Post office 5 Keizer Dr, Porter's Lake; 08.30–17.15 Mon–Fri, 08.30–noon Sat

What to see and do Built in 1850, the **Acadian House Museum: L'Acadie de Chezzetcook** (*79 Hill Rd, West Chezzetcook; 902 827 5992; www.acadiedechezzetcook.ca; Jul–Aug 10.00–16.30 Tue–Sun; CAN$3*) retains the character of a typical Acadian home from the period. On show are clothes, documents, tools, photos and artefacts – including a mid 19th-century-style outdoor oven. There's also a sweet little tea room, **La Cuisine de Brigette** (*902 827 3431; Apr–mid Dec 09.00–16.00 daily;* **$**) – try the Acadian fishcakes.

MUSQUODOBOIT HARBOUR Musquodoboit (pronounced 'Muska-dobbit') Harbour pips Sheet Harbour (pages 385–7) as the largest community between Dartmouth and Canso (population: approx 1,000), a distance of some 200km. Unless you're sure that you'll reach Sheet Harbour when the relevant shops or services are open, stock up here.

The Mi'kmaq name '*Moosekudoboogwek*' means 'suddenly widening out after a narrow entrance at the mouth'. The harbour itself is sheltered from the Atlantic Ocean by a long barrier beach system and is an incredibly productive estuary. The varied coastal scenery includes sandy beaches, salt marshes, saline ponds, dunes, eel grass beds, mudflats and mature coastal coniferous forest.

Large numbers of birds flock to this region every year to feed and rest during their long migration, and in 1987, Musquodoboit Harbour was added to the official 'List of Wetlands of International Importance' in recognition of its importance as a habitat for diverse waterfowl populations. Birds apart, there's a railway museum and good hiking.

Musquodoboit Harbour is accessible **by car**, being on Highway 7, approximately 45km/28 miles from Halifax and 69km/43 miles from Sheet Harbour.

Where to stay, eat and drink

Old Riverside Lodge B&B (3 rooms) 98 Riverside Av; ☏ 902 889 3464; **tf** 1 877 859 3674; www.oldriversidelodgebnb.com; ⊕ May–Oct; off-season by reservation. A c1853 lodge with original hardwood floors. Continental / hot b/fast inc. **$$**

✕ Harbour Fish 'N' Fries 7886 Hwy 7; ☏ 902 889 3366; ⊕ Apr–mid Dec 11.00–19.30 daily. Not the most exciting of exteriors, a seafood eatery with a few tables in & outside a simple building. The fried clams & fish & chips are very good but you're quite limited if deep-fried food is not for you (in which case, choose the lobster roll). That aside, quality is generally high & prices low. $

Dobbit Bakehouse 7896 Hwy 7; ☏ 902 889 2919; ⊕ 07.00–17.00 Mon–Fri, 08.00–17.00 Sat, 09.00–17.00 Sun. Excellent artisan bakery with 3 small tables indoors (& a picnic table outside).

Turnovers, squares, tasty assorted North American & European breads, & good beverages – try the 'choffee'! $

Uprooted Market & Café 7992 Hwy 7; ☏ 902 889 9189; uprootedmarketcafe.ca; ⊕ 09.00–18.00 Mon–Fri except Wed, 09.00–16.00 Sat & Sun. Market & café focusing on locally grown food & locally produced goods. The café serves healthy (& tasty!) soups, salads & sandwiches & Laughing Whale coffee. $

Well & Good 11 East Petpeswick Rd; ☏ 902 889 9004; wellandgoodns.ca; ⊕ summer 07.00–15.00 Wed–Fri, 08.00–14.00 Sat & Sun; off-season check website. This 'well-being centre' serves fresh smoothies plus smoothie 'specials' (eg: 'Green Monkey' – spinach, banana, almond milk, peanut butter, dates, carob powder & hemp), energy bars, salads, wraps, etc. $

Other practicalities

$ Royal Bank 7907 Hwy 7; ☏ 902 889 2626; ⊕ 09.30–17.00 Mon–Fri

✉ **Post office** 7901 Hwy 7; ⊕ 08.30–16.30 Mon–Fri (til 20.00 Thu)

ℹ **Tourist information** Main St, Musquodoboit Harbour; ☏ 902 889 2689; ⊕ late Jun–late Aug

09.00–18.00 daily. In the former Waiting Room of the Railway Museum complex.

Musquodoboit Harbour Public Library 7900 Hwy 7; ☏ 902 889 2227; ⊕ 10.00–17.00 Tue & Fri, 14.00–20.00 Wed&Thu, 10.00–14.00 Sat

What to see and do

The **Musquodoboit Railway Museum** (*Main St, Musquodoboit Harbour;* ☏ *902 889 2689;* ⊕ *late Jun–late Aug 09.00–18.00 daily; admission free*) is housed in the beautifully restored – and brightly painted – c1916 Canadian National Railways Station and three vintage rail cars. You don't need to be a train buff to enjoy a brief visit: there is a caboose and a huge old snowplough, and exhibits of the history of Nova Scotia's railways. Railway enthusiasts will also find photographs, maps, posters, tickets and artefacts relating to the history of the railway in the province and, in particular, this region.

The death of the province's railways (box, opposite) has brought some benefits – a section of the old line has been converted into the splendid 14.5km **Rail Trail**, part of the Musquodoboit Trailways network. Leading off the main trail are worthwhile side-trips, such as the Admiral Lake Loop, Bayer Lake Loop, and Gibraltar Loop. The trail crosses the Musquodoboit River on a long trestle bridge and then follows an old stagecoach road before reaching the shore of Bayer Lake. Access the trail from the museum car park.

Also worth a stop is the Sunday **Musquodoboit Harbour Farmers Market** (*Bingo Hall at Eastern Shore Community Centre, 67 Park Rd; www.mhfarmersmarket.ca; ⊕ May–mid Oct 09.00–13.00 Sun*).

Detours from Musquodoboit Harbour

Martinique Beach A worthwhile side-trip (12km each way) from Musquodoboit Harbour will take you along the shoreline of beautiful Petpeswick Inlet. You'll pass little jetties, fishing boats and neatly stacked lobster pots *en route* to the province's longest sand beach, much of which lies within the **Martinique Beach Provincial Park**. This has picnic tables and small parking areas at regular intervals along the first 1,500m from which boardwalks lead between the dunes to the stunning 5km beach.

Across the access road is a large wetland, popular with canoeists and kayakers. Part of the beach and wetland is a bird sanctuary, teeming during the spring and autumn migrations and attracting wintering Canada geese, black ducks, herons and osprey. The endangered piping plover nests on the beach and entry to sensitive areas is restricted during nesting season.

To get there **by car**, take East Petpeswick Road from Musquodoboit Harbour.

Meaghers Grant Highway 357 leads north (inland) off Highway 7 along the lovely, fertile Musquodoboit Valley, one of the province's principal farming areas. The country villages, rich rolling green farmlands and forested hills make this a very pleasant drive: in the autumn, the colours are breathtaking. Among these villages is Meaghers Grant, a small community, 22km/14 miles from Musquodoboit Harbour, which offers a few reasons to stop. First and foremost, it is home to 18- and nine-hole courses including **River Oaks Golf Club** (see River Oaks Country Lodge for contact details), whose design is one of the more successful attempts at blending fairways, greens and nature. Bird sightings (including bald eagles) are common, and you might be lucky enough to see otters, beavers, muskrats, deer or even moose. Green fees are CAN$45–50. The **River Oaks Country Lodge** (*8 rooms; 3856 Meaghers Grant Rd; ☎ 902 384 2033; www.riveroaksgolfclub.ca; ⊕ mid May–mid Oct; $*) is right by the golf course. Some units have kitchenettes, and there is a deck, a pool (in season), and a licensed restaurant (⊕ *mid May–mid Oct, daily; $–$$*), where the menu includes soups, pasta and seafood.

In addition to the Musquodoboit, both the Stewiacke and the Shubenacadie rivers are easily accessible, and all three are excellent for canoeing. **Meaghers Grant Canoe Rentals** (☎ *902 384 2513;*) will drive you to your chosen put-in spot on the

Eastern Shore **LAWRENCETOWN TO SHEET HARBOUR**

9

latter so that you can paddle downstream to your vehicle. The best time of year is late spring, while the waters are still high and the weather has warmed up a bit. Be prepared – you will pass through virtual wilderness.

Just north of Meaghers Grant, a left turn on to Highway 212 will quickly bring you to the 1,200ha **Dollar Lake Provincial Park**. The eponymous lake has a white-sand beach, and the park offers picnic and camping facilities (*119 sites; 5265 Old Guysborough Rd;* ✆ *902 384 2770; parks.novascotia.ca/content/dollar-lake;* ⊕ *mid Jun–early Oct;* **$**). The park is criss-crossed with logging roads and tracks, offering a good variety of lakeside and forest walking trails.

OYSTER POND The Mi'kmaq called Oyster Pond '*Pajedoobaack*' – 'wave washed'. In days gone by, bivalves were abundant, hence the current name. A sawmill was built on the water's edge, a dam constructed across the 'pond's' mouth, and the water was channelled with the intention of powering the mill. The good news was that this all worked well, and the mill's owners sawed their way to prosperity. The bad news was that playing with nature prevented salt water from entering the pond at high tide. As a result, Oyster Pond had plenty of freshly cut lumber – but no more oysters. The community is now home to a small, yet fascinating museum. Incidentally, a recently constructed upmarket resort and marina on the waterfront at nearby Head of Jeddore only lasted a couple of seasons before its doors closed.

Oyster Pond is on Highway 7, 68km/42 miles from Halifax, 13km/8 miles from Musquodoboit Harbour and 50km/31 miles from Sheet Harbour.

🏠 Where to stay, eat and drink

🏠 **Salmon River Country Inn** (7 rooms) 9931 Hwy 7; ✆ 902 889 2233 or 902 221 7080; salmonrivercountryinn.ca; ⊕ May–Nov. This comfortable C1855 riverside inn – German spoken – has a decent restaurant (lunch & dinner) focusing on seafood & German specialities such as *sauerbraten* (**$$**). Room rate includes continental b/fast. **$$**

🏠 **Jeddore Lodge & Cabins** (12 units) 9855 Hwy 7, Salmon River Bridge; ✆ 902 889 3030; tf 1 888 889 3030; www.jeddorelodge.com. 2 B&B rooms (b/fast inc) & 10 1- & 2-bedroom cabins, some with fireplaces & verandas overlooking the river & harbour. Outdoor pool (seasonal). The licensed dining room (⊕ *check for hours;* **$$**) offers salads, BBQ ribs/chicken, sandwiches & seafood. **$**

Å **E & F Webber's Lakeside Resort** (66 sites,plus camping cabins) 738 Upper Lakeville Rd; ✆ 902 845 2340; tf 1 800 589 2282; www. webberslakesideresort.com; ⊕ mid May–mid Oct. Full hook-ups, unserviced sites, camping cabins, lake swimming & canoe rental. 7km from Salmon River Bridge. **$**

What to see and do The **Black Sheep Gallery** (*1689 W Jeddore Rd, West Jeddore;* ✆ *902 889 5012; www.blacksheepart.com;* ⊕ *mid Jun–mid Sep 11.00–16.00 Tue–Sun; mid Sep–mid Jun by chance or appointment*) is a fascinating gallery specialising in folk art. Artists whose work is on display include Maud Lewis, Joe Norris and Charlie Tanner. For more on folk art, **Barry Colpitts** (*15359 Hwy 7, East Ship Harbour;* ✆ *902 772 2090; www.barrycolpitts.ca;* ⊕ *by chance or appointment*) is a renowned exponent of the genre.

In the early 1900s, the tiny house and small farm that now make up the **Fisherman's Life Museum** (*58 Navy Pool Loop;* ✆ *902 889 2053; fishermanslife.novascotia. ca;* ⊕ *Jun–Sep 10.00–17.00 Mon–Sat, 13.00–17.00 Sun; admission CAN$3.90*), comprising a restored farmhouse, garden and outbuildings, were once home to an inshore fisherman, his wife and 12 daughters. The Myers family lived a simple life, supplementing their meagre fishing income with a small farm operation. Inside the house, guides in period costume hook rugs, prepare food using the old wood stove or tell stories about the land, the sea and life a century ago.

In 1817, a William Kent built a house on Kent Island, and always claimed it was haunted. The house was torn down in 1903, and a lighthouse constructed on the site in 1904. For many years, Kent's descendants operated their house adjacent to the lighthouse as a B&B, and there were several reports of supernatural activity in and around the lighthouse. A few years ago, a medium staying at the B&B announced that not only was the lighthouse haunted, but the haunter was also the ghost of Admiral Horatio Nelson. The remarks were taken with a pinch of sea salt, but a couple of years later, when researching the family history, the current Kents discovered that William, who built the house, had sailed with Nelson, serving as navigator aboard Nelson's HMS *Victory* at the Battle of Trafalgar in 1805 when Horatio met his death.

The lighthouse is not open to the public. You can see it by turning onto Ostrea Lake Road from Highway 7 at Smith Settlement 4km east of Musquodoboit Harbour and following the road along the eastern side of the water, then turning onto Kent Road. It is worth continuing to Pleasant Point for lovely views of the harbour mouth.

Lovers of things floral won't want to miss **Harbour Breezes** (*10099 Hwy 7, Salmon River Bridge;* ☏ *902 889 3179; harbourbreezes.ca;* ⊕ *mid May–early Sep daily*), a garden centre with a magnificent display of daylilies, and wonderful Jeddore Harbour views from the hillside garden.

Held in September, the **Pirate Days Festival** (*www.novascotiapirates.ca*) is a day of pirate-themed fun for all the family.

LAKE CHARLOTTE This community was named in honour of Princess Charlotte Augusta of Wales, who died in 1817 shortly after the area was settled. Situated on Highway 7, it is 15km/9 miles from Musquodoboit Harbour and 50km/31 miles from Sheet Harbour. The main attraction here is the community-owned **Memory Lane Heritage Village** (*Clam Harbour Rd;* ☏ *902 845 1937;* ☏ *1 877 287 0697; www. heritagevillage.ca;* ⊕ *mid Jun–mid Sep 11.00–16.00 daily; off-season by appointment; admission CAN$8*), which takes a nostalgic look at rural coastal village life in the 1940s. Most of the 18 c1894–1949 buildings – including the two-seater outhouse – were 'rescued' from around the region, restored, and moved here. There is also a general store, homestead, barn, one-room schoolhouse, industry buildings including boat shop, fish store and gold-mining complex. Hands-on demonstrations, soundscapes, immersive exhibits using a smartphone or tablet, and costumed guides bring the village alive. Eat in the replica 1940s' cookhouse with fresh baked bread and beans, served daily. If you're here in June, you can see a range of antique vehicles here at the **Antique Car Show**.

CLAM HARBOUR Clam Harbour boasts one of the province's prettiest beaches,

The community of Ship Harbour (on Hwy 7 between Lake Charlotte and Tangier) is home to the **AquaPrime Mussel Ranch** (*14108 Hwy 7;* ☏ *902 845 2993;* ⊕ *08.00–16.00 Mon–Fri, but best to call ahead to check*), where you can learn how mussels are grown, harvested and sold: informal (free) tours are offered subject to staff availability.

which – as a result of a warmer-than-average tidal stream – is usually the best swimming beach on the Eastern Shore. The beach park has a hiking trail, a lifeguard and canteen (weekends in season), showers and changing rooms. There is also a picnic area with tables tucked between trees: to reach it, turn right at the end of the access road. The beach is unlikely to be crowded for 364 days of the year. However, several thousand visitors (incredible considering both the Eastern Shore's population and tourist numbers) stop by for the August one-day **Clam Harbour Beach Sandcastle Sculpture Contest** (*www.halifax.ca/sandcastle; CAN$10 to enter, free-to-enter children's competition*), where competitors enthuse about the beach's 'perfect' sand in the same way skiers rave about 'champagne' snow. Not only can designs have minute, perfect features, but the sculptures also remain in place for hours without collapsing or weathering. This area is one reputed to have a larger than average number of foggy days, but fingers crossed that the sun will shine on the broad crescent of sand for your visit.

To get there **by car**, follow Clam Harbour Road for about 8km/5 miles south from Lake Charlotte.

TANGIER This small community (population: 115) once serviced several gold mines. It is now home to an excellent sea kayaking company, **Coastal Adventures** (*84 Mason's Point Rd;* ☎ *902 772 2774; www.coastaladventures.com*), which is also one of the only places offering kayak rentals along the entire Eastern Shore. Come for expert advice, half- and full-day kayak excursions that include visits to uninhabited islands, and a range of longer (multi-day) packages. Also just off Highway 7 at Mason Point Road is the simple **Prince Alfred Arch**, erected to commemorate the (1861) visit to the local gold mine by Queen Victoria's son.

Tangier is easy to reach **by car** as it is located on Highway 7, 47km/29 miles from Musquodoboit Harbour and 20km/12 miles from Sheet Harbour. You'll find a post office just west of town (*17276 Hwy 7;* ⊕ *07.30–12.30 & 13.00–14.00 Mon–Fri*).

⌂ Where to stay, eat and drink

⌂ **Paddler's Retreat** (4 rooms) 84 Mason's Point Rd; ☎ 902 772 2774; e info@ coastaladventures.com; www.coastaladventures. com; ⊕ mid Jun–mid Oct; off-season by reservation. Under the same management as Coastal Adventures (above), this laid-back c1860s' old fisherman's home is the obvious choice for anyone going on a kayaking trip. 3 rooms share a bathroom, 1 has en suite. Wi-Fi & outdoor hot tub. Full country b/fast inc. **$**

⋀ **Murphy's Camping on the Ocean** (50 sites) 308 Murphy's Rd, Murphy Cove; ☎ 902 772 2700; www.murphyscamping.ca; ⊕ mid May–mid Oct. Located on a headland just off Hwy 7, 7.5km west of Tangier, with open & wooded campsites (serviced & unserviced), boat rentals, scenic boat tours & numerous other activities including a nightly campfire & mussel boil. Another great base for sea kayakers. **$**

100 WILD ISLANDS

Close to Tangier lies a fascinating, virtually undeveloped archipelago of islands, which feature white sand beaches, bogs, barrens and forest. These islands have retained their pristine nature and changed very little since well before Europeans arrived, a fact recognised by the **Nova Scotia Nature Trust** (*www. nsnt.ca*). They have launched the CAN$7million-plus 100 Wild Islands Legacy Campaign to preserve and protect 46,000 acres of wilderness – stretching from Clam Harbour to Mushaboom Harbour – for future generations.

TAYLOR HEAD PROVINCIAL PARK This beautiful park (📞 902 772 2218; *friendsoftaylorhead.com* or *parks.novascotia.ca/content/taylor-head;* ⊕ *mid May– mid Oct;* but see box, below) occupies a narrow 6.5km peninsula, jutting in to the Atlantic like a huge rocky finger. It encompasses 16km of unspoilt and virtually untouched coastline, varied habitats rich in flora and fauna, and fascinating geology. In season, the park offers unsupervised swimming, changing rooms, several picnic areas, interpretive panels and vault toilets.

The west side of the peninsula is rugged and windswept: as a result of the salt spray and nearly constant winds, white spruce and firs are stunted, almost flattened to the rocky ground. The more protected east side has sandy coves lapped by calmer waters. Several rocky barrens covered with dwarf shrubs and lichens are found in the southern portion of Taylor Head, and peat-filled open bogs are scattered throughout the park.

This is one of only a few locations in Nova Scotia where sand volcanoes (small cone-shaped geological features) are found. Other special features, called flute marks, appear as ripples in the bedrock and indicate that strong ocean currents once moved large volumes of sediment rapidly across what was the sea floor. Parallel northeast–southwest quartzite ridges that show the direction of bedrock folding can still be seen at Taylor Head, and the beach and sand dunes at Psyche Cove were formed by sand deposits from the erosion of glacial till and bedrock.

The park is home to a variety of mammals, including white-tailed deer, racoons and muskrats. Seals have been spotted on nearby rocks, and there have also been sightings of pilot whales and dolphins offshore.

For most, though, it is the park's **walking and hiking** trails that are the big draw: many people rate them among the finest coastal trail systems on North America's eastern seaboard. Possibilities include the 2km Beach Walk, and the Headland Trail, a wonderful 8km figure-of-eight hike taking in boardwalks and bogs, forest dripping with moss, and of course stretches of the shoreline.

A 5km unpaved road from Highway 7 hugs the west side of the peninsula before crossing to sheltered Psyche Cove. At the end of the road is a series of small parking areas with beach access.

The park is accessible **by car**, just off Highway 7, 14km/9 miles from Tangier and 12km/7 miles from Sheet Harbour.

SHEET HARBOUR Roughly halfway between Halifax and Canso, the town (population: 825) lies between the outflows of the West and East Sheet Harbour

---

GET IN WITH A LITTLE HELP FROM THE FRIENDS

The provincial government does not have the resources to keep provincial parks open for more than a relatively short season. This is not always a problem, as you can see the highlights of many parks out of season by parking outside the closed gate and walking in. Taylor Head's highlights, however, are a long way from the gated entrance. The **Friends of Taylor Head Provincial Park** (*www.friendsoftaylorhead.com*) is a non-profit society, and for the last few years its members have managed to keep the park gate open until early December – a real bonus for out-of-season visitors. The group also coordinates and hosts many free park activities (eg: birdwatching, hikes, astronomy nights and workshops for children). See website for details.

rivers at the head of a long narrow bay. After Musquodoboit Harbour, it is one of the biggest communities along the Eastern Shore.

Sheet Harbour was founded in 1784 by Loyalist refugees and British veterans of the American Revolution and became a prosperous centre for the lumber industry and consequently a shipbuilding centre. In recent years, the government has made an effort to make Sheet Harbour into a major port and chief supply depot for the gas platforms off Sable Island (pages 398–401).

In town at the **MacPhee House Community Museum** (*Hwy 7 at the West River Bridge;* \ *902 885 2092;* ⊕ *late May–Sep 09.00–17.00 daily; off-season by appointment; admission free*), the *Life before Plastic* exhibit illustrates Eastern Shore life in the days before modern technology. There are some interesting curios that may intrigue and challenge young and old alike. August visitors shouldn't miss the **Seaside Festival,** a two-week festival with a range of events including parades, Fun Day and Kids' Activity Day.

Sheet Harbour is on Highway 7, 120km/75 miles east of Dartmouth and 65km/46 miles west of Sherbrooke, and therefore convenient to reach **by car.**

⌂ **Where to stay, eat and drink** There are plans that a new Sheet Harbour microbrewery, the Sober Island Brewing Company (**f** *soberislandbrewing*), which started up in 2016, may tie up with the Henley House Pub.

⌂ **Fairwinds Motel & Restaurant**
(10 rooms) 22522 Hwy 7; \ 902 885 2502;
fairwindsmotelsheetharbour.ca. A traditional
sgl-storey motel; some rooms have sea views. The
restaurant (⊕ *07.00–20.30 daily; $*) offers good
service & reliable food (splendid fish & chips).
Licensed bar. Deck overlooks the sea. **$**
⋏ **East River Lodge Campground** (40 sites)
200 Pool Rd; \ 902 885 2057; ⊕ May–Oct.
Serviced & unserviced sites. **$**

✖ **Henley House Pub** 22478 Hwy 7; \ 902 885
3335; **f**; ⊕ May–Dec (check for days/hours),
Jul–Aug daily (check for hours). Restaurant & pub
in a c1916 former family house. Deck with lovely
harbour view. Daily specials, weekend brunch. The
maple curry chicken penne is recommended. Live
music on some w/ends. **$$**
✖ **Il Porto** 22808 Hwy 7; \ 902 885 3111; **f**;
⊕ 11.00–19.00 daily (20.00 Fri). Mediterranean (inc
Greek & Italian) dishes, plus Cajun, Creole, etc. Burgers,
pizza & seafood. Good lobster rolls. Small deck. **$$**

Other practicalities
$ Scotiabank 22540 Hwy 7; \ 902 885 2310;
⊕ 10.00–17.00 Mon–Fri

✛ **Eastern Shore Memorial Hospital** 22637
Hwy 7; \ 902 885 2554

GOLDEN DUFFERS

Between 1862 and 1976, 1.1 million ounces of gold were mined from 65 gold districts throughout Nova Scotia, but the province has experienced more than one relatively short-lived gold rush over the past 150 years. Most recently, July 2014 saw the opening – to great fanfare – of the Dufferin Mine, and Quebec-based owner Ressources Appalaches (RA) announced, 'the return of the Dufferin Mine to production will begin another exciting chapter in Nova Scotia's gold-mining history'. At the beginning of October in the same year, the company ceased production and three months later RA defaulted on CAN$11 million in loans and the mine was put into receivership. In another twist, RA (now renamed Resource Capital Gold) announced that it had paid US$9.5m for a 90% stake in the mine, and was aiming to start production early in 2017.

✉ **Post office** 22526 Hwy 7; ⊕ 08.00–11.30 & 12.30–17.00 Mon–Fri

i **Tourist information** Hwy 7 at the West River Bridge; ☎ 902 885 2595; ⊕ summer 10.00–17.00 daily. In the MacPhee House Museum (page 386).

PORT DUFFERIN AND THE BAY OF ISLANDS The small community of Port Dufferin (13km/8 miles east of Sheet Harbour and 18km/11 miles west of Moser River) was named after the Marquis of Dufferin, Governor-General of Canada 1872–78. It offers beautiful views out to sea from the Salmon River Bridge area. If you turn along the waterside just by the bridge, there's a small look-out: continue on this road (signposted Smiley's Point) and a 2km drive will bring you to a small jetty and parking area also offering tranquil coastal vistas.

Many of the next stretches of Highway 7 offer wonderful panoramas of wooded peninsulas and tiny coves, and a sea dotted with dozens and dozens of uninhabited wooded islands. The region between Beaver Harbour and Ecum Secum is known as the Bay of Islands.

Small fishing communities dot the highway and in autumn the forests are ablaze with red maple and birch, the brilliant colours reflected in the rivers, lakes and coves. **Moser River** (on Hwy 7, 18km/11 miles east of Port Dufferin and 35km/22 miles west of Liscomb) has a waterfront park on the estuary that is a favourite spot for birdwatchers. Seaward, you'll see hundreds of small islands, popular with sea kayakers and yachtsmen. The Moser was once famous for its abundance of Atlantic salmon, which the old timers will tell you, could 'be scooped up in buckets' as they travelled upstream to spawn.

Necum Teuch (whose name derives from the Mi'kmaq for 'sandy river bottom') is 5km past Moser River on Highway 7. It was home to Angella Geddes, author of several popular children's books, most famous of which is *Necum Teuch Scarecrows*, which has been translated into German and French. In addition to writing about them, she created a large collection of articulated scarecrows – many of which represented local people – that used to adorn her house and garden. Geddes passed away in 2006, and the figures are all but gone.

LISCOMB GAME SANCTUARY

From Sheet Harbour, Highway 374 heads north for 130km to Stellarton. For much of the way, this remote road passes through a game sanctuary established in 1928 to protect wildlife, particularly moose and woodland caribou. We are not talking safari parks here, but over 43,000ha of remote forest, logging roads, rivers and lakes and no services.

The rugged landscape is dotted with ancient drumlins (page 224) and dips that have filled with water. The 'protected area' was cloaked in old-growth boreal forest, but sadly much of it has been logged as although the legislation that created the sanctuary protected the animals themselves, it had little thought for their habitat.

In recent years, environmentalists and conservationists have campaigned to extend the sanctuary's boundaries right up to the Atlantic coast and, more importantly, to change the designation to 'wilderness area' (page 13). Not only has this met with little success thus far, but there have also been reports that logging activity has actually increased.

Within the sanctuary boundary, four small wilderness areas have been established, including Boggy Lake Wilderness Area, where a chain of lakes are ideal for extended – true back-country – canoe trips.

Eastern Shore **LAWRENCETOWN TO SHEET HARBOUR**

9

If you thought that Necum Teuch was an odd name, the next community, 5km further east, is **Ecum Secum** (this name derives from the Mi'kmaq 'Megwasaagunk', and means 'a red house'). At Ecum Secum Bridge, turn right and follow the side road to Mitchell Bay, where there is a beautiful Anglican church and cemetery overlooking the water. Stay on this road and it will take you back to Highway 7.

LISCOMB MILLS This isn't a community as such, more some fine hiking trails and a resort. Accessed from the parking area and trailhead immediately east of the Liscombe Lodge's entrance are a couple of relatively challenging hikes. The 9.6km return **Liscomb River Trail** follows the river's edge upstream to a swinging suspension bridge, which spans a 20m waterfall. Near the waterfall is a fish ladder comprising 15 pools separated by concrete weirs, designed to aid salmon in their annual migration. The best time to see them 'climbing' the ladder is from early June to October (peaking in July). Return to the trailhead along the river's other bank. From the same trailhead, the rugged 2.9km loop **Mayflower Point Trail** heads to the mouth of the river opposite Rileys Island before returning along and above the riverbank.

By car, Liscomb Mills is 47km/29 miles east of Sheet Harbour, and 7km/4 miles west of Liscomb. Liscomb is 18km/11 miles east of Sherbrooke.

Where to stay, eat and drink

Liscombe Lodge Resort & Conference Centre (68 units) 2884 Hwy 7, Liscomb Mills; 902 779 2307; www.liscombelodge.ca; ☼ mid May–mid Oct. Not on a beach but boasting a lovely riverside setting. Rather than one of the 5 cottages or 30 lodge rooms, choose a riverfront chalet & wake to the sound of birdsong. Complimentary use of good-sized indoor pool & sauna, canoes & bicycles, or hike the trails (take repellent). The lodge's restaurant (☼ mid May–mid Oct 07.00–21.00 daily; $$–$$$) is famous for its 'Planked Salmon Dinner' – the fish is cooked over an open fire as the Mi'kmaq did in years gone by.

Arrive early to secure a coveted window table. More casual dining is offered in the Lone Cloud Lounge (☼ mid May–mid Oct 11.00–21.00 daily; $$–$$$), or head for Sherbrooke (see below), 24km along Hwy 7. B/fast not inc. $$$

Birchill B&B & Guest House (3 units) 5254 Hwy 7, Liscomb; 902 779 2017; www.birchillbb. com; ☼ May–Oct. If resorts don't do it for you, try one of the B&B rooms (b/fast inc) or the 1-bedroom cottage 7km east of Liscomb Mills (the B&B is on a hill, the cottage on the Spanish Ship Bay waterfront). Hot tub & free use of kayaks. $

SHERBROOKE This town on the St Marys River has a hospital, a few places to stay and eat, a bank, post office, convenience store and a little supermarket. Most visitors come to see the living museum (see opposite).

How times change. Long renowned far and wide for its salmon, the river was a favourite fishing spot of baseball legend Babe Ruth and many other famous celebrities and anglers. In recent years the population of Atlantic salmon has decreased dramatically, and fishing for the species is now strictly prohibited.

Sherbrooke was founded in the early 1800s at the farthest navigable point of the St Marys River. Gold was discovered in the area in the late 1860s and was mined until 1890. Lumber was processed and exported, and there were shipbuilding operations. However, the mines closed and shipbuilding ceased. By the late 1960s, there were few visitors apart from anglers. The town was beginning to die until ambitious locals, with help from the Nova Scotia Museum, began a big restoration project. The result is the Eastern Shore's most popular attraction: the Living Museum (pages 389–90).

Easy to reach **by car**, Sherbrooke is on Highway 7, 80km/50 miles from Sheet Harbour, 209km/130 miles from Halifax and 60km/37 miles from Antigonish.

Where to stay, eat and drink
Sherbrooke Village museum also has a tea room (see below).

⌂ **Sherbrooke Village Inn Motel**
(19 units) 7975 Hwy 7; ☎ 902 522 2228; sherbrookevillageinn.ca. Cottages, a family house, a B&B suite (b/fast inc) & motel-type units. The licensed dining room (⊕ *mid May–Oct 07.30–19.00 daily (summer til 20.00)*; **$$**) focuses on seafood & most dishes are made without use of a deep fryer. **$$**

⌂ **St Marys River Lodge** (5 rooms) 21 Main St; ☎ 902 522 2177; www.riverlodge.ca; ⊕ Apr–Oct; off-season by reservation. Under Swiss management, the lodge itself – across the road from the river & right by the museum – has 5 guestrooms, all with private bathrooms. Full b/fast inc. **$**

⋏ **St Marys Riverside Campground** (24 sites) 3987 Sonora Rd; www.riversidecampground.ca; ☎ 902 522 2913; ⊕ Jun–Sep. Open tent & RV sites, laundromat, pool (in season). **$**

✘ **Beanie's Bistro** 27 Main St; ☎ 902 522 2044; f; ⊕ Apr–Nov 08.00–16.00 daily. Excellent, funky b/fast & lunch (eg: locally smoked-salmon sandwich) spot. Brunch (⊕ *Jul–Oct 10.00–14.00 Sun*). Locally sourced ingredients where possible. Pity it is not open in the evening. **$–$$**

✘ **House of Jade** 8164 Main St; ☎ 902 522 2731; ⊕ Jun–Sep 11.30–19.45 Tue–Sun; Oct–May noon–19.00 Wed–Sun. Canadian & Chinese standards. The won ton soup is a stand-out. **$–$$**

Other practicalities
$ Royal Bank 6 Main St; ☎ 902 522 2800; ⊕ 10.00–15.00 Mon–Fri

✚ **St Mary's Memorial Hospital** 91 Hospital Rd; ☎ 902 522 2882

✉ **Post office** 15 Main St; ⊕ 08.30–17.00 Mon–Fri, 09.00–13.00 Sat

ℹ **Tourist information** 7975 Hwy 7; ☎ 902 522 2400; ⊕ early Jun–mid Sep 09.30–17.00 daily. At the entrance to Sherbrooke Village.

Sherbrooke Library 11 Main St; ☎ 902 522 2180; ⊕ 11.00–16.00 Mon–Tue & Thu, 09.30–16.00 Fri, 10.00–13.00 Sat

What to see and do
An unusual living museum, **Sherbrooke Village** (*Main St*; ☎ *902 522 2400*; tf *1 888 743 7845*; *museum.gov.ns.ca/sv*; ⊕ *Jun–Sept 09.30–17.00 daily; admission CAN$13.75*) reflects Nova Scotia as it was during its industrial boom in the late 1800s/early 1900s and comprises more than 80 restored buildings, 29 of which are open to the public, and which are integrated with the town itself. It is the largest Nova Scotia Museum site and unlike (say) Memory Lane (page 383), the buildings here are on their original sites. Every morning at 09.30 (*Jun–Sep*), this part of the town is closed to traffic, and the clock goes back a century. Period-costumed, knowledgeable guides help maintain the feeling that you have indeed been transported back in time as they tend to the crops, stroll through the town, staff the buildings and demonstrate such skills as pottery, weaving, candle making, blacksmithing and wood turning. Tree lighting and procession, Christmas crafts, concerts, dinner theatre, Victorian tea and more can be seen at the **Old-fashioned Sherbrooke Christmas** festival, which takes place in November.

The **St Marys River Education and Interpretive Centre** (*8404 Hwy 7*; ☎ *902 522 2099*; *www.stmarysriverassociation.com*; ⊕ *Jun & Sep–Oct 09.00–16.00 Mon–Fri; Jul–Aug 09.00–16.30 daily; admission by donation*) has exhibits relating to fishing, wildlife, river enhancement and stabilisation projects, and the history of fishing. There is also a small aquarium.

Eat at the **Sherbrooke Hotel's tea room** – the menu is unpretentious, and – bearing in mind that it caters to something of a captive market – offers good value. Be sure to follow the Sonora Road on the east bank of the river for a few hundred metres from the main restoration area to hear the rush of water and smell the scent of lumber freshly cut by the village's authentic, photogenic water-powered **sawmill**. Across the street in the **stamp mill**, you can see how gold ore was mined, crushed and processed during the gold rush. If you visit out of season, this is still a nice place to wander even when the village is not officially 'open'.

The **St Marys River Smokehouses** shop (*8000 Hwy 7*; ✆ *902 522 2005*; *www. thebestsmokedsalmon.com*; ⊕ *09.00–17.00 Mon–Fri*) is located at the western end of town. An array of both hot smoked- and cold smoked-salmon products are made here: the oven-smoked salmon strips, flavoured with pepper, maple syrup, or 'all-dressed', are particularly good.

PORT BICKERTON Lighthouse fans will want to break their journey in this small community, just west of the Country Harbour ferry. A 2km unpaved road leads to the **Port Bickerton Lighthouse Interpretive Centre & Gift Shop** (*630 Lighthouse Rd*; ✆ *902 364 2000*; *www.portbickertonlighthouse.ca*; ⊕ *Jul–Sep 09.00–17.00 daily*; *admission CAN$3*), with two lighthouses standing on a windswept, often fog-enshrouded bluff at the end of the headland. The newer of these is a fully automated working lighthouse dating from 1962. The older, built in 1930, is now a lighthouse museum with an original foghorn and well-laid-out display about the province's 170-plus lighthouses. Climb up the narrow staircase for a panoramic view of the wild and beautiful coastline and walk to a sandy beach. If you're looking for somewhere different to stay, the former lightkeeper's house (sleeps 4) is rented out on a weekly basis between May and October.

For the princely sum of CAN$7, you and your vehicle can enjoy a pleasant – albeit just 7-minute – boat ride on the **Country Harbour Ferry** (*on Hwy 211, 7km from Port Bickerton*; ⊕ *24hrs daily; Jul–Sep departs east side on hr & ½hr, west side quarter past & quarter to, 08.00–18.00, departs east side on the hr, west side on the ½hr 18.30–07.30; Oct–Jun departs east side on the hr, west side on the ½hr; CAN$7 each way*). If you are going east, it is well worth checking that the ferry is running before heading this way – ask at a local tourist office or (✆ *902 387 2200*). The alternate route via Country Harbour Cross Roads is longer of course, but you would also have to add on the 30km backtrack from the ferry dock. If you want to stay nearby, camp on the eastern side at the pleasant waterside Salsman Provincial Park (*40 sites; 15641 Hwy 316; parks.novascotia.ca/content/salsman*; ⊕ *mid Jun–mid Sep*; **$**), which also has a picnic site and a boat launch.

Port Bickerton is on Highway 211, 29km/18 miles from Sherbrooke and 90km/56 miles from Canso, and accessible **by car**. As with much of the Eastern Shore, expect little in the way of services.

MORE GOLDEN TALES

History books state a farmer, Nelson Nickerson, found gold in 1861 while he was haymaking. The story locals tell is that a woman picking wild flowers was attracted by a shiny piece of quartz which she took home. A passing traveller later saw the quartz, recognised its significance, and casually asked the woman where she'd found it. Armed with this information, he took his leave, found himself a pick and shovel and put Goldenville (on Hwy 7, 5km west of Sherbrooke) on the map. The tiny community's c1900 Presbyterian Church now houses the **Goldenville Gold Mining Interpretive Centre** (*Goldenville Rd*; ✆ *902 522 4653*; ⊕ *Jun–Aug 10.00–17.00 Wed–Sun; admission CAN$2.50*), which tells of the history of gold mining in Nova Scotia.

Just offshore from Drum Head, which is on Highway 316 between the Country Harbour Ferry and Tor Bay, is Harbour Island: its southern end is named 'Saladin Point' after a vessel which ran aground here in 1844. More interesting than the fact that the *Saladin, en route* from Chile to London, was carrying a cargo of guano, copper and silver is that the vessel beached because her captain, officers and many of the crew had been butchered by mutineers who had overlooked the fact that they had not spared any skilled navigators. The four mutineers were rescued – and sent to the gallows.

TOR BAY Originally named 'Port Savalette' after a French fisherman, Tor Bay is worth a stop for its lovely provincial park (*parks.novascotia.ca/content/tor-bay*; ⊕ *late May–early Oct*). Situated on an isthmus along a peninsula that forms the southern boundary of the bay, the small day-use park has a boardwalk that leads to a sandy beach, from which a short trail heads to a rocky headland where covered interpretive boards describe the geology of the region. There are other (almost always empty) beaches on the other side of the headland, and the park also has picnic facilities.

Accessible **by car**, Tor Bay is just off Highway 316, 22km/14 miles from Guysborough, 33km/21 miles from Country Harbour and 52km/32 miles from Canso.

🏠 Where to stay, eat and drink

🏠 **Seawind Landing Country Inn** (13 rooms) 159 Wharf Rd, Charlos Cove; 📞 902 525 2108; **tf** 1 800 563 4667; www.seawindlanding. ca. On Hwy 316, about 15km east of Tor Bay, the picturesque Acadian fishing village of Charlos Cove is home to this establishment, which occupies a 8ha peninsula with over 900m of ocean frontage, including a couple of lovely secluded beaches. Most of the rooms offer sea views. Gift shop showcasing local artists, & boat tours to deserted islands (Jul–Sep). Pets welcomed. The inn has an excellent dining room open to non-guests by reservation (⊕ *summer 07.30–10.00 & 18.00–21.00 daily; off-season call to check; $$$*), with a regularly changing menu of fresh locally sourced ingredients. Try, for example, bourbon-glazed pork tenderloin or scallops in a vermouth cream sauce. The Bailey's *crème brûlée* is a delicious dessert. **$$**

CANSO Situated at the entrance to Chedabucto Bay, Canso is sheltered from the ocean by round Grassy Island (page 393). The town is located at the extreme eastern point of mainland Nova Scotia and – were it not for a little bit of Labrador – would have the honour of being the closest point on the North American mainland to Europe. For a while Canso has been in need of a cash injection, but at least the waterfront's old Whitman Wharf had a recent makeover.

To reach Canso **by car**, the town is at the eastern end of Highway 16, 46km/29 miles from Guysborough, 105km/65 miles from Aulds Cove, 114km/71 miles from Antigonish and 320km/199 miles from Halifax.

History There is evidence that the French and the Basques were making annual visits to fish in the Canso area perhaps a

Nova Scotia's first direct transatlantic telegraphic connection was established in 1874 when the Direct United States Telegraph Company laid a cable between Tor Bay and Ballinskelligs in Ireland's Waterville Bay. A plaque in the park's car park commemorates the event.

century before 1605, the 'official' year of Canso's first permanent settlement. They built temporary shelters and came ashore to salt and dry their abundant cod catches. In any case, Canso is thought to be the oldest fishing village in the Maritimes, and one of the oldest settlements in Nova Scotia. It was one of the most coveted anchorages for the cod-fishing industry during the 16th and 17th centuries, offering shelter and a relatively ice-free harbour well positioned for markets in western Europe and the Caribbean.

From the 1680s on, New Englanders used the area for trade and fishing with increasing frequency. They decided to establish and fortify a community on Grassy Island (page 393) in 1718. Soon after, the wood-and-earth Fort William Augustus was constructed. The settlement met its end quite suddenly in the summer of 1744 when a French expedition from Louisbourg (pages 363–4) attacked and burned all the buildings to the ground. The following year, New Englanders used the island as a staging point for their attack on Louisbourg. After the fall of Louisbourg, the French threat faded and Grassy Island was abandoned. It lay virtually untouched until reclaimed as a Canadian National Historic Site in 1977.

In the 18th century, there was talk that Canso, a thriving commercial centre and major fishing port, would become Nova Scotia's capital but this did not happen, partly because of its somewhat remote location.

Where to stay, eat and drink

Last Port Motel (13 units) 10 Hwy 16; 902 366 2400; www.lastportmotel.com. A clean, traditional-style standard motel outside the town centre. Licensed restaurant (⊕ *summer 10.00– 19.00 daily; winter 16.00–19.00 daily; $*), serving decent food including good fish & chips. **$**

Cape Canso RV Park (33 sites) 1639 Union St; 902 366 2937; ⊕ Jun–Oct. Geared to motorhomes (sites are serviced), but there are a few grassy spots on which to pitch a tent. **$**

Seabreeze Campground (74 sites & 4 cottages) 230 Fox Island Rd; 902 366 2532;

tf 1 866 771 2267; www.seabreezecampground. com; ⊕ mid May–mid Oct. A quiet, beautifully located site overlooking Chedabucto Bay, approx 10km west of Canso. Wooded & open serviced & unserviced sites, 4 fully equipped cottages. **$**

AJ's Dining Room, Lounge & Pub 237 Main St; 902 366 2281; ⊕ 10.00–21.00 daily, later on summer w/ends. Decent pub food, good pizza & poutine – the closest Canso comes to nightlife, & occasional live music. **$**

Harbour View Bakery & Café 1315 Union St; 902 366 2180; f; ⊕ summer

STANFEST

Over the first weekend in July, thousands of music fans descend on Canso for the **Stan Rogers Folk Festival** (tf *1 888 554 7826; www.stanfest.com*), or, more simply, Stanfest. Born in Ontario, Stan Rogers spent many of his summers in Nova Scotia's Guysborough County when growing up. His songs often had a Celtic feel, and some were in the style of sea shanties. Following his death in an air accident in 1983, he was nominated posthumously for a Juno (the Canadian equivalent of the Grammy) Best Male Vocalist award.

Since the decision in 1997 to hold a festival in Canso in his memory, the event has been a roaring success. The ever-growing outdoor event features around 40 acts from around the world performing on six stages. It may have 'folk' in the title, but expect to hear just about every main musical genre.

There is limited accommodation in the area, so most visitors camp at the special festival campground. In 2016, a tent camping pass cost CAN$75 (*CAN$92 for an RV*) and entry to the concerts CAN$149 for the entire weekend.

noon–19.00 daily, check off-season hours.
Soup, salads, wraps, diner-style food, pies &
other sweet treats. Good service & generous
portions. $

Other practicalities
$ **Bank of Montreal** 28 Main St; ☏902 366
2654; ⊕ 10.00–15.00 Mon–Fri
✚ **Eastern Memorial Hospital** 1746 Union St;
☏902 366 2794
✉ **Post office** 1315 Union St; ⊕ 08.00–17.00
Mon–Fri, 11.00–15.00 Sat

ℹ **Tourist information** Whitman Hse, 1297
Union St; ☏902 366 2170; ⊕ Jun–Sep 09.00–
17.00 daily. In the Canso Museum (below).
Canso Branch Library 130 School St; ☏902 366
2955; ⊕ noon–17.00 Mon–Thu, 10.00–15.00 Fri
Canso Co-op 111 Water St; ☏902 366 2182;
⊕ Mon–Sat, hours vary. Groceries, necessities
& more.

What to see and do Housed in the magnificent three-storey Whitman House
(box, below), the **Whitman House Canso Museum** (*Whitman Hse, 1297 Union St;*
☏*902 366 2170;* ⊕ *Jun–Sep 09.00–17.00 daily; admission free*) has local history exhibits
covering Canso and eastern Guysborough County, including period furniture and
many works by Canso folk artist Mel Schrader. There are wonderful views of the
town, harbour and fuel tanks from the widow's walk atop the corner tower.

The waterfront **Canso Islands and Grassy Island Fort National Historic Sites of
Canada** (*1465 Union St;* ☏ *902 366 3136 or off-season 902 295 2069; www.pc.gc.ca/
eng/lhn-nhs/ns/canso/index.aspx;* ⊕ *Jul–early Sep 10.00–18.00 daily; admission &
boat fare by donation*) describes the region's history. Here you can see a scale model
of the island before the French attack, a short video, and life-sized dioramas of
three island properties. Park boats leave on demand (weather permitting) from
the adjacent wharf for the 15-minute trip to Grassy Island where you can wander
around, or take a self-guided (or free guided) tour of the ruins of 18th-century
fortifications and remains of a colonial New England fishing station. Most traces
of the church, fort, gun batteries, barracks and houses have gone, leaving just
foundations and a few flattened remnants of the 18th-century fortifications. Go
prepared: there are no services on the island.

There is also excellent **hiking** in the area. Follow the signs from town to take the
Chapel Gully Trail (Chapel Gully is actually a saltwater inlet), a well-maintained
easy 10km loop hike through diverse forest, over rocks and on long boardwalks.
You'll find picnic tables, look-outs and numerous bird-feeders. There is also a
shorter loop but offering fewer coastal views. Both loops take you across a 40m
footbridge that spans the gully. This is also a popular area for birdwatchers.

WHITMAN HOUSE

In 1885, wealthy merchant and businessman Clement H Whitman supervised
construction of a rectory for the Baptist minister. However, the building work
went so far over budget that the Baptist congregation withdrew from the
project. Undeterred, Whitman poured more and more of his own money in,
using the best materials he could find. When the house (one of the costliest
in the province) was completed, he moved in – and generously gave his old,
far more modest home to the Church for use as a rectory. The house was
sold following Whitman's death in 1932, and after that resold many times.
Apparently, if you'd come along at the right time, you could have picked it up
for less than CAN$500. It now houses the Canso Museum.

9

If you take Union Street to its end, you can follow a rugged unpaved road to **Glasgow Head** enjoying wonderful views of the mouth of Canso Harbour, lighthouse and islands *en route*. When you reach the road end, choose between a swim in a manmade pond sheltered from the direct coastal waters by a rock barrier, and the spectacular cove on the other side of the barrier. If it's not too windy, the sandy knoll that separates the two areas is excellent for a picnic.

Two other lovely local beaches (you'll need a car or bike) are those at **Fox Island**, just off Highway 16, 11km from Canso, and at **Black Duck Cove Day Use Park** (*1609 Dover Rd;* ⊕ *mid May–mid Oct*), approximately 10km from Canso.

The surrounding waters make another great **sea kayaking destination**; however, unless your accommodation offers kayak loan or rental – and very few do – you'll need to wait until Guysborough (pages 394–7) or have rented one back in Tangier (page 384).

Festival-wise, the **Stan Rogers Folk Festival** takes place here in July (box, page 392). At the **Canso Regatta**, boat races, dances, parades and concerts are held over an August weekend.

QUEENSPORT AND HALFWAY COVE These two tiny communities lie on Highway 16 between Canso and Guysborough – Queensport is 23km/14 miles and Halfway Cove 34km/21 miles from Canso; Halfway Cove is 15km/9 miles and Queensport 24km/15 miles from Guysborough, and convenient to reach **by car**.

Lighthouse fans will want to pop in to the **Out of the Fog Lighthouse Museum** (*Hwy 16;* ☏ *902 358 2108; www.outofthefog.ca;* ⊕ *mid Jun–late Sep 10.00–18.00 Thu–Mon*) at Half Island Cove. Here, a varied and extensive collection of lighthouse- and fishing-related artefacts and memorabilia can be seen. Displayed in two rooms of a former schoolhouse, exhibits include working fog horns and numerous lenses. The community also offers a combination petrol station/grocery store/take-away (open seven days). Queensport has a beach and picnic area just off Highway 16, and just offshore on Rook Island is the photogenic c1937 **Queensport Lighthouse**.

South of Highway 16 and carved by glaciers millions of years ago, the 10,000ha **Bonnet Lake Barrens Wilderness Area** is dotted with lakes, marshes, granite barrens and coastal spruce-fir forest. You won't find a restaurant along this stretch of Highway 16 – head back to Canso, or on to Guysborough.

GUYSBOROUGH Lying at the head of lovely Chedabucto Bay, Guysborough has a few things going on (mostly thanks to one man's vision; box, page 396) including

---

PRINCE HENRY SINCLAIR

Some people – many of whom are members of The Prince Henry Sinclair Society of North America – believe that Prince Henry Sinclair landed at Chedabucto Bay in 1398. In 1996, they erected a monument in the pretty picnic area at Halfway Cove to commemorate their belief. The Prince – whose other titles included 1st Earl of Orkney, Baron of Roslin, and Lord of Shetland – is thought by some to have undertaken voyages of discovery in the late 14th century to what is now Greenland, Nova Scotia and the USA. Some claim that the Mi'kmaq deity Glooscap is none other than Sinclair. We do know that his grandson, William Sinclair, was the builder of Rosslyn Chapel, just outside Edinburgh, Scotland, well known to Freemasons and fans of *The Da Vinci Code*.

A native of this region, Rob Carter returned to the area from northern California a few years ago, and couldn't understand why more people were not aware of what a great destination this is. Consequently, he organised and created the Lost Shores co-operative marketing map that highlighted the natural beauty and unhurried pace of life in eastern Guysborough County, and also started up the online **Lost Shores Gallery** (*902 358 2939;* *lostshoresgallery*) showcasing aerial photos of the region shot from a drone. Realising that the region's scenery and low-traffic roads were ideal cycling country (bikes can be rented in Guysborough; page 397), a huge cycling event – the inaugural **Lost Shores Gran Fondo** (*lsgf.ca*) – was organised for September 2016. The cyclefest (that will hopefully become an annual event) included a 90km loop through 15 fishing communities, a 50km route from Guysborough to the Queensport lighthouse and back along the south shore of Chedabucto Bay, a 30km loop around the Milford Haven inlet and a 30km mountain-bike loop following the Trans Canada Rail Trail along the Salmon River.

some excellent places to eat, a brewpub, marina, golf course, kayak rentals and fine hiking/cycling trails in the area. On the main street, several businesses are located in beautifully restored historic buildings backing on to the waterfront. The **Old Court House**, which houses the tourist office and a museum, is one block up the relatively steep Queen Street from Main Street. Close by is a golf resort with a distillery/brewery.

To get to Guysborough **by car**, it is on Highway 16, 46km/29 miles from Canso, 59km/37 miles from the Canso Causeway, 70km/43 miles from Antigonish and 281km/175 miles from Halifax.

History First European settlement dates from 1636 when Nicolas Denys (box, page 349) established a fishing station here and called it 'Chedabouctou', after '*Sedabooktook*', the Mi'kmaq name for the area, meaning 'running far back, or deep extending harbour'. Fort St Louis was built, and by 1683, the community had become home to over 150 Acadians. In 1690, the fort was sacked by privateers from New England: the last Acadians left as a result of the Expulsion in 1755.

Subsequently, the largest group of settlers came at the end of the American Revolution when lands were granted to Loyalists. Guysborough was named in honour of Sir Guy Carleton, commander-in-chief of the British forces in America and the Governor-General of Canada during the 1780s.

⌂ Where to stay

⌂ **Des Barres Manor Inn** (10 rooms) 90 Church St; *902 533 2099;* **tf** *1 888 933 2099;* www.desbarresmanor.com. Built for a Supreme Court judge in 1837, this beautifully restored mansion is set in immaculate landscaped grounds. Rooms are large & furnished with antiques. All in all, this is the region's best upmarket accommodation. Full gourmet b/fast inc May–Oct, continental b/fast only Nov–Apr. **$$$**

⌂ **Osprey Shores Golf Resort** (13 rooms) 119 Ferry Lane; *902 533 3904;* **tf** *1 800 909*

3904; www.ospreyshoresresort.com; ⊕ May–mid Oct. As the name suggests, the motel-style rooms are most popular with golfers. Outdoor pool (seasonal). Ask about 'Stay & Play' packages. The licensed clubhouse lounge (⊕ *May–mid Oct 08.00–19.00 daily;* **$**) serves sandwiches & beverages. Continental b/fast inc. **$$**

⌂ **Pepperlane Manor B&B** (4 rooms) 22 Court St; *902 533 1884,* *902 870 2400;* www. pepperlane.ca. Wonderful views from guest rooms (3 have en-suite bathrooms, 1 a private bathroom) in Elaine & Greg's delightful, recently renovated c1874 house. Common room area, with kitchenette, recliners & large-screen TVF. Rate includes excellent b/fast. **$$**

⋔ Boylston Provincial Park campground (35 sites) Hwy 16; parks.novascotia.ca/content/ boylston; ☉ early Jun–early Sep. 5km north of

Guysborough, this site offers exceptional views of the harbour & Chedabucto Bay from a hillside above the wide Milford Haven River with picnic facilities & a basic 35-site wooded campground & occasional concerts in season. Prince Henry Sinclair (box, page 394) is once again commemorated, here by a wooden prow-shaped monument. **$**

✕ Where to eat and drink

✕ Des Barres Manor Inn Contact details above; ☉ reservations required. You can sit on the lovely outdoor deck when the weather is clement, or inside by the fire. The menu captures the flavours & traditions of this Nova Scotia region. Excellent wine list & a true fine-dining experience. **$$$**

✕ BIG G's Pizza 111 Main St; ☎902 533 1886; www.biggspizza.ca; ☉ daily. Not just good pizza but burgers, sandwiches, pita wraps & more. Generous portions – & delicious! **$–$$**

✕ Days Gone By Bakery & Restaurant 59 Main St; ☎902 533 2672; www.daysgoneby.ca; ☉ approx mid Feb–mid Nov 08.00–20.00 daily. Buy fresh-baked bread & pastries to take away, or sit at one of the pine tables to enjoy all-day b/fast, or healthy salads, soups & excellent-value daily

specials such as pan-fried haddock or roast turkey dinner. Occasional live music. Licensed. **$**

✕ Rare Bird Pub 80 Main St; ☎902 533 2128; www.rarebirdpub.com; ☉ Jun–mid Oct 11.30–22.00 Wed–Sun. A tastefully restored c1866 heritage building offering good pub fare, including burgers, salads, & chowders. Patio looks out over the water. Quench your thirst with one of the pub's own Rare Bird craft beers brewed seasonally in small batches. Occasional live music. **$**

✕ Skipping Stone Café & Store 74 Main St; ☎902 533 2460; www.skippingstonestore.com; ☉ daily. Beautifully restored old building, patio overlooking marina & harbour. Café features light b/fasts, soups, sandwiches, locally roasted Full Steam coffee, & locally made baked goods/ice cream. **$**

Shopping and other practicalities There's a small independent supermarket in the **Chedabucto Centre** (*9996 Hwy 16*) on the south side of town. Both the **Days Gone By Bakery** and the **Skipping Stone Café** have a selection of gifts and crafts.

A DISTILLERY ON PARK LANE?

I am not sure that Glynn Williams – Toronto-based multimillionaire and former engineer – plays monopoly the same way that everyone else does. Having first visited this area almost three decades ago, he bought an oceanfront farmhouse and started spending summer vacations there. He formed the Authentic Seacoast Company and in 2005 bought what is now the Des Barres Inn (page 395). Guysborough's Rare Bird Pub & Eatery and Skipping Stone Café have since become part of the portfolio, as have Full Steam coffee, Harbour Belle baked goods, and the Osprey Shores Golf Resort (a 15-minute walk from downtown Guysborough). At the golf resort, the company has recently opened (June 2016) the state-of-the-art CAN$10 million Authentic Seacoast Distillery & Brewery (*75 Ferry Lane;* ☎*902 533 2078; authenticseacoastdistillery.com; tours (inc tastings)* ☉ *late Jun–mid Oct 14.00 daily (rest of year by appointment), CAN$20*), apparently the first distillery in the world to be located within a golf resort. Products include Sea Fever and Fortress rum, Glynnevan whisky and Rare Bird craft beer. Visitors can tour the facility and learn about the town's connections with the history of beer and spirits.

$ Royal Bank Main St; ✆902 533 3604; ⊕ 10.00–17.00 Mon–Fri

✚ Guysborough Memorial Hospital 10560 Hwy 16; ✆902 533 3702

✉ Post office 120 Main St; ⊕ 08.30–17.00 Mon–Fri, 10.30–16.30 Sat

ℹ Tourist information 106 Church St; ✆902 533 4008; ⊕ Jun–mid Oct 09.00–17.00 Mon–Fri, 10.00–17.00 Sat & Sun. In the Old Court House Museum (below).

Cyril Ward Memorial Library 27 Pleasant St; ✆902 533 3586; ⊕ noon–17.00 Mon–Thu, 10.00–14.00 Fri & Sat

What to see and do It's worth checking the schedule to see if your visit to the **Chedabucto Place Performance Centre** (*27 Green St;* ✆ *902 533 2015; chedabuctoplacetheatre.com*) might coincide with a show at this excellent 300-seat venue, which opened in 2007.

The c1843 church-like **Old Court House** (*106 Church St;* ✆ *902 533 4008; www. guysboroughhistoricalsociety.ca;* ⊕ *Jun–mid Oct 09.00–17.00 Mon–Fri, 10.00–17.00 Sat & Sun*) houses the local museum. Serving as both courthouse and town hall for 130 years until 1973, this is one of the country's oldest preserved courthouses. Displays include information on early Acadian and black settlements in the area, a collection of domestic tools and early photographs. There's a reading room with historical and genealogical information.

The magnificently situated **Osprey Shores Golf Resort** (page 395) offers wonderful Chedabucto Bay views from every hole, and in 2016 a green fee deal of CAN$46 for all-day golf was offered (with discounts for extra rounds). What is said to be the world's first distillery on a golf course opened here in summer 2016. The state-of-the-art facility, **Authentic Seacoast Distilling Company** (box, page 396), produces Glynnevan Canadian rye whisky and some rums. Tours are offered in summer and by appointment throughout the year.

If you're keen to go **canoeing**, **kayaking** and **cycling**, reasonably priced rentals are available from the **Skipping Stone Café & Store** (page 396). Whereas the entire 44km **Guysborough Nature Trail**, which connects Guysborough with Cross Roads Country Harbour (on Hwy 316, 25km/15 miles northwest of the eastern terminal of the Country Harbour ferry), might be too daunting for a leisurely **hike**, a walk along the first part of this trail, which follows the path of a railbed that never became a railway, is still worthwhile. Pick up the trail opposite the Fire Station on Queen Street (*Hwy 16*). The **Boylston Provincial Park** (page 396) is also worth a visit

Come Home Week (🅵 *GuysboroughComeHomeWeek*) attracts previous residents and visitors in the last week of July, with various events including races, dances and barbecues.

ON TO MULGRAVE Between Guysborough and Mulgrave, Highway 344 follows the western bank of the Strait of Canso. At Port Shoreham (19km/12 miles from Guysborough), a small provincial park features a boardwalk to the 1.5km sand and pebble beach, picnic tables overlooking the sea, changing rooms and toilets. Further along Highway 344, plans are under way for construction of a huge marine container terminal at Middle Melford (approx 12km/7.5 miles south of Canso).

Eastern Shore **LAWRENCETOWN TO SHEET HARBOUR**

9

MULGRAVE Other than a tourist office, neighbouring heritage centre, library and a look-out, there is little to delay you in Mulgrave. Aulds Cove (page 313), a 5-minute drive away, has accommodation and dining options.

In 1833, ferry services were established, carrying passengers from Mulgrave to Port Hawkesbury. Following the completion of the eastern extension of the Inter-Colonial Railway in 1882, passengers got off the train here to board a ferry across to Cape Breton Island. Mulgrave saw great prosperity and became one of the region's principal commercial hubs. That all changed when the Canso Causeway was completed in 1955: almost immediately, rail and much of the road traffic by-passed the town, severely hitting the social and economic life of the community. But things have improved in recent times. One consequence of the causeway's construction was the creation of the deepest ice-free harbour on the coast of North America, and a superport has been constructed at Mulgrave.

The **Mulgrave Heritage Centre** (*54 Loggie St;* ✆ *902 747 2788;* ☉ *early Jul–late Aug 09.00–17.00 daily; admission CAN$2*) is housed in an edifice built to resemble one of the old ferries. Displays on the Canso Causeway (box, page 315), World War memorabilia, and railway and fishing industry history can be seen here. It is located within the **Venus Cove Marine Park** home to a picnic area, playground, boardwalk and floating dock on a small cove. At the south end of town the **Scotia Ferry Look-off** offers a good vantage point from which to watch the Strait of Canso shipping and interpretive boards tell of the pre-Causeway ferries. At the **Scotia Days Festival** in **July**, there are five days of dances, dinners, races, music and more, culminating in a last-night firework display.

To get to Mulgrave **by car**, it is on Highway 344, 5km/3 miles from Aulds Cove, 54km/34 miles from Guysborough.

Other practicalities

✉ **Post office** 433 Main St; ☉ 08.30–17.15 Mon–Fri, 09.00–13.00 Sat
ℹ Tourist information 54 Loggie St; ✆ 902 747 2788; ☉ early Jul–late Aug 09.00–17.00 daily. In the Mulgrave Heritage Centre building (see above).

Mulgrave Library 390 Murray St; ✆ 902 747 2588; www.ecrl.library.ns.ca; ☉ see website for opening hours

SABLE ISLAND NATIONAL PARK RESERVE

One of Nova Scotia's most fascinating parts – and one of Canada's newest national parks – is one of the most difficult (and costly) to visit. Not to be confused with Cape Sable Island in the southwest of the province, Sable Island is a 42km-long windswept treeless and rockless crescent of land a maximum of 1.3km wide in the Atlantic Ocean approximately 290km southeast of Halifax. The closest landfall is Canso, and that is over 160km away.

Some of the island's many sand dunes approach 25m in height, and shift slowly towards the east. Maintained by precipitation, what is known as a 'freshwater lens' underlies Sable Island. Where this lens is exposed to the surface, it does so in the form of freshwater ponds (normally in the west of the island), which provide fresh water for the island's inhabitants. In the centre of the south side of the island was the site of brackish Lake Wallace; I say 'was' because this geographical feature has all but disappeared, having been filled in by blowing sand. As waves break over the beach head, they flood dips in the land and there may be some residue as the sea water cause the lake's waters to burst through the sand and drains back into the ocean. In winter and spring, the only obvious vegetation is marram grass, but in summer and autumn the island becomes almost lush with wild flowers and berries.

The island was once home to breeding colonies of the Atlantic walrus, but National Park Reserve designation came over a century too late for them. Hunted for their tusk ivory, they were last recorded here in the late 1800s. Today, Sable Island is home to the world's largest breeding colony of grey seals, which pup between late December and early February. A far smaller breeding population of harbour seals also calls the island home. However, the island's most famous inhabitants are its wild horses (box, below). This is also part of an important migratory flyway, and over 350 species of bird have been recorded here. Over 15 species have been recorded as breeding here in the spring and summer: one, the Ipswich sparrow, is thought to breed only on Sable Island.

Sable Island is close to one of the major shipping routes between Europe and North America. Because it lies directly in the path of most storm systems that track up the Atlantic coast, it is often hit by strange weather patterns. Being low-lying and treeless, it would have been very difficult for mariners to spot the island before it was too late – even more so in foggy conditions or after dark. The island was designated a National Park Reserve (NPR) in October 2011: the designation ensures that the island receives the highest level of protection for its natural and cultural features.

Parks Canada and Environment Canada's Meteorological Service maintain a year-round presence on the island with personnel based at Main Station. The operational hub of island activities and programmes, the station houses weather monitoring equipment, staff accommodations, workshops, emergency supplies, power generation, water treatment, and communications equipment.

HISTORY There are disputes over the 'discovery' of the island with three unsubstantiated claims by the French and Portuguese in the early and mid 16th century. In 1598, the Lieutenant-General of New France landed on Sable Island, leaving some 50 or 60 convicts with a few provisions whilst he sailed off to find a safer place to anchor. Strong winds made it impossible for him to return to the island and instead he made a brisk journey back to France. It is hard to imagine how anyone survived on the treeless windblown island without proper shelter or provisions: incredibly 11 castaways were picked up by a relief expedition in 1603.

SABLE ISLAND'S HORSES

Seals are quite common on the beach and in the surrounding waters, and over 350 bird species have been sighted, but the island's most famous residents are equine.

There is much speculation over how the horses first came here – records suggest that a clergyman from Boston brought some here in 1737, but historians say that those would have been appropriated by fishermen or privateers. It is thought that another Bostonian, Thomas Hancock, shipped 60 horses to the island in 1760, and that those were the ancestors of today's herds. If this is true, where Hancock obtained the horses is also unclear; one suggestion is that they had belonged to Acadians deported from Nova Scotia In 1755. The fact is that between 350 and 400 wild horses now run free on Sable Island.

One of the world's few truly wild horse populations is naturally controlled by the island's food and water supply. The horses fatten up on the relatively lush and plentiful summer vegetation: in winter they rely on marram grass. They supplement their diet with seaweed and kelp that washes up on the beaches.

9

Access to the island was first restricted in 1801 (and has been ever since) to try to stop the plunder of shipwrecks, and later to protect the island's unique environment. That year also marked the beginning of human presence on the island when Canada's first life-saving station was created. It wasn't until the 1870s that the government decided to erect a couple of lighthouses at each end of the island – it has been necessary to move these several times due to the constantly shifting shoreline. The lighthouses are no longer used for naval navigation, and the only permanent residents are four scientists, monitoring the weather and environment, and studying the wildlife.

Vast reserves of offshore undersea gas were found off Sable Island in the 1990s. In 1999, the first wells were opened – the drilling platforms can be clearly seen

SHIPWRECKS AND GHOSTLY TALES

The cool Labrador Current flows into the Atlantic Ocean and meets the warm Gulf Stream flowing from the southeast. Not only does this result in a far higher than average number of foggy days, but is also thought to be the cause of an immense whirlpool. The Gully, the largest undersea canyon in eastern North America, might also be a contributing factor.

Since the early 17th century, there are records of over 350 vessels which have come to grief on and immediately around Sable Island. It's impossible to estimate how many others failed to be recorded. Not without reason has it long been known as the 'Graveyard of the Atlantic'. Today, with modern navigational equipment, few boats run aground on Sable Island: the last wreck recorded was a luxury yacht in July 1999. But remains from centuries of shipwrecks are buried in the sand, appearing and disappearing as the wind shifts the grains.

Isolated, windswept and frequently foggy, and with restricted access: not much might grow on the Graveyard of the Atlantic but it has proved fertile for those who like to tell a good yarn, and although they might not admit it, many a Maritimer believes the island to be haunted. Stories circulated that pirates and bandits used the island as a base from which to lure ships into trouble, allowing the buccaneers to steal anything of value from the stricken vessels, and those on board. Almost as many ghost stories are told about the island as ships that have been wrecked there.

For example, it is said that a dead mother was washed ashore, clutching a baby which somehow still clung to life, albeit very weakly. The baby was taken to the nearest house, and the mother buried on the beach. No-one was surprised when the baby died a day or two later. After that there have been many reports of sightings of a sobbing female spirit wandering the beach as if looking for something.

Some survived wrecks, others were not so lucky. From time to time, bodies would be washed ashore on a strip of Sable Island's shore that became known as the 'haunted beach'. Those living on the island would regularly check the beach for bodies: if any were found, the corpse would be sewn up into a bag made from old sailcloth, and then left on the shoreline to be picked up on the supply boat's next visit – the shifting sand was too unstable for permanent burials.

In the mid 1990s, a scientist reported hearing the sound of piano music floating across the dunes. He knew that no-one else on the island would be playing a radio or CD, and also knew that although there had been pianos on the island in the past, there certainly weren't any at that time.

from the island (when it is not foggy) – and the gas is transported to the mainland via a 225km pipeline. One of the many benefits of the 'National Park Reserve' designation was the introduction of a ban on any drilling within one nautical mile of the island. Park officials, scientists and environmentalists continue to keep a close watch on any unwelcome side effects from the drilling process – and keep their fingers crossed.

GETTING THERE AND AWAY Although Sable Island is accessible **by air** and **by sea**, that doesn't begin to tell the full story.

The most favourable travel conditions exist between August and October, since fog is often thick from late June to early August, and can impede air and boat access. Weather conditions at other times of year can make travel to Sable Island especially unpredictable. At the time of writing, visitation is limited to same day, i.e. no overnight travel is permitted. Visitors must pack in and pack out everything they require.

Anyone planning to visit the island must first register with Parks Canada. Details required include the names and number of people in the party, dates and mode of transportation to and from the island and logistical support required (aircraft landing, boat landing, accommodations, etc).

By air Air services are provided by **Sable Aviation** (*902 499 7941; www. sableaviation.ca*), which operates a five-passenger plane for the (approx) 75-minute flight from Halifax International Airport. The company is not permitted to sell individual seats, so visitors must charter the entire aircraft (sometimes travellers try to organise groups – try the Sable Island Aircraft Charter Facebook page). As the plane must return to Halifax the same day, all visits are day trips only.

In addition, the island has no permanent runway: the plane lands and takes off on the island's south beach. Island personnel must assess and mark a runway based on the condition of the beach at the appropriate time – flooding of the beach after a severe storm, for example, can interrupt air service to the island for days or weeks at a time.

Costs are likely to change, but in 2016 chartering the plane for the day and paying all the compulsory extras (including taxes) involved with the flight would cost in the region of CAN$7,000.

By sea The chance of dense fog, the ever-changing sandbars, and potentially rough seas around the island (not for nothing was it known as the 'Graveyard of the Atlantic') don't encourage sea arrivals. There are no wharf facilities so vessels must anchor offshore and use a Zodiac or other small boat for a beach landing, and you must register with Parks Canada if you wish to visit. They will determine if it is possible.

In recent years companies such as **Adventure Canada** (tf *1 800 363 7566; www. adventurecanada.com*) and **One Ocean Expeditions** (tf *1 855 416 2326; www. oneoceanexpeditions.com*) have begun to offer a Sable Island visit on one of their cruises each year.

CONTACTS AND RESOURCES Since April 2012, **Parks Canada** (*www.pc.gc.ca/eng/ pn-np/ns/sable/index.aspx*) has been the main point of contact for co-ordinating access to the island, and has a detailed section on Sable Island National Park Reserve on its website. The **Sable Aviation** website (*www.sableaviation.ca*) also has useful Q&A information. For further information, see www.greenhorsesociety.com.

9

Appendix

FURTHER INFORMATION

BOOKS Note that many of these titles are out of print but often pop up in (real or online) used bookshops.

Architecture

Archibald, Stephen and Stevenson, Sheila *Heritage Houses of Nova Scotia* Formac, 2003

Penney, Allen *Houses of Nova Scotia: An Illustrated Guide to Architectural Style Recognition* Nova Scotia Museum, 1989

Autobiography

Haines, Max *The Spitting Champion of the World* Penguin, Canada, 2007. Growing up in Antigonish in the 1930s–50s.

Maclean, Angus Hector *God and the Devil at Seal Cove* Petheric Press, 1976

Fiction, historical true crime, and poetry

Bishop, Elizabeth *The Complete Poems (1927–79)* Chatto and Windus, 1983. A number relate to her time in Nova Scotia.

Buckler, Ernest *The Mountain and the Valley* New Canadian Library, 1989

Clarke, George Elliot *Whylah Falls* Raincoast Books, 2001

Coady, Lynn *Hellgoing* Anansi, 2013

Conlin, Christy Ann *Heave* & *The Memento* Anchor Canada, 2002 & Doubleday Canada, 2016

Eaton, Evelyn *Quietly My Captain Waits* Formac, 2001

Fitch, Sheree *The Gravesavers* Doubleday Canada, 2005. Based on the SS *Atlantic* disaster – for readers aged ten plus.

Haliburton, Thomas Chandler *The Clockmaker* BiblioLife, 2009

Hill, Lawrence *The Book of Negroes* (aka *Someone Knows My Name*) Harper Collins, 2007. The story of an African-born slave and her experiences before, during and after coming to Nova Scotia.

Jobb, Dean *Empire Of Deception* Harper, 2015

Joe, Rita *The Poems of Rita Joe* Abanaki Press, 1978

MacLennan, Hugh *Barometer Rising* New Canadian Library, 2007. Compelling romance set against the horrors of wartime and the Halifax Explosion.

MacLeod, Alistair *No Great Mischief* Vintage, 2001. Cape Breton Island-set Scottish family saga.

McKay, Ami *The Birth House* Vintage Canada, 2007

Mian, Sarah *When the Saints* Harper Avenue, 2015

Mills, Dana *Someone, Somewhere* Gaspereau Press, 2013

Raddall, Thomas Head *The Governor's Lady,* Nimbus, 1992

Skibsrud, Johanna *The Sentimentalists* Douglas & McIntyre, 2010

Folklore

Creighton, Helen, and others *Bluenose Ghosts, Bluenose Magic, Traditional Songs from Nova Scotia* Nimbus, 2009

History

Bradley, Michael *Holy Grail Across the Atlantic* Hounslow Press, 1988

Bruce, Harry *An Illustrated History of Nova Scotia* Nimbus, 1997

Cameron, Silver Donald *The Education of Everett Richardson: The Nova Scotia Fishermen's Strike, 1970–71* McClelland & Stewart, 1977

Campey, Lucille H *After the Hector: The Scottish Pioneers of Nova Scotia and Cape Breton 1733–1852* Dundurn Group, 2008

Choyce, Lesley *Nova Scotia: Shaped by the Sea* Pottersfield, 2007

Finnan, Mark *The Story of Sir William Alexander* Formac, 1997. The story of the first Nova Scotian.

Goodwin, William B *The Truth About Leif Ericsson and the Greenland Voyages* Kessinger, 2007

Hannay, James *The History of Acadia (1605–1763)* J&A McMillan, 1879. Very rare.

Kimber, Stephen *Sailors, Slackers & Blind Pigs: Halifax at War* Random House, 2003. The story behind Halifax's infamous VE Day riots

Kitz, Janet *Shattered City: The Halifax Explosion and the Road to Recovery* Nimbus, 2008

Ledger, Don, Style, Chris & Strieber, Whitley *Dark Object: The World's Only Government-Documented UFO Crash* Dell Publishing, 2001

MacDonald, Laura M *Curse of the Narrows* Walker & Co, 2005. The Halifax Explosion.

MacNeill, Blair H *Ferry Tales: Stories of Village Life* Pronto, 2000. Stories from Digby Neck.

Mann, William F *The Knights Templar in the New World: How Henry Sinclair Brought the Grail to Acadia* Inner Traditions Bear & Company, 2004

Perkins, Charlotte *The Romance of Old Annapolis Royal* Historical Association of Annapolis Royal, 1985

Pohl, Frederick *Prince Henry Sinclair: His Expedition to the New World in 1398* Nimbus, 1997

Raddall, Thomas Head *Halifax, Warden of the North* Nimbus, 2007

Raddall, Thomas Head *The Rover: Story of A Canadian Privateer* MacMillan, 1966

Saunders, Margaret Marshall *Beautiful Joe* Lulu.com, 2007

Mi'kmaq

Choyce, Lesley and May, Rita (eds) *The Mi'kmaq Anthology* Pottersfield, 1997

Joudry, Shalan *Generations Re-Merging* Gaspereau Press, 2014

Knockwood, Isabelle *Out of the Depths* Fernwood Publishing, 2001. The experiences of Mi'kmaq children at school in Shubenacadie.

Holmes Whitehead, Ruth *Six Micmac Stories* Nimbus, 1983

Lacey, Laurie *Micmac Medicines Remedies and Recollections* Nimbus, 1993

Nowlan, Alden *Nine Micmac Legends* Nimbus, 1983. Mi'kmaq Glooscap legends retold

Paul, Daniel N *We Were Not The Savages* Fernwood Publishing, 2006. Nova Scotia's history from a Mi'kmaq perspective.

Spicer, Stanley T *Glooscap Legends* Nimbus, 2007. The life history of Glooscap.

Natural history

Ferguson, Laing *The Fossil Cliffs of Joggins* Nova Scotia Museum, 1988
Maybank, Blake *Birding Sites of Nova Scotia* Nimbus, 2005
McLaren, Ian *All the Birds of Nova Scotia* Gaspereau Press, 2012
O'Connor, D'Arcy *The Secret Treasure of Oak Island* The Lyons Press, 2004
Parker, Mike *Guides of the North Woods: Hunting & Fishing Tales* Nimbus, 2004
Sibley, David *The Sibley Field Guide to Birds of Eastern North America* Knopf Publishing, 2003
Thurston, Harry *Dawning of the Dinosaurs: The Story of Canada's Oldest Dinosaurs* Nimbus, 1994
Zinck, Marion (ed) *Roland's Flora of Nova Scotia* Nimbus, 1998. Two volumes.

Sports and activities

Conrod, Gary *The Nova Scotia Bicycle Book* Available from Atlantic Canada Cycling (✆ 902 423 2453; *www.atlanticcanadacycling.com*), 1995. The accommodation listings are out of date but the rest of the book is still very useful.
Cuningham, Scott *Sea Kayaking in Nova Scotia* Nimbus, 2013
Dill, C *Canoe Routes of Nova Scotia* Canoe Nova Scotia Association, 1983
Haynes, Michael *Hiking Trails of Nova Scotia* Goose Lane Editions, 2012
Paine, Albert Bigelow *The Tent Dwellers* Kessinger, 2005
Smith, Andrew L *Paddling the Tobeatic: Canoe Routes of Southwestern Nova Scotia* Nimbus, 2004
Watt, Walter *Nova Scotia By Bicycle* Available from Bicycle Nova Scotia (*bicycle.ns.ca*), 2004

Travel writing

Bird, Will R *This Is Nova Scotia* and *Off-Trail in Nova Scotia* Ryerson Press, 1950 and 1956 respectively. Motoring around Nova Scotia in the 1950s.
Crowell, Clement W *Novascotiaman* Nova Scotia Museum, 1979
Day, Frank Parker *Rockbound* University of Toronto Press, 1998. Based on East Ironbound Island near Blandford.
Dennis, Clara *Down in Nova Scotia* and *More about Nova Scotia* Ryerson Press, 1946 and 1937 respectively. Motoring around Nova Scotia in the 1930s.
Howe, Joseph *Western and Eastern Rambles: Travel Sketches of Nova Scotia* University of Toronto Press, 1973
Richardson, Evelyn *We Keep a Light* Nimbus, 1995. Set on Bon Portage Island near Shag Harbour.
Spicer, Stanley T *Masters of Sail* Ryerson Press, 1968

WEBSITES
Driving in Nova Scotia

www.novascotia.ca/sns/rmv/safe/handbook.asp Nova Scotia drivers' handbook.
www.novascotiagasprices.com Petrol costs.

Facts

www.cbc.ca/news/canada/nova-scotia Provincial, national and international news.
clean.ns.ca, www.ecologyaction.ca and nsenvironmentalnetwork.com Environmental groups.
destinationhalifax.com/experience-halifax/lgbt and gay.hfxns.org Useful information for gays.
nsgna.ednet.ns.ca Genealogy.
www.statcan.gc.ca Canada's official national (and provincial) statistics.
www.weatheroffice.gc.ca and www.theweathernetwork.com/ca Weather forecasts for locations all over the province.

Natural history

maybank.tripod.com/BSNS/BSNS.htm Birding sites of Nova Scotia. The website is no longer updated (its creator is no longer with us) but most of the info is still valid.
www.nsbirdsociety.ca The Nova Scotia Bird Society.
nswildflora.ca Nova Scotia Wild Flora Society.

Sports and outdoor activities

www.cyclenovascotia.ca and **bicycle.ns.ca** Cycling.
ckns.ca Canoeing and kayaking.
nsgeocaching.com and **geocachingnovascotia.ca** Geocaching.
www.nsga.ns.ca and **www.golfnovascotia.com** Golf.
novatrails.com and **www.hikenovascotia.ca** Hiking.
www.surfns.com and **haliwax.com** Surfing.

Travel information and accessible travel

accessadvisor.weebly.com and **www.accesstotravel.gc.ca**
www.bbcanada.com Inns and B&Bs across Nova Scotia.
www.cbsa-asfc.gc.ca Canadian Border Services Agency – customs and immigration.
maritimebus.com The major coach operator.
www.novascotia.com Official Nova Scotia tourism site.
www.viarail.ca VIA Rail Canada schedules and prices.

UPDATES WEBSITE

You can post your comments and recommendations, and read the latest feedback and updates from other readers online at www.bradtupdates.com/novascotia.

FOLLOW BRADT

For the latest news, special offers and competitions, subscribe to the Bradt newsletter via the website www.bradtguides.com and follow Bradt on:

f BradtTravelGuides
🐦 @BradtGuides
📷 @bradtguides
📌 bradtguides

Index

Entries in **bold** indicate main entries; those in *italics* indicate maps

413